WHAT THE BIBLE IS ALL ABOUT

WHAT THE BIBLE IS ALL ABOUT

An easy to use survey of God's Word that shows you how to put each Biblical book in perspective ■ helps you learn with illustrations, outlines, daily readings and many other study aids ■ explains how the Bible was written and why ■ gets you into the Bible and gets the Bible into you

HENRIETTA C. MEARS
Foreword by Billy Graham

Regal
Books
A Division of G/L Publications
Ventura, California, U.S.A.

The foreign language publishing of all Regal books is under the direction of GLINT. GLINT provides financial and technical help for the adaptation, translation and publishing of books in more than 85 languages for millions of people worldwide.

For more information write: GLINT, P.O. Box 6688, Ventura, CA 93006.

Twenty-seventh Printing, 1980

Published by Regal Books
A Division of G/L Publications
Ventura, California 93006
Printed in U.S.A.

Library of Congress Catalog Card No. 79-92452

Cloth: ISBN 0-8307-0512-0
    Code Number: 51 024 21
Trade Paper: ISBN 0-8307-0473-6
    Code number: 54 047 03

PREFACE

Sailing across the Ionian Sea from old Corinth in Greece, I was asked to prepare these words. Could there be a more suitable setting in which to sound the authority of God's Word! At Corinth Paul continued a year and six months teaching the Word of God (Acts 18:11). He used the direct approach of identifying with the people and "reasoning in the synagogue" about the Living Word who had come as the fulfillment of the written Word.

This is a bewildering age. Men lack a sense of direction in destiny. They have lost their moorings. They are floundering in their quest for faith and salvation. They are lonely in the midst of millions.

The message of God's Word is the total answer to man's total need. It is the Good News of forgiveness, faith, peace, purpose and heaven. In the Bible man discovers what he is to believe and where he is going.

One of the greatest needs today for Christians is to become acquainted with the Scriptures in daily study and meditation. Through dependence upon the Holy Spirit and the prayerful reading of God's Word, His eternal truth grips our hearts with a dynamic force. We gain a sense of destiny and direction. We need to understand the Word of God, and the study of "What the Bible Is All About" will help bring this essential understanding of God's essential revelation of Himself.

Cyrus N. Nelson

Regal Books Division of Gospel Light Publications

FOREWORD

Millions of people today are searching for a reliable voice of authority. The Word of God is the only real authority we have. His Word sheds light on human nature, world problems and human suffering. But beyond that, it clearly reveals the way to God.

The message of the Bible is the message of Jesus Christ who said, "I am the way, the truth, and the life" (John 14:6). It is the story of salvation; the story of your redemption and mine through Christ; the story of life, of peace, of eternity.

Our faith is not dependent upon human knowledge and scientific advance, but upon the unmistakable message of the Word of God.

The Bible has a great tradition and a magnificent heritage. It contains 66 books written over a period of several hundred years by many different men. Yet the message, divinely inspired by the Holy Spirit, is clear throughout. The 66 books become one.

The Bible is old; yet it is ever new. It is the most modern book in the world today. There is a false notion that a book as ancient as the Bible cannot speak to the needs of modern man. Men somehow think that in an age of scientific achievement, when knowledge has increased more in the past 25 years than in all preceding centuries put together, this ancient Book is out of date. But to all who read and love the Bible, it is relevant for our generation.

It is in the Holy Scriptures that we find the answers to life's ultimate questions: Where did I come from? Why am I here? Where am I going? What is the purpose of my existence?

One of the greatest needs in the church today is to come back to the Scriptures as the basis of authority, and to study them prayerfully in dependence on the Holy Spirit. When we read God's Word, we fill our hearts with His words, and God is speaking to us.

William Lyon Phelps, called the most beloved professor in America, and one-time president of Yale University, made the oft-quoted statement, "I thoroughly believe in a university education for both men and women; but I believe a knowledge of the Bible without a college course is more valuable than a college course without the Bible."

One of the greatest tragedies today is that, although the Bible is an available, open book, it is a closed book to millions—either because they leave it unread or because they read it without applying its teachings to themselves. No greater tragedy can befall a man or a nation than that of paying lip service to a Bible left unread or to a way of life not followed.

The Bible, the greatest document available for the human race, needs to be opened, read and believed. A recent survey indicates that only 12 per cent of the people who say they believe the Bible actually read it every day; 34 per cent read it only once a week, and 42 per cent read it only once in a great while.

This book, *What The Bible Is All About*, will help make the reading and study of God's Word interesting, challenging and useful. We commend it to you.

Billy Graham

CONTENTS

UNDERSTANDING
the BIBLE

*The Bible
Portrays Jesus Christ,
the Saviour
of the World*

"Behind and beneath the Bible, above and beyond the Bible, is the God of the Bible."

The Bible is God's written revelation of His will to men. Its central theme is salvation through Jesus Christ.

The Bible contains 66 books, written by 40 authors, covering a period of approximately 1600 years.

The Old Testament was written mostly in Hebrew (a few short passages in Aramaic). About 100 years before the Christian Era the entire Old Testament was translated into Greek.

The New Testament was written in the Greek language. Remember our English Bible is a translation from these original languages.

The word "Bible" comes from the Greek word "biblos."

The word "testament" means "covenant," or agreement. The Old Testament is the covenant God made with man about his salvation before Christ came. The New Testament is the agreement God made with man about his salvation after Christ came.

In the Old Testament we find the covenant of law. In the New Testament we find the covenant of grace which came through Jesus Christ. One led into the other (Galatians 3:17-25).

The Old commences what the New completes.

The Old gathers around Sinai,

The New around Calvary.

The Old is associated with Moses,

The New with Christ (John 1:17).

The authors were kings and princes, poets and philosophers, prophets and statesmen. Some were learned in all the arts of the times and others were unschooled fishermen. Other books soon are out of date but this Book spans the centuries.

Most books must be adapted to age but old and young alike love this Book.

Most books are provincial and only interest the people in whose language it was written, but not this Book. No one ever stops to think it was written in what are now dead languages.

Old Testament Books

(5) Law	(17) Prophetical
(12) Historical	(5 Major)
(5) Poetical	(12 Minor)

New Testament Books

The New Testament was written to reveal to us the character and teachings of Jesus Christ, the mediator of the New Covenant, by at least eight men, four of whom, Matthew, John, Peter and Paul, were apostles; two, Mark and Luke, were companions of the apostles; and two, James and Jude, were brothers of Jesus. The books were written at various times during the second half of the first century.

The books in the New Testament may be grouped thus:

(4) Gospels	(21) Epistles
(1) History	(14 Pauline)
(1) Prophecy	(7 General)

The Old Testament begins with God (Genesis 1:1).

The New Testament begins with Christ (Matthew 1:1).

From Adam to Abraham we have the history of the human race.

From Abraham to Christ we have the history of the chosen race.

From Christ on we have the history of the Church.

"Most people's knowledge of history is like a string of graduated pearls without the string," said an historian. This statement seems to be especially true of Bible history. Many people know the Bible characters and the principal events, but they are hopelessly lost when they are called upon to connect the stories in order. Anyone who has experienced the thrill of learning to place the individual characters in their right setting as to place and time, can realize the difference it makes in his enjoyment of God's Word.

Pick up the "pearls" in the Scriptures and string them into order from Genesis to Revelation so that you can "think through" the Bible story.

Old Testament — Principal Characters

Here is a list of 40 principal characters whose combined story forms the history of the Old Testament.

1. God	22. Saul
2. Satan	23. David
3. Adam	24. Solomon
4. Noah	25. Elijah
5. Abraham	26. Elisha
6. Isaac	27. Kings of Israel (19)
7. Jacob	
8. Joseph	**28-30. Kings of Judah (20)
9. Pharaoh	
10. Moses	***31-34. Prophets
11. Aaron	35. Nebuchadnezzar
12. Caleb	36. Cyrus
13. Joshua	37. Zerubbabel
*14-19. Judges (15)	38. Ezra
20. Ruth	39. Nehemiah
21. Samuel	40. Esther

You will see that in the study of the first book, Genesis, the first eight characters will be located. What a vast page of history is written around them.

New Testament — Principal Characters

1. John the Baptist
2. Christ
3-14. Disciples (12)
15. Stephen
16. Philip
17. Paul
18. James, brother of Jesus

---

*Big Six—Othniel, Deborah, Barak, Gideon, Jephthah, Samson
**Jehoshaphat, Hezekiah, Josiah.
***Isaiah, Jeremiah, Ezekiel, Daniel.

Old Testament — Principal Places

The twelve principal places around which the history of the Old Testament is written are:

1. Eden
2. Mount Ararat
3. Babel
4. Ur of the Chaldees
5. Canaan
6. Egypt (with Joseph)
7. Sinai
8. Wilderness
9. Canaan
10. Assyria (captivity of Israel)
11. Babylon (captivity of Judah)
12. Canaan (Palestine—return of the exiles)

As you build the story of the Bible around these places, you have the whole history in chronological order.

Still another way to "think through" the Bible is by following the "Great Facts" in order.

Old Testament — Principal Facts

1. Creation, Genesis 1:1–2:3
2. Fall of man, Genesis 3
3. Deluge, Genesis 6–9
4. Babel, Genesis 11:1-9
5. Call of Abraham, Genesis 11:10–12:3
6. Descent into Egypt, Gen. 46;47
7. Exodus, Exodus 7–12
8. Passover, Exodus 12
9. Giving of the Law, Exodus 19–24
10. Wilderness wanderings, Numbers 13;14
11. Conquest of the promised land, Joshua 11
12. Dark ages of the chosen people, Judges
13. Anointing of Saul as king, I Samuel 9:27;10:1
14. Golden age of Hebrews under David and Solomon, United Kingdom, II Samuel 5:4;5; I Kings 10:6-8.

15. The Divided Kingdom—Israel and Judah, I Kings 12:26-33
16. The Captivity, II Kings 17;25
17. The Return, Ezra

New Testament — Principal Facts
1. Early life of Christ
2. Ministry of Christ
3. Church in Jerusalem
4. Church extending to the Gentiles
5. Church in all the world

Principal Periods
I. Period of the Patriarchs to Moses—Genesis
   A. The godly line
      Leading events:
      1. Creation
      2. Fall
      3. Flood
      4. Dispersion
   B. The chosen family
      Leading events:
      1. Call of Abraham
      2. The descent into Egypt—bondage
II. Period of Great Leaders: Moses to Saul—Exodus to Samuel
   A. Exodus from Egypt
   B. Wandering in wilderness
   C. Conquest of Canaan
   D. Rule of the Judges
III. Period of the Kings—Saul to the Captivities—Samuel, Kings, Chronicles, the Prophetical Books
   A. The United Kingdom
      1. Saul
      2. David
      3. Solomon
   B. The Divided Kingdom
      1. Judah
      2. Israel

IV. Period of Foreign Rulers—Captivities to Christ—Ezra,
    Nehemiah, Esther, Prophecies of Daniel and Ezekiel
    A. Captivity of Israel
    B. Captivity of Judah
 V. Christ—The Gospels
VI. The Church—Acts and the Epistles
    A. In Jerusalem
    B. Extending to the Gentiles
    C. In all the world

Remember that in God's Word the foundation of Christianity is laid in the revelation of the one and only true God. God chose a people (the children of Israel) to show forth this truth and to preserve a record of Himself.

The Bible tells us of the origin of sin and how this curse separated man from God. We discover how utterly impossible it was for the law to bring to man the salvation that he needs, for by the deeds of the law could no flesh be justified, for *all have sinned* (see Romans 3:20,23). Then we find the promise of a Saviour, One who was to come *to seek and to save that which was lost and give his life a ransom for many* (Luke 19:10; Matthew 20:28). We see all through the ages one purpose is evident, that of preparing a way for the coming of the Redeemer of the world.

There is no royal road to learning and certainly there is no royal road to knowledge of the Bible. The Spirit of God will lead us into all truth, to be sure, but God's command is that we study to be approved, workmen unashamed. (See II Tim. 2:15.)

You must give to the Bible attention with intention, and it is intention that will necessitate attention. Perhaps there is so little attention in Bible reading today because there is so little intention. We must come to it with a purpose, with a clearly defined object; we must know what we are about.

Many say, "The Bible is so great. I don't know where to commence and don't know how to go on." This is often said quite earnestly and sincerely. And it is true that, unless we have some method, we shall assuredly lose the very best results, even though we may spend much time upon the Book.

6

Campbell Morgan once made the statement, "The Bible can be read from Genesis 1 to Revelation 22 at pulpit rate in 78 hours." A lawyer challenged him on that. Morgan told him to go on and try it before he challenged. The lawyer went home and read the Bible in less than 80 hours.

Do you want to read the Bible through? Leave 80 hours for it. Plot out that time. How much time can you give each day? How many days a week? This is a highly practical proposition and should be seized by the very busiest. We are all busy and must take time for it. If we are going to know the Bible, we must give time to it and arrange for it. We must adjust our lives so that time is made. Unless we do, we shall never come into any worthy knowledge of the Word; for it is impossible from pulpit ministry to get that knowledge of the Word which is possible and is indeed needful. The Bible reveals the will of God so as to lead man into it. Each book has a direct teaching. Find out what it is and conform to it. This is our purpose. We are going to consider a book in each chapter.

Now the Bible, although it is a library, is also "the Book." It is a story, a grand story that moves on from commencement to finish. Here surely is something that is phenomenal in literature. Suppose, for instance, you were to cover the great fields of knowledge, such as law, history, philosophy, ethics and prophecy, and you were to bring these different subjects all together and bind them up into one book. What, to begin with, would you call the book? Then what unity could one possibly expect to find in such a jumble of subjects? Such an infinite number and variety of themes and styles as are found in the Bible, brought together across not a few generations in the history of the people, but across centuries, makes the likelihood of any unity being present amazingly small. No publisher would risk publishing such a book, and if he did, nobody would buy it or read it. That is, however, what is done in the Bible.

Interesting Facts About the Bible

LAW in the books of Moses
HISTORY in Samuel, Kings, Chronicles and other books
PHILOSOPHY in Job and Ecclesiastes

POETRY in the Psalms and Song of Solomon

PROPHECY in Isaiah, Ezekiel, Jeremiah and the minor prophets

DOCTRINE in the Epistles

REVELATION in the Apocalypse and Daniel

Remember, these were given to us by 40 different men over a period of about 1600 years. All these are brought together and bound and are called "the Book." We can begin at Genesis and read on through to the end. There is no jar. We can pass from one style of literature to another as easily as though we were reading a story written by one hand and produced by one life, and indeed we have here a story produced by one Mind (II Peter 1:21) though not written by one hand.

While divine, it is human. The thought is divine, the revelation is divine, the expression of the communication is human. *Holy men* [human element] *of God spake as they were moved by the Holy Ghost* [divine element] (II Peter 1:21).

So we have here a book unlike all others. The Book, a divine revelation, a progressive revelation, a revelation of God to man communicated through men, moves on smoothly from its beginnings to its great end. Away back in Genesis we have the beginnings, in the Revelation we have endings, and from Exodus to Jude we see how God carried out His purpose. We can't dispense with any part of it.

Bible history takes us back into the unknown past of eternity and its prophecies take us into the otherwise unknown future.

The Old Testament is the foundation; the New Testament is the superstructure. A foundation is of no value unless a building be built upon it. A building is impossible unless there be a foundation. So the Old Testament and New Testament are essential to one another.

"The New is in the Old contained,
 The Old is in the New explained.
 The New is in the Old latent,
 The Old is in the New patent."

The Old Testament and New Testament constitute a divine library, one sublime unity, origins in past to issues in future, processes between, connecting two eternities.

One Book, One History, One Story

The Bible is one book, one history, one story, His story. Behind 10,000 events stands God, the builder of history, the maker of the ages. Eternity bounds the one side, eternity bounds the other side, and time is in between—Genesis, origins, Revelation, endings, and all the way between God is working things out. You can go down into the minutest detail everywhere and see that there is one great purpose moving through the ages, the eternal design of the Almighty God to redeem a wrecked and ruined world.

The Bible is one book, and you cannot take it in texts and expect to comprehend the magnificence of divine revelation. You must see it in its completeness. God has taken pains to give a progressive revelation and we should take pains to read it from beginning to end. Don't suppose reading little scraps can ever be compensation for doing deep and consecutive work on the Bible itself. We must get back to the Book and then we will not tolerate such work. One would scorn to read any other book, even the lightest novel, in this fashion.

Another way we can study the Bible is by groups—law, history, poetry, major and minor prophets, Gospels, Acts, Epistles and Revelation. Here again we find great unity for "in the volume of the book it is written of Me," says Christ. Everything points to the King!

Each book has a message, and we should endeavor to discover what that message is. Read until you discover the message of the book. For instance, in John it is easy to discover the purpose. It is stated in John 20:31. It is not always given as clearly but the truth may be found.

In one sense we should treat the Bible as we treat any other book, and there is a sense in which we should not do that. When we get a book from the library, we would never treat it as we do the Bible. We would never think of reading just a paragraph, taking some ten minutes, reading a little at night and then reading a little in the morning, and so spending weeks, perhaps months, in reading the book through. No interest could be maintained in any story by such procedure. Take a love story, for instance; we would naturally begin at the beginning and read right through to the end, unless we turned back to the finish to see how the story ended.

A Love Story

Do you come to the Bible with such eagerness? Do you read with that purpose and persistence? The Bible is not a book of texts—it is a story—it is a revelation, to be begun and pursued and ended as we start and continue other books. Don't trifle with the Bible. Don't divide it into short devotional paragraphs and think you have understood its messages. Don't trifle with it. It may be excusable for some poor soul who can hardly read to open the Bible and take whatever his eyes light upon as the message of God. Many people do that but the Bible isn't to be misused in that manner. We must come to it in a common sense fashion. Believe that every book is about something and read and reread until you find out what that something is.

First we read the Book, not read books *about* the Book, nor turn to the comments. They will come in good time, perhaps, but give the Book a chance to speak for itself and to make its own impression; to bear its own testimony. A man was given one of those Bibles with the text at the top of the page with all the rest comments. It was given by a friend who meant well. When asked later how he was getting on, he said that the text did throw a mighty lot of light on the comments. Comments too often set one off the track instead of putting him on.

Don't wish to put on colored glasses of man's opinions and then read through the interpretation put on it by other minds. Let the Spirit of God Himself teach you. Each has a right to read it for himself. *No scripture is of any private interpretation* (II Peter 1:20). Read it seeking for illumination. It is a revelation, and He will flash light upon the page as you come humbly.

We have been studying the Bible piecemeal. Now we must turn to the reading of books as wholes and not tinker with texts. No part of any book will give you the whole message of the book.

The Word of God is alive and every part is necessary to the perfection of the whole. We don't say that every part is equally important. If you were to ask me whether I would give up my finger or my eye, of course I would part with my finger. So with the Word of God. All is necessary to make a perfect whole, but some portions are more precious than others. You can't take away the Song of Solomon and have a perfect revelation. No one says the Song of Solomon is comparable with John's Gospel, but both are parts of an organism and that organism is not complete if any part is missing.

The Bible is a whole and can't be tampered with. To add anything to it or take anything from it would mar its absolute perfection (Rev. 22:18,19). The canon of Scripture is closed. Other works throw valuable light upon it, but this stands unique, alone, and complete, and these parts all partake of the perfection of the whole.

Read a Book a Week

So we come to these books as complete in themselves, yet bearing in mind their vital relation to what precedes and what succeeds. We should read them one at a time. Read a book in a week. Now don't suppose that this is impossible. It is not. How much time do you spend reading in 24 hours? How much time on newspapers? magazines? How much time do you give to fiction? to other reading? And how much time do you give to television? Now the longest of these books doesn't take longer than some of you devote to reading in one day.

There are some of the larger books in the Old Testament, such as Genesis, Exodus, Deuteronomy, Isaiah, that might take some hours to read with care, and if that be too much, divide them into seven equal parts, but put your reading into strict limits. Don't give yourself time to lose the impression made by the first reading before you get to the second and don't suppose that you can grasp the content and intent of any book at a single reading.

You don't suppose that as you walk down the corridors of a gallery and look at the pictures you see the gallery. You see some pictures on the wall, but you don't know what they are about. You must sit in front of a picture and study it.

More Interesting Facts About the Bible

God, man, sin, redemption, justification, sanctification. In two words—*grace, glory*. In one word—*Jesus*.

Christ quotes from 22 Old Testament books:
In Matthew, 19 O.T. quotations

> Mark, 15
> Luke, 25
> John, 11
> Hebrews, 85 (quotations and allusions)
> Revelation, 245

"Christ quotes the very passages most avoided by the Bible's critics—the flood, Lot, manna, brazen serpent, Jonah," said D. L. Moody.

Number of verses—31,102
Number of words—775,693
Longest chapter—Psalm 119
Shortest chapter—Psalm 117

It is a curious fact that Ezra 7:21 contains all the letters of the alphabet except j.

Longest verse—Esther 8:9
Shortest verse—John 11:35
Longest book in Old Testament—Psalms
Longest book in New Testament—Luke

CHRIST, THE LIVING WORD

The Old Testament is an account of a nation (the Hebrew nation). The New Testament is an account of a Man (the Son of man). The nation was founded and nurtured of God in order to bring the Man into the world (Genesis 12:1-3).

God Himself became a man so that we might know what to think of when we think of God (John 1:14; 14:9). His appearance on the earth is the central event of all history. The Old Testament sets the stage for it. The New Testament describes it.

As a man Christ lived the most perfect life ever known. He was kind, tender, gentle, patient, and sympathetic. He loved people. He worked marvelous miracles to feed the hungry. Multitudes, weary, pain-ridden and heartsick, came to Him, and He gave them rest (Matthew 11:28-30). It is said that if all the deeds of kindness that he did were written, the world would not contain the books (John 21:25).

Then He died—to take away the sin of the world, and to become the Saviour of men.

Then He rose from the dead. He is alive today. He is not merely an historical character, but a living Person—the most important fact of history, and the most vital force in the world today. And He promises eternal life to all who come to Him.

The whole Bible is built around the story of Christ and His promise of life everlasting to men. It was written only that we might believe and understand, know and love, and follow HIM.

The Bible — God's Written Word

Apart from any theory of inspiration, or any theory of how the Bible books came to their present form, or how much the text may have suffered in passing through the hands of editors and copyists; or what is historical and what may be poetical; assume that the Bible is just what it appears to be. Accept the books as we have them in our Bible as units, study them to know their contents. You will find there is a unity of thought which indicates that One Mind inspired the writing of the whole series of books; that it bears on its face the stamp of its Author; that it is in every sense the WORD OF GOD.

Minimum Daily Requirements/Spiritual Vitamins

Sunday: GOD-GIVEN   II Timothy 3:10-17
Monday: SHOULD BE TREASURED   Deut. 11:1-9,
   Josh. 1:8,9
Tuesday: SHOULD BE KEPT   Psalm 119:9-18
Wednesday: A LAMP   Psalm 119:105-117
Thursday: FOOD   Isaiah 55:1-11; Matt. 4:4
Friday: FULFILLED   Luke 24:36-45
Saturday: COMPLETE   Revelation 22:8-21

UNDERSTANDING GENESIS

Genesis Portrays Jesus Christ, Our Creator God

Genesis is the seed-plot of the Word of God. The title Genesis, which is Greek, means "origin," and the first word in the Hebrew of Genesis is translated "in the beginning"—words which indicate both the scope and the limits of the book. It tells us the beginning of everything except God. Another thing to notice is that it tells only of beginnings. There is no finality here. Upon its truths all the future revelation of God to man is built up.

Satan appears to have special enmity for the Book of Genesis. No wonder the Adversary has bent his attacks upon it. It exposes him as the enemy of God and the deceiver of the human race; it foretells his destruction; it depicts his doom (Genesis 3).

Without Genesis our knowledge of a creating God would be pitifully limited; we would be woefully ignorant of the beginnings of our universe.

Genesis Is the Book of Beginnings

1. The beginning of the world   Genesis 1:1-25
2. The beginning of the human race   Genesis 1:26–2
3. The beginning of sin in the world   Genesis 3:1-7
4. The beginning of the promise of redemption Genesis 3:8-24
5. The beginning of family life   Genesis 4:1-15
6. The beginning of a man-made civilization Genesis 4:16–9:29
7. The beginning of the nations of the world   Genesis 10,11
8. The beginning of the Hebrew race   Genesis 12–50

Adam began with God, and fell through disobedience (Genesis 3).

Abel began with God by the blood of sacrifice (Genesis 4:4).

Noah began with God by way of the ark (Genesis 6:8, 14,22).

Abraham began with God when he built altars (Genesis 12:8).

These all made new beginnings for the race.

Genesis is the record of the beginnings of all these things. No wonder that when men, because of spiritual blindness (Ephesians 4:18), reject God's revelation in this peerless record of beginnings, they worship chance as the creator, beasts as their ancestors, and fallen humanity as the flower of natural evolution!

Genesis begins with "God" but ends "in a coffin." This book is a history of man's failure. But we find that God meets every failure of man. He is a glorious Saviour. We find that where sin abounded, grace did much more abound (Romans 5:20).

Genesis gives us at least 2000 years of record. It is not entirely history; it is a spiritual interpretation of history. In two chapters God flashes on the wall an account of the creation of the world and of man. From there on we see the Story of Redemption. God is bringing lost man back to Himself.

We have noted Satan's reasons for attacking this majestic book. Its authorship by Moses, its scientific accuracy, and its literal testimony to human sin as deliberate disobedience to God have all been bitterly assailed. The Word of God, however, definitely declares Genesis to be one of the living oracles delivered to Moses. To its infallible truth and its testimony to the Messiah, our Lord Jesus set His seal (John 5:46,47).

When Genesis goes, a divine Creator, a divine creation, a divinely promised Redeemer, and a divinely inspired Bible must also go. Around its sacred pages is the protection of the Holy Spirit of God who inspired its words. If there were more study of Genesis instead of so much argument about it, its truth would be clearer. Many origins are recorded in the first eleven chapters: natural universe, human life, sin, death, redemption, civilization, nations, and languages.

16

The remainder of the book from Genesis 12 deals with the beginnings of the Hebrew race, first in its founding through Abraham, then in its subsequent development and history through the great figures of Isaac, Jacob and Joseph. This great Hebrew nation was founded with a definite purpose that through it the whole world should be blessed. God promised Abraham, a believer in Him, that his descendants:

1. Should inherit the land of Canaan (Genesis 12:1-3).
2. Should become a great nation.
3. Through them all nations should be blessed.

God repeated these promises to Isaac and Jacob (Genesis 26:1-5; 28:13-15).

Seven Great Names and Messages are:

Bow with Abel at the cross of the slain lamb.

Catch step with Enoch and walk with God.

Believe God and launch out with Noah on God's waters.

Go forth with Abraham in faith.

Dig wells with Isaac and get down to divine resources.

Climb ladders with Jacob and see God.

Be true like Joseph and live with God.

Won't you make a book of Genesis (beginning) and of new love to your Lord in your own life?

Genesis answers the great questions of the soul, as:

1. The eternity of God.
2. Where did man come from?
3. Whence came sin?
4. How can sinful man get back to God? (Abel's sacrifice)
5. How can man please God? (Abraham's faith)
6. How can we have power with God and man? (Jacob's surrender)

There are three words which also might give us the outline of Genesis:

1. Generation—*In the beginning God* ... (Genesis 1:1)
2. Degeneration—*Now the serpent* ... (Genesis 3:1)
3. Regeneration—*Now the Lord* ... (Genesis 12:1)

Genesis is the record of human failure, first in an ideal environment (Eden), then under the rule of conscience (from the fall to the deluge), and finally under patriarchal rule (Noah to Joseph). In every case of human failure, however, God met man's need with marvelous promises of sovereign grace. It is therefore fitting that the Bible's first book should show us the failure of man under every condition met by the salvation of God.

Hints of the Messiah

Remember, Jesus Christ is the center of the Bible. He is somewhere on every page. In Genesis we see Him in type and prophecy in:

Seed of woman ....Genesis 3:15
Skins of slain beasts...Genesis 3:21
Abel's blood sacrifice necessary ....Genesis 4:4
The entrance into the ark of safety....................Genesis 7:1,7
The offering up of Isaac ....Genesis 22
Joseph lifted from pit to throne ......Genesis 37:28; 41:41-44

PATRIARCHAL PERIOD

The period of the patriarchs is the groundwork and basis of all history. It covers the time from Adam to Moses. In consequence of the failures on the part of men during this early period, God called out an individual. He put aside the race and called a man, Abraham, who was to become the father of the Hebrew nation. We enter into this period in Genesis 12.

There are five patriarchal fathers, Abraham, Isaac, Jacob, Joseph and Job, for the Book of Job must be put after the Book of Genesis and before the Book of Exodus. Job certainly lived before Moses and we read of Moses in Exodus 2.

God called out Abraham and made a covenant with him, known as the Abrahamic Covenant. Be familiar with this covenant (Genesis 12:1-3). If you are not, the whole study of the chosen people (in fact, the whole Old Testament) will have little meaning. God repeated that covenant to Abraham's son, Isaac, and again to his grandson, Jacob (Genesis 26:1-5; 28:13-15). He repeated it to no one else.

These three, therefore, are the Covenant Fathers, and that is why you read in Scripture *I am the God of thy fathers, the God of Abraham, and the God of Isaac, and the God of Jacob* (Acts 7:32). He never adds anyone else. God gave His covenant to these three and it is for them to communicate it to others. What is the covenant (Genesis 12:1-3; 26:1-5; 28:13-15)?

FROM FAMILY TO NATION

A very large proportion of the story of Genesis is devoted to Joseph (Genesis 37-48). Why? Because Joseph is the link between the family and the nation. Up to the time of Joseph it is a family, the family of Abraham, Isaac, and Jacob. Some seventy souls are found at the end of the Book of Genesis, constituting the family of Jacob. But still it is a family with which God is dealing. Read about this family and the blessings that Jacob gave to each of his sons in Genesis 49.

The moment we turn over the page and step into Exodus it is a nation, not a family. During the long period from the end of Genesis to the opening of Exodus this nation has developed. Joseph is the link between the family and the nation.

Joseph is a character presented without fault—not that he hadn't faults, but his faults are not recorded. He was a man of flesh and blood like ourselves. God honored him, for there are at least 130 parallels between the life of Joseph and the life of Jesus. He is therefore the messianic patriarch, the patriarch who reflected the Christ Himself.

WHO WROTE GENESIS?

The age-long Hebrew and Christian position is that Moses, guided by the Spirit of God, wrote Genesis. The book closes something like three hundred years before Moses was born. Moses could have received his information only by direct revelation from God or from historical records to which he had access, that had been handed down from his forefathers. (Amos 3:7) See what Jesus said about Moses (Luke 24:27; John 7:19).

Every year there are being dug up in Egypt and Palestine evidences of writing in Moses' day and of the historical truth of what is recorded in the Pentateuch. Moses was educated in the palace of Pharaoh and *was learned in all the wisdom of the Egyptians,* (Acts 7:22) which included the literary profession.

Moses did make use of writing (Exodus 34:27; Numbers 17:2; Deut. 6:9; 24:1,3; Josh. 8:32).

WHO WROTE THE CREATION STORY USED BY MOSES?

No doubt it was written long before, maybe by Abraham, or Noah, or Enoch. Who knows? Writing was in common use before the days of Abraham. In Ur, as in every important city in Babylon, there were libraries with thousands of books, dictionaries, grammars, reference works, encyclopedias, works on mathematics, astronomy, geography, religion and politics. No doubt Abraham had received traditions or records from Shem about the story of creation and the fall of man, and of the flood. Abraham lived in a society of culture, books and libraries. He no doubt made careful and accurate copies of all that happened to him and of the promises God had made to him. He put it down on clay tablets in the cuneiform writing to be handed down in the annals of the nation he was founding.

CREATION (Genesis 1; 2)

As the book begins we see these words untarnished by the ages, *In the beginning God created the heaven and the earth.* In these few simple words we have the Bible declaration of the origin of this material universe. God called all things into being by the word of His power. He spoke and worlds were framed. (Hebrews 11:3) Interpretations of the method of God may vary but the truth of the fact remains.

God's creative work was progressive:
1. The world of matter (Genesis 1:3-19)
2. The system of life (Genesis 1:20-25)
3. Man, the crown of creation (Genesis 1:26,27)

Who was the God mentioned so many times in the first thirty-one verses of Genesis? Read John 1:1 and Hebrews 1:1. Here we see that the One who redeemed us by His precious blood, our Saviour, was the Creator of this universe. Someone has said that God the Father is the architect; God the Son, the builder, and God the Holy Spirit, the beautifier of the universe. We find the Holy Spirit in Genesis 1:2.

In chapter one we have the account of creation in outline, in chapter two part of the same in detail. The detail concerns the creation of man, for the Bible is the history of the redemption of man.

Know this, God created man in His own image to have fellowship with Himself. Man cut himself off from God by sin. It is only when sin is removed that we can have fellowship again. This is why Jesus Christ came to this earth: that he might *bear our sins in his own body on the tree* (I Peter 2:24). Read in I John 1 how sin keeps us not only from fellowship with God but with one another. I John 1:9 tells us what we can do to have a restored fellowship.

THE FALL (Genesis 3; 4)

Adam and Eve were created in a state of innocence but with the power of choice. They were tested under the most favorable circumstances. They were endowed with clear minds and pure hearts, with the ability to do right. God gave them His own presence and fellowship (Genesis 3:8).

Satan, the author of sin, acting through a serpent, tempted them to doubt God's Word. They yielded to the temptation and failed in the test. Here sin entered the world. Satan still influences men to disobey God. The results of their sin are enumerated in Genesis 3. They were separated from God, the ground was cursed, and sorrow filled their hearts.

In mercy God promised One who would redeem men from sin (Genesis 3:15). The seed of the woman (the virgin-born Jesus) would come to destroy the works of the devil (I John 3:8).

Genesis 3:21 contains a picture in miniature of the whole plan of redemption for man through the shed blood of our Substitute. The "coats of skin" could not have been obtained except through the death of an innocent victim. The verse throws light on Hebrews 11:4. There is no covering for sin except by blood.

Immediately after "the fall" men began to offer sacrifices unto the Lord. No doubt these sacrifices were ordered of God. They were for the purpose of keeping before man the fact of his fall and of the coming Sacrifice. It would be by the shedding of this blood that he was to be redeemed from sin and death (Hebrews 9:22).

Two of the sons of Adam, Cain and Abel, brought their sacrifices unto the Lord. *Cain brought of the fruit of the ground.* Abel *brought of the firstlings of the flock.* Abel's offering was accepted while Cain's was rejected. From our knowledge of the Word it is quite evident that it was not accepted because it was not typical of the Sacrifice that was afterwards offered on Calvary. Cain became angry with his brother Abel and in his wrath killed him.

The first writing began when God put a "mark" or "sign" on Cain (Genesis 4:15). That mark stood for an idea and the people knew what it stood for. Thus "marks," "signs," "pictures," came to be used to record ideas, words, or combinations of words. These pictures were made on pottery or hard clay tablets, painted or engraved. This is the kind of writing found in the lowest levels of the pre-historic cities of Babylonia. The oldest known writings are pictures on clay tablets.

Long before God gave the law to Moses (Exodus 20), we find several very definite ordinances given in the Book of Genesis. At the very beginning God had instituted the Sabbath (Genesis 2:1-3) and marriage (Genesis 2:24).

The law of the tithe was evidently observed. Read Abraham's words in Genesis 14:20, and Jacob's words in Genesis 28:22. God has evidently made man realize from the very beginning that he was only a steward of all that he had.

THE FIRST CIVILIZATION

This civilization before the flood is called the antediluvian civilization. It perished in the judgment of the flood. It was the civilization started by Cain. It ended in destruction.

The Bible teaches and the archaeologist confirms that the people of the world before the flood were not mere savages. They had attained to a considerable degree of civilization. Everything in material civilization is touched on in Genesis 4:16-22. While not much is known about the antediluvians, yet some of their actual places of abode have been discovered and some relics of their handwork which have been uncovered give evidence of a civilization such as the Bible seems to describe.

In three cities, Ur, Kish, and Fara, the layer of silt left by the flood has been found by Professor Woolley, an archaeologist sent out by the British Museum and Pennsylvania University. Underneath the flood deposit in Ur layers of rubbish full of stone and flint instruments, colored pottery, seals and burnt brick, were found. The same is true of the other two cities.

Turn to Genesis 4:16-22 and see what is mentioned of their civilization in the Scriptures.

First, herdsmen. *And Adah bare Jabal: he was the father of such as dwell in tents, and of such as have cattle* (Genesis 4:20).

Second, musicians. *And his brother's name was Jubal: he was the father of all such as handle the harp and organ* (Genesis 4:21).

Third, artificers and manufacturers. *And Zillah, she also bare Tubal-cain, an instructor of every artificer in brass and iron* (Genesis 4:22).

Fourth, builders. *And Cain knew his wife; and she conceived, and bare Enoch: and he builded a city, and called the name of the city, after the name of his son, Enoch* (Genesis 4:17).

The civilization founded by Cain may have been equal to that of Greece or Rome, but God's judgment was upon it. Why? (Genesis 6:5-7).

THE FLOOD (Genesis 5–9)

The account of the flood in the Bible is very plain and straightforward. The story is not told because it is startling or interesting, but because it is an incident in the history of redemption which the Bible relates. Evil had grown rampant. It threatened to destroy everything that was good. Only one righteous man remained, Noah. God sent the flood to restore good upon the earth.

Adam and Eve had yielded to an outward temptation, but now men had yielded to temptation which was within. *And God saw that the wickedness of man was great in the earth, and that every imagination of the thoughts of his heart was only evil*

23

BIBLE LANDS

CASPIAN SEA

PERSIAN GULF

ARARAT?

RIVER TIGRIS

GARDEN OF EDEN?

RIVER EUPHRATES

ARABIA

ASIA MINOR

CANAAN

MEDITERRANEAN SEA

EGYPT

RED SEA

continually (Genesis 6:5). God was going to separate the righteous from the wicked. He was taking the first step toward a chosen nation.

After the fall God gave the world a new beginning but soon the wickedness of man increased until there remained but one righteous man, Noah.

God had been long-suffering in His patience with men. The Holy Spirit had striven with men. Noah had warned them for 120 years while he was building the ark. Even after Noah and his wife and his three sons and their wives, taking with them two of every unclean animal and fourteen of every clean animal, had entered into the ark of safety, there was a respite of seven days before the flood came, but God's mercies were refused and so men had to perish (Genesis 6; 7). Noah was saved from the flood by the ark (a perfect type of Christ, our Ark of safety). When he came out, the first thing he did was to erect an altar and worship God (Genesis 8:20).

Out of the fearful judgment of the earth by the flood, God saved eight persons. He gave the purified earth to these men with ample power to govern it (Genesis 9:1-6). He gave them control of every living thing on earth and sea. For the first time God gave man human government. Man was responsible to govern the world for God. The greatest responsibility God gave is the taking of a life for a life (Genesis 9:6). God established capital punishment for homicide. God has never changed this for world government. God never substituted life imprisonment. This was man's way out.

Sir Charles Marston, as a decipherer of ancient clues, outclasses all the great detectives of modern fiction. In his search for race-rebuilding material, he has unearthed thousands of witnesses in stone and pottery. The truth concerning the Scripture comes out whenever he wields spade or pen. Sir Charles, often called an "archaeologist with a purpose," serves to silence the critics of the Bible. Records of many persons that scientists have said never existed have been brought to light; many places that they said were only Bible names have been unearthed.

Marston tells us that the scene of the events recorded in the first chapters of the Book of Genesis appears to be laid around

25

the river Euphrates. The surrounding country is called Shinar, or Chaldea, or Mesopotamia. We have known it as Babylonia; today, it is called the kingdom of Iraq.

It is a land of sandy deserts through which the great Euphrates flows down to the Persian Gulf. But the deserts are studded with the ruins of ancient cities, and scored with the channels of old irrigation canals; the sand has submerged all.

Excavations have revealed the ruins of a vast civilization which existed in 5000 B.C. These evidences of an era, until lately almost forgotten, have been left by two great peoples— the Sumerians, and the Semites. The Semites take their name from Shem, the eldest son of Noah, and the Hebrew race, from which Abraham sprang, was a branch of this people.

Archaeological discovery in Mesopotamia bares evidence of the flood, both in the cuneiform writings and in the actual flood deposits. The cuneiform libraries seem to have given us ample accounts of, and references to, this catastrophe. A clay prism has also been found on which are inscribed the names of the ten kings who reigned before the flood.

Dr. Langdon's expedition found evidences of the flood at Kish near ancient Babylon.

Dr. Woolley's discoveries of the deposits were made while excavating Ur of the Chaldees, a good deal farther south, about half-way between Baghdad and the Persian Gulf. The excavations at Kish revealed two distinct flood strata, the one nineteen feet below the other.

Dr. Langdon associates the Ur deposits with the lower level of Kish. He reports that Babylonian and Assyrian scribes frequently refer to the age "before the flood." One king praises himself as one "who loved to read the writings of the age before the flood."

BABEL (Genesis 10; 11)

After the flood the world was given a new start. But instead of spreading out and repeopling the earth as God had commanded, they built the great tower of Babel in defiance of God. They thought they could establish a world-wide empire that would be independent of God. In judgment God sent a confusion of tongues and scattered them abroad.

The race was then divided into nations speaking different languages according to Noah's three sons, Shem, Ham and Japheth. Shem's sons settled in Arabia and to the east; Ham's sons settled in Africa; Japheth's sons settled in Europe.

The great Jewish historian, Josephus, declares that the tower of Babel was built because the people did not want to submit to God.

As we read the story in Genesis 11:1-9, the narrative seems to imply that the people were at cross purposes with God. As a result there was this confusion of tongues and dispersion abroad. A difference in language tends to separate people in more ways than one and to check progress in commerce, in arts and in civilization.

Man tried to glorify himself, but it is God's purpose that man shall only glorify Him. If you read Genesis 10 and 11, you will find the basis upon which the nations were divided according to the three sons of Noah—Shem, Ham and Japheth. You will also find the reason for the division.

The main body of Noah's descendants seems to have migrated from Armenia, where Noah's family left the ark, back toward the plain of Babylonia where they built the tower.

THE CALL OF ABRAHAM (Genesis 12–38)

In spite of the wickedness of the human heart, God wanted to show His grace. He wanted a chosen people:

1. To whom He might entrust the Holy Scriptures.
2. To be His witness to the other nations.
3. Through whom the promised Messiah could come.

He called a man named Abram to leave his home in idolatrous Ur of the Chaldees to go to an unknown land where God would make him the father of a mighty nation (Genesis 12:1-3; Hebrews 11:8-19). This begins the history of God's chosen people, Israel.

Wherever Abraham went, he erected an altar to God. God signally honored him by revealing Himself to him. He was called a "friend of God." God made a covenant with him that

27

EGYPT, CANAAN
SINAI PENINSULA

HITTITES

REHOB? •

MEDITERRANEAN SEA

DOTHAN •

SHECHEM •

CANAAN

RIVER JORDAN

JERICHO •

ASHDOD •
GAZA •

HEBRON •

ESHCOL •

GOSHEN

BEERSHEBA •

WILDERNESS
OF ZIN

EDOM

RAAMSES (RAMESES) •

SUCCOTH •
• PITHOM

• PI-HAHIROTH

AMALEKITES

KADESH-BARNEA •

MT.
SEIR

MT. HOR ?

MT.

WILDERNESS
OF PARAN

MIDIAN

RIVER NILE

MARAH? •

ELIM? •

WILDERNESS
OF SIN

EGYPT

REPHIDIM? •

MT. HOREB
(MT. SINAI)

RED SEA

28

he should be the father of a great nation and that through him the nations of the earth would be blessed (Genesis 12:1-3). His family became God's peculiar charge. God dealt with them as with no other people. The Jews are always spoken of as God's chosen people.

Through Isaac, Abraham's son, the promises of God were passed down to Jacob, who, despite his many faults, valued God's covenant blessing. He was enthusiastic about God's plan of founding a nation by which the whole world would be blessed. Jacob in his wanderings suffered for his sin, and through chastening came out a great man. His name was changed to Israel, a prince with God (Genesis 32:28). This is the name by which God's chosen people were called—Israelites. His twelve sons became the heads of the twelve tribes of Israel. Read Genesis 49.

DESCENT INTO EGYPT (Genesis 39–50)

Isaac and Rebecca made the mistake of playing favorites with their two sons. Isaac favored the hunter, Esau. Rebecca favored the quiet Jacob. Jacob did the same thing in the treatment of Joseph, which aroused jealousy in the other sons. Joseph is one of the outstanding noble characters of the Old Testament. It was through Joseph that Jacob's family was transplanted into Egypt. Joseph's life is one of the most perfect illustrations in the Bible of God's overruling providence. He was sold as a slave at seventeen. At thirty he became ruler in Egypt; ten years later his father, Jacob, entered Egypt.

After Isaac's death and after Joseph had been sold into Egypt, Jacob and his sons and their children, numbering seventy in all, went down into that land because of a famine. Here they were exalted by the Pharaoh that was reigning at that time. When he learned that they were shepherds, he permitted them to settle in the land of Goshen where they grew in number, wealth and influence under the "shepherd kings."

God knew that it was necessary that the Israelites leave Canaan until they had developed national strength so that they would take possession of the land of Canaan. God wanted to safeguard them against mingling and intermarrying with the idolatrous races then in the land.

Read Jacob's dying words to his twelve sons (Genesis 49). We see here again the promise of Shiloh who is to be the coming ruler. Remember, Christ is called *the Lion of the tribe of Judah* (Revelation 5:5).

The Book of Genesis ends in failure. The last words are *in a coffin in Egypt*. Only death marks the pathway of sin; *the wages of sin is death* (Romans 6:23). The people needed a Saviour!

There are eight names mentioned in Genesis that we should remember in order: God, Adam, Satan, Noah, Abraham, Isaac, Jacob, Joseph.

There are six places of supreme importance in connection with the history of Genesis—Eden, Mount Ararat, Babel, Ur of the Chaldees, Canaan (promised land), Egypt.

MASTER THE CONTENTS OF EACH BOOK

On the following pages you will find a bit of rhyme which will give you a clue to the contents of each book of the Bible.

OLD TESTAMENT

Pentateuch

In Genesis the world was made,
  In Exodus the march was told;
Leviticus contains the law,
  In Numbers are the tribes enrolled;
In Deuteronomy again
  We're urged to keep God's law alone.
And these five books of Moses make
  The oldest writings that are known.

Historical Books

Brave Joshua to Canaan leads,
  In Judges oft the Jews rebel;
We read of David's name in Ruth,
  And First and Second Samuel;
In First and Second Kings we read
  How bad the Hebrew state became;

In First and Second Chronicles,
    Another history of the same.
In Ezra captive Jews return,
    While Nehemiah builds the wall;
Queen Esther saves her race from death.
    These books "Historical" we call.

Poetical Books

In Job we read of patient faith,
    In Psalms are David's songs of praise;
The Proverbs are to make us wise;
    Ecclesiastes next portrays
How vain fleeting earthly pleasures are;
    The Song of Solomon is all
About the love of Christ, and these
    Five books "Poetical" we call.

Prophetical Books

Isaiah tells of Christ to come,
    While Jeremiah tells of woe,
And in his Lamentations mourns
    The Holy City's overthrow.
Ezekiel speaks of mysteries,
    While Daniel foretells kings of old;
Hosea calls men to repent;
    In Joel, judgments are foretold.
Amos tells of wrath, and Edom
    Obadiah is sent to warn,
While Jonah shows how Christ should rise,
    And Micah where He should be born;
In Nahum, Nineveh is seen,
    In Habakkuk, Chaldea's guilt;
Zephaniah, Judah's sins,
    Haggai, the temple's built.
Zechariah tells of Christ,
    And Malachi, of John, his signs.
The Prophets number seventeen,
    And all the books are thirty-nine.

NEW TESTAMENT

Matthew, Mark, Luke and John
 Tell of Christ, His life they trace;
Acts shows the Holy Spirit's work;
 And Romans how we're saved by grace.
Corinthians instructs the church,
 Galatians shows God's grace alone;
Ephesians, how we are "in Christ,"
 Philippians, Christ's joys made known.
Colossians portrays Christ exalted.
 And Thessalonians tells the end.
In Timothy and Titus both,
 Are rules for pastors to attend.
Philemon pictures charity,
 And Hebrews clearly shows how all
.The Jewish law prefigured Christ;
 Fourteen Epistles, penned by Paul.
James shows that faith by works must live,
 And Peter urges steadfastness,
While John exhorts to Christian love;
 And those who live it, God will bless.
Jude shows the end of evil men,
 While Revelation tells of heaven.
These end the whole New Testament,
 In all, they number twenty-seven.

Minimum Daily Requirements/Spiritual Vitamins

 Sunday: CREATION   Genesis 1:1-5; 26–31; 2:7-22
 Monday: FALL   Genesis 3:1-24
 Tuesday: DELUGE   Gen. 6:1-7; 7:7-24; 8:6-11;
   18–22; 9:1-16
 Wednesday: BEGINNING OF LANGUAGES
   Genesis 11:1-9
 Thursday: THE ABRAHAMIC CALL AND COVENANT
   Gen. 12:1-9; 13:14-18; 15:1-21;
   17:4-8; 22:15-20; 26:1-5; 28:10-15
 Friday: STORY OF JOSEPH   Genesis 37:1-36; 42
 Saturday: JACOB'S FINAL BLESSING   Genesis 49

CHAPTER 3

UNDERSTANDING EXODUS

Exodus
Portrays Jesus Christ,
Our Passover Lamb

Exodus follows Genesis in much the same relation as the New Testament stands to the Old Testament. Genesis tells of man's failure under every test and in every condition; Exodus is the thrilling epic of God hastening to the rescue of man. It tells of the redeeming work of a sovereign God.

Exodus is pre-eminently the book of redemption in the Old Testament. It begins in darkness and gloom, yet ends in glory; it commences by telling how God came down in grace to deliver an enslaved people, and ends by declaring how God came down in glory to dwell in the midst of a redeemed people.

Exodus, which is Greek, means "way out." Without Genesis the Book of Exodus has no meaning. It begins with the word "Now" which really means "And." The story is just continuing. This book, like many other books of the Old Testament, begins with the word "And." This seems to point to the fact that each author was not just recording his own story but only his part of a great drama which began in the events of the past and looked forward to that which would come. Take the five books of Moses—Genesis, Exodus, Leviticus, Numbers, Deuteronomy. Each book is about something and those five things are vitally related to one another.

SOME THINGS TO REMEMBER IN EXODUS

1. The Great Hero, Moses

The book gives us the story of Moses, the great hero of God. Moody said that Moses spent

40 years thinking he was somebody

40 years learning he was nobody

40 years discovering what God can do with a nobody.

See Hebrews 11:23-29.

2. The Law

The last half of the book (19–40) teaches us that the redeemed must do the will of their Redeemer, consecrating themselves to His service, and submitting to His control. Therefore, the moral law is given, followed by the ceremonial law which was provision for the violator of the moral law.

3. The Tabernacle

God gave the tabernacle as a detailed picture of the Redeemer to come, in His many offices, and as a dwelling place for His visible glory on earth. Its wonderful typology is rich in Christian truth.

THE BONDAGE (Exodus 1:1-22)

As this book opens—three and a half centuries have passed since the closing scene of Genesis. The Book of Genesis is a family history. The Book of Exodus is a national history. We have no account of what happened during this long period of silence. The patriarch, Abraham, died when Jacob, his grandson, was fifteen years old. Jacob's favorite son Joseph had been sold as a slave into Egypt and had risen to great power and influence. The sons of Jacob had gained great favor because of their brother Joseph. There were only seventy persons that went down into Egypt, but before they left Egypt the people had grown into a nation of 3,000,000.

When Joseph died and a new dynasty came to the throne in Egypt, the wealth and great numbers of the children of Israel made them objects of suspicion in the eyes of the Egyptians. The Pharaohs, wishing to break with them, reduced them to a slavery of the worst sort. This was hard for a people who had lived as free men with every favor upon them. They remembered the promises God had given to Abraham and his descendants, and it made this bondage doubly hard to understand (Genesis 12:1-3, etc.).

The story told in the books of Exodus, Leviticus, Numbers and Deuteronomy shows that God did not forget the promise which He made to Abraham—*I will make of thee a great nation* (Genesis 12:2).

34

The family records of Abraham, Isaac and Jacob no doubt had been carried into Egypt, and there became a part of Israel's national annals. Through the long years of bondage, they clung to the promise that one day Canaan would be their home.

We will see God coming down to deliver the people from Egypt (Exodus 3:7,8). Now the individuals and families had been organized into a nation. God was going to give them laws with which to govern themselves. He was going to take them back to the land which He promised them.

THE EXODUS (Exodus 3–4)

Think of the preparation that had to be made for moving so great a host, *six hundred thousand on foot that were men, beside children. And a mixed multitude went up also with them; and flocks, and herds, even very much cattle* (Exodus 12:37,38).

No doubt it was a well-organized expedition. Moses had appealed to Pharaoh again and again to let the children of Israel go (Exodus 5:1; 7:16). The plagues and the negotiations that Moses had to make with Pharaoh must have lasted for nearly a year. This gave the children of Israel time to gather their things together. The plagues taught the children of Israel some great things, besides forcing Pharaoh to let the children of Israel go.

In the construction of any great edifice a blueprint has to be drawn and a pattern made. Our salvation was designed by God before the foundation of the world (Ephesians 1:4). We find the pattern in the Book of Exodus. Exodus is the historical picture of divine grace in the redemption of man by God to Himself by Jesus Christ, who is at once our great Apostle (Moses) and High Priest (Aaron) (Hebrews 3:1).

The story of Exodus is repeated in every soul that seeks deliverance from the enmeshing and enervating influence of the world. From this point of view, the book is human, from the first verse to the last. The things that happened were by way of figure, and they were written for our admonition. We study Exodus in order to see God's way of delivering sinful man, and His gracious purposes in thus rescuing him.

THE PASSOVER (Exodus 12–19)

Exodus 12 gives us the thrilling story of the Passover, the clearest Old Testament picture of our individual salvation through faith in the shed blood of our Lord Jesus Christ. In this chapter is the basis for calling Christ the *Lamb of God, Christ our Passover,* and the many tender references to His crucifixion as the death of our own Passover Lamb.

For even Christ our passover is sacrificed for us (I Corinthians 5:7).

As the Passover chapter is the heart of the book, so is the whole book a pattern of our salvation.

The Passover is the prominent feature of Exodus. (chapter 12) Perhaps the children of Israel did not know the significance of this feast the night before they left Egypt, but they believed God and obeyed.

God had sent ten plagues on Egypt in order to make Pharaoh willing to let His people go. Almost a year had passed and with each plague there was a hardening of Pharaoh's heart. Finally God said that the first-born in all Egypt should die. It would have fallen on the Hebrews, too, had they not killed the paschal lamb and been protected by its blood of redemption (Exodus 12:12,13).

Every person should study the divine order of the Passover as it is given in Exodus 12.

1. Take a lamb

Hebrews 9:28; Isaiah 53:6; John 19:14; I Cor. 5:7.

Not the spotlessness of the living lamb saved them (Hebrews 9:22; I John 1:7; Revelation 1:5). It was not Christ's sinless life that saves us but His death on the cross.

2. Sprinkle the blood

It is not enough for the lamb to be slain. The blood was sufficient but not efficient unless applied.

Every Israelite individually had to apply it to his own household. Notice over the doorway, not under. What have you done with the blood, the blood of our Passover Lamb who died on Calvary? (Exodus 12:22; John 1:12).

The hyssop—a common weed but obtainable by everyone—typical of faith. The blood on the lintel is that which saved. Not what they thought about it, but what they did with it counted. *When I see the blood, I will pass over you* (Exodus 12:13).

Not blood in the basin but blood applied saves a soul. Not all the blood shed on Calvary's cross can save a soul from death unless it is applied, then—*When I see the blood, I will pass over you.*

Not feelings—not personal worthiness, but one thing saved them—*the blood* (Hebrews 9:22).

3. Eat the lamb

After the blood was shed and sprinkled, then there was direction for nourishment, etc. So with us. Salvation first, then feeding—fellowship, worship, walk and service.

Feeding did not save them, but blood first; then nourishment was possible (John 6:54-58). *My flesh is meat indeed.*

4. Remove the leaven

Search me . . . and see if there be any wicked way in me (Psalm 139:23,24). Leaven is always a type of sin. *Leaven of the Pharisees* (Matthew 16:6). *Purge out therefore the old leaven* (I Corinthians 5:7).

Leaven of unrighteousness must be removed from our lives if we are to eat with God.

5. Bitter herbs

Christ tasted the bitter cup for us and some bitterness, we, too, must suffer. *No chastening for the present seemeth to be joyous* (Hebrews 12:11).

The lamb was to be feasted upon not raw, not unbaked, but a suffering lamb who passed through fire. Nothing was to be left —eaten in haste and nothing remaining. Not a bone broken! Christ's body was broken but not His bones (Psalm 34:20; John 19:36).

6. Be ready to leave

They ate the food standing—not knowing whither they would go. All provision was made for the journey. What a contrast that night!—peaceful feasting in the houses of Israel; awful mourning in the houses of Egypt!

We have read here of the Passover. Now comes the Passage. The Passover sealed them. The Passage of the Red Sea steeled them. They left Egypt under the blood, marked men. They passed through the Red Sea directed, determined men. God led them out and shut the door behind them!

When I came forth out of Egypt (Exodus 13:8). When did you come out? (Remember, Egypt is a type of the world.)

THE GIVING OF THE LAW (Exodus 20–24)

In Exodus 20–24 we see the law given, broken and restored. Up to this time in Israel's history all has been grace and mercy. God had heard the cry of their bondage and answered them. God selected a leader and trained him. God defeated their enemies. God fed them and yet they rebelled. Now a new order of things is brought about at Sinai.

The law demands nothing short of perfection. The Psalmist says, *The law of the Lord is perfect.* (See Psalm 19:7-11.) Only one Man since it was given has been able to keep it perfectly. Christ not only kept the law but He paid the complete penalty for the broken law. Christ suffered that we might be spared. (See Hebrews 9:13-15; 10:1-22; I Peter 1:18-20.)

If man could not keep the law, why was it given? That we might know our exceeding sinfulness. The law did not make man sin, but it showed him that he was a sinner. The physician comes and looks at a child and the symptoms reveal that he has measles. He gives him some medicine that makes him break out. The doctor did not make the child have measles, but he proved that measles was there. (Read Galatians 4:4,5; Romans 8:1-4; 3:19-28.)

The law is God's mirror to show us our exceeding sinfulness. *Wherefore the law is holy, and the commandment holy, and just, and good* (Romans 7:12)

There are two mountain peaks which stand over against each other in God's Word.

1. Mount Sinai with all of its horror thundered forth the law. (Read Exodus 19.)

2. Opposite this God places Calvary. Calvary took away all the fire and thunder and made possible a meeting place between God and the sinner.

We each have a choice as to how we shall approach God, either by law or by blood (Heb. 12:18-29).

There was no provision made in the law for failure. It is all or nothing—the whole law or a broken thing. One hole in a bowl, one crack in a pitcher, unfits it for its purpose. One flaw in a character mars the perfection God requires under the law.

Laws may be divided into two parts:

1. Laws regarding man's attitude toward God.

2. Laws regarding man's attitude toward his fellow men.

We are told that God gave all these words (Exodus 20:1). God gave the whole testimony and man assumed the whole responsibility of keeping it. Read what he says in Exodus 19:8. Why did Israel accept the law rather than cry for mercy? Human pride always makes us think that we can please God by ourselves. Before Israel even received the law or started to keep it, they were dancing around the golden calf, and worshiping a god they had made (Exodus 32:1-10,18).

THE BUILDING OF THE TABERNACLE (Exodus 25–40)

Exodus 25–40 gives us one of the richest veins in inspiration's exhaustless mines. We must use our imagination and reason as we enter the holy precincts and gaze upon the significant furniture. God told Moses He wished a sanctuary or holy dwelling place which should point to Christ and tell of His person and work.

The Outer Court

Herein we see the brazen altar on which the burnt offerings were sacrificed. Remember, Christ is our sin-offering (Exodus 27:1-8).

The laver was there for the cleansing of the priests before they could enter into the holy place to render their service. (Exodus 30:18)

The Holy Place

Herein was the golden candlestick (Exodus 25:31-40), typifying Christ, the Light of the world, and the table of shewbread (Exodus 25:23-30), for Christ is the Bread of life, and the golden altar of incense (Exodus 30:1-10), symbolizing Christ's intercession for us.

Holy of Holies

Now if we draw back the beautiful veil (which typifies the body of Christ), we will see the Ark of the Covenant, the symbol of God's presence. Into this holy of holies, the high priest came only once a year to sprinkle the blood of atonement. The Book of Hebrews tells us that Christ is not only our High Priest but that he was our atonement, and so we can go into the holy of holies (the presence of God) at any time with boldness.

The Tabernacle Itself

The tabernacle, with the cloud of glory over it, taught the people that God was dwelling in their midst (Exodus 25:8).

The tabernacle was the common center and rallying point which could be moved from time to time. Critics say that the account of the tabernacle and its wonderful structure could not be true. They say that the times were too primitive, but research has given abundant evidence of great skill in such matters long before the Exodus. Fine linen was used in many ways. Fine work in gold has been discovered in the tombs dating back to as early as the twelfth dynasty, and Moses lived in the eighteenth dynasty.

DON'T FORGET

Redemption was not an afterthought with God. Ephesians 1:4.

The Law was broken in the people's hearts before it was broken by Moses' hand.

Over against Sinai is Calvary!

God's mirror reveals but never cleanses.

The blood of the Lamb makes us safe; our trust in God's Word makes us sure.

God's plan will never be frustrated.

Minimum Daily Requirements/Spiritual Vitamins

Sunday: BONDAGE   Exodus 1:1-22
Monday: THE CALL OF MOSES   Exodus 3–4
Tuesday: THE PLAGUES   Exodus 7:20–11:10
Wednesday: THE PASSOVER   Exodus 12:1-51
Thursday: THE LAW   Exodus 20:1-26
Friday: THE WORSHIP   Exodus 25:1-9;
        28:1-14,30-43
Saturday: MOSES' COMMISSION RENEWED
        Exodus 33:12–34:17

CHAPTER 4

UNDERSTANDING
LEVITICUS

*Leviticus
Portrays Jesus Christ,
Our Sacrifice
for Sin*

"Get right," say the offerings; there are five of them: burnt offering, meal offering, peace offering, sin offering, trespass offering.

"Keep right," say the feasts; there are eight of them: Sabbath, Passover, Pentecost, Trumpets, Atonement, Tabernacles, the Sabbath year, and Jubilee.

Leviticus is called the Book of Atonement (Leviticus 16:30-34).

God says, *Be ye holy as I am holy.* (See Leviticus 11:44,45; 19:2; 20:7,26.)

A PICTURE BOOK

The Book of Leviticus is God's picture-book for the children of Israel to help them in their religious training. Every picture pointed forward to the work of Jesus Christ.

The title of Leviticus suggests the subject matter of the book —the Levites and the priests and their service in the tabernacle. It is also called the Book of Laws.

We remember how God had given Moses, in the Book of Exodus, the exact instructions as to how to build the tabernacle and about the institution of the priesthood to carry on the service in this holy place.

You notice Leviticus begins with "And." As this book opens the children of Israel are still at Mount Sinai. God is continuing to give His instructions for orderly worship in the tabernacle.

In Genesis we see man ruined.

In Exodus, man redeemed.

In Leviticus, man worshiping.

This book is a timely book for it insists on keeping the body holy as well as the soul. It teaches that the redeemed ones must be holy because their Redeemer is holy. It gives us not only the key for our spiritual life and its holy walk, but it surprises us with real lessons in hygiene and sanitation for the care of the body. The Jews are wonderful evidence of the result of this latter in their long and vigorous lives.

It is a divine book. The opening verse affords us the clue to the whole, *The Lord called unto Moses, and spake unto him out of the tabernacle of the congregation.* Leviticus is God speaking to us through the tabernacle and its meaning.

It is a personal book. The second verse intimates this, *if any man of you bring an offering unto the Lord.* Notice, He expects each person to bring his own gift. The way is often as important as the gift. Have you an offering for the Lord? Then this book will appeal to you.

THE FIVE OFFERINGS

One of the most important questions in life is "How may an unholy people approach an holy God?"

At the very beginning of the book we see God making provision for His people to approach Him in worship. This book shows redeemed Israel that the way to God is by sacrifice and the walk with God by separation.

Isn't it strange that deep down in every heart there is a sense of guilt and the feeling of a need of doing something to secure pardon or gain the favor of the one wronged? The pagan brings his sacrifice to the altar of his gods, for he realizes that he cannot do anything about his sin himself. He must make an atonement for it. The mothers of India used to throw their babies into the Ganges to appease their gods. The British government put a stop to this.

The pagan cannot see beyond his sacrifice. When we look at the sacrifices in this book, we find that they are only a type. They point to the Perfect Sacrifice for sin, which was to be made on Calvary.

All the sacrifices in this book point to *the Lamb of God, which taketh away the sin of the world* (John 1:29).

Sin may be forgiven, but it must receive its penalty. *The*

wages of sin is death (Romans 6:23). Sin keeps us from drawing near to God. He is too pure to behold evil.

There can be no fellowship between God and the sinner until sin has been dealt with; the only way is sacrifice. *Without shedding of blood is no remission* (Hebrews 9:22).

There are five offerings described in Leviticus. God wants us to understand the awful reality of sin, so He asks for a sacrifice each day.

Here is a list of the offerings, with a key-word to identify them. Learn this simple outline to fix in mind the first six chapters of Leviticus.

Burnt Offering..........."Surrender" of Christ for the world (Lev. 1).

Meal Offering..........."Service" of Christ in life (Lev. 2).

Peace Offering..........."Serenity" of Christ in life (Lev. 3).

Sin Offering.............."Substitute" of Christ for sin (Lev. 4–5:13).

Trespass Offering.."Satisfaction" by Christ for demands of God (Lev. 5:14-6:7).

THE BURNT OFFERING (Leviticus 1)

The offerings start with the burnt offering and end with the trespass offering.

The burnt offering is a type of Christ offering Himself without spot to God. There were daily burnt offerings. Christ offered Himself in the sinner's stead (Leviticus 1:4).

This was an offering of dedication. Why first? Because sacrifice comes first. No one begins with God until he has yielded all to God. (See Leviticus 1:3.) This was the most common sacrifice in the ancient temple.

Dedication is man's part.

Consecration is God's part.

We dedicate ourselves to God.

He consecrates us—to His service.

"Consecrate me now to Thy service Lord,
By the power of grace divine;
Let my soul look up with a steadfast hope,
And my will be lost in Thine."

We sing, "Take my life and let it be consecrated, Lord, to Thee." (This is a burnt offering.)

MEAL OFFERING (Leviticus 2)

This is the sacrifice of daily devotion.

As the burnt offering typifies Christ in death, so the meal offering typifies Christ in life.

The fine flour speaks of the character of Christ—His perfection in thought, in word, in action.

Let us feed on the perfect meal offering.

We must come to Him first with our whole burnt offering. Then we keep coming with our continual meal offering. It is our very best, our gift of life. Notice, the slain offering must come first. Abel brought it. Cain did not.

PEACE OFFERING (Leviticus 3)

Christ is our peace. (See Ephesians 2:14.) He hath *made peace through the blood of his cross* (Colossians 1:20).

This offering represents fellowship and communion with God. It is an offering of thanksgiving.

SIN OFFERING (Leviticus 4; 5)

This shows us Christ on the cross in the sinner's stead.

In this offering we see an acknowledgement of sin, *If a soul shall sin . . . let him bring* (Lev. 4:2,3). This offering is for expiation. In the other offerings the offerer comes as a worshiper, but here as a convicted sinner. God holds us accountable for our sin. We are like criminals who have been tried, found guilty, and sentenced to death.

Though placed last, the sin and trespass offerings are included in all that goes before. The only reason burnt offerings, meal offerings or peace offerings can be made is that the blood of pardon has been shed. God has accepted the one offering of His Son, which every lesser offering typified.

The heathen brings a sacrifice to his god; the Christian accepts the sacrifice from his God.

TRESPASS OFFERING (Leviticus 5:14–6:7)

Christ has even taken care of our sin against others.

The blood of the trespass offering cleanses the conscience, and sends the trespasser back to the one he has wronged, not only with the principal but with the fifth part added (Lev. 6:5).

The injurer is forgiven and the injured becomes an actual gainer.

It is a grave error to suppose that you are safe and right if you live up to your own conscience. God has scales. We can never comprehend His holiness.

None of these sacrifices forgave sin. They only pointed forward to the true Sacrifice, God's very own Son (Hebrews 10).

You will notice that bullocks, oxen, goats, sheep, turtle doves and pigeons were mentioned for sacrifice. The offering was determined by the ability of the one who brought it.

What we bring is our sin; what Christ brings is the offering and the atonement for sin.

THE PRIEST (Leviticus 8–10)

We have been studying the great subject of sacrifice, but no man could bring his own sacrifice to God. He must bring it to the priest and he in turn would offer it to God.

God chose one tribe out of the twelve to care for the tabernacle. This was the tribe of Levi. One family of Levites, Aaron's, should be the priests. The priests had charge of the sacrifices and were supported by the tithes of the people.

The priest went from man to God with the prayers and praises of the people. He stood for them and pleaded their cause.

The burdened Israelite who desired to approach God brought his animal to the court of the tabernacle. At the altar of burnt offerings he laid his hand on the animal's head to express his penitence and consecration. The animal was killed and its blood sprinkled on the altar.

The priest representing the worshiper then came to the laver, in which he washed his hands, thus indicating the clean life that should follow the forgiveness of sins. He entered the holy place, passed by the sacred furnishings, the candlestick, the table of shewbread, and came to the altar of incenses, where prayer was offered.

THE HIGH PRIEST

One day in the year the high priest passed beyond the veil

that separated the holy and the most holy place and stood before the mercy seat, with the blood of the atonement, to intercede for the people.

The priest could not consecrate himself. Moses acted for God in this service. Each priest presented his body a living sacrifice for service just as Paul wants us to do in Romans 12:1,2.

The priests had charge of the sacrifices. The Levites were their assistants. They took care of the tabernacle, formed choirs, were guides and instructors in the temple.

Notice the opening of Leviticus 10. At the very beginning of the history of the work of the priesthood, there were evidences of failure. Nadab and Abihu, two sons of Aaron, offered strange fire before the Lord *which he commanded them not,* and they were swiftly slain by fire.

We read in Leviticus 10:3 that Aaron held his peace. He was their father, but he dared not question God. We talk too much before God. We must learn to walk softly in the divine presence. The other priests were solemnly charged to show no signs of mourning and to abide at their posts.

The priests were the ministers of the sacrifices that we have just been studying. Each was a picture of the great sacrifice of Christ for the sin of the world.

OUR GREAT HIGH PRIEST

Animal sacrifices are no longer necessary because all sacrifices were fulfilled in Christ. Therefore priests are no longer necessary. Christ Himself is the great High Priest for man (Hebrews 2:17; 4:15). He is the only Mediator between God and man. There is no one who can put himself between God and man. We are all kings and priests (I Peter 2:5).

Christ is our High Priest and He is at the right hand of the Father today making intercession for us. We approach God by Him and Him alone. (See Hebrews 10:12; 7:25; John 14:6.)

When we see Christ as Sacrifice, we see beauty and completeness.

When we see Christ as Priest, we see His divine perfection *touched with the feeling of our infirmities* (Hebrews 4:15).

As Sacrifice He establishes the relationship of His people with God.

As Priest He maintains that position.

We read of this perfect and eternal priesthood in the Book of Hebrews. Heaven, not earth, is the sphere of Christ's priestly ministry. He never appeared in the temple on earth to offer sacrifice. He went there to preach and teach but not to sacrifice. Except in the sense that all believers are priests (I Peter 2:5), there is no such thing as a priest on earth. The believer is a spiritual priest. It is not necessary that any child of God go before any man on earth to obtain entrance into the presence of God. Every Christian has the right to enter because he knows Jesus Christ. The Lord said, *I am the way* (John 14:6). *Let us therefore come boldly unto the throne of grace, that we may obtain mercy, and find grace to help in time of need* (Hebrews 4:16).

The God-appointed priests belonged to the tribe of Levi.

THE EIGHT FEASTS

As the first part of the book has to do with offerings and the offerers, so the last part of the book deals with feasts and feasters.

Five great festivals are mentioned in Leviticus 23.

The sacrifices spoke of the blood that saved.

The feasts spoke of the food that sustains.

Both are of God.

The sacrifices correspond to the cup of the Lord's Supper that reminds us of Christ's death on the cross whereby we are redeemed. The bread of the Communion witnesses to his life of which we are partakers.

THE FEAST OF THE SABBATH (Leviticus 23:1-3)

The Sabbath was given the foremost place. It was a perpetually recurring feast to be obeyed through the whole year on every seventh day. It was a day of worship and rest, celebrating the finished work of God in creation (Genesis 2:2,3). Christians celebrate the first day of the week or the day our Lord arose from the grave (Luke 24:1; Acts 20:7; I Cor. 16:2). Thus we celebrate the finished work of redemption.

THE FEAST OF THE PASSOVER (Leviticus 23:4,5)

The Passover spoke of redemption and was celebrated every spring at our Easter time. It was the Fourth of July for the children of Israel. They did not celebrate it by fireworks and parades but by a great service of worship to God. Every Jew who could, made his way to Jerusalem.

It lasted one day, but the feast of unleavened bread which immediately followed lasted seven days. With these the year commenced.

The Jews were still celebrating this feast when our Lord was on this earth. Read in the Word the times that He went to the Passover feast (Luke 2:41-52; Matt. 26:19; John 13). The Jews today celebrate this same feast. They are still looking for their Messiah.

THE FEAST OF PENTECOST (Leviticus 23:15-22)

This feast was observed fifty days after the feast of the first fruits. This feast of the first fruits typified Christ's resurrection and ours (I Cor. 15:20). It was fifty days after Christ's resurrection that the Holy Spirit descended upon the disciples and the Church was born. Pentecost was the birthday of the Church. The death and resurrection of Christ had to be accomplished before the descent of the Holy Spirit.

THE FEAST OF THE TRUMPETS (Leviticus 23:23-25)

This was the New Year's day of the children of Israel. It was celebrated in the fall about October. This feast points forward to the future gathering of the dispersed people of Israel (Zechariah 14).

THE DAY OF ATONEMENT (Leviticus 23:26-32)

This was the greatest day in the history of God's chosen people. On this day the sins of the nation were confessed. Confession is always the first step toward righteousness. It reveals a right attitude toward sin. It leads to a desire for forgiveness. God says, *If we confess our sins, he is faithful and just to forgive us our sins, and to cleanse us from all unrighteousness* (I John 1:9).

On this day Jehovah's relationship to His people was established—all the sins, failures and weaknesses of the people were atoned for. The blood was shed and the sins of the people were covered so that God could take up His abode in the midst of His people in spite of their uncleanness.

We learn in Leviticus 16 that God was hidden behind a veil in the tabernacle and man was at a distance. Read Leviticus 16:2. The way was not yet made open for man to approach God. Now we *have boldness and access* (Eph. 3:12). We can run into God's presence at any time for Christ has made the way possible for us. In the Book of Leviticus, God was shut in from man and man was shut out from God.

This was the only day in the year when the high priest was permitted to enter the holy of holies. He went in with an offering for the atonement of the sin of the people. Atonement means "cover." This offering "covered" the sins of the people until the great sacrifice on Calvary was made. None of these offerings "took away" those sins.

THE FEAST OF TABERNACLES (Leviticus 23:33-36)

This was the last feast of the year. It commemorated the time when the children of Israel lived in tents during their wilderness journey. It was celebrated in the fall of the year and lasted an entire week. The people lived in booths out-of-doors and heard the reading of the Law.

The Feast of the Passover and the Feast of Tabernacles kept before the children of Israel the marvelous way in which they were delivered from Egypt and were sustained in the wilderness. God did not want them to forget the way in which the gods of Egypt were utterly discredited and the great nation of Egypt humbled.

The Feast of Tabernacles recalled to their mind that by their own disobedience they were compelled to wander forty years in the wilderness, but in spite of their unbelief God was faithful in caring for them and in bringing them to their inheritance. These days reminded them of their dependence upon Jehovah and the blessings that would come if they would be obedient to His will.

THE SABBATIC YEAR (Leviticus 25)

This was the year of meditation and devotion. It was a year-long Sabbath. The purpose and character of the Sabbath was magnified. God impressed it upon the minds of the people, keeping them from any kind of labor for the extent of a year. This He did every seven years.

God wanted to impress upon them that the very land was holy unto Him. This is why Palestine is called the Holy Land. There was quiet over the whole land during these days. All breathed the spirit of rest and meditation. All industry ceased. Every day was like the Sabbath, and the minds of the people were kept on the things of the Lord. The Law was read. There were no debts to worry or mar the spirit of the people during this holy year. This time exerted a tremendous influence upon the lives of the people.

THE YEAR OF JUBILEE (Leviticus 25:8-24)

This was celebrated every fiftieth year. It was inaugurated on the Day of Atonement with the blowing of trumpets. As in the sabbatic year the land was not cultivated. All slaves of Hebrew blood were freed. The blowing of the trumpets that ushered in the year released every bondman. Jewish writers tell us that the year of jubilee was observed at the time of the fall of Judah in 586 B.C. References are made to this in Isaiah 5:7-10; 61:1,2; Ezekiel 7:12,13; 46:16-18.

Another outstanding event was the restoration to the original owner of all land that had in any way been taken away. That is, it was returned to the family to whom it had been assigned in the original distribution. What a wise provision it was from an economic standpoint. But God no doubt had a more far-reaching plan bearing upon the coming of the Messiah. Every tribal and family register must be carefully kept so that the rights of all would be protected. This would apply to Judah, the tribe from which the Messiah was to come. From these registers our Lord's natural descent could be exactly traced.

This book is for a redeemed people, showing how God is to be approached and worshiped. The Book of Exodus is the book of redemption, but the Book of Leviticus tells how the re-deemed ones can worship God.

Only through the blood of Christ can we have access to God.

God demands a holiness which Christ alone can give, for "He is our Holiness."

In Genesis we see man ruined.

In Exodus, man redeemed.

In Leviticus, man worshiping.

SEVENS IN LEVITICUS

Every seventh day was the Sabbath. Every seventh year was a sabbatic year.

Every seven times seven years was followed by a year of Jubilee.

Pentecost was seven weeks after the Passover.

In the seventh month were the feasts of trumpets, tabernacles and atonement.

Pentecost lasted seven days. Passover lasted seven days.

This book, like Revelation, is built around a series of seven.

Minimum Daily Requirements/Spiritual Vitamins

Sunday: BURNT OFFERING   Leviticus 1

Monday: THE PRIESTS   Leviticus 8

Tuesday: PURE FOOD LAWS   Leviticus 11

Wednesday: THE DAY OF ATONEMENT
Leviticus 16

Thursday: THE FEASTS OF JEHOVAH   Leviticus 23

Friday: GOD'S PLEDGE   Leviticus 26

Saturday: DEDICATION   Leviticus 27

CHAPTER 5
UNDERSTANDING NUMBERS

*Numbers
Portrays Jesus Christ,
Our "Lifted-up One"*

The children of Israel were saved to serve. So is every child of God today.

Beware of unbelief! The apostle Paul says to us, *Ye did run well; who did hinder you* (Galatians 5:7)? Unbelief hinders blessing. God tells why we cannot enter into his blessings (Hebrews 3:19).

This book might be called the Wilderness Wandering from Sinai to the border of Canaan, the land of promise, covering about forty years.

Numbers is also called the Book of the March and the Roll Call (Numbers 33:1,2).

It might, too, be called the Book of Murmurings because from beginning to end it is filled with the spirit of rebellion against God. Read what God says about this in Psalm 95:10.

Numbers is indeed the book of the wilderness, recording the pitiable failure of Israel at Kadesh-barnea, and the consequent wanderings and experiences of the people in the wilderness. It records the pilgrimage, warfare, service, and failure of the second generation of the nation after the Exodus from Egypt. This, however, is not all the message of Numbers. The first ten chapters give us the divine legislation; chapters eleven to twenty tell the story of the nation's failure; but the closing chapters of the book record Israel's return to Jehovah's favor and final victory, even in the wilderness.

While the annals of many powerful nations of that same time are lost to the world, these of a comparative handful of people are preserved. The reason for this is because the Messiah who would redeem the world was to come from this people. This is the reason God was so patient with them. He wanted to preserve them for Himself. In I Corinthians 10, we learn that the things which happened to them were "examples" unto us. In other words their whole history was an "object lesson" to us, illustrating God's dealing with us today.

The key thought is discipline. Numbers is the fourth book of Moses. Someone has said that the order of the books is as follows:

1. In Genesis we see man ruined.
2. In Exodus, man redeemed.
3. In Leviticus, man worshiping.
4. In Numbers, man serving.

This is the order the Lord lays down. Only a saved man can serve and worship God. Remember, we are saved to serve. We are not saved by good works but we are saved *unto good works* (Ephesians 2:10). The law can bring us to the land of promise but only our divine Joshua (Christ) can bring us in. Paul says that the law is the schoolmaster to bring us to Christ (Galatians 3:24). The law cannot save us, for we are saved *not of works, lest any man should boast* (Ephesians 2:9).

Leviticus deals with the believer's worship.

Numbers deals with the believer's walk.

In Leviticus we see the believer's privileges.

In Numbers the wilderness is the drill field.

If you know five names, you will master the story of the Book of Numbers.

Moses, the great leader.

Aaron, the high priest, Moses' brother.

Miriam, who was Moses' and Aaron's sister.

Joshua and Caleb, the two spies who dared to believe God, the only men of their generation who lived to enter Canaan.

The geography of the book takes us:

1. From Sinai to Kadesh
2. From Kadesh around back to Kadesh
3. From Kadesh straight to Canaan
   (Follow this on your map)

GOD'S SCHOOL

The children of Israel learned

1. That they must trust God and not man in the day of crisis

(Psalm 37:5). Read Numbers 13:26–14:25.

2. That God would supply all their need according to His riches (Philippians 4:19).

He gave them food. Numbers 11:6-9

He gave them meat. Numbers 11:31-33

He gave them water. Numbers 20:8

He gave them leaders. Numbers 1:1,3

He gave them a promised land. Numbers 14:7,8

3. That they must worship God according to His instructions.

It was God's plan that the children of Israel should go straight into the land that He had promised them, the land of Canaan, but the people would not. God said that all those at Kadesh over twenty years old, except Joshua and Caleb, would have to die. A new generation arose during the forty years of wandering, but at the end the nation was about as strong in numbers as the day they left Egypt. (Read Numbers 26.)

PREPARATION FOR THE JOURNEY (Numbers 1–12)

As the book opens we see the children of Israel in the wilderness of Sinai. The Law had been given, the tabernacle had been built, and the priests had been assigned to their service. Now God was going to prepare the nation for its work. The teachings of this book are very applicable to the Christian life.

Order is heaven's first law. We see God numbering and arranging the tribes (chapters 1 and 2), choosing and assigning duties to the priests and Levites, (chapters 3 and 4). God is the author of order.

The thought of God numbering His people and gathering them about Himself is most precious to our hearts. He dwelt in the camp. The twelve tribes guarded the tabernacle of the Lord. The Levites encamped directly around the court, and Moses and Aaron and the priests guarded the entrance whereby God was approached.

The circumference of the camp arranged in this way and facing the tabernacle is supposed to have been twelve miles. What an imposing sight the camp must have been to the outward eye, in the midst of the desert, with God stretching over them in a cloud by day and fire by night (Numbers 9:15-23).

He was their night lamp and their day shade. Their shoes did not wear out nor their garments wax old. Think of 600,000 men, twenty years old and upward, and about 3,000,000 men, women and children in this great camp! But the most glorious thing was that God was in the midst.

In the first chapter, Moses is commanded to take a census. The Lord knows all by name that are His (II Tim. 2:19; Phil. 4:3). Even the hairs of our head are numbered. How wonderful to know that God cares for each of His children!

For Christians, too, there is a census, for Christ numbers His jewels and knows them who are His. *A book of remembrance was written before him* (Malachi 3:16).

In this chapter we find the declaration of their pedigree. Can you trace your genealogy to the risen Lord? Are you sure of your pedigree? (John 1:12).

GOD WAS THERE

Here were about 3,000,000 people on a sterile desert, not a blade of grass, not a drop of water, no visible means of support. How were they to be fed? God was there! How were they to trace their way through a howling wilderness where there was no path? God was there!

God's presence provides everything! What? Are all these 3,000,000 to be fed on air? Who has charge of the commissary? Where is the baggage? Who is to attend to the clothing? etc. God was there! In faith's arithmetic God is the only figure that counts.

No one had gone before to blaze a trail for the children of Israel. There was not a footprint, not a landmark. It is much like our life as a Christian today. We are passing through a trackless desert—a moral wilderness. There is no trail. We would not know where to walk except for one little sentence from the lips of the Lord, *I am the way* (John 14:6). He will guide us step by step. There is no uncertainty, for He said, *He that followeth me shall not walk in darkness* (John 8:12).

God gave His children a cloud to guide them by day and a pillar of fire by night. It is interesting to see how they were guided a step at a time. They did not know when they were to go and when to stop, but the Ark of the Covenant (signifying God's presence) went on before, the pillar of cloud always leading (Numbers 10:33).

Sin crept into this well-ordered camp life. The people began to murmur against God. God sent judgment of fire (Numbers 11:1-3). Then they complained about their food (11:4). It seemed monotonous. They longed for the garlic and onions of Egypt and they wanted fish. As a result of their complaining, God sent them quails for thirty days. They made gluttons of themselves *and while the flesh was yet between their teeth, ere it was chewed, the wrath of the Lord was kindled against the people, and the Lord smote the people with a very great plague* (Numbers 11:33). Many became ill and died.

Then we read of the sin of Aaron, the high priest, and Miriam, the sister of Moses. God had chosen Moses to be the leader of this great people and Aaron and Miriam were only his assistants. Jealousy crept into their hearts. They wanted more honor. Read of Miriam's terrible punishment. She was smitten with leprosy for seven days (Numbers 12:1-16).

We find the invitation of God's marching host to the people round about them, *Come thou with us, and we will do thee good: for the Lord hath spoken good concerning Israel* (Numbers 10:29). Can we say this, do we say it, to those about us?

The ark of the covenant is the Word of God in the midst.

The sound of the silver trumpet is the witness of a faithful prophet.

The pillar of fire and of cloud is the comfort and guidance of the Holy Spirit.

The tabernacle and its ordinances make the worship of the sanctuary.

Christ "the Apostle and High Priest" of our profession gives significance to it all.

We are just humans making many mistakes and capable of wandering far. God has given us these heavenly attendants and guides. Who does not need them? Who can make progress without them? Invite others to join our band and go with us. We should always be taking someone by the hand and inviting him to go with us.

WILDERNESS WANDERINGS (Numbers 13–20)

After one year at Mount Sinai the Israelites journeyed to Kadesh. This is at the southern border of the promised land. Afraid to enter they turned back and wandered in the wilderness to the south and east till all that generation died. They did not travel all the time but remained in some places with their flocks and herds grazing on the surrounding hills. When the cloud lifted, they marched. They finally approached Canaan from the east of the Dead Sea.

Think of the lost years from Kadesh back to Kadesh because men would not believe God. After two years in the wilderness, the children of Israel could have gone into the land of promise immediately had it not been for the sin of unbelief. They listened to the discouraging words of most of the spies.

When the spies came back and told them about the giants in the land and the high walled cities, their hearts failed them. They would not listen to Joshua and Caleb who agreed with all that was told, but added, *Let us go up at once, and possess it; for we are well able to overcome it* (Numbers 13:30). But the people would not trust God. They said, *Let us return into Egypt* (Numbers 14:4).

When they refused to enter Canaan, the door was closed to them. It meant wandering in the wilderness for forty years. God said that He would not allow any of those who were over twenty years old to enter Canaan, except Joshua and Caleb.

At the beginning, the journey from Sinai to Kadesh was a swift and jubilant one! Then came sad doubt and delay. Hesitant Israel was plunged down into the wasting years of wilderness wanderings. Sadly Moses reminded them of it, *And the space in which we came from Kadesh-barnea, until we were come over the brook Zered, was thirty and eight years; until all the generation of the men of war were wasted out from among the host* (Deut. 2:14).

Eleven days from the land of promise! But they turned back. They could have made eleven days of progress, but they chose forty years of wandering.

60

God opens doors and no man closes, and He closes doors and no man opens (Isa. 22:22; Rev. 3:8).

God opened the door and about three million souls walked out of Egypt; He closed the door when the Egyptians tried to follow.

God took the children of Israel out of Egypt so that He could take them into Canaan, the land of promise. God did not want the children of Israel just to come out of Egypt. He wanted to have them come in to the promised land. This they could have done in comparatively a few days; not more than two or three weeks. You remember the spies made the trip and returned within forty days. As we have already seen, their fear disqualified them to take over the land of promise.

Oftentimes it is our fear that keeps us from enjoying all that God wants to give us. We fear what others will say. We fear what might happen if we put our trust completely in Christ.

One of the reports of the spies was that there were giants in the land and that the Israelites were as grasshoppers in their sight (Numbers 13:33).

This record tells the story of many a Christian life and in part the story of every life. Giants of selfishness and greed, far outranking the Anakims, oppose our advance! But when the returns are all in, the fact remains that there is One with us stronger than they!

Like the ten, we can be pessimists; or like the two, optimists. Like the ten, we can put difficulties between us and God and say we are not able, or like the two, we can put God between the difficulties and ourselves and say we are able!

We start out with high hope in the enthusiasm of our first love. Yonder lies the land of possibilities and achievement. Then the giants appear—giants of opposition from without; giants of fear from within. Our faith fails. We forget God. We compare our difficulties with our own strength rather than committing them to the great arm of God. Then we turn back into the wilderness of half trust, half victory and whole despair.

Numbers 33 is the pitiful log book of this journey, *And they departed from Hazeroth, and pitched in Rithmah. And they departed from Rithmah, and pitched at Rimmon-parez. And they departed from Rimmon-parez, and pitched in Libnah,* etc., to the end of this dismal chapter! Going, going, pitching, and departing but never arriving anywhere. An endless circle of aimless wandering with no success. When we doubt God we find this to be our experience, too. We feel defeated and discouraged. We wander around but never accomplish anything. It is like a swinging door—lots of motion but getting no place.

Before this scene ends we find Israel murmuring again, this time because of the shortage of water. They complained bitterly to Moses and Aaron and said they wished they had never been brought out of Egypt. The land was dry and parched and there was no water to drink. Moses and Aaron again went to God. He told Moses to take his rod and speak to the rock before the people, and the rock would give forth water.

Moses' patience was at an end. The people had complained about everything. In a fit of anger he called the people rebels and instead of speaking to the rock he struck it. The water gushed out. Even though Moses disobeyed, God was faithful and kept His promise. That stream may still be flowing. In this district the Turkish army put a pipeline and got their water during World War I. Kadesh-barnea is a beautiful oasis. Ruins of the ancient city of Kadesh are to be found here today.

Is it not sad that even children of God fail under testing? Moses' error was great, yet it showed him to be just like us. Moses put himself up as God—*Hear now, ye rebels; must we fetch you water out of this rock* (Numbers 20:10)? This dishonored Jehovah God. Because Moses smote the rock a second time (see first time, Exodus 17:5,6) instead of speaking to it, he was not permitted to enter the promised land. Christ, like the rock, was to be smitten once for our sins (I Cor. 10:4). He need not be smitten again.

There are three ways of knowing men, a rabbi in the Talmud says:

> In their cups
> With their cash
> In their wrath

How true it is that ill-behavior at the table discloses bad

culture; ill-conduct in business reveals the unscrupulous; ill-speaking in wrath proclaims the ignoble.

AARON'S ROD THAT BUDDED

One of the important things that we have not covered is this incident in Numbers 17.

Aaron's priesthood had been questioned so God Himself was to confirm it. The head of each tribe laid up a dead rod. God put life into Aaron's. So we find that all the authors of the religions of the world have died—even Christ died—but only Christ was raised from the dead and exalted to be our High Priest (Hebrews 4:14; 5:4-10).

ON TO CANAAN (Numbers 21–36)

As this scene opens we discover that all the Israelites who left Egypt had died except Moses, Aaron, Joshua, Caleb, Miriam, and the children who were under twenty years of age when the spies entered the land. Why was this?

Finally, while they were yet in Kadesh, Miriam, Moses' sister, and Aaron, his brother, now over 100 years old, died.

Israel was to move on again. They started from Kadesh-barnea, this time with faces set resolutely toward the land of promise. The way was difficult, much harder than before, but faith had been renewed, discipline had done its work, and the arm of God went forth conquering and to conquer.

GOD'S SECOND BEST

Learn here the lesson of God's second best. He offers the perfect way and we refuse it. It is gone forever. Every male over twenty years of age who refused to go into the land of promise the first time (except Joshua and Caleb who believed God) died in the wilderness. Not one of them entered the land.

But God is kind, and He sets before us another way, a second best; it may even be a third, for His mercy is wonderful. He forgives us seventy times seven. He brings us through, provides for us, never failing in His grace, but, oh, how much we miss and how many burdens we have to bear by not taking the first and the best. How costly this is!

Israel was complaining again, although over and over again

God had proven to them that His way is best. Discontent and murmuring seem to have been ingrained habits of the children of Israel. Grumbling is the easiest thing in the world to learn. "No talent, no self-denial, no brains, no character is required to set up the grumbling business," are the words written in a large business office.

What's the use of grumbling? It never makes a heavy burden light. It never subtracts from ills. Instead it always adds to them.

They battled with the Canaanites and became discouraged. Then they grumbled because they had to march around the land of Edom instead of through it. They growled again against God and against Moses because they loathed the manna (Numbers 21:5). They never were content.

This time God sent fiery serpents among the people, which caused suffering and death. After they confessed their sin, Moses prayed for the deliverance of his people. God did not take away the serpents but told Moses to make a brass serpent and fasten it to a pole so that all could see it. As soon as they looked, they would live. (See Numbers 21:6-9.)

The Bible reveals that the whole human family has felt the serpent's sting of sin which means death. The only way man can live is by looking to the One who took upon Himself the likeness of men and was lifted up on the cross to take the sting of death upon Himself. If we look on Him, our Saviour, we shall live (John 3:14,15).

Minimum Daily Requirements/Spiritual Vitamins

Sunday: THE GUIDING CLOUD   Numbers 9:15-23
Monday: THE REPORT OF THE SPIES
        Numbers 13:16-33
Tuesday: ISRAEL'S UNBELIEF   Numbers 14:1-45
Wednesday: WATER FROM THE ROCK
        Numbers 20:1-13
Thursday: THE BRAZEN SERPENT   Numbers 21:1-9
Friday: BALAAM'S BEAST   Numbers 22:1-41
Saturday: THE CITIES OF REFUGE
        Numbers 35:6-34

CHAPTER 6

UNDERSTANDING
DEUTERONOMY

*Deuteronomy
Portrays Jesus Christ,
Our True Prophet*

"Observe to do" is the word of Moses to the people. He wanted them to be *doers of the word, and not hearers only* (James 1:22).

This book shows the blessings of obedience and the curse of disobedience.

Everything depends on obedience—life itself, possession of the promised land, victory over foes, prosperity and happiness. We find this book teaching the inflexibility of the law. "Thou shalt" and "thou shalt not" occur over and over again—"a blessing if ye obey" and "a curse if ye will not obey."

The Book of Deuteronomy is a collection of the orations and songs of Moses which he gave as his farewell to the children of Israel. These noble orations were given as he stood on the great divide between his earthly and heavenly life. He was looking from Pisgah's top over a century of the past crammed full of epoch-creating events. Then he turned his gaze upon the future of the people he was about to leave.

The book contains a most interesting and instructive summary of the wilderness history of Israel, and, in the last chapter we find an account of Moses himself. Carefully compare Moses' review of the events with the account itself given in Exodus and Numbers. It will be found that Deuteronomy gives the divine rather than the human view. Compare Deuteronomy 1 with Numbers 13; 14.

Deuteronomy is a Book of Remembrance. The name Deuteronomy means "second law" which indicates that the law is repeated. This Moses did to remind the people what God had done for them and what they were to do to serve Him when they reached the promised land. It omits the things that relate to the priests and Levites and includes the things that the people should know.

This book is the last of the five books of Moses. You often hear these five books called the Pentateuch, meaning five books.

Genesis tells of the beginnings of the chosen nation Israel.

Exodus relates the organization of the people into a nation and the giving of the law.

Leviticus tells the way this people were to worship God.

Numbers gives a story of the wanderings of this people.

Deuteronomy relates the final preparation for entering the promised land.

Deuteronomy covers only about two months, including the thirty days of mourning for Moses.

Moses delivered his counsels probably within a period of seven days and about a month before the passage of Jordan (Deut. 1:1-3).

Moses was the writer but not the author of the Pentateuch. See chapter two. Over five hundred times in these first five books we find expressions like these, *The Lord spake, . . . God said etc.* Who is the divine Author of the Bible? (II Peter 1:21).

THE SAVIOUR'S FAVORITE BOOK

The Christian heart always quickens its beat when it comes to Deuteronomy, for this book was a favorite with our Saviour. From this book He quoted in His conflict with the adversary. These passages were His weapons with which He repelled the tempter: Matt. 4:1-11; Luke 4:1-13; and Deut. 8:3; 6:16; 6:13; and 10:20. Thus this Book of Deuteronomy, God's book on obedience, Moses' last charge to his people, seems to have about it the peculiar blessing and protection of Christ Himself.

You will come to appreciate the full force and magnetic beauty of Deuteronomy only as you read its pages. Read it through in a single sitting.

Nothing in literature matches the majesty of its eloquence; nothing in the Old Testament has any more powerful appeal for the spiritual life. No book in all the Word of God pictures better the life which is lived according to God's will, and the blessings showered upon the soul who comes into the richness and fullness of spiritual living along the rugged pathway of simple obedience.

Jesus often quoted from Deuteronomy. In fact, it is almost invariably from this book that He quotes. He took Deuteronomy as His code of conduct (Luke 4:4,8,12). He answered the devil in the hour of temptation from its writings. These were His weapons with which He repelled the tempter (Matt. 4:4,7,10; also Deut. 8:3; 6:16; 10-20).

Why do men pick flaws in the Bible and leave Homer, Virgil, Horace, and others alone? The Bible reveals men and their wicked hearts. Man does not want to be told that he is a sinner.

If you want a taste of heaven on earth become familiar with Deuteronomy. Catch step with Moses and march ahead by way of the Honey Land. (Canaan, *a land flowing with milk and honey* Exodus 3:8.)

"Brethren," a man once said, "when I get to the gates of heaven, if they shut me out, I'll say, 'Anyhow, I had a good time getting here.' "

Are you having a good time on your way to heaven? God *hath blessed us with all spiritual blessings in heavenly places in Christ* but we must appropriate and possess them by faith (Ephesians 1:3).

MOSES' FIRST ADDRESS — "LOOKING BACK"
(Deuteronomy 1–4)

As the book opens we see the children of Israel on the border of the land of Canaan, in a place where eleven days' journey, some forty years ago, could have brought them. Yet it had taken them forty years. How slowly they covered the ground! What windings and turnings! How often we have to go over the same ground again and again. We marvel at Israel's slowness. We can rather marvel at our own! We, like they, are kept back by unbelief. We should be ashamed at the time it takes us to learn our lessons! God is such a faithful teacher. He never lets us pass on to another grade until we are ready.

How deplorable is unbelief! God never fails us when we put

our trust in Him, but He cannot do many mighty works because of our unbelief (Matthew 13:58).

Several hundred years before, God had promised to Abraham and his seed a rich and wondrous land upon whose borders they were standing (Genesis 17:8). Now they were ready to enter in after all the years of anticipation and hope. The closing chapters of Numbers found them camped by the Jordan, waiting to go over into the goodly land itself.

As we shall see, God is putting the conditions of their entering and holding the land before the children of Israel in Deuteronomy. We see all these conditions summed up in one great word: Obedience.

The children of Israel entered the promised land under the conditions of the law.

The Book of Deuteronomy is one long plea for hearty obedience to God based on two grand motives of love and fear. *And now, Israel, what doth the Lord thy God require of thee, but to fear the Lord thy God, to walk in all his ways, and to love him, and to serve the Lord thy God with all thy heart and with all thy soul* (Deut. 10:12).

In the first four books of the Pentateuch God is choosing Israel. Now He is letting Israel choose Him.

THE PEOPLE

Only Caleb and Joshua were left from that generation that had come out of Egypt. All the others had died. The younger men who now lived had suffered hardships in the wilderness wanderings and were ready and anxious for conquest! But Moses must rehearse the law to them. He knows his work is finished, for God has told him another will lead them into Canaan (Numbers 20:12).

Moses, the grand old man, was now one hundred and twenty years old. We see him giving his farewell address to the people whom he had led these past forty years. He stood erect and spoke with a clear tone, for it is said that *his eye was not dim, nor his natural force abated* (Deut. 34:7).

Moses gives the children of Israel a look back. He recalls the history of Israel and reviews their wanderings. He reminds them of God's faithfulness and urges them to be grateful and obedient. He likens God's care of them to a loving father who cherishes his little ones, lest they should be lost in the wilderness, or be injured by the heat of the sun. He supplied all their needs; they lacked nothing (Deut. 2:7).

He spoke to his beloved people in the most earnest and eloquent way and appealed to them to serve and obey God. His words still echo down the corridors of time!

Moses' work was done, He had spent the last forty years of his life in delivering his people from the bondage of Egypt, in guiding them through the many dangers that confronted them. He trained them, gave them forms of government, laws, religious institutions and molded them into a nation.

The children of Israel were now at the end of their journey, in the plain east of the Jordan, overlooking the land they had come so far to possess. It lay before them in the glories of the springtime. But the impassable Jordan river rolled between, and walled cities rose up in seemingly impregnable strength. The Israelites were like young men leaving school or college, and about to enter upon their life's work.

MOSES' SECOND ADDRESS — "LOOKING UP"
(Deuteronomy 5–26)

In Deuteronomy 12:1 we see the key to this section. *These are the statutes and judgments, which ye shall observe to do in the land.* Israel was going into a new land and everything would depend on their constant and intelligent obedience to God who was giving them the land. God wanted to teach Israel the love which is the real fulfilling of the law (Romans 13:8-10; Matthew 22:37-40).

Moses now sets forth the law simply and clearly so that it would take a living hold of the people. God says, "You are My people; I love you. I have chosen you; I am in the midst of you. I will protect you. I am only asking you to obey Me for your good." He says *Be ye holy; for I am holy.* Since God's people are His, He wants them to walk in the world in the way that befits them, separating themselves from evil (chapter 14). They should show charity toward their fellows (chapter 15).

69

They must gather together to worship (chapter 16). See Hebrews 10:25.

Today people are careless about church-going and worship. This speaks of spiritual decay. God demands discipline. (See Deut. 17.)

In Deuteronomy 18, God tells us of the great Prophet, the Lord Jesus Christ. He alone knows the future. In this day, many are turning to enchanters, soothsayers, fortune-tellers, mediums, consulters with familiar spirits and the black art of sorcery of every description. Spiritualism is rampant today! If you want to know what God thinks about the modern seance look up Isaiah 8:19,20; Lev. 19:31; 20:6; and study the dark story in I Samuel 28 in the light of I Chronicles 10:13.

God showed the Israelites that their highest duty was to exhibit the spirit of loving obedience. They were to be thankful, yes, really thankful. They were to be full of joy and gladness. Why shouldn't they be joyful in the best land on earth, and with such a God as Jehovah? Surely they ought to be glad and love their God with all their heart.

But Moses' heart was burdened because he knew that Israel had a hard heart and the people were selfwilled (Deut. 31:24-29). How many children in these days of ours (see their description by Paul in II Timothy 3:1-9), should die, under the solemn command of Deuteronomy 21:18-21?

Note this! A disobedient child who is rebellious toward his parents is an abomination in God's sight.

If we read Deuteronomy 21:22,23 and compare it with John 19:31, we see why Christ was *accursed* as He hung between heaven and earth on the cross. In Galatians 3:10-13 we read that He is cursed because He was bearing our sin (II Cor. 5:21). What effect did this have upon Paul? (II Cor. 5:14,15).

MOSES' THIRD ADDRESS — "LOOKING OUT"
(Deuteronomy 27–33)

We see Moses giving the people some solemn warnings. He first spoke of the blessings that the children of Israel could enjoy if they would be obedient. He then told them the results of disobedience. Misfortune would follow them in everything they would undertake—in business, in farming, and in health. They would suffer for their disobedience to God (Chapter 28:15 to end of chapter).

Deuteronomy 28 is a most remarkable chapter. It traces what Israel might have been through obedience (1-14) and is yet to be in the millennial age to come. (See Isaiah 60–62; Zech. 14:8-21; Jer. 31:1-9; Deut. 30:1-10; Rom. 11:25-31.)

Verses 47-49 tell of the Roman invasion, A.D. 70, under Titus. This was indeed a bloody page of history!

Verses 63-67 describe the Jew today. God spoke this more than 3000 years ago. Chapter 28 leaves Israel where that nation is today—"scattered." (Verse 64)

1. "Scattered"—He shall be scattered from one end of the earth to the other. Today the Jew is everywhere—there are German Jews, Russian Jews, Italian Jews, American Jews, etc.
2. "Restless"—No rest for the Jew in these countries (Verse 65).
3. "Sorrowful"—The Jew today has a trembling heart and sorrow fills him. Think of the way he has been treated in many countries! (Verses 65-67). God foretold all this of him!

Moses spoke to Joshua, his personal attendant through the wilderness. He was one of the spies who dared to believe God. He was now 80 years old and Moses committed to him the leadership of this great people! Read his words in Deuteronomy 31:7,8.

The charge that Moses gave to the people and to Joshua was built on one great fact, "The Lord is with you; be strong." If God is present, fear is baseless!

This grand old man, one hundred and twenty years of age, stood a witness to the grace of God. He sang a song for Israel (Chapter 32). Moses had celebrated the deliverance of Israel from Egypt with a song (Exodus 15), and now he closed his life's work with another. He wrote a third which we know as the ninetieth Psalm. Christians have always had a song! And in heaven throughout the ages everyone will sing!

MOSES' FUNERAL

After the song and final words of blessing, Moses went up to Nebo's heights and there God showed him the promised land toward which his face had so long been set. Moses died there and God buried His servant in the valley and was there to comfort him. God buries the workman but carries on the work.

Whether Moses himself wrote Deuteronomy 34 by revelation or whether Joshua added it later is immaterial. Moses climbed Mt. Pisgah, saw the promised land and never came back. We know he died there and the Lord buried him. No one knows where. Someone said, "God buried his burial."

The horde of slaves made into a nation by Moses wept for him thirty days. Had it not been for their perversity they might still have had him with them.

Why do you think Moses' grave was hidden? No doubt it would have become the object of superstitious idolatry.

We read of Moses again in the Gospels. One day Jesus took Peter, James and John and climbed up Mt. Hermon in the northern part of Palestine. Then Moses and Elijah appeared and talked with Jesus about His coming death (Matthew 17:1-3).

Minimum Daily Requirements/Spiritual Vitamins

Sunday: FORWARD MARCH   Deut. 1:6-46
Monday: INSTRUCTIONS   Deut. 5:1-33; 6:4-18
Tuesday: THE MESSIAH, PROPHET   Deut. 18:15-22
Wednesday: GOD'S COVENANT   Deut. 30:1-20
Thursday: THE SONG OF MOSES   Deut. 32:1-44
Friday: GOD'S BLESSINGS   Deut. 33:1-29
Saturday: THE DEATH OF MOSES   Deut. 34:1-12

UNDERSTANDING JOSHUA

*Joshua
Portrays Jesus Christ,
Captain of
Our Salvation*

Possess the land, which the Lord your God giveth you to possess it (Joshua 1:11). It is God's to give! It is ours to possess!

When we open the Book of Joshua, we are beginning the second division of the Old Testament, the books of History. No book has more encouragement and wisdom for the soldier of the cross than this Book of Joshua. It is full of spiritual truth.

Joshua is the Book of Conquest or the Battlefield of the Canaan Heritage. This book relates the settlement of the children of Israel in Canaan, proving God's faithfulness in keeping His promise with Abraham. What was that promise? (Genesis 12:1-3).

This book bears the name of Joshua, the hero of this great conquest. The name Joshua was originally Hoshea, meaning salvation, or Jehoshua, God's salvation. Joshua is called the servant of Jehovah, one by whom God issued His orders, and by whom He accomplished His purposes—God's prime minister.

For all you know, God may have set His heart to appoint you a captain of His army, or to make you a standard bearer in the legion of His cross. Are you getting ready?

This book goes on where Deuteronomy leaves off. It is a continuation of the history of the chosen people.

The chosen people were led out of bondage by Moses, and led into the promised land by Joshua. In this book, Israel not only overcomes the enemy but occupies the land which God promised them.

MOSES—ANTICIPATION

**Moses passed through the Red Sea.
Moses led Israel from bondage.
Moses gave a vision of faith.**

Moses told of an inheritance.
We see anticipation in Deuteronomy.

Joshua completes what Moses began! God never leaves His work unfinished. Remember the great Craftsman always has another tool sharpened and ready for use. Service awaits everyone. You can always honor God best by taking up your task with a strong and resolute heart that trusts God.

The nation that was led out by Moses was led in by Joshua!

Moses was dead, but the march must continue! God's voice was still speaking to Joshua. Yes, God's voice is still speaking today and if we listen we will hear Him speak to us.

The apostle Paul is dead, but the cross he preached abides. Men may perish, but the true Leader, though invisible, is on the field and will never fail!

"Moses is dead!" Then the march must be halted! Without the leader the followers were left forlorn. There was gloom in the camp. Joshua was appalled by the magnitude of his task. To go forward under such conditions would mean failure.

JOSHUA—REALIZATION

Joshua passed over Jordan.
Joshua led Israel into blessing.
Joshua led them into a life of faith.
Joshua led them into possession.
We see realization in Joshua.

When great hearts fail, faint hearts will flee! The poor Israelites were ready to turn back into the desert and dig their graves among the sand dunes where the bones of their fathers were buried. They could not invade this land filled with giants and take their walled cities. The conquest of the land was impossible!

Who talks like that? Not God! A million men may die! No man is indispensable to the God of heaven. The greatest that ever lived is only a servant and when he completes his task, God has another to follow in his train.

To destroy slavery was the great motive that nerved Livingstone to his heroic life in Africa. For thirty years he toiled, pushing his way through the jungles, over 30,000 miles, to give

Christ to the black people and to discover the source of the Nile. He thought that this would give him greater weight when he would plead at home for the cause of the African slave. But others discovered the source of the Nile; others freed the slaves. He died alone with God in the wild African forests. But his heroic Christian death touched the hearts of his countrymen as not even his life had done, and Christian Britain determined to finish his work and free the African slave.

So it is in all our work in the world, especially in our Christian service. We are just a part in a mighty whole. Do your little part and do not care if it is not singled out in the completed whole. The waters of the brook are lost in the river.

God had been getting Joshua ready for years. He was born in slavery in Egypt but God led him out and made him a co-laborer of Moses. He was always a valiant captain. He was the one that was almost stoned to death because he urged the children of Israel to advance into Canaan forty years before (Numbers 14:6-10).

Tomorrow some great judge or merchant or statesman will die. The young person who is ready for the place will find the mantle falling on his shoulders. Success is readiness for opportunity!

Remember as we study this Book of Joshua that: God gives —man takes. This book deals with overcoming the enemy and occupying the land. God says, "Take it all."

This book seems to fall into two great parts. If you can only remember this much of an outline, you will remember the most important things:

A. Conquest of the promised land. Chapters 1-12.

B. Occupation of the promised land. Chapters 13-24.

MOBILIZATION OF THE ARMY (Joshua 1; 2)

Open your Bible to the text, Joshua 1; 2. We find the children of Israel right on the border of the land of promise, near the banks of the Jordan. (Boundaries of the promised land, as given in Joshua 1:4. Wilderness on the south, Lebanon mountains on the north, Euphrates River on the east, Mediterranean on the west.)

75

Joshua is the leader of the children of Israel now! Moses is dead! Joshua stands with bowed head and a lonely heart, for his wise counselor and friend has gone. But God said to him, *I will not fail thee, nor forsake thee. Be strong and of a good courage; be not afraid, neither be thou dismayed: for the LORD thy God is with thee whithersoever thou goest* (Joshua 1:5,9). We hear God say, *Moses my servant is dead; now therefore arise, go over this Jordan* (Joshua 1:2).

Moses must die before the children of Israel could go into Canaan. Moses could not even enter Canaan himself, to say nothing of bringing anyone else in. Israel had to wait until Moses was out of the way. To the Christian, Moses represents the law. Joshua represents Christ. Christ alone can lead us into the inheritance that is ours. Paul says, *Not of works, lest any man should boast* (Ephesians 2:9). Oh, that all Christians would simply lean on their faithful Joshua and follow Him only! Christ wants to lead us into what He has purchased on the cross for us. It takes Moses and Joshua together to present to us typically the finished work of Christ.

We see an anxious crowd of people all waiting to enter the land they had so long been promised. Can you picture the row on row of tents and all the people wondering when Joshua would say, "Go." Joshua sent men through the camp to tell them that in three days they would cross the Jordan, and to be prepared for the journey (Joshua 1:10,11).

God called Joshua to lead the children of Israel into the promised land. We have the words which must have come to him in answer to a prayer for help in his great undertaking. *I will be with thee: I will not fail thee, nor forsake thee* (Joshua 1:5). These words are just as true for us.

GOD SAYS SOME VERY IMPORTANT THINGS HERE

1. **Set your foot down.**

   Every place that the sole of your foot shall tread upon, that have I given unto you, as I said unto Moses (Joshua 1:3).

2. **Take it all.**

   From the wilderness and this Lebanon even unto the great

river, the river Euphrates, all the land of the Hittites, and unto the great sea toward the going down of the sun, shall be your coast (Joshua 1:4).

Not until Solomon's day, some five hundred years later, was this fully realized (II Chron. 9:26), but it was coming all the time. Queen Victoria was made Empress of India long before her royal grandson actually occupied all its borders.

3. Be on the move.

Moses My servant is dead; now therefore arise, go over this Jordan (Joshua 1:2).

4. Take the sword.

This book of the law shall not depart out of thy mouth (Joshua 1:8).

5. Go in for a full life.

Go in to possess the land, which the Lord your God giveth you to possess it (Joshua 1:11).

The Book of Law was Joshua's Bible. Our Bible is far more complete and we know more about God's will because Christ has interpreted it for us. Do we meditate upon the Word? Do we turn from it to the right or to the left? Read God's words to Joshua (Joshua 1:7).

Joshua called the officers together and gave them detailed directions. Hear these men speak. *All that thou commandest us we will do, and whithersoever thou sendest us, we will go* (Joshua 1:16). They were ready for any service.

We see both Joshua and the people prepared for the journey. Remember, Joshua had been one of the twelve spies who had been sent into Canaan forty years before. Now he sends two scouts to bring a report of the land. Read the story of Rahab and the spies in Joshua 2.

Joshua asked them especially to find out the strength of Jericho for this was the first stronghold they would have to attack after crossing the river. The spies aroused suspicion but were saved from death by Rahab who hid them under flax that was spread on the roof of her house. The spies learned from Rahab that all the city was in terror of the Israelites and they promised that they would spare her and her household when the city was taken. Rahab let them down over the city wall on which her house was built, and they returned to tell Joshua the good news that *all the inhabitants of the country do faint because of us* (Joshua 2:24).

Rahab hung a scarlet cord out of her window that her house might be marked and spared when the city was destroyed. The red speaks of safety through the blood (Hebrews 9:19-22). *And she bound the scarlet line in the window* (Joshua 2:21). "There are hints of redemption from every casement window of God's Word," someone has said. Rahab was saved not by character but by blood! We find this woman's name in the genealogy of Jesus (Matthew 1:5).

The Canaanites, the people of the land, were the descendants of Canaan, the son of Ham. They were a wicked and idolatrous people. God had warned them in the destruction of Sodom and Gomorrah, but they had not changed a bit. Now God was going to destroy their power and give their land to the Israelites.

FORWARD MARCH (Joshua 3-5)

Read Joshua 3-5. Encouraged by the report the spies had brought, the Israelites moved from their encampment at Shittim, six miles from the Jordan, to a spot within a mile of the swollen stream. At dawn the officers passed through the camp and ordered all to watch the Ark and follow it at a distance of two thousand cubits, *that ye may know the way by which ye must go: for ye have not passed this way heretofore* (Joshua 3:4). The great leader, Joshua, instructed the people to sanctify themselves, for on the morrow the Lord would do wonders among them. (See Joshua 3:5.)

The children of Israel had followed the cloud in the wilderness. Now they would follow the Ark of the Covenant which represented the presence of Jehovah.

The long journey in the desert was over, and the mystery of an unknown country and an unknown life lay before them. The people grew serious. It was the impressiveness of a new experience. Life is always opening new and unexpected things to us. There is no monotony in the life of a Christian.

At the beginning of the Exodus from Egypt there was a crossing of the Red Sea. Now at the close of the Exodus, there is a crossing of the Jordan river. Both were most memorable events in the history of the children of Israel. Of all the great host that crossed the Red Sea, only Caleb and Joshua remained of their generation. Why?

It was the time of the overflow of the Jordan, and the people of Jericho must have thought it impossible for them to cross or they would have been there to oppose them. There were no bridges and only a few fords, and these not passable at this season of the year. The spies had crossed and recrossed by swimming, no doubt. But how could a great host with women and children and baggage cross?

God has a way. He gave the directions for the people to follow. Martin Luther said, "I know not the way He (Christ) leads me, but well do I know my Guide."

Remember how Christ told the man with the withered arm to do what he could not do—yes, to stretch it forth. The man made the attempt to do the impossible and Christ made it possible. The way to stretch forth the palsied arm was to stretch it forth. The way to cross the Jordan was to cross it. Joshua told the priests to take up the Ark and step into the Jordan, when the river was overflowing all its banks. When the soles of their feet touched the waters of the Jordan, they stood on dry ground. And all Israel passed over on dry ground (Joshua 3:9-17). With men this is impossible, but with God all things are possible. God is always doing the impossible. God's biddings are His enablings.

A man once said, "If God tells me to jump through a stone wall, it would be my duty to jump; it would be God's duty to remove the wall!"

What was the Ark? The symbol of the divine Presence. And Christ is the reality of the divine Presence. He says, *Lo, I am with you alway* (Matthew 28:20).

He goes before us and says, *Follow me,* and He sends His Holy Spirit to whisper in our ear and say, *This is the way, walk ye in it.* The living Ark of the Covenant is still our guide. He will guide us in the little as well as the great things of life. Yes, *the steps of a good man are ordered by the Lord* (Psalm 37:23).

The Bible tells us of the crossing of the river. From the river bed, *the place where the priests' feet stood firm,* the stones were taken and piled up on the other shore as a lasting memorial of the wonders God did for them (Joshua 4:3). No formal prayer is recorded, but memorial stones are set up. The people wanted to perpetuate the memory of their great Deliverer.

THE FALL OF JERICHO (Joshua 6)

Jericho was not far from the Jordan and about a short twenty-minute walk from the encampment at Gilgal. The author has stood on the site of the city of Joshua's conquest whose massive walls have been unearthed. The modern Jericho, or Ericha, as the village is called, is a mile away from the ancient stronghold, which was destroyed, and rebuilt in the reign of Ahab.

A man, passing by a building which was being torn down, stopped to look at a laborer who was pulling away on a rope fastened to the top of the wall.

"Do you think that you are going to pull that thick wall down that way?" he finally asked in amazement.

Between his tugs the man answered, "It doesn't look that way to me, but I guess the boss knows what he's about."

And the boss did know, for the wall had been undermined, and after an hour of tug after tug the great wall vibrated, swayed, and fell down flat.

The walls of Jericho had to come down so that the Israelites might proceed to conquer the promised land, for Jericho was the key to southern Canaan. How could this be brought about? To the Israelites God's directions seemed strange, but like that laborer they kept steadily at the part assigned them. They were confident that their Leader knew what they did not, and that they would soon enter the city. What was their task? Read Joshua 6.

The wall was in two parts. On a natural rock foundation a massive six-foot-thick wall was erected. Enormous blocks were employed in some parts of this outer wall. The inner wall was separated from the outer wall by a space of from twelve to fifteen feet and was itself twelve feet thick. The fortification wall proper was built of clay bricks. The wall originally reached perhaps a height of about thirty feet. A most imposing structure this fortification must have been; visible over the plain for miles! After several thousand years the buttressing of the wall did not show a single fissure. The only advantage of modern construction over this is the use of cement. Thousands of people must have been employed to construct this wall.

The procession of priests, Ark, men and trumpets that marched around the city daily were the only visible means for its capture. How futile must such a march have seemed to the people of Jericho, yes, and to the Israelites themselves. But God knew what He would do.

Some would try to explain that the fall of Jericho was no miracle but a simple scientific fact. God knew that a certain vibration would destroy the wall. It was struck in the sound of the trumpet and shout, and the wall fell before the Israelites.

Whether this is the case or not, the miracle remains that the wall fell. God accomplished the destruction with or without "scientific" means. The glory is the Lord's, not Joshua's. When the people obeyed the command of the Lord given by Joshua, they saw God's power.

The fall of Jericho before the blast of Joshua's rams' horns was a miracle so stupendous that the rationalist can but discredit it. The Israelites believed that they were following God's plan. The seven trumpets, leading a procession seven days, and seven times on the seventh day, showed the Israelites that this was Jehovah's plan of conquest as directly as an American flag would inform people today that the property over which it waved was under the protection of the United States. God put an invisible band around the foundation of that city wall and tightened it, and when God does that to the foundation of any structure, national or personal—beware!

It is not hard work that is needed; it is the want of vision that makes us fail. It is easy to blow a trumpet, a little thing to walk around a wall. The hard thing is to see the good in it. Say, "Lord, one step is enough for me."

No one wants long delays. We love to see things happen. If there must be six days of weary traveling around the walls, the seventh day will come when the walls will fall. God gives us victories through ways that seem utterly foolish to us. (See I Cor. 1:17-29.)

CAMPAIGN AT AI (Joshua 7; 8)

The capture of Jericho gave the Israelites a chance to enter central Canaan. The next place strategically important was Ai, which commanded the entrance into the valley leading into western Canaan.

As he had done in the case of Jericho, Joshua sent spies to Ai to learn the situation. Made overconfident by their recent success, they gave poor counsel on their return, saying, *Two or three thousand go up and smite Ai; and make not all the people to labor thither; for they are but few.* The small force was sent up the steep ascent, but when the garrison at Ai sallied forth and attacked them, the Israelites fled without striking a blow. In the disaster all saw the withdrawal of God's guiding hand. They soon learned that they could not trust in their own strength alone. *Not by might, nor by power, but by my Spirit, saith the Lord* (Zechariah 4:6).

One man's sin caused Israel's defeat. (Israel had become a nation and no one could act alone.) Achan had hidden the wedge of gold. Read the story in Joshua 7. Beware of the wedge of gold! (Joshua 7:13). Achan alone was guilty, yet we read: *Israel hath sinned, and they have also transgressed my covenant which I commanded them: for they have even taken of the accursed thing, and have also stolen, and dissembled also* (Joshua 7:11).

No one's sins affect himself alone. None of us lives to himself. One stricken with smallpox can infect an entire schoolroom. A few influenza germs can infect a whole nation. The sin of one becomes the sin of the community.

Every sin you commit will hunt you down, find you out, and make you pay. Know this, there has never been one sin committed on this earth for which the man who committed it did not suffer. You may escape the law of man. You cannot escape the law of God.

SOUTHERN CAMPAIGN (Joshua 10)

The Israelites went out a second time to Ai. This time they were victors. The taking of Ai shows real military strategy. In working for the Lord there must always be a recognition of the value of the best in human reason, but strategy without obedience is worth nothing. Moody said, "Work as if everything depended upon you, and pray as if everything depended upon God."

The fame of Israel began to spread far and wide. The kings of Canaan formed a league against the oncoming hosts. But we read of the treaty with the Gibeonites who played a trick on the Israelites. As a result Joshua condemned the Gibeonites to become the *hewers of wood and drawers of water* (Joshua 9:21).

Then Joshua routed the allied army. Read about the hail storm and the prolonged daylight which God sent to help His warrior (Joshua 10:10,11,13).

Joshua says, *Sun, stand thou still.* This is his way of saying that God stopped the earth from rotating on its axis for twenty-four hours in answer to his prayer. Professor Totten of Yale has given us calculations which he has published to show that one day in the earth's history was more than twenty-four hours long.

Sun, stand thou still upon Gibeon (Joshua 10:12). Ordinary things come to a standstill when God's work is on.

NORTHERN CAMPAIGN (Joshua 11)

After all of southern Canaan was in Israel's possession, a new confederacy had to be faced and conquered. The northern kings had joined together and tried to break the power of the conquering Israelites. But in divine strength Joshua routed them all. This did not all happen at once. Scripture says that it took *a long time*. At last the land rested from war (Joshua 11:23).

Jerusalem is so named here for the first time in the Bible. To think that since then it has become possibly the most famous place in the world! The Crusaders shed rivers of blood trying to capture it. General Allenby walked in with head uncovered and took this citadel without a sound of a cannon! It is a city with a great past history and a bright future history.

PALESTINE
ISRAEL AND JUDAH

DAMASCUS

SIDON

TYRE

PHOENICIANS

DAN

KEDESH

ARAM

MEDITERRANEAN
SEA

SEA
OF
GALILEE

GOLAN?

MT.
TABOR

RIVER KISHON

MT.
CARMEL

WELL OF
HAROD

VALLEY OF
JEZREEL

BROOK CHERITH?

MT. GILBOA

ISRAEL

RAMOTH-GILEAD
(RAMOTH)

SHECHEM

RIVER JABBOK

RIVER JORDAN

APHEK

EBENEZER?

SHILOH

BETHEL

AMMON

RAMAH

GILGAL

EKRON

GIBEAH

PHILISTINES

JERUSALEM

JERICHO

ASHDOD

BEZER?

BETH-SHEMESH

BETHLEHEM

ASHKELON

MT. NEBO

GATH?

TEKOA

HEBRON

GAZA

EN-GEDI

JUDAH

MOAB

GERAR?

ZIKLAG

DEAD
SEA

BEERSHEBA

84

EDON SEIR

Here Christ will reign when He comes again in power and great glory (Luke 21:27).

We see God judging these wicked people, the Canaanites. Until recently it was supposed that Canaan was at this time a country of semi-barbarians. Now we know that as early as 3500 B.C. Canaan was subject to Babylonian rulers, and the Babylonian language and civilization had been adopted there. Next came Egyptian domination, and we know the high culture of Egypt. Tell-el-Amarna tablets, dating 1400 B.C., before the conquest of Canaan by the Israelites, are many of them letters to the Pharaoh of Egypt, written in the Babylonian language by tributary princes in Canaan. "At that period Canaan had already behind it a long civilized past. The country was filled with schools and libraries, with richly furnished palaces, and workshops of artisans. The cities in the coast had their fleets, partly of merchantmen, partly of warships, and an active trade was carried on with all parts of the known world."

DIVISION OF THE LAND (Joshua 13–24)

Joshua was an old man now, about ninety years of age, and he realized that the conquest of the land was by no means complete. There yet remained *much land to be possessed.* In order that the children of Israel might do this, he divided it among them.

"This is Judah's; this is Asher's; this is Simeon's; and this is Benjamin's," we hear the people saying as the scene opens. They said this even while the Amorites, the Jebusites, and the Hittites were in open possession of the promised land (Joshua 13). The division made of the land was the announcement on faith of certain things which under God's guidance they proposed to realize by the long struggle which followed.

Alas for the dull-eyed persons whose aspirations never get a foot in advance of their present achievements. Unless we keep a vision before us and dream dreams, we will never win either materially or spiritually. This is just what the Israelites did. They reached out into a hoped-for but unknown future, when they divided up great stretches of country which was still in the hands of their foes!

85

Though all this land was alloted to the various tribes, it was not all conquered until the time of David. All that was subdued at this time was the mountainous land; the cities and the plains were hardly touched.

The strong did not take the best part of the land because they were strong, leaving the fragments for the weak. Neither did the rich purchase the choicest spots, leaving the poor the more undesirable sites. They tried to determine God's will in the matter. God cares about distribution of goods.

Do you see any application of this principle today? God cares about the inequalities of condition of His children. He cares that the weak are thrust aside by the shrewd and strong. There is a will of God concerning all the questions of hours and wages, capital and labor. God is concerned in a more equal division of His blessings in this world, when He rules that *they shall sit every man under his vine and under his fig tree* (Micah 4:4).

When the assignment was made by lot no one could be jealous. They met before the Ark of Jehovah, the symbol of His presence.

Unto the Levites he gave none inheritance among them (Joshua 14:3). You remember that this tribe was set apart for the sacred service of the priesthood.

CALEB'S POSSESSION (Joshua 14)

Caleb now was eighty-five years old! Joshua and he were alone among the spies because they had dared to trust God! How many spies did Moses send into Canaan? How many of their names do you remember? No doubt these two are the only ones. Two trusted God and these are the only names we know. As a reward for obedience, these were the only ones in their generation who were permitted to enter Canaan.

Caleb asked his friend Joshua for the high and walled cities! He added, *if so be the LORD will be with me, then I shall be able to drive them out, as the LORD said* (Joshua 14:12). He valued his inheritance because of the hard work it offered and the opportunity that it gave him for conquering it! Joshua's recognition of his friend, and of his right to a choice possession was quick and generous. He granted him the mountain and blessed his aged friend.

Caleb was old but he gloried in the hardness of the task. One of Helen Keller's teachers said she was the happiest person she had ever met even though she was deaf, dumb and blind. Her teacher attributed it to her having overcome so much. Caleb was the happiest man in the camp because he had overcome so much and yet had fields to conquer! Horace Mann said, "Difficulties are things which show what men are."

The Lord has never promised His children that they will have an easy time serving Him. In fact, Christ said, *In the world ye shall have tribulation* (John 16:33). The promise is not for ease; the promise is for victory. Christ says, *I have overcome the world*. We grow in adversity, for we learn to trust the Lord more. Paul said to Timothy, *Endure hardness, as a good soldier of Jesus Christ* (II Timothy 2:3).

"General Booth, tell me what has been the secret of your success all the way through," begged Dr. J. Wilbur Chapman of the head of the Salvation Army.

Slowly General Booth replied, "I will tell you the secret. God has had all there was of me."

Caleb said, *I wholly followed the LORD* (Joshua 14:8).

We might call attention to the fact that the cities of refuge that God planned, spoken of in Numbers and Deuteronomy, are now set apart (Numbers 35).

JOSHUA'S FAREWELL (Joshua 24)

Joshua had become an old man. He knew that he could not live much longer. He wanted to give the people some last words of admonition.

He called first the leaders and then all the people together and urged them to remember the power and faithfulness of God and admonished them to be faithful to Him. *Now therefore fear the LORD, and serve him* (Joshua 24:14). He warned them against apostasy. He said, *Choose you this day whom ye will serve; whether the gods which your fathers served that were on the other side of the flood, or the gods of the Amorites*. Then he

87

added, *As for me and my house, we will serve the LORD* (Joshua 24:15).

It is a good thing to have people make an open confession and commit themselves to a solemn promise. These older men who had made an open confession were true to their promises.

It is a great help for young people to stand and make a public confession of Christ and unite with the church. You have made a definite commitment which gives you something to live up to. See what Paul says about confession, Romans 10:9,10.

The people said that day, *Nay; but we will serve the LORD.*

JOSHUA DIES

At one hundred and ten years of age the grand old man, Joshua, died. The book closes with death. We see three graves. Joshua's, the great leader of Israel; Eleazer's, the priest; and Joseph's, whose bones the children of Israel had carried with them from Egypt and which were now buried in the land of promise.

Here is a great tribute to a great leader, *And Israel served the LORD all the days of Joshua* (Joshua 24:31).

The great walls of Jericho fell flat after the host of the Israelites marched around the city seven times. The outer wall was six feet thick and the inner wall twelve feet. The two walls were fifteen feet apart and both were about thirty feet high. The two walls were linked together by houses built across the top. The remains seem to show that the outer wall fell outwards and down the slope, quite flat, dragging the inner wall and the houses with it. This made it possible for the invaders to enter *every man straight before him . . . they burnt the city with fire.*

This information is based on the discoveries of Dr. John Garstang, director of the British School of Archaeology in Jerusalem, at Jericho, 1929-1936. Great layers of charcoal and ashes and ruins of the walls reddened by fire, with pottery and scarab, give evidence that the great conflagration occurred in the fourteenth century B.C.

Under the ashes and fallen walls they found foods—wheat, barley, dates and the like—turned to charcoal by the intense heat. There was every evidence of the sudden destruction of the population.

Read what Joshua says about this: *Walls fell down flat,* etc. (Joshua 6:20). Rahab's *house upon the town wall* (Joshua 2:15).

Canaan, or the Promised Land, was 180 miles long and approximately 40 miles wide. The boundaries were the wilderness on the south, the Lebanon ranges on the north, the Euphrates on the east, and the Mediterranean on the west.

It was the center of mighty civilizations that made ancient history:

Egypt—300 miles to the south.

Nineveh—700 miles northeast.

Babylon—700 miles east.

Persia—1000 miles east.

Greece—800 miles northwest.

Rome—1500 miles northwest.

STRICTLY PERSONAL

Do not pray for an easy task. Pray to be stronger!

The greatness of a man's power is the measure of his surrender. It is not a question of who you are, or of what you are, but whether God controls you.

I wholly followed the Lord. (Caleb)

Be sure—be sure—be sure your sin will find you out.

God commands a complete out-and-out for him.

Facts do not change; feelings do.

It is not enough to light a fire; you must put fuel on it.

Minimum Daily Requirements/Spiritual Vitamins

Sunday: JOSHUA'S COMMISSION   Joshua 1;2

Monday: CROSSING THE JORDAN   Joshua 3

Tuesday: THE FALL OF JERICHO   Joshua 6

Wednesday: THE SIN OF ACHAN   Joshua 7

Thursday: OCCUPATION OF THE LAND   Joshua 11

Friday: CALEB'S POSSESSION   Joshua 14

Saturday: JOSHUA'S FAREWELL   Joshua 24

CHAPTER 8

UNDERSTANDING JUDGES and RUTH

Jesus Christ,
Our Deliverer Judge;
Our Kinsman-Redeemer

Someone has called the Book of Judges the account of the Dark Ages of the Israelitish people. The people forsook God (Judges 2:13) and God forsook the people (Judges 2:23).

The infidel Ingersoll spoke so much of "the liberty of man, woman and child." It was a godless liberty. You see this kind in this Book of Judges.

Judges covers the period after the death of their great leader, Joshua, to the ascension of Saul to the throne of Israel. The people were ruled by judges whom God raised up to deliver His oppressed people. We read, *In those days there was no king in Israel* (Judges 17:6). It covers the history of the first three hundred and fifty years in the land of promise. It gives us a record of great exploits.

It was a new hour in the history of Israel. Remember, Israel had come from a long era of bondage in Egypt to a period of forty years when she lived in tents and wandered in the wilderness. Now the march was over. The nomads were to become settlers in a land of their own. The change was not as easy for them as they expected it to be. The Book of Judges is in a way another book of beginnings where we see a new nation adjusting her national life. It is filled with struggle and disasters but the moral courage of the people grew.

There is a decided monotony in the description of each successive stage of sin in Israel, but there is an equally remarkable variety in the instruments and methods of deliverance which God used. There is something different in the story of each judge.

There are fifteen judges—Othniel, Ehud, Shamgar, Deborah,

Barak, Gideon, Tola, Jair, Jephthah, Ibzan, Elon, Abdon, Samson, Eli and Samuel. (Abimelech, a petty ruler, was not called of God to judge.)

There were three types of Judges:

1. The Warrior-Judge as Gideon and Samson.
2. Priest-Judge as Eli.
3. Prophet-Judge as Samuel.

The chief judges were Deborah, Gideon, Samson and Samuel.

Just how long these judges ruled we do not know but it is believed about three hundred and fifty years. No doubt the judges were not just one governor after another. They were probably raised up as deliverers on different occasions, in different parts of the land and there could have been overlapping of the time of their rule.

There is a phrase running through the whole book—*Every man did that which was right in his own eyes* (Judges 17:6). Mark this phrase every time you find it. We find the people falling away from Jehovah and worshiping the gods of the nations round about them (Judges 2:13). They forgot that God had chosen them for a purpose—to tell the world the truth that there is but one true God. In punishment for their sins God would deliver them into the hand of that nation. Then under the oppression of these new enemies they would cry to God for mercy and He would hear them and send a judge to deliver them. And so the book is full of rebellion, punishment, misery, and deliverance. It has a minor key throughout.

The book begins with compromise and ends with confusion. This is what happens in every unsurrendered life!

After one has read Judges, you may think that the whole of these three or four hundred years were spent in rebellion and sin. But if you read it carefully, you will see that only about one hundred out of these possibly three hundred and fifty years were spent in disloyalty to God.

One thing we learn in the Book of Judges is that a people who spend much of their time in disobedience to God make little progress during their lifetime. The Book of Numbers recounts the forty years of wandering in the wilderness, but this book repeats again and again a record of departure from God.

This book is in sharpest contrast to Joshua.

In Joshua	In Judges
Joy	Sobs
Heavenly vision	Earthly in emphasis
Victory	Defeat
Progress	Declension
Faith	Unbelief
Freedom	Servitude

Professor Moorehead, D.D., gives an outline for Judges which is easy to remember. "Seven apostasies, seven servitudes to seven heathen nations, seven deliverances!"

We read of man's constant failure and God's constant mercy.

Read this book through this week. It can be done in an hour or two. To learn just the great facts of the Bible, however necessary this is, will never satisfy the Christian and make him a real blessing to others. We must know what God is teaching us.

Study carefully the following:

1. The wickedness of the human heart (Judges 2:11-13,17,19; 8:33-35; 10:6; 13:1).
2. God's delight in using the weak things (I Cor. 1:26-29). Note the stories of:
   Left-handed assassin Ehud (Judges 3)
   Deborah, a woman (Judges 4; see also Judges 9:53)
   Gideon, from an obscure family in the smallest tribe (Judges 6)
   Shamgar, a rustic with an ox goad (Judges 3:31)
   Gideon's little pitcher-armed band (Judges 7)
   The jaw bone used by Samson (Judges 15:14-19)
3. The Holy Spirit in Judges.
   Othniel—*The Spirit of the LORD came upon him* (Judges 3:10).
   Gideon—*The Spirit of the LORD clothed himself with Gideon* (see note on Judges 6:34, A.S.V.).
   Jephthah—*The Spirit of the LORD came upon Jephthah* (Judges 11:29).
   Samson—*The Spirit of the LORD began to move him* (Judges 13:25; see also 14:6; 15:14, etc.).

Over the Book of Judges as a guide to its spiritual interpretation might be written Zechariah's great word (Zechariah 4:6) —*Not by might, nor by power, but by my spirit, saith the LORD of hosts.*

The critics of the Bible would have the history of God's chosen people start here in these dark days of the judges as a wild, lawless, nomadic people, developing finally into a higher civilization. Just because Israel failed to keep God's law does not mean there was no law. Just as today, because the people of this world disregard the Ten Commandments and put aside the teachings of Christ, it does not prove that these words were never spoken.

Men would love to believe that man's trend is upward. But God's Word shows us plainly that the natural course is downward.

ISRAEL'S FAILURE (Judges 1–3:4)

Joshua had died (Judges 1:1). Much of the promised land must be conquered. The first act of the children of Israel was to seek God's will as to how they should commence the final conquest. They began well. They consulted God.

God appointed Judah, the kingly tribe (Judges 1:2). The work began in earnest but it ended in weakness. The people did not obey God.

Israel's troubles were due directly to her disobedience to God. They did not exterminate the enemies in the land but rather worshiped the idols of the people and became corrupted in their morals.

The children of Israel went into the land and settled where they wanted and began to raise enough for their living. Soon an enemy would come along, catch the tribe off guard, and take the people captive. Their enemies were "fifth columnists" within. God had told His people to do away with them.

Chapter one is a failure chapter. They did not drive out the enemy as God had commanded. *Neither did Ephraim drive out the Canaanites . . . Neither did Zebulun drive out the inhabitants . . . Neither did Asher drive out the inhabitants . . . Neither did . . .* six times in succession.

94

This records a series of disobediences. So, of course, chapter two is a chapter of defeat and failure. God gave them up to their own will. God said, *Ye shall make no league with the inhabitants of this land; ye shall throw down their altars; but ye have not obeyed my voice . . . Wherefore . . . they shall be as thorns in your sides* (Judges 2:2,3). The children of Israel brought on their own judgment and became their own executioners. Several times Israel was on the verge of being exterminated, but God intervened.

Sometimes we wonder why God didn't remove all the enemies from the promised land before He let the children of Israel go in. But God had a definite reason (Judges 3:1-4).

God uses the results of our lack of faith in Him to prove to us our sin and weakness. He does not forget His covenant (no merit of ours), and He allows our very weakness, our guilty weakness, to drive us back to Him.

God wanted the chosen people to realize that they were a holy people. They must not mix with the wicked nations about them. They must continually separate themselves. God knew that separation makes men strong. Christians today must remember that they cannot mix with the world. They must keep close to God and war against sin and unrighteousness. God wants us to be good warriors. Read Ephesians 6:10-18 and see the armor He provides.

And so we see that a false toleration toward a people so utterly corrupt resulted in the undoing of God's chosen people. See the result of this disobedience, Judges 2:20-22.

THE JUDGES (Judges 3:5–16:31)

This scene gives us the picture of seven failures, seven servitudes and seven deliverances. The Israelites intermarried with the heathens, worshiped at their shrines, and practiced their vices.

First Oppression, Judges 3:7-11.

    Sin—Idolatry
    Punishment—Eight years
    Deliverer and Judge—Othniel

Second Oppression, Judges 3:12-31.
   Sin—Immorality and idolatry
   Punishment—Eighteen years
   Deliverer and Judge—Ehud and Shamgar

Third Oppression, Judges 4; 5.
   Sin—Departed from God
   Punishment—Twenty years
   Deliverer and Judge—Deborah and Barak

Fourth Oppression, Judges 6–8:32.
   Sin—Departed from God
   Punishment—Midianites for seven years
   Deliverer and Judge—Gideon

Fifth Oppression, Judges 8:33–10:5.
   Sin—Departed from God
   Punishment—Civil war, etc.
   Deliverer and Judge—Tola and Jair

Sixth Oppression, Judges 10:6–12:15.
   Sin—Idolatry increased
   Punishment—Philistines and Ammonites, eighteen years
   Deliverer and Judge—Jephthah (and successors)

Seventh Oppression, Judges 13–16.
   Sin—Departed from God
   Punishment—Philistines, forty years
   Deliverer and Judge—Samson

Joshua had no successor. After his death, each tribe acted independently. There was no capital and no fixed government.

There was no unity of action except in the time of danger, when the tribes combined for their own good. When the people sinned against God, their enemies defeated them and ruled them. When in their distress they sought the Lord, He sent great leaders called judges, who delivered them.

But this scene is not only filled with servitude, it also records deliverances, for God was always near His people, and when they cried, He answered. God is always brooding over His disobedient children. He promises us that He will never leave us nor forsake us. We see defeat on man's part but deliverance on

God's part. *Where sin abounded, grace did much more abound* (Romans 5:20).

We see His dealings with His own rebellious people, whom He has crowned with His best blessings and upon whom He has lavished His tender love. We find the patience of God and His constant readiness to respond to the least sign of penitence in His people (Judges 3:9,15; 4:3-7; 6:6-12; 10:15,16).

He repeated His mercy again and again although it was never appreciated. If you think on these things, it will draw you nearer to this God of mercy and love and grace. Look up, repent and trust God.

We have found that God fulfilled His purpose for Israel by leaving around them in Canaan a circle of strong tribes unlike each other. It is said, *These are the nations which the LORD left, to prove Israel by them . . . to know whether they would hearken unto the commandments of the LORD.*

One of the best known nations was the Philistines who settled on the coast plain. They were a maritime people much like the Danish invaders of Saxon England, sea-rovers and pirates, ready for any fray that promised land and gain. In wealth and civilization they no doubt presented a real contrast to the Israelites, and their equipment gave them great advantage in war. Even in the period of the judges there were imposing temples in the Philistine cities. The Hebrews feared the Philistines and did not mix freely with them. They only met in war.

FIRST APOSTASY (Judges 3:7-11)

We find the Israelites settling among the Syrian nations. They seemed too ready to live at peace with these other nations and to yield not a little for the sake of peace. (Read the few verses 3:5-8 to see what they did.) They intermarried to make their position safer. They traded with the Amorites, Hivites, Perizzites. They determined on boundary lines to make things run smoothly. Next they accepted their neighbor's religion (Judges 3:7), and then his bad customs. But soon the Mesopotamians began to oppress them (Judges 3:8). The Israelites then realized that they had a God from whom they had departed. Israel was a prodigal people. They had left the God whose presence before had assured them victory. For eight years they were under the oppression of these northern nations. Year by year conditions grew worse.

It was from the far south that God sent help in answer to their pitiful cry (Judges 3:9). The deliverer was Othniel, who was Caleb's nephew. No doubt he had had frequent skirmishes with the Arab marauders from the wilderness. *The Spirit of the LORD came upon him, and he judged Israel, and went out to war* (Judges 3:10). First he prayed, then went out to battle. When we see an army bow in prayer, as the Swiss did at Morat, the Scots at Bannockburn, and General MacArthur's troops in the Philippines, we have faith in their spirit and courage for they are feeling their dependence on God!

Othniel's first concern was to put away the idolatry of Israel and teach them the law of the Lord and remind them of their calling as a nation. Soon success and victory was theirs (Judges 3:10-11).

Othniel, the first of the judges, was one of the best. He pointed Israel to a higher level of reverence for God and His plans. Forty years of rest followed.

No man can do real service for his country who does not fear God and love righteousness more than country.

SECOND APOSTASY (Judges 3:12-31)

God used different kinds of men to deliver His people. Israel's second judge, Ehud, is in marked contrast to Othniel, the judge without reproach.

The long peace which the country enjoyed after the Mesopotamian army had been driven out let the people fall into prosperity and to lapse again into spiritual weakness (Judges 3:12). This time the Moabites led the attack. The punishment lasted for eighteen years. Again the people cried to God, and Ehud, with whom Shamgar's name is associated, was the deliverer (Judges 3:15). This left-handed Benjamite chose his own method of action and assassinated the Moabite king. His crime is one that stinks in our nostrils. But eighty years of rest for Israel followed (Judges 3:30).

Shamgar, the man of the ox-goad, follows in line (Judges 3:31).

THIRD APOSTASY (Judges 4; 5)

Now a prophetess arises in Israel (Judges 4:4). She was one of those rare women whose heart burns with enthusiasm when men's hearts are despondent. Many a queen has reigned with honor and wisdom, and often a woman's voice has struck a deep note which has roused nations.

Israel had been oppressed for twenty years (Judges 4:3). The oppression was terrible under Sisera. Again they cried and God heard. This time the story of deliverance is filled with romance and song. Deborah, the daughter of the people, had gained the confidence of the people to such a degree that they had appointed her as judge.

Deborah called Barak to help her. Together they delivered Israel from their oppression. The land had been so filled with Canaanite spoilers that the highways could not be used. War was everywhere, and the Israelites were defenseless and crushed; but God delivered them.

After Jabin, king of Canaan, was defeated and his nine hundred chariots turned into ploughshares, we might expect that Israel would at last make a real start to accomplish her true career. The tribes have had their third lesson and should know by now the danger of leaving God. Without God they were as weak as babes. Will they not now bend themselves to Him? Not yet. Not for more than forty years. The true reformer had not yet come. Deborah's work was not in vain. She was destroying the heathen altars and improving the land. Everywhere they were ploughing new ground, building houses, repairing roads. But they were falling into the old habit of friendly association with the Canannites.

Following deliverance from this servitude the land rested for forty years.

FOURTH APOSTASY (Judges 6–8:32)

But a fourth apostasy came (Read Judges 6:1). This time the deliverer was Gideon, a humble farmer. The Midianites had held the Israelites under bondage for seven years. So terrible was it that the people hid themselves in caves and dens and were hunted in the mountains (Judges 6:2). Again they cried unto the Lord. Gideon was called to act as deliverer. He broke down the altar of Baal and restored the worship of God. The story of the conflict is one of the most fascinating in history. Everyone knows the story of Gideon and his band of three hundred with their pitchers and horns. Refresh yourself with this story (Judges 7:7-24).

After the great victory over the Midianites, they sought to make Gideon king. He refused. Gideon was not perfect. We find in the record some things that he should not have done, but he did have faith in Jehovah that God could honor, and He gave his name a place in the Hall of Faith in Hebrews 11.

In 1926-28 excavations were made by Xenia Seminary and the American School under the direction of Melvin Grove Kyle and Albright. They found in a city built by Othniel (1500 B.C.) many hidden grain pits, showing how insecure life and property were in those days. There was no organized defense against the Midianites who made constant raids upon the Israelites. The people took refuge in dens and caves.

FIFTH APOSTASY (Judges 8:33–10:5)

A fifth time we see the people falling into the sin of idolatry by worshiping the Baalim almost immediately upon the death of Gideon. The record is: *As soon as Gideon was dead, that the children of Israel turned again, and went a whoring after Baalim* (Judges 8:33). How often the personal influence of the hero is everything while he is alive but confusion follows on his death.

Gideon was one of the most successful judges to maintain order, and *the country was in quietness forty years*. But no sooner was Gideon's funeral over than discord began. There was no rightful ruler to follow. Gideon left many sons but not one of them could take his place. Abimelech, a son of Gideon, unprincipled and brutal, secured the allegiance of the men at Shechem and usurped the position of king. He ruled three years in tyranny. He was slain by a woman and a period of forty-five years of quietness followed under the dictatorship of Tola and Jair.

The men who are busy are the men who have moved the world upward!

SIXTH APOSTASY (Judges 10:6–12:15)

In the sixth apostasy we find the people almost entirely given over to idolatry. Their condition was appalling. God sent judgment this time from the Philistines for eighteen years. At last, sorely distressed, they cried to God. For the first time it is recorded that He refused to hear them and reminded them of how repeatedly He had delivered them (Judges 10:13). The true attitude of Jehovah toward them is found in this statement—*His soul was grieved for the misery of Israel* (Judges 10:16).

Deliverance came through Jephthah. The Hebrews have always produced men of passionate religious fervor. The Arab of the present day is much the same. He can be excited to a holy war in which thousands perish. With the battle cry of Allah and his Prophet, he forgets fear. He is both fierce and generous. He rises to great faith, then sinks to earthly passions. We have the type in Deborah, David, Elijah and Jephthah. Jephthah's history is full of interest. He was a man of heroic daring. Read the story of his vows and victories, especially the vow that he made concerning his only child (Judges 11:30-40). After his great victory Jephthah judged Israel but six years.

SEVENTH APOSTASY (Judges 13–16)

The seventh apostasy opens with the words, *Israel did evil again in the sight of the Lord* (Judges 13:1). This time they were disciplined by the Philistines under whose awful oppression they lived for forty years. Here we read the story of Samson. It is a story filled with opportunity and failure. This man was appointed of God before birth, to deliver Israel from the Philistines (Judges 13:5).

In those days everything was dependent upon physical strength. That was what made a leader great. In this case God used it to begin the deliverance from the Philistines. Everything should have been in Samson's favor, but he entered into an unholy alliance which meant his downfall. The final fall occurred at Gaza. (Read Judges 16.) Nothing is more pathetic than Samson, blind and bound, grinding in the house of the Philistines, when he ought to have been delivering his nation from them (Judges 16:20,21).

The story ends with Samson and is taken up in I Samuel. The remaining chapters, and the Book of Ruth, have their chronological place in this period.

THE APPENDIX (Judges 17–21)

These last chapters give us a picture of anarchy and confusion. Israel had forsaken God and now we see the depths into which they have sunk. Read Judges 17:6 and you will find the reason for it all.

First, we find confusion in the religious life of the nation (Judges 17,18).

Second, we find confusion in the moral life of the nation (Judges 19).

Third, we find confusion in the political life (Judges 21).

These events no doubt took place soon after Joshua's death. It gives us a picture of the internal condition of the chosen people. The story of the backsliding of individuals is followed by the backsliding of the nation.

The last chapter proves that the children of Israel had lost the way to God's house, so low had they sunk. We find faithlessness, failure and forfeiture! But God loves His own.

The history of the church through the ages has been like this with Luther, Knox, and Wesley as deliverers. The biography of many a Christian in just the common run of life is like this. God opens doors and gives us grace for great tasks. Then we forget Him and begin to have our interests in the world about us. This brings loss and defeat. But God hears our cry of repentance and restores us to favor again.

UNDERSTANDING RUTH

This delightful story should be read in connection with the first chapters of Judges as no doubt it gives us an idea of the domestic life of Israel at that period of anarchy. Samuel may have been the author of this book, but no one knows where or when it was written. It records the events during the rule of Gideon or Jephthah. This book, written on a separate scroll, was read at Pentecost, the harvest festival.

Ruth was the great-grandmother of David. This book establishes the lineage of David, the ancestor of Christ. It tells of the beginning of the Messianic family, within the Messianic nation into which over a thousand years later the Messiah was to be born.

There are some interesting things to notice in this book. Ruth was a Moabitess. These people were descendants of Lot. They were heathen. God, in establishing the family which was to produce the world's Saviour, chose a beautiful heathen girl, led her to Bethlehem and made her the bride of Boaz. This is God's grace. He adopts the Gentiles into Christ's family. Of course, we know that although Ruth was born a heathen, through her first husband, or Naomi, she learned of the true God.

Boaz was the son of Rahab, the harlot found in Jericho. See Matthew 1:5. So we see that David's great-grandmother was a Moabitess and his great-grandfather was half Canaanite. This is found in the blood-line of the Messiah.

Minimum Daily Requirements/Spiritual Vitamins

Sunday: ONLY PARTIAL VICTORIES   Judges 1–2:5
Monday: INSTITUTION OF THE JUDGES
            Judges 2:16–3:11
Tuesday: DEBORAH AND BARAK   Judges 4:4–5:31
Wednesday: GIDEON, THE FARMER   Judges 6:1-16; 7:16-25
Thursday: JEPHTHAH'S TERRIBLE VOW
            Judges 11:12-40
Friday: SAMSON, THE STRONG MAN
            Judges 15 and 16
Saturday: THE STORY OF RUTH   Book of Ruth

CHAPTER 9

UNDERSTANDING I SAMUEL

I Samuel
Portrays Jesus Christ,
Our King

We enter now our study of the king books. Let us look at the six before us:

I Samuel—Man's choice—Saul.
II Samuel—God's choice—David.
I Kings—Solomon and Israel.
II Kings—Israel's kings.
I Chronicles—Solomon and the temple.
II Chronicles—The kings and the temple.

Royal history begins with the Book of Samuel. The long period of the rule of the judges ends with Samuel. When Samuel came into power, the people were in an awful state. They had practically rejected God, and we hear them clamoring for an earthly king (I Samuel 8:4-7). This book begins the five hundred year period of the kings of Israel (approximately 1095-586 B.C.).

The events recorded in I Samuel cover a period of about one hundred and fifteen years from the childhood of Samuel through the troublous times of Saul to the beginning of the reign of the king whom God chose, David. In the personal lives of these three men this book gives us an exceedingly graphic picture of these times. Samuel was the last of the judges; Saul was the first of the kings. The record brings us up to the time when David is ready permanently to establish the monarchy and God is ready permanently to establish David's throne (Psalm 89).

The book may be divided under the names of three of its chief characters—Samuel (1–7), Saul (8–15), and David (16–31). The history of this book is presented to us in the attractive cloak of biography. Everyone likes a true story.

We all have known and loved the stories recorded in I Samuel from the time we were little children. Who does not know the story of the boy Samuel (chapter 3), and David and Goliath (17), and the friendship of David and Jonathan (18)?

This book, of course, is named for its most prominent figure, Samuel. Probably he wrote the greater part of it through chapter 24. Nathan and Gad finished it (I Chronicles 29:29 and I Samuel 10:25).

SAMUEL, THE KING MAKER (I Samuel 1-7)

Samuel—"asked of God!" That is the meaning of his name. This book opens with the record of Hannah, Samuel's mother, praying for a son whom God could use. Samuel, the last of the judges, was God's answer to this prayer. *But Samuel ministered before the LORD, being a child* (I Samuel 2:18).

Throughout Samuel's long and useful life, he was God's man. He was pre-eminently a man of prayer. This first book which bears his name is a marvelous study in the place and power of prayer, illustrated from life. He was a child of prayer (I Samuel 3:1-19); he brought victory to his people through prayer (7:5-10); when the nation wanted a king, Samuel prayed unto the Lord (8:6); intercessory prayer was the keynote of his life (12:19-23).

It was in the dark and troublous times of Israel that we hear the prayer of faith from the lips of a simple trusting woman, Hannah. She asked God for a son whom she could dedicate to Him for service (I Samuel 1:9-19).

When Samuel was born, Hannah brought him to the tabernacle at Shiloh. Although the corruption of the priesthood was appalling, Samuel was protected and grew as a boy in the fear of the Lord (I Samuel 1:24-28; 2:12-26; 3:1-21).

Eli was both judge and priest at this time. He had ruled for forty years. He was an indulgent father and as a result his two sons, Hophni and Phinehas, also priests, were allowed to act in a most disgraceful manner. As a result there was moral corruption, and God warned Eli of the downfall of his house.

Fungus growth in a tree usually is not detected for a long time. Everything seems right outwardly; but when the crash suddenly comes, the state of the tree is seen. Israel had been sinning for a long time. At length the catastrophe came in the disaster recorded at this time (I Samuel 4).

During the next invasion of their enemies, the Philistines, Israel was defeated, the Ark was taken and Eli's sons were killed. When Eli heard all this, the old man, now ninety-eight years of age, died of the shock (I Samuel 4).

A CONSTANT THREAT

Read the history of the Philistines' possession of the Ark.

This mention of the Philistines is the first since Judges 13–16. The bondage lasted forty years (Judges 13:1), and seems to have come to a close in the days of Samuel (I Samuel 7:13,14), about his twentieth year as judge (I Samuel 7:2). The battle with this enemy probably was fought about four miles northwest of Jerusalem.

The Philistines were Israel's powerful enemies living to the southwest on the coast. Perhaps this renewed action on their part was due to the death of Samson. The battle soon went against Israel. They wondered why God had deserted them. While warring against God, they asked God to war for them. Read the account of the revival at Mizpeh (I Samuel 7).

We cannot win while we war against God! Apart from the immediate causes, rebellion against God is the root reason for tragic wars today. Civilization in general has not been seeking first and always the glory and will of God. The United States has failed to meet this test, as well as all other nations. Civilized nations have failed, as they were bound to do, and they always will fail as long as God is left out.

Though this life is bound to be a fight, it may always be a winning fight if we enlist under the banner of the Captain of our Salvation and make His will our will. *We are more than conquerors* (Romans 8:37).

A POOR SUBSTITUTE

After Israel's first defeat by the Philistines, did they do right by looking to the Ark of God for protection? (I Samuel 4:3-7,10).

The Ark of God was a very poor substitute for the God of the

Ark. Many people think that when they wear religious symbols, or perform religious rituals, or give money to charitable causes that they will be safe. They think that these things are a charm, or talisman, to bring them victory. Can you give some illustrations of this?

"Man's extremity is God's opportunity!" Although at the time the loss was terrible, yet God overruled for good. Through Samuel God provided (1) deliverance from the Philistines, (2) preparation for the kingdom, (3) a permanent sanctuary instead of a tabernacle at Shiloh, (4) a better priesthood.

SAMUEL, THE PROPHET

Samuel was the last of the judges, the first of the prophets, and the founder of the monarchy. Beside this, he started a school of the prophets, a kind of seminary. The record of this great man's life is beyond reproach. It is hard to find a single mistake that Samuel made.

God always gives us the best we will take, *for his mercy endureth forever*. We are free human agents. We can choose for ourselves; but we may well tremble at the consequences. We must choose God's best or our own way.

A TIMELY REVIVAL

And the LORD appeared again in Shiloh (I Samuel 3:21). God revisited Shiloh! For Shiloh had been left. Read Judges 21:19-21. The place of worship had been turned into a place of feasting and dancing. Shiloh was the location of the house of God from the days of Joshua to Samuel. David moved it to Jerusalem. The Ark was removed by the Philistines in Samuel's childhood and from then on Shiloh ceased to be of great importance (I Samuel 4:3,11).

WHAT BROUGHT THE REVIVAL?

Three things:
1. A praying mother, chapter 1.
2. A chastened people, chapter 2.
3. A faithful prophet, chapter 3.

We need a praying band of Christians, a people brought to a sense of their need, and a consecrated preacher to bring about revival. Under the Philistine rule Israel had no definite center of worship. Samuel grew into manhood and assumed the leadership for which he had been born. The first hopeful sign after Israel's long rebellion and defeat was that they had a sense of need. They began to want God. They *lamented after Jehovah*. The Jews are going to do this again some day (Zechariah 12:10,11) when Christ *whom they have pierced* returns to this earth and reveals Himself to His own people.

God cannot do much for people who do not feel that they need anything. God pities that person. There are those who think they are "all right."

"Well," said Samuel, "if you really mean business, you've got to show me. Do something. Prove it. How? Put away your strange gods." (See I Samuel 7:3.) "Put away" might be translated "cut it out." If you mean business, God will mean business. Religion is not just a matter of emotion but also of the will.

It is often easy for us to "talk big," but it is another question to live up to what we say. We often make promises to God that we never keep. How sad that sometimes our lives shout, "Lie!" to what our lips say.

The people began to lament and Samuel took advantage of this and called on them to return to their God and put away their idols. Samuel erected an altar and called it Ebenezer (I Samuel 7:12). Ebenezer means "stone of help." Christ our victory is called "the stone" in both the Old Testament and the New (Daniel 2:35; Matthew 21:42).

In just a brief paragraph we find the actual story of Samuel's judgeship. His home was at Ramah. From here he was a circuit rider covering his territory once a year to Bethel, Gilgal, and Mizpeh, and overseeing and administering the affairs of the people (I Samuel 7:15-17). We find missionaries doing this today. They choose some place as home center and then move out through the surrounding country.

Samuel established a school for the prophets at his home in Ramah. This was the beginning of the "order" of the prophets, or seers. When the Ark was taken, the priests were scattered.

This is when Samuel retired to his home in Ramah. Through Samuel, God introduced a new way of dealing with Israel. He called prophets through whom He would speak. It was with Samuel that prophecy became a definite part of the life of Israel. Samuel gathered groups about him called *Sons of the Prophets*. They were found in Shiloh, Gilgal, Bethel, Samaria and Ramah. (See Acts 3:24.)

Samuel's greatest ministry was the organization of the kingdom. The independent tribes were now going to be formed into a nation. In order to survive among other strong nations, Israel must become powerful. They had refused to take God seriously and obey Him as He had commanded them so He permitted Samuel to find a king for them. The people wanted to be "like all the nations." God wanted them to be unlike the other nations. In Deuteronomy 17:14-20 God had prophesied that Israel should have a king, but He did not want them to become independent of Him.

SAUL, THE KING CHOSEN (I Samuel 8–15)

God never intended Israel to have any king but Himself. He would send them great leaders and these in turn would receive their orders directly from Him. But Israel in her falling away had become restless. They wanted a king like the other surrounding nations. We find God granting their request. Here is a great lesson. We either can have God's best or His second best, His directive will or His permissive will.

Saul, their first king, was a failure. He was handsome to look at, he was tall and of a noble mien. He started out splendidly. He proved to be an able military leader. He defeated the enemies about him—the Philistines, the Amalekites and the Ammonites.

Saul was humble at first, but we find him becoming proud and disobedient to God. No man had a greater opportunity than Saul and no man ever was a greater failure. His jealousy of David bordered on insanity.

Inasmuch as Saul was granted to Israel as king in response to Israel's sinful demand for a king, contrary to God's will, did Saul ever really have a chance to "make good" in God's sight? Could he possibly have succeeded under such circumstances?

110

Was he not condemned by God to failure even before he started as king?

We find the answer clearly in God's Word. In I Samuel 12:12-15 the prophet of God tells Israel that, although they had demanded their king in defiance of God (verse 12), if both they and their king would fear Jehovah and serve Him, all would be well. Note what follows this word of Samuel (verses 16-18). Then we see the fact that Israel confesses her sin in asking for a king (verse 19), and Samuel reassures Israel, promising blessing if they serve God.

The only reason why any soul is ever rejected by God is because that soul has first rejected God. God takes the initiative in love. We *love him, because he first loved us* (I John 4:19). Man takes the initiative in sin (I Samuel 15:23).

NOTE FOUR THINGS IN SAUL'S ORDINATION

1. Divine Ordination (I Samuel 9:3-20). He went out with a bridle and came back with a scepter.
2. Prophetic Ordination (I Samuel 10:1). Samuel was his tutor and friend. What an advantage but it was thrown away. How often we do this today!
3. Spiritual Ordination. *The Spirit of God came upon him* (I Samuel 10:10). He GRIEVED this Spirit; then he QUENCHED Him. If the Holy Spirit is to remain, He must be loved and obeyed.
4. Popular Ordination. *And all the people shouted, and said, God save the king* (I Samuel 10:24)!

NOTICE!

1. Saul's presumption at God's altar (I Samuel 13:11-13).
2. Cruelty to his son Jonathan (I Samuel 14:44).
3. Disobedience in the matter of Amalek (I Samuel 15:23).
4. His jealousy and hatred of David (I Samuel 18:29).
5. His sinful appeal to the witch of Endor (I Samuel 28:7).

SAUL'S CAMPAIGNS

1. Against the Ammonites

Beginning of reign . . . against unsurmountable obstacles . . . army mobilized with great haste . . . Ammonites completely ruined . . . Saul's prestige as king strengthened.

2. Against the Philistines

Saul's sin in assuming function of priest . . . God rejected Saul . . . bravery of Jonathan and single companion created panic among Philistines . . . enemy routed.

3. Against the Amalekites

Saul drove enemy into desert . . . marred success by disobedience . . . seized valuable property . . . lied to Samuel . . . prophet repeated that God had rejected him.

4. Against the Philistines

Saul in constant warfare with Philistines . . . boy David appeared after his anointing . . . met Goliath, giant of Philistines . . . slew him . . . panic caused . . . David won distinction.

5. Against David

Blind jealousy drove Saul to seek David's life . . . David became an outcast . . . David repeatedly delivered . . . Saul, David's enemy till his death . . . David's immortal friendship with Saul's son, Jonathan.

6. Against the Philistines

Battlefield plains of Esdraelon . . . when dark Saul made his visit to the witch of Endor . . . Samuel called up . . . defeat and death announced . . . Israel completely defeated . . . Saul and three sons slain.

GIVE GOD HIS RIGHT-OF-WAY

All through the years Samuel mourned for Saul. When he failed, Samuel was faithful in warning him, then in loneliness he mourned over him. Multiplied verses tell the story. (See I Samuel 15:35.)

In a battle with the Philistines, Saul and his three sons met death. Here a life so full of promise ended in defeat and failure. Saul had not obeyed God absolutely. For instance, if I should sell one thousand acres of land and would reserve one acre in the center, I would have the right to go over those one thousand acres to get to mine. One trouble with us is that we reserve a room for Satan in our hearts and he knows he has his right-of-way. This was the trouble with Saul.

Think of the difference between the end of Saul of Tarsus (Paul) and Saul the king! One put God first, the other himself!

God is showing in this book that He must be all in all; that His children have no blessing apart from Him.

The morning of Saul's life was bright but soon the sky became overcast. Then his sun set in the blackest storm clouds. Follow carefully his rise, his reign, and his ruin.

DAVID, THE KING PROVEN (I Samuel 16–31)

As the third division of the book opens we see Samuel mourning for Saul. God rebukes him and tells him to arise and anoint the new king (I Samuel 16:1).

David, "the apple of God's eye," was one of the greatest characters of all times. He made great contributions to the history of Israel both spiritually and nationally.

In this book we see David as a shepherd lad, a minstrel, an armorbearer, a captain, the king's son-in-law, a writer of psalms, and a fugitive. He was anointed three times and was to be the founder of the royal line of which the King of kings came.

David, Jesse's son and the great-grandson of Ruth and Boaz, was born in Bethlehem. He was the youngest of eight sons. When David was only eighteen, God told Samuel to anoint him king to succeed Saul. As a boy he tended his father's sheep, and we read of his brave deeds in defending them from wild beasts.

As a harpist, David's fame reached the king. Saul's melancholy caused David to be called into the court to play. One of the most charming stories of real love in friendship is found between David and Jonathan, Saul's son.

When David was promoted to a high command in the army, his great success roused the jealousy of Saul who determined to kill him. He made five attacks on David's life (I Samuel 19:10,15,20,21,23,24). But God preserved David. *If God be for us, who can be against us* (Romans 8:31)? David was delivered from all these dangers. Read David's words in Psalm 59. Read Psalm 37.

These were trying days for the young man David who had been appointed to the kingly office. It was natural that he should go to Samuel for protection. All this was training for the one whom God was preparing for the throne. He not only learned how to handle men but how to handle himself. He became independent and courageous. He learned, too, in those trying days, to trust God, not men. He always awaited God's time.

He was an outcast for no wrong that he had done but because of the insane jealousy of Saul. David grew under his trials and afflictions. Instead of letting Saul's hatred harden his heart, he returned love for hate.

He learned to be a warrior those days, too. He was to become the head of a great nation, and God was training him for active service.

AN OUTCAST BECOMES KING

Finally David took refuge in flight. During this time Samuel died. Twice was Saul's life in David's hand but both times he spared Saul. Feeling that he should *perish one day by the hand of Saul,* he took refuge among the Philistines. Psalm 56 was written then. After Saul and his sons were killed by the Philistines David's exile ended.

The closing chapter of our book is draped in black. It gives the closing picture of one of the most disastrous failures. Saul died on the field of battle by his own hand. Advantages and opportunities in youth never guarantee success in manhood. One must keep true to God. Saul's undoing was not so much disobedience, as half-hearted obedience (I Samuel 15). He was a victim of human pride and jealousy.

Minimum Daily Requirements/Spiritual Vitamins

Sunday: SAMUEL, "ASKED OF GOD"   I Samuel 1–3
Monday: SAMUEL, THE PROPHET   I Samuel 4–7
Tuesday: SAUL, THE KING   I Samuel 8–12
Wednesday: SAUL, THE SELF-WILLED
    I Samuel 13–15
Thursday: DAVID ANOINTED   I Samuel 16–18
Friday: DAVID'S ADVENTURES
    I Samuel 19; 20; 22; 24
Saturday: DEATH OF SAMUEL AND SAUL
    I Samuel 25; 26; 31

UNDERSTANDING II SAMUEL

*II Samuel
Portrays Jesus Christ,
Our King*

We must not only crown Christ as King of our life, but we must set Him on His rightful throne.

The Book of I Samuel records the failure of man's king, Saul. II Samuel describes the enthronement of God's king, David, and the establishment of the "House of David" through which the Messiah, Jesus Christ, should later come. When Christ comes again, He will sit upon the throne of David (Isaiah 9:7; Luke 1:32).

The Book of II Samuel is occupied with the story of David as king (II Samuel 5:3). It does not tell the whole story, for it begins with I Samuel and runs into I Kings. I Chronicles deals with it from another standpoint.

It will make it easy to remember the contents of this book if we study it as a biography. David now occupies the field of view. He comes into his own. Let us begin with I Samuel 16.

DAVID'S PREPARATION AND DISCIPLINE

These were the testing days. David was

1. Called from the sheepcote (I Samuel 16:11-13)
2. Given victory over Goliath (I Samuel 17)
3. Persecuted by Saul (I Samuel 18 to the end)

The children of Israel had clamored for a king. God first gave them one after their own heart, Saul. Then He gave them one after His own heart, David.

This is the substance of II Samuel:

1. David was made king over Judah, II Samuel 1-4
2. David was made king over all Israel, II Samuel 5-24

Notice the blessedness of the life that recognizes the "Lord's anointed," and puts the true King on the throne of the heart.

Such a life is sheltered. *Thou wast he that leddest out and broughtest in Israel* (II Samuel 5:2).

Such a life is nurtured. *Thou shalt feed my people Israel* (II Samuel 5:2; see also Psalm 23:1,2).

Such a life is victorious, with Christ's own victory. *And thou shalt be a captain over Israel* (II Samuel 5:2).

Jesus says, *Follow Me*. If we obey, it means He will shield us and shepherd us and make our victory sure!

If we read II Samuel 7:18-22; 8:14,15, we find David at his very best, when he was at the height of his prosperity. It shows what he had become and what he might have continued to be if only he had remained faithful to God.

David was a man after God's own heart—not because of boasted perfection but because of confessed imperfections. He hid himself in God. Read what God tells us to do when we sin, I John 1:9.

The story of David the shepherd is found in I Samuel 16 and 17; then we see him as a prince in the court, I Samuel 18–20; and finally an exile in chapters 21–31.

There is no one found anywhere in God's Word who is so versatile. He is David, the shepherd boy, the court musician, the soldier, the true friend, the outcast captain, the king, the great general, the loving father, the poet, the sinner, the broken-hearted old man, but always the lover of God. We find him as a sort of Robin Hood of the Bible. We love the stories of his daring courage, his encounter with lions and bears and the giant.

He was a man of wonderful personal power and charm. Can you find, as you read this book, the record that portrays the following qualities which stand out so clearly?

1. Faithfulness   4. Courage
2. Modesty   5. Big-heartedness
3. Patience   6. Trustfulness

7. Penitence

It would be well to compare Saul and David and roughly measure their stature one against the other. Both were kings of Israel. Both reigned about the same length of time, forty years.

Both had the loyal support of the people, and both had the promise of God's power to back them. Yet Saul was a failure and David was a success. Saul's name is a blot on Israel's history, and David's name is honored today both by Jew and Gentile.

What is the reason for the difference? It is well for us to find out, for these same factors may work in your life and mine, and we may deliberately choose the forces which shall carry us on either course.

Saul had a brilliant start and for a while made good. But with success came pride. (Read Proverbs 16:18.) Thirty-five years of his reign was spent in insecurity and failure. He had lost hold upon God. He finally died a suicide in a lost battle and left his kingdom at war with their neighbors and divided in their loyalty (I Samuel 31).

The immediate link between the last chapter and this ought to be reviewed. After David had spared Saul (I Samuel 26), he realized that his life was in danger, but he made the great mistake of associating himself with the Philistines instead of quietly trusting God (I Samuel 27). Meanwhile, the closing scenes and final tragedy of Saul's life took place (I Samuel 28–31). David's lament over Saul's death showed his attitude. Everything was clear now for David to fulfill the divine purpose and become king of Israel.

I AND II SAMUEL

Now II Samuel draws our attention. Really there is no division between the first and second books. Originally the two books were one, covering the period from the beginning of Samuel's life to the end of David's. But II Samuel is occupied wholly with David.

There is no parallel account to that in II Samuel 2 of David's succession to the kingdom of Judah, but I Chronicles 11 and 12 give a vivid picture of the men of Israel as they came to make David king over the whole land. Saul was the people's choice; David was God's choice.

After the results of Gilboa when both Saul, the king, and Jonathan, his beloved friend, lay dead, David naturally desired to know what was to be the next step. So David sought guidance of God (II Samuel 2:1). David did not ask about being a king, but only as to the place whither he should go. The nation of Israel needed a leader and the divine answer was that he should go up to the city of Hebron (verse 3).

Hebron was one of the most ancient cities (Numbers 13:22). It was in existence in Abraham's day. When Canaan was conquered it became the possession of Caleb and was one of the cities of refuge (Joshua 14:13-15; 21:11-13). This was David's capital for the first seven years of his reign. This made it still more important. It was fifteen miles south of Jerusalem, in the center of Judah, and a strong place. It was especially suitable as a capital of the new kingdom, with the Philistines on the one side and the followers of Saul on the other.

David seemed every inch a king when he spared the life of Saul. He was willing to wait for God to tell him that he would surely prevail (I Samuel 26). He was on the heights. David's training seemed complete.

The devil would rather throw a man when he is on the heights; he falls farther and harder. He threw David. For David now passed into one of the worst periods of his life and stayed there for almost a year and a half (I Samuel 27:1). David fell from a mountain peak of spiritual victory and privilege to a black valley of defeat and he deliberately chose to stay there, weak and discouraged, for a long time. (Yet the instant he turned to God, God gave him a sweeping victory over his enemies. When he asked God's guidance, God directed him to Hebron, where he was promptly made king).

David's faith had collapsed. Without God's counsel he left the country of God's people, went to live in the land of the enemy, hopelessly certain of dying at Saul's hand unless he would escape. He joined Achish, king of Gath, who gave him Ziklag in which to live (I Samuel 27:1-7).

David lied to Achish to win his favor, saying that he had raided the people of Judah when he had not. David met calamity. At last he flung himself upon God. He *encouraged himself in the LORD his God* (I Samuel 30:6). He asked God what to do. God answered and under His guidance he had a real victory (I Samuel 30).

Notice what happened at almost exactly the same time in the lives of Saul and David. Saul, an unrepentant sinner, went down to death, dragging his family and his country with him (I Samuel 31:3-7). David, a repentant sinner, is given a glorious victory over the enemy and many are saved with him (I Samuel 30:17-20). We are all sinners. Which ending do we want for our lives?

Read David's sorrowful lament over Saul and Jonathan, II Samuel 1:17-27.

How did Saul meet his death? (I Samuel 31:4).

Why is suicide wrong?

Can it ever be justified?

What motive prompts suicide?

Who fell in the same battle with Saul? (I Samuel 31:2)

What was David's attitude when he heard of their deaths?

Might one not expect him to have been glad for Saul's death?

Still in Ziklag in the enemy's country, David asked God just what he should do, but not whether he was to be king (II Samuel 2:1). He obeyed God and returned to Hebron where the men of Judah made him their king. Study the facts of II Samuel 2:8 to 4:12. Amid fighting and civil war and intrigue, David does not lift a finger to secure the kingdom of Israel. The opposition steadily weakens itself and his cause steadily grows stronger. Seven and one-half years after ascending Judah's throne, David was made king of Israel.

Why are we assured of David's success when he is made king? Saul chose the way of self; David chose God's way. Because of this, God calls him a *man after his own heart*. Notice after Saul's death David made no effort to seize the kingdom by force. After Judah claimed him as king, it was seven and one-half years before Israel crowned him. David knew that it was God's plan that he should be king of Israel but he was willing to wait.

Some people grow under responsibility; others swell. We

learn from Saul's failure that the surrendered life is the only secure and truly successful life.

DAVID'S RISE — SUPREMACY AND RULE (II Samuel 1–10)

As this book opens we find David just returning to Ziklag after his great victory over the Amalekites. He had come back weary in body but refreshed in spirit because of his great success. No doubt he was wondering what had been the outcome of that great battle at Mount Gilboa. His dearest friend, Jonathan, and King Saul, were in that battle.

David was not kept in suspense long. An Amalekite from the camp of Israel came running that great distance, Bedouin style, to tell David of the disaster. No doubt the story the messenger told was fabricated and David dealt severely with him. (Read II Samuel 1:1-16.)

David's age was now thirty (II Samuel 5:4), and never did a man at that age, or any age, act in a nobler way. His generous heart not only forgot all that Saul had done but remembered all that was favorable in Saul's character. Recall some of the things Saul had done against David.

How beautiful is this spirit of forgiveness! See that spirit when men nailed Christ to the cross, (Luke 23:34), and when men stoned a martyr to death (Acts 7:60). David wrote a song for this occasion called "The Song of the Bow." It is filled with extreme tenderness when it speaks of his beloved friend (II Samuel 1:19-27).

The death of Saul did not end David's troubles. He had formed an alliance with Achish. He had gone as near to the position of a traitor to his country as he could without actually fighting against it.

His own tribe, Judah, was by far the friendliest. They knew better how cruelly Saul had hunted him down. This is why he had thrown himself into the hands of Achish.

David inquired of God where he should set up his kingdom, and God told him in Hebron. No sooner had David gone up to the city than the men of Judah came, and anointed him king over the house of Judah. Although it was not all that God had promised David, it was a large installment, for Judah was the royal tribe.

David's start was slow and discouraging. But David had faith in God. He was patient and was willing to wait for God to lead. He was humble before God and man. He was humble in his success, and when he sinned he genuinely repented. David's was a great career. He used every talent God gave him for the glory of his Creator and built up the people of God's choice. He brought Israel to the height of her glory, extending her boundaries from the Mediterranean to the Euphrates by conquest of battle. He left a rich heritage to his race—a heritage that included power, wealth, honor, and songs and psalms. But above all he left an example of loyalty to God.

Will we not all adopt David's plan of life? He started right! He began with God. He committed every plan into His keeping (Psalm 37:5). David never forgot that God was supreme. When he sinned, he bowed in penitence and sorrow, and God forgave him.

The men of Judah who came to meet David were probably the elders of his own tribe. They came to elect him as king, and although he had been anointed privately by Samuel to indicate that God had chosen him, it was natural and necessary to repeat the anointing in public as the outward and visible inauguration of his reign.

You remember Saul was anointed privately, too (I Samuel 10:1). Anointing with oil meant a divine appointment. Saul was set apart for the service of king. He was given the right to rule the people.

However, David's kingship was not acknowledged by all of the people. Abner, the captain of Saul's army, at once took steps to appoint Saul's son to take his place.

The earnest efforts of David to ward off strife and bring the people together in recognizing him as king were all in vain. The spirit of Saul, which was so antagonistic to David, was perpetuated in Abner, who was determined to center the kingdom of Israel around the house of Saul, not of David (II Samuel 2:8-10).

The people did not consult Jehovah, but merely tried to stem the popular tide in David's direction.

Civil war followed, but finally everything turned to David and he was made king of all Israel. The monarchy in Israel was never an absolute autocracy (I Samuel 10:25; I Kings 12:3).

In the prime of his life, thirty years of age, David entered upon his complete inheritance. This was the task God intended him to do. He reigned forty years in all, including seven and one-half years in Hebron over Judah and thirty-three years in Jerusalem over the whole land. The fortress of Jerusalem was still in the hands of the Jebusites but was captured early in David's reign (II Samuel 5:6-10).

One of the great results of David's kingship was the unity of the whole nation under him as leader. He brought the various conflicting elements into one group. We find a united people under a young leader united to God. The Hebrews needed only to have kept on following David's leading down the years to have gone on from greatness to greatness. They had only to follow David's greater Son to have gone on from glory to glory!

David trusted God with all his heart and leaned not to his own understanding. He acknowledged God in all his ways and God did direct his path (Proverbs 3:6). How did David obtain guidance? By asking for it. Just how God gave the answer we are not told. God has assured us that if we ask He will answer (I John 5:14,15; Jer. 33:3). God never breaks His word. We have to make decisions almost every hour of our life. Shall I continue this course in my life? Shall my vacation be spent at home, traveling, at rest? Would we take false steps if He made the decisions for us? Could we fail?

There was long war between the house of Saul and the house of David: but David waxed stronger and stronger, and the house of Saul waxed weaker and weaker (see II Samuel 2 and 3). The cause of its weakness was that God was against it.

After seven and one-half years of opposition David finally won the heart of all Israel by his justice and great spirit. He was left now without a rival. Representatives of all the tribes came to Hebron to anoint him king of the whole nation (II Samuel 5).

From the anointing of David as king at Hebron, we go with him to the field of battle.

The first thing that engaged David was the capture of Jerusalem, the stronghold of Zion. Since the days of Joshua, Jerusalem alone had defied the attack of Israel. It was an impregnable fortress. David thought it was best suited to be his nation's capital. This became the residence of David and the capital of his kingdom.

What is the city of greatest importance as far as God is concerned? The record of how it came for the first time completely into the possession of God's people is given in II Samuel 5:6-9; I Chronicles 11:4-8.

After David had established the capital at Jerusalem, he wished to bring the Ark of God into the new ruling center. He realized the people's need of God. But we are not told that he consulted God. A real tragedy followed. What was it? (II Samuel 6:1-19). What do you know of God's directions for carrying the Ark?

It is not what we think but what God says that is important. Uzzah's human opinion was that it was all right to take hold of the Ark to keep it from falling. He was sincere, but it was directly contrary to what God said. He died. We can always know what God has said if we are willing to pay the price of knowing by studying His Word and trusting what He says (John 7:17).

What was the greatest thing David did for his people?

He captured Jerusalem, built it bigger and stronger, conquered the Philistines and unified the people. But all this would be of little use without putting God at the center. This is really what gave the nation unity and power. Neither a nation nor an individual can be great without Christ in its heart.

All the events in David's reign that followed the capture of Jerusalem may be summed up in these words, *David waxed greater and greater: for the LORD of hosts was with him* (I Chronicles 11:9). God had been getting David ready for this reign. Training is difficult. It is good to bear the yoke in youth. Many a great man can testify to this.

The first concern of David when he settled in Jerusalem was the bringing up of the Ark of the testimony. His attempt to place the Ark in Mount Zion failed through want of due reverence on the part of those carrying it, but after three months it was duly placed in the tabernacle. (Read the story in II Samuel 6.)

David was an active man. He was fond of work. His wars with outside nations had ceased. Now he sought to find what he could do to improve and beautify his kingdom. He compared the elegance of his own palace with the tabernacle where Jehovah dwelt. He thought this difference ought not to be. He called Nathan the prophet and consulted him about building a temple for Jehovah. At first it seemed as though God would let him do this, but God had a different purpose for David. Read what God told Nathan to tell to David (II Samuel 7:4-17).

David's spirit is again revealed in his submission to God's plan for him. God allowed him to gather materials for his son to use.

God's servants do not take it ill that the Lord thwarts their plans and desires. A real servant learns what God's will is and yields his will to his Master's!

Don't pass over the sweet story of David's treatment of crippled young Mephibosheth when he found he was his best friend's son (II Samuel 9).

David was powerful in every art of war, although his heart was inclined to peace. Chapter ten recounts some perilous undertakings. This story gives the closing account of David's rise to power and prepares for the terrible story of his fall.

Under David's rule Israel reached its high-water mark. It has been called Israel's golden age. There were no groves, no idol worship, no worldly functions when "the sweet singer of Israel," the "shepherd boy of Bethlehem," commanded the ship of state. His merchant caravans crossed the deserts and his routes went from the Nile to the Tigris and Euphrates, and Israel prospered in those days. When Israel was right with God, she was invincible against all odds.

DAVID'S FALL (II Samuel 11–20)

We wish the life of David could have ended before chapter II was written. The golden era has passed away and what is left is a checkered tale of sin and punishment. In all of God's Word there is no chapter more tragic or more full of warning for the child of God. It tells the story of David's fall. It is like an eclipse of the sun. His sins of adultery and virtual murder were a terrible blot on David's life. He became a broken man. God forgave him but the Word says, "The sword never departed from his house." He reaped just what he had sown. We see the harvest in his own house and in the nation.

Look over the steps in David's fall. You will find the steps downward in rapid succession.

First, he was idle (II Samuel 11:1,2). It was the time for a king to go to war but he was not there. He remained in Jerusalem in the place of temptation. At evening-time he arose from off his bed and walked on the roof of his house. He was in that idle, listless mood which opens one to temptation. He saw the beautiful Bathsheba and he wanted her. His first sin was in the fact that he saw. Don't look on evil. Ask God to keep your eyes. Refuse the admission of sin into your mind. If David had nipped the temptation in the bud, he would have saved himself a world of agony and awful sin. Instead of driving it out of his mind, he cherished it.

Next, *he sent and inquired* (II Samuel 11:3). He makes inquiry about this woman and then *he took* (v.4). He brings her to his house. He forgets what is due to the faithful soldier whose wife she is.

But the next step is far worse—his sin against Uriah, one of the bravest of his soldiers. He must get rid of him. He makes Joab his confidant in sin, his partner in murder.

This sin was the more terrible because it was committed by the head of the nation. This one had been signally favored by God. He was no longer a young man. He had passed through many experiences. Then, too, the excellent service of Uriah entitled him to rewards, not death.

Why do you suppose that this tragic story is given in the

Bible? It bears the character of a beacon, warning the mariner against some of the most perilous rocks that are to be found in all the sea of life. Never neglect watching and praying. An hour's sleep left Samson at the mercy of Delilah. Don't fool with one sin even in thought. The door may be opened to a dangerous brood. It doesn't take a whole box of matches to start a fire. One will do it!

SIN PUNISHED

A year later the prophet Nathan visited David and charged him with his sin. We can imagine the anguish of David's heart that year. We read of David's sincere repentance (Psalm 51). God told David that his child should die because of his sin. See how David accepted this punishment (II Samuel 12:13-32). When the child died, David arose and worshiped God.

"A living sorrow is worse than a dead one," says a proverb. The death of his child was a grievous sorrow to David, but the living sorrow which he endured through his beloved son Absalom we cannot imagine. The rebellion of this young man is full of tragedy. Absalom was a handsome young man, but he was treacherous. He weaned away his father's subjects by treachery. He sat at the city gate and told the farmers what he would do if he were their ruler. When men bowed in honor, he kissed their hand. He drove a beautiful chariot drawn by prancing horses. He became a favorite.

Through a spy system he stole the kingdom from his father. When David left Jerusalem, Absalom gathered his army in Hebron and marched triumphantly into the city. Finally David prepared for battle with Absalom. During the fray Absalom was caught by his long hair in the trees of the forest.

Absalom was heartless and cruel. David suffered alike in the day of Absalom's victory and in the dark hour of his defeat and slaying. Read his lament over Absalom when he heard the news of his death (II Samuel 18:19-19:4).

DAVID'S LAST DAYS (II Samuel 20-24)

After the rebellion was crushed, King David returned to his kingdom. New officers were installed and reconstruction began on every hand. We see David's sin in numbering the people, because God had not told him to. The land was punished with a three-day pestilence.

He gathered great provisions for the building of the temple and directed his son Solomon to build it. David was only seventy years old when he died.

David was a mighty king and warrior. He ranked with Abraham, Moses and Paul. His great spirit is revealed to us in the psalms which he wrote. But he sinned. The story does not end here, because he repented. Read the great confession in Psalm 51.

This is the *man after God's heart*. We need to understand David's life in order to understand and use the Psalms. We must know, too, why Christ was called the *Son of David* (See Acts 13:22,23). David stands halfway between Abraham and Christ.

David had his faults. He did much that was very wrong, but he kept his nation from going into idolatry. Although his private sins were grievous, he stood like a rock for Jehovah. He sinned, but he repented and gave God a chance to forgive and cleanse him. He illustrates the conflict that Paul describes in Romans 7. He was a great saint even though he was a great sinner.

David took a chaotic nation and established a dynasty that was to last to the time of the captivity, a period of over 450 years. There never was a greater warrior or statesman than David. He made Israel the dominant power of western Asia.

The last verses of II Samuel 24:18-25 tell of King David's buying Araunah's threshing floor. He erected an altar there. This has special significance for it is on this site the great temple of Solomon was later built. On this sacred spot today stands the Mosque of Omar. It is a most galling thing to the Jews to have this sacred ground in the hands of the Moslem. The Jew cannot step his foot on the former temple area, the most hallowed spot in all the world to him.

Do not pray for an easy task. Pray to be stronger! The greatness of a man's power is the measure of his surrender. It is not a question of who you are, or of what you are, but whether God controls you.

Consider, what constitutes a missionary call? How does God call men today?

The angel of Jehovah generally comes when you are busy (Judges 6:11,12).

—Saul was out hunting the livestock.
—David was tending sheep.
—Disciples were fishing.
—Luther was a busy pastor.
—Washington was a farmer-surveyor.
—Lincoln was a country lawyer.
—Frances Willard was a school teacher.
—Moody was a shoe salesman.
—Carey was a cobbler.

You say, "Those men outside the Bible never saw an angel!" How do you know they didn't? God speaks to men in many different ways and surprises us as much as He surprised the young Hebrew farmer, Gideon.

Minimum Daily Requirements/Spiritual Vitamins

Sunday: DAVID MOURNS FOR JONATHAN AND SAUL
II Sam. 1:1-27

Monday: DAVID, KING OF JUDAH
II Sam. 2:1-32; 3:1

Tuesday: DAVID, KING OF ALL ISRAEL
II Sam. 5:1-25

Wednesday: DAVID'S HOUSE ESTABLISHED
II Sam. 7:1-29

Thursday: DAVID'S SIN   II Sam. 11:1-27

Friday: DAVID'S REPENTANCE   II Sam. 12:1-23;
Psalm 51

Saturday: DAVID NUMBERS THE PEOPLE
II Sam. 24:1-17

CHAPTER 11

UNDERSTANDING KINGS and CHRONICLES

*Kings and Chronicles
Portray Jesus Christ
As King*

If we reject God, He will reject us. If we obey God, He will bless us. *In those days the LORD began to cut Israel short* (II Kings 10:32).

In the original Hebrew in which these books were written I and II Kings formed one book, I and II Samuel another, and I and II Chronicles a third. When they were translated into the Greek language, they were divided by the translators because the Greek required one third more space than the Hebrew and the scrolls on which they were written were limited in length.

Probably the author of the Book of Kings was Jeremiah. The book was written while the first temple was standing.

I and II Kings are just a continuation of the Books of Samuel. As their name suggests, they record the events of the reign of Solomon and then of the succeeding kings of Judah and Israel. They cover a period of four hundred years and tell the story of the growth and then decay of the kingdom. We see the kingdom divided. We see both Israel and Judah led into captivity. The Southern Kingdom (Judah) had twenty kings, and the Northern Kingdom (Israel) had nineteen kings.

These are the two most important books of history in the world. Every day expeditions are digging up the records of history about which nothing has been written outside the Books of the Kings. At first they may seem dry to you, but the lives of the kings, and the stories in these books prove:

1. *God is no respecter of persons* (Acts 10:34).
2. When our all is on the altar, God never keeps us waiting for the fire (I Kings 18:38). What is the spiritual meaning of this?

129

3. The final captivity was because of disobedience to God. It was prophesied before (Deut. 28:49). What has God said about the individual who forgets Him?

Kings begin with King David and end with the king of Babylon.

Kings open with the building of the temple and end with the burning of the temple.

Kings open with David's first successor to the throne of his kingdom, Solomon, and end with David's last successor, Jehoiachin, released from captivity by the king of Babylon.

Kings open with the building of the temple and end with the Babylonian captivity and the destruction of the temple.

Remember these Books of Kings cover practically the whole rule of the kings over God's chosen people. During Solomon's reign the kingdom reached the height of its grandeur. With the death of Solomon, the kingship really ceased to be the medium through which God governed His people. The period of the prophets is introduced at this time by the great Elijah. I Kings ends with the story of this prophet. II Kings centers around Elisha. The decline of the kingdoms is given until we see both Israel and Judah led into captivity.

THE SPLENDID REIGN OF SOLOMON (I Kings 1–10)

As the scene opens we find *king David now old and stricken in years*. He was prematurely aged for he was only seventy. His son Solomon was but nineteen. Because of David's feebleness we find a rebellion started against him. Adonijah's attempt to get his father's throne was natural because he was the oldest surviving son (II Samuel 3:4). This rebellion called for prompt action which Nathan, the prophet, took. David saw that Solomon was the most fit to succeed him. Solomon was God's choice (I Chronicles 22:9; I Kings 2:15). It was clear that the choice of Solomon was popular (I Kings 1:39,40). Adonijah soon saw that opposition was useless. Because of this rebellion, Solomon was crowned before David's death (I Kings 1:30,39,53).

Solomon received his religious training from Nathan the prophet. This wise prophet loved Solomon and gave him the name Jedidiah, "God's darling" (II Samuel 12:25). Solomon's reign began in a blaze of glory. It was splendor without surrender. And as with Saul, Solomon's life ended in an anti-climax.

His heart was not perfect with the LORD his God, as was the heart of David his father (I Kings 11:4). Remember, God wants our hearts!

Yet Solomon was a magnificent king; his throne was the grandest the world had ever seen and his life was filled with happenings of marvelous significance. His kingdom of 60,000 square miles was ten times as great as that which his father had inherited.

A CHARACTER STUDY

I. Solomon a great and good man

1. His rearing was under the religious and wise Nathan who gave him the pet name, Jedidiah, "God's darling" (II Samuel 12:25).

2. His kingship was clear. All the city rang with the glad cry, *Solomon sitteth on the throne of the kingdom* (I Kings 1:46).

3. His charge from his father was full of promise (I Kings 2:1-9).

4. His choice of wisdom from God was a divine choice (I Kings 3).

5. His cabinet was greater than any king of Israel ever had (I Kings 4).

6. His lifework was the building of the temple. Several million dollars was expended in erecting it. Its service of dedication has gone down on record because of its sublimity.

7. The kingdom he established realized at last, after four hundred years, the broad dimensions outlined to Joshua (Joshua 1:4).

8. The wealth and glory of Solomon's reign fairly took the breath of the Queen of Sheba. *There was no more spirit* [breath] *in her* (I Kings 10:5).

9. His beauty of person is hinted in Psalm 45.

10. His ardent affection is seen in the songs that bear his name (Songs of Solomon).

Solomon was a great and glorious king but we soon find the note of decline.

II. Solomon the Weak and Erring One

1. Unlike his father David, he dealt cruelly with his brother Adonijah (I Kings 2:24,25).

2. Like Saul, his heart was lifted up in pride (I Kings 10:18-29).

3. Led by his heathen wives, he fell into idolatry (I Kings 11). *Be ye not unequally yoked together with unbelievers* (II Cor. 6:14).

Solomon did not display spiritual wisdom. The Book of Ecclesiastes, with its note of despair, is a confession of it. He did not have a heart at peace with God.

After David's final words of admonition to his son to be absolutely loyal to Jehovah, the king died, having reigned for forty years.

When the young Princess Victoria learned early one morning that she had become Queen of England, the first thing she did was to ask the Archbishop of Canterbury to pray for her. The Archbishop and Lord Chamberlain knelt down together and prayed that grace, strength and wisdom might be given to her throughout her reign. Governing is a serious business. Solomon realized its seriousness, as a young man, and began his reign with prayer.

God appeared to Solomon in a dream early in his reign and asked him to make a choice of anything that he might wish. The young king's wise choice revealed his feeling of inability to do all that was put upon him. What was his request of the Lord? God gave him the wisdom for which he asked. What is God's promise to us? (James 1:5). *Ask what I shall give thee* (I Kings 3:5). This is the high privilege of every man. Each one's life tells what he has asked for. What is your choice?

The youth had not been swept off his feet by his father's praise when David twice called him a wise man (I Kings 2:6-9). Solomon asked for a "hearing heart." Have we a heart that listens to the Spirit's voice?

Solomon was the wisest man the world ever saw until the coming of Him who could say of Himself, *a greater than Solo-*

mon is here (Matthew 12:42). All the earth acknowledged Solomon but when the greater than Solomon came His own received Him not (John 1:11). That is tragedy. But have you received Him?

First Solomon organized his leaders. He gathered around him a wise company of officers of state, each having his own department for which he was responsible. This led to days of tremendous prosperity in the kingdom.

The greatest undertaking of Solomon's reign was the building of the temple. This was what his father David had longed to do. The immense foundation of great hewn stones upon which Solomon's temple was built remains till this day under the Dome of the Rock. One stone alone is thirty-eight feet, nine inches long. The huge stones, the fragrant cedar wood and gold covering gave it unusual splendor.

The temple site was an historic spot. On Mount Moriah Abraham offered up Isaac (Genesis 22:2). We saw how David secured Araunah's threshing floor and here today the Dome of the Rock stands, the sacred spot of the Mohammedans. No Jew is allowed to step his foot upon this "holy" ground. So we see the Jews gathering from near and far to wail at the wall outside this area, to pray for mercy, and to ask God for deliverance from their enemy. The great stones which form this ancient wall were the foundation stones of Solomon's temple.

Men used to have to make pilgrimages to the temple to meet God. But now we know a wonderful truth that our bodies are the temples of God (I Cor. 3:16; 6:19). Is your body a real temple? God wishes to live in you, but He cannot if you are defiled with sin.

There are three earthly temples mentioned in Scripture. The first is Solomon's, which was destroyed by the Babylonians about 587 B.C. (II Kings 25:8,9). The second was Zerubbabel's (Ezra 5:2; 6:15-18). This was not comparable in elegance to Solomon's. The third was Herod's temple erected on a grander scale in B.C. 20 and completed in A.D. 64. This temple was destroyed by Titus in A.D. 70. The Mosque of Omar now stands on this site.

PALESTINE
TRIBES OF ISRAEL

LEBANON MTS.

SIDON

TYRE

DAN

SYRIANS

NAPHTALI

MEDITERRANEAN
SEA

ASHER

ZEBULUN

SEA OF GALILEE

MANASSEH

ISSACHAR

MANASSEH

MT. EBAL   SHECHEM   MAHANAIM?

MT. GERIZIM

RIVER
JORDAN

EPHRAIM   GAD

JOPPA

BETHEL   GIBEON

BENJAMIN   **AMMON**

DAN   GIBEAH

JERICHO

JERUSALEM

PHILISTINES   BETHLEHEM

GATH?   REUBEN

HEBRON

JUDAH

GAZA

DEAD SEA

ZIKLAG

JESHIMON
VALLEY

BEERSHEBA   **MOAB**

SIMEON

EDOM SEIR

THE GLORY OF SOLOMON'S REIGN

Read I Kings 9:1-28 and 10:14-29 to find the possible, not to say the probable, dangers to Solomon in all this wonderful glory. Note his high position, his great wisdom, his countless riches. It is hard not to forget God in the hour of such prosperity. One thinks only of his possessions. It was this very glory that led to Solomon's downfall.

Because of his backsliding God raised up enemies to vex Solomon. The Book of Ecclesiastes describes the futility of life to Solomon at this time.

The Queen of Sheba witnessed Solomon's reign at its zenith and saw the fulfillment of David's prayer for his son, offered about a year before his death.

Solomon's reputation probably had spread through the voyages of his navy (I Kings 9:21-28). The fame of Solomon was associated with Jehovah. His fame concerning the name of the Lord was the thing that interested her Majesty, the Queen of Sheba. She was impressed by (1) Solomon himself, with his wisdom and wealth, I Kings 10:1,7; (2) his servants, verse 8; and (3) his God, verse 9.

THE KINGDOM TORN ASUNDER (I Kings 11-16)

Solomon reigned forty years, the second great period of the complete kingdom (I Kings 11). At first all went well, but later there was serious trouble. You note that Saul, David and Solomon each reigned forty years (Acts 13:21; II Samuel 5:4; I Kings 11:42).

Taxes under Solomon's reign had weighed the people down. Luxury and idolatry had broken down their morale. The kingdom now was to be divided. A rise to such prosperity and power as Solomon enjoyed had its dangers. It cost money and meant increased taxation that grew into burdens which were unbearable and which bred the seeds of unrest and revolution.

Solomon set up a great establishment in Jerusalem, built his famous temple, bringing in foreign workmen and materials to do it, and then he built himself a palace that dazzled his own subjects and his foreign visitors.

During this time there was corruption and graft, and under all these burdens the people grew restless and rebellious.

Consider the events leading up to the division. For years there had been jealousy between the Northern Kingdom (Israel) and the Southern Kingdom (Judah). The cause for the jealousy went back three hundred years and was due mainly to the jealousy between the tribes of Ephraim and Judah. Note the blessings that Jacob gave to Ephraim (Genesis 48:17-22; 49:22-26). And from the time of Joshua, who was of that tribe, Ephraim took a leading place. The transfer of authority to Judah came under David, who was of the tribe of Judah. All this tribal jealousy was intensified by the hardships felt by the people through Solomon's high-handed actions. His demands created oppression and his unfaithfulness to God demanded judgment (I Kings 11:26-43; 12:4).

When Solomon's son, Rehoboam, threatened to levy heavier burdens upon the people, his unwise headstrong action added fuel to a fire which had been gathering and burning for nearly three hundred years from the time of the judges.

The revolt of the ten tribes immediately followed (I Kings 12:16), though the two tribes of Judah and Benjamin remained loyal (I Kings 12:17). This tension led to the appointment of Jeroboam as king of the northern section (Verse 20).

SECRET OF DECLINE

A new name of great importance appears in the pages of this story: Jeroboam. This young man, of low origin, had risen to notice because of faithful service and deeds done. The prophet Ahijah made a startling revelation to Jeroboam. Using Oriental imagery, he took off his new coat and tore it into twelve strips and then he said to Jeroboam, *Take thee ten pieces: for thus saith the LORD, the God of Israel, Behold, I will rend the kingdom out of the hand of Solomon, and will give ten tribes to thee* (I Kings 11:31).

The kingdom was divided. The judgment was upon Solomon for his long years of luxury and pride and power. Every ruler should look ahead and see toward what rocks he may be steering his kingdom, and whether or not he is heading toward the day when his power shall be taken out of his hand.

Have we not seen, in our day, men rising to great wealth and power in which they have piled up millions, stripped to nothing and fleeing from outraged justice?

Things do not happen by accident. There is a cause at the root of every revolution. The event may come as suddenly as an explosion, or as the eruption of a volcano, but somewhere secret causes were at work undermining the structure. The French Revolution had its roots down under centuries of oppression.

Religious apostasy had been gnawing like a deadly worm at the root of Israel's life. One day the tree fell. Nothing destroys a nation's life like religious decline. Take the sun out of the sky and there will be no grass, or flowers, or orchards. Take God out of our sky and there will be no homes, or schools, or social life.

SIN BRINGS DIVISION

Though they didn't know it, the people were carrying out the divine purpose (I Kings 12:15; 11:29-33). God could not overlook the disobedience of Solomon to His clearest commands.

The kingdom of God's chosen people was divided. It has been divided for almost 3,000 years. It was divided through sin. We see this kingdom go to pieces and finally into captivity (II Kings 17 and 25). It is part of the gospel, the Good News, that those two great sections of divided Israel are going to be united again on this earth at Christ's return in glory. (Read the wonderful passages in Isaiah 11:10-13; Ezekiel 37:15-28.)

THE MINISTRY OF ELIJAH (I Kings 17-22; II Kings 1:1-2:2)

Elijah was a bolt of fire that God let loose upon wicked Ahab and idolatrous Israel. He flashed across the page of history, as sudden and terrible as a flash of lightning. *Elijah the Tishbite, who was of the inhabitants of Gilead,* is his brief biography by which he was introduced. His name Elijah means *Jehovah is my God.* It fitted him perfectly. He was the most outstanding of the prophets. Follow his sudden appearance, his undaunted courage, his zeal, the heights of his triumph on Mount Carmel, the depths of his despondence, the glorious rapture into heaven in the whirlwind, his reappearance on the Mount of Transfiguration.

He was a striking character from the highlands of Gilead. His long thick hair hung over a cloak of sheepskin. Jehovah sent him to do away with the awful worship of Baal during the reign of Ahab who had married the wicked heathen princess, Jezebel. Suddenly emerging from the desert and standing before the corrupt king in the splendor of his court, the stern prophet boldly said, *As the LORD God of Israel liveth, before whom I stand, there shall not be dew nor rain these years, but according to my word* (I Kings 17:1). He was given power to shut up the heavens so there would be no rain for three and a half years. He called down fire from heaven before the prophets of Baal at Mount Carmel. He was the evangelist of his day, thundering out warnings to this idolatrous people. The events in this great career will intrigue you. Read them over.

THE MINISTRY OF ELISHA (II Kings 1-9)

Elisha succeeded Elijah. He was beneficent in contrast to the fiery Elijah. Elijah trained Elisha as his successor. Elisha's ministry lasted fifty years. Most of his miracles were deeds of kindness and mercy. Elisha had a great influence upon the kings of the day and although he did not approve of what they did, he was always coming to their rescue.

Elijah and Elisha are in marked contrast to one another:

Elijah, the prophet of judgment, law, severity.

Elisha, the prophet of grace, love, tenderness.

Baal worship was introduced by the wicked Jezebel and after thirty years was exterminated by Elijah, Elisha and Jehu.

THE CORRUPTION OF ISRAEL (II Kings 1-17)

Jeroboam, the ruler of the northern kingdom, Israel, made Shechem his capital. It seemed the natural place because it was in the center of the land.

It was the custom, according to the law, to go up to Jerusalem regularly to worship (Deut. 12:11,14; 16:6,15,16; I Samuel 1:3,7). Jeroboam was afraid to have his ten tribes journey to Jerusalem, the capital of Rehoboam's kingdom, to worship God, so he made two golden calves and placed them in convenient spots—Bethel (Genesis 28:11-19) in the south, and Dan (Judges 18:29,30) in the northern end of the kingdom, so the people would not have to go to Jerusalem.

Over twenty times he is described as *Jeroboam, the son of Nebat, who made Israel to sin.* Beware of man-made religion. We must worship where and how God tells us!

God says, *Not forsaking the assembling of ourselves together, as the manner of some is* (Hebrews 10:25). God knows we need fellowship in worship to keep the spiritual coals alive, but we hear people say constantly that they can worship better alone in the woods or by the sea. Learn now to do what God asks you to do. Remember, a request from a king is a command!

After 256 years the people were carried into captivity by the king of Assyria (II Kings 17). Many of God's prophets had warned Israel of captivity but they would not turn from their idolatry to Jehovah.

The Assyrians were great and cruel warriors. They built their kingdom on their pillage from other countries. Their practices were horrible. They skinned men alive, cut out their tongues, put out their eyes, dismembered their bodies and then made mounds of the skulls of men to instill fear! For three hundred years Assyria was a world empire.

THE CAPTIVITY OF JUDAH (II Kings 13–25)

The Southern Kingdom tried to conquer the Northern Kingdom. For eighty years there was continuous war between them. But they failed. Then there was a period of eighty years of peace between these two kingdoms following the marriage of the son of Jehoshaphat (southern king) to the daughter of Ahab (northern king). Finally there was a period of fifty years when they intermittently warred with one another until the captivity.

In the Southern Kingdom there was only one dynasty (Davidic) from King Rehoboam to Zedekiah. The great prophets of that day were Isaiah, Nathan, Jeremiah, Joel and Zephaniah.

About 136 years after the Northern Kingdom had been taken into captivity by Assyria, the Southern Kingdom was taken captive by Nebuchadnezzar, king of Babylon. Jerusalem was destroyed, the temple burned and the princes led away. The people had forgotten God and refused to listen to the warnings of the prophets. God wanted His people to learn the lesson of obedience and dependence upon Him.

In I Kings we see the kingdom of Israel, filled with pride and arrogance, falling apart. In II Kings, sinning yet more, Israel goes into captivity. Surely the way of the transgressor is hard. The history of the Jews is a record of God's dealings with disobedient children. In all His punishment He is kind and merciful for He loves them still.

The secret of the downfall of the Jewish people is found in II Kings 3:2, *And he wrought evil in the sight of the LORD.* Be loyal and true to God. It does not pay to do evil.

The moving figures and powerful factors of those days were the prophets Elijah and Elisha. Elijah was the strength of Israel. Jezebel and Ahab had frightened the people into submission. But Elijah stood. Read I Kings 17:1 where he said, *As the LORD God of Israel liveth, before whom I stand.* And there he stood for God, like a rock, in face of all the weakness of Israel. We ask today, *Where is the LORD God of Elijah* (II Kings 2:14)? Would that we might see some of this old-time power.

Elijah was the champion of the Most High. He brought God to the people. He was the pastor-evangelist of Israel's day.

NOTE: There is a great difference between the fall of Israel and Judah. Israel was scattered throughout the nations for an indefinite period, but God specified the length of Judah's captivity to seventy years. Judah was to return to Jerusalem which she did later. The Messiah was to come out of Judah and God was preparing the way for Him to come to Palestine and not to Babylon or Assyria.

God was using even the rulers of foreign nations to work out His plan. Cyrus, king of Persia, for example, was going to issue a decree which would allow the Jews to return to their homeland, Palestine.

Look up the following questions:

What was Solomon's greatest work? Describe it.

What books of the Bible did Solomon write?

Why was the kingdom divided after Solomon's death?

Describe the kings of Israel. How did this kingdom end? Who were her conquerors? (Know this.) Who were Israel's prophets?

Describe the kings of Judah. Who took Judah captive and where was she taken?

UNDERSTANDING I CHRONICLES

The History of Judah

It is through such books as the Chronicles that we get the history of the Jewish nation. Through this nation our Lord came to earth. God chose this people for the fulfillment of His great promises and purposes. He is still their God (Romans 11:1), and He has His purposes yet to be fulfilled in them. In the light of this truth books such as the Chronicles take on new meaning and power.

UNDERSTANDING II CHRONICLES

A Book of Revivals!

Great revivals under:

1. Asa...II Chronicles 15
2. Jehoshaphat.............................II Chronicles 20
3. Joash...II Chronicles 23; 24
4. Hezekiah...................................II Chronicles 29–31
5. Josiah..II Chronicles 35

Jesus Christ is portrayed as King in the books of Kings and Chronicles.

Minimum Daily Requirements/Spiritual Vitamins

Sunday: BUILDING AND DEDICATING THE TEMPLE
I Kings 6:1-14; 8:22-53
Monday: SOLOMON'S GLORIOUS REIGN
I Kings 10:1-29
Tuesday: THE KINGDOM DIVIDED   I Kings 12:1-33
Wednesday: THE PROPHET ELIJAH
I Kings 17:1–18:46
Thursday: ELIJAH AND ELISHA   II Kings 2:1-22
Friday: THE CAPTIVITY OF ISRAEL (THE NORTHERN KINGDOM) II Kings 17:7-23
Saturday: THE CAPTIVITY OF JUDAH (THE SOUTHERN KINGDOM) II Kings 25:1-21

UNDERSTANDING EZRA and NEHEMIAH

Ezra and Nehemiah Portray Jesus Christ, Our Restorer

Again we find that Ezra and Nehemiah were one book in the Hebrew Bible as were the two books of Samuel and Kings. These books tell the story of the return of God's chosen people after the exile. They give the record of one of the most important events in Jewish history—the return from exile in Babylon.

The time covered by these two books is about one hundred years.

Both books begin at Babylon and end at Jerusalem.

Both center around the man of God who wrote it.

Both stories begin with a Persian king's decree.

Both tell of building as their chief theme.

Both books contain a long prayer of humiliation and confession in the ninth chapter.

Both end with the purification of the people.

KEYNOTE OF EACH LIFE

Ezra 7:10—Ezra's keynote

Nehemiah 6:3—Nehemiah's keynote

The purposes of God may sometimes seem delayed, but they are never abandoned. *Remember . . . the word that thou commandest thy servant Moses,* prayed Nehemiah (Neh. 1:8). The Books of Ezra and Nehemiah tell the story of how God remembered and how He brought back His people from exile. Jeremiah 29:10-13 tells us of this remembrance.

During the captivity, the prophets, Jeremiah and Ezekiel, told the Jews of their restoration and predicted that they would return to their own land and rebuild Jerusalem. Jeremiah, the prophet, told them this would happen at the end of seventy years. *For thus saith the LORD, that after seventy years be accomplished at Babylon I will visit you, and perform my good word toward you, in causing you to return to this place* (Jeremiah 29:10). You remember that the Books of Kings ended with the story of the captivity of first the northern kingdom of Israel and then the southern kingdom of Judah.

Daniel was carried away captive to Babylon at the time of the captivity of Judah. The last incident in the history was the story of Daniel in the lions' den (Daniel 6:16-24). This happened about ten years before Cyrus became king over Babylon. Daniel was an old man now when these present events took place.

The rebuilding of the national life of the Jews covered one hundred years.

There are two periods of time that are very important.

1. Twenty years (537-517 B.C.) from the first year of Cyrus to the sixth year of Darius when the people under Zerubbabel, the governor, and Joshua, the priest, rebuilt the temple. For this period read Ezra 1–6; Zechariah and Haggai; the first chapters of I Chronicles; the last two verses of II Chronicles; Psalms 126; 137; and the reference to Cyrus in Isaiah 44:23 to 45:8.

2. Twenty-five years (458-433 B.C.) when Nehemiah, the governor, and Ezra, the priest, rebuilt the wall of Jerusalem and restored the city. Malachi was the prophet of this day.

Ezra gives the record of both of these periods.

Nehemiah tells of the second period, the building of the walls.

The book of Ezra has both a backward and a forward look.

Looking Backward

We find a second exodus for captive Israel. The first exodus was out of Egypt. This second exodus was from Babylon. This time Ezra is leader in the place of Moses. He, like Moses, is an inspired writer and leader. Both men were great organizers, lawgivers, and teachers raised up to fulfill God's gracious purpose and bring captive Israel out of bondage. Both of these great leaders dealt with Israel in a strong and merciful way.

Looking Ahead

In history it is like the landing of our Pilgrim Fathers on a

144

bleak and hostile shore. They came in timid, struggling relays back to Jerusalem. But God gave them a foothold. It was His city and it is His city still. He will again bring back His own; He will raise up Zion out of ruins.

CAPTIVITY AND RESTORATION

The Jews were taken captive first by Assyria (II Kings 17), then by Babylon. (II Kings 25) They were restored to their own land under the Persian Empire. The Babylonians had been conquered by the Medes and Persians. The ten northern tribes who were carried away to Assyria never returned.

In 537 B.C. The first Jews returned to Jerusalem from Babylon.

In 516 B.C. Temple restored.

In 479 B.C. Esther became queen of Persia. (She was wife of Xerxes.)

In 458 B.C. Ezra led second expedition from Babylon.

In 445 B.C. Nehemiah built wall of Jerusalem.

RETURN UNDER ZERUBBABEL AND REBUILDING THE TEMPLE (Ezra 1-6)

As the book opens (Ezra 1:1-6), we find Cyrus, king of Persia, making a proclamation throughout his kingdom permitting the Jews who were captives in his kingdom to return to Jerusalem.

Two hundred years before, God had prophesied that He would do this. He named Cyrus as the one He would use. The record of this remarkable prophecy, which calls a king by his name two hundred years before he was born, is found in Isaiah 44:28; 45:1-4. No doubt this proclamation of Cyrus was due in part to the fact that he saw these words of Isaiah.

Daniel's influence in the court was very powerful. He had been the Disraeli of the court in Babylon. He was one of the princes carried away by Nebuchadnezzar to his court. Now he was an old man.

At Cyrus' first call (537 B.C.), (Ezra 1:1-4) no more than 50,000 Jews availed themselves of the opportunity of returning to Jerusalem under Zerubbabel. Notice from this time the

Israelites are called Jews because most of them were of the tribe of Judah and the name Jews comes from Judah.

Cyrus gave back to Zerubbabel the golden vessels which Nebuchadnezzar had taken from the temple in Jerusalem (Ezra 1:5-11). They started back over seven hundred miles of trackless desert from Babylon to Jerusalem.

At the time of the captivity, seventy years before, only the better classes were taken into Babylon. The rest were left in their own land to suffer (Jeremiah 24:5-8; 44:15). Now everyone does not return; only the earnest and pious Jews go back. It was a time of real sifting among the people. Most of them after seventy years had built homes and established themselves and were content to remain in Babylon. They did not care to face the dangers and hardships of returning across the desert and arriving in a city that had been destroyed.

How like the Jews of today when thousands are returning again to Palestine from all over the world! Those who have prospered in other lands do not care to go back to make a new start in Jerusalem.

Although the leaders were from the tribe of Judah, no doubt there were representatives from the whole of Israel. Only those who loved God were ready to make the attempt. Many of the Jews had been born in Babylon during the seventy years. These were not considered captives but exiles.

Everything is taken care of when God is in charge. Not only money for rebuilding the temple in Jerusalem, but traveling expenses and all other needs were provided by God at Cyrus' direction (Ezra 1:4,6). Someone has said that God used Babylon as the safety deposit vault for the silver and gold vessels of the temple.

The names of those who returned are given in chapter two. They laid the foundation of the temple the first thing upon returning. It was a time of great rejoicing. It is interesting to notice that before they built homes for themselves they first thought of a house for the Lord. They did not build the temple first but the altar (Ezra 3:2).

The place where sin must be dealt with must come first in

146

every life. The heart must be right if God is to bless. The altar was the center of the Jew's religion, the cross the center of the Christian faith.

Read about the hindrances to the work (Ezra 4:1-22). Hindrances to all real work for God are to be expected. The church must not have the help of the world.

The opposition disheartened them. They needed Haggai's message. Refer to the Book of Haggai. Haggai and Zechariah, the prophets, encouraged the people from within the ranks (Ezra 4:23–5:17), and within four years the temple was complete and dedicated (Ezra 6).

Zerubbabel's temple was very plain and simple. It was not the sumptuous edifice that Solomon's was. In fact, it was in such contrast to the elegance of the first temple that the old men who had seen Solomon's temple wept aloud. But it was God's house and so the people thanked God and took courage.

RETURN AND REFORMATION UNDER EZRA (Ezra 7–10)

Ezra appears in person in the seventh chapter (458 B.C.). At least sixty years after the Jews had first returned to Jerusalem he led a second expedition from Babylon to reinforce the struggling colonists in Palestine. Ezra received a commission from Artaxerxes, the king, (Ezra 7:11–8:14) who half-blindly aided in accomplishing God's plans for His people. Read Ezra 7:25 and find how impressed the king was with Ezra's love of God's Word. Oh, that we might live in such a way that others would learn to have respect for God's Book!

This contingent under Ezra consisted of 1700 Jews. It took them four months to make the journey, and it was financed by King Artaxerxes (Ezra 7:12-26). Thirteen years later this same king authorized Nehemiah to build the walls of Jerusalem. (Nehemiah 2) Cyrus, Darius and Artaxerxes, the three Persian kings, were very friendly to the Jews.

Tradition tells us that Ezra was the founder of the synagogue worship which arose in the days of the captivity. Because the temple had been destroyed and the people were scattered, they needed some place to worship God. Each Jewish community had its place of worship and instruction. After the Jews returned to their homeland, these centers were not only at home but in other lands where they had been scattered.

The Old Testament history closes about one hundred years after the Jews returned from their captivity. Alexander the Great (336-325 B.C.) broke the Persian hold and world power passed from Persia to Greece. Alexander showed consideration to the Jews, as we find in history.

EZRA, THE SCRIBE

Of Ezra it is said he *prepared his heart to seek the law of the LORD, and to do it, and to teach in Israel statutes and judgments* (Ezra 7:10). His name means "help." He belongs to the great triumvirate of the Old Testament times (Moses, Samuel, Ezra). He wrote and worked to keep the record intact and to hold Israel, God's chosen people, to her divinely appointed mission. We are indebted to Ezra for the literary and ecclesiastical renaissance of that day. He did a work in forming the scripture canon for which he was appointed of God. Tradition makes him the president of a council of 120 men who formed the Old Testament canon.

In addition to Ezra's outstanding ministry of the Word, he probably wrote portions of I and II Chronicles, and Psalm 119 which is a wonderful poem on the Word of God. As we have said, he instituted the synagogue worship which is the parent of our own form of worship, and assisted by the Great Synagogue of which he was president, settled the canon of Old Testament Scripture. It was under Ezra that we see the great revival of Bible study.

Ezra was the Thomas Jefferson of his time, laying the constitutional foundations for the future. To him we are indebted for codifying Israel's laws and the formation of her scripture canon.

When Ezra returned to Jerusalem, he found things even worse than he had expected. Although the people had not returned to idolatry, they had intermarried with the people of the land and had done everything that the heathen had taught them (Ezra 9:1-4). The princes and rulers were the worst offenders. Ezra rent his garments and literally pulled out his hair in grief! Read Ezra's touching prayer and confession (9:5-15).

EZRA'S PRAYER

As Ezra was praying and weeping before God, a great congregation assembled. What happened? (Read Ezra 10:1-44.) The people who had gathered about him through the long hours of the day came to a consciousness of the greatness of their sin as they saw how it affected Ezra. Finally one of their number spoke and acknowledged the sin. At once Ezra led them into a sacred covenant with God. Read what God says about confession of sin (I John 1:9).

NEHEMIAH'S PRAYER

Turn now to Nehemiah 9 and you will find the prayer of Nehemiah. Prayer is the most important privilege of a Christian. Nehemiah's prayer began where Ezra's ended—with utter surrender to God. (Compare Neh. 9:1,2 with Ezra 9:15; 10:1.)

God had definitely promised to bring the Jews back after seventy years in Babylon (Jer. 25:11,12; 29:10). We read in the very first verse of Ezra that it was to fulfill this word that *the LORD stirred up the spirit of Cyrus* to proclaim the restoration. (Look this up!) But it is through prayer that God wishes to have His will brought to pass. The restoration was wholly undeserved by Israel but purposed in "God's heart of mercy."

See the results of this restoration of God's people to their land again:

First, through the rebuilding of the temple, God opened the door of fellowship with Himself. Through the seventy years of suffering they were ready to return and build and wait until He, the true Servant, should come.

Second, He renewed His promise of a coming Redeemer. It was prophesied that the Redeemer would be associated with Palestine.

Third, to make ready for the *fullness of the time* when Christ should come, as spoken of by Paul in Galatians 4:4.

UNDERSTANDING NEHEMIAH

REPAIRING THE CITY'S WALL (Nehemiah 1-7)

Nehemiah was the cupbearer at the court of King Artaxerxes.

This was a position of high honor. But in this position of familiarity with the king, he had not forgotten his people. The news that was brought to him about Jerusalem made him very sad. This sadness could not be wholly hidden and the king detected it. The Jews had been back home for one hundred years, but had made no attempt to build Jerusalem beyond the restoration of the temple because their enemies made it almost impossible.

Artaxerxes' step-mother was Esther, the Jewess, who no doubt was still alive. It may have been that Nehemiah received his appointment through her influence. He was loyal enough to his people to leave the luxury of a king's court and go back to rebuild Jerusalem, the capital of his homeland. The king gave consent. We find even today Jews everywhere long to see Jerusalem flourish and turn their faces there as their homeland.

When Nehemiah reached Jerusalem in 445 B.C., Ezra had been there for thirteen years. Ezra was a priest and had been teaching the people the Word of God. But Nehemiah was a civil governor. He had come with the authority of the king of Persia to build the walls of Jerusalem. After he had been there only three days, he went up and viewed the walls at night. When he saw their dilapidated condition, he encouraged the people to begin building immediately. The work was accomplished in fifty-two days by assigning a portion of the wall to each family. Their attitude was expressed in the sentence, *The people had a mind to work* (Nehemiah 4:6). Nehemiah was a real engineer.

First the Samaritans, the enemies of the Jews, derided them. They hindered their work so that the Jews had to keep watch night and day. Their derision turned to anger and Nehemiah divided the men into two groups, one keeping watch while the other worked.

Then opposition rose within the ranks. Some of the Jews became tired and complained that there was so much rubbish that the walls could not be built. All this rubble had to be removed in a thick canvas pad on the carrier's back; there were, of course, no wheelbarrows nor cars to convey the material. Then, the complaint arose that the rich were demanding usury which the poor were unable to pay.

Again the enemies tried by craft to bring Nehemiah away from his building, but Nehemiah only prayed and again he foiled his enemy. The Persian kings were ever the friends of the Jews.

Nehemiah gave the city of Jerusalem into the charge of his brother Hanani (Nehemiah 7:1-4). When he took a census (7:5-73) the whole number was 42,360 besides 7,337 servants and 245 singing men and women.

REPAIRING THE PEOPLE'S MORALS (Nehemiah 8-13)

All the people gathered together in the street before the water gate in the city of Jerusalem and requested Ezra, the scribe, to bring out the book of the Law of Moses. He stood upon a pulpit of wood and read and explained the Law to the people (Nehemiah 8:1-13). This public reading brought true repentance to the people and a great revival broke out. When Josiah found the book of the Law, a great reformation started. When Martin Luther read the Bible, the Protestant Reformation began. We need to have the Word read today!

Their captivity in Babylon cured the Jews of idolatry. You remember up to that time, in spite of all the warnings of the prophets, the people would worship the idols of the peoples around them. But from the days of the captivity to the present (about 2500 years) the Jews have never been guilty of this sin. The Jews had intermarried with the idolatrous neighbors and this was the reason for their sin. Intermarriage of Christians with those who do not believe is a dangerous thing today. Paul says, *Be ye not unequally yoked together with unbelievers* (II Corinthians 6:14).

Remember, Nehemiah left a life of ease and luxury and security for a life of toil and danger and heartbreaks. He was a reformer! And no one appreciates the man who tries to reform him.

Nehemiah was a man of prayer. We do not find a blot on his character. He was fearless and courageous.

The Important Thing . . . in the study of the Bible is to find how Jesus Christ is portrayed in each book.

THE BIBLE portrays Jesus Christ, the Saviour of the World.

GENESIS portrays Jesus Christ, our Creator God.

EXODUS portrays Jesus Christ, our Passover Lamb.

LEVITICUS portrays Jesus Christ, our Sacrifice for Sin.

NUMBERS portrays Jesus Christ, our "Lifted-Up One."

DEUTERONOMY portrays Jesus Christ, our True Prophet.

JOSHUA portrays Jesus Christ, Captain of our salvation.

JUDGES portrays Jesus Christ, our Deliverer Judge.

RUTH portrays Jesus Christ, our Kinsman Redeemer.

I AND II SAMUEL portray Jesus Christ, our King.

KINGS AND CHRONICLES portray Jesus Christ as King.

EZRA AND NEHEMIAH portray Jesus Christ, our Restorer.

Minimum Daily Requirements/Spiritual Vitamins

Sunday: JEWS RETURN TO JERUSALEM   Ezra 1–3

Monday: DISCOURAGEMENT AND JOY   Ezra 4–6

Tuesday: EZRA'S EXPEDITION   Ezra 7–10

Wednesday: NEHEMIAH REBUILDS THE WALL
Neh. 1–3

Thursday: OVERCOMING OPPOSITION   Neh. 4–6

Friday: NEHEMIAH REBUILDS THE MORALS
Neh. 7–9

Saturday: REFORMING THROUGH RELIGION
Neh. 11–13

A QUICK LOOK AT THE OLD TESTAMENT

GENESIS THROUGH NEHEMIAH

—— OUTLINE OF OLD TESTAMENT HISTORY ——

I. **PERIOD OF PATRIARCHS: Adam to Moses**......Genesis
II. **PERIOD OF GREAT LEADERS: Moses to**
   Saul ....Exodus—I Samuel
III. **PERIOD OF KINGS: Saul to the Babylonian**
   Captivity......Samuel, Kings, Chronicles, prophetical books
IV. **PERIOD OF FOREIGN KINGS: Captivity to coming**
   of Christ..........Ezra, Nehemiah, Esther, Ezekiel, Daniel

I. Period of Patriarchs: Adam to Moses

Bible account found in Book of Genesis.
We find in this period:
1. God's chosen men.
2. God's chosen family.
3. God's chosen people—the tribes of Israel.

1. God's Chosen Men

In the beginning we find no nations. God chose men who made Him known, but the earth became more and more wicked (Genesis 6:5).

The chosen men were:
   Adam, created in God's image
   Seth, his godly son
   Enoch, who walked with God
   Noah, who built the ark
   Shem, (Noah's son) and his descendants
The important events during this time were:
   Creation --(Genesis 1; 2)
   Fall ---(Genesis 3)
   Flood --(Genesis 6-8)
   Babel and the dispersion...................................(Genesis 11)

Four great nations were established as a result:

Egypt in North Africa

Phoenicia on the Mediterranean

Chaldea between the Tigris and Euphrates rivers

Assyria, north of Chaldea

2. God's Chosen Family

The race had failed (Genesis 6:5) so God limited His promises to a single family. He called Abraham to become the father of this nation.

The important events are:

Abraham called......................(Genesis 12:1–25:11)

Jacob chosen.........................(Genesis 25:19–36:43)

Joseph cherished.....................(Genesis 45; 46)

3. God's Chosen People

Twelve tribes become a nation.

II. Period of Great Leaders: Moses to Saul

Bible account given in Exodus to I Samuel.

We find in this period:

1. The Exodus
Exodus

2. The wilderness wandering
Exodus, Leviticus, Numbers, Deuteronomy.

3. Conquest of Canaan
Joshua

4. The rule of the judges
Judges

III. Period of Kings: Saul to the Babylonian Captivity

Bible account given in Samuel, Kings, Chronicles and the Prophets. Tribal life developed into national life.

We find in this period:

1. The united kingdom
Saul

David

Solomon

154

2. The divided kingdom
Kings of Israel—Northern Kingdom
Kings of Judah—Southern Kingdom
The fall of the Northern Kingdom
The fall of the Southern Kingdom

IV. Period of Foreign Kings: Captivity to Christ

Bible account in Ezra, Nehemiah, Esther, Ezekiel and Daniel. God was preparing the land, the people and the world for the coming Christ.
We find in this period:
1. Restoration under Persian kings.

REVIEW THE BOOKS OF THE BIBLE by stating how Christ is portrayed in each one.

Survey Quiz

Who Are the Following?

1. THIS MAN (a) was never born; (b) never had a birthday; (c) owned a great estate; (d) was perfect physically; (e) was a great zoologist, gave every animal a name.

(ADAM)

2. THIS MAN (a) was father of the oldest man in the world; (b) lived a godly life in one of the most wicked generations in the world; (c) was the only man in 3,000 years who did not die; (d) walked into heaven.

(ENOCH)

3. THIS MAN (a) was radiant with righteousness in the midst of moral darkness, and saved his family of seven by his faith in God; (b) was a great ship builder, but built a huge ship on a desert, miles from the sea; (c) never had to launch his ship into the sea—the sea came to it and lifted it to the top of a mountain; (d) gathered the greatest collection of animals the world has ever known; (e) had sons who were the fathers of the nations of the world.

(NOAH)

4. THIS MAN was akin to a covered wagon pioneer: (a) he left a great city of culture at God's request and traveled across a trackless desert; (b) he left a beautiful home and lived in a

PALESTINE
ISRAEL AND JUDAH

DAMASCUS

SIDON

TYRE

DAN

ARAM

KEDESH

PHOENICIANS

MEDITERRANEAN
SEA

MT.
TABOR

SEA
OF
GALILEE

GOLAN?

RIVER KISHON

MT.
CARMEL

WELL OF
HAROD

VALLEY OF
JEZREEL

BROOK CHERITH?

MT. GILBOA

ISRAEL

RAMOTH-GILEAD
(RAMOTH)

SHECHEM

RIVER JABBOK

APHEK

EBENEZER?

SHILOH

BETHEL

AMMON

RAMAH

GILGAL

EKRON

GIBEAH

RIVER JORDAN

JERUSALEM

JERICHO

PHILISTINES

ASHDOD

BETH-SHEMESH

BETHLEHEM

BEZER?

ASHKELON

MT. NEBO

GATH?

TEKOA

HEBRON

GAZA

JUDAH

EN-GEDI

MOAB

GERAR?

ZIKLAG

DEAD
SEA

BEERSHEBA

156

EDON SEIR

tent for one hundred years; (c) he was called "a friend of God"; (d) he was the father of a great nation; (e) his son was born after he was one hundred years old; (f) angels visited him.

(ABRAHAM)

5. THIS MAN (a) and his young friend believed God when no one else would; (b) was a great general; (c) did not have to build a bridge to transport his army into the land that he wanted to conquer; (d) used trumpets instead of bombers and priests instead of trained soldiers to destroy a city.

(JOSHUA)

6. THIS MAN (a) was an adopted child; (b) lived amidst the wealth of the day; (c) enjoyed unlimited education; (d) in spite of this, chose to identify himself with the poor people from whom he came rather than with the rulers with whom he lived; (e) was forced to live in a desert for forty years; (f) was chosen as the leader of 3,000,000 people and led them out from under the bondage of the strongest ruler of his day without firing a shot; (g) made slaves become rich overnight; (h) was the meekest man on earth and yet he lost his temper; (i) talked with God; (j) died an unknown death; (k) was buried by no man.

(MOSES)

Did You Know This?

Between chapters 6 and 7 of Ezra, three great world-battles (Salamis, Thermopylae, and Marathon) were fought; and two great world-leaders (Confucius and Buddha) died! Time elapsed: 58 years! (516-458 B.C.)

In the Old Testament, Esther (which takes place in above named period) follows Nehemiah; in history, the events in Esther occur 30 years before Nehemiah!

The purposes of God are sometimes delayed; but never abandoned!

CHAPTER 14

UNDERSTANDING ESTHER

Esther
Portrays Jesus Christ,
Our Advocate

You have heard of the great Xerxes, king of Persia, the Ahasuerus of the Book of Esther, of his famous expedition against Greece, and how the Greeks defeated his tremendous fleet at the battle of Salamis in 480 B.C. Historians tell us that this was one of the world's most important battles. From parallel passages in Herodotus we find that the feast described in the first chapter of Esther was the occasion for planning the campaign against Greece, (third year of his reign). Esther replaced Vashti in the seventh year of his reign (Esther 2:16) when Xerxes was seeking comfort after his disastrous defeat.

In the midst of this famous chapter in world history occurs the beautiful and charming Bible story of Esther. Although God's name is not mentioned in the Book of Esther, every page is full of God, who hides Himself behind every word. If you miss the name of Jehovah here, remember that this book had to pass through the hands of the Persian censor. Although they could eliminate His name, they could not eliminate God.

Matthew Henry, the great Bible commentator, says, "If the name of God is not here, His finger is." Dr. Pierson calls it, "The Romance of Providence." God has a part in all the events of human life.

The world today cannot get rid of God; neither could Israel. He has never let His people go in the past and He will never let them go in the future. He followed them in their captivity into Babylon. When the prophets were silent and the temple closed, God was still standing guard. When the kings of earth feasted and forgot, God remembered, and with His hand He wrote their doom or moved their hand to work His glory.

This book opens with a feast of the world's prince—Ahasuerus; it closes with the feast of God's prince—Mordecai. For a while Haman is exalted; at last, Mordecai. As you read this story, the upsets in human history and the final triumph of God's chosen people.

Esther is like Joseph and David. God had each one hidden away for His purpose. When the day came, He brought them to the front to work out His plan. God hid Joseph away in a dungeon in Egypt but when He was ready, He placed him in the position of prime minister of that country. God always has someone in reserve to fulfill His purposes. Sometimes it is a man like Joseph, or Moses. Sometimes it is a woman like Hannah, or Esther, or Mary. Recall men in history whom God seems to have prepared and kept for the hour.

Esther stands out as God's chosen one. She is a sweet and winsome person. She has come to the kingdom for just such a time as this. (See Esther 4:14.) We see her taking her life in her hand. As she goes in for her people's sake unto the king, she says, *and if I perish, I perish* (Esther 4:16).

Two beautiful girls join hands in behalf of God's people. They are Ruth and Esther. Ruth becomes the ancestress of the Deliverer of Israel and Esther saves the people so that the Deliverer might come. God had been carefully protecting this nation through the centuries for the purpose of blessing the whole world. It could not be wiped out before it had brought the Saviour into the world. This was not according to God's plans. Therefore God kept this nation according to His promise to Abraham.

In what period this story was written and who was its author, are unknown facts. In point of time, it is placed between chapters six and seven of the Book of Ezra. Comparatively few, not more than 50,000, of the captive Jews had returned from Babylon under the edict of Cyrus. Many were born in Babylon and had established themselves in business there and were not inclined to cross the desert and begin all over again in the land of their fathers. If they had all returned to Jerusalem, the Book of Esther would not have been written.

The Book of Esther is named for a Jewish orphan who became a Persian queen. This book and Ruth are the only books in the Bible which bear the name of a woman. The name "Esther" means "Star of the East."

Someone has said that all the events of this book center around three feasts:

1. Feast of King Ahasuerus..Esther 1; 2
2. Feast of Esther ....Esther 7
3. Feast of Purim..Esther 9

REJECTION OF VASHTI (Read Esther 1)

The great feast to which Vashti refused to come, as has been learned from the inscriptions, was held to consider the expedition against Greece, for which Xerxes spent four years in preparation. King Ahasuerus of the story was Xerxes, the famous Persian monarch (485-465 B.C.).

As this book opens the king was entertaining all the nobles and princes of his kingdom in the royal palace at Shushan. The banquet was on a colossal scale. It lasted 180 days (Esther 1:4). The men were feasting in the gorgeous palace gardens and the women were entertained by the beautiful Queen Vashti in her private apartment.

Shushan was the winter residence of the Persian kings. Remember Nehemiah was in the palace in Shushan (Neh. 1:1). In 1852 its site was identified by Loftus, and in 1884 a Frenchman named Dieulafay continued the excavation. He definitely located the places mentioned in the Book of Esther—the "inner court," the "outer court," the "king's gate," the "palace garden." He even found a die, or "pur," which they used to cast lots.

When the king and princes were in the midst of their drunken revelry, the king called for Vashti, so that he could show off her beauty. Of course, no Persian woman would permit this. It was an affront to her womanhood. Drunkenness had outraged the most sacred rules of Oriental etiquette. The seclusion of the harem was to be violated for the amusement of the dissolute king and his boon companions. Vashti refused. This made the king a laughing stock. To defend himself, he deposed the queen. (See Esther 1:12-22.)

Remember modesty is the crown jewel of womanhood. Never be false to your pure ideals. Men are bound to protect this crown jewel in womanhood. Modesty seldom rises in a breast that is not enriched by nobler virtues.

CROWNING OF ESTHER (Read Esther 2)

The minute Ahasuerus saw Esther, he made her his queen. The little Jewish orphan girl, brought up by her cousin Mordecai, was lifted to the Persian throne. At this time the Persian Empire comprised over half the then-known world.

Between chapters one and two, Ahasuerus made his historic attack on Greece with an army of 5,000,000 men, suffering a terrible defeat.

Two years after Xerxes (Ahasuerus) fought the famous battles of Thermopylae and Salamis he married Esther. She was his queen for thirteen years. Esther, no doubt, lived for many years into the reign of her stepson, Artaxerxes. Under this king, Nehemiah rebuilt Jerusalem. It was Esther's marriage to this famous Persian monarch that gave the Jews enough prestige at this court and made it possible for Nehemiah to rebuild Jerusalem. (See Nehemiah 2:1-8.)

The great palace of Xerxes at Persepolis, where Esther no doubt spent much of her time, has been excavated. The description of it, even in its ruin, is magnificent. The city itself was destroyed by fire by Alexander the Great, in 331 B.C. It has been buried in the sands of the desert ever since. In 1930 the Oriental Institute of Chicago received permission from the Persian government to excavate and restore the palace as completely as possible.

To make the story of this Jewish girl more real and interesting, let us give you a little description of this palace. The foundation of the palace was a platform fifty feet high and covered an area of two and a half acres. Underneath was a vast sewer system miles in length through which one may walk today. The walls of the palace were covered with the most magnificent carvings and reliefs and sculptures. Two large rooms in the Louvre display these treasures. When the rubbish was finally cleared away, they found these carvings preserved, as fresh

162

and beautiful as they were when Queen Esther walked through the corridors and looked upon them.

The second chapter describes the scene in this palace. Richly colored awnings were stretched across from marble pillars to silver rods, shading the exalted guests as they reclined on gold and silver seats while they feasted gluttonously and drank heavily day after day (Esther 1:5-8).

There was a grand audience hall where men came from the four corners of the earth to pay their honor to the great king, Esther's husband. The giant columns still rise in their grandeur, speaking of the former glory of the palace. This was the place to which Esther was brought as queen.

Note: Here, parenthetically, occurs the story of Mordecai's saving the king's life. This account figures prominently later in the book (Esther 2:21-23).

PLOTTING OF HAMAN (Read Esther 3; 4)

We see a form casting a shadow across the picture. This scene is one of sorrow and mourning. In Esther 3–5 we read of the ascendancy of a man by the name of Haman. He was a wicked man whose day of triumph was short and whose joy endured but for a moment. (See Job 20:4,5.) We see him becoming the chief minister of the king.

Haman was the Judas of Israel. He was a wicked monster in the life of God's chosen people. During the reading of the Book of Esther in a Jewish synagogue at the Feast of Purim, the congregation may be found taking part in a chorus at every mention of the name of Haman, "May his name be blotted out," while boys pound stones and bits of wood on which his hated name is written.

When Haman appears in the Book of Esther, he had just been exalted to the highest position under the king of Persia (Esther 3:1). The high honor turned his head. He swelled with vanity and was bitterly humiliated when a porter at the gate did not do homage to him as to the king (Esther 3:2). Haman was simply an Oriental despot's favorite.

Inflated with pride, he could not endure the indifference of even his meanest subject. The little fault of Mordecai was magnified into a capital offense. Mordecai, a Jew, could not give divine honor to a man! Haman became so enraged that he wanted to have a wholesale massacre of all the Jews in the kingdom (Esther 3:6). To determine the day his enemies should be destroyed, he cast lots, which fell on the thirteenth day of March, just ten months away (Esther 3:7). Haman tried to prove to the king that all the Jews were disloyal subjects. He offered to pay the king a $19,400,000 bribe (Esther 3:9). The king signed a royal decree that meant that every man, woman, and child who were Jews should be killed and all their property should be taken. Compare this treatment with that used by the Nazi regime.

Imagine the fasting and praying and the weeping in sackcloth that took place among the Jews (Esther 4:1-3).

Queen Esther saw it all and inquired of Mordecai what it meant. He gave her a copy of the king's decree which told the sad story. Then he added, *And who knoweth whether thou art come to the kingdom for such a time as this* (Esther 4:14)?

It would do well for each one of us to pause and ask himself this same question. Why has God allowed me to live at this particular hour? To do what is right may mean that we must jeopardize our lives. Then we must face the issue and answer with this young queen, *And if I perish, I perish.*

VENTURE OF ESTHER (Read Esther 5)

Queen Esther answers the challenge of Mordecai. She, who had been placed in the palace on flowery beds of ease, had not succumbed to the luxury of her surroundings. She chose a course at terrible danger to herself for the sake of her oppressed people, the Jews.

There is one thing to do always. Do what is right and leave the rest to God. God prepares men for emergencies. Failure is not sin; faithlessness is. There is a time to act. "There is a tide in the affairs of men which taken at the flood leads on to fortune." Act when God speaks.

The beauty of Esther was that she was not spoiled by her great elevation. Though she became the queen of a great king, she did not forget the kind porter who brought her up from

164

childhood. When she once accepted her dreaded task, she proceeded to carry it out with courage. It was a daring act for her to enter unsummoned in the presence of the king. Who could tell what this fickle monarch would do? Think what he had done to Vashti!

When she had been received by the king, she used her resources. She knew the king's weakness for good living so she invited him to a banquet. Read what happened that night when the king could not sleep. (See Esther 6:1-11.) How was Haman trapped? (Esther 6:6). At the second banquet Esther pleaded for her own life. She had Haman on the spot.

The king granted Esther's wish. Haman was hung on the very scaffold which he had prepared for Mordecai, and Mordecai was elevated to the place of honor next to the king.

As you study God's Word, you will find that through the ages Satan has ever tried to destroy, first, God's people, the Jews, then the church, and even Christ Himself. But God has thwarted his plans. Even the *gates of hell shall not prevail against* His Church. God will triumph! Christ has won the victory!

DELIVERANCE OF THE JEWS (Read Esther 6-10)

The Book of Esther closes with the account of the establishment of the Feast of Purim and the lifting of Mordecai to the place made vacant by Haman (Esther 10:3). The Jewish porter became the second man, just under the king of Persia. The Feast of Purim was to be celebrated annually. It is always inspired by the dramatic story of Esther.

The Feast of Purim celebrated even today sets the seal upon the accuracy of the story. The feast does not celebrate the downfall of Haman so much as the deliverance of the people.

This feast celebrates a deliverance of the Jews from a fearful danger. It was a Thanksgiving Day for the chosen people. Although they had forsaken God, He had spared them. Deliverance seems to be the keynote of Jewish history. God has always delivered this nation from danger and servitude. Even yet, God will deliver His people in the hour of their trouble.

This Book of Esther is an important link in a chain of events that tell of the re-establishment of the Hebrew nation in their own land in preparation of the coming of the Messiah into the world. The Jews had escaped extermination. It was God's purpose that they should be preserved to bring forth the Saviour of the world.

The character of Ahasuerus illustrates how unlimited power often is crushed and dissolved beneath the weight of its own immensity. The man who is exalted to the pedestal of a god is made dizzy by his own altitude.

King Ahasuerus (Xerxes of Herodotus) was punished with childishness. This silly monarch decorated a tree with the jewelry of a prince in reward for its fruitfulness. He flogged and chained the Hellespont as a punishment for its tempestuousness. Such actions are akin to insanity.

CHARACTER STUDY OF ESTHER

Esther is a sweet and attractive character.

Beautiful and modest..........................Esther 2:15

Winsome ....Esther 2:9-17; 5:1-3

Obedient ....Esther 2:10

Humble ....Esther 4:16

Courageous ....Esther 7:6

Loyal and constant................Esther 2:22; 8:1-2; 7:3-4

DON'T FORGET

There is always one thing to do—do what is right and leave the rest with God.

So will I go in unto the king, which is not according to the law: and if I perish, I perish (Esther 4:16).

God meets emergencies with human lives which He has redeemed and prepared.

Who knoweth whether thou art come to the kingdom for such a time as this? (Esther 4:14).

Prayer moves the hand that moves the world. A devoted woman moved a determined monarch.

Surely the wrath of man shall praise thee (Psalm 76:10).

Those who walk in holy sincerity with Christ may walk in holy security among men.

God's pioneers leave all—to gain all.

166

Minimum Daily Requirements/Spiritual Vitamins

Sunday: REJECTION OF VASHTI   Esther 1
Monday: CROWNING OF ESTHER   Esther 2
Tuesday: PLOTTING OF HAMAN   Esther 3; 4
Wednesday: VENTURE OF ESTHER   Esther 5
Thursday: MORDECAI EXALTED   Esther 6
Friday: ESTHER'S FEAST   Esther 7; 8
Saturday: DELIVERANCE OF THE JEWS
           Esther 9–10

UNDERSTANDING JOB

*Job
Portrays Jesus Christ,
My Redeemer*

We have finished reading the historical books of the Old Testament—Joshua through Esther. Now we open the books of poetry—Job, Psalms, Proverbs, Ecclesiastes and Song of Solomon. These books tell of the experiences of the heart.

Job's key word is "tried." *He knoweth the way that I take: when he hath tried me, I shall come forth as gold* (Job 23:10).

Trials and suffering are not always for our punishment but sometimes for our education and training. The athlete is not put under strict discipline for punishment but merely to make him ready for the race. Christ is ever preparing us for the race that is set before us. (See Hebrews 12:1,2.)

Job is no doubt one of the most wonderful poems ever written. Tennyson called it "the greatest poem, whether of ancient or modern literature." The scene in this amazing book is laid in the patriarchal days. For all we know this book may be one of the most ancient pieces of finished literature in existence. It is one of the oldest, if not the oldest, books in the Bible. The Word of God settles the fact that Job was a real person. God speaks through the prophet Ezekiel and says, *Though these three men, Noah, Daniel, and Job, were in it, they should deliver but their own souls* (Ezekiel 14:14; see also 14:20). If you doubt Job's existence, you will have to refute Noah and Daniel.

It is fitting that the oldest book should deal with the oldest problems. Among these is, "Why do godly people suffer?" This is the theme of the book. People have always asked why God permits good people to suffer. Haven't you wondered yourself why some good person has to die of an awful disease or has to be confined to a bed of pain? The drama of Job offers a solution to these problems. We believe it gives God's answer.

It is easy to become confused about this problem of suffering. Remember the disciples of Christ thought that suffering was the result of sin in a life. (Read John 9:2.) The book of Job gives an entirely different reason for the suffering of Job. In this case, Job was being honored by God. It was the truth that God could trust Job to remain faithful to God in spite of everything. How wonderful it would be if you and I learned to thank God for all that happens to us.

This book should first be read as a narrative. The story of Job is a simple one. It opens with a scene in heaven, and then tells of Job's fall from prosperity to poverty. This is followed by the great discussion between Job and his four friends, Eliphaz, the religious dogmatist, much like an ancient Pharisee; Bildad, who sought to comfort Job with worn-out platitudes; and Zophar, who thought he had a corner on all religious wisdom. Then comes Elihu, the impetuous youth. Finally, the climax is reached when God speaks. Job answers, at last in a humble spirit, and the problem is solved. This is the story of the book.

Next, we should study the problem of the book. It may be stated, "Why do the righteous suffer?" We find:

(1) The shallow view of Satan—that the children of God love and serve Him because it pays in riches and honor (Job 1:1–2:8). Satan said that Job's godliness was selfishness, that he served God for profit, that when prosperity ended, he would be no more godly. He received permission to test Job (Job 2:6). Satan added, "Who wouldn't serve God for a handsome income of so many thousand a year? Watch him when his prosperity ends."

(2) The scarcely less-false view of Eliphaz, Bildad and Zophar (who agreed for the most part) that the unrighteous suffer because of their sins and the righteous are rewarded. Hence they reasoned that Job must have sinned, and this suffering was his punishment. Job was a great sufferer; therefore he must have been a great sinner. They said, *Who ever perished, being innocent* (Job 4:7)? But Job knew that his heart was true to God, and he could not accept the accusation of his friends. He showed

them that their conclusion was false and that the wicked often prospered in the world (Job 24:6).

(3) Elihu had a far more just answer of the problem but his eloquent discourse was marred by conceit. He defended God and saw in affliction the chastisement of a loving Father. But this did not explain the reason of suffering to Job. Elihu argued that suffering was God's discipline to bring His sons back into fellowship with Himself. He believed that suffering was sent to keep us from sinning.

(4) Jehovah explained to Job (by revealing Himself to him) that when men see God something always happens. The godly are allowed to suffer that they may see themselves first. Read Isaiah 6:1-5; Genesis 17:1-3; Daniel 10:4-8. When we come to the end of ourselves, God can lift us up. Job was a good man, but self-righteous. Read Job 29:1-25 and you will find the personal pronouns "I," "my" and "me" fifty-two times. It reminds one of Romans 7.

God has a wise purpose in all of our suffering. God wants to show His manifold wisdom (Ephesians 3:10). He wants the trial of our faith to work patience. He wants to bring out the gold as by fire. He wants to reveal real character. Furthermore we have an unseen cloud of witnesses gathered in the great stadium of heaven to watch us in the conflict (Hebrews 12:1,2).

How little did Job realize that so much hung on his steadfastness and trust in God when he said, *Though he slay me, yet will I trust in him* (Job 13:15). I wonder if we realize today the issues which hang upon our faithfulness to God. If God could only find more of us who would trust Him, how much we might encourage others to trust!

THE SAVIOUR AND SUFFERING

The problem of suffering has had much light thrown upon it from the New Testament—especially from the cross of Christ. Here we see the world's most righteous Man, the world's greatest Sufferer. We know now that the righteous suffer with the wicked today because of sin which fills the world with misery. We know there are natural consequences of sin, for the godly as well as the sinner. We have already noted that chastening is sometimes for training and correction. There is a suffering which Christians must endure for Christ's sake and the Gospel's.

The Book of Job is a commentary on I Corinthians 11:31,32; Hebrews 12:7-11; Luke 22:31,32; I Cor. 5:5. The chief subject of the Book of Job is the riddle of all times, "Why do the righteous suffer?" But it deals with a wide scope of knowledge—the power of Satan, telling of his might and the limit of his authority; the fact of the resurrection; and many of the latest scientific discoveries.

The Book of Job tells us much about human suffering. Job's friends, as thousands do today, made the mistake of thinking that all suffering was God's way of punishing sin. They asked, *Who ever perished, being innocent* (Job 4:7)?

Do you know of any good person today who is suffering? Of course you do. One of the greatest saints I ever knew was blind; another was so poor that we, as children, carried him things to eat and saved our money to buy him clothes. We gave material things to him, but he gave spiritual blessings to us.

God allowed Stephen to be stoned (Acts 7:59) and Paul to have a thorn in his flesh to buffet him (II Cor. 12:7). Even Jesus knew suffering.

Job's friends concluded that Job must have sinned greatly to account for such exceptional suffering. Let us find out what God proved.

What was Job's attitude toward God? He first had access to God through the blood of the sacrifice (Job 1:5). Then he walked with God in integrity of heart and life.

Job had a conscience right toward God. He knew his heart was true and so he could accept the accusations of his friends. He finally could show them that their conclusion was wrong and that the wicked often prosper in this world (Job 24:6).

God trusted Job; therefore He assigned to him this great problem of suffering. Because He loved Job, He allowed him to be chastened, for *whom the Lord loveth He chasteneth* (Hebrews 12:6). When Job was in the midst of his anguish, he realized that it is only the gold that is worth putting into the fire. Any-

172

thing else would be consumed. James said, *Count it all joy when ye fall into divers temptations; knowing this, that the trying of your faith worketh patience* (James 1:2,3).

When Job was prosperous and upright and benevolent, he was in danger of becoming self-confident, and could easily forget that he only held his power and place in this world as a steward of God. God does not give us great gifts just to please ourselves. The Westminster Confession tells us that the chief end of man is to glorify God. *Even Christ pleased not himself* (Romans 15:3). He came to glorify the Father.

God Dealt with Job:
1. He was broken (Job 16:12,14; 17:11).
2. He was melted (Job 23:10).
3. He was softened so he could say, *The hand of God hath touched me* (Job 19:21). *God maketh my heart soft* (Job 23:16).

Do you ever sing, "Spirit of the Living God, fall afresh on me. Melt me; mold me; fill me; use me"? Do you know what it might mean for you? This is what happened to Job.

Job never really saw himself until he saw God. This is true of every life. See how it affected Isaiah when he, as a young man, saw God (Isaiah 6:1-9).

Job was all ready to reason with God, as many do today, about His dealings with him. He could not understand Him. It was a vision of God Himself that completed the work in Job and brought him to the dust.

Listen to God speak of Job, *Shall he that contendeth with the Almighty instruct him* (Job 40:2)? Think of trying to instruct the God of this universe! The wisdom of man is only foolishness with God. Hear Job's answer. *Behold, I am vile* [absolutely worthless]; ... *I will lay mine hand upon my mouth* (Job 40:4).

God kept dealing with Job till he came to the very end of himself! Hear him speak again, *Therefore have I uttered that I understood not; things too wonderful for me, which I knew not ... I have heard of thee by the hearing of the ear: but now mine eye seeth thee. Wherefore I abhor myself, and repent in dust and ashes* (Job 42:3-6).

We find Job a chastened, softened servant. God turned the tide and his prosperity was given back to him doubled—twice as many sheep and oxen, asses and camels! He rejoiced again in his sons and daughters, just the same number as before.

Job no longer asked a question but made a statement. *I know that my redeemer liveth, and that he shall stand at the latter day upon the earth: and though after my skin worms destroy this body, yet in my flesh shall I see God* (Job 19:25,26).

Job's vision of a future life that had been uncertain before was clear now. We had heard him asking a question that multitudes have asked, *If a man die, shall he live again* (Job 14:14)? Paul answered this question in the great resurrection chapter of the Bible, I Corinthians 15. Jesus answered it in His statement, *He that believeth in me, though he were dead, yet shall he live* (John 11:25).

What a wonderful vision of the future life we have in these words! What a prophecy of the coming of the Saviour!

Job was *a perfect and an upright man, one that feareth God, and escheweth evil* (see Job 1:8).

1. He was "perfect"—complete, all-round.
2. He was "upright"—Hebrew word means "straight."
3. He "feared God"—this is the beginning of wisdom.
4. He "eschewed evil"—this is his moral conduct.

Job was right with man and with God, and remember it was God who said this. God added, *There is none like him in the earth* (Job 1:8). What an honor God gave to Job to use these words to describe him!

As the book opens we see Job surrounded by wealth, family, position and friends. Let us watch this man whom God said was perfect! We see this man visited by Satan. A swift succession of calamities followed. Remember these things did not come because of anything wrong in this man Job. All of Job's friends thought that the reason for his trouble lay in himself. But God had made it very plain in the opening of the book that this was not true.

Watch this man stripped of his wealth and reduced to poverty! His children are taken! Health is gone! Then he loses the confidence of his wife! Finally his friends go!

SATAN AND THE SAINT (Read Job 1:6–2:10)

In Job 1:6 the "sons of God" presented themselves before the King. The "sons of God" mean angelic beings, the messengers of God. The mystery is that Satan was among them. He was angelic, but he had fallen. There was no hint that he was out of place or that he had forced himself into the audience-chamber.

In contrast to the Almighty we have the figure of the adversary, or Satan. Let us stop and study this person for a while. Satan, as the adversary, is depicted with great clearness, representing a real being, not an imaginary one. We cannot help but contrast the Satan of the Book of Job with the grotesque, gigantic, awful figure depicted by the poets. The Bible tells us that Satan comes as *an angel of light* to deceive and to tempt (II Corinthians 11:14).

Our strange idea of the devil is derived from Dante's Inferno where he attempted to paint this monster of hell. His enormous size depicted by Dante is matched by his hideousness. We find, too, a picture of Satan given by Milton. His description is magnificent but it has little justification from Scripture. This regal archfiend has no kinship with the Satan of the Book of Job. Neither is Mephistopheles of "Faust" the true picture, although, no doubt, Goethe's picture of a cynical devil, gaily damning a mind, is based on the Book of Job.

Satan could bring up the hosts of Sabeans and Chaldeans and have them carry away the oxen and asses and camels of Job (Job 1:13-17). He could slay the sheep by lightning, and cause the wind to kill Job's children, and even smite Job himself with boils. Remember, he is the prince of the power of the air (Ephesians 2:2).

Know this besides! Satan has great power, but there are limits to his might. Satan is mighty, but God is Almighty! He can break through only where God allows (Job 1:10). What a comfort it is to know that no calamity can come to us that the Father does not allow. He who has *shut up the sea with doors, . . . and said, Hitherto shalt thou come, but no further: and here shall thy proud waves be stayed* (Job 38:8,11), will never let us be tempted above that we are able. (See I Cor. 10:13)

Remember, Satan is so held by the Almighty that he can only strike where he is given permission (Job 1:12).

1. Job rent his clothes (Job 1:20).

It is worthwhile for us to learn that we are meant to feel grief. Sorrow has its use in our life. We are told not to "despise the chastening of the Lord" but to be "exercised" thereby.

Jesus wept! Christ does not destroy our natural emotions. Jesus told the women of Jerusalem to weep for themselves and for their children.

2. Job recognized that loss and sorrow are the laws of life.

We have to learn that all possessions are transient. We are losing something every moment. We cannot stop and weep over everything that is taken from us. We have to learn a hard lesson—that we can live on in spite of all our losses. Begin to learn while you are young that nothing is necessary but Christ.

Only pure gold can stand the fire. All dross is burned up. God, the great metallurgist of heaven, puts us in the fire, but He watches and tries us Himself. He trusts no other. When the fire has burned long enough to destroy the impurities, He pulls us out.

GOD AND SATAN

God speaks to Satan, *Whence comest thou?* What a tragedy in the answer! *From going to and fro in the earth, and from walking up and down in it* (Job 1:7). Remember, this reveals the "endless restlessness of evil." *Be sober, be vigilant; because your adversary the devil, as a roaring lion, walketh about, seeking whom he may devour* (I Peter 5:8).

God speaks again, *Hast thou considered my servant Job* (Job 1:8)?

What do you think God meant by "considering" Job? It is a strong word, as if he had been watching his every act. "Have you been trying to find a flaw?"

Satan says, *Doth Job fear God for nought?* He seems to imply—"I'm trying to find out why this fellow is so perfect. There is a reason." *Hast not thou made an hedge about him, . . . and about all that he hath on every side?* That was the truth, of course. Then he added, *Thou hast blessed the work of his hands.* This was true also. *And his substance is increased in the land.* Yes, all this was correct.

But Satan went on, *But put forth thine hand now, and touch all that he hath, and he will curse thee to thy face.* Satan's charge against Job was that a man only serves God for what he can get out of it. Really Job is not so much on trial here as God. It is not a question of Job's loyalty so much as it is one of God's power. Is God able to keep *that which we have committed unto him* (II Timothy 1:12.)?

This same thing is being said today! Some say that ministers are preaching the gospel for what they can get out of it; that heathens are turning to Christ because it gives them food and shelter.

So God says, "all right, try it out! Take everything away from Job and see what happens!"

Do you see that the real conflict here was between God and Satan? God was proving the truth about His statement of Job's integrity in following Him.

When the trials came, Job did not understand the meaning of all his suffering. He knew it was not because he had sinned, as his friends said. He wondered what God was doing. We will not always understand what God is working out on the battleground of our hearts, but know this: there is a reason and value to everything that God allows and that *all things work together for good to them that love God, to them who are the called according to his purpose* (Romans 8:28).

Job proved that Satan's statement concerning God's children was a lie, that is, that they only serve Him for what they can get out of it.

Don't always try to find the reason for your trials and experiences. Sometimes we will have to wait for the answer. We wonder why God takes a Borden of Yale when he is only a young man at the threshold of a life of service, and allows an old, drunken, apparently good-for-nothing to live.

Man will never find the answer to all of God's dealings. Men may be honest and sincere as far as they go, as were Job's friends, but God's ways are past finding out. God never allowed the devil to prove that God blundered when He made man, by suggesting that men only serve God for what they can get out of Him.

Do not be surprised to find hypocrites in every congregation of God's children. Satan comes to do mischief to saints. He distracts our attention. He sets us to criticising. He sows dissension in the congregation. He excites the pride of preachers and singers, of givers and those who publicly pray. He chills our spirit and freezes our prayers. Yes, when the Word is being sown, the fowls of the air come to pluck it away (Matthew 13:3-23).

Remember, you can never walk before God and try to lead a godly life, without Satan coming in to walk with you—accusing you, finding fault and vexing you.

What Kind of a Man Was Job?

He was a perfect man..........................Job 1:1
He was a prosperous man.....................Job 1:2-4
He was a praying man.........................Job 1:5
He was a popular man....................Job 29:21,25
He was a proven man.....................Job 42:10,12

JOB AND HIS FRIENDS (Read Job 2:11–37:24)

Get acquainted with Job's friends. Let us introduce you to them. First there is courtly Eliphaz, then argumentative Bildad, and blunt Zophar, and the youthful Elihu.

This is a familiar scene. Everyone has a reason to offer as an explanation for his experiences and problems. Job's four friends came. Do you know Job was rich in friends? Generally when a man loses his wealth and position and health, he has no friends left.

There are things we can say in favor of these men although their words of "comfort" were anything but that. The first is that they came at all. They were friends who stuck through adversity. When all the multitude of acquaintances had forgotten Job, they came.

You notice they kept still for seven days. This is good! They seemed to be trying to find out the reason for all of Job's troubles before they spoke. Someone has said that instead of talking about Job, they came and talked with him.

They all had a reason; they wished to tell Job why they thought he was suffering as he did. They all agreed that he must have sinned miserably to have caused this suffering.

Eliphaz backs his argument by a dream (Job 4:1–5:27); Bildad, by some old proverbs (Job 8); Zophar, by experience and reason (Job 11). Elihu came nearest the truth when he argued that suffering was God's discipline to bring the soul back into fellowship with God; but it was not the whole truth.

God called Job "perfect and upright." His friends were wrong in charging him with sin as the only possible cause of his calamities.

WRETCHED COMFORTERS

The chief question returns: "Why does God permit the righteous to suffer?" Job cries out from the ashes, "I cannot understand it. It doesn't seem right."

Job's wife, looking on discouraged, says, "Something is wrong. Your religion is a failure. Curse God and die." This literally means, "say goodbye to God." It is the voice of despair.

Eliphaz adds, shaking his head, "God never makes a mistake. What have you done to bring this on yourself?"

Bildad says, "God is just. Confess your sin."

Zophar next speaks, "God is all-wise. He knows man."

Elihu, God's man, says the wisest thing, "God is good; look up, and trust Him, for He is God."

THE RIGHTEOUS COMFORTER

Jehovah now is heard from the whirlwind *I will demand of thee, and declare thou unto me* (Job 40:7).

Now Job speaks himself: *I know that thou canst do everything, and that no thought can be withholden from thee* (Job 42:2). Then comes the great confession, *I have heard of thee by the hearing of the ear: but now mine eye seeth thee. Wherefore I abhor myself* ["count myself out"], *and repent in dust and ashes* (Job 42:5,6).

179

This is the victory of submissive faith. When we bow to God's will, we find God's way. Stoop to conquer. Bend to obey. This is the lesson of Job.

The philosophy of Job's friends was wrong. Job was glad to see them and he could pour out his troubles to them, but they did not understand him.

Job even lost his friends! He had tried to explain, but he was misunderstood. Only God understands!

JEHOVAH AND JOB (Read Job 38–42)

The scene begins with God gloriously revealing Himself. In a series of approximately sixty questions, God is saying, in effect, who can do all these things but Myself? God is thus revealed to Job, and Job to himself.

As so often is true with us, when Job came into the presence of God, he forgot the speech he thought he would make! (Job 40:4,5). There was no arguing with God. Finally, Job went flat down on his face, repenting in "dust and ashes" (Job 42:6). This is the only place to learn God's lessons—on your face, with your mouth shut!

Jehovah explains to Job (by revealing Himself to him) that when men see God something always happens. The godly are allowed to suffer that they may see themselves. Read Isaiah 6:1-5. When Isaiah saw himself as he really was, he fell on his face undone and cried out, *I am a man of unclean lips.*

Did you ever think that you looked all right until some friend dropped in to invite you to go some place with him? When you saw how immaculate your friend looked, you immediately realized how you needed a good grooming. So often this is true in the presence of Christ. The very immaculateness of His Person makes us feel sinful. Measure your life by His life and you will feel as Job did.

In Job 42 We Find:

1. A Consciousness of God.......................verse 5
2. A Collapse of Job...........................verse 6
3. A Commission to serve.......................verse 8

As you read the chapter, you see that Job enjoyed a double portion of prosperity from the hand of God. God allows His children to suffer in order to reveal character, to set forth an object lesson, and to bring to light some hidden sin. In Job's case, that hidden sin was self-righteousness.

This book well illustrates the text of Romans 8:28. How wonderful to hear of the patience of Job and to have seen how that the end of the Lord is pity and mercy. A morning of joy always follows the night of sorrow.

Job found God in his trouble. Many know God as a Creator and believe in His greatness, but they do not really know God. The more we understand His ways the more we will love Him and put our trust in Him.

Job is rich:

1. In philosophy

Ancient as the book is, it is filled with a divine record of human philosophy, and blind gropings of human wisdom. Human reason has never been able to go beyond Job's friends in explaining the great mysteries of human experience on natural grounds. (See I Cor. 2:14 and Col. 2:8.)

2. In gems of spiritual truth

Be sure to read the following references: Job 1:21; 5:17; 13:15; 14:14; 16:21; 19:23-27; 23:10; 26:7-14; 28:12-28; 42:1-6. These are some of the most frequently quoted and best loved passages in the Bible.

Minimum Daily Requirements/Spiritual Vitamins

Sunday: SATAN AND SAINT   Job 1:1-2–2:13
Monday: BILDAD THINKS JOB A HYPOCRITE
Job 8:1-22
Tuesday: JOB ANSWERS HIS FRIENDS
Job 12:1-25
Wednesday: JOB'S FAITH   Job 19:1-29
Thursday: JOB AND ELIHU   Job 32:1-22;
37:23, 24
Friday: GOD SPEAKS TO JOB   Job 38:1-18
Saturday: JOB VINDICATED AND HONORED
Job 42:1-17

CHAPTER 16

UNDERSTANDING
PSALMS

Psalms
Portrays Jesus Christ,
Our All in All

O come let us sing unto the LORD: let us make a joyful noise to the rock of our salvation (Psalm 95:1). Here we take this view of the Psalms in panorama. The sights that catch and hold our attention are so numerous as to defy exhaustive treatment in one short chapter.

Give unto the LORD the glory due unto his name; worship the LORD in the beauty of holiness (Psalm 29:2). This is the key verse to the Book of Psalms. The door into the temple of praise and prayer is open. Go in with the psalmist to rest and pray. It is a real privilege to go apart during the rush of earthly things.

No doubt Psalms is the best loved book in the Old Testament. Someone has called it the solid gold of Christian experience. Slip in wherever you will and you will find a treasure. Every Psalm is a direct expression of the soul's consciousness of God. With which Psalms are you familiar? Pause a moment to think.

The Hebrew title of this book is "Praise," or the "Book of Praises," which indicates that the main contents of the book are praise, prayer and worship. The name "Psalms" comes from the Greek. We find that the early Christian fathers called it the Psalter.

The Psalms is the National Hymn Book of Israel. It contains one hundred and fifty poems to be set to music for worship. Worship is the central idea. The Psalms magnify and praise the Lord, exalt His attributes, His names, His word, and His goodness. Every human experience is related to Him.

We see the life of the believer pictured in all of its experiences of joy and sorrow, victory and failure.

The Psalms are full of Christ. They describe the whole program of His suffering and death. Let us look and see!

We have Christ's own warrant for looking for Him in the Psalms. He said, *All things must be fulfilled, which were written in the . . . psalms, concerning me* (Luke 24:44).

His prophetic office is found in Psalm 22:22
His priestly office in Psalms 40:6,8; 22; 49; 110
His kingly office in Psalms 2; 21; 45; 72
His sufferings in Psalms 22 and 69
His resurrection in Psalm 16

Another extremely useful classification of the Psalms may be made according to the subjects of the individual Psalms:

Instruction 1; 19; 39
Praise 8; 29; 93; 100
Thanksgiving 30; 65; 103; 107; 116
Penitence 6; 32; 38; 51; 102; 130; 143
Trust 3; 27; 31; 46; 56; 62; 86
Distress 4; 13; 55; 64; 88
Aspiration 42; 63; 80; 84; 137
History 78; 105; 106
Prophecy (Psalms of the Messiah) 2; 16; 22; 24; 40; 45; 68; 69; 72; 97; 110; 118

AUTHORSHIP

We speak of the Psalms as the Psalms of David. He has been considered the principal writer. He gives the keynote and his voice rises highest in the sacred choir. But there were other authors besides him. Seventy-three of the one hundred and fifty Psalms are assigned to him, and fifty are anonymous. The ninetieth Psalm is by Moses. Two are by Solomon, the seventy-second and one hundred and twenty-seventh. Besides these, Asaph, David's choir leader, the sons of Korah, a family of official musicians, and Jeduthun wrote some. But let us not be too engrossed in finding who penned them. Let us rather read and enjoy these grand expressions of praise. They are of God for you. Sing them and make them your own. Catch David's note and spirit. He had marching songs, prayer songs, rally songs, hilltop songs, confession songs. Sing as you march. Keep step with David and David's Lord all the way.

There are numerous quotations from this book found in the

New Testament. At least twenty of these are in direct reference to Christ and His life and death.

MAN, HIS STATE OF BLESSEDNESS, FALL, AND RECOVERY
(Read Psalms 1–41)

1. Man blessed..Psalm 1
2. Man fallen from his high position and
   at enmity with God.....................................Psalms 2 and 14
3. Man restored by his blessed Redeemer,
   the Man Christ Jesus................................Psalms 16–41

In this section we have a collection by David of the Psalms which he wrote. Psalm 1 tells us of the road to success. Everyone wants to prosper. No one wishes to fail. The Psalmist says that everyone may prosper. Think of it! It will be well for every young person to master the rules for success laid down here.

Things Not to Do

1. Refuse to walk in the counsel of the ungodly; do not take their advice or follow the pattern of their lives.

2. Refuse to stand in the way of sinners. Standing is even a lower step. When you stand in sin, it shows that you have been brought under the spell of evil.

3. Refuse to sit—to take the scorner's seat is to take the most despicable place possible. He sits idly watching the struggles of his fellows and cares not that many are losing the fight. You ask him, "Isn't there great need in this world?" "I suppose," he answers, but just sits and plays the cynic. He is sure "that every minister, missionary, or Christian worker is either a fool or a hypocrite."

Things to Do

1. Read the Bible.
2. Delight in it.
3. Meditate upon it.

The more you read the Word the more you want to. As one great Christian leader has said, "The gospel feeds you, then it makes you hungry." It never grows stale. You cannot read it too often or too much.

Things That Result

When the Christian has followed the "don'ts" and "dos," what results? Three things:

"Planted"—*like a tree planted* [transplanted] *by the rivers of water*—the settled and steadfast life in a luxuriant soil.

"Purposive"—he *bringeth forth his fruit in his season*—the productive life.

"Prosperous"—*his leaf also shall not wither*—the abiding, happy life.

Other psalms in this group that show the final blessings of man because of the glorious work of the Man Christ Jesus are Psalms 22; 23; 24.

Psalm 22 tells of the Good Shepherd giving His life for His sheep. We see the cross and hear the cries of our dying Saviour. As you read this Psalm, you will recognize the facts.

Psalm 23 tells of the great Shepherd keeping His sheep. We read *The LORD is my shepherd; I shall not want.* He promises to guide and provide and keep me.

Psalm 24 tells of the chief Shepherd in His glory rewarding His sheep. He is my King and He is coming to reign in power and great glory.

PSALM 22

This Psalm gives a picture of Calvary. We see the crucifixion portrayed here more clearly than in any other part of the Old Testament. The Psalm opens with the cry of our Lord in the darkest hour of His life; *My God, my God, why hast thou forsaken me?* It closes with, *he hath done this.* The original Hebrew means, *It is finished*—the last cry of the Saviour.

Psalm 22:6, *I am a worm, and no man; a reproach of men, and despised of the people.* This tells us of the offense of the cross!

Read and Compare These Verses:

Psalm 22:1..Matthew 27:46
Psalm 22:6,7..Luke 23:35,36
Psalm 22:6-8......................................Matthew 27:39,41,43
Psalm 22:12,13....................................Matthew 27:36,44
Psalm 22:28..I Cor. 15:23,24

Poured out like water . . . my heart is like wax; it is melted (**Psalm 22:14**). This depicts excessive perspiration due to physical torture. It also means the breaking of Jesus' heart.

He tells us why His heart was broken. *Reproach hath broken my heart* (**Psalm 69:20**). *But one of the soldiers with a spear pierced his side, and forthwith came there out blood and water. And he that saw it bare record, and his record is true: and he knoweth that he saith true, that ye might believe* (John 19:34, 35).

Jesus died of a broken heart. He bore the reproach and shame for others. The bearing of our sins which hid Him from His Father's face, broke His heart. Death by a broken heart is very rare. It is caused by intense agony of suffering.

My tongue cleaveth to my jaws (**Psalm 22:15**). This verse describes intense thirst. The account in the New Testament said, *Jesus . . . that the scripture might be fulfilled, saith, I thirst.* Yes, Psalm 69:21 says, *In my thirst they gave me vinegar to drink.* Read John 19:28,29.

They pierced my hands and my feet (**Psalm 22:16**). Crucifixion! The Roman method of death by crucifixion is described here. The Jewish law did not know of this method. These words give the description of death by crucifixion—"bones out of joint"—bones of hands, arms, shoulders out of joint due to nailing to the cross and straining of bone and muscle.

They part my garments among them, and cast lots upon my vesture (**Psalm 22:18**). Even the act of the soldiers is described here. See Matthew 27:35.

ISRAEL (Read Psalms 42–72)

1. Her Ruin..Psalms 42–49
2. Her Redeemer.....................................Psalms 50–60
3. Her Redemption ....Psalms 61–72

Here in this section we find additional psalms compiled by Hezekiah for use in the temple. It opens with "a cry" from the depth of oppression. See Psalms 42-49. It ends with the King reigning over the redeemed nation. *He shall have dominion also from sea to sea, and from the river unto the ends of the earth* (**Psalm 72:8**). Read this glorious Psalm.

PSALM 51

There are several psalms of penitence, but the chief is Psalm 51. It is a psalm of David. If you turn to II Samuel 11 and 12, you will find the story of David's sin. When you read this, notice three things that David said. When Nathan the prophet was telling David the story of the despicable fellow who took the only lamb belonging to the poor man, we hear him say to David: *Thou art the man.* David did not try to dodge the issue but said, *I have sinned against the LORD.* Then Nathan reassured him, saying, *The LORD also hath put away thy sin* (see II Samuel 12:13).

We think it strange when we read that David was *a man after his* [God's] *own heart.* When we compare what other kings would have done under the same circumstances, we are not so surprised. But David confessed and said, *I have sinned against the LORD* (II Samuel 12:13). That is what sin is— breaking God's law.

You notice in the Psalm these words, *Against thee, thee only, have I sinned, and done this evil in thy sight.* This Psalm is a prayer of contrition and confession. He cries for mercy from a God whom he knows is merciful and full of loving kindness.

We learn from this Psalm that we must confess our sin to God (I John 1:9) and that God is just to forgive. Whenever a man is sincere in his confession to God, He will cleanse his sin.

THE SANCTUARY (Read Psalms 73–89)

In the Psalms of this third section we see the sanctuary mentioned, or referred to, in almost every one. (See Psalm 84:1.) It is concerned almost entirely with material used in worship service, and needs little comment.

We see God's counsels in relation to the sanctuary. The sanctuary is seen from its ruin to its restoration in the fullness of blessing. In this section we also find a compilation of Josiah.

THE EARTH (Read Psalms 90–106)

Blessing needed..Psalms 90–94
Blessing anticipated..Psalms 95–100
Blessing enjoyed..Psalms 101–106

188

The first of this group of Psalms was written during the wanderings in the wilderness. The Psalms are not arranged in chronological order.

Read the opening verses of Psalms 90 and 91 together. *LORD, thou hast been our dwelling place in all generations. He that dwelleth in the secret place of the most High shall abide under the shadow of the Almighty.* If God is our dwelling place on this earth, we shall live in confidence, sheltered by the Almighty. Christ says, *If ye abide in me, and my words abide in you, ye shall ask what ye will, and it shall be done unto you* (John 15:7). The secret of a godly life is abiding in the Almighty. When the devil attacked the Lord, he quoted from Psalm 91. But Christ was victorious because He lived in the place described by this same Psalm. We are told that there is a point of perfect calm at the center of a cyclone. There may be raging stormy snares, pestilences, terror by night, darkness and destruction, but when the soul is abiding under the shadow of the Almighty, it is safe.

If you wish to praise the Lord for His goodness, read Psalm 103. It is full of worship, adoration, praise and thanksgiving. This is great exercise for the soul.

THE WORD OF GOD (Read Psalms 107–150)

All the teaching in these Psalms is grouped around the Word of God. This section opens with Psalm 107 which gives the key. *He sent his word, and healed them.*

Psalm 119 is the great Psalm of the whole book. It extols the Word of God which is the great revelation of the heart and mind of the Lord. This book is *sweeter also than honey and the honeycomb* and above *gold, yea, than much fine gold* (Ps. 19:10). Almost every verse speaks of God's word, or law, or precepts, or statutes.

Value God's Word

1. It blesses little children..................................Matt. 19:14
2. It strengthens young men..................................I John 2:14
3. It sanctifies and cleanses all who read it............Eph. 5:26
4. It protects the widows..................................Ex. 22:22-23
5. It honors the aged..................................Lev. 19:32
6. It offers eternal life to everyone..................................John 3:36

189

Praise is the highest duty that any creature can discharge. Man's chief end is to glorify God. There is no heaven either here or in the world to come for people who do not praise God. If you do not enter into the spirit and worship of heaven, the spirit and joy of heaven cannot enter you!

The Psalms begin with the word "blessed." This word is multiplied in this book. The book seems to be built around this first word. There is not one "woe" in the entire Psalms.

How can we make the Psalms our own in experience?

Why do you like the Psalms?

What Psalms can you quote?

Probably no other book has so largely influenced the turning points in men's lives, given expression to their deepest experiences, and woven itself into the very fiber of their character, as the Book of Psalms.

THE POSITION OF THE BOOK

Hold your Bible in your hand and turn to the middle of the book. It is the Psalms. Not merely is this true physically. There is a deeper truth. It is central also in human experience.

This book is used by Hebrew and Christian alike even in our day. The Psalms were for use in the temple, for which many were prepared. They were written for the heart to worship God out under the open heavens, or in the pit of despair, or in a cave of hiding. When you find yourself in deep need, you can always find a psalm which expresses your inmost feeling. Or, if you have an abounding joy, the words are there for you, too.

It is the book for all who are in need, the sick and suffering, the poor and needy, the prisoner and exile, the man in danger, the persecuted. It is a book for the sinner, telling him of God's great mercy and forgiveness. It is a book for the child of God, leading him into new experiences with the Lord. It tells of God's law in its perfection and pronounces blessings upon the one who will keep it.

Minimum Daily Requirements/Spiritual Vitamins

Sunday: PSALMS OF LAW   Psalms 1; 19
Monday: PSALMS OF CREATION   Psalms 29; 104
Tuesday: PSALMS OF JUDGMENT   Psalms 52; 53
Wednesday: PSALMS OF CHRIST
        Psalms 22; 40; 41
Thursday: PSALMS OF LIFE   Psalms 3; 31
Friday: PSALMS OF THE HEART   Psalms 37; 42
Saturday: PSALMS OF GOD   Psalms 90; 139

UNDERSTANDING PROVERBS, ECCLESIASTES, SONG OF SOLOMON

*Jesus Christ,
Our Wisdom;
The End of All Living;
The Lover of Our Souls*

Happy is the man that findeth wisdom, and the man that getteth understanding (Proverbs 3:13).

The books classed as poetical are Job, Psalms, Proverbs, Ecclesiastes, and Song of Solomon. These are not "poetical" in the sense that they are fanciful or unreal but in form only. There is no meter or rhyme, but rather a thought rhyme expressed in parallelism—repeating the same thought in different words.

In Psalms we find the Christian on his knees.

In Proverbs we find the Christian on his feet.

The Psalms are for the Christian's devotions.

The Proverbs are for the Christian's walk.

The Psalms are for the closet of prayer.

The Proverbs are for the business place, home and playground.

We find in Proverbs that godliness is practical. Every relationship in life is mentioned. We find our duty to God, to our neighbors, the duty of parents and children, our obligations as citizens.

The Jews likened Proverbs to the outer court of the temple; Ecclesiastes to the holy place; the Song of Solomon to the holy of holies. Remember that the altar of burnt offering and the laver of cleansing were in the outer court. If we come to the Book of Proverbs with a cleansed and surrendered heart and mind, we will get most out of the book.

The Book of Proverbs takes us out in the court of the congregation where the people are. Here they live their daily lives, and jostle each other in the highways of life. This is a book for everyday instruction. It deals with the practical affairs of life. The author, Solomon, wrote more wisely than he lived. Solomon wrote four hundred years before the seven wise men of Greece. The wise give heed to the commands of God and obey them. The foolish ignore God's will. This book divides men into two classes—wise and foolish.

AUTHOR

Notice how the book opens—*The proverbs of Solomon.* Solomon was a great king, famous for his wisdom and riches. He wrote 3,000 proverbs, 1,005 songs. (See I Kings 4:31,32.) Solomon was peculiarly qualified to write this book. God had given him *wisdom and understanding exceeding much, and largeness of heart, even as the sand that is on the sea shore* (I Kings 4:29). Solomon was a philosopher; he was a scientist of no mean ability. He was an architect of a temple that was one of the wonders of the world, and then, too, he was a king.

That Solomon was the author of this book implies no more than that he gathered these sayings already current among the people, given by the Holy Spirit through the centuries, and put them into the orderly arrangement that we have today. See what Solomon said about this in Ecclesiastes 12:9, where, it is recorded—*he gave good heed, and sought out, and set in order many proverbs.*

Someone has said that they were a collection of maxims, woven into a didactic poem around a general topic, wisdom.

Several names are given in the book regarding authorship:

Solomon..Proverbs 1:1; 25:1
The wise..Proverbs 22:17
Men of Hezekiah..Proverbs 25:1
Agur..Proverbs 30:1
King Lemuel and his mother............................Proverbs 31:1

This book is filled with words of wisdom. There is one terse saying after another. Men have tried to add to them and failed. A brilliant lawyer tried it once. He thought he could write a few before breakfast. He came away from his task humbled and baffled and glorying in the marvelous wisdom of God.

DIVISIONS OF THE BOOKS OF PROVERBS

The book closes with one of the most beautiful chapters in the Word (Proverbs 31). This is a chapter on woman's rights. *Give her of the fruit of her hands; and let her own works praise her in the gates.* Wherever Christ goes womanhood is lifted up. In heathen countries, where Christ is not known, woman is never more than a chattel or slave. In Christian lands, woman is made a queen.

This book presents a system of conduct and life. You cannot find any agnosticism here. God is taken for granted! Be wise and find God's way for your life! This book is to provide rules for the righteous life.

The real power and beauty in this book lies hidden in the true meaning of the word "wisdom." It is evident that this word means more than an excellent attribute. It is found that the wisdom of Proverbs is the Incarnate Word of the New Testament. Christ found Himself in this book (Luke 24:27).

Wisdom is represented as dwelling with God from all eternity. *I was set up from everlasting, from the beginning, or ever the earth was . . . When he prepared the heavens, I was there: when he set a compass upon the face of the depth: . . . when he appointed the foundations of the earth: then I was by him, as one brought up with him:* [I was as His designer] (see Proverbs 8:23-31). Compare these with John 1:1,2; Heb. 1:2; Col. 2:3.

When you read the Book of Proverbs put Christ instead of wisdom in the verse. (See I Cor. 1:30.) You will see a wonderful power in this book. *And we know that the Son of God is come, and hath given us an understanding, that we may know him that is true* (I John 5:20).

The purpose of the Book of Proverbs is stated clearly at the beginning. See Proverbs 1:2-4. We find that the first of all duties is the fear of God (Proverbs 1:7). *Receive the instruction of wisdom, justice, and judgment, and equity.* This is the true college spirit—education of self. *Give subtilty to the simple, to the young man knowledge and discretion.* Plain common sense is needed in life. Don't be a fool!

God wants to give us of His wisdom—the wisdom which created heavens and earth, that we might use it in all of life (James 1:5). This would put an end to all the confusion and evil in this world, wouldn't it? Human wisdom can never solve life's problems. Only God knows the ways of men. *The fear of the LORD is the beginning of wisdom* (Psalm 111:10).

COUNSEL FOR YOUNG MEN (Read Proverbs 1–10)

"Sermons For Sons"

"Wise Up!"—Worship is the first step to wisdom (1:7).

"Walk Straight!"—The "straight and narrow" has the lowest accident rate (2:20).

"Directions"—Ask God about everything: He knows every road (3:6).

"Watch Your Step!"—Every step helps mold character; step well (4:26).

"Flee Flattery"—"Smoother than oil" is modern terminology. Most young men understand it (5:3).

"God's Black List"—Pride, lies, murder, deceit, mischief, betrayal, discord (6:17-19).

"A Bad Woman"—Read carefully Proverbs 7:15-27.

"Riches"—Rubies of wisdom command highest prices on the market of character values (8:11).

"More Fun"—Nothing you ought not to do is ever "more fun." Wait till you see what results (9:17,18).

"Wanted! Silence"—Wordy men seldom are wise men (10:19).

This whole book is extremely practical. It would be well for us all to give it closer study for our guidance in daily life. *In all thy ways acknowledge him, and he shall direct thy paths* (Proverbs 3:6). This means straighten them. This is the Lord's rule for our feet. The way of evil . . . *avoid it, pass not by it, turn from it, and pass away* (Proverbs 4:15). This is God's "Stop! Look! Listen!"

The fear of the Lord spoken of here is not a fear of fright but a fear of a son who is afraid he might grieve his father's love. It is the fear coming from love, the fear of displeasing the Lord, that leads to godliness. We shall not begin to be wise until our lives are in right relation with Christ, the fount of all wisdom. *Wisdom is the principal thing; therefore get wisdom: and with all thy getting get understanding* (Proverbs 4:7).

God wants *to give subtilty to the simple*, [or open-minded], *to the young man knowledge and discretion* [advisement](Proverbs 1:4). Don't be a fool. God wants you to have plain common sense. The most uncommon thing in the world today is common sense.

In Proverbs 4:23-26, we find that the whole body is included:

Keep thy heart..Verse 23

Put away a froward mouth...Verse 24

Let thine eyes look right on...Verse 25

Ponder the path of thy feet...Verse 26

The duty of parents to chastise their children is enforced, and is based upon God's chastening of His children (Proverbs 3:11,12). One of the signs of the last wicked days upon the earth is given by Paul as "disobedient to parents." (See II Timothy 3:2.) What happened to Eli and his boys because he allowed his sons to sin?

The young are warned against the influence of bad companions, against impurity and intemperance, against anger, strifes, and quarrels. (See Proverbs 1:10-19; 4:14-19; 19; also chapters 3; 10; 13; 15; 16; 18.)

There are many sins of the tongue. We use it too freely. We lie and are deceitful in dealings with others. Much is said about guarding the tongue, for in the tongue is the power of life and death. (See Proverbs 12:22; 18:21.)

As we read this book, we find the author pleading with us to shun evil companions, pride, envy, intemperance, sins of the tongue and idleness. All these things would be impossible to do unless we had Christ, the Wisdom of God, within us.

Read about pride and its consequences in Proverbs 8; 11; 16; 19. See Proverbs 16:18. The Lord wants us always to be humble before Him and not to esteem ourselves better than others. Every truly great person is humble.

COUNSEL FOR ALL MEN (Read Proverbs 11–20)
"Messages for Men"

"False Economy"—A gift is never lost; only what is selfishly kept impoverishes (11:24).

"Fools"—You cannot convince a fool of his folly; only a wise man will accept a rebuke for foolhardiness (12:15).

"Lying"—Righteousness and lying are enemies; to a wicked man they are synonymous (13:5).

"Answers that Heal"—Two people ought not to get angry at the same time (15:1).

"Clean Sin"—A man deep in wickedness will invent "pretty names for sin" (Spurgeon) (16:2).

"To Win Friends"—A friendly man will have friends; being a relative does not insure being a friend (18:24).

"Drink Up!"—When you decide for strong drink, don't be surprised when it decides against you (20:1).

He that withholdeth corn, the people shall curse him (Proverbs 11:26). This reveals the sin of the grain speculator. It is a warning to the speculators of our day.

The just man walketh in his integrity: his children are blessed after him (Proverbs 20:7). Douay says: "He leaves behind him blessed children." This is a good man's legacy to the world. Godly parents are a blessing to children (Proverbs 20:7) and should instruct them in the right way (Proverbs 22:6).

There has never been a time when men did as well as they knew how. However imperfect their instructions, they have never lived up to them. The last thing a man could complain of is a lack of good advice.

Who has heart trouble? Who has woe? Sorrow? Contentions? (Read Proverbs 20; 23; 31.) No sin is more severely denounced in Scripture than that of drunkenness. *Know ye not that the unrighteous shall not inherit the kingdom of God? . . . Nor thieves, nor covetous, nor drunkards, nor revilers, nor extortioners, shall inherit the kingdom of God* (I Cor. 6:9,10). The words in

Proverbs are *apples of gold in pictures of silver* (Proverbs 25:11). Study the picture, but do not miss the apples of gold depicted here.

Proverbs is an intensely practical book, exposing a series of traps that would ensnare us. *There is no wisdom nor understanding nor counsel against the LORD* (Proverbs 21:30). At last we see God's will and God's way! Hasten it, O Lord!

COUNSEL FOR KINGS AND RULERS (Read Proverbs 21–31)

"Self-Control"—A guarded mouth makes for a serene soul (21:23).

"Reputation"—Choose a good name rather than great riches. Your name goes on; your wealth stops at death (22:1).

"Soberness"—Red wine is colorful but calamitous (23:31).

"Counsel"—The sober judgment of a sane thinking group is more reliable than your own opinion (24:6).

"Women"—Better solitude on top of the house than sojourning in the house with a nagging woman (25:24).

"Gossip"—Fire goes out when fuel gives out; scandal stops when mouths are stopped (26:20).

"Tomorrow"—There is never a tomorrow, only today. Get it done now, for now soon becomes then (27:1).

"Understanding"—Rank does not guarantee an understanding heart (28:16).

"Bribes"—Seek justice and your land shall stand; accept bribes and it will fall (29:4).

"Security"—A trust in God is the only safe soul-armor (30:5).

UNDERSTANDING ECCLESIASTES

Jesus is the beginning of all in Proverbs;
He is the end of all in Ecclesiastes, the "summum bonum" of life.

Wisdom in Proverbs is piety.

Wisdom in Ecclesiastes is prudence and sagacity.

Ecclesiastes is the soul's autobiography or the book of experience.

"Vanity" is the key word. See Ecclesiastes 2:11.

You do not have to go outside the Bible to find the merely human philosophy of life. God has given us in the Book of Ecclesiastes the record of all that human thinking and natural religion has ever been able to discover concerning the meaning and goal of life. The arguments in the book, therefore, are not God's arguments, but God's record of man's arguments. This explains why such passages as 1:15; 2:24; 3:3,4,8,11,19,20; 8:15 are at positive variance with the rest of the Bible.

The writer is Solomon, and the book is a dramatic autobiography of his experience and reflections while he was out of fellowship with God. Solomon may have been wise, but he did not follow his own wisdom. Ecclesiastes has its origin in his tragic sin of forsaking God and seeking satisfaction in philosophy and science "under the sun," that is, based only upon speculation and thought. The inference of the book that *all is vanity and vexation of spirit* is, therefore, inevitable, and the message of Ecclesiastes is that, apart from God, life is full of weariness and disappointment.

The problem which faced Solomon was how he could find happiness and satisfaction apart from God (Eccl. 1:1-3). He sought satisfaction in science (Eccl. 1:4-11), but could get no answer. He sought it in philosophy (Eccl. 1:12-18), but in vain; he found pleasure (Eccl. 2:1-11), mirth (v. 1), drinking (v. 3), building (v. 4), possession (vs. 5-7), wealth and music (v. 8), all empty.

He tried materialism (Eccl. 2:12-26), fatalism (Eccl. 3:1-15), and deism (Eccl. 3:1–4:16), but these likewise were vain. Natural religion (Eccl. 5:1-8), wealth (Eccl. 5:9–6:12), and even morality (Eccl. 7:1–12:12) proved equally fruitless.

The conclusion is in Ecclesiastes 12:13, and is the best thing possible to man under the law. It is interesting to notice the place of youth in the argument (Eccl. 11:9–12:1). We must begin young to know God if we are to find life worth living.

Remember, Ecclesiastes only shows us the best that man can do apart from God's gospel of grace.

The name Ecclesiastes means "preacher." This is so named because it contains the meditations and sermons of the wise man, Solomon.

CONFESSION (Read Ecclesiastes 1–7)

The great question: "Is life worth living?" is presented. Solomon has tested it to the full. No man could better do it or better tell it—and the answer he gives is not reassuring for the life that now is.

Try wisdom! (Eccl. 1). What better thing is there in all the world? Solomon declared, *I gave my heart to know wisdom.* Yet he was forced to cry out, *Vanity of vanities! . . . For in much wisdom is much grief: and he that increaseth knowledge increaseth sorrow* (Eccl. 1:17,2,18). This is always true of mere earthly wisdom. *The fear of the Lord is the beginning of real wisdom* (Ps. 111:10).

Try pleasure! (Ecclesiastes 2) *I said in mine heart, Go to now, I will prove thee with mirth, therefore enjoy pleasure: and, behold, this also is vanity* (Eccl. 2:1). This is his deliberate conclusion. God made us all to be joyful. He has given us a thousand avenues of enjoyment. Let us not sacrifice true happiness for questionable pleasure. Always make your recreation a re-creation.

Philosophy has failed says the preacher, so let merriment be tried. Music, dance, wine (not to excess), the funny story, the clever repartee: these are now cultivated. Clowns are now welcomed to the court, where only grave philosophy had been. The halls of the palace resounded with laughter and gaiety. Yet after a while all this palled on the king's taste. He even goes so far as to say that laughter is mad and mirth inane (Eccl. 2:1-2). Cheerfulness is admirable. A hearty laugh in its place is delightful but the person who is always giggling is a bore.

Try architecture! (Ecclesiastes 2:4). Now he becomes practical. He attends to great works of state. Aqueducts, pools, palaces and other public buildings occupy his thoughts. Now the court fools are frowned upon and great architects are welcomed to the palace. But the excitement incident to building soon fades away.

Try gardening! (Ecclesiastes 2:5,6). Vineyards, gardens, orchards, rare flowers, tropical plants are all the rage. Jerusalem and the vicinity bloom like the Garden of Eden. Soon it is like a new toy for a child, that pleases for a while but is soon tossed away.

Try cattle breeding and art collecting! (Ecclesiastes 2:7 and 8). Then the king tries cattle breeding, art collecting, and even becomes an amateur musician (v. 8). Choruses and orchestras gather in the royal palace. But even though "music hath charms," it is powerless to charm with permanent happiness.

Try just living the weary round of life—with discretion! (Ecclesiastes 3). But again, "What profit?" Vanity of vanities!

Try the stoic's philosophy! (Ecclesiastes 4). Surely this also is vanity. He wails, *vanity and vexation of spirit* (Eccl. 4:16)!

Try ritualism—formal religion! (Ecclesiastes 5). Be sure to *pay that which thou hast vowed* (Eccl. 5:4). This, too, is vanity.

Try wealth! (Ecclesiastes 6). Solomon had it. He was *a man to whom God hath given riches*. What is the good of it? *God giveth him not power to eat thereof, but a stranger eateth it: this is vanity, and it is an evil disease* (Eccl. 6:2). Many agree with Solomon in the emptiness of pleasures, but they think that money is the supreme goal in life. Jesus told us to seek first the kingdom of God and His righteousness, and all these things would be added.

Try reputation! (Ecclesiastes 7). *A good name is better than precious ointment; and the day of death than the day of one's birth* (Eccl. 7:1). It doesn't last long in this world. Men are soon forgotten when they die. Vanity still!

ADMONITION (Read Ecclesiastes 8–12)

Now comes a turning point. Ecclesiastes 8:12 says, *Yet*

surely I know that it shall be well with them that fear God. The full meaning of this is in the last chapter—*Fear God, and keep his commandments: for this is the whole duty of man* (Eccl. 12:13).

The "Preacher," as he is called, has been looking out and back and around. Now he looks up and he sees God and is satisfied.

The phrase *under the sun* (Eccl. 1:3) is found twenty-eight times in this little book. The "under-the-sun-life" is hardly worth living; but above the sun, and in the heavenlies that Paul describes, it is glorious (Ephesians 1).

Dr. Pierson well said, "The key to Ecclesiastes is that a man is too big for this world." We find in this book that we can never find satisfaction and happiness in this world. True happiness apart from Christ is impossible. We find dissatisfaction among the poor and rich alike, among the ignorant and learned, among people and kings.

Ecclesiastes closes with a call to the young! Lay the foundations early. *Remember now thy Creator in the days of thy youth.* This book is given as a danger sign, that we may be spared having to learn the bitterness of life by finding the cisterns we have sought to be empty. The greatest proportion of men and women who are living to serve God have chosen Him in childhood.

UNDERSTANDING SONG OF SOLOMON

The Song of Solomon has been called the Christian's Love Song. Key text is Song of Solomon 6:3.

This is a song of love in marriage in Oriental language and imagery. The persons are Solomon and the Shulamite maid and the daughters of Jerusalem. The idea of the love of husband and wife sets forth the love between Jehovah and His people. This is seen in many passages in the Bible. Moreover, Solomon as a lover was a type of Christ. See Ephesians 5. Personal love to Christ is the greatest need of the church today. The knowledge of sin forgiven and of Christ's redeeming work has drawn us to Him.

Minimum Daily Requirements/Spiritual Vitamins

Sunday: GET WISDOM   Proverbs 1–4
Monday: TO SONS   Proverbs 5–7
Tuesday: GOOD AND BAD   Proverbs 15–17
Wednesday: WISE WORDS   Proverbs 20; 22; 31
Thursday: ALL IS VANITY   Ecclesiastes 1–3
Friday: ONLY GOD SATISFIES   Ecclesiastes 11; 12
Saturday: JOYFUL COMMUNION
           S. of Sol. 1:1-7; 2:1-7

CHAPTER 18

UNDERSTANDING ISAIAH

Isaiah
Portrays Jesus Christ,
the Messiah

The key note of Isaiah is "salvation." Isaiah's name means "salvation of Jehovah."

INTRODUCTION TO THE PROPHETICAL BOOKS

The poetical books belong to the golden age of the nation. The prophetical books belong to the dark ages of God's chosen people.

The prophets were men whom God raised up during the dark days of Israel's history. They were the evangelists of the day, the religious patriots of the hour. Read what God says about them in II Kings 17:13. *Yet the LORD testified against Israel, and against Judah, by all the prophets, and by all the seers, saying, Turn ye from your evil ways, and keep my commandments and my statutes, according to all the law which I commanded your fathers, and which I sent to you by my servants the prophets.* We read everywhere in the New Testament that God spoke through the prophets. The period of the prophets in Israel covered five hundred years from the ninth to the fourth century B.C. Then the voices of the prophets were silenced until John the Baptist. These prophets spoke fearlessly to kings and people alike of their sins and failures.

The office of prophet was instituted in Samuel's time. When the kingdom was divided and Judah and Israel were established as separate monarchies, the great prophets appeared. There were four major and twelve minor prophets.

There are seventeen prophetical books in the Old Testament. They are subdivided into major and minor prophets. This difference is made not because of their importance but because of the amount of material written.

The captivities of Israel (the northern kingdom) and of

Judah (the southern kingdom) are largely the theme of the Old Testament prophets. The record of these is found in II Kings 17:1-23; 24:11-25:21. These are called the Assyrian and Babylonian captivities. Some of the prophets served before the exile and some afterwards. These are called pre-exilic and post-exilic prophets.

PRE-EXILIC PROPHETS

The prophets during the exile (or "pre-exilic") in order of their writings were: Obadiah, Joel, Jonah, Amos, Hosea, Isaiah, Micah, Nahum, Habakkuk, Zephaniah and Jeremiah.

The prophets to Israel during this period were Jonah, Amos and Hosea. The prophets to Judah were Obadiah, Joel, Isaiah, Micah, Nahum, Habakkuk, Zephaniah and Jeremiah.

EXILIC PROPHETS

The prophets during the exile (or captivity in Babylon) were Ezekiel and Daniel. They prophesied to all the Israelites. Jeremiah extended for a while into this period. Those who prophesied after the exile were Haggai, Zechariah and Malachi.

Prophets According to Time:

6 lived in the time of Israel's destruction by Assyria—Joel, Jonah, Amos, Hosea, Isaiah, Micah.
7 lived in the time of Judah's destruction by Babylon—Jeremiah, Ezekiel, Daniel, Obadiah, Nahum, Habakkuk, Zephaniah.
3 lived in the time of the Restoration to their own land—Haggai, Zechariah, Malachi.

Prophets According to Special Messages:

3 to Israel—Amos, Hosea, Ezekiel.
2 to Nineveh—Jonah, Nahum.
1 to Babylon—Daniel.
1 to Edom—Obadiah.
9 to Judah—Joel, Isaiah, Micah, Jeremiah, Habakkuk, Zephaniah, Haggai, Zechariah, Malachi.

THE PROPHETS — THEIR MESSAGE

The prophet's chief duty was to deal with the moral and religious life of his own people during his day. The prophet was never sent while the nation was walking in obedience to God. All of the writings are rebukes because of the bad condition that existed at that very time. There was nothing general about the prophet's denunciations.

The prophet was always a Hebrew. He not only spoke of judgment that would come to pass to the people because of their sin but he was also a foreteller of future events. The events of which he spoke concerned the nation of Israel in the main. Other peoples were mentioned only as they came in contact with Israel.

Let us note some of the prophecies of the future which are recounted. Hold these in mind as you study their writings.

1. The dispersion and captivity of God's chosen people.

Everywhere the prophet tells that the Jew is to be scattered among the nations of the world.

2. The coming of the Messiah.

The Jew is still looking for his Messiah.

3. The restoration of the chosen people to their own land under the coming Messiah, David's greater Son.

The Jews are returning from the four corners of the earth to dwell in their own promised land. Every Jew has a longing in his heart to be a part of a great nation. Now Israel is a nation.

4. The reign of the Messiah over the whole earth.

Even though we see the final collapse of God's people, at first Israel, then Judah being led into captivity, nevertheless God revealed that the ending of His nation did not end His plans. There is yet to be a glorious future when the Prince of Peace shall reign over His people and sway His scepter *from sea to sea, and from the river unto the ends of the earth* (Psalm 72:8).

When you read the Gospels, you find this phrase constantly, *that it might be fulfilled.* We find in examining these passages that God fulfills prophecy literally. Learn to interpret the meaning of the words of the prophets in a literal, natural way. Do not force a spiritual interpretation and read out all the real meaning. There are figurative passages, of course. But you will find that as soon as you determine the meaning of the figure that that, too, will have its literal fulfillment. This method makes the study of the prophets a simple one. Remember, the Church is not in the prophets at all. This is the "mystery" that God kept until He wished it to be revealed (Ephesians 3:3,11,12).

The prophets speak only of the earthly ministry of Christ and say nothing of His *called out ones* (ecclesia). This was announced by Jesus Himself (Matthew 16:18; Eph. 3:3-10).

THE PROPHETS — THEIR CHARACTER

The prophets were fearless men. They denounced the sins of their day. They called men away from idols back to God. It is true that the prophets were concerned about the moral and political corruption of the nation but the fact that the people were worshiping idols was their greatest concern. The nation had a wrong attitude toward God. Christ gave us a succinct statement of what our attitude should be. *Love the Lord thy God with all thy heart* (Luke 10:27). God knows that what a man's attitude is toward God will affect his whole moral life. Creed always determines conduct. This is true, not only of individuals, but of nations. The adage "it makes no difference what a man believes" is completely refuted in the prophets.

The prophets exposed the cold formalism of their religion. They constantly reminded the people that Jehovah was the only true God. They pointed men to the law. They were statesmen of the highest order. They were prophets in that they came to tell forth what God said. They were not only "forth-tellers" but "fore-tellers."

So important is prophecy in God's Word that it occupies about one third of the whole Bible. Prophecy is God's revelation of His plans to His children.

Campbell Morgan says that there were three elements in the message of the prophets:

1. A message to their own age—directly from God.
2. A message of predicted future events.

(a) The failure of God's chosen people and God's judgment upon them and the nations around them.

(b) The coming of the Messiah and His rejection and final glory.

(c) The Messianic Kingdom ultimately to be established on the earth.

3. A living message to our own age—eternal principles of right and wrong.

The Spirit of God spoke by the prophets. *As he spake by the mouth of his holy prophets which have been since the world began* (Luke 1:70). Read II Peter 1:21; Jer. 1:9; Ezek. 2:7 to find how the message was given.

Read what Christ said of the prophets (Luke 24:25-27).

The prophecies concerning Christ Himself are so definite that it gives great assurance to us that the Bible is the Word of God.

God puts a telescope before the eyes of the prophets and lets them look far into the future. Especially do we find this spirit of expectation in Isaiah. We hear the prophet cry, "He is coming!" Isaiah was a man of vision. Read the opening words. *The vision of Isaiah the son of Amoz, which he saw concerning Judah and Jerusalem* (Isaiah 1:1).

Isaiah was a man who certainly spoke boldly to his own time, but as a prophet he spoke of the future as well; hence he is the prophet for all times. We sit at his feet today and following his index finger as it points into the future, we hear him say, "Lo, your King!"

This great statesman was the prophet of the southern kingdom of Judah. He lived at the time that the northern kingdom of Israel was destroyed by Assyria. Isaiah was the one whose voice saved the kingdom of Judah during these trying hours.

It is interesting to note that this is also the time of Romulus and Remus and the founding of Rome. The traditional date of the building of Rome is 753 B.C., just a few years after the birth of the prophet, Isaiah. About this time Sparta and Athens in Greece were founded.

The prophets were the most unpopular men in their day for they dealt with the moral and religious conditions of the hour! Generally the state was bad. Prophets were sent when the nation was out of step with God—when they were walking in disobedience. The words which the prophets used to rebuke or exhort the people were very pointed. They were for the very people to whom they addressed themselves. Truth is seldom popular with the sinner.

Let us find the scriptural definition of a prophet. Look in Deuteronomy 18:18. *I will raise them up a Prophet from among their brethren, like unto thee,* [Moses] *and will put my words in his mouth; and he shall speak unto them all that I shall command him.* Also verse 19, *And it shall come to pass, that whosoever will not hearken unto my words which he shall speak in my name, I will require it of him.*

Although the prophets spoke to their own age, as we have already noted, they were ever looking forward to future events. Besides this, we find abiding principles stated for all times. They foretold the failure of the chosen people and the coming of the Messiah. Each showed how God was to bring to pass His purposes through the Messiah. We see today how the Jews have failed. *He came unto his own, and his own received him not* (John 1:11). They rather cried, *Crucify him!* The Messiah came to establish His kingdom but the Jews said, *We have no king but Caesar* (John 19:15). They rejected Him. But His kingdom will yet be established over the whole earth.

Isaiah told of the judgment that must fall on Judah because she would not fulfill her mission in the world. But through the whole book we find the ultimate triumph of God's plan through His appointed Servant, the Lord Jesus Christ, who would bring in final victory through suffering and death (Isaiah 53).

AUTHOR

This book of Isaiah is written with two distinct emphases. Because of this some Bible scholars believe that there was more than one author. This need not be the case. It is the work of one man with two messages. In the first of the book he pictured Israel. In the last of the book, the prophet beheld Jesus bearing our load of sin, and he told the story; then he beheld Christ exalted and glorified and shouted of his vision from the house-top. It is the same prophet all the time but suiting his language to the theme at hand.

The only way to understand Isaiah is to understand the prophet's Christ. It is far more important that we be familiar with the truths of the book than the theories of its authorship. Don't let anyone interpret the Book for you who does not know its Author.

Isaiah is a miniature Bible in structure. This book has sixty-six chapters, just as the Bible has sixty-six books. There are two great divisions, just as there are in the Bible, with thirty-nine chapters in the first (like the Old Testament) and twenty-seven chapters in the second (like the New Testament).

The Old Testament opens with God's case against man because of his sin. Isaiah opens the same way (Isa. 1:18). The first section closes with the prophecy of the coming King of Righteousness and the redemption of Israel (34–35), just as the prophets close the Old Testament with the prediction of His coming kingdom. The second part of Isaiah (chapter 40) opens with *the voice of him that crieth in the wilderness,* (John the Baptist) and is concerned with the person and work of Jesus Christ. The New Testament opens in exact accord with this. John the Baptist, the forerunner of Jesus is announced (John 1:6,23). Isaiah ends with the vision of new heavens and a new earth wherein dwelleth righteousness. The New Testament closes with this same view in Revelation. This striking similarity between Isaiah and the whole Bible is unforgettable when once mastered.

Isaiah is like a jewel case; and the fifty-third chapter is the jewel. This has a central position in the group of the chapters to which it belongs. As you see, it is located in the second division of the book or the last twenty-seven chapters. In the very middle of this precious group of twenty-seven chapters lies the fifty-third. This is the chapter that tells of the Saviour, who *hath borne our griefs* [sins], *and carried our sorrows.* Chapter 53 is a wonderful one to store in your memory. Each verse is a nugget of golden truth. This is the chapter that pictures Christ, our suffering Redeemer.

TWO COMINGS OF CHRIST

We see Christ in this book and hear the prophet crying, "He is coming!" and "He is coming again!" He is coming as Saviour, pictured in the fifty-third chapter, in humiliation as our sin-bearer. He is coming again in power and great glory, pictured in chapter 34.

As we look through the telescope, we see two mountain peaks with a valley between. One is called Calvary; on its hilltop is a cross. But as we look farther we see another peak. It is radiant with the light of a crown! This hill is Olivet. The eye of the ancient seer went farther than the sufferings of Calvary; his eye caught the kingdom and the glory that should follow!

Isaiah speaks of Christ's death when he says, *Though your sins be as scarlet, they shall be as white as snow; though they be red like crimson, they shall be as wool* (Isaiah 1:18). Again, *He is despised and rejected of men* (Isaiah 53:3). This speaks of the first time when *He came unto his own, and his own received him not.* When He will come again we shall hear, *Arise, shine; for thy light is come, and the glory of the LORD is risen upon thee* (Isaiah 60:1). Then he tells us of His coming kingdom. *And it shall come to pass in the last days, . . .* (Read Isaiah 2:2-5).

Life of Christ, Portrayed in Isaiah

Birth ....Isaiah 7:14; 9:6
Family ....Isaiah 11:1
Anointing ....Isaiah 11:2
Character ....Isaiah 11:3,4
Simplicity of Life ....Isaiah 7:15
Gentleness ....Isaiah 42:1-4
Death ....Isaiah 53
Resurrection ....Isaiah 25:8
Glorious Reign ....Isaiah 11:3-16; 32

Isaiah was a man of royal blood. He was a young aristocrat from a princely line. His father, Amoz, was the younger son of Joash, king of Judah. He was brought up in the court and had high standing with the people of Jerusalem. He not only was a prophet, but he married a prophetess (Isaiah 8:3,18). His training was of the best. After his labor of sixty years, tradition tells us that he died a martyr in the reign of Manasseh at the age of 120.

Isaiah was a special messenger to Judah. Look over II Kings

15–20 and note the moral and political rottenness of Judah and Israel, and the danger from the surrounding Gentile nations. Assyria was strong and aggressive, striving for world power. Egypt was on the south, and Palestine was the road between these two enemies. Both Assyria and Egypt aimed at a world empire. Therefore Palestine became the battleground of the ages.

Isaiah did not fail in his ministry. He laid bare the sins of his people and called them to repent and turn to God. "Come back to God," he cried. But his chief theme was "the Coming One." It was Jesus. He saw Christ's near first coming and His far away second coming, but in all he saw Christ.

Johannes Kepler, in failing to bring the heavenly bodies into satisfactory adjustment with one center, at last conceived of the ellipse with two foci and everything fell into harmony. So when in our reverent study of God's Word we catch the dual center of Christ on the cross and Christ on the throne, then the Word shines clear and we begin to see what the prophet saw, the world's Redeemer, coming first in humiliation, then again, in power and great glory.

4 Words to Judah

Rebellion—*Ah, sinful nation* (Isaiah 1:2-4,10-15,21-23)
Retribution—*Ye shall be devoured* (Isaiah 1:5-8,15,20,28)
Repentance—*If ye be willing and obedient* (Isaiah 1:16-19,27)
Restoration—*Zion shall be redeemed* (Isaiah 1:9,18,24-31)

Judah thought that in keeping up all outward observances in their religious service that all would be well. Isaiah denounced their hypocrisy (Isaiah 1:15). He told them of forgiveness if they would repent, but promised them a sword if they continued in their rebellion against God.

Because of their sin and their forsaking God, Judah was facing judgment (Isaiah 1:1-31; 2:6–3:26). Yet there is a glorious future for Judah when Christ comes again. Jerusalem is to be the capital of the coming kingdom (Isaiah 2:1-5; 4).

God's truths of redemption go beyond our reason, but they do not insult our reason; they rather appeal to it. To worship aright in the presence of God, we must be right in the presence of men.

UNDER UZZIAH AND JOTHAM (Read Isaiah 1–6)

Read Isaiah 1:1 and you will discover that Isaiah was prophet during the reigns of Uzziah, Jotham, Ahaz and Hezekiah. During this time the statesman prophet preached in Jerusalem.

Now turn to Isaiah 6:1-13 and you see that Isaiah received his real commission in the year that King Uzziah died. No doubt he had written chapters 1–5 before this time. The long reign of fifty-two years that was so glorious during the greater part ended in gloom. For the last four years of his life Uzziah was a leper. He was shut off from all the business of state, and the kingdom was under the regency of his son Jotham. The early chapters of Isaiah fit the situation perfectly.

When Isaiah preached that God was about to abandon Judah, it may have seemed too cruel, but the Lord is infinitely more concerned with the purity of His people than with their prosperity.

Uzziah was a leper and Jotham was regent (II Kings 15:5). "Azariah" is another spelling of "Uzziah." Uzziah's reign did not directly affect Isaiah's prophecy.

Jotham, Uzziah's successor, is only mentioned twice in the book (Isaiah 1:1; 7:1). It does not seem that Isaiah was active during his reign. It is with the reign of the next two kings, Ahaz and Hezekiah, that Isaiah's prophecy deals.

Ahaz reigned sixteen years and Hezekiah reigned twenty-nine years. Ahaz was a wicked king, and more, he was an idolater. Hezekiah was for the most part a good king and he did much to remove idolatry from the people.

ISAIAH'S MESSAGE

Isaiah warned Judah of her folly and rebellion (Isaiah 1:2-9). They separated themselves from God by the sins of greed, heathen alliances, and idolatry (Isaiah 2:6-9). God called them a fruitless vine. God had tried patience, then punishment; now they must be destroyed by heathen kings.

God called Isaiah just as He called Moses, Joshua, Gideon or Paul. Isaiah's commission came at the tragic death of the grand old King Uzziah (Isaiah 6:1). His call was a never-to-be-forgotten experience. It taught him his own unworthiness and gave him his real commission to a sinning, needy world calling out for help. It came to him in the form of a "vision." For years Isaiah preached and told of doom and deliverance. Hardship and peril awaited him but God gave him a victorious strength. He was the man of the hour. Let us look at the steps leading from the opening of the vision to his final commission.

SECRET OF ISAIAH'S LIFE

This experience of Isaiah's should be every disciple's experience. The secret of all of Isaiah's power lay in this vision in the temple, *I saw the Lord!*

Conviction—*Woe is me . . . I am undone* was the cry brought on by the sense of sinfulness before God's holiness (Isaiah 6:5).

Confession—*A man of unclean lips.* A broken and a contrite heart is precious to the Lord (Isaiah 6:5).

Cleansing—*Thy sin purged.* After confession, a flying seraph cleansed his lips with a hot coal from off the altar (Isaiah 6:7).

Consecration—*Here am I; send me* (Isaiah 6:8).

Commission—*Go.* God's command (Isaiah 6:9).

UNDER AHAZ (Read Isaiah 7–14)

And it came to pass in the days of Ahaz . . . (Isaiah 7:1). Ahaz was utterly bad. He was an open idolater. For this sin God allowed Rezin, king of Syria, and Pekah, king of Israel, to invade his kingdom. Isaiah had been silent under Jotham but this invasion brings him to the front in his ministry. *Then said the LORD unto Isaiah, Go forth now to meet Ahaz* (Isaiah 7:3). He appealed to him to put his trust in God for help rather than call in Tiglath-Pileser from Nineveh.

God sent the prophet to encourage Ahaz. Beside predicting the Assyrian invasion in Isaiah 8, the prophet saw an end to all of Israel's troubles through the birth of the Christ-child who shall rule over the kingdom of David in righteousness forever and forever. He gave Ahaz a "sign" that Judah was not to perish—the prophecy of Immanuel, the Virgin's Son, Jesus Christ. *Therefore the Lord himself shall give you a sign; Behold, a virgin shall conceive, and bear a son, and shall call his name Immanuel* (Isaiah 7:14). Read these important words in Isaiah 7:10-16. Ahaz refused the evidence upon which his faith might have been established. He pursued his own plans with Assyria and that nation on which they now leaned was to become the means of their punishment (Isaiah 7:17-20).

Then followed the sentence of doom upon king and land (Isaiah 8:6-22). With nations, this is God's policy: doom for idolatry.

In Isaiah 9:6,7 we find another great prophecy concerning Christ. *For unto us a child is born, unto us a son is given: and the government shall be upon his shoulder: and his name shall be called Wonderful, Counsellor, The mighty God, The everlasting Father, The Prince of Peace. Of the increase of his government and peace there shall be no end, upon the throne of David, and upon his kingdom, to order it, and to establish it with judgment and with justice from henceforth even for ever. The zeal of the LORD of hosts will perform this.* The Son to be given, the child to be born, was to sit on David's throne. Remember the "throne of David" is as definite as the "throne of the Caesars." Yes, Christ will sit on the throne of David. Hear the angel's words to Mary, *He shall be great, and shall be called the Son of the Highest: and the Lord God shall give unto him the throne of his father David: and he shall reign over the house of Jacob for ever* (Luke 1:32,33).

We find present woe and future glory strangely mixed in Isaiah 10. But in Isaiah 11 we see the picture of the glory of the future kingdom which Christ is coming to establish on this earth. Some day He is coming to Jerusalem to sit upon the throne of David and peace shall cover the earth *as the waters cover the sea.*

In this kingdom the people will worship the Lord Jehovah. The prophet says, *Sing unto the LORD; for he hath done excellent things* (Isaiah 12:5).

In Isaiah 13 we see great Babylon's doom. She was to carry Judah away captive but the prophet sees her destruction. God is keeping His promise to Abraham. *And I will bless them that bless thee, and curse him that curseth thee: and in thee shall all families of the earth be blessed* (Genesis 12:3). God always brings a curse on any nation that afflicts Israel. You can follow this truth through history. God often allows nations to punish Israel for her national sins but retribution is inevitable (Deut. 30:5-7; Isa. 14:1,2; Joel 3:1-8).

Read every word of Isaiah 11 and 12, which gives a picture of this coming King and kingdom.

1. The King Himself..Isaiah 11:1
2. His anointing..Isaiah 11:2
3. His righteous reign..Isaiah 11:3-5
4. His glorious kingdom...Isaiah 11:6-9
5. His gathering together of His people from the
   four corners of the earth................................Isaiah 11:10-16
6. His kingdom worship..Isaiah 12

When it was my privilege to drive out to old Babylon and look over the ruins of that once magnificent city and see the absolute devastation, I thought of Isaiah's prophecy concerning this city found in Isaiah 13:19-22. God said that *Babylon, the glory of kingdoms, the beauty of the Chaldees' excellency, shall be as when God overthrew Sodom and Gomorrah. It shall never be inhabited, neither shall it be dwelt in from generation to generation: neither shall the Arabian pitch tent there; neither shall the shepherds make their fold there. But wild beasts of the desert shall lie there; and their houses shall be full of doleful creatures; and owls shall dwell there, and satyrs shall dance there. And the wild beasts of the islands shall cry in their desolate houses, and dragons in their pleasant palaces: and her time is near to come, and her days shall not be prolonged.*

This is true today. There is not even the tent of an Arab pitched there. Only bats and owls make their home in its ruins. Not a shepherd is seen on the plains. There is only desolation. Yes, God's Word is true!

In Isaiah 14:28 we read that King Ahaz died. But Isaiah warns the people that his death must not be hailed as the end of their burdens. Even worse oppressors than Ahaz were yet to come (Isaiah 14:28-32).

UNDER HEZEKIAH (Read Isaiah 15–66)

The reign of Hezekiah occupied one of the most important periods in all of Israel's history. Hezekiah was a godly king. The

Assyrian armies, like a dark storm cloud, were threatening the northern frontiers. Before Hezekiah had completed his sixth year, Samaria had fallen beneath this invader. This success only whetted the Assyrian appetite for further conquest. Eight years later Judah was invaded. The first invasion was by Sargon and the second by his son, Sennacherib. Assyrian history tells us this. The critical year in Hezekiah's reign was the fourteenth (Isaiah 36:1). It was then we have the Assyrian invasion, the king's mortal sickness and his recovery, and the final withdrawal of Assyrians from the land. (This covered a period of about four years.)

These stony-hearted Assyrian warriors came year after year, blazing with steel and banners. The watchmen on the walls of Jerusalem could see them advance by the smoke of the burning towns and cities.

King Hezekiah stripped the temple of its treasures and took the gold from its doors and pillars in order that he might send them 300 talents of silver and 30 talents of gold to buy them off (II Kings 18:13-16). In desperation, help from Egypt was sought. But nothing availed in face of the fury of these Assyrians.

Finally the Assyrians built their camp fires around the city of Jerusalem and demanded its surrender. Read the intensely dramatic account of the parleyings between the Assyrian general and the chiefs of Jerusalem.

See the account of the swift and terrible disaster that fell upon the Assyrians as they were slain by a mysterious visitation in their camp (Isaiah 37:36-38).

Isaiah denounced the alliance with Egypt and said it was relying *on horses* and trusting *in chariots, because they are many; and in horsemen, because they are very strong* (Isaiah 31:1).

Is it not true that we today have put our trust in the "horses and chariots" of war's machinery? Have we not multiplied our horses and chariots beyond the wildest dreams of Egypt and Babylon? We have hitched all the forces of nature to our chariots. We have armored tanks and jet airplanes, battleships and atomic submarines. We have added nuclear missiles and I.C.B.M.'s! War has been turned into a hideous prospect of devastation and death.

We need to hear the prophet say today, *Woe to them that go down to Egypt for help; and stay on horses, and trust in chariots* (Isaiah 31:1). How great need there is today for those who will *remember the name of the LORD our God* (Psalm 20:7), who know the *saving strength of his right hand* (Psalm 20:6)!

History reveals a graveyard of the nations that have gone down to death through their own moral rottenness. Egypt, Babylon, and Rome are memorable examples of this.

God wants us to recognize Him in national affairs. He calls His people to turn *unto him from whom* [ye] . . . *have revolted* (see Isaiah 31:6). As a people we must get right with God before we can get right with other nations.

The kingdoms of Judah and Israel had become so weakened by idolatry and corruption that the enemies swept down upon them from the north "like a wolf on the fold." First, Israel rolled in the dust under the tramp of the terrible Assyrian hosts (722 B.C.), and then Judah fell with the Babylonians thundering at her gate and breaking down her walls (586 B.C.). Both kingdoms ended and her people were carried into captivity. Isaiah lived and prophesied in Jerusalem at this time.

Isaiah spent his life trying to get Judah to become acquainted with God and His Word. He wanted them to trust wholly in God's guidance. Isn't this a worthy aim for any minister today?

GLORIOUS FUTURE—RESTORATION!

This part of the book, chapters 46–66, is called the "Book of Consolation" because Isaiah tells in glowing terms not only of the restoration of Judah but the coming of Jehovah's "Servant" to be the Messiah King.

The restoration is assured for they must return to their own land to prepare the way for the coming Messiah, the Servant of Jehovah, who is to redeem His people.

Isaiah 53 gives us a perfect picture of our suffering Redeemer. *Surely he hath borne our griefs, and carried our sor-*

219

rows (verse 4). *All we like sheep have gone astray; . . . and the LORD hath laid on him the iniquity of us all* (verse 6). He was the substitute for the sinner.

Can you repeat verse five and say, *He was wounded for* [my] *transgressions, he was bruised for* [my] *iniquities: the chastisement of* [my] *peace was upon him; and with his stripes* [I] *am healed?* It is accepting this great fact that makes you a child of God. He was wounded, bruised, pierced—not for His own sins, but for ours. He bore on His own body the sins of the world.

Isaiah 60–66 tells of the coming kingdom—the future glory of Israel. God's goodness to redeemed Israel is seen in chapters 61 and 62. He promises an era of prosperity in chapters 63–65.

Minimum Daily Requirements/Spiritual Vitamins

Sunday: GOD'S CASE AGAINST JUDAH
Isaiah 1:1-18

Monday: ISAIAH'S COMMISSION   Isaiah 6:1-13

Tuesday: CHRIST—ISRAEL'S HOPE
Isaiah 7:10-16; 9:1-21

Wednesday: THE COMING KINGDOM
Isaiah 11:1-16

Thursday: A GREAT GOD   Isaiah 40:1-31

Friday: CHRIST OUR SUBSTITUTE   Isaiah 53:1-12

Saturday: A GLORIOUS SALVATION
Isaiah 55:1-13

UNDERSTANDING JEREMIAH and LAMENTATIONS

Jeremiah and Lamentations Portray Jesus Christ, the Righteous Branch

Here is the story of a diffident, sensitive lad who was called from the obscurity of his native town to assume, at a critical hour in the nation's life, the overwhelming responsibilities of a prophet. Jeremiah came from the village of Anathoth some three miles from Jerusalem. This gave him the advantages of the Holy City. His father, Hilkiah, was a priest. (Some think that this was "Hilkiah the priest" in II Kings 22, who brought the Book of the Law to the notice of the king, Josiah, which started the great revival in the kingdom.) He inherited the traditions of an illustrious ancestry. His early life was, no doubt, molded by strong religious influences. God had something better for Jeremiah than to spend his life as a priest serving at the altars. God appointed this young man to be a prophet of the Lord in this most trying hour in the history of the chosen people.

God often chooses unlikely instruments to do His work. He chose the sensitive, shrinking Jeremiah for what seemed a hopeless mission, with the words: *Say not, I am a child: for thou shalt go to all that I shall send thee, and whatsoever I command thee thou shalt speak. Be not afraid of their faces: for I am with thee to deliver thee* (Jeremiah 1:7,8). This is what a prophet is—one that "tells forth" what God says. Although many prophets told of future events, it is not necessary that they do so to be a prophet.

Jeremiah, unlike many of the prophets, has much to say concerning himself. He tells us that he was a priest by birth (Jeremiah 1:1). He was called by the Lord to be a prophet at an early age (Jeremiah 1:6). He pleaded, first, his youth (only twenty-one), second, inexperience, and third, his lack of eloquence (Jeremiah 1:6) as reasons for not accepting the call. Are these not just the excuses that youth makes today for not obeying Christ?

Jeremiah was assured that Jehovah ordained him to this work before his birth (Jeremiah 1:5). God tells us in Ephesians 2:10 that we were created unto good works before God even laid the foundation of the world. God has a plan for each one of our lives. (Read Jeremiah 1:1-8.) He was not allowed to marry, for God had a special mission for him in life (Jeremiah 16:1,2). Jeremiah prophesied during the time when Israel had been taken into captivity and Judah was in her declining days.

Soon after Josiah's death the kingdom of Judah hastened to its end. Judah was reduced to practical vassalage to Egypt at the battle of Carchemish. About twelve years later Nebuchadnezzar, king of Babylon, took Jerusalem and began the deportation of all the princes and men of station which ended in the complete captivity of Judah eleven years after. A few of the poorest were left in the land. Jeremiah kept on with his ministry among them until they went into Egypt. They did this in spite of divine warnings. Jeremiah followed them into Egypt and the last we hear of him he was still rebuking his people. There are conflicting traditions concerning his death. Tertullian says that the Jews in Egypt stoned him to death. According to the Jews, he escaped to Babylon and died there.

He was called to be a prophet in the thirteenth year of the reign of King Josiah (Jeremiah 1:2). No doubt his early ministry, and that of the prophet Zephaniah, were among the influences that led to the reforms under the young King Josiah. Jeremiah prophesied for more than forty years. He began his ministry sixty years after the death of Isaiah, the great evangelical prophet.

Jeremiah was contemporary with the prophetess Huldah, and Habakkuk, Zephaniah, Ezekiel and Daniel and perhaps even Nahum.

Jeremiah's message was never a popular one. At one time he barely escaped with his life (Jeremiah 26:7-16). At another

222

time his enemies beat him and put him in prison. Men have always treated God's witnesses thus.

It is almost impossible to outline this book chronologically. Some of the first messages are found later in the book and some of the last messages are first. He wrote on a great roll. No doubt he had given his messages many times to the people and had repeated them often before he began to write. His faithful scribe, Baruch, wrote them down. After he had written one of his discourses, some other message given years before might come to his mind and he would record it, possibly without dating it. He would fill up his parchment as he unrolled it. Later on, when he wished to write down another incident, or record another message, he would have to begin on the roll where he left off, whether it fitted in chronologically or not. This is important to remember.

ANALYSIS OF JEREMIAH

Because the Book of Jeremiah is not arranged chronologically a division of the book is difficult. The analysis is more moral than structural.

Jeremiah Prophesies Concerning:

1. JUDAH
{ Captivity
{ Restoration

2. CITIES
{ Jerusalem
{ Babylon
{ Damascus

3. GENTILE NATIONS
{ Egypt
{ Philistia
{ Moab
{ Ammon
{ Edom
{ Elam
{ Babylon

4. MESSIAH

Jeremiah uses many symbols given him by Jehovah in teaching the people. On one occasion he wore a rotted girdle; another time he put a yoke on his neck, like an ox; again, he broke a bottle in the presence of the ruler; he bought a field and buried the deed. The interpretation is given in the text.

Here Is a List of Object Lessons Found in the Book

Christ is pictured in Jeremiah as:

Fountain of Living Waters............................Jeremiah 2:13
Great Physician...Jeremiah 8:22
Good Shepherd....................Jeremiah 31:10; 23:4
The Righteous Branch...............................Jeremiah 23:5
David the King..Jeremiah 30:9
The Redeemer ....Jeremiah 50:34
Lord our Righteousness..........................Jeremiah 23:6

Jeremiah was the ninth of the prophets. He prophesied to the southern kingdom of Judah, before the exile and during the trying days of the captivity. He saw five kings upon the throne of Judah: Josiah, Jehoahaz, Jehoiakim, Jehoiachin, and Zedekiah. He was to Josiah what Isaiah had been to Hezekiah. (Read II Kings 21:1-25 to find the history of Jeremiah's time.)

Three Great Events in Jeremiah's Life:

1. Battle of Megiddo, between Judah and Pharaoh-Necho of Egypt in which good King Josiah was killed.

2. Battle of Carchemish, near the same spot, about four years later, during Jehoiakim's reign. He had become a vassal of Egypt. In this battle the Egyptians were defeated by Babylon under Nebuchadnezzar and the first deportation of Jews followed.

3. Capture of Jerusalem by Nebuchadnezzar, destruction of city and temple, and exile of greater part of those who were left to Babylon.

There was a great contest for world supremacy in the day of Jeremiah. Assyria had been in the place of leadership for 300 years. Now she was growing weak; Babylon was ascending in power. Egypt, too, was striving for supremacy. In 607 B.C. Assyria was defeated by Babylon. In 605 B.C. Egypt was crushed in the battle of Carchemish, and Babylon became the world's master. In the few years that followed she invaded Jerusalem and took the Jews captive. False prophets swarmed the city of Jerusalem in these days. They flattered the king and prophesied to him whatever they thought he wanted to hear.

CALL AND COMMISSION OF JEREMIAH (Read Jeremiah 1)

This unique tragedy opens in the little village of Anathoth. At twenty-one, Jeremiah was becoming aware that God had ordained him before his birth to be a prophet. (See Jeremiah 1:5.) God has a plan for the life of every person. Some see clearly how their lives are to be used. Many learn to wait upon God and trust Him for the outcome. These latter cannot understand the ways of the Lord, but they believe His promises. Jeremiah must have been one of these. He must have wondered what God had planned for him. But because he let the Lord have His way, his life affected all of Israel.

We hear Jeremiah speak, *Ah, Lord God! behold, I cannot speak: for I am a child* [like a young man] (Jeremiah 1:6). He protests and shrinks from the task God gave him and begs to be excused. Notice Jeremiah's reluctance to undertake the task.

A prophet is simply God's messenger-boy delivering not his own ideas, but conveying to the last detail God's thoughts. (Compare Jeremiah's call with Moses'. Exodus 4:10-12.) God had called Jeremiah to be a prophet and he had entered bravely upon the task, but now he is overwhelmed at the thought of hurting anyone. He would rather live at peace with them.

Jeremiah is saying, in effect, "I have not yet reached the years of maturity," for in Oriental society a young man has no role to play until he is of age. (Read Matthew 11:25.) His prophetic message would not be received. Would not his career be cut short by those he provoked? Would they not try to kill him?

The young man is only too conscious of his inexperience, and he almost makes "the great refusal." But God knows how to overcome his hesitancy. He made the young Jeremiah conscious of a Divine Call. He made him see that the work to which he was commissioned was not his own.

The path of duty is the path of safety! While Jeremiah is pondering, a hand touches his mouth and we hear a voice saying, *Behold, I have put my words in thy mouth* (Jeremiah 1:9). No longer could he complain of inability to speak. God promises to put the message into the mouth of His prophets. (See what Christ said to His disciples in Matthew 10:20.) Then Jeremiah heard the voice add, *See, I have this day set thee over the nations and over the kingdoms, to root out, and to pull down and to destroy, and to throw down, to build, and to plant* (Jeremiah 1:10).

SECRET OF NATIONAL POWER

What God asks us to do, He fits us for, and what He fits us for He asks us to do. That was quite a position for just a poor country preacher.

The church and the minister who have answered God's call today are still in a place of power. They need no other weapons than the promise of God, and they really control the building and the breaking, the planting and the plucking of the community.

Jeremiah's commission was world-wide, including not only his own country, but all nations and kingdoms of Egypt, Ammon, Moab, Tyre and Sidon. His commission was to root out, and to pull down, to destroy and to throw down. He must root out the idolatry and pride, but he must finally "build and plant."

226

Jeremiah was to go only to those persons or peoples to whom the Lord sent him. And he was to say only what the Lord commanded him to say. This must be true of us also if we are to be true workers together with God.

JEREMIAH'S RELUCTANCE

Jeremiah, like men today, was engaged in the Lord's work because God said he must. He had heard the "Thou shalt" of heaven. Although at first the cost may be great, the gain in after years cannot be estimated. Jeremiah was shrinking and offered every excuse for his unfitness, but the task was forced upon him. *Thou shalt go* (see Jeremiah 1:7). He hated the limelight. He loved the simple life. He wanted to live in the country, but the Lord had work for him in the cities. Jeremiah had to choose between his desires and God's will.

Because he was forced into the task that was so distasteful to him, in later years he cried, *Woe is me, my mother, that thou hast borne me a man of strife and a man of contention to the whole earth* (Jeremiah 15:10)! God told Jeremiah, *Be not afraid of their faces, for I am with thee to deliver thee* (Jeremiah 1:8). He was not a public speaker, and he shrank from bearing such an unwelcome message to so undisciplined a people. How often he must have thought of that promise of God when he was haled before princes and rulers. We like to carry good news but to bear bad is always hard. We are afraid of the faces of people. When they register pleasure, we feel safe. When they show disgust, we melt before them.

THE TOUCH OF GOD'S HAND

The LORD put forth his hand (Jeremiah 1:9). Compare this story of Jeremiah's call with that of Isaiah's (Isaiah 6:7). Paul says that prophecy is a spiritual gift (I Cor. 14:1). The touch of God's hand was a tangible pledge for Jeremiah that God was with him. He could not get away from it.

The Word of the Lord is a power that carries out His will and accomplishes what He wishes (Isaiah 55:11; Heb. 4:12). Against this power nothing can stand. It is a hammer that breaks rocks in pieces (Jeremiah 23:29). God's Word shows its power in two ways—in destruction and in construction. We see this in God's words to Jeremiah. If men accept God's Word, it will give life; if they reject it, it will bring condemnation (John 3:36).

BEFORE THE FALL OF JERUSALEM (Read Jeremiah 2–39)

The prophecies of Jeremiah before the fall of Jerusalem were made in this order: (Long silences divide these.)

Prophecies in the reign of Josiah.........................Jeremiah 2–12
Prophecies in the reign of Jehoiakim.....Jer. 13–20; 25:1-27:11
Prophecies in the reign of Zedekiah.......Jer. 21–24; 27:12-39:18

REIGN OF JOSIAH

The LORD said also unto me in the days of Josiah the king . . . (Jeremiah 3:6). The first twelve chapters cover the prophecy of this period.

Jeremiah 2–6. These chapters tell of Judah's sin and give God's call to repentance. Judgments are predicted.

Jeremiah 7–9. Again we read of threatenings. We see the prophet's grief.

Jeremiah 10–12. Here we see idolatry and disobedience continued. The Lord's disappointment in His people is shown.

In the early years of his ministry, during the reign of Josiah, Jeremiah's message, for the most part, was a warning to Judah and a call to her to repent. (Read Jeremiah 3:6,12,13,22,23.) He spared nothing in exposing the moral rottenness of the people. (Read Jeremiah 7:1-26.) He warned them of coming judgments if they would not return to God. He especially told them of the danger from the north (Jeremiah 4:6). He said that the avengers would come like a raging lion from the thicket (Jeremiah 4:7). They would sweep over the land with chariots like the whirlwind and with horses swifter than eagles, spread terror before them and leave ruin in their train (Jeremiah 4:13).

In Chapter 26 we see Jeremiah taking a stand on the same spot as in Jeremiah 7. On this occasion he nearly lost his life. The address in Chapter 7 was probably given during the reign of Josiah himself.

It is probable that for some time after his call Jeremiah continued to reside in Anathoth, but before long he was compelled to leave the home of his birth and take up his residence in Jerusalem. The men of his home town had made a conspiracy to put him to death (Jeremiah 11:18-23). The disloyalty of his neighbors, and especially his own relatives, came as a painful shock to the unsuspecting prophet. But Jehovah told him that this was only the beginning of his troubles and it was a time of preparation for still greater trials in the days to come (Jeremiah 12:5,6). Jeremiah's chief enemies were the priests and the prophets (Jeremiah 26:7,8). They had a large following among the people. It is sad to notice that the principal opposition to the message of God came from the professedly religious people. It was the same in our Lord's case, and it is often the same today. You remember that the Pharisees and Sadducees always were taking counsel how they might kill Jesus. Jesus tells us that today if we live godly lives we will suffer persecution. Men hate God and they will hate His children.

We do not know much of Jeremiah's work during the later years of Josiah's reign. No doubt he was in great sympathy with this young reformer, but he realized that his work did not go deep enough. In the death of the good King Josiah, at the battle of Megiddo, Judah suffered a calamity from which she never recovered. It was in this battle that Judah made a noble attempt to withstand the Egyptian army advancing against Assyria under Pharaoh-Necho.

King Josiah was succeeded by his younger brother Jehoahaz whom "the people of the land" placed on the throne instead of the older brother Eliakim. But Jehoahaz was allowed to reign for only three months. He was deposed by Necho and carried off in chains to Egypt, where he died. Necho now virtually was overlord of Judah. He appointed Jehoiakim to be ruler.

REIGN OF JEHOIAKIM

Dr. Graham Scroggie says that prophecies in Jehoiakim's reign recount the events in this order:

Jeremiah chapters 26; 46–49; 25; 36:1-8; 45; 36:9-32; 14;

15; 16; 17; 18:1–19:13; 19:14–20:1; 35; 22:1–23:8; 23:9-40; 13.

In substance Jeremiah predicted the judgment of the nations and Judah. He reproved the false prophets. He foretold the Babylonian captivity. He suffered for his message.

It was a sad day for Judah when Jehoiakim ascended to power. It was a bad day for Jeremiah, too. Read what God said to Jeremiah at the beginning of Jehoiakim's reign (Jeremiah 26:1-7). Jehoiakim was a bad ruler. He was proud, selfish, covetous and vindictive. He weighed the land down with taxes to meet the demands of his Egyptian conqueror (II Kings 23:35). He was indifferent to the suffering of his people. He devoted most of his time to enlarging and adorning his palace and carried out his costly schemes with incredible meanness.

Jehoiakim reigned eleven years and after his death, his son, a youth of eighteen, came to the throne. But Jehoiachin's reign was short (about three months and ten days) because Nebuchadnezzar's army soon appeared at the gates of Jerusalem; and after a three-month siege, the city was captured. He took with him many of the princes and the flower of the people to Babylon. Among them was Jehoiachin and the queen-mother. None were left *save the poorest sort of the people of the land* (II Kings 24:14).

It was then that Jeremiah first mentioned the seventy years' captivity (Jeremiah 25:1-14). God told them just how long they must remain in exile. (Read Daniel 9:2).

Jeremiah did not hesitate to denounce even the king in his shameless wrongdoing. In Jeremiah 22:13-19 we see him verbally putting Jehoiakim in stocks and then releasing the lash of a righteous scorn, predicting that he would die without being mourned, and would be buried with the burial of an ass.

The reformation under Josiah only touched the surface. The work was abandoned after his death and the nation, in Jehoiakim's reign, fell back into the worst form of idolatry.

Jeremiah's mission was to endeavor to turn his people back to God. During the reign of Josiah he began to prophesy the dreadful calamity threatening them from the north (Jeremiah

230

4:6) if they would not return to God. Jeremiah told Judah that her salvation was still possible, but each year her sin grew worse and her doom more certain.

Standing in the temple Jeremiah told the people that the temple would be destroyed and Jerusalem itself would become a desolation. Jeremiah's hearers were shocked. (See Jeremiah 26:7-9.) They called his words blasphemy.

They said, *This man is worthy to die; for he hath prophesied against this city* (Jeremiah 26:11). The Jewish people always remembered that they were the chosen people of God. God had given them privileges, hence they concluded that God would not proceed to do such things as Jeremiah said He would do against the people whom He had chosen (Amos 3:2). God had consecrated the temple as an abode for His Name, therefore they thought He would not let it be destroyed by enemies. This is quite false. Let us not entertain this spirit ourselves. We think we are God's children, therefore He must forgive us, He must make us win in battle and put our enemies to rout.

Jeremiah was charged with being unpatriotic. The cry then would have been "Un-Judaistic!" as today it is "Un-American!" For his opponents it was, "My country, right or wrong." For Jeremiah it was, "God's will in my country" (Jer. 26:12-15). It is not so much a question of what we think is right, as it is that we learn what God considers to be the best for us and our country. God said to Jeremiah, *Be not afraid . . . for I am with thee* (Jeremiah 1:8). We may have to endure ostracism and ridicule for Christ's sake, but His promise is sufficient.

The priests and prophets, aided by the people, laid hold on Jeremiah and threatened him with death. But Jeremiah was delivered from the hand of his enemies. (Read Jeremiah 26:15-24.)

The fourth year of Jehoiakim was one to be remembered because it was in this year that Jeremiah first put his prophecies in writing on a roll (Jeremiah 36:1,2). Baruch, his intimate friend, who was such a comfort to him through his trials, took down the prophet's words.

We next see the prophet in a dimly lighted dungeon. What happened? The rulers had bound him so they would no longer be troubled by the word of the Lord. But the Lord told Jeremiah to write the words down. There he was, with his loyal friend Baruch at his side busily writing the words on the roll as the prophet spoke them. *And Baruch wrote from the mouth of Jeremiah all the words of the LORD, which he had spoken unto him, upon a roll of a book. And Jeremiah commanded Baruch, saying, I am shut up; I cannot go into the house of the LORD: Therefore go thou, and read in the roll, which thou hast written from my mouth, the words of the LORD in the ears of the people* (Jeremiah 36:4-6).

What Baruch was to read were *the words of the Lord.* He read them in the temple (Jer. 36:6,8).

INVESTIGATING COMMITTEE

The Royal Investigating Committee immediately sent for Baruch and commanded him to read the roll again (Jeremiah 36:14,15). They decided the roll must be brought to the king. *We will surely tell the king of all these words* (Jeremiah 36:16). Knowing full well the character of this ruler, they advised Jeremiah and Baruch to go into hiding before the roll was read in the royal presence (Jeremiah 36:19).

They asked Baruch, *Tell us now, how didst thou write all these words at his mouth? Then Baruch answered them, He pronounced all these words unto me with his mouth, and I wrote them with ink in the book* (Jeremiah 36:17,18). Then the princes wanted the king to see it.

The scene changes. We are no longer in the dark dungeon, but in the winter palace of Jehoiakim, surrounded by all the luxury of an Eastern court. The king is sitting before his hearth. A fire is burning. Jehudi is reading the roll of Jeremiah. All are listening intently. When three or four pages had been read Jehoiakim could stand no more. With penknife and angry hands the roll was cut to pieces and thrown into the fire. The very act of Jehoiakim seemed to symbolize the doom of the city, the temple, and all the people of Judah. They had heard God's Word and had rejected it. (See Jeremiah 36:20-26.)

Of course Jeremiah and Baruch were ordered to be seized but God had "hid them" (Jeremiah 36:26). How often God does this for His children. He hides us under His wings, and in the hollow of His hand far from harm.

Now the Lord commanded Jeremiah to take another roll, and to write *all the words of the book which Jehoiakim, king of Judah had burned in the fire; and there were added besides unto them many like words* (see Jeremiah 36:27,32).

Jeremiah stood in the temple gate and spoke boldly for righteousness and God. He uttered a series of accusations against Judah and warnings of God's inevitable judgment of sin. But he always made an appeal to turn back to God and receive forgiveness. We see him standing in the gate hurling thunderbolts into the faces of the false worshipers but always holding up the pardon of God.

Jeremiah's was a moral battle, and a moral battle is harder to fight and keep fighting.

AFTER THE FALL OF JERUSALEM (Read Jeremiah 40–52)

In the fourth year of Jehoiakim's reign Nebuchadnezzar invaded Judah, and it was then that Daniel and his companions were carried away to Babylon and Jehoiakim himself was put into chains.

Nebuchadnezzar placed Zedekiah, Jehoiakim's brother, on the throne in place of Jehoiachin. Only the poor were left in Jerusalem now. Jeremiah likens them to bad, worthless figs, in contrast to those who had gone who were good figs. (See Jeremiah 24.) The picked men of the nation were carried away. You remember that Daniel afterwards became prime minister of Babylon. The men who were left were so weak and degenerate that the prophet could see nothing but doom for Jerusalem.

Zedekiah was disposed to be friendly to Jeremiah, but he was a weak man and had no courage to make decisions of his own. He was like clay in the hands of the princes who surrounded his throne. The remnant of men who were left were not qualified to govern. They had taken the places of the real nobility of the nation, but they were in great contrast to those who had been carried into captivity.

Jeremiah incurred the displeasure of the prophets who had gone to Babylon because, in a letter to the exiles, he directly opposed their prediction of an early return from captivity. (See Jeremiah 29:1-14.) Neither did the prophets in Jerusalem like it because they thought that soon they could throw off the yoke of Nebuchadnezzar. Zedekiah's advisers were in favor of throwing off the Babylonian yoke and looking to Egypt for help, but Jeremiah kept insisting that the Chaldeans would certainly capture the city. (See Jeremiah 37:3-10.) Finally Zedekiah broke his covenant with the king of Babylon. Nebuchadnezzar swiftly marched against Jerusalem and the final siege began.

As the siege proceeded, the hostility of Jeremiah's enemies became more intense. They charged him with desertion and thrust him into prison. They even petitioned the king to put him to death. (See Jeremiah 38:4.) Weakling that he was, Zedekiah gave Jeremiah over into the hands of the princes. Then for some reason they shrank from killing him. But they chose a worse thing for Jeremiah; they lowered him with cords into a miry dungeon, and left him to die of starvation and exposure. But God was with him and raised up a friend to deliver him. An Ethiopian, Ebed-melech, heard of Jeremiah's plight and made his way to the king. Gaining permission, he rushed to the dungeon and lowered a quantity of "old rotten rags" for the prophet to put under his armpits beneath the cords, for Jeremiah had "sunk in the mire" and the work of getting him out would mean a great strain. (See Jeremiah 38:6-13.)

After Jeremiah's deliverance Zedekiah, driven by fear, visited Jeremiah to find out what was in store for him. Jeremiah could only promise him doom for the city. Jeremiah still insisted that the king should surrender to Nebuchadnezzar, but Zedekiah was afraid of the princes. (See Jeremiah 38:14-28.)

After eighteen months of siege, Jerusalem was taken, Zedekiah's sons were put to death before his eyes, and afterwards he himself was blinded and carried in chains to Babylon. (See Jeremiah 39:1-7.) Jeremiah was given the choice of going to Babylon where freedom and honor awaited him, but he chose to cast his lot with the remnant left in the land. (See Jer. 39:11,12; 40:1-16.)

We can see how close Jeremiah was to the affairs of Judah during her captivity. He had seen the condition of Judah's decline after Josiah's good reign till the day of Zedekiah. He saw the people carried away captive and witnessed the destruction of Jerusalem and the temple.

We find in chapter 24 one of the first discourses of Jeremiah in Zedekiah's reign. Jeremiah urged Judah to submit to Babylon in accordance with God's will, but without effect. (See Jeremiah 21:1-10.) Jeremiah never ceased urging this submission to Babylon, so much so that his enemies accused him of being a traitor. King Nebuchadnezzar of Babylon regarded his stand and made him an offer of any honor he would accept, besides saving his life. (See Jeremiah 39:11,12.)

At the same time Jeremiah was crying out against Babylon for her heinous crime in destroying God's children, he told them that Babylon would be demolished and would be in ruins forever. (See Jer. 51:37-43.) This is literally true of this wonder city of the ancient world. Read again Isaiah 13:17-22 along with Jeremiah 51:37-43.

By the time of Christ, Babylon's power had gone, and in the first century A.D. it was mostly in ruins. Its bricks have been used in building Baghdad and repairing canals. For centuries it has lain in heaps of desolate mounds. Only beasts of the desert inhabit it. This is a remarkable fulfillment of prophecy. When this writer stood and looked over its ruins, it was hard to believe that once this was a city of wonder and beauty, filled with luxury and gross extravagance, unsurpassed in the history of the world, for today it is only a heap of fallen bricks.

In 606 B.C. the first deportation of the Jews to Babylon occurred. It was this year that Jeremiah was ordered to write the predictions he had made and to have them read to the people.

These predictions are scattered throughout chapters 24-49 and concern the future of the Jews, the Babylonian captivity, and the coming Messiah.

Teachers may wish to know the order of the prophecies during Zedekiah's reign. Dr. Scroggie is our authority in this. Chapters 24; 27; 28; 29; 49:34; 51:1; 21; 34; 37; 38; 39:15-18; 32; 33; 30; 31; 39:1-14.

PREDICTIONS

1. Concerning God's future dealings with Judah (Jeremiah 23; 31).

2. Conquest of land by Nebuchadnezzar, king of Babylon (Jeremiah 20:4).

3. Judah's exile or captivity in Babylon and return after seventy years (Jeremiah 25 and 26).

4. Concerning the Messiah (Jeremiah 23:6; 30:4-11; 33:14-26).

5. Israel will be scattered among all the kingdoms of the earth (Jeremiah 24).

6. Final recovery of Israel (Jeremiah 23:1-40; 32:37-41; Ezekiel 37:21,22).

Jeremiah got his messages to the people by speaking to them as they thronged to the feasts. Often he did symbolic things to attract their attention. When he was shut up in prison he dictated his messages to Baruch, the scribe, who wrote them down and read them to the people. The roll of Jeremiah that Jehoiakim burned no doubt took Jeremiah and Baruch about one and one-half years to prepare. Writing in those days was not like it is now. It was a long and laborious task.

In the days when David's throne was tottering and Judah was going into captivity the prophet announced the coming Christ, King of the house of David, a righteous Branch. *In his days Judah shall be saved, and Israel shall dwell safely: and this is his name whereby he shall be called, the LORD our righteousness* (Jer. 23:6).

Judah's future redemption through Christ is given in chapters 30; 31. The Jews are scattered today but God is bringing them back. (See Jeremiah 30:10,11; 31:10.)

Jeremiah 23 is dear to the Jews, God's chosen people, and dear to the heart of God. It tells of the future of Judah, redeemed through the work of their Messiah. Jesus, the Good Shepherd, is promised (vs. 1,3). He will gather His sheep from every corner of the earth and they will return to their own country, the promised land. This will take place when the King shall come and sit upon the throne of David (v. 5).

Judah's History in a Word

"Chosen"—Jeremiah prophesied to God's chosen people, Judah, before their exile into Babylon.

"Captured"—He warned them of their captivity if they would not listen to Jehovah.

"Carried Away"—They sinned until God allowed them to be carried away by Nebuchadnezzar into Babylon. God tells them they must remain captive seventy years. (See Jeremiah 25:1-14; Daniel 9:2.)

"Coming Messiah"—But God will not allow His children to remain scattered through the nations of the world forever. Some day the Jews will be gathered to their own land and the good Shepherd will appear. (See Jeremiah 33:14-17.)

Finally those left in Jerusalem all fled to Egypt in spite of God's warning against it. (See Jeremiah 43.) They asked Jeremiah to pray for guidance, but when it was given they refused to obey it. The prophet and Baruch were compelled to accompany them. Even in Egypt we find the prophet carrying out his commission. He prophesies the conquest of Egypt by Nebuchadnezzar. (See Jeremiah 43:8-13.) The Jews who dwelt in the Nile valley were practicing idolatry and Jeremiah warned them against this wickedness. When they refused to listen to his warning, and went on worshiping these other gods, Jeremiah told them that the judgment of God would fall. (See Jer. 44:26-28.)

This is the last we hear of Jeremiah. How long he lived in Egypt afterwards we know not. Other prophets had at least occasional successes to cheer their hearts in the midst of difficulties, but Jeremiah seemed to be fighting a losing battle to the very end. Disaster, failure and hostility were rewards for his work. He preached to deaf ears and seemed to reap only hate in return for his love for his people. In life he seemed to accomplish little. He was brokenhearted. But God hath given us a record that makes him one of the greatest of all the prophets.

Jeremiah's life was one of deepening gloom. He had to watch the people and city which he loved fall from sin to sin. And all the time he had no hope that things might change. How deeply he felt all this can be seen in his Lamentations. Hudson Taylor one time wrote that "God delights to trust a trustworthy child with a trial." How God must have trusted Jeremiah! We have seen the bitter opposition he had to meet. Now we have to watch the hatred of his enemies reaching a climax in a savage demand for his death. *Let this man be put to death.* This came from the princes. (See Jer. 38:4.)

Being confined in the court of the guard attached to the royal palace, Jeremiah had opportunities of talking to the soldiers on duty as well as to the citizens who came along. (See Jeremiah 37:21.) To every one he declared the Word of the Lord. (See Jeremiah 37:6-10.) That message was that it was foolish to resist the Chaldeans. It would only result in destruction. This was so galling to national pride that the princes named in Jeremiah 38:1 resolved to kill Jeremiah. Yet King Zedekiah was convinced that Jeremiah was right.

Of course Jeremiah "weakened the hands" of the people. (See Jeremiah 38:4.) The people were convinced that resistance was useless, since God had said that Jerusalem would be captured and burned by the Chaldeans. People and soldiers were unwilling to sacrifice their lives any longer in defending the city.

We find in chapters 40—44 prophecies given by Jeremiah after the fall of Jerusalem.

1. To the remnant in Judah.....................Jeremiah 40:1–43:3
2. To the remnant in Egypt....................Jeremiah 43:4—44:30

A bit of history is recorded in chapter 52 which gives the facts about the captivity of Judah.

JEREMIAH AND HIS TIMES

The prophecy of Jeremiah comes out of the turmoil in Judah preceding and during the Babylonian captivity like the song of a lark on the battlefield of Flanders. It is like a beautiful symphony of sorrow, God's oratorio of tears and consolation, as His great heart of love weeps over the people He is chastening. The message of the book deals with the certainty of God's judgment because of sin, yet the tenderness and eternity of His boundless love. The prophecies are not chronological, but each prophecy is bound up with the history of the times, under the five kings Josiah, Jehoahaz, Jehoiakim, Jehoiachin, Zedekiah,

238

and finally with the captivity. Jeremiah is concerned with backsliding. Judah had forsaken the Lord, and through Jeremiah God sent warnings of impending judgments, beseeching His people to return to His commandments.

NUGGETS OF TRUTH FROM JEREMIAH

Jeremiah was God's prophet, speaking God's words. Read of his marvelous call, Jeremiah 1:4-10. Scores of times Jeremiah cries, *Thus saith the Lord.* Once he adds, *O earth, earth, earth, hear the word of the Lord!* The book abounds in golden passages: 6:16; 9:23-24; 10:10-13; 17:7-8; 18:1-6; 20:9; 22:29; 23:5-6. The golden chapters are 31 and 33. It is hard to find words in any language of more touching beauty.

Christ appears in Jeremiah. His virgin birth is definitely mentioned in 31:22. He is wonderfully pictured in 23:5-6. His future kingdom is lavishly described: chapters 31 and 33. The whole book is a series of messages, each of which was spoken to fit the need of the moment. Therefore these messages are like *apples of gold in pictures of silver* (Proverbs 25:11), and when we apply them to ourselves, we discover that they meet our needs just as they met the needs of Jehovah's wandering people.

THE BOOK OF LAMENTATIONS

Here is another of the Bible's exquisite books of poetry. It is commonly attributed to Jeremiah. Five beautiful, distinct poems are bound together in the book. It is not all sorrow. Above the clouds of the poet's weeping over the sins of his people, God's sun is shining. In Lamentations 3:22-27 the light breaks through to throw a shining rainbow across the murky sky. God's grace always shines above the clouds of sin (see Romans 5:20), and it will always shine in the heart which is trusting in God through faith in the Lord Jesus Christ who gives *beauty for ashes, the oil of joy for mourning, and the garment of praise for the spirit of heaviness* (Isaiah 61:3).

Minimum Daily Requirements/Spiritual Vitamins

Sunday: JEREMIAH WARNS JUDAH Jer. 1:1-10; 2:1-13; 3:12,22,23; 4:14-19; 6:1-30

Monday: A REBUKE Jer. 7:1-15; 9:1-16; 17:5-18

Tuesday: THE POTTER Jeremiah 18:1-17

Wednesday: THE FAITHLESS SHEPHERDS Jeremiah 23:1-40

Thursday: REPENTANCE AND RESTORATION Jeremiah 24; 25

Friday: ISRAEL'S LAST DAYS Jeremiah 30:18–31:40

Saturday: THE OVERTHROW OF JUDAH Jeremiah 52:1-34 COMFORT TO THE SORROWING Lamentations 1–5

CHAPTER 20

UNDERSTANDING EZEKIEL

Ezekiel
Portrays Jesus Christ,
the Son of Man

Ezekiel, the faithful preacher to the exiles in Babylon, is the author of this book.

Jeremiah, the great prophet whom we have just finished studying, was the last of the prophets in Jerusalem before the exile. His ministry was still going on when the end came. Recall the story. The young prophet Ezekiel was already at work among the exiles in Babylon. God had prepared a witness to the people in their captivity. God needed a voice to warn the people and to remind them of the reason why all these calamities had befallen them. For twenty-two years Ezekiel dealt with the discouraged captives to whom God had sent him.

The word of the Lord came unto me (Ezekiel 24:15). This phrase occurs forty-nine times in Ezekiel. God's greatest communications can only be made by his servants whose own hearts have been broken. The instrument in God's hands must himself be ready to share in suffering with others. Jesus' body was broken for us.

Ezekiel is for the Jew today. It tells God's chosen people that God will fulfill His sure promises. Their land, their city, their temple will be restored to them. It reveals God's plan for them.

Ezekiel is for the Christian today. It is a book of the times, for God's time is always revealed by His dealing with the Jew. Israel is beginning to return to her land and divine history is being made. The nation now exists officially. When the Jew moves, we know God is getting ready to act.

You find little of Ezekiel in the Gospels or Epistles. But look in Revelation. Ezekiel and John seem to lock arms across the centuries, and looking into the future they see the unfolding of a new heaven and a new earth. Ezekiel, the prophet, peering forward with rapt gaze, half whispering, says, *And above the firmament that was over their heads was the likeness of a throne, as the appearance of a sapphire stone: and upon the likeness of the throne was the likeness as the appearance of a man above upon it* (Ezekiel 1:26). And John, a little nearer, revealing God's vision to him, says in clearer tones these thrilling words, *And, behold, a throne was set in heaven, and one sat on the throne. And he that sat was to look upon like a jasper and a sardine stone* (Revelation 4:2,3).

This book is named after its author as are the other books of the prophets. Like Jeremiah, Ezekiel was not only a prophet but he was a priest as well. He was a prophet during the captivity. When he was twenty-five years old, he was carried captive to Babylon in 597 B.C. with the upper class of people, eleven years before the destruction of Jerusalem. This means that for eleven years 10,000 exiles were living in a concentration camp in Babylon while Jeremiah and the folks at home tried to "carry on" at Jerusalem. For five years the captives had no preacher. Then Ezekiel began to serve them. He immediately tried to remove their false hopes of an early return to Palestine. He tried to prepare them for the news of the tragic destruction of their beloved Jerusalem. He lived at the same time as Daniel and Jeremiah. Jeremiah remained among the Jews in Jerusalem. Ezekiel lived with the exiles in Babylon, and Daniel lived in the court of the rulers in Babylon.

Daniel and a few other Jewish boys had been brought to Babylon in 606 B.C. Ezekiel came nine years later. Ezekiel found that Daniel had attained a high position in the palace of Nebuchadnezzar, although he was only a youth. No doubt Daniel helped ease the lot of the captives because of his station. Ezekiel and Daniel were both young men of about the same age. Jeremiah was older. He had been prophesying for about thirty years in Jerusalem when Ezekiel was taken away. No doubt Ezekiel had been Jeremiah's pupil while he was in the Holy City and we find him preaching to the captives in Babylon the same things that Jeremiah had preached. He told them of their sin and their certain judgment. He reiterated their folly in relying on Egypt.

EZEKIEL'S DAY

The kingdom of Israel had been taken captive 120 years before by the king of Assyria. Then God brought judgment upon the southern kingdom of Judah. Nebuchadnezzar had come to Jerusalem and carried away ten thousand of the chief men of the southern kingdom and some of the royal seed, including Daniel and Ezekiel. (See II Chronicles 36:6,7; Daniel 1:1-3; II Kings 24:14-16.) The people of Israel had been living in constant trouble. It took Nebuchadnezzar twenty years to completely destroy Jerusalem. He could have done it sooner but he wanted tribute money. Then, too, Daniel was his court favorite and he may have been influenced by his young prime minister. He was finally forced to devastate Jerusalem because the city persisted in allying herself with Egypt. It was a tragic hour for Jerusalem when her walls were laid flat, her houses burned, the temple destroyed and her people dragged away as captives.

God had told of Judah's captivity by Babylon more than one hundred years before it happened. (See Isaiah 39:6; Micah 4:10.) The seventy years of its duration was foretold by Jeremiah. (See Jeremiah 25:11,12.) It is interesting to notice that God told them the exact time of their exile. But the captivity did not bring the people of Judah back to God. This judgment of God only seemed to drive the people into greater wickedness. They worshiped idols and set up groves in the hills and defiled the sanctuary of Jehovah. (See Ezekiel 5:11.) Ezekiel began his prophecies to them.

Ezekiel's Babylonian home was by the Chebar river. It was a ship canal which branched off from the Euphrates above Babylon, the most beautiful city of the world, filled with palaces, gardens, temples and bridges, making it an outstanding show place of the East. Chebar was probably one of many canals we know the Babylonian monarchs had dug. Ezekiel was among the captives digging the canal. Tradition tells us that the little village of Kifil (which is the Arabian for Ezekiel) was the town where Ezekiel lived, died and was buried. Tel-abib, where a colony of captive Jews dwelt, was near at hand. Ezekiel lived with these. He was fifty miles from Babylon. No doubt he often

243

visited Daniel in the palace. The Jews presented a pitiable picture—no temple, national life gone, little opportunity for business. To such an audience Ezekiel devoted the best years of his life.

Ezekiel has a style and method of preaching all his own. He uses symbols, as in the mimic siege of Jerusalem (Ezekiel 4), visions (Ezekiel 8), parables (Ezekiel 17), poems (Ezekiel 19), proverbs (Ezekiel 12:22,23; 18:2) and prophecies (Ezekiel 6; 20; 40–48).

Ezekiel is an artist. He paints strange pictures for us. They are mystifying and full of terror and sometimes hard to be deciphered. They glow with life and action. He talks of sin and punishment, of repentance and blessing.

AN EXILE AMONG EXILES

God told Ezekiel to go to the people in captivity. He was a captive ministering to captives. We must get alongside people to help them. This was our Lord's way. God tells Ezekiel to speak *whether they will hear, or whether they will forbear* (Ezekiel 3:11). Ezekiel's responsibility was to deliver God's message. The results were not in his hands.

Soon after Ezekiel was born a great reformation of popular worship and social life was aroused. This was caused by the inspiration of the Book of Deuteronomy, which had just been published (621 B.C.). But the reformation was only superficial. The religious decline was crowned by political disaster and Jerusalem was taken after an eighteen-month siege amid horrors untold. The temple, on which such a passion of love had been lavished, was reduced to ashes and the people deported to Babylon.

THE GLORY OF GOD

The "glory of God" seems to be the key phrase to Ezekiel. It occurs twelve times in the first eleven chapters. Then it does not occur again until the forty-third chapter. The *glory of the Lord* was grieved away from the temple at Jerusalem by the idolatry of the people. God says, *Ye have defiled my sanctuary, therefore I will make thee waste.* In Ezekiel 8 we see Ezekiel in a vision transported to Jerusalem and he sees four kinds of idolatry which were practiced in the courts of the Lord's house, even to the worshiping of the sun, with their backs to the sanctuary, while their faces were to the East. We see *the glory of the Lord* gradually grieved away from the inner sanctuary by the sin of idolatry, and the brightness filled the court. Then it departed to the threshold and rested over the cherubim. As the cherubim rose from the earth, *the glory of the Lord* abode above their pinions and mounted with them, forsaking the city and removing to the mountains (Ezekiel 10).

Young Christians, this is just what can happen to us. We can grieve the Holy Spirit and resist Him until He is quenched and our heart becomes like a ruined temple bereft of its glory. There are so many blighted Christian lives from which the radiance has gone through disobedience.

We grieve the Spirit when we do not allow ourselves time to read the Word or pray. We limit the Spirit when we refuse to be clean channels through which He can work. We resist Him by allowing idols to be in our hearts. Remember, your body is the temple of the Holy Spirit. Does His presence glow in your life?

In the Old Testament the glory of God refers to the light that shone between the cherubim in the holy of holies as the evidence of the presence of God. Ezekiel opens with this heavenly glory in the vision (Ezekiel 1). The book ends with earthly glory (Ezekiel 40–48). Ezekiel's visions given in between tell of the departing of this glory (Ezekiel 9:3). First it left the cherubim for the threshold of God's house (Ezekiel 10:4), thence to the east gate (Ezekiel 10:18,19) and finally clear away from the temple and city to the Mount of Olives (Ezekiel 11:22,23). Thus gradually, reluctantly, majestically, the glory of the Lord left the temple and Holy City. Then captivity came.

This was Ezekiel's message to the nation. Their captivity was a result of their sin, and before they could hope for return to their land they must return to their Lord. This message reaches its climax in the impassioned cry of Ezekiel 18:30-32.

God's judgment on sin is certain and severe. His redemption is equally certain when it is welcomed by the human heart. Ezekiel's message closes with the promise of future glory. Ezekiel 37 is the great classic of Israel's hope. The closing

245

vision of the temple is equally significant. The glory of the Lord returns (Ezekiel 43:2-6) and fills the house of the Lord (Ezekiel 44:4).

Ezekiel's prophecy is intensely practical for nation and church. As Israel's captivity was the result of sin, so we must remember that sin is a reproach to any people. A nation's troubles are the result of national apostasy from God.

The same is true of the church of Christ. The glory of the Lord left the house of the Lord because of the sins of God's people. It is also true of individual Christian experience. God's blessing returns to His people when His people return to Him.

EZEKIEL AND THE CAPTIVITY

It seems that God called Ezekiel that He might explain and justify His action in allowing His children to be taken into captivity. They had been wicked and stiff-necked; they were guilty of unspeakable sin and abomination. When other nations did what Israel had done, God had wiped them out. But all of God's dealings with Israel were for correction. They should say, *I know, O Lord, that thy judgments are right, and that thou in faithfulness hast afflicted me* (Psalm 119:75). He was punishing His children for their sin and was teaching them great lessons. He said a remnant would survive. *They shall know that I am God* was His purpose. And it is true that with all their sins, the Jews have never been idolaters since the captivity! They insisted upon it before, in spite of the warnings of God, but never after they had come out of Babylon.

God set Jeremiah to be a strong tower of strength in the land of Judah. In the same way He set Ezekiel to be a tower among his own captive people by the river Chebar, in the land of the Chaldeans. He told Ezekiel that as *adamant harder than flint* had He made his forehead (Ezekiel 3:9). Strength characterized the ministry of the prophet whose name means "God will strengthen."

EZEKIEL — A HOME MISSIONARY

Ezekiel was sent to his own people. It is sometimes easier to go as a missionary to China or India than to speak to the members of your own household or your own friends.

246

Perhaps God is speaking to us as He spoke to Ezekiel—*Thou art not sent to a people of a strange speech and of an hard language, but to the house of Israel . . . Go, get thee to them of the captivity, unto the children of thy people, and speak unto them* (Ezekiel 3:5,11). It was a difficult task to speak to false prophets, elders, shepherds and princes, but God commanded it.

EZEKIEL — A WATCHMAN

God told Ezekiel to be a watchman. He told the prophet not to fear the people but give them warning and that if he did not do it, He would require their blood at his hands. (Read Ezekiel 3 and 33.) These chapters state plainly our personal responsibility in giving out the gospel message. Paul was so faithful in doing this that he could say, *I am pure from the blood of all men* (Acts 20:26).

EZEKIEL — THE SIGN

To be God's sign to the people, Ezekiel underwent the loss of all personal interests. He stood ready to do anything God asked of him in order to demonstrate the plan of God for His people, and God asked some extraordinary things of him. He shut himself up in his house (3:24). He was placed in weird positions (4:4-8). He ate his food by weight (4:10). He sacrificed personal appearance (5:1), smote with hand or struck with foot (6:11), and even moved personal and domestic goods out of his house to show the removal of Israel into captivity (12:2-7). God may never ask these of us, but He may ask us to do things that cross our wills and desires. Will He find us as obedient as Ezekiel? Christ seeks for such—*I sought for a man among them, that should make up the hedge, and stand in the gap before me for the land, that I should not destroy it: but I found none* (see Ezekiel 3:15; 22:30).

JUDGMENTS ON JUDAH'S ENEMIES

In Ezekiel 25–32 we hear pronouncements of doom on surrounding nations. We remember Isaiah gave warnings in chapters 13–23. Jeremiah gave warnings in chapters 46–51. Each mentioned different nations. Ezekiel warned Ammon, Moab, Edom, Philistia, Tyre, Sidon, Egypt.

The remarkable thing about these prophecies is that they were given at a time when these cities and nations were strong and powerful. Each one has passed into a state of utter desolation, as Babylon, or has been put into a place of insignificance among world powers. Many of the specific prophecies have already been fulfilled to the most minute detail. *Righteousness exalteth a nation: but sin is a reproach to any people* (Proverbs 14:34).

VISIONS OF EZEKIEL

Ezekiel is a prophet of visions. The key text of the book shows this: *As I was among the captives . . . the heavens were opened, and I saw visions of God* (Ezekiel 1:1). It is urgent that you scan all these visions before you enter into further detailed study.

Vision of the Cherubim (Ezekiel 1:1–3:13)

In this vision "four living creatures" appear, having unusual faces, but each with the general appearance of a man. The main purpose of the vision is twofold—to commission Ezekiel for service, and to impress upon him the need for assimilating the words God spoke to him and giving them to the people. Note "the roll of a book" which he ate in his vision (3:1). The unswerving obedience to God's will of the creatures symbolized the obedience expected of Ezekiel. Their movement as a single unit is the picture of God's will perfectly executed. Ezekiel and Revelation are often alike in symbolism. "The man" upon the throne (1:26) is the Son of God. The "bow that is in the cloud" spoke of the covenant God made with Noah (1:28). The "fire" (1:4,13,27) bespoke God's Spirit. In Revelation, all these appear. Christ figures prominently in all the symbolism.

Vision of Glory and Godlessness (Ezekiel 8–11)

Before the siege of Jerusalem, Ezekiel is given an extended vision which shows the people's abominations in defiling the sanctuary, and the contrasting glory of God. "Abominations" occur all the way through the section. "Glory" stands in sharp contrast. God was trying to show why Israel was to be led into captivity (8:17,18).

Vision of the Burning Vine (Ezekiel 15)

The vine becomes a symbol of Judah, and the burning of a useless vine which bears no fruit is the destruction of the people of God. The abominations of Jerusalem are so great as to warrant the most severe punishment. This vision of doom is followed by the parable of the unfaithful wife. Israel was Jehovah's "bride," who had forsaken God to go whoring after other gods. Love of idols, rather than the love of God, caused Israel's downfall (Chap. 16).

Vision of Dry Bones (Ezekiel 37)

In this vision, a great valley is seen, filled with dry bones, said to be the "whole house of Israel" (37:11). The main lesson of the vision is the restoration of God's people. He takes them from among the heathen and gathers them out of all countries through which, as bones without flesh, they have been scattered. It is a picture also of the power of God to raise those who have not only been scattered, but dead in sins. This "new birth" was explained to Nicodemus. God promises it here to Israel. They are to be brought forth, filled with God's Spirit, and brought to their land.

PARABLES AND SIGNS IN EZEKIEL

These, as well as visions, abound in Ezekiel. The more outstanding ones command great interest. 1—The parable of the two eagles (chap. 17) reveals the king of Babylon (v. 12) and the king of Egypt. The "highest branch" of the cedar (v. 3) corresponds to Jehoiachin carried captive to Babylon. The "seed of the land" was Zedekiah (v. 5). The "tender twig" (v. 22) Jehovah will plant is the Messiah, the future King of David's line through whom all nations will learn to know God. Jeremiah tells also of the "highest branch." (Jer. 23:5,6. See also Isaiah 11:1; Zech. 3:8; Isaiah 53.) For "the mountain of the Lord," see 17:22; 20:40; Micah 4:1,2; Isaiah 2:2,3. 2—Chapters 20–23 include several parables, prominent among which is that of the two sisters Aholah and Aholibah. They represent Israel's and Judah's deterioration into idolatry. 3—The parable of the boiling caldron (chap. 24) symbolizes the holocaust in Jerusalem at the hands of the invading Babylonians. Much fuel, hot fire, boiled flesh, and burnt bones show the intensity of the siege (vs. 5,10). 4—Two sticks—one Judah, the other Israel—are shown as ultimately reunited under the Shepherd King of God's people—Christ (37:24). This is one of the important "signs."

PREDICTIONS BEFORE THE SIEGE OF JERUSALEM — AGAINST JUDAH (Read Ezekiel 1–24)

As the book opens we see Ezekiel, a young man of about 30, captive, yet being commissioned by God for a great service.

Like the prophets generally, Ezekiel entered upon his ministry only after he had a vision and a call from God. Read of Jeremiah's call in Jeremiah 1:4-10. Turn to Isaiah 6 and review the facts of Isaiah's commission. Ezekiel opens with the description of the experiences of the prophet when he was called.

A QUICK PANORAMA OF EZEKIEL

The pivot of the book is the destruction of Jerusalem.

I. Pre-Siege . . . (1-24)

Ezekiel began six years before the destruction of Jerusalem with his prophecies and kept predicting its certainty until it occurred.

II. Siege . . . (25-32)

After that his prophecies deal with Judah's enemies and the overthrow of these heathen nations.

III. Post-Siege . . . (33-48)

Finally the restoration and reestablishment of Judah is pictured.

Ezekiel gives us a very dramatic picture of his vision and call to service. The Holy Being who appeared to him could go everywhere. He was all powerful, could see everything and could rule the entire universe by His mighty hand.

The vision which he saw was unusually complicated and elaborate. Notice how many times Ezekiel uses the words "appearance" and "likeness." He knows he is trying to describe things impossible to picture.

The prophet saw a fiery cloud approaching. From out of the glow were four living creatures, suggested by the cherubim of the temple. (See I Kings 6:23-28; Genesis 3:24; Psalm 18:10.) Each had four wings and four faces: that of a man, a lion, an ox and an eagle, symbolizing intelligence, dignity, strength and speed. They faced east, west, north and south suggesting that all parts of the universe are open to the gaze of God. The wings showed that there was no spot inaccessible to divine power. There were eyes in the wheels—wheels so equipped cannot miss their way. We see a symbol of the omnipotence (all power), omnipresence (all present), and omniscience (all knowledge) of God.

The mysterious whir of the mighty wings was followed by an equally mysterious silence. The wings dropped. The chariots stopped. Above the heads of the creatures was a crystal floor on which rested a sapphire throne, and on the throne Almighty God Himself, a figure of supernatural brilliance and glory. The terror of divine majesty was softened by the sight of a lovely rainbow around the throne. Little wonder that when Ezekiel saw this vision he fell prostrate. The vision was to destroy all self-confidence that the prophet might have.

THE CALL

Following the vision the awful silence was broken by the Almighty upon the throne. The prophet was receiving his call. God told the prostrate prophet to rise and accept his commission for service. God wants more than inactive submission. He wants loving service. God called Ezekiel "son of man." One hundred times this phrase is used. Ezekiel was called to declare the message of God—a message of doom to the people. (Read Ezekiel 2:1-10.) This doom was justified by their rebellion. Ezekiel had every temptation to "rebel" but he went without flinching to speak the word.

The prophet's authority is suggested by the symbolic swallowing of a book-roll. He must make the message his own. He

251

must "eat it." (Read Ezekiel 3:3.) Bitter as its contents were to his mouth, they were sweet as honey, for it is sweet to do the will of God and to be trusted with tasks for Him.

Then the whir of the wings and the roar of the wheels was heard when the glory of Jehovah rose from the place and the chariot departed, leaving the prophet in a state of bitterness and heat of spirit. In this mood he found his way to Tel-abib, a colony of his fellow exiles and remained for a week in a state of utter stupefaction.

THE WATCHMAN

At the end of the week he received another message from God. This time it was more explicit. He was called to be a watchman. *I have made thee a watchman . . . give them warning from me. . . . If thou givest him [wicked man] not warning . . . his blood at thy hands I will require. Yet if thou warn the wicked . . . thou hast saved thyself* (see Ezekiel 3:16-21).

God places a great responsibility on His watchmen. How can we be so careless in the light of such words as these? How can we go to sleep and fail to warn others of their sins? Let us answer this challenge and heed this warning.

Ezekiel 33:7 says, *I have set thee a watchman.*

As a watchman Ezekiel must warn individual men of the coming catastrophe which he so clearly sees. It is not enough to warn the crowd. He must deal with individuals, good or bad, who compose the crowd and tell them to turn from their evil ways.

God impressed Ezekiel with individual responsibility. Each one must repent. Each one must hear the Word. How true this is today of every person. Each one must accept Christ for himself. No one can do it for another. *But as many as received him, to them gave he power to become the sons of God, even to them that believe on his name* (John 1:12). (See John 3:16; 5:24; 3:36.)

252

FOUR SYMBOLS OF COMING DOOM OF JERUSALEM

1. The Siege of Jerusalem . . . . Ezekiel 4:1-3

Ezekiel cannot speak, but he is a prophet still and he can preach, if not by word, by symbol. (See Ezekiel 3:22-27.)

2. The Exile—Its Duration . . . . Ezekiel 4:4-8

This section is curious. Remember Ezekiel was a sign. He lay upon his side to symbolize the years of punishment the Jews were to suffer in exile—a day for a year.

3. The Hardships of the Exiles . . . . Ezekiel 4:9-17

The horrors of famine due to siege are symbolized here by the prophet's food and drink, carefully measured out—about one-half pound of food a day and a pint of water.

4. The Fate of the Besieged . . . . Ezekiel 5:1-17

This last symbol, the knife and razor, is the most terrible of them all. It suggests the completeness of the destruction.

All of these visions and symbols reveal the method of Ezekiel's prophecy. This is the method used in Daniel and Revelation.

The prophet was shown the way the people had profaned the temple of Jehovah. This justified, to the new generation, the national punishment. (See Ezekiel 8:1–11:12.)

The prophet pled that Jehovah spare a remnant and Jehovah promised to be a "little sanctuary" to them in the land of their exile. He promised to restore them finally. (See Ezekiel 11:13-21.)

The next chapters reveal the past sins of both Samaria and Jerusalem, and the punishment, and instructions in righteousness for the elders of Israel. (See Ezekiel 11:22–24:27.) God says, *I will give them one heart . . . a new spirit I will put within them . . . they shall be my people . . . I will be their God* (see Ezekiel 11:19,20). God wants a religious experience of the heart. God will give His people a new spirit. (See Ezekiel 18:31; 36:26.)

PREDICTIONS DURING THE SIEGE OF JERUSALEM —
JUDGMENT AGAINST JUDAH'S ENEMIES
(Read Ezekiel 25–32)

Ezekiel's gloomy predictions are completed. (Ezekiel 1–24) With the news of the fall of Jerusalem he immediately begins to prophesy about the future restoration of Israel. God often reveals a bright picture of Israel's future against the backdrop of divine judgment. (See Ezekiel 33–48.) But before Israel is restored to her land those who are her enemies must be put out of the way. So at this point we hear of the future doom of these foreign powers. First we hear of her near neighbors who have insulted and harassed her and then of the more distant and more powerful ones. God pronounces His judgment upon Ammon, Moab, Tyre, Sidon and Egypt for their sins against Israel. All of these powers were ancient enemies of Israel. They dated back before the days of the monarchy. From Israel's petty neighbors with their petty spite, Ezekiel turns to the great empires of Tyre and Egypt. They, too, must go. In a passage of great literary power, Ezekiel describes the brilliance of Tyre, the extent of her commerce, the pity and terror inspired by her fall.

Ezekiel 29–32 tells of the collapse of Egypt. The mighty Nebuchadnezzar with his terrible army will deal a crushing blow and Egypt will be devastated.

PREDICTIONS AFTER THE SIEGE OF JERUSALEM —
JUDAH'S RESTORATION (Read Ezekiel 33–48)

We now can look into the future and see the final restoration and glory of Israel. God will gather together His scattered people. God says over and over, "I will, I will."

Shepherds of Israel had proven faithless to the people, the flock had been scattered; but now Jehovah will set up a Shepherd, "my Servant David." (Read Ezekiel 34:23,24.) This, no doubt, refers to the Davidic Covenant and to the seed of David, the Messiah. Look up this series of passages: II Samuel 7:16; Psalm 89:20-36; Isaiah 7:13,14; 9:6,7; 11:1-12; Jeremiah 23:2-7; Ezekiel 37:21-28; Hosea 3:4,5; Luke 1:30-33; Acts 2:29-31; 15:14-17. All this reveals that the future blessing of

Israel will come with the Messiah, David's Son. When the Jews rejected Jesus, they did not thwart God's plan or defeat His purpose for in Acts we read that He was raised from the dead to sit on David's throne, and He will return for that purpose (Acts 2:30).

The restoration that Ezekiel tells about does not refer to the feeble remnant that returned to Jerusalem after the seventy years of captivity (see Ezra and Nehemiah) for it is a restoration from all nations (Ezekiel 36:24).

Ezekiel sees a vision of all this. There is a valley of dry bones (See Ezekiel 37:1-14.) The "bones" are the Jews who shall be alive at the restoration of the nation. The "graves" are the nations where they are dwelling but "buried." God first will bring them into their own land. Then they will be converted—a nation shall be born in a day. The Spirit will give them life. The revival of national life is possible! It is not beyond the power of God. Even dry bones, without sinew and flesh, are made to live. The Holy Spirit can bring life. This truth is seen everywhere when the Spirit comes with His quickening power. (See Genesis 2:7; Rev. 11:11.) Israel shall multiply as they return to their own land. This restoration of Israel will be a national one. They shall look on Him whom they have pierced and mourn because of Him. And a nation shall be born in a day. (See Zechariah 12:10; John 19:37; Rom. 11:26.) The resurrection in this chapter is not of the individual Jew but of the whole nation.

Ezekiel 38 opens with the doom of *Gog, the land of Magog, the chief prince of Meshech and Tubal*. The reference is to the northern (European) powers, perhaps headed up by Russia. (Read these passages in connection with Zechariah 14:1-9; 12:1-4; Matthew 24:14-30; Revelation 14:14-20; 19:17-21.) Before the curtain falls we read the description of the kingdom during the coming millennial age. This is what the thousand-year reign of Christ on earth is called when He shall sit upon the throne of David, in Jerusalem. (See Revelation 20:6.) All the prophets tell us of what a glorious day this will be for both Jew and Gentile. We read of the temple, the worship, and the final possession of the land given to Abraham and to his seed according to the covenant God gave to him. (See Genesis 12:1-3; 13:14,15; 15:18; 17:3-8.)

GOLDEN TRUTH ABOUT THE GOLDEN AGE

Back here in the Old Testament, while the Jews were in what seemed hopeless captivity, God declares constantly that He will restore the Jews to their own land, set up the throne and the kingdom of David through David's greater Son. With His reign will come such earthly and spiritual blessings as have not been known since the world began. This is the golden truth about the golden age which is coming to pass here on this earth. (Read Ezekiel 34:22-31.)

Gabriel's prophecy at Jesus' birth in Luke 1:30-33 will be literally fulfilled through David's Son, the Lord Jesus Christ. This promise of a Messianic King and Kingdom must be carefully distinguished from our Lord's spiritual rule over hearts and lives. The words of Gabriel to Mary still wait complete, literal fulfillment. (See Ezekiel 34:23,24; 37:24; I Kings 14:8; Jeremiah 30:9.)

The appearance of the Messiah will usher in a glorious future. God will make a covenant of peace. (Read Leviticus 26:6; Jeremiah 31:31; Ezekiel 37:26.) Wonderful blessings are promised to His people. They will be assured of absolute protection from heathen nations ("evil beasts") because they are possessed by none other than God Himself. (See Ezekiel 34:31.)

Minimum Daily Requirements/Spiritual Vitamins

Sunday: THE PROPHET'S CALL   Ezekiel 2:1–3:9
Monday: THE PROPHET A WATCHMAN
     Ezekiel 3:10-27
Tuesday: ISRAEL SHALL BE SAVED
     Ezekiel 11:14-21; 28:25,26
Wednesday: ISRAEL'S SINS   Ezekiel 22:3-31
Thursday: ISRAEL'S FUTURE   Ezekiel 34:1-31
Friday: ISRAEL'S RESTORATION   Ezekiel 36:1-38
Saturday: VISION OF THE DRY BONES
     Ezekiel 37:1-14

CHAPTER 21

UNDERSTANDING DANIEL

Daniel
Portrays Jesus Christ,
the Smiting Stone

Children [young men] *in whom was no blemish, but well favored, and skillful in all wisdom, and cunning in knowledge, and understanding science, and such as had ability in them* (Daniel 1:4)—these are some of the men with whom this books deals. They were skilled in God's wisdom as opposed to man's. They had an understanding of God's revelation which unlocks the mysteries of human science. They had ability in them such as God gives to live the overcoming life!

Chief among these princely young men was the incomparable Daniel. He stands in God's Word as the man who dared to keep a clean heart and body (Daniel 1:8), and the man therefore whom God chose as a channel for His message to the Gentile nations of the world. A large part of this book is concerned with the thrilling personal life of this peerless captive prince of Judah.

Daniel was in the palace at Babylon the same time that Ezekiel was toiling in a slave gang. If Daniel's was the easier life in many of its material aspects, it may also be considered by far the more perilous.

Ezekiel's work during these dreary exile years was to proclaim to his people God's truth and to explain the real meaning of the miseries that had befallen them. Daniel's task was to share in the actual government of Babylon.

Daniel has been called the prophet of dreams. God revealed to him His secrets. *Then was the secret revealed unto Daniel in a night vision* (Daniel 2:19). Daniel, like Ezekiel, looks far into the future. He is quoted most in Revelation. One cannot understand the great signs of Revelation without looking at their meaning in Daniel.

Daniel belonged to a family of high rank. He was taken captive to Babylon during the first invasion by Nebuchadnezzar at about the age of sixteen. Ezekiel was taken captive eight years later during the second invasion. Daniel lived to be over ninety years of age. He saw the Babylonian kingdom fall, and the Medo-Persian empire established. He held high positions under kings Nebuchadnezzar, Belshazzar, Darius, and Cyrus.

Daniel's whole life from the time of his captivity was spent in the great and glamorous city of Babylon, the ancient Hollywood. He spent sixty-nine years in a vile court. There he lived a life without blame and well favored. Ezekiel refers to him as a model of righteousness, in Ezekiel 14:14-20; 28:3.

Although Daniel was a captive, he rose to be prime minister of Babylon. The wonderful thing is that he always remained true to Jehovah God.

DANIEL — BOOK OF DEVOTIONS

This book is packed with heart-touching devotional passages for the personal Christian life:

The surrendered life..Daniel 1:1-21
Light amidst darkness......................................Daniel 2:20-22
Triumph through trial......................................Daniel 3:17-25
The reward of service......................................Daniel 5:17
Prayer and confidence in God............................Daniel 6:10-24
Confession of sin..Daniel 9:3-19
The wisdom of soul-winning..............................Daniel 12:3

Daniel was among the great on this earth. The historical portions of his own book hint it. Ezekiel, nearest to him in his own day and therefore knowing him best, ranks him as one of the world's triumvirate of virtue—Noah, Daniel and Job. (See Ezekiel 14:14.)

Daniel was also great in heaven. God broke the silence of the skies twice over to cry out, *O Daniel, a man greatly beloved, O man greatly beloved* (Daniel 10:11,19). Furthermore, no position, no matter how difficult, found him without trust in God. God is able, in all temptations, to keep us from falling (Jude 24), unless we have deliberately placed ourselves, with Peter, at the fire of the enemy.

God honored Daniel in his prayers. Marvelous in power that they were, God sent a special embassy of angels from the throne, with the thrilling words, *I am come for thy words* (Daniel 10:12). God exhibited His power in a remarkable way in Daniel's life and Daniel never introduced himself or his own actions, except as illustrations of that power.

Daniel was the companion of kings. He was a leader of men. He was a pioneer in reform. He started the first Society of Total Abstinence. (See Daniel 1:12.) Daniel was, like Joseph, God's candle, shining in heathen darkness. He was chief statesman in the first empire of the world, chief adviser of a great monarch, and a great protector of his own people. God gave him favor and love in the sight of the court official, Ashpenaz. Even proud Nebuchadnezzar seemed to have had real affection for Daniel.

The feelings of Darius toward Daniel are revealed when he finds what a trap has been set for him. He is *sore displeased with himself, and set his heart on Daniel to deliver him* (Daniel 6:14).

No doubt Cyrus was greatly influenced by the aged statesman. Daniel probably showed him the prophecy that Isaiah had written concerning him one hundred years before he was born. This made Cyrus issue the decree for the rebuilding of the temple at Jerusalem. (See II Chron. 36:22,23; Ezra 1.)

In the book which Daniel wrote, we see him pre-eminently as a prophet of God. He drew back the curtain and unveiled, as no one had ever done before, the hidden things of the future. Indeed, we are seeing more and more that his great prophecies are only history written before it occurred. It was the world's great annals in anticipation.

This book reveals the power of God and His universal sovereignty. God's power is contrasted with world-power.

God the Keeper—Daniel 1—God's power in keeping Daniel and his companions. They were given understanding and wisdom above all the wise men of Babylon.

God the Revealer of Secrets—Daniel 2—God's power in revealing the dream of Nebuchadnezzar to Daniel. None of the wise men of Babylon could do this.

God the Deliverer—Daniel 3—God's power in delivering Daniel's three companions from the fiery furnace. These young men stood up alone, against a nation, with the calm assurance that God would deliver them, yet adding, *but if not, be it known unto thee, O king, that we will not serve thy gods, nor worship the golden image.* This occurred after they had been in Babylon about twenty years and God was demonstrating, in this most dramatic way, His power over all of the gods of this country.

God the Potentate—Daniel 4—God's power in dealing with a mighty heathen monarch, Nebuchadnezzar. God struck him while the proud king was boasting of his power as he was strolling on the roof of his magnificent palace. He was driven from his kingdom to dwell among beasts—victim of a strange form of insanity.

God the Judge—Daniel 5—God's power is shown in the awful judgment revealed to Belshazzar, son of Nabonidus, by the handwriting on the wall. That night the king was slain by the Persian army and his city taken.

God the All Powerful—Daniel 6—God's power revealed in the deliverance of Daniel from the lions' den. Remember, Daniel was an old man. When he was a young man of about twenty, he was honored by the highest office in the whole empire. Now at ninety he was thrown into the den of lions. It seems that even the lions honored him.

God used the times of captivity to reveal His power among the nations of the world. When the chosen people were captives in Egypt, He worked miracles and wonders by the hand of Moses and showed, not only to the Israelites, but to the Egyptians, that the Lord God is Almighty.

Now, during the Babylonian captivity, God uses this as a special occasion to manifest His power. We find these great world monarchs confessing that He is the Living God, the Most High, the King of Heaven. He visits His children even in exile, and shows them again that He is mighty to save.

Unlike the other prophets Daniel deals more fully with the Gentile nations than with his own Jewish nation. The other prophets only mention the Gentiles as incidental to something concerning Israel. But Daniel gives us the history of the Gentile powers from Babylon to the end. The prophecies are considered among the most remarkable in the whole Scriptures.

The Book of Daniel is divided into two great sections:

1. Historical—narration ....Daniel 1–6
2. Prophetic—revelation ....Daniel 7–12

REIGN OF NEBUCHADNEZZAR (Read Daniel 1–4)

This scene opens upon a little company of four young men, Daniel, Hananiah, Mishael, and Azariah (also called Shadrach, Meshach, Abed-nego). They had been taken captive from Jerusalem by Nebuchadnezzar and carried away to his palace in Babylon. Daniel was only about sixteen years old, Nebuchadnezzar little older. He came to the throne about the time that Daniel was taken captive into Babylon, and was the most powerful and distinguished king of the Babylonian empire. Daniel's career was marked by its extent in time and its greatness in accomplishment.

Daniel was carried to Babylon during the first deportation of the captives. He gained a high position in the kingdom and was influential through the seventy years of his captivity. He saw his captive brothers return to Jerusalem under the decree of Cyrus. He saw world-ruling Babylon pass away and a new empire arise. Even at the age of ninety he received a position of high distinction in the court of Persia.

Daniel and his friends lived in an atmosphere of loose morals and low standards even though they were in a palace. Yet we read that they kept themselves apart from the evil of that court—true to God in a day when everything was against them. Evils much like those of today were rampant everywhere in the courts of royalty.

Listen to what these brave youths said when they faced their first temptation in the court of the Babylonian king. *We will not defile ourselves with the king's meat* . . . and they did not. It was to young men like these that God could tell His secrets and demonstrate His power. Remember, "the secret of the Lord is with them that fear Him."

These youths met every emergency and were victors. We will find them in three difficult positions:

1. In the court of a powerful emperor
2. In the fiery furnace
3. In the den of lions

In this first scene we find them in the luxurious heathen court. The youths were brought very quickly face to face with a serious practical difficulty. This was a real test for these chaps. As favored ones, they had been put into one of the apartments in the palace and given many of the delicacies of the king's table. They were to be trained in state affairs and equipped for high positions. It was hard indeed to refuse the king's meat and ask for a simpler fare. It would look as if they had no choice in the matter. Many of us would have argued that way. They asked to be able to prove that their faces would be satisfactory. And God gave them favor in the eyes of their companions. Remember, we ought always to obey God rather than men. The king's meat had probably been offered in sacrifice to idols, (Exodus 34:15; I Cor. 10:20), and the flesh food would have been killed with the blood left in the animal which was unclean (Lev. 3:17; 7:26).

There was nothing priggish about Daniel. It was something to make a man like Ashpenaz love him. Notice how loyal his companions were to him. This is a fine trait. Success did not turn Daniel's head. He was a man to whom, early in his career, men turned.

We are told that God gave them knowledge and skill in all learning and wisdom: and Daniel had understanding in all visions and dreams. This was God's reward. God's power is shown through His dealing with Daniel and his three companions in all the wisdom and understanding which He gave them.

There was a stir in the palace. Nebuchadnezzar had dreamed a dream and not one of the wise men of the kingdom could tell him what it was. A decree had been sent forth that all the wise men should be slain, and Daniel and his friends were sought. But Daniel was not afraid. God would tell him the dream and give him the meaning of it.

Daniel called his prayer partners (Daniel 2:17) and they presented their problem before God. *Then was the secret re-*

vealed unto Daniel in a night vision (Daniel 2:19). God never disappoints faith.

THE DREAM OF WORLD EMPIRES

Nebuchadnezzar's dream and the interpretation teaches us some very interesting things about the history of the world from that time till the "end of this age." This period the Bible calls "the times of the Gentiles" because God has put aside His own people, the Jews, for a time and has passed over the government of the world to the Gentiles.

Daniel 2 has been called the "ABC of Prophecy." It stretches out before us the most complete picture in all the Scriptures of what is to come to pass—"the future."

God revealed His plan of the future to a heathen monarch in a dream. (Read Daniel 2:29.) After Nebuchadnezzar had dreamed, he forgot! But it worried him. No one could tell him his dream but one who knew "the God of heaven." (Master the outline of history given in this second chapter.)

Picture a great image. The head was of gold. its breast and arms of silver, the belly and thighs of brass, and its legs of iron, with its feet and toes of iron and clay. Then a Stone cut out without hands smited the image and broke it to pieces; and the Stone became a great mountain and filled the whole earth. (This Stone was no other than Jesus Christ.)

God first reveals the Gentile powers. Four great empires were to succeed each other in the government of the world from Nebuchadnezzar to the end. God says, *Thou art this head of gold.*

The breast and arms of silver represented the Medo-Persian empire which overthrew Babylon and became its successor. Its power began with Cyrus under whom the Jews returned to Jerusalem. (See Ezra 1:1,2.)

Then the belly and thighs of brass represented Greece, which overturned the Medo-Persians. It pictures the Grecian rule "over all the earth" under Alexander the Great.

DANIEL'S HISTORICAL SUMMARY

Daniel tells us what each metal represents. Daniel 2:38 says that the head of gold is Babylon. In Daniel 8:20 we find that the Medo-Persians are to follow. Then in Daniel 8:21 it states that Greece is to follow Persia. Daniel 9:26 indicates a fourth world-power. From then on we find an ever-dividing kingdom and a government ever weakened in its power and represented by toes of iron and clay that cannot hold together. More is said of the fourth Gentile government than of the others. Maybe it is because it is the last. There will be a division into many kingdoms, as the toes. There is deterioration represented by the feet and toes being part iron and part clay which cannot hold together. This last government will be the weakest. It will not be completely unified, and will finally end in chaos.

KINGDOM OF CHRIST

In the "Stone" cut out without hands we see the kingdom of Christ, whose kingdom shall never be destroyed, bringing to an end all the other kingdoms. Christ will come and set up a kingdom which will last forever. (Read Daniel 2:44,45.) If you wish an interesting study, see what the Word says about the "Stone." Psalm 118:22; Isa. 8:14; 28:16; Zechariah 3:9.

Remember at the time Nebuchadnezzar dreamed his dream the Persian kingdom did not exist. It was merely a Babylonian satrapy. It would have seemed impossible that a strong Grecian empire would rise. Only wandering tribes inhabited the Hellenic states. The city of Rome was only a little town on the banks of the Tiber. Yet God told Daniel what would come to pass.

Notice that the metals in the image deteriorate in value—gold, silver, brass and iron. This reveals the weakening in the power of each succeeding empire. Finally we will find a condition of iron mixed with brittle clay, suggesting attempted unions between a democratic and an imperialistic form of government. Name the forms of government that exist today. Do these resemble the toes of clay, "brittle" and not holding together?

Many ask, "When will this Stone fall?" We know not the day nor hour but the King is coming with power and great glory with all His holy angels to establish His kingdom.

The great King Nebuchadnezzar fell on his face and worshiped Daniel, and declared that his God was the God of all gods. But we find as we go on in the story that this wonderful revelation of God had little real effect upon Nebuchadnezzar. It did not bring him to his knees before God.

THE FIERY FURNACE

As the curtain is pulled back again we face a very tense moment. (See Daniel 3.) Nebuchadnezzar had set up a golden image on the plain of Dura and had commanded all peoples to fall down and worship it. If any refused, he should be cast into a fiery furnace.

But there were three in the throng that refused to obey the king. Yes, here they are again, after twenty years, Shadrach, Meshach and Abed-nego. Spies reported their disobedience. These three knew what God had said. *Thou shalt not make unto thee any graven image . . . Thou shalt not bow down thyself to them* (Exodus 20:4,5). They were fearless in the presence of this eastern despot.

The story of the fiery furnace is a familiar one. What was the wonderful thing about that scene? Yes, the Son of God was with them. What effect did this have on Nebuchadnezzar? He was filled with great admiration for the miraculous power of the God of these men. But still he does not bow to worship God in humility. He calls Jehovah "their God." Remember God wants us to say, "My Lord, and my God." Christ said, "When ye pray, say, our Father." This scene demonstrated, in a most dramatic way, before the dignitaries of the far-flung empire, the power of the Most High God. The erecting of an image will be repeated by the beast, the Antichrist, last head of Gentile world-dominion. (Read Revelation 13:11-15; 19:20.)

THE KING DREAMS AGAIN

This time the king has another dream (Daniel 4:4-27). In Job 33:14-17 the Bible says, *God speaketh once, yea twice, yet man perceiveth it not. In a dream, in a vision of the night, when deep sleep falleth upon men . . . and sealeth their instruction, that he may withdraw man from his purpose, and hide pride from man.*

God has spoken often to men in dreams to reveal His will when the Bible was not open to them. God spoke to Nebuchadnezzar once and gave him the image representing the Gentile kingdoms, and showed him his doom. But he did not repent. Then God spoke to him again from the fiery furnace, where He revealed His power to him. But still his proud heart felt no repentance.

Now we find God speaking to Nebuchadnezzar for the third time in the dream of the great tree which was cut down (Daniel 4:4-27). This was a warning to Nebuchadnezzar of his coming madness. God was trying to bring this proud king to the end of himself. But a year later we see him a madman, his mind gone. He fancied himself a beast (Daniel 4:28-34). All this because he had set himself up as a rival against Almighty God. Hear him say, *Is not this great Babylon, that I have built for the house of the kingdom by the might of my power, and for the honor of my majesty* (Daniel 4:30)?

Through his insanity, Nebuchadnezzar's eyes were opened and his conscience was touched. He confessed to the greatness of God and bore his testimony to the goodness of God (Daniel 4:34). He learned that man is not the architect of his own fortune.

REIGN OF BELSHAZZAR (Read Daniel 5; 7; 8)

The following outline may help you to know who Belshazzar was, and where he came from . . .

Nebuchadnezzar—reigned to 562 B.C.

Merodach—dissolute son of Nebuchadnezzar, reigned two years.

Neriglizzar—brother-in-law of Merodach and his murderer, followed with a four-year reign. No successor.

Nabonidus—son of Nebuchadnezzar's second wife, ascends throne in 556 B.C. Other name "Labyretus."

Belshazzar—son of Nabonidus, co-regent with him. Medes, imprisoning Nabonidus, press on to capture revelling Belshazzar, and Babylon.

As chapter 5 opens we see a great banquet hall with a thousand lords sitting about the tables. It was "ladies' night." All the king's sweethearts were there besides the thousand lords. Often the presence of ladies seems to inspire a man to do something spectacular. So as an extra feature, Belshazzar had sent for the sacred golden and silver vessels which his grandfather Nebuchadnezzar had stripped from the temple in Jerusalem. He showed them just how little he regarded the God of Israel. As they looked, behold, golden and silver vessels adorned the tables! They had been taken out of the "temple of the house of God" in Jerusalem. The last prince of Babylon, Belshazzar, drank wine to the idols in these sacred vessels.

God shows His power in the awful handwriting on the wall. Daniel was called in to explain the meaning. The prophet fearlessly condemned this foolish and sensual young king. Read the details of the divine interruption in Daniel 5.

A bad reign came to a sudden end. *In that night was Belshazzar the king of the Chaldeans slain.* We are not told how, but we learn from Xenophon and Herodotus and Berosus the strange story of the fall of the great city.

Many of the tablets from Babylon, recently found, tell us that the Persian army took Babylon without a battle. Four months later Cyrus entered the city. Darius probably received the kingdom from Cyrus as his vice regent over some part of it.

DANIEL'S VISION

During the first year of Belshazzar's reign, Daniel had a vision of four wild beasts, which symbolized the four kingdoms pictured in Nebuchadnezzar's dream (Daniel 7). Picturing them as beasts gives us a hint as to the moral character of these empires for they are represented by ferocious wild beasts. How history's wars reveal the true heart of nations!

In Nebuchadnezzar's dream-image we have man's view of the magnificence of these kingdoms. In Daniel's dream we have God's view of the same. See who Daniel says these four beasts are in Daniel 7:17-23. The first, or Babylon, was like a lion with eagle's wings. Jeremiah likened Nebuchadnezzar both to the lion and eagle. (See Jeremiah 49:19-22.) Persia was the bear, the cruel animal who delights to kill for the sake of killing. The third was a leopard or panther, a beast of prey. His four wings portray swiftness. Here we see the rapid marches of Alexander's army and his insatiable love of conquest. In thirteen short years he had conquered the world. The fourth beast was different from all the rest. He was *dreadful and terrible, and strong exceedingly; and it had great iron teeth* (Daniel 7:7).

This vision of the four beasts covers the same ground as the great image of Daniel 2. Compare them carefully.

The "little horn" coming up among the ten is the Antichrist yet to come. We see him represented in Revelation as the beast coming up out of the sea. (See Daniel 7:15-25.) The saints will be oppressed by Antichrist, the last world ruler before Christ comes (Rev. 13:1). Rule of the dictators is beginning to hint at the extent of the power and authority possible to this last great dictator, the Antichrist. This period terminates the great tribulation. (See Revelation 5-18.) This is the period during which the judgments of God are to come upon the earth for the rejection of Jesus Christ.

Two years later in Daniel 8 we have another vision of the ram and the he-goat. Belshazzar was still on the throne. This vision includes only two of the four kingdoms, Persia and Greece. (See Daniel 8:20,21).

The kingdom of Medo-Persia is overthrown by the king of Greece. It contains the prophecy of the division of the latter kingdom on the death of Alexander between his four generals. Daniel had this vision at Shushan, the capital of Persia, where seventy years later the events recorded in Esther took place.

REIGN OF DARIUS (Read Daniel 6; 9)

One of the most difficult questions in the Old Testament is the identity of "Darius the Mede" (Daniel 5:31). He must have been someone appointed by Cyrus, and the statement that he "took the kingdom" confirms this. Some think that he was the father or grandfather of Cyrus, known otherwise as Astyages; and thus allowed to act as king until his death. Others think that he was a commander in the army of Cyrus, named Gobryas, and the difference between this and Darius in the original would be slight.

Twenty-three years after the death of Nebuchadnezzar, his great city, Babylon, fell into the hands of a conqueror, the Medes.

Even under these new rulers, Daniel was in a place of power. The jealousy of the other officials was aroused by the preference given to Daniel, and a plot to destroy him was quickly formed. *Then the presidents and princes sought to find occasion against Daniel* (Daniel 6:4). Of course they did. He "okayed" all their tax receipts and they soon found that Daniel would not allow any graft. They had always "knocked down taxes." If Daniel didn't let them "get by," how were they going to get along with the high cost of living in Babylon? So Daniel had trouble because he would not stand in with the political crowd.

They used his religion to set their trap, with the very same result as always when men are fools enough to try to trip the Lord's faithful children. (See I Peter 3:12,13; Deut. 9:3.) Remember there is always access to God through prayer in Christ. We may speak not just three times a day but whenever the need arises. The Lord Jesus invites us to pray. (Read again John 14:13-15.)

All unconsciously the king was induced to pass the decree solely for Daniel's destruction. Just imagine, if you can, a David, an Alexander, a Caesar, a Peter the Great, a Napoleon, a Queen Victoria, or any other strong ruler letting a cabal of his court trick him into sacrificing a favorite if he did not want to! Signing that law without finding out what was back of it was inexcusable. When he found the trap he had walked into, he should have broken the promise. "A bad promise is better broken than kept."

The envy of these men no doubt was due to Daniel's ability and his Jewish blood. This spirit of "Anti-Semitism" is in fulfillment of God's prophecies that the Jews would be hated. It continues rampant even in modern times.

Daniel's conduct in face of danger was quite deliberate. He knew he had to deny his religion or be prepared to die for it. There was nothing different in his actions. He prayed as was his custom. His example would influence the other Jews. By drawing attention to himself, he might reduce the danger for others. Daniel's faith during this ordeal was glorious and just what we would expect from a man ripened in years with God.

The officials knew that the king would not lift a finger against Daniel, so they had to trap the king. What was their bait? Notice the subtle appeal to the king's pride.

The law of Medes and Persians was unchangeable. (See Esther 1:19; 8:8.) The king saw that he had been deceived, and realizing the injustice of putting Daniel to death, did his best to avoid carrying out the law.

Contrast the edict of Darius before and after Daniel's deliverance from the den of lions (Daniel 6:26-27). Over the vast realm a proclamation went, declaring the power and greatness of Daniel's God. This scene closes with Daniel's prospering during the reign of Darius, and also on to the reign of Cyrus.

Daniel was thrown into the den of lions, but he fell into the hands of the living God. The world cannot breed a lion that God cannot tame. Shutting lions' mouths of difficulty and temptation is God's specialty.

Notice that Daniel prayed with thanksgiving. (Read Daniel 6:10; Philippians 4:6,7.) When Daniel found out that the writing was signed, he did not fall down in terror and agony, but he praised God. *Commit thy way unto the Lord; trust also in him; and he shall bring it to pass* (Psalm 37:5).

REIGN OF CYRUS (Read Daniel 10–12)

It was during the reign of Cyrus that the decree was sent out for the captives to return and build the walls of Jerusalem. (Read Ezra 1:2-4.) Daniel, now nearly ninety years old, was too aged to return. No doubt he was needed among the exiles in Babylon. Daniel had outlived all the friends and companions of his youth. Now he saw the Israelites gathering in the streets of Babylon and the aged man watched the last caravan leave the west gate of the city to return to Jerusalem. Daniel was concerned about his people. We will see how he was comforted in his perplexity. In Daniel 10 we see the vision of the glory of God.

THE LAST DAYS

In Daniel 11 we find the vision which concerns the near future of the kingdom in which Daniel was so great a personage. Three kings were yet to come in the Medo-Persian empire. Then

Alexander, the mighty king of Greece, would appear. (See Daniel 11:2,3.) His empire would be divided among his four generals as had already been predicted. The course of affairs is followed down to Antiochus Epiphanes, the "little horn" of Daniel 8. His desecration of the sanctuary is again mentioned. (See Daniel 12:11.)

Beginning with Daniel 11:36 we see the description of the final "little horn" of Daniel 7.

The great tribulation follows. How is it described in Daniel 12:1? This is a time of unparalleled trouble. Our Lord spoke of it in Matthew 24:21. What does He say? Mention is made of two resurrections. (Read Daniel 12:2.) These two will be one thousand years apart. (See Revelation 20:1-6.) The first is the resurrection of the saints at Christ's coming to life everlasting. This is followed by one thousand years, called the millennium. Then the resurrection of the wicked to shame everlasting. *Many of them that sleep in the dust of the earth shall awake, some to everlasting life, and some to shame and everlasting contempt* (Daniel 12:2). Those now that *turn many to righteousness* are given significant rewards, showing us the necessity of diligence in soul-winning during our wait for Christ's return. (See Daniel 12:3.)

DANIEL'S 70 WEEKS

The Scripture

Seventy weeks are determined upon thy people and upon thy holy city, to finish the transgression, and to make an end of sins, and to make reconciliation for iniquity, and to bring in everlasting righteousness, and to seal up the vision and prophecy, and to anoint the most Holy.

Know therefore and understand, that from the going forth of the commandment to restore and to build Jerusalem unto the Messiah the Prince shall be seven weeks, and threescore and two weeks: the street shall be built again, and the wall, even in troublous times.

And after threescore and two weeks shall Messiah be cut off, but not for Himself: and the people of the prince that shall come shall destroy the city and the sanctuary; and the end thereof shall be with a flood, and unto the end of the war desolations are determined.

And he shall confirm the covenant with many for one week: and in the midst of the week he shall cause the sacrifice and the oblation to cease, and for the overspreading of abominations he shall make it desolate, even until the consummation, and that determined shall be poured upon the desolate (Daniel 9:24-27).

The Meaning

"Week," as used here, is a poor English equivalent. "Week" means a period, doubtless of 7 years. If there be 70 seven-year periods, this is 70 x 7, or 490 years.

The Divisions

Scripture divides these 70 weeks into 3 divisions (Daniel 9:24-27) with a parenthetic time lapse for the present "Gentile rule."

"7 WEEKS"—49 years, began at the command to build and restore Jerusalem under Ezra and Nehemiah.

"62 WEEKS"—434 years, began at the building of the wall of Jerusalem, continues to the Crucifixion. Christ is *cut off, but not for Himself* (Daniel 9:25,26). At this point, after 483 years, the clock of Israel's national life stops.

("GENTILE RULE"—an unknown number of years, intervenes after the 69th week. We are in this period now, awaiting the coming of Christ.)

"70th WEEK"—7 years, not yet begun, during which God deals with Israel exclusively. Beginning after the coming of Christ, Antichrist takes power, covenants with the Jews, breaks it after half the week is up. This ushers in the time of trouble of Daniel 12:1—the Great Tribulation of Revelation. When will the 70th week begin?

Minimum Daily Requirements/Spiritual Vitamins

Sunday: DANIEL THE CAPTIVE   Daniel 1; 2
Monday: NEBUCHADNEZZAR, THE PROUD KING
    Daniel 3; 4
Tuesday: BELSHAZZAR'S REIGN   Daniel 5; 7; 8
Wednesday: DARIUS' REIGN   Daniel 6; 9
Thursday: GOD'S GLORY   Daniel 10
Friday: THE CONFLICT OF KINGS   Daniel 11
Saturday: DANIEL'S LAST MESSAGE   Daniel 12

UNDERSTANDING HOSEA, JOEL, AMOS

Jesus Christ,
Healer of the Backslider;
Restorer;
Heavenly Husbandman

With the study of Hosea's prophecy we enter upon twelve books known as the minor prophets. Remember the difference between the major and minor prophets is not a matter of importance but of the amount of material writen.

Hosea was sent to the ten northern tribes called "Israel." He prophesied in the reign of Jeroboam II of Israel. He lived in this northern kingdom, when the splendors of Jeroboam's brilliant reign of forty-one years were beginning to fade into the black midnight of Israel's captivity. He prophesied during the eighth century B.C. This was a stirring time in the world's history. Rome and Carthage were both founded during this period. Phoenician sea traffic founded the latter great city. The big Phoenician westbound ships made their terminus Tarshish, a Phoenician colony in southern Spain. But during the time of Hosea they ran northward to the tin mines of Cornwall.

Another important fact in this period was the religious reformation that Gautama introduced in India which has issued in Buddhism. It was a time of stir and change. It presented many things akin to those of the sixteenth century after Christ.

Hosea's contemporaries were Amos, Isaiah and Micah. He has been called the Jeremiah of the northern kingdom. You remember Jeremiah prophesied to Judah. In Hosea "Israel" means the ten tribes that formed the northern kingdom. "Judah" means the tribes of Judah and Benjamin that formed the southern kingdom. Hosea was not trained in a seminary (school of the prophets), but he was a layman called by God to give the distinct message to Israel that God loved them.

ISRAEL'S UNFAITHFULNESS (Read Hosea 1–3)

The hero of this book, Hosea, is one of the greatest lovers in all literature. We find his love so strong that even the worst actions of an unfaithful wife could not kill it. Read Hosea 1:1 for a bit of the personal history of the prophet. We hear God speaking His first words to Hosea Himself (Hosea 1:2). Whose son was he? The scene is laid during the closing years of the prosperous reign of Jeroboam II who was king of Israel. This statesman-prophet must have preached sixty or seventy years up to the time of the captivity of his people. The people had given no heed to Amos. Hosea knew that the country was due for a downfall, but they were not disposed to listen to him.

Turn to II Kings 15-17 and read the page of history that covers the period of the prophet. As we have already stated, it was a very unsettled time. Sin was rampant. The golden age of Jeroboam II was passing and a dark cloud hung over Israel. On the death of Jeroboam, six kings followed in quick succession. Within twenty years, four were assassinated. About the middle of Hosea's ministry a great part of the nation was carried away by the Assyrians. At the end of Hosea's life the kingdom of Israel came to an end with the fall of Samaria. The prophet lived to see his prophecies fulfilled.

We know little about Hosea other than that he had a very sad home life. The book pictures this man as gentle, frank and affectionate. He had a deep loving nature that made him attached to his home.

A STRANGE LOVE STORY

As chapter 1 opens we see a young man marrying a girl unworthy of him. He loved her truly. God told him to do something which would have been very repulsive to him. What was it? (Hosea 1:2,3). It was a severe test. But as in the case of Isaiah, he was to be a sign for Israel.

Hosea is told to marry a woman worthless in character, in fact, a harlot. God was using this for a sign to His people of how they remained the object of Jehovah's love, in spite of their sinfulness. This all seems very strange to us. But God was making this picture of His redeeming grace. Grace is unmerited favor. Here we see Israel so undeserving of Jehovah's love, yet still He is lavishing it upon them. God has not chosen the righteous but sinners. *But God commendeth his love toward us, in that, while we were yet sinners, Christ died for us* (Romans 5:8). God's dealings with Israel picture His dealings with us now. *All these things happened unto them for ensamples: and they are written for our admonition, upon whom the ends of the world are come* (I Cor. 10:11).

Hosea obeyed God and *went and took Gomer* (Hosea 1:3). His name was hers. Home, reputation, God's favor, comfort, were Gomer's. All that he had he gave her. In return, Hosea's name, domestic reputation, love were all sacrified on the altar of a shameful and worthless woman. How like our Lord Jesus this is! He not only came to us while we were yet in sin but He died the death of shame on Calvary for us that all He had might be ours. (See Titus 2:14.)

Gomer ran away from home and left her young husband, Hosea, with two little boys and a daughter to care for. Lured away by the sin about her, she fell into the moral cesspool of the day and finally was carried off a slave. Through it all Hosea was true to her. Still loving her, he tried everything to win her back to a happy family life. But she would not. What a sad picture of man's stubbornness! What a wonderful picture of God's love!

Just as Hosea was married to an unfaithful bride, Gomer, so God was married to unfaithful Israel. This experience of Hosea helped him to understand God's heart of love as He yearned over wayward Israel to come home to Him. No doubt there were tears in his voice for there was tragedy in his life. He had thrown himself wholly into his mission.

Who best can suffer, Best can do.—Milton

GOD'S BRIDE

God frequently uses marriage to symbolize His relation to Israel. *As the bridegroom rejoiceth over the bride, so shall thy God rejoice over thee* (Isaiah 62:5). And, *I am married* [a

277

husband] *unto you* (Jeremiah 3:14). Israel is Jehovah's bride while the Church is the Lamb's bride. God said of Israel, *I will betroth thee unto me forever* (Hosea 2:19). God had been true to His bride, the Jews. He had loved them, and protected them, and lavished every gift upon them. But they left God and went after other gods. They disobeyed His laws. Like Hosea's wife, they had broken their marriage vows and had fallen into slavery, sin and shame. Israel, like Gomer, had forgotten who had given her past blessings in abundance. (See Hosea 2:8.)

G. Campbell Morgan says, "Sin in the last analysis, in its most terrible form, is infidelity to love. It hurts God. It destroys the sinner."

There are differing interpretations of this part of the Book of Hosea. Some believe that Hosea was told by God to marry a sinful woman, which was done; others, that God told Hosea to marry a woman who did not go into sin until after the marriage; still others that this experience of Hosea's was only a vision, not an actual experience. In any case the undefeatable love of a true husband, to whom God likens Himself, is shown; and Israel's strange, sad, persistent backsliding is revealed.

BACKSLIDING A HISTORICAL FACT

But why should Israel's backsliding seem strange to us? Isn't it exactly what we all know about by personal experience? The history of man has been a history of backsliding, and will continue to be so, during the ages.

Creation of Man (Genesis 1:28). Man was started at the top but soon he was moving toward the bottom.

Fall of Man. Man went steadily downhill from the expulsion from Eden (Genesis 3:23) to the time of the flood.

Human Government (Genesis 8:20). Man went downhill until he tried to ignore God in exalting himself (Genesis 11:4) and the judgment of the confusion of tongues fell upon him.

Promise to Abraham (Genesis 12:1). Israel, God's chosen people, went down until they found themselves at the bottom of the hill in bondage in Egypt.

Mosaic Law Given (Exodus 19:8). Israel, during its entire national history had its ups and downs. Hosea's day pictures it.

The Word shows us that, until the end, men will sin, will break God's heart of love; but a wonderful and patient God has endured this through the centuries.

In Hosea 3:4 the present state of the Jews is described. Read it! Read it!

Ever since the destruction of Jerusalem by Titus (A.D. 70), the Jews have answered the description given here by Hosea. They have been a nation of wanderers over the face of the earth, going from nation to nation, and city to city. They are scattered, despised and often hated people. (See Deut. 28:63-65.) But notice what is happening to them today. Hosea 3:5 describes the Jew's glorious future. King, prince, sacrifice, image, ephod, and teraphim all are then restored in Christ. The Jew has a glorious future!

ISRAEL'S NATIONAL SIN AND CHASTISEMENT
(Read Hosea 4-10)

Here we hear a voice from the north where Israel dwelt (Hosea 4:1). Two hundred years before, the ten tribes had seceded from Judah and set up an independent kingdom called Israel. They began immediately worshiping idols. God had sent Elijah, then Elisha, to warn them, but in vain. They refused to return to God. Now we hear a new voice. It is Hosea! *Return unto the LORD* (Hosea 6:1)! is the much needed cry of the prophet. Return unto God and He will return unto you, is his message.

Hosea, whose name means "salvation," was poet laureate to the king. But he was more than that. He was God's voice to the people. They did not care to hear his message for his appeal was to a backslidden nation in behalf of a God grieved by His children's sins. It is well to remember that there is a name of Israel always connected with sin or backsliding. It is used thirty-seven times in this book—it is Ephraim. *O Israel, return unto the LORD thy God; for thou hast fallen by thine iniquity* (Hosea 14:1).

279

It is not more liberty we need today, but more loyalty. Do not give God ready-made plans for Him to bless. Do not make your plans and then come to Him for approval. Let Him make the plans. Israel had foolishly made their own decisions. They had become stiff-necked. God will not do anything with a rebellious spirit and a defiant will.

God's Word is a mirror. What is a mirror really for? Is it to see how well you look? No! I believe it is to see the flaws—to see what is wrong so you may correct it. *Wherewithal shall a young man cleanse his way? by taking heed thereto according to thy Word* (Psalm 119:9). *Hear the word of the LORD, ye children of Israel: for the LORD hath a controversy with you.* (Hosea 4:1).

Israel's Blacklist of Sin

"Falsehood" ....Hosea 4:1
"Licentiousness" ....Hosea 4:11
"Murder" ....Hosea 5:2
"Robbery" ....Hosea 7:1
"Oppression" ....Hosea 12:7

God's Figures for Sin

An adulterous wife...Hosea 3:1
A wine-inflamed drunkard.......................................Hosea 4:11
A backsliding heifer...Hosea 4:16
As troops of robbers..Hosea 6:9
Adulterers ....Hosea 7:4
Hot as an oven..Hosea 7:7
A cake not turned (half baked)................................Hosea 7:8
Like a silly dove...Hosea 7:11
Like a deceitful bow...Hosea 7:16
Swallowed up ....Hosea 8:8
A vessel wherein is no pleasure..............................Hosea 8:8
A wild ass..Hosea 8:9

ISRAEL'S HOPE (Read Hosea 11–14)

Light breaks over these last chapters. They give us a picture of Israel's ultimate blessings in the future kingdom. We get a glimpse into God's heart of love when He, as a father, says, *When Israel was a child, then I loved him, and called my son out of Egypt* (Hosea 11:1).

GOD'S CHOICE

As God looked over the vast and glittering expanse of empire, He did not choose Israel for His people because they were the greatest or richest of the nations of the world (Deut. 7:6-8). He rather chose a weak, unattractive slave child to be the object of His love and care and blessings (Hosea 11:1).

There lay Babylon in all her glory. She was then a strong and mighty nation and gave great promise of a powerful future. To the south was the glory of Egypt, wrapped in the rich and jewelled web of centuries which we are just now unwrapping. Even today our eyes are dazzled as we look on their splendors. The Hittites, to the north, had a culture and power, and the ships of the Phoenicians were plowing the seas. But God did not choose these. He chose a slave child in Egypt who was making bricks without straw in his awful bondage, upon whom He could lavish His love and blessing (Ex. 3).

We can never understand God's choices. He chooses the weak things of the world to confound the things that are mighty. (See I Cor. 1:27.) Whenever any one loves God, it is because He loved him first. (See I John 4:19.)

ISRAEL'S SIN

But Israel, the child who had been outwardly adopted in history at the time of the Exodus from Egypt, began to grow persistently disobedient and rebellious. The more the prophets warned them the farther they went away from God. They showed no gratitude to God for all the blessings of their land. But in their freedom they forgot God and fell into sin and idolatry and were plunging into captivity (Hosea 11:2). Israel finished her training in the slave markets of Assyria and Babylon. (Read Hosea 4:6,7.)

God has been good to us and set His love upon us and has sent us prophets and teachers and put us in the midst of resources and luxury. But the more they warn us the more we are prone to turn away, and the greater our education and learning, the more sufficient we become unto ourselves. Nations today are educating themselves away from God. So did Israel. God taught Israel that when people refuse light, the light is withdrawn. (See Hosea 5:6.)

We must understand God's attitude toward sin. He says, *The wages of sin is death* (Romans 6:23). *Be not deceived; God is not mocked: for whatsoever a man soweth, that shall he also reap* (Galatians 6:7).

God reveals to His children through Hosea that knowledge always creates responsibility. This truth is taught also by the apostle Peter. He says, *It had been better for them not to have known the way of righteousness, than, after they have known it, to turn from the holy commandment delivered unto them* (II Peter 2:21). It is a dangerous thing to play with God's grace.

THE GRACE OF GOD

We find grace abounding in the Old Testament as well as in the New.

Jehovah says to Israel here, *I drew them with cords of a man, with bands of love* (Hosea 11:4). Christ drew us with cords of a man when He became man and died for us. *I, if I be lifted up from the earth, will draw all men unto me* (John 12:32).

God has agonized over His rebellious people and will not give them up. His mercy is kindled and He says, *I will heal their backsliding, I will love them freely . . .* (Hosea 14:4). *But where sin abounded, grace did much more abound* (Romans 5:20).

God has threatened Israel with His wrath, but now God offers them grace. God appeals to Israel to return and repent. (See Hosea 14:1-3.) Then He gives them a promised blessing. (Read Hosea 14:4-8.)

In Hosea 1:11 God tells Israel that one day Judah and Israel shall be gathered together and have one head. They are looking for this Messiah to come who will be their ruler. God again promises this in Hosea 3. Read Hosea 9:17 to see the condition of the Jew today—*wanderers among the nations*. God will do more than forgive their backsliding; He will cure them and remove the cause.

Hosea 14 is the greatest chapter in the Bible for backsliders. Read the wonderful words of the Lord to backsliding Israel in Hosea 14:4, *I will heal their backsliding, I will love them freely: for mine anger is turned away from him*. God's great heart is bursting with love, but our sins keep Him from telling us all that is there. As with Israel, you may know the joy of barriers broken down and love poured out. *I will be as the dew unto Israel: he shall grow as the lily* (Hosea 14:5). The dew speaks of the presence of the Holy Spirit. See how God pictures His abiding joy in His people after they are healed.

UNDERSTANDING JOEL

Joel is considered by some to be one of the earliest of all the prophets whose writings have come down to us. He possibly would have known both Elijah and Elisha in his youth.

His personal history is stated in one verse, *The word of the LORD that came to Joel the son of Pethuel* (Joel 1:1). His name means "Jehovah is my God." His ministry was to Judah. Remember Hosea prophesied to Israel.

Joel has been called "the prophet of religious revival." He knew that revival must follow repentance. "A rent heart is followed by a rent veil and heaven." He tried to bring his people to this place. We will find access to the throne of grace and know the presence of the Holy Spirit when we truly repent.

The land of Israel had just suffered a terrible plague of locusts. They had devoured every green thing, leaving only desolation in their trail. Joel believed that this had been a judgment sent by God, because of the sin of His people. He was the first to prophesy the outpouring of the Spirit upon all flesh (Joel 2:28). Joel appears just a little before Hosea, only he speaks to the southern kingdom of Judah, while Hosea speaks to the northern tribes. His message is to us all today.

THE PLAGUE — THE WARNING (Read Joel 1)

Appalling famine, caused by an awful plague of locusts, followed by a prolonged drought, devastated the land. People and flocks were dying for lack of food and water.

Joel spoke to Judah. Using the present judgment of a plague of locusts he called his people to repentance. He wanted to spare them from greater judgments at the hands of hostile armies. The locust was a type and forerunner of the devastation they would bring.

Graphically he described the plague, calling the old men to confirm the fact that there had never been one like it before (Joel 1:2). Drunkards felt the effect of it, for the vines had been destroyed (Joel 1:5). Priests had no meat-offering, nor drink-offering of wine to offer (Joel 1:9). Cattle and sheep cried in the fields (Joel 1:20). Joel urged the people to call a fast (Joel 1:13). Then he continued to describe the plague.

Joel called the people to consider the cause of the calamity. They must mourn with true penitence if they wished to be spared further judgment. (Read Joel 2:12-17.) Desperate, they were ready to listen to anyone who could explain their plight. It was a great hour for the preacher, for now, in their extremity, men would turn to God.

THE FAST — THE PROMISE (Read Joel 2)

The blast of the ram's horn calling an assembly for a great fast opens this chapter (Joel 2:1). Everyone is there—old and young alike. Even brides and bridegrooms on their wedding day attend (Joel 2:16). The priests come in black sackcloth, and bow to the ground and cry to God within the sanctuary. *Spare thy people, O LORD,* and to the people, *Rend your heart, and not your garments, and turn unto the LORD your God* (Joel 2:13). It was an event to bring the people back to God.

The locusts had made an Eden into a desolate wilderness (Joel 2:3). For one who has not seen it, an army of locusts is an incredible thing. They fill the air and darken the sun like an eclipse (Joel 2:2). They spread for miles over the land. Armies of "soldiers" with leaders in front advance, destroying everything that is green. In a few minutes every leaf and blade is

destroyed. Others following strip the bark from the trees (Joel
1:6,7). The people dig trenches and kindle fires and beat and
burn to death heaps of insects, but the effort is utterly useless.
A land that has been devastated by locusts takes years to re-
cover (Joel 1:17-20). Their flight is heard for miles much
like a roaring fire (Joel 2:5). The land over which they pass
looks as if it had been fire-swept (Joel 2:3). After the country
is stripped, they go into cities and like mailed horsemen, they
march into houses and consume everything that can be consumed (Joel 2:4,7-9). God's promise, *I will restore to you the
years that the locust hath eaten* (Joel 2:25), becomes more
graphic in the mind when one sees the desolation wrought
by the consuming insects.

THE PROMISE OF PENTECOST

The prophet assures the people that God will indeed send
both temporal mercies (Joel 2:18-27) and spiritual blessings
(Joel 2:28-32). Yes, and God will send deliverance from the
sky! *And it shall come to pass afterward, that I will pour out my
spirit upon all flesh; and your sons and your daughters shall
prophesy, your old men shall dream dreams, your young men
shall see visions: And also upon the servants and upon the
handmaids in those days will I pour out my spirit* (Joel 2:28,
29). Here is the prophecy of Pentecost.

Spiritual deliverance is the great central promise of the Book
of Joel. Other prophets have foretold details concerning the
Lord's life on earth, and even His future reign. To Joel was
committed the privilege of telling that He would pour out His
Spirit upon all flesh. He tells us that the blessing will flow forth
from Jerusalem. (Read Joel 2:32; 3:18.) This prophecy we
are definitely told was fulfilled at Pentecost. Peter said, *This is
that which was spoken by the prophet Joel* (Acts 2:16). Read
all of Acts 2.

There is a lesson for us today. The church is in a desolate
condition. It has been laid waste by many spiritual foes, well
described in Joel 1:4. There are famine and drought on all sides.
The call goes to Christians today to go into the dust before the
Lord in true repentance of heart. This repentance must begin

with ministers and elders. If we will return unto the Lord, He will fulfill His promise to us by His outpouring of the Holy Spirit and then He will restore *the years that the locust hath eaten.* This great outpouring on Israel is future (Ezekiel 36:23-33). The great need in pulpit and pew today is the power of the Holy Spirit.

THE DAY OF THE LORD

The day of the LORD, spoken of five times in this short book, refers to judgment. It tells of a series of judgments, the present locusts, the armies of invasion which were about to come as a scourge of God upon the land, and the final day of the Lord described in the third chapter of Joel. *The day of the LORD* is the period of time from the return of the Lord in glory until the new heavens and the new earth. (See Isaiah 2:17-20; 3:7-18; 4:1,2; 13:6-9; Jer. 46:10; Malachi 4:5; I Cor. 5:5; I Thess. 5:2; II Thess. 2:2; II Peter 3:10.) *The day of the LORD* is at least one thousand years in length. (Read Revelation 20:4.)

THE BLESSING — THE FUTURE (Read Joel 3)

Joel, Judah, the Future

Enemies—Overthrown! ....Joel 3:1-15

Jerusalem—Delivered! ....Joel 3:16,17

Land—Blessed! ....Joel 3:18

Judah—Restored! ....Joel 3:19-21

Only God could have told Joel of the return of the Jews from captivity. Joel not only saw the return from Babylon, but the last regathering of the Jews from among the Gentile nations. He also tells of the judgment of the nations after the battle of Armageddon (Joel 3:2-7). (Read Matthew 25:32 and Rev. 19:17-21.) Man's day of decision is over. God's hour of destiny has arrived.

After Israel has been restored and the nations of the earth have been judged (Joel 3:1,2) then will the everlasting kingdom be set up (Joel 3:20). Once again Palestine, the land of promise, will be the center of power and the gathering place of the nations for judgment. Christ will return to establish His rule as sovereign. God will dwell in Zion. (See Joel 3:17.)

BOOK OF AMOS

Amos was from Tekoa, a small town about twelve miles south of Jerusalem. He was not a prophet nor the son of a prophet. (See Amos 7:14.) He was not a priest nor a member of the prophets' school. He was a sheepherder and dresser of the sycamore trees. He must have been educated, for his book shows literary skill. Perhaps he traveled extensively selling his wool. The places he mentions may have been scenes of his visits.

In Amos we find one of many instances in the Bible of God calling a man when he was occupied in his daily work (Amos 1:1). God called him, shepherd's crook in hand, and sent him forth to gather his straying people. Remember David was caring for his sheep and Gideon was at the threshing floor when they received their commissions.

On the wild uplands of Judah, beyond Tekoa, Amos received his training as a prophet straight from the hand of God. His beautiful writing abounds with illustrations from his mountain home. Like David, he had gazed on the stars and looked beyond to their Creator. He was not a courtier like Isaiah, nor a priest like Jeremiah, but just an ordinary working man. Though a native of Judah he prophesied in and about Israel.

Amos was not the only prophet of his day. God had sent a great galaxy of messengers to save His people from the destruction they were inevitably facing. No doubt, as a boy, he had known Jonah, and possibly Elisha. Hosea was his co-worker. These men surely knew each other well. Maybe they had gone on evangelistic campaigns together. When Amos' work was coming to a close, Isaiah and Micah appeared. These men, when boys, might have heard Amos preach on one of his tours. These younger prophets would have received much from this champion of Jehovah.

Amos prophesied while Uzziah was on the throne of Judah, and Jeroboam II was king of Israel. This was a time of great prosperity. The old boundaries of the kingdom of David were gained back. Money poured in and armies were victorious. Amos and Hosea were prophets to Israel (northern kingdom) and Isaiah and Micah to the southern kingdom of Judah.

Under these two kings mentioned above the two kingdoms reached the summit of their prosperity (II Chronicles 26 and II Kings 14:25). Assyria had not yet risen as a conquering world power. The idea of the approaching doom of their kingdoms seemed utterly improbable to Israel. They were enjoying a period of peace. The surrounding nations were not strong enough to give them trouble. (See Amos 6:1-13.) All they thought of was pleasure and having a good time (Amos 2:6-8; 5:11,12; 6:4-6). God tried to arouse His people to a sense of their danger, hence He sent two witnesses, Hosea and Amos.

Amos feared God so much that he feared no one else at all. "Amos proclaimed a message so far ahead of his time that most of the human race, and a large part of all Christendom have not yet caught up with it," so says a modern student of Amos, the herdsman of Tekoa, whose daring words date back some eight hundred years before our Lord.

Such courage was no more heeded in Israel's time than in ours today. Of course you will find among the evils which Amos denounced some of the very same that prevail in our day. Here you find his voice raised against intemperance, in a far larger sense than merely excessive use of wine. Were he speaking primarily to our day, he would raise his voice in thundering tones against this abuse which has increased practices of intemperance unknown and undreamed of by the luxurious lives of Israel. But the secret of all such sin is revealed in Amos' words because the children of Israel have rejected the law of Jehovah, and have not kept His statutes.

The law of our beloved country will be kept when we learn to keep the law of God. The law of God is fulfilled in love.

Character Sketch

Amos was humble—in not hiding his station in life.

Amos was wise—in not preaching over the heads of the people.

Amos was clever—in catching people's fancy by judging their enemies first.

Amos was fearless—in not tickling the ear, but telling the truth.

Amos was faithful—"Thus saith the Lord" was his message.

This raw young herdsman, Amos, had a certain rugged frankness about him that was refreshing. He always hit straight from the shoulder (1:2). He didn't fail to tell even King Jeroboam II what he should do. God wanted someone to bear His message courageously, and Amos did not fail Him. Israel needed a prophet who would tear the scales from their eyes and let them know the sure consequences of their idolatry, and Amos fearlessly set them forth. God abhors sin. Sin must be punished. Men must suffer!

Jeroboam had brought Israel to the zenith of her power. The kingdom was flourishing and was at peace with her enemies. About the most unpopular man would be a "calamity howler," and Amos knew that is what they would call him if he delivered God's message. David before Goliath could not have been more courageous than Amos before Jeroboam, the idolater, "who made Israel to sin." Hear him in some of his unique figures of speech.

Neither shall he stand that handleth the bow (2:15), Amos prophesied. Jeroboam's stalwart archers were accustomed to press forward upon the enemy. They never gave in. What foolishness to talk of the unerring archers of Israel failing to stand anywhere at anytime!

And he that is swift of foot shall not deliver himself, Amos went on. What? Shall Israel's fleet-footed runners be using their speed to run away from battle? Has this insolent prophet gone crazy?

Neither shall he that rideth the horse deliver himself, thunders the messenger. There were no horsemen in all the world like Jeroboam's invincible cavalry.

But the climax is reached in these words of Amos, *Thus saith the LORD; as the shepherd taketh out of the mouth of the lion two legs, or a piece of an ear; so shall the children of Israel be taken out that dwell in Samaria in the corner of a bed* (3:12). This sounded like mockery! The idea of powerful Israel being likened to a poor sheep—or rather the fragments of a poor eaten sheep!

Yet this is what came to pass! In less than fifty years Israel was utterly destroyed, and the pitiful remnant of her people were not even as the leg of a sheep taken from the jaw of the devourer. Such is the picture of God's abhorrence of sin.

To every question as to why great empires have fallen, the answer is sin. The secret of a great man's undoing is sin. Let Amos help you see sin in its true light.

If a ship at sea follows a wrong course, what happens? Yes, some sort of trouble, and wreckage in the end. But what of a captain that follows a wrong course knowingly? Something is wrong with his mind. No wonder prophets like Amos spoke plainly in warning people about the wrong course of sin.

JUDGMENT AGAINST NATIONS (Read Amos 1; 2)

This simple country preacher left his home in Judah and traveled twenty-two miles to Bethel in the northern kingdom to preach to the kingdom of Israel. Why did God send him to Bethel? Surely Jerusalem needed his ministry. But God wanted the kingdom of Israel to have a strong word of warning. Bethel was the religious capital of the northern kingdom. Idolatry was there. They had substituted calf-worship for Jehovah. The people felt no need of preaching. (See I Kings 12:25-33.)

Amos started his preaching to the assembled crowds at Bethel, for it was a sacred feast day, by proclaiming the Lord's judgment upon six neighboring nations—Damascus (Syria), Gaza (Philistia), Tyrus (Phoenicia), Edom, Ammon, and Moab. Then he came nearer home and pronounced judgment against Judah (Amos 2:4), and against Israel itself (Amos 2:6), and finally the whole nation (Amos 3:12). Amos' approach was clever. We are always willing to hear of our enemy's doom. Our own is harder to swallow, but we are forced to take it with our enemy.

When the people doubted his authority, Amos gave a series of seven questions to show that the Lord revealed His secret to him. Therefore he must prophesy (Amos 3:3-8).

Amos denounced the sin of Israel more graphically than Hosea (chapter 2). He spoke of their careless ease and luxury, their oppression of the poor, the lying and cheating that existed, and worse than all, their hypocrisy in worship. The Lord grieved over His people not heeding His warnings. *Yet have ye not returned unto me, saith the LORD* (Amos 4:6). Then the invitation, *Seek ye me, and ye shall live* (Amos 5:4).

The book opens with judgments on the nations surrounding Israel:

Damascus threatened because it had invaded Israel (Amos 1:3; II Kings 10:32,33).

Gaza and Tyrus for conspiracy with Edom in its invasion of Judah (Amos 1:6,9; II Chron. 21:16,17; 28:18).

Edom for continuing hostility (Amos 1:11; compare Obadiah 10-12).

Ammon for attacking Gilead (Amos 1:13).

Moab for heathen practices (Amos 2:1; II Kings 3:27).

Judah for neglect of God's law (Amos 2:4; II Chron. 3-19; II Kings 25:9).

Israel for her unrighteousness (Amos 2:6; II Kings 17:17-23).

The nations of the world, no matter how powerful they may be, cannot withstand the judgments of God. God sets up kingdoms and brings them down. The mighty power of the Pharaohs has come to naught. Napoleon thought he could rule the world but he languished in St. Helena. The Kaiser thought he could act independently of God and he was soon brought low. In World War II there were monarchs who thought they could stamp out God's chosen people and set themselves up as rulers of the earth, but hinderers of God's ultimate plan are always brought low (Psalm 2).

JUDGMENT AGAINST ISRAEL (Read Amos 3–6)

Amos was called to tell of certain punishment (Amos 3). If men will reject the repeated warning of God, they must be punished (Amos 5).

Amos told Israel they were greedy, unjust, unclean, and pro-

fane (Amos 2:6-12) and that they defended and excused themselves on the ground that they were God's chosen people
(Amos 3:2). He reminded them that this made their sin the
greater. The Israelites looked at their relationship to God differently. They saw it as merely an outward and formal thing.
They boasted that they were the chosen nation and no real evil
could befall them. We see many professing Christians today in
the same danger. They imagine their salvation is secured by
their being members of a church. They are conferring a favor
upon God and He cannot condemn them. (Read Amos 5:21,23,
24.)

The first of God's punishments concern the sins of six of the
heathen nations that surround Israel. Then the prophet passes
on to Judah and Israel. The sin of Judah had been her contempt
of God's law, expressed in her idolatry. Only during the exile
was Judah freed of this sin. The punishment of Judah was fulfilled in the destruction of Jerusalem by Nebuchadnezzar
(Amos 2:5).

Amos condemned Israel. Israel was a chosen nation. They
knew God's law. Therefore their sin was the greater. Amos told
them about their injustice in the administration of the law. They
sold the righteous for silver. He enumerated their evil oppression.
They had forgotten righteousness. The rich were cruel and they
longed to see the poor oppressed. Even among Christians today
we find wealth often counts more than character. Nothing is
more dangerous in the church than influence and power given to
those who have wealth but no Christian scruples.

Amos called the women of his day "kine of Bashan" because
they only cared for luxury and worldly pleasures (Amos 4:1).
This is the prophet's picture of the cruel, heartless, brainless
women—a herd of kine, heavy, heedless animals treading on all
in their way as they seek to gratify their appetites.

Even the religious sacrifices and feasts of the people became
an abomination. God said, *I hate . . . your feasts* (see Amos
5:21). When they made their pilgrimages from Gilgal to Bethel,
they only sinned the more for it was merely an outward form
mixed with idolatry (Amos 5:4-6). God demands conduct

worthy of Himself, not just empty sacrifices. Amos called attention to how God had sent drouth, plagues and earthquakes. Still they did not repent.

God always warns before a punishment, yes, and offers a way of escape. God denounces sin, but He offers a remedy for sin. Israel's rejection of repeated warnings should lead them to prepare for God's judgment (Amos 5). If Israel had sought the Lord, the "day of the Lord" spoken of in Amos 5:20 would not have overtaken them. They did not seek Him and Assyrian fighters ushered in that day.

Amos Tells of Israel's Coming Judgment in 5 Visions

The Devouring Locust..Amos 7:1-3

In the first vision the prophet sees green fields, and, *behold he* [God] *formed grasshoppers* . . . and they destroyed the grass. Amos prays: *By whom shall Jacob arise?* [Who will deliver her?] God answers: *It* [the famine] *shall not be.*

The Consuming Fire..Amos 7:4-6

In this vision, fire so terrible as to consume the waters and the land is seen. Amos prays: *By whom shall Jacob arise?* God answers: *It also* [the fire] *shall not be.*

The Searching Plumbline..Amos 7:7-11

In this vision Amos sees God measuring the city for destruction. The measuring revealed how far out of line Israel was. This time Amos has not the heart even to pray. Israel's judgment was certain—*I will not again pass by them any more.*

The Summer Fruit-Basket..Amos 8

"Summer fruit" of the fourth vision was that which was "soon to perish." The basket revealed the sad truth that Israel, like a basket of overripe fruit, looked fine, outwardly, but was rotting at the heart. The guilty nation was "ripe" for judgment.

The Lord at the Altar..Amos 9:1-10

The last vision shows God standing upon the altar, bidding Amos to break the doorposts and shower the fragments over the peoples' heads. All the worshipers are to be scattered and slain by the sword. This speaks of final dispersion. The visions end with judgment, but God closes the book with a bright outlook.

VISIONS REGARDING THE FUTURE (Read Amos 7–9)

We do not know how long Amos preached in Bethel but we know that throngs heard his fearless message. When he spoke of the doom of the surrounding nations, they were drawn to him and they cheered him to the last echo.

Then Amaziah, the priest of Bethel, could not stand up against Amos' preaching. So backed by the king, the priest rebuked Amos. Listen to the report he sent to the king: *Amos hath conspired against thee in the midst of the house of Israel: the land is not able to bear all his words. For thus Amos saith, Jeroboam shall die* (Amos 7:10,11). Amaziah told Amos to go back and mind his own business.

Amos was silenced by the false prophet. He was driven from Israel. Freedom of speech was not given the true prophet of God. Neither Elijah nor Amos were safe in Israel. When Amos found that Israel would not hear him, he returned to Judah and put his writings in a book so all the people could read and understand it.

Amos, as do most of the prophets, tells us of a bright future for God's chosen people. The whole land will once more be a kingdom under the house of David (Amos 9:11,12). The tabernacle of David, now torn down, shall be rebuilt (Acts 15:16,17). Israel shall be restored to her land and prosper. A happy people shall dwell in a happy land.

Always keep in mind that the Jew, today scattered over the face of the world, is being gathered back to her land of promise. National prosperity will again flourish. Jerusalem shall be the capital of a mighty kingdom. Converted Israel shall be God's witnesses (Amos 9:13-15).

Men need such dealing as Amos gives at times when sin abounds. We get to be too tender and gentle with the common sins of the people. We forget how to denounce; we lose the power of righteous indignation.

Not so with Amos, plumbline prophet that he was. The crooked wall always hates the straight line. So men hated Amos. They will hate us if we speak out. Nevertheless learn to speak, no matter what it costs. Recall here the Man with the scourge of small cords purging the temple (John 2:13-16).

Repentance is not just an easy or jaunty turning to God and saying, "I'm sorry." Not even the truest repentance can remit sin. Redemption is costly. Christ has paid the price. Salvation is the establishment of a personal relationship between the individual person and God. Nothing can take the place of that. (See John 1:12.)

Minimum Daily Requirements/Spiritual Vitamins

Sunday: ISRAEL'S WILFUL IGNORANCE   Hosea 4
Monday: ISRAEL'S GLORIOUS FUTURE
    Hosea 3; 14
Tuesday: PUNISHMENT AND BLESSING   Joel 2
Wednesday: THE RESTORATION OF ISRAEL   Joel 3
Thursday: PERSONAL ADMONITIONS
    Amos 3:1-7; 4:6-12
Friday: THE PROPHET'S INTERCESSION
    Amos 7:1-17; 8:1-7
Saturday: FUTURE KINGDOM BLESSINGS
    Amos 9:1-15

CHAPTER 23

UNDERSTANDING OBADIAH, JONAH, MICAH

Jesus Christ,
Our Saviour;
Our Resurrection and Life;
Witness Against
Rebellious Nations

Petra is one of the wonders of the world. It was a city unique of its kind among the works of men. It perched like an "eagle's nest" (Obadiah 4) amid inaccessible mountain fastnesses. Its only approach was through a deep rock cleft more than a mile long with massive cliffs more than seven hundred feet high rising on either side. The city was able to withstand any invasion. We are told that its temples numbered a thousand. They were cut out of the pink rock on the side of the massive cliffs. The dwellings were mostly caves hewn out of the soft red sandstone (Obadiah 3,6) and placed where you can hardly believe it possible for a human foot to climb.

South of the Dead Sea and on the western border of the Arabian plateau lies a range of precipitous red sandstone heights, known as Mount Seir. It is here that Esau settled after he had sold his birthright to his brother Jacob. Having driven out the Horites (see Genesis 14:5-6), he occupied the whole of the mountain. Read Deuteronomy 2:12. These Horites are first spoken of in the time of Abraham (Genesis 14:5,6). Sela, or Petra, "Rock," was their capital. Today it is called "the silent city of the forgotten past."

The descendants of Esau were called Edomites. They would go out on raiding expeditions, and then retreat to their impregnable fortress where they kept alive in their hearts a bitter enmity toward the Jews, that began with Jacob and Esau. They never failed in helping any army who attacked the Jews. During the period of the Maccabees they became bitter enemies of the Jews. And in the time of Christ, through Herod they obtained control of Judea. They disappear from the pages of history after the destruction of Jerusalem by Titus in A.D. 70.

This book is the shortest in the Old Testament. It contains only twenty-one verses, but it includes two important themes—the doom of the proud and rebellious and the deliverance of the meek and humble.

It is directly spoken to Edom and Zion and represents Esau and Jacob, the two sons of Isaac. But it appeals to us all with our two natures—the earthly represented by Esau on one side, so proud and bold, and the spiritual, by Jacob, chosen and set apart by God. The story of the bitter family feud that takes us back to the days of the two brothers, Jacob and Esau, unfolds before us.

THE DOOM OF EDOM (Read Obadiah 1–16)

Of the prophet who wrote this book we know nothing. His contemporary was Jeremiah. We find the occasion of this prophecy as we read it in Obadiah 11—*In the day that thou* [the Edomites] *stoodest on the other side, in the day that the strangers carried away captive his forces, and foreigners entered into his gates, and cast lots upon Jerusalem, even thou wast as one of them.* No doubt, it was the awful day when Nebuchadnezzar took Jerusalem and reduced it to a desolate heap. The Edomites had helped the marauders by catching the fleeing Israelites, treating them with cruelty, and selling them as slaves.

This prophecy was written because of this confederacy against Jerusalem in which Edom took the part of the enemy (Obadiah 7-14). Against this people the prophecy of the unknown prophet Obadiah, "a worshiper of Jehovah," was directed. Edom looked on while Jerusalem was being plundered. They seemed to manifest fiendish delights in the calamity that overtook its inhabitants.

We read the denunciation of the selfish, indifferent and presently hostile spirit of nearby Edom! She, holding the attitude of Esau, remained aloof and allowed Jerusalem to be despoiled. She even became party in the destruction and went in for her part of the spoils.

God had commanded Israel, *Thou shalt not abhor an*

Edomite; for he is thy brother (Deut. 23:7). But Edom had shown an implacable hatred to Israel from the time that Israel was refused a passage through Edom on the way to Canaan (Numbers 20:14-21) to the day of the destruction of Jerusalem by the Chaldeans, when Edom cried, *Raze it, raze it* (Psalm 137:7).

Because of the pride and cruel hatred of Edom, her utter destruction was decreed (Obadiah 3,4,10). Nothing could save the guilty nation. The people were driven from their rocky home five years after the destruction of Jerusalem, when Nebuchadnezzar, passing down the valley of Arabah, which formed the military road to Egypt, crushed the Edomites. They lost their existence as a nation about 150 B.C., and their name perished with the capture of Jerusalem by the Romans. *As thou hast done, it shall be done unto thee* (Obadiah 15).

ZION'S DELIVERANCE (Read Obadiah 17–21)

The book closes with the promise of deliverance for Zion. *And the house of Jacob shall possess their possessions* (Obadiah 17). The first step in the future reestablishment of the Jews is the recovery of what was previously their own.

God's chosen people had just been carried into captivity by Nebuchadnezzar; the holy land was deserted; and God had told Edom of her doom. Jeremiah gave this same prophecy in chapter 49. Both Jeremiah and Obadiah had probably said these things many times. Five years later Edom fell before the same Babylon she had helped. She would be as though she had never been, swallowed up forever. This was the prophecy against Edom. But Israel shall rise again from her present fall. She will possess not only her own land, but also Philistia and Edom. She will finally rejoice in the holy reign of the promised Messiah. God's chosen people, the Jews, shall possess their possessions and among the dearest to them is their Holy Land. Obadiah, as the other prophets, predicts the coming of the day of the Lord and the establishment of Messiah's kingdom. Remember a Christian, too, is an heir of promises to be fulfilled when Christ comes. The believer possesses all things in Christ. (Read II Cor. 6:10.)

God's judgment on Edom as Israel's notable enemy should warn nations today that God has not cast off His people and that nations that oppress them will surely bring down His judgments. (Read Genesis 12:3.)

UNDERSTANDING JONAH

Jonah was a native of Gath-hepher, a town about an hour's distance from Nazareth. Jewish legend tells us that he was the son of the widow of Sarepta whom Elijah brought to life. Whether this is true or not we do not know, but he probably was a disciple of the great Elisha and succeeded him as a prophet.

Jonah lived in the reign of Jeroboam II and aided him in making the northern kingdom of Israel very powerful and prosperous. (See II Kings 14:25.) Jonah was a famous statesman.

For the past half century we have been living in an age that has created a certain attitude toward the Book of Jonah. It is impossible to open the book and take a reading from it anywhere without people's thoughts centering upon a fish! Men have been so busy with tape lines trying to find the dimensions of the fish's belly that they seem to have had no time to plumb the depths of the teaching of the book. Be sure to read this short book through. Many stumble over this book. Few know it.

God is in this book. He is taking care of His prophet. God is working. Find the statement four times concerning Him.

God Prepared

A great fish	Jonah 1:17
A gourd	Jonah 4:6
A worm	Jonah 4:7
A vehement east wind	Jonah 4:8

Jonah is the test book of the Bible. It challenges our faith. Our attitude toward Jonah reveals our attitude toward God and His Word. Is the story of Jonah mere naturalism or supernaturalism? Right here we stand or fall.

Jesus Christ Himself made the book of Jonah important. When He was asked for a sign to prove His claims, He would give the people only the sign of the prophet Jonah. (Read Matthew 12:38-40.)

There are two events of great importance in Jonah. One is the great fish swallowing Jonah and the other the possibility of such a large heathen city as Nineveh being converted by an obscure foreign missionary in just a few days. See what Jesus said in Matthew 12:41.

AN OBSTINATE PROPHET (Read Jonah 1; 2)

As the book opens God is speaking to Jonah, giving him his commission. *Arise, go to Nineveh, that great city, and cry against it; for their wickedness is come up before me* (Jonah 1:2).

God is very definite with His orders. He told Jonah to arise and go. *But Jonah rose up to flee unto Tarshish from the presence of the LORD, and went down to Joppa* (Jonah 1:3). He said "no" to God. Why did he flee? Read Jonah 4:2. Jonah knew that Assyria was Israel's dreaded enemy. Just at this period in history Assyria seems to have been somewhat weakened in power. It was then that God told him to go to the capital of that hostile country and pronounce judgment against it for its great wickedness. Jonah fears that Nineveh may repent and be spared impending doom. If Assyria falls, Jonah's own beloved Israel may escape judgment at Assyria's hands. Jonah has the spirit of a national hero. He decides to sacrifice himself in order to save his people, but his heroism is sadly misguided.

Nineveh was one of the greatest cities of the world, situated on the east bank of the Tigris, four hundred miles from the Mediterranean. It was the capital of Assyria (Genesis 10:11,12). The stronghold of the city was about thirty miles long and ten miles wide. It was marvelous in appearance. There were five walls and three moats (canals) surrounding it. The walls were one hundred feet high and allowed four chariots to be driven abreast. There were palaces great and beautiful with the finest of gardens. Fifteen gates guarded by colossal lions and bulls opened into the city. There were seventy halls decorated magnificently in alabaster and sculpture. The temple in the city was in the form of a great pyramid which glittered in the sun. The city was as great in wickedness as it was in wealth and power. Intellectual attainments were almost incredible.

As soon as Jonah fled, God began to act. He *sent out* [or hurled] *a great wind into the sea, and there was a mighty tempest in the sea* . . . (Jonah 1:4). God loved Jonah too much to let him prosper. Failure never relieves us of responsibility to serve.

Read events that took place before the throwing of Jonah into the sea (Jonah 1:3-15). Jonah was cast into the sea, but he was gripped by the hand of God (Jonah 1:17). God's way is best. If we don't accept it, He forces strange things upon us.

The story of Jonah 2 tells us how Jonah came to the end of himself. After much praying he confessed that he could do nothing by himself. *Salvation is of the LORD* (Jonah 2:9). Then God could afford to set him at liberty (Jonah 2:10).

AN OBEDIENT PROPHET (Read Jonah 3; 4)

God gave Jonah another chance to be of service. *And the word of the LORD came unto Jonah the second time.* How foolish he was to make the Lord repeat His call! How much better to obey at once!

God said again, *Arise, go unto Nineveh, that great city, and preach unto it the preaching that I bid thee* (Jonah 3:2).

It was not easy for Jonah to go through the streets and cry, *Yet forty days, and Nineveh shall be overthrown* (Jonah 3:4). There was no mercy in his message. There was no tear in the prophet's voice. He was obeying God but his heart was unchanged. (See Jonah 4:1-3.) The common people of Nineveh repented first. Then the nobles followed. This is always true. Revival starts among the people. Think of a city like Chicago repenting and turning to God in one day because of the preaching of a modern prophet. It would be a miracle of the ages. But this is what happened when Jonah preached in his day.

OBEDIENT BUT PERPLEXED

Look at him sulking, as he sits out on the hill on the east side of the city under a gourd that God "prepared" for a shadow over his head, waiting to see what God would do (Jonah 4:6).

The book ends abruptly! But we must notice two things in this book. First, Jonah is a type of Christ in His death, burial and resurrection. *As Jonas was three days and three nights in the whale's belly; so shall the Son of man be three days and three nights in the heart of the earth* (Matthew 12:40). Second, Jonah is also a type of Israel—disobedient to God, swallowed by the nations of the world, who will yet give her up when Christ comes. Then shall Israel be witnesses of God everywhere.

No doubt, two things hindered Jonah when God told him to go to Nineveh—his pride of self and his scorn of the rest of the world. God took this out of him in the fish's belly.

Jonah, Type of Israel

Jonah was called to a world mission. So was Israel.

Jonah refused to fulfill his mission by obeying God. So did Israel.

Jonah was punished by being cast into the sea. Israel by being scattered among the nations.

Jonah was preserved. So is Israel.

Jonah repented and was cast out of the fish and restored to life. Israel shall be cast out by all the nations and restored to her former position.

Jonah, obedient to God, goes on his mission. Israel in obedience shall become a witness to all the earth.

Jonah was blessed in that Nineveh was brought to salvation. Israel shall be blessed in the conversion of the whole world.

UNDERSTANDING MICAH

Micah was a country preacher who lived in the days of Isaiah and Hosea. His home was about twenty miles south of Jerusalem in the town of Morasthite on the Philistine border. He was preaching there the same time that Isaiah was preaching in

Jerusalem and Hosea in Israel. Micah was a prophet of the common people and of country life; Isaiah preached to the court in the city of Jerusalem. Micah knew his fellow countrymen well. Read what he says his real equipment is. *But truly I am full of power by the spirit of the LORD, and of judgment, and of might, to declare unto Jacob his transgression, and to Israel his sin* (Micah 3:8). Micah prophesied concerning Samaria, the capital of Israel, and Jerusalem, the capital of Judah, but the burden of his prophecy was for Judah. The times in which he lived were difficult. Oppression was within the walls and foes were coming from without. The condition was the same both in the kingdom of Judah and in the kingdom of Israel. The kings Jotham, Ahaz and Hezekiah, reigned during Micah's day.

The prophet denounced the social sins of his day (Micah 2:2). Micah felt keenly these social evils. He saw the unfair treatment of the poor by the rich. He felt that these sins cried up to heaven. No class was free from corrupting influences; princes, priests and people alike were all affected. (Read Micah 2:2,8,9,11; 3:1-3,5,11.) Micah makes them all smart under the lash. Micah wanted the people to know that every cruel act to one's fellow man was an insult to God. God is offended by the conduct of the people and the rulers. In spite of the state of things the people tried to carry on their religious observances. Micah shows the uselessness of all this (Micah 6:7,8).

The northern kingdom of Israel was taken into captivity during Micah's lifetime. Israel would not heed the warning of the prophets. Judah did, and was spared for one hundred fifty years. Micah knew that national sins would lead to national downfall. *Righteousness exalteth a nation: but sin is a reproach to any people* (Proverbs 14:34).

The Book of Micah seems to be divided into three parts, each beginning with, "Hear ye" (Micah 1:2; 3:1; 6:1). And each closes with a promise.

1. A promise of deliverance................................Micah 2:12,13
2. A promise to overthrow the
   enemies in the land...................................Micah 5:10,15
3. A fulfillment of promise to Abraham................Micah 7:20

Catalogue of National Sins

Passages Concerning Christ

Micah Is Quoted on Three Occasions

By the elders of Judah—Jeremiah 26:18 quoting Micah 3:12.

By magi coming to Jerusalem—Matthew 2:5,6 quoting Micah 5:2.

By Jesus when sending out the twelve—Matthew 10:35,36 quoting Micah 7:6.

See also Isaiah 2:2-4; 41:15; Ezekiel 22:27; Zephaniah 3:19.

GOD'S REMNANT

The word "remnant" is used often by the prophets. What does it mean? Remnant means the small part of the nation that God always preserves for Himself. (See Micah 2:12; 4:7; 5:3,7,8; 7:18.)

A MESSAGE TO THE PEOPLE CONCERNING ISRAEL'S SIN (Read Micah 1; 2)

As the book opens we hear the cry, *Hear, all ye people;*

305

Hearken, O earth, and all that therein is: and let the Lord GOD be witness against you (Micah 1:2).

God is not asleep. He knows the sad condition of His people. He will sit in judgment upon His people. Yes, the Lord was coming to call Israel to judgment because of her wrongs. Samaria and Jerusalem were pronounced guilty before the great Judge of the universe. Captivity and exile were their fate. God rebuked them for social injustice, unfaithfulness, dishonesty, and idolatry. What were their sins? (See Micah 2:1-11; 1:6-9.)

Micah told them that Samaria, the capital of Israel, would fall. (See Micah 1:6,7.) A similar judgment would come upon Judah. Judah's sin is described as an incurable wound. Some kinds of disease are cured only by destruction. All Judah's people shall be taken captive, for God finds incurable oppression, violence and injustice. Notice the towns of Judah mentioned in the last verses of Micah. Look at the map and you will see that they all surround the prophet's hometown.

The idolatry of Israel spread rapidly to Jerusalem and the strong city of Lachish (Micah 1:13). It was this awful spread of idolatry and all its terrible evils, to Judah, under King Ahaz, that Micah especially denounced. The oppression of the poor (Micah 2:2), and women and little children being driven from their homes (Micah 2:9) were also rebuked by the prophet. The sins of the people are stated in blunt frankness in Micah 2:1-11. God will bring suffering and shame upon them for their unscrupulous use of power.

More and more we are realizing the social value of the gospel of the Lord Jesus Christ. Wherever this gospel goes we find conditions bettered and a brotherhood which is based on sonship. Heart worship of God always issues in practical demonstrations of changed lives. Missionaries all bear witness of this in a most wonderful way.

A MESSAGE TO THE RULERS CONCERNING THE COMING CHRIST (Read Micah 3–5)

Hear . . . O heads of Jacob, and ye princes of the house of Israel (Micah 3:1). What does God say of them? Read Micah 3:1-4. God likens their covetousness and self-aggrandizement, even at the price of blood, to cannibalism. The leaders are devouring the poor, defenseless people (Micah 3:2,3).

The nation was ready to collapse and the princes and priests were responsible for it. God denounces the sin of the rulers (Micah 3:9), the bribery among the judges (Micah 3:11), false weights and balances. God describes these men in Micah 3:5. *The prophets that make my people err, that bite with their teeth, and cry, Peace.*

Micah, brokenhearted, tells of God's judgment upon Judah for their sins. Jerusalem and its temple will be destroyed (Micah 3:12; 7:13). The people of Judah will be taken captive to Babylon (Micah 4:10). But he seems to hasten over words of judgment, and to linger over the message of God's love and mercy. God will bring His people back from captivity (Micah 4:1-8; 7:11; 14-17). Micah was a prophet of hope. He always looked beyond doom and punishment to the day of glory when Christ Himself shall reign, when peace shall cover the earth. God gives the promise. The Messiah will come. He will be born in Bethlehem (Micah 4:8; 5:2-4).

Then Israel will be gathered from the nations into which she has been scattered (Micah 4:6). Oh, that the Prince of Peace might come soon and make all these things come to pass. We pray with John on the isle of Patmos, *Even so, come, Lord Jesus* (Rev. 22:20).

Little Bethlehem, smallest among the towns of Judah, shall be signally honored by the birth of God's Messiah, Jesus Christ, our Lord. His victories shall not be won by might nor by power but by His Spirit. He comes as a little babe to bring salvation to a world so in need of a Redeemer. This seven-hundred-year-old prophecy from Micah 5:2-5 led the wise men to Jerusalem to seek the new King.

A MESSAGE TO THE CHOSEN PEOPLE CONCERNING GOD'S ARGUMENT (Read Micah 6; 7)

Hear ye, O mountains, the Lord's controversy, and ye strong foundations of the earth: for the Lord hath a controversy with his people, and he will plead with Israel (Micah 6:2). God is pictured as one bringing a law-suit against His people.

They had ignored God. He told them to remember how good He had been to them and how He had kept His covenant with them (Micah 6:3).

The people, conscience-smitten, asked how they could please God. Frantically they asked if burnt offerings would do (Micah 6:6,7).

Man is always trying to get back in the good graces of God with some outward religious service or some material goods. But remember *the sacrifices of God are a broken spirit: a broken and a contrite heart, O God, thou wilt not despise* (Psalm 51:17). God wants righteous conduct, and a real personal experience of Him in each life. Because of unrighteous conduct the people had to suffer unbelievable consequences. God is a righteous Judge (Micah 1:3,5; 3:12). What does the apostle Paul tell us to do in return for God's mercies? (Read Romans 12:1,2.) The best way to get back in God's graces is to accept God's grace.

SIMPLE ESSENTIALS OF REAL RELIGION

The Old Testament gives us a definition of religion. What does God require of thee? (Read Micah 6:8.)

How does this compare with man's present-day definitions of "religion"?

Do justly—good ethics in all of life.

Love mercy—consideration for others, when justice has not been done.

Walk humbly with thy God—personal experience with God.

Paul would call this *the mind of Christ. Let this mind be in you, which was also in Christ Jesus* (Philippians 2:5). If our religion is only a great creed, grand cathedrals and elaborate rituals, then we have nothing. All must be filled with the mind of Christ. We must *worship him in spirit and in truth* (John 4:24). Christ wants us to have more than a beautiful creed even if it is spiritual and true. He wants this spirit of Christ to be lived out through our daily lives and to be exhibited in all our conduct, in our homes, and in our business. Can our religion stand this test?

It is interesting that when Christ summed up the same matter (Matthew 23:23), He used the words judgment, mercy and faith. He thus equated *faith* with *walking humbly with our God,* an apt comparison.

God's Government

Jerusalem, capital of Christ's Kingdom............Micah 4:1,2
Universal, extent of Christ's Kingdom...................Micah 4:2
Peace, keynote of Christ's Kingdom ....Micah 4:3
Prosperity, blessing of Christ's Kingdom............Micah 4:4
Righteousness, basis of Christ's Kingdom ......Micah 4:5; 4:2

Minimum Daily Requirements/Spiritual Vitamins

Sunday: DOOM AND DELIVERANCE   Obadiah 1–21
Monday: A FISH STORY   Jonah 1; 2
Tuesday: AN OBEDIENT PROPHET   Jonah 3; 4
Wednesday: A MESSAGE TO THE PEOPLE
        Micah 1; 2
Thursday: A MESSAGE TO THE RULERS
        Micah 3; 4
Friday: THE BIRTH AND REJECTION OF THE KING
        Micah 5
Saturday: A MESSAGE TO THE CHOSEN PEOPLE
        Micah 6; 7

UNDERSTANDING NAHUM, HABAKKUK, ZEPHANIAH

Jesus Christ,
a Stronghold
in the Day of Trouble;
the God of My Salvation;
a Jealous Lord

Nahum, the writer of this book, was a native of Elkosh. In Assyria, near the ruins of Nineveh, there is a tomb which the natives point to as Nahum's. But most authorities think that this Elkosh was in Galilee. Today it lies in ruins.

In name and in message "Nahum" means "comfort" for Judah. *The LORD is good, a stronghold in the day of trouble; and he knoweth them that trust in him* (Nahum 1:7). Deliverance for Judah and destruction for their enemy, Assyria, was God's great theme for His people. That Capernaum, where Christ the Comforter wrought so many works, means "village of Nahum" (comfort) is noteworthy. Nearby is the town where he was born, Elkosh.

Nahum was probably a native of Galilee, and lived at the time of the good King Hezekiah and the great prophet Isaiah. No doubt, when the cruel Assyrians invaded his country and carried away the ten tribes of Israel, he escaped into the southern kingdom of Judah. He probably took up his residence in Jerusalem, where seven years later, he witnessed the siege of that city by Sennacherib that ended with the miraculous destruction of the Assyrian host. You remember 185,000 perished in one night, as II Kings 19:35 records. It may be that Nahum 1:2 refers to this. Shortly after this event Nahum wrote his book.

The theme of this book is the destruction of Nineveh, the city that Jonah warned. Nineveh is a culprit and God is sending Nahum to declare His righteous judgment upon her. In judging Nineveh, we see God judging a sinning world. Nahum was written about one hundred fifty years after the revival of

Jonah's day when the city of Nineveh was brought to repentance in "dust and ashes." Mercy unheeded finally brings judgment.

No doubt the Ninevites were sincere then, but it did not last. They were guilty of the very sins of which they had repented. Nineveh, the glory of the Assyrians, had come to a complete and deliberate defiance of the living God. They were not just backsliders! They deliberately rejected the God they had accepted (II Kings 18:25,30,35; 19:10-13).

God sent Nahum to predict the final doom and complete overthrow of Nineveh and her empire. This empire had been built up by violence. The Assyrians were great warriors. They were out on raiding expeditions continually. They built their state on the loot of other people. They did everything to inspire terror. They said they did this in obedience to their god, Asshur. God was going to doom her to perish in a violent and extraordinary way. All this came to pass about eighty-six years later. Read of her beast-like violence and cruelty (Nahum 2:11,12).

Assyria had enjoyed a brilliant epoch of three hundred years in which she was a world-empire. Nineveh was the capital of this mighty empire. It was in 721 B.C. that she destroyed Israel and threatened Judah, but God was going to see that Assyria's doom was final. The message of Nahum shows what God can do with a wicked and rebellious people. He will utterly destroy them.

The doom of the city was delayed some one hundred and fifty years after Jonah preached, but it fell at last. Nahum's prophecy was not a call to repentance but the statement of certain and final doom. Read Nahum 1:9; also 3:18,19. Her name should be utterly cut off (Nahum 1:14). God would dig her grave.

THE JUDGE (Read Nahum 1:1-7)

In Nahum 1 we see God the holy Judge on the bench of the court of heaven judging the wicked city of Nineveh. The case is presented. This God is a just God, therefore He must avenge all crimes.

There is a two-fold revelation of the character of this Judge of all the world. We find a sublime and powerful statement of those attributes of God which constitute the basis of all His actions toward men. This lesson gives us an excellent opportunity of presenting the attributes of God.

Study the prophet's vision of God in Nahum 1:2,3,7. Find the words that are used of Him. As Judge:

1. Jealous
2. Vengeful ("revengeth")
3. Furious
4. Wrathful
5. Great in power
6. Will not acquit wicked
7. Indignant (Nahum 1:6)

As Father:

1. Slow to anger
2. Good
3. A stronghold in the day of trouble
4. Knowing them that trust Him.

The first seven words of the vision are awe-inspiring, *God is jealous, and the LORD revengeth*. To think of a God like this makes us examine ourselves. We will find that there is no righteousness in us. How this thought drives us into the loving arms of a Saviour who is our "covering for sin" and clothes us with the robes of His righteousness.

Notice God did not bring judgment on Assyria in hot haste. He had been patient for a long time. He is *slow to anger*, but God sent ruin. He is a God of absolute justice. He is the Lord, the Lord God, merciful and gracious, long-suffering and forgiving iniquity, yet He will by no means clear the guilty. Jonah had dwelt on the first side of God's character, love (Jonah 4:2). Nahum brings out the second, the holiness of God which must deal with sin in judgment (Nahum 1:2,6). This holy Judge is *just, and the justifier of him which believeth in Jesus* (Romans 3:26) because His holy law has been vindicated in the cross of Christ.

THE VERDICT (Read Nahum 1:8-14)

Nahum 1:8-14 states the battle-and-destruction sentence upon corrupt Nineveh. She has been weighed in the balance and found wanting.

Look at the Verdict of Nineveh

1. Condemned to utter destruction..................Nahum 1:8,9
2. Captured while defenders were drunk...........Nahum 1:10
3. Name blotted out...Nahum 1:14
4. God to dig her grave......................................Nahum 1:14

We cannot read this without being struck by the solemnity of it all. Nahum told of this destruction as prophecy. We look at it today as history. Yes, the Judge has brought everything to pass. Today the traveler finds this great city Nineveh of the past still lying in ruins.

This book gives us the picture of the wrath of God. Read the second verse again, *God is jealous, and the LORD revengeth; the LORD revengeth, and is furious; the LORD will take vengeance on his adversaries, and he reserveth wrath for his enemies.* This is a picture of God and of God acting in wrath. It is not pleasant to be reminded that God is a God of anger as well as a God of love. But remember both attributes are His. He is a holy God. He hates sin. He will bring judgment upon it.

THE EXECUTION (Read Nahum 2; 3)

Read what God says in these short chapters. We find a picture of Nineveh's siege, fall and desolation. All that God can do with a rebellious and defiant nation is to destroy it.

The picture of the siege and fall of Nineveh, and the desolation which followed are described with graphic eloquence in Nahum 2; 3. God would make an end of her with an overrunning flood; her name would be utterly cut off, and He would dig her grave. The mustering of the armies around Nineveh, and the marshalling of the forces within the city are pictured in such a way that the prophet makes his hearers see all the horrid sights of the tragic scene.

Outside the walls the Medes have gathered. Shields are brilliantly painted. Robes are of purple. Terrible spears glitter in

314

the sun. Knives on their chariot wheels flash in the light. Inside the city pandemonium reigns! Too late the king tries to rally his drunken nobles to defend the beloved city. But the Tigris has caused a flood which has washed away most of the wall which had seemed to them an impregnable bulwark. This aided their enemies. Queen Huzzab is taken captive, and her maidens, like a flock of doves, moan around her.

The cries of the Medes are heard as they shout to one another, *Take ye the spoil of silver; take the spoil of gold: for there is none end of store and glory out of all the pleasant furniture.* The city is looted while the people stand with their knees smiting together for fear. Nineveh shall no longer terrify the nations because God has made an end of her. This will happen to all wicked nations of the earth.

The Medes and Babylonians completely destroyed Nineveh in 607 B.C. It occurred at the zenith of her power. According to Nahum's prophecy, it came true that a sudden rise of the Tigris, carrying away a great part of the wall, assisted the attacking army of the Medes and Babylonians in its overthrow (Nahum 2:6). It was partly destroyed by fire (Nahum 3:13,15).

So deep and effectively did God dig Nineveh's grave that every trace of its existence disappeared for ages and its site was not known. When Alexander the Great fought the battle of Arbela nearby in 331 B.C., he didn't even know there had ever been a city there. When Xenophon and his army of 10,000 passed by two hundred years later, he thought the mounds were the ruins of some Parthian city. When Napoleon encamped near its site, he, too, was not aware of it.

This city had one denunciation more, given a few years later by Zephaniah (Zephaniah 2:13). In 607 B.C. the whole was fulfilled. So complete was the destruction that all traces of the Assyrian Empire disappeared. Many scholars thought the references to Nineveh in the Bible were only mythical. It seemed that no such city ever existed. In 1845 Layard confirmed the suspicions of the Englishman, Claud James Rich, who in 1820 thought the mounds across the Tigris from Mosul were the ruins of Nineveh. The ruins of the magnificent palaces of the

Assyrian kings, and thousands of inscriptions were unearthed which give to us the story of Assyria as the Assyrians wrote it themselves. And so the magnificent capital of the wealthiest and most splendid city in the world of its day has been discovered and the Bible account has been confirmed.

SOWING AND REAPING

As Nineveh sowed, so must she reap. This is God's law. Nineveh had fortified herself so that nothing could harm her. With walls one hundred feet high and wide enough for four chariots to go abreast, a circumference of eighty miles, and adorned by hundreds of towers, she sat complacently. A moat one hundred and forty feet wide and sixty feet deep surrounded the vast walls. But Nineveh reckoned without Jehovah. What are bricks and mortar to God! The mighty empire which Shalmaneser, Sargon and Sennacherib had built up, the Lord threw down with a stroke. The inventions of civilization are powerless against heaven's artillery.

Nineveh is a type of all nations that turn their backs on God. In our day, proud civilizations are staking everything upon the strength of manpower and machines and there is a terrible disregard of God. We find that Nineveh was overthrown because of her sin (Nahum 3:1-7) and that her great wealth and strength was not sufficient to save her (Nahum 3:8-19). Oftentimes nations depend upon might and power to survive. They forget that it is *not by might, nor by power, but by my spirit, saith the Lord of hosts* (Zech. 4:6). The person or nation that deliberately and finally rejects God, deliberately and finally and fatally elects doom. Beware of this!

Hear Peter's words of warning spoken hundreds of years later—*The Lord is not slack concerning his promise, as some men count slackness; but is longsuffering to us-ward, not willing that any should perish, but that all should come to repentance. But the day of the Lord will come as a thief in the night; in the which the heavens shall pass away with a great noise, and the elements shall melt with fervent heat, the earth also and the works that are therein shall be burned up* (II Peter 3:9,10).

UNDERSTANDING HABAKKUK

Watch and see..Habakkuk 1
Stand and see..Habakkuk 2
Kneel and see..Habakkuk 3

We know little about this prophet of faith except that he asked questions and received answers. He, like many men today, could not reconcile his belief in a good and righteous God with the facts of life as he saw them. He was troubled with an eternal "Why?" Even today a man of faith finds himself bewildered at many things that are going on round about him. We ask, "Why does God allow such awful crimes to go unchecked? Why doesn't God stop men in their mad rush if He is all-powerful?"

The question, "Why do the wicked prosper?" is discussed. It seems to contain a complaint to God that He should destroy His own nation for their wickedness by a nation even much more wicked. (See Habakkuk 1:13.) We even see the prophet complaining of the lack of justice in God's management of the world. Why is God silent in times of disaster? (Habakkuk 1:13).

Habakkuk, in all his difficulties, went to God in prayer and waited patiently for His answer. (Habakkuk 2:1) He went on the watch-tower and listened to God. Campbell Morgan says that when Habakkuk looked at his circumstances he was perplexed (Habakkuk 1:3), but when he waited for God and listened to Him, he sang (Habakkuk 3:18,19).

Habakkuk was a prophet (Habakkuk 1:1), but we find something else of interest about him. He was one of the Levitical choristers in the temple (Habakkuk 3:19) or helped in the arranging of the services.

We learn much about him as a thinker and a man of faith from his own words. He was a contemporary with Jeremiah at home and with Daniel in Babylon.

The world-empire of Assyria had fallen just as Nahum had prophesied. Egypt and Babylon had then contended for the place of power. At the battle of Carchemish, 605 B.C., in which King Josiah was killed, the Babylonians were conquerors and the great kingdoms of the Babylonians and Chaldeans were united under Nebuchadnezzar. Habakkuk knew only too well that Judah must fall before this great rising power. But one question arose in his mind and troubled him greatly. Why should any nation as wicked as Babylon conquer a nation like Judah which was less evil? It seemed to him that it was just a matter of evil triumphing over evil. What good could come of this? God had to show him His ultimate plan. Judah needed punishment. God was using Babylon to correct Judah, but Babylon's turn would come. Babylon would be utterly blotted out. As for God's people there was yet to be a glorious future and a kingdom where Jehovah Himself would prevail.

This book seems to be a dialogue between Jehovah and the prophet. Two conversations are recorded and the book closes with a hymn and doxology which reveal that all the questions have been answered and there is a new confidence in God.

HABAKKUK'S COMPLAINT (Read Habakkuk 1)

This scene opens with the cry of a man who has a problem he cannot solve. *O Lord, how long shall I cry, and thou wilt not hear* (read Habakkuk 1:1-4)!

Habakkuk was confused and bewildered. It seemed to him that God was doing nothing to straighten out the conditions in the world. He had lived during the days of the great reformation under the good King Josiah. He had seen Assyria fading in power and Babylon, under Nebuchadnezzar, rising to a place of supremacy. The world about him was in an upheaval. Violence abounded and God was doing nothing about it.

But worse, he saw his own land, Judah, full of lawlessness and tyranny. The righteous were oppressed (Habakkuk 1:4,13). The people were living in open sin. They were worshiping idols (Habakkuk 2:18,19). They were oppressing the poor. Habakkuk knew that the day was dark. He knew that this sin was leading to an invasion of Jerusalem by a strong enemy.

Habakkuk asked his question of God. He didn't call a committee or form a society to solve the problem of the day. He went straight to Jehovah and stated his problem. Then God answered *I will work a work in your days, which ye will not believe, though it be told you* (Habakkuk 1:5). God told Habakkuk that He was not indifferent to His people. He wanted Habakkuk to look beyond the present. He was already working. God called the Chaldeans to the work of punishing Judah. They were a cruel scourge which swept over the land to destroy it (Habakkuk 1:5-11).

God's answer horrified Habakkuk. He could not understand how God would allow such awful means to bring about the punishing of His people, Judah. How could He use such a cruel scourge? How was it possible for God to use such an enemy to punish His own people when He Himself is so pure and holy? Listen to Habakkuk's challenge to God to defend His actions (Habakkuk 1:13).

The nations have always been God's object lessons, illustrating His moral laws (Habakkuk 1:12).

GOD'S REPLY (Read Habakkuk 2)

As this scene opens we see Habakkuk facing the great moment of his life. Watch him as he climbs up on the watchtower to wait for God. He expects God to answer him (Habakkuk 2:1).

Everything lies in ruins around the prophet. Chaldea is coming up to destroy what is left. There is only One to whom he can turn so he waits expectantly for God. God gives an answer. Read God's answer in Habakkuk 2:2-20. God admits the wickedness of the Chaldeans, but declares that they will destroy themselves finally by their own evil. Pride and cruelty always bring destruction. Men sometimes have to wait to know what the final outcome will be. God sometimes takes ages to show His plans. *One day is with the Lord as a thousand years, and a thousand years as one day* (II Peter 3:8). God's testing always reveals what men are. He burns out the dross. It may seem that the Chaldeans are prospering for a time but they are doomed. *The just shall live by his faith.* Habakkuk 2:4 is the heart of the book.

There are five "woes" in Habakkuk 2. Find what they are. Remember evil will perish. Only righteousness will remain before God.

319

HABAKKUK'S SONG (Read Habakkuk 3)

Habakkuk is the prophet who sang in the night. Listen to the magnificent melody with which his prophecy closes—*Although the fig tree shall not blossom, neither shall fruit be in the vines; the labour of the olive shall fail, and the fields shall yield no meat; the flock shall be cut off from the fold, and there shall be no herd in the stalls: Yet I will rejoice in the LORD, I will joy in the God of my salvation* (Habakkuk 3:17,18). This ode was set to music and sung at the public worship by the Jews.

After a sincere prayer (Habakkuk 3:1-16) God's glory appears. God always responds to the cry for help from His people. Habakkuk realizes that God is in control of this universe and that He is working out His own purpose in His own time. Habakkuk learns that he can trust implicitly in God. He realizes that he can see only a small part of God's plan at one time. One must wait for God to reveal His entire program. One must know God's way is best.

God cannot always give us a satisfactory answer because our finite minds cannot grasp the thoughts of the infinite. His thoughts are high above our thoughts, and His ways above our ways (see Isaiah 55:9) but we can trust God, always! *All things work together for good to them that love God, to them who are the called according to his purpose* (Romans 8:28).

Remember, God does not promise that He will unravel every problem, but He does assure us that we can put our trust absolutely in Him. (Read Psalms 37:5 and II Timothy 1:12.)

One of the texts in Habakkuk has great significance in the history of the Reformation. Do you know the story of the young monk, Martin Luther, who rose to his feet as he was crawling up the Sancta Scala in Rome? He remembered these words, *The just shall live by his faith* (Habakkuk 2:4). Not by works! This started him out on his great crusade which brought about the Reformation.

Find where Habakkuk 2:4 is quoted in the New Testament: Romans 1:17; Galatians 3:11; Hebrews 10:38. Mark them.

UNDERSTANDING ZEPHANIAH

Little is known of Zephaniah, the writer of this book. Two facts of his personal history appear in the first verse of the prophecy. We learn that very likely he was a prince of the royal house of Judah, being a descendant of Hezekiah. He was in a position to denounce the sins of the princes for he himself was an aristocrat. He lived in the reign of the good King Josiah. His name means "hidden of Jehovah."

Zephaniah began his ministry as a prophet in the early days of the reign of Josiah (641-610 B.C.). Fifty years had elapsed since the prophecy of Nahum. Three of Hezekiah's descendants had succeeded him (II Kings 20; 21). Two wicked and idol-worshiping kings had preceded Josiah on the throne and the land was overrun with evil practices of every kind. Social injustice and moral corruption was on every hand. The rich had amassed great fortunes by grinding the faces of the poor. The condition was as bad as it could be when King Josiah, only sixteen years of age, undertook to promote a religious revival. He became one of the most beloved of the kings of Judah. He took a hatchet and hewed down the altars and images. How the words of Zephaniah must have encouraged the reformers!

Zephaniah depicts God as both loving and severe. The following verses give us these two characteristics: Zephaniah 1:2; 3:17.

Zephaniah foretold the doom of Nineveh (Zephaniah 2:13). Who else had prophesied her doom? This came to pass in 612 B.C.

We hear Zephaniah denouncing the various forms of idolatry—Baal and Malcham or Molech all being condemned (Zephaniah 1:1–2:3). This idol worship was destroyed during Josiah's reign. No doubt Zephaniah was mainly responsible for the revival under Josiah. He was the pioneer in this Reform Movement. Tradition tells us that Jeremiah was his colleague.

As you start reading this book, you are appalled at its contents. There is nothing but denunciations, dire threats, and wrath. Cowper says that punishment and chastisement is "the graver countenance of love" *for whom the Lord loveth he*

chasteneth, and scourgeth every son whom he receiveth
(Hebrews 12:6). We see in all of this a proof of God's love.
The book begins with sorrow but ends with singing. The first of
the book is full of sadness and gloom, but the last contains one
of the sweetest songs of love in the Old Testament.

Zephaniah showed that

1. A faithful remnant would be delivered from captivity.

2. The heathen shall be converted.

3. One day man could worship God anywhere, not only in
Jerusalem (Zephaniah 2:11; see John 4:21).

God is searching out the people. *I will search Jerusalem with
candles, and punish the men that are settled on their lees*
(Zephaniah 1:12).

JUDAH SEARCHED (Read Zephaniah 1)

Jehovah is in the midst of the land for judgment. (See
Zephaniah 3:5 and 1:17.) He first searches Judah and pronounces doom on all those who are worshiping idols. The land
must be freed from idolatry. Jehovah cannot allow such abomination to remain. We see the rulers are denounced as is every
class of sinner (Zephaniah 1:7-13).

1. The idol worshipers..Verses 4, 5
2. Those who swear by God one time and at
   another time by Molech..Verse 5
3. Those who turned back from the Lord....................Verse 6

Upon all these shall God bring a blast of fire. It shall strike
the whole earth, but especially upon the inhabitants of Jerusalem. The "day of the Lord" is a day of dread. He calls the
people to tremble at God's presence. He is "in the midst" of the
land to judge her.

The "day of the Lord" is mentioned seven times in the
prophecy. Almost without exception when "day" is used in
Scripture it means a period of time. If a number is used before
it, like 40 days, 3 days, then it is a day of twenty-four hours.
But when you use "day" alone, like the day of the Puritan, or
Lincoln's day, you mean the time in which they lived. So when
the Word says "the day of the Lord," it means a time of the

322

Lord's special working. To the Jews of Zephaniah's day it meant the time when God would deal with His people in punishment and captivity. The future day of the Lord is the period of the great tribulation and the millennium. (See Revelation 6:1-17.) Judah was taught that "the day of the Lord" was coming when there would be a special reckoning.

THE NATIONS SEARCHED (Read Zephaniah 2)

After the prophet calls the people to seek God (Zephaniah 2:1-3) that they may be *hid in the day of the LORD's anger,* he declares that nothing can save the nation from doom but real repentance. *Seek ye the LORD, . . . seek righteousness, seek meekness* is his admonition. Then he turns to the five heathen nations, Philistia, Moab, Ammon, Ethiopia and Assyria. They shall be visited with the wrath of God because of their pride and scorn toward the Lord's people (Zephaniah 2:10). The desolation of Nineveh is described in wonderfully accurate terms (Zephaniah 2:13-15). These began to be accomplished in the conquests of Nebuchadnezzar.

The judgment on Israel's local enemies is literally fulfilled (Zephaniah 2:4-15). The judgment on Israel's enemies over this wide world is yet to be fulfilled. Read God's Word in Zephaniah 3:8; 2:10,11. God says the idols of their enemies shall be broken up, and the heathen shall worship God, every one in his own country (Zeph. 2:11). Instead of all having to make a pilgrimage to Jerusalem, they may worship God anywhere.

The Jews taught that Jerusalem was the place of worship. The Samaritan declared that Mount Gerizim ought to be the religious center, but Zephaniah taught that spiritual worship did not depend upon a place but on the Presence of God. Men have always tried to establish sacred places and shrines. Rome and Mecca have long been "holy" spots among hundreds of other places. Men have undergone every hardship to worship at these shrines. In India, thousands make the pilgrimage to Benares, the Hindus' most sacred spot, to worship and to bathe in the Ganges, and to carry back with them its sacred water.

323

ISRAEL RESTORED (Read Zephaniah 3)

The prophet concludes with the most wonderful promises of Israel's future restoration and of the happy state of the purified people of God in the latter days (Zephaniah 3). The redeemed remnant will return cleansed, humbled, trusting and rejoicing with their offerings to Zion. They will be established in their land with God "in their midst" (Zephaniah 3:15,17). Zion then shall be a delight among nations and a blessing to the whole earth as was foretold in the promise God made originally with Abraham. (See Genesis 12:1-3.)

The rejoicing of Zephaniah 3:14-20 must refer to something beside the day when the remnant will return after the captivity of Babylon. Judah's worst judgment followed that return. She has seen little but misery every since. Neither did anything like this occur at Christ's first coming. It must refer to the day when the Lord Himself shall sit on the throne of David, when His people shall be gathered from the four corners of the earth (Zephaniah 3:19). This prophecy shall be blessedly fulfilled in the kingdom age when Christ comes to this earth to reign in power and great glory.

Minimum Daily Requirements/Spiritual Vitamins

Sunday: THE JUDGE AND THE VERDICT   Nahum 1
Monday: THE EXECUTION   Nahum 2; 3
Tuesday: HABAKKUK'S COMPLAINT   Habakkuk 1
Wednesday: GOD'S REPLY   Habakkuk 2
Thursday: HABAKKUK'S SONG   Habakkuk 3
Friday: COMING JUDGMENTS   Zephaniah 1; 2
Saturday: THE KINGDOM BLESSINGS   Zephaniah 3

324

CHAPTER 25

UNDERSTANDING HAGGAI, ZECHARIAH, MALACHI

Jesus Christ, the Desire of All Nations; the Righteous Branch; Sun of Righteousness

Note: The greater number of Old Testament prophets spoke before the captivity. During the captivity, Ezekiel and Daniel prophesied. After the return Haggai, Zechariah and Malachi prophesied. This makes it easy for you to remember. Just two during the exile, three after, then twelve of the seventeen before.

Haggai, Zechariah and Malachi are the last of the prophetic books. Each of these prophets belongs to the period after the exile. They prophesied to the Jews after they had returned to Jerusalem. Nebuchadnezzar had captured Jerusalem and had completely destroyed the temple. This had not brought the Jews to national repentance. In reading Ezra, we find that when Cyrus, king of Persia, issued a decree permitting all the captives to return to Jerusalem and to rebuild their temple that only about 50,000 returned. Most of these were priests and Levites and the poorer among the people. Although the Jews increased in power and in numbers, they never established their political independence. They were a subject people under Gentile rulers from this time on.

About sixteen years before, the Jews had returned to their own land under Zerubbabel and had begun to build the temple (Nehemiah 12). But their enthusiasm soon waned. They made no progress beyond laying the foundation. The Samaritans and their enemy neighbors were determined that Jerusalem should not be rebuilt. This meant that the work lay unfinished for fifteen years. During these years each person became interested in building his own private house. It was then that Haggai arose and gave his message. He encouraged the people to build the temple again. This time it was finished in four years. It seemed incredible that God's people should have waited so long to do the very thing they came back to do.

We know little of Haggai except that he worked with Zechariah during the days following the exile. He prophesied two months before Zechariah. Zechariah prophesied for three years and Haggai prophesied for four months.

Haggai is the first voice to be heard after the exile. His name means "my feast." His book is a collection of four brief messages written between August and December.

Each message is specifically dated. These dates, rather than places and characters, dominate the scenes. These were given in "the second year of Darius," 520 B.C. Confucius, the Chinese philosopher, was flourishing in China at this time. The book is dominated by one central purpose. Haggai is determined to persuade the people to rebuild the temple. It is no easy task to move a discouraged nation to rise up and build a temple. But he did it.

A MESSAGE OF REBUKE (Read Haggai 1:1-11)

A poor handful of people had returned to Jerusalem from Babylon where they had lived in captivity. With a colossal task before them of rebuilding the temple and restoring the worship of Jehovah, the Jews labored under the same old sins, idolatry, intermarrying with idolatrous neighbors. They were few in number, poor, harassed by enemies and worse, they had lost the inner strength that comes from a joy in the Lord. (Read Nehemiah 8:10.)

Because of all this the work dragged and the people lost heart and became selfish. Neglecting the Lord's house, they had become more interested in building homes for themselves than for God (Haggai 1:4). God would not allow this to go on and so he sent punishment as a result. Poor crops, droughts, scanty trade, misery and turmoil made their spirits fail (Haggai 1:6).

They were working and slaving but finding no real joy (Haggai 1:6,9-11).

We see the effect of Haggai's challenge. His stern call to duty proved to be a good tonic. Zerubbabel, the governor of Jerusalem, Joshua, the high priest, and the people arose and began the work of rebuilding the temple (Haggai 1:12-15). How did God respond to their repentance? (Haggai 1:13).

God sometimes allows hardships because of our indifference to Him. Crops had failed and business was depressed because of the sin of the Jews. But God wants us to keep up the church. Without churches sin and vice will grow. When men forget to love God, they forget to love their fellow men, too. We should beautify God's house. (See II Samuel 7:2.) We are not to live in fine homes and allow the church building to be in ruins.

A MESSAGE OF COURAGE (Read Haggai 2:1-9)

Note: How long after the first message was this one given? (Haggai 1:1; 2:1). For the history of this period read Ezra 3:8-13.

As the people were building, a new discouragement seized them. The older ones, remembering the splendor of the temple of Solomon, were greatly disappointed in this new temple. It did not measure up in any way, they thought. How inferior in size and costliness of the stones! How much smaller in extent was the foundation itself! How limited were their means! And besides, this second temple would not have the things that made the first one so glorious—the Ark, the Shekinah, and all that went with the service of the high priest. These pessimists dampened the enthusiasm of the builders.

But Haggai came with a word of cheer that God was to pour His resources into that new building. The living God was to be in the midst of this new temple. *The desire of all nations shall come: and I will fill this house with glory, saith the LORD of hosts* (Haggai 2:7). *The glory of this latter house shall be greater than of the former, saith the LORD of hosts: and in this place will I give peace, saith the LORD of hosts* (Haggai 2:9). What a comfort this must have been to the Jews in their exile.

327

A MESSAGE OF ASSURANCE (Read Haggai 2:10-23)

This message of cleansing and blessing was delivered three months after the temple was started. By the use of questions and answers Haggai showed the people their impurity. He made them realize their sinfulness. He showed them the reason their prayers were not answered was because they had put off so long the completing of the temple. They had spoiled all that they had done because of their guilt. If they would renew their zeal, they would find God would bless them. Haggai heard their complaints of seeing no visible signs of blessings although they had been working for three full months. Haggai showed them that the land had been rendered useless by their neglect but God was working and it would be different now. *From this day will I bless you* (read Haggai 2:18,19). God begins when we begin.

UNDERSTANDING ZECHARIAH

Zechariah is a book of the future. It is a Book of Revelation of the Old Testament.

THE CHOSEN PEOPLE AND THE TEMPLE
(Read Zechariah 1-8)

We now find Judah still a remnant, Jerusalem far from restored, the Gentile nations at ease round about her. (See Zechariah 1:14-16.) Zechariah, a young prophet who had stood alongside the aged Haggai, strengthened the children of Israel as they built the temple and warned them not to disappoint God as their fathers had done. He pictured God's love and care for His people. He quickened their hopes by painting in glowing colors the time of perpetual blessing that was coming to Israel in the far off ages.

Zechariah, like Haggai, was a prophet to the remnant of the Jews who returned from Babylon after the 70 years of captivity. The Jews, once a powerful nation as God had planned them to be, were now a pitiful and insignificant remnant, dwelling in their promised land only because of the courtesy of a foreign ruler. Both Haggai and Zechariah tried to tell the people that it would not always be so. One day the Messiah would come and God's chosen people would rise into power.

Zechariah was the prophet of restoration and glory. Born in Babylon, he was priest as well as prophet. Zechariah, whose name meant "Jehovah remembers," prophesied for three years. The glorious future, rather than the sad present, was his message. He was a poet, while Haggai was a plain, practical preacher.

Zechariah's keen enthusiasm for the rebuilding of the temple kept the people at the task of finishing the work. Serious crop failures and business depression among the Jewish people had made them so discouraged that only Haggai's blunt and consistent hammering kept them at the work. They needed a new voice. Zechariah's was that one. He threw himself into the work of helping his great friend Haggai.

Zechariah does not condemn the people but presents in glowing pictures the presence of God to strengthen and help. He especially encourages the governor, Zerubbabel, who was conscious of his own weakness. Hear what Zechariah says, *Not by might, nor by power, but by my spirit, saith the LORD of hosts* (read Zechariah 4:6-10). He promised that the mountains of difficulty would be removed. How marvelously this truth was fulfilled at Pentecost when God filled men with His power.

The King Cometh

Zechariah foretells the Saviour more than any other prophet except Isaiah.

Christ the Branch...Zechariah 3:8

Christ my Servant..Zechariah 3:8

Christ's entry in Jerusalem on a colt.............Zechariah 9:9

Christ, the good Shepherd................Zechariah 9:16; 11:11

Christ, the smitten Shepherd.........................Zechariah 13:7

Christ betrayed for 30 pieces of silver....Zechariah 11:12,13

Christ's hands pierced...................................Zechariah 12:10

Christ's people saved..........................Zechariah 12:10; 13:1

Christ wounded in the house of His friends....Zechariah 13:6

Christ's coming on Mount of Olives............Zechariah 14:3-8

He who ascended from The Mount of Olives shall so come in like manner as He went. Read Acts 1:11.

Christ's coming and coronation............................Zechariah 14

TWO SEARCHLIGHTS

Someone has said to read the visions of this book aright you must get two lights upon them—the light of the cross and of the crown. Otherwise you will find these pictures of Zechariah to be without perspective or background. The prophet, looking far into the future, saw the Messiah of the days to come as one Person, but in two aspects. First, he saw Him in humiliation and suffering, and again, in majesty and great glory.

The Jew ignores the Christ of the cross. The Christian, too often, ignores the Christ of the crown. Both are wrong!

Zechariah seems to let the glory of Christ glow in all his teaching and preaching.

Visions of Zechariah

Of the Minor Prophets, Zechariah alone majors in visions. *I saw by night, and behold . . .* (1:7,8)

The Angelic Horseman...(1:7-17)

Here is a picture of Israel today, outcast, but not forgotten by God.

The Horns and Blacksmiths...(1:18-21)

The overthrow of Israel by her enemies is foreseen.

The Measuring Line...(2)

The coming prosperity of Jerusalem is seen. The city, walled in by the presence of God, is great in extent and blessed by His favor.

Joshua, the High Priest...(3)

Filthy garments clothing the priest, and representing Israel's sin, are removed, replaced, and the Branch, Christ, introduced.

The Golden Candlesticks...(4)

Israel is shown as God's future light-bearer. Olive trees, anointed of God, speak of Zerubbabel, the ruler, and Joshua, the priest.

The Flying Roll..(5:1-4)
Wicked governments receive God's curse in this unique picture.

The Ephah..(5:5-11)
Borne away on divine wings, wickedness is removed.

The Four Chariots...(6:1-8)
"Administrative forces of righteousness"—Dr. G. Campbell Morgan.

THE CORONATION SCENE

The visions are followed by a symbolic act of crowning the high priest. (See Zechariah 6:9-11.) Gold and silver brought from Babylon was wrought into a crown and placed on the head of Joshua, the high priest. By this act the two great offices of the priest and king are united. This is a type of Christ the King who will sit on His throne of glory as a priest when He returns to earth to set up His millennial kingdom.

Two years later we find a committee from Bethel waiting on Zechariah to ask him if the national fasts should be kept. (See Zechariah 7; 8.) The Jews themselves had instituted these fasts. They had been used to fasting on their great anniversary days. Zechariah warned them against cold formalism in their religious observances. He urges them to change their fasts into feasts of joy and be practical in their righteousness. God says, *To obey is better than sacrifice, and to hearken than the fat of rams* (I Samuel 15:22).

Fasting is only profitable as an outward sign of an inward confession of sin. Merely refraining from eating will never bring a blessing. God wants a humble and a contrite heart.

THE MESSIAH AND THE KINGDOM
(Read Zechariah 9–14)

These chapters are full of promises of the coming Messiah and a worldwide kingdom. The prophet no longer pictures a city rebuilt on its old foundations, but a glorious city whose wall is the Lord. It is not armed for war, but is a city filled with peace, for the Prince of Peace reigns. He shall come the first time as the lowly One, riding upon a humble beast. (Read Zechariah 9:9.)

But we see this lowly One becoming a mighty Sovereign. (Zechariah 14:8-11) The Messiah in all His glory and might shall put all the enemies under His feet and He shall establish His kingdom in Jerusalem and sit upon the throne of David. *His dominion shall be from sea even to sea, and from the river even to the ends of the earth* (Zechariah 9:10).

If one would follow these chapters more closely, he would discover victory over all the enemies of Israel. Chapter 11 reveals the Shepherd who would seek to save Israel but is rejected. He is sold for thirty pieces of silver, the price of a slave. This all foreshadowed Christ and His betrayal by Judas. Chapter 12 gives us the prophecy of the siege of Jerusalem by the Antichrist and his armies in the last days. Then we see the repentance of the Jews (verse 12) when they shall see Him whom they have pierced. The fountain shall be opened to the house of David for sin and uncleanness. (Zechariah 13:1) Then the return of the Messiah upon the Mount of Olives, which shall cleave asunder by an earthquake (Zechariah 14:4) reminds us of the day when He left the earth at that same spot with the promise of His return. (See Acts 1:11.) Finally He shall be King over the whole earth and all people shall be holy unto Him. (Zechariah 14:9-20)

The Blessings of the Kingdom of Christ

1. The extent of His Kingdom......................Zechariah 14:9
2. Abundant rain...Zechariah 10:1
3. Outpouring of the Spirit on Israel..........Zechariah 12:10
4. Revelation of the "pierced" Messiah......Zechariah 12:10
5. Changes in Palestine.....................Zechariah 14:4,5,10,11
6. Kingdom set up on earth......................Zechariah 14:9-15
7. Jerusalem center of worship..............Zechariah 14:16,17

UNDERSTANDING MALACHI

We have now come to the last book in the Old Testament. It sums up much of the history of the Old Testament. Martin Luther called John 3:16 "The Little Gospel." In the same way we might speak of Malachi as the "Little Old Testament." Malachi is the bridge between the Old and New Testaments. To show this read Malachi 3:1. Who is "My messenger"? Read John 1:23 and Luke 3:3,4. A silence of 400 years lies between the voice of Malachi and the voice of one crying in the wilderness, *Prepare ye the way of the Lord.*

The Old Testament closes with the word "curse." The New Testament closes with blessing—*The grace of our Lord Jesus Christ be with you all. Amen.*

By this time, a hundred years or more had passed since the Jews had returned to Jerusalem after the captivity in Babylon. Malachi is the last prophet to speak to Israel in her own land. Israel here means all the remnant of Israel and Judah that returned after the exile. The first enthusiasm after the return from Babylon had spent itself. Following a period of revival (Nehemiah 10:28-39), the people had become cold religiously and lax morally.

The prophet Malachi came as a reformer, but he encourages while he rebukes. He dealt with a people perplexed, with spirits failing, whose faith in God seemed to be in danger of collapse. If they had not already become hostile to Jehovah, they were in real danger of becoming skeptical.

Malachi means "the messenger of the Lord." Like the forerunner, John the Baptist, of whom he prophesies, he was but a voice.

THE SINS OF THE PRIESTS (Read Malachi 1:1-2:9)

The skeptical attitude aroused among the people showed itself in religious coldness and social laxity. This is always true. The priests became irreverent and neglectful. Read Malachi 1:6,11,12. God said, *Where is mine honor? . . . O priests, that despise my name.* The prophet rebukes these careless priests for offering worthless animals in sacrifice to God that they would not offer to the governor. They stood in marked contrast to God's ideal for the priesthood. They had completely lost sight of their high calling and deserved the ignominy heaped upon them. They refused to work except for money. God's condemnation begins with the leaders (Malachi 2:1-9). As long as the priests were openly unfit, what could be expected from the people at large? This resulted in a carelessness among God's people in keeping themselves separate from the heathen nations. Mixed marriages with women of outside tribes became common. Some men had not hesitated to divorce their Israelitish wives to make this possible (Malachi 2:10-16).

THE SINS OF THE PEOPLE (Read Malachi 2:10–3:18)

What would you think of a person who deliberately held something before his eyes and then complained that he could see nothing? What would you suggest might quickly solve the difficulty? Well, this is just what Malachi had to do. The Jews declared that Jehovah did not love them as He said (Malachi 1:2). They could not see that His love had been of any special advantage to them.

Another result of this laxity of loyalty to God was in the growing prevalence of social sin (Malachi 3:5). Malachi 3:7 reveals the religious indifference and skepticism of the people. Amid all the hypocrisy of the day there were those in the Jewish community (a remnant) who still feared God and remained faithful. If we turn to Malachi 3:16, we will find this. Malachi longed to develop a strong body of enthusiastic believers who could influence his people's future. It is interesting to note that God bent His ear to hear His people speak about Him (Malachi 3:16).

Spiritless routine worship.............................Malachi 1:6-8
Evil associations..Malachi 2:10-12
Questioning Jehovah's justice...................Malachi 2:17–3:6
Robbing God..Malachi 3:7-12
Impatience in waiting...............................Malachi 3:17–4:3

These were the sins which Malachi rebuked. Are they yours, too? Suppose we do find some of these sins in our daily lives, what are we to do? Confess them to Jehovah. Israel was troubled about the result of her confession. Malachi had to encourage the people by assuring them of Jehovah's wonderful love and giving the beautiful promise of Malachi 3:7. Turn to it and mark it in your Bible.

The children of Israel could depend on Jehovah to forgive. It was this same picture of the Father that Jesus gave when he told of the prodigal's return. The father, seeing the boy while yet a great way off, ran out to meet him. This is ever God's attitude.

The Jews had been cured of idolatry, but they had grown careless and indifferent about many things. They had neglected the house of God. The priests had become lax. They were bringing inferior sacrifices to the temple. They had robbed God of their tithes and offerings. They fell into social sins. They had become so selfish and covetous that Malachi dared boldly to challenge them with these words, *Will a man rob God* (Malachi 3:8)?

The key that opens God's big blessing windows is your recognition of His ownership by giving back to Him a proper share of the money or the property that He permits you to acquire. *Bring ye all the tithes into the storehouse.* The tenth (or tithe) is the outward recognition that everything belongs to God. We are to bring Him our whole selves, body, soul and spirit. Then He will accept us and open the windows of heaven to pour out His blessings.

COMING THINGS (Read Malachi 3; 4)

Why does God permit such things? This attitude of the people was probably due to the feeling that the glowing promises of Haggai and Zechariah and of the other prophets had not been realized. They said that Jehovah did not seem to distinguish between good and bad men (Malachi 2:17). He blesses all alike, and evil men often flourish at the expense of their fellows (Malachi 3:14,15). What's the use of being good? Is this not one of the standing complaints of those who think they are good men? They say, "What is God doing that He permits such things?" The answer to such a complaint is that Jehovah does care. He showed this to them by saying that one day He will send His messenger (John the Baptist) to prepare His way, then He will come in person "suddenly" and sit in judgment and separate the evil from the good (Malachi 3:1). His judgment will be searching and effective *like a refiner's fire,* like *fullers' soap* (Malachi 3:2,3). When God really gets ready to act, what will He do? The action will be final. (Malachi 3:1-3).

We find the burden of God's message by Malachi to His people stated in the second verse of the book, *I have loved you, saith the LORD*. What a message to a people who had sinned as Israel had and had spurned the love of Jehovah God. God is always sending His messenger before Him to prepare His way (Malachi 3:1). He wants all His children to honor and adore Him. He longs to have us obey and worship Him. But who can stand the day of His appearing? And who can endure His purifying fire (Malachi 3:2)? God's messenger will be a witness revealing our cruelty, our lies, our injustices, our double dealing. This can be said of us today just as much as of the Jews of old. Jehovah's representative comes and finds us robbing Him of His due. (Read Malachi 3:2-5.) Yet, Jehovah God is unchanging. He never forgets His promises of undying love and everlasting mercy.

Oh, how we need God's Malachi today to be sent before Him, to prepare His way so that God's people may honor and adore Him. Malachi cries, "Back to God's house! Back to God's Word! Back to God's work! Back to God's grace!"

Each one may be like Malachi, a herald of the Christ whose coming we now await. Each one who loves and looks for Him may help prepare His way by his very manner of living and work.

Think of the needs of this day, the needs of the church and the world. Is not formalism a just charge today against our churches—an outward observance without a wholehearted love? Are not we, too, offering gifts that cost nothing? Are we not robbing God in the matter of tithes?

Close by reading aloud Malachi's solemn declaration concerning the second advent of Christ for which we wait, Malachi 3:16–4:3. Yes, the Sun of Righteousness will come with healing in His wings.

Minimum Daily Requirements/Spiritual Vitamins

Sunday: HAGGAI'S MESSAGE   Haggai 1; 2
Monday: VISIONS   Zechariah 1–6
Tuesday: FASTS   Zechariah 7; 8
Wednesday: RESTORATION OF JUDAH AND ISRAEL
Zechariah 9–11
Thursday: THE MESSIAH   Zechariah 12–14
Friday: SINS OF PRIESTS AND PEOPLE   Malachi 1; 2
Saturday: MESSAGE OF HOPE   Malachi 3; 4

A QUICK LOOK AT THE OLD TESTAMENT
ESTHER THROUGH MALACHI

Esther
> THEME OF BOOK: Jesus Christ is portrayed as our Advocate.
>
> OUTSTANDING LESSON: God will deliver His children!

Job
> THEME OF BOOK: Jesus Christ is portrayed as our Redeemer.
>
> OUTSTANDING LESSON: Why do the righteous suffer?

Psalms
> THEME OF BOOK: Jesus Christ is portrayed as our All in all.
>
> OUTSTANDING LESSON: Praise God!

Proverbs
> THEME OF BOOK: Jesus Christ is portrayed as our Wisdom.
>
> OUTSTANDING LESSON: Get wisdom!

Ecclesiastes
> THEME OF BOOK: Jesus Christ is portrayed as the End of all living.
>
> OUTSTANDING LESSON: Try wisdom!

Song of Solomon
> THEME OF BOOK: Jesus Christ is portrayed as the Lover of our souls.
>
> OUTSTANDING LESSON: Love God!

Isaiah
> THEME OF BOOK: Jesus Christ is portrayed as the Messiah.
>
> OUTSTANDING LESSON: Salvation is of God!

Jeremiah

> THEME OF BOOK: Jesus Christ is portrayed as the Righteous Branch.
>
> OUTSTANDING LESSON: Go and tell!

Lamentations

> THEME OF BOOK: Jesus Christ is portrayed as the Righteous Branch.
>
> OUTSTANDING LESSON: God's grace always shines!

Ezekiel

> THEME OF BOOK: Jesus Christ is portrayed as the Son of man.
>
> OUTSTANDING LESSON: Judgment and Restoration!

Daniel

> THEME OF BOOK: Jesus Christ is portrayed as the Smiting Stone.
>
> OUTSTANDING LESSON: God is Sovereign!

Hosea

> THEME OF BOOK: Jesus Christ is portrayed as the Healer of the backslider.
>
> OUTSTANDING LESSON: Return unto God!

Joel

> THEME OF BOOK: Jesus Christ is portrayed as the Restorer.
>
> OUTSTANDING LESSON: Repent for "the day of the Lord" is coming.

Amos

> THEME OF BOOK: Jesus Christ is portrayed as the Heavenly Husbandman.
>
> OUTSTANDING LESSON: Prepare to meet your God!

Obadiah

> THEME OF BOOK: Jesus Christ is portrayed as our Saviour.
>
> OUTSTANDING LESSON: Possess your possessions!

Jonah

> THEME OF BOOK: Jesus Christ is portrayed as our Resurrection and Life.
>
> OUTSTANDING LESSON: Arise and go!

340

Micah

> THEME OF BOOK: Jesus Christ is portrayed as a Witness against rebellious nations.
>
> OUTSTANDING LESSON: Hear Him!

Nahum

> THEME OF BOOK: Jesus Christ is portrayed as a Stronghold in the day of trouble.
>
> OUTSTANDING LESSON: Beware, the Lord avenges!

Habakkuk

> THEME OF BOOK: Jesus Christ is portrayed as the God of our salvation.
>
> OUTSTANDING LESSON: Live by faith!

Zephaniah

> THEME OF BOOK: Jesus Christ is portrayed as a Jealous Lord.
>
> OUTSTANDING LESSON: God is mighty to save!

Haggai

> THEME OF BOOK: Jesus Christ is portrayed as the Desire of all nations.
>
> OUTSTANDING LESSON: Build for God!

Zechariah

> THEME OF BOOK: Jesus Christ is portrayed as the Righteous Branch.
>
> OUTSTANDING LESSON: Turn to Him!

Malachi

> THEME OF BOOK: Jesus Christ is portrayed as the Sun of Righteousness.
>
> OUTSTANDING LESSON: Repent and return!

FOUR HUNDRED YEARS OF SILENCE

By the time Old Testament history ended, a few of the Jews, chiefly of the tribe of Judah, had returned to Palestine under Zerubbabel, and about eighty years later another company had returned with Ezra. They were living peaceably in their own land with the Temple rebuilt and religious ceremonies set up.

The last three books of history in the Old Testament—Ezra, Nehemiah and Esther—give us the story of this time. They cover one hundred years following the decree of Cyrus the king, allowing the Jews to return to their land (536–432 B.C.). (Read Ezra 1:1-4.)

From Nehemiah to the beginning of New Testament times, four hundred years passed by. During this period no Biblical prophet spoke or wrote. In fact, it is called the "period of silence." As we come to the year when Jesus was born, it is important that we know some of the things that happened from the days of Nehemiah and Malachi to that time.

THE SEPTUAGINT

Before the death of Alexander the Great, he divided his empire among his four generals, for he had no heirs to his throne. Egypt, and later Palestine, went to his general, Ptolemy. Great numbers of Jews at this time settled in Egypt, as well as other centers of culture, spreading everywhere the knowledge of their God and their hope of a Messiah.

It was during this time, about 285 B.C., that the Old Testament was translated into Greek. This version of the Scriptures is called the "Septuagint," meaning seventy, because seventy noted Hebrew scholars did this great work. You will find it referred to by Roman numerals LXX.

THE JEWS PERSECUTED

Now the Syrian kingdom arose. In the conflicts between Syria and Egypt, Antiochus Epiphanes, king of Syria, seized Palestine. He began a bitter persecution of the Jews. The Jews were forbidden by Antiochus Epiphanes to worship in the Temple and were compelled to eat the flesh of swine, which God through Moses had forbidden (Leviticus 11:1-8). Many Jews refused and a period of martyrdom began.

The cruelties of this terrible king, Antiochus Epiphanes, brought about the revolt of the Maccabees under the leadership of Mattathias. Aroused by the patriotism and religious ardor of Mattathias, a group of patriotic Jews gathered about him and began an insurrection that spread rapidly. When he died, his son Judas took his place. In an attempt to crush this rebellion under the Maccabees, Antiochus was defeated in three deadly conflicts. The cause of Judas had seemed hopeless because his followers were untrained and without equipment, and they were opposed by the trained soldiers of a powerful king. But this band of ragged but loyal Jews, inspired by an undying faith in God, came out victorious!

THE ROMAN TRIBUTE

In 63 B.C. Rome gained possession of Palestine, preparing the way and the time for Jesus to be born. The Jews had some political liberty, but were required to pay a yearly tax to the Roman government.

CHAPTER 27

UNDERSTANDING
The GOSPEL

*The Gospel
Portrays Jesus Christ,
Our Saviour and Lord*

THE GOSPELS

Dr. Van Dyke said, "If four witnesses should appear before a judge to give an account of a certain event, and each should tell exactly the same story in the same words, the judge would probably conclude, not that their testimony was exceptionally valuable, but that the only event which was certain beyond a doubt was that they had agreed to tell the same story. But if each man had told what he had seen, as he had seen it, then the evidence would be credible. And when we read the four Gospels, is not that exactly what we find? The four men tell the same story each in his own way."

WHY CALLED SYNOPTIC

The word gospel is derived from the two Anglo-Saxon words God, meaning good, and spell, meaning tidings or history. The four writers of the Gospels are called evangelists, from a Greek word meaning bringer of good tidings. The first three Gospels, Matthew, Mark and Luke are called the Synoptic Gospels because, unlike John, they give a synopsis of Christ's life. The word synopsis is from the two Greek words meaning a view together, a collective view. So these three Gospels may be viewed together.

The Synoptic Gospels are striking in their similarities. They are equally striking in their differences. The Synoptics narrate His ministry chiefly in Galilee; but John's Gospel stands in a class by itself. He tells of Christ's ministry in Judea. The Synoptics narrate His miracles, parables and addresses to the multitudes; John presents His deeper and more abstract discourses, His conversations and prayers. The three portray Christ in action; John portrays Him in meditation and communion.

He is here! The promised One has come! The One whom all the prophets have foretold, Jesus Christ, the Lord.

Every prophet in the Old Testament assured God's chosen people again and again that a Messiah should come who would be the King of the Jews. They therefore looked forward with passionate longing and patriotism to the coming of that King in pomp and power.

Expect to find in the Gospels *Him of whom Moses in the law, and the prophets, did write, Jesus* (John 1:45). But know that you will find Him infinitely more beautiful in person than any prophet's vision of Him.

We read in Isaiah 7:14: *Therefore the Lord Himself shall give you a sign; Behold, a virgin shall conceive, and bear a son, and shall call his name Immanuel* [God with us]. This is just the One that the evangelists tell us about. The Gospels present Jesus in our midst. John says, *The Word was made flesh, and dwelt among us* (John 1:14). Think of God coming down to live with men! It seems that the Gospels are the center of the whole Bible. All that the prophets have said leads us to our Lord's earthly life and work, and all that follows in the Epistles proceeds from them. The Gospels are the source.

The Gospels tell us WHEN and HOW Christ came.

The Epistles tell us WHY and FOR WHAT Christ came.

Notice where the four Gospels are placed. They stand at the close of the Old Testament and before the Epistles.

THE BIBLE AT A GLANCE

Dr. Wm. H. Griffith Thomas suggests that we remember four words to help us link together the whole of God's revelation.

PREPARATION . . . In the Old Testament God makes ready for the coming of the Messiah.

MANIFESTATION . . . In the four Gospels Christ enters the world, dies for the world, and founds His Church.

APPROPRIATION . . . In the Acts and Epistles, the ways are revealed in which the Lord Jesus was received, appropriated, and applied in individual lives.

CONSUMMATION . . . In the Book of Revelation, the outcome of God's perfect plan is revealed.

346

WHAT IS THE GOSPEL?

Gospel means "good news." The good news concerning Jesus, the Son of God, is given us by four writers, Matthew, Mark, Luke and John, although there is but one Gospel, the glad story of salvation through Jesus Christ our Lord. The word "gospel" is never used in the New Testament of a book. It always means "good news." When we speak of the Gospel of Luke, we ought to understand that it means the good news of Jesus Christ as recorded by Luke. Nevertheless, from the earliest times, the term "gospel" has been applied to each of the four narratives which record the life of Christ.

No doubt originally the good news was oral. Men went from one place to another, telling the glad story by word of mouth. After a while a written record was necessary. More than one attempted this, with no success. See what Luke says in Luke 1:1-4: *Forasmuch as many have taken in hand to set forth in order a declaration of those things which are most surely believed among us, Even as they delivered them unto us, which from the beginning were eyewitnesses, and ministers of the word; it seemed good to me also, having had perfect understanding of all things from the very first, to write unto thee in order, most excellent Theophilus, that thou mightest know the certainty of those things, wherein thou hast been instructed.*

There is but one Gospel, with four presentations. Four pictures of one Christ are given. The combined gospel records set forth a Personality rather than present a connected story of a life.

WHY FOUR GOSPELS?

As everyone knows, there are four Gospels, but the question at once arises, "Why four?" Why wouldn't one straightforward, continuous narrative have been enough? Would not this have been simpler and clearer? Might this not have saved us from some of the difficulties which have arisen in what some have said are conflicting accounts?

The answer seems plain. Because one or two would not have given us a portrayal of the life of Christ. There are four distinct offices of Christ portrayed in the Gospels. He is presented as:

King in Matthew, Servant in Mark, Son of Man in Luke, Son of God in John.

It is true that each of the four Gospels has much in common with the others. Each deals with Christ's earthly ministry, His death and resurrection, His teachings and miracles, but each Gospel has its differences. We at once see that each of the writers is trying to present a different picture of our one Lord.

Matthew deliberately adds to his account what Mark omits. There is a lack of completeness as to His life history in any one of the four Gospels. Hear what John says in 21:25: *And there are also many other things which Jesus did, the which, if they should be written every one, I suppose that even the world itself could not contain the books that should be written.*

There are deliberate gaps which none of the evangelists professes to fill in. For instance, all omit any account of the eighteen years of Christ's life between the ages of twelve and thirty. Although each Gospel is complete in itself, it is very selective; only a few of His miracles are described and only a portion of His teachings are given. Each evangelist has recorded that which is relevant and pertinent to his particular theme.

In the National Gallery in London there are three representations on a single canvas of Charles I. In one his head is turned to the right; in another, to the left; and in the center we find the full-face view. This is the story of this production. Van Dyck painted them for Bernini, the Roman sculptor, that he might by their help make a bust of the king. By combining the impressions so received, Bernini would be better able to produce a "speaking" likeness. One view would not have been enough.

It may be true that the Gospels were intended to serve the very purpose of these portraits. Each presents a different aspect of our Lord's life on earth. Together we have the complete picture. He was a King, but He was the Perfect Servant, too. He was the Son of Man, but we must not forget He was the Son of God.

There are four Gospels with one Christ, four accounts with one purpose, and four sketches of one Person.

JESUS IN THE FOUR GOSPELS

Master this outline and you will be familiar with the contents of the Gospels for life.

KING . . . Matthew presents Jesus as King. Written primarily for the Jew, He is the Son of David. His royal genealogy is given in chapter 1. In chapters 5–7, in the Sermon on the Mount, we have the manifesto of the King, containing the laws of His kingdom.

SERVANT . . . Mark depicts Jesus as Servant. Written to the Romans, there is no genealogy. Why? Men are not interested in the genealogy of a servant. More miracles are found here than in any other Gospel. Romans cared little for words; far more for deeds.

MAN . . . Luke sets forth Jesus as the perfect Man. Written to the Greeks, His genealogy goes back to Adam, the first man, instead of to Abraham. As a perfect Man, He is seen much in prayer and with angels ministering to Him.

GOD . . . John portrays Jesus as the Son of God. Written to all who will believe, with the purpose of leading men to Christ (John 20:31), everything in this Gospel illustrates and demonstrates His divine relationship. The opening verse carries us back to "the beginning."

Dr. Griffith Thomas gives the pictures of the Gospels in this way:

Matthew is concerned with the coming of a Promised Saviour.

Mark is concerned with the life of a Powerful Saviour.

Luke is concerned with the grace of a Perfect Saviour.

John is concerned with the possession of a Personal Saviour.

Let us present another answer to the question, "Why four Gospels?" Scripture answers much for us. Scripture uses numbers with precision, accuracy and real meaning. You know that seven is the perfect number; three is the number of the Godhead; forty is the number of testing. Four is the number of the earth. Look at a few illustrations. There are four points of the compass, north, east, south and west. There are four seasons of the year, spring, summer, autumn and winter. In the parable of the Sower, our Lord divided the field into four kinds of soil.

Later He said, *The field is the world.* If four is the earth number, how fitting that the Holy Spirit should have given us four Gospels in which to depict the earthly ministry of the Heavenly One.

When we draw nearer, we see then good reason for four Gospels. Christ is the one glorious Theme of them all, but each of the writers is absorbed with some special feature in Christ's character and office. Each evangelist takes some office and develops it with convincing power. It is the unfolding of this particular view of the work of Christ that stamps the design on each book.

Let us pause to say this. All the Gospels are bound up with the promises of the Messiah in the Old Testament. We cannot explain the Gospels apart from the great Messianic prophecies in the Old Testament.

The prophets have portrayed a magnificent picture of the Messiah. They have told of His offices, mission, birth, suffering, death, resurrection and glory. Let us consider the names and titles which the prophets have bestowed upon Him.

He is called the King. Psalm 72; Isaiah 9:6,7; 32:1; Jeremiah 23:5; Zechariah 9:9; 14:9. These passages, among many others, tell of the kingly office of the Messiah. The prophets tell much of His kingdom and its extent, and of Christ's ultimate triumph.

He is called the Servant of Jehovah. Isaiah 42:1-7; 52:13-15; 53.

He is called the Man, the Son of Man. Genesis 3:15; 22:18; Isaiah 7:14-16; 9:6.

He is called God. Isaiah 9:6; 40:3-5; 47:4; Jeremiah 23:6.

It is as these four that Jesus is set forth in the Gospels.

TYPES OF MEN THEN AND NOW

Christ was going to be presented to widely different types of men, who made up the world. Each race was capable of appreciating one particular kind of presentation more than another.

THE JEW—There were four classes of people in Jesus' day that represent four types of men today. Take the Jew first. He had his special training. He was steeped in Old Testament Scrip-

350

ture and the prophets. Matthew writes the story of Jesus' life on earth especially for this people. If the Jew was to be impressed, it would have to be by one of his own race. His teacher must be a man versed in the Old Testament, and in the customs of the Jews. They must know that this Jesus came to fulfill the prophecies of the Old Testament. Over and over again we read in Matthew, *That it might be fulfilled . . . as was spoken by Jeremiah the prophet.*

We have the same type of person today. They revel in prophecies fulfilled and unfulfilled. They seek to know what the prophets have spoken, and how it is brought to pass.

THE ROMAN—Next came the Roman, the master of the world at that time. Mark writes especially for him. The Romans knew nothing about Old Testament Scripture. They were not interested in prophecy being fulfilled. But they were vitally concerned over a remarkable Leader who had appeared in Palestine. He had claimed more than ordinary authority, and had possessed extraordinary powers. They wanted to hear more about this Jesus—what sort of a person He really was, what He had said, and what He had done.

The Roman liked the straightforward message of one like Mark. One thousand three hundred and seventy-five times the word "and" is used in Mark. It moves on in a beauty and force all its own. Mark's Gospel is filled with deeds, not words. Clearly it is the Gospel of the Ministry of Christ.

The Roman of Jesus' day was a type of the average businessman of today. He is not concerned at first about the genealogy of a king, but with a God "who is able", a God who can meet man's every need. Mark is the businessman's Gospel.

THE GREEK—Then there is Luke. This Gospel was written by a Greek doctor, to his own countrymen who were lovers of beauty, poetry and culture. They lived in a world of large ideas. Their tastes were fastidious. The Gospel of Luke tells of the birth and childhood of Jesus. It gives the inspired songs connected with the life of Christ. We find the salutation of Elizabeth when Mary visited her (Luke 1:42-45). We hear the song of the virgin mother (Luke 1:46-55). Even Zacharias burst into praise when speech was restored to him (Luke 1:68-79). At the Saviour's birth a chorus of angel voices ring out (Luke 2:13,14), and then the shepherd's song of praise to God in Luke 2:20 is heard.

The Greek is the type of the student and idealist today who is seeking after truth for he believes that is the goal of happiness.

ALL MEN—John is written to all men, that they might believe that Jesus is the Christ. Christ is portrayed as the Son of God. This Gospel is filled with extraordinary claims that attest His divine character and mission.

The "all men" of John's day were like the masses today who need Christ. They include the "whosoever" who will believe on the Lord Jesus because they have a sense of need and want to receive the gift of eternal life through Jesus Christ the Lord.

KEYS TO THE GOSPELS
Front Door Keys

God has hung the key to the Gospel of Matthew right over the entrance. The book opens thus: *The book of the generation of Jesus Christ, the son of David, the son of Abraham* (Matthew 1:1). This shows His covenant position as the Son of Abraham, (see Genesis 12:1-3), and His royal position as Son of David.

Matthew is presenting Christ as King; he gives the royal genealogy in the first seventeen verses. A king is not chosen by popular ballot, but by birth.

Turn now to Mark. See how this book opens. No genealogy is given. The reason is that Jesus is portrayed as a Servant, and no one is interested in the pedigree of a servant.

Turn to Luke. Is there a genealogy given? See Luke 3:23. Matthew traces Christ's line back to Abraham and David, to show He was a Jew and of the royal line. Luke traces His line back to Adam. Christ is presented as the ideal Man. He was of the line of Adam.

Turn to John. How does this book open? No genealogy, but *In the beginning was the Word, and the Word was with God, and the Word was God.* Christ is portrayed as God in John.

Back Door Keys

Now let us see how the Gospels close. Turn to Matthew 28:18-20. Hear the KING commanding and commissioning His disciples. The Messiah is still on earth, for it is on earth and not in heaven that the Son of David shall reign in glory. *All power is given unto me in heaven and in earth. Go ye therefore, and teach all nations . . . to observe all things whatsoever I have commanded you: and, lo, I am with you alway, even unto the end of the world.*

Now look at the close of Mark. It is very significant and appropriate. *And they went forth, and preached everywhere, the Lord working with them . . .* (16:20). Jesus, the Servant, is pictured as still laboring with His disciples.

Luke ends in a different way. Jesus, the perfect Man, is ascending to the Father. Notice what Luke says in 24:51: *He was parted from them, and carried up into heaven.* Not that He ascended, but was carried up into heaven. He is still a Man in resurrection and ascension glory.

The closing verse of John is significant: *And there are also many other things which Jesus did, the which, if they should be written every one, I suppose that even the world itself could not contain the books that should be written* (21:25). Truly, *Never man spake like this man* (7:46)! for He was the very Son of God.

Minimum Daily Requirements/Spiritual Vitamins

Sunday: THE KING CHRIST JESUS
Matthew 2:1-12; 21:1-11

Monday: THE SERVANT CHRIST JESUS
Mark 10:35-45; 2:1-22

Tuesday: THE MAN CHRIST JESUS   Luke 4:1-13;
John 19:4-13

Wednesday: THE GOD-MAN   John 1:1-18; 3:1-16

Thursday: OUR REDEEMER, JESUS CHRIST
John 19:16-42

Friday: THE MASTER, JESUS CHRIST
Matthew 4:18-25

Saturday: OUR MASTER, JESUS CHRIST
John 21:1-17

UNDERSTANDING MATTHEW

Matthew Portrays Jesus Christ, The Promised Messiah

Matthew has a special object in his Gospel, to show the Jews that Jesus is the long-expected Messiah, the Son of David, and that His life fulfilled the Old Testament prophecies. The purpose is given in the first verse. Matthew is *the book of the generation of Jesus Christ, the son of David, the son of Abraham.* This statement links Christ with two of the great covenants that God made with David and Abraham. God's covenant with David consisted of the promise of a King to sit upon his throne forever (II Samuel 7:8-13). God's covenant with Abraham promised that through him should all families of the earth be blessed (Genesis 12:3). David's son was a King. Abraham's son was a Sacrifice. Matthew opens with the birth of a King, and closes with the offering of a Sacrifice.

From the beginning, Jesus is associated with the Jewish nation. Matthew used wisdom in not alienating the Jews who might read the story. He is convincing them that this One fulfilled every prophecy spoken concerning their promised Messiah. He quotes freely from the Old Testament, more than any of the other evangelists. Twenty-nine such quotations are given. Thirteen times he says that this or that event took place *that it might be fulfilled which was spoken of the Lord by the prophet.*

Matthew links us up with the Old Testament. On every page he is trying to connect the Gospel with the prophets and show that all of their teaching is being fulfilled in the person and kingdom of Jesus Christ.

It is difficult for us to appreciate how great the transition is from the old to the new. It seemed to the Jew that he must give up his tradition and orthodoxy and accept another creed.

Paul, especially in Galatians, show
they were not giving up their old
giving up types and shadows for the

quainted with Jewish history and cus-
ning and fishing and the housekeeping of
en parables in chapter 13. He knew this
ld strike responsive chords in the hearts of

atthew, get a clear and comprehensive view of
the entil el. Keep in mind the Messianic character of this
Gospel. Note the balance between Jesus' ministry and teaching.
We find the genealogy of the King; His birth in Bethlehem, the
city of David, according to Micah's prophecy (Micah 5:2); the
coming of the forerunner, John the Baptist, as Malachi predicted (Malachi 3:1); the ministry of the King; His rejection by
Israel; and the promise of His coming again in power and glory.

The author is no doubt a Christian Jew (Matthew 9:9;
10:3). Matthew, "gift of God," was a tax collector at Capernaum, under the Roman law, when Jesus chose him as one of
the twelve disciples. His name is found in all the lists of the
twelve, though Mark and Luke give his other name, Levi. The
only word the author speaks about himself is that he was a "publican," which was then a term of reproach, as the term "poli-
tician" so often denotes today. The other evangelists tell about
the great feast he gave Jesus, and record the significant fact that
he left all and followed Him. No doubt he was a man of means.

THE POSITION OF MATTHEW

Matthew breaks the silence of 400 years, between Malachi's
prophecy and the announcement of the birth of Jesus. Israel
was under the domination of the Roman Empire. No man of
"the house of David" had been allowed to sit upon the throne
for over 600 years.

Herod was not the king of Israel, but a governor of Judea,
appointed by the Emperor of Rome. The man who really had
the throne-rights of the house of David was Joseph, the carpenter, who became the husband of Mary. See the genealogy of

Joseph in Matthew 1, and notice especially one name, Jechonias (Jeconiah), in verse 11. If Joseph had been Jesus' father according to the flesh, He could never have occupied the throne, for God's word barred the way. There had been a curse on this royal line since the days of Jeconiah. In Jeremiah 22:30 we read, *Thus saith the Lord, write ye this man childless, a man that shall not prosper in his days: for no man of his seed shall prosper, sitting upon the throne of David, and ruling any more in Judah.* Joseph was in the line of this curse. Hence, if Christ had been Joseph's son, He could not have sat on David's throne.

But we find another genealogy in Luke 3. This is Mary's line, back to David, through Nathan, not Jeconiah (Luke 3:31). There was no curse on this line. To Mary, God said, *Fear not, Mary, for thou hast found favor with God. And, behold, thou shalt conceive in thy womb, and bring forth a son, and shalt call His name JESUS. He shall be great, and shall be called the Son of the Highest: and the Lord God shall give unto him the throne of his father David: And he shall reign over the house of Jacob forever; and of his kingdom there shall be no end* (Luke 1:30-33).

Now the silence is broken and the coming of the Messiah declared.

The Book of Matthew follows after the Old Testament and is the beginning of the New. It is the connecting link between the books. It is written for the Jews, and it is fittingly placed. It takes for granted that the course of events is known to its readers. The Old Testament had closed with the chosen nation looking for their long-promised King, their Messiah. Matthew's Gospel shows that Jesus was that King. It is the Gospel of Fulfillment.

Matthew presents the Lord Jesus in a distinctly Jewish relationship. Only in this one of the four Gospels do we find a record of the Messiah's declaration, *I am not sent but unto the lost sheep of the house of Israel* (Matthew 15:24). What did His own people do with Him? (See John 1:11.)

In numerical position, the Book of Matthew is the fortieth in the canon. Thirty-nine books in the Old Testament, then Matthew. Forty is always a number of testing or probation in Scripture. Jesus was tempted of the Devil forty days; Israel was in the wilderness forty years; David was king forty years; Moses was in a palace forty years, then on the back side of a desert for forty years. What other instances of this number forty do you remember in Scripture? Look it up in your concordance.

In this fortieth book of the Bible, Israel is in the place of probation and testing, by the presence of the Messiah in their midst. Christ is presented as King to the Jews, and they reject Him, not only as their Messiah, but as their Saviour (Matthew 16:21).

COMING OF THE KING (Read Matthew 1:1–2:23)

Jesus would have made any book of notables. Matthew is the Gospel of the Messiah, God's anointed One. The main purpose of the Spirit in this book is to show that Jesus of Nazareth is the predicted Messiah, the Deliverer, of whom Moses and the prophets wrote. *His goings forth have been . . . from everlasting* (Micah 5:2). He is the child that was to be born, the Son given, of whom Isaiah speaks (Isaiah 9:6) who shall be called *Wonderful, Counsellor, The mighty God, The everlasting Father, The Prince of Peace.*

All the maps of the world and all the calendars of time tell of Christ's birthplace and birthday. Jesus was born in Bethlehem of Judea (Micah 5:2; Matthew 2:1), in the days of Herod the king. We know this place and this king. We don't have to build the story out of the imagination. We are given names and dates. Christianity is an historical religion. The Gospel does not begin with, "Once upon a time," but starts with *Bethlehem in Judea.* The town is there, and we can know the very place where Jesus was born.

The time is definite, *in the days of Herod the king.* History knows Herod. There is nothing mythical about this monster of iniquity.

These statements are facts and no critic or unbeliever can doubt them. The Gospel narrative sets its record in the solid foundation of history. We are not building our faith on a myth, but substantial fact. This thing was not done in a corner, but in the broad day, and it is not afraid of the geographer's map and the historian's pen.

The story of the birth of Jesus, in Matthew, differs from the record in Luke. They complement each other. While there is much untold, God has told us all we need to know. Jesus' earthly life began in a stable. His cradle was a manger. His family and associates were humble folk. He came as a helpless babe. How human was our Lord! But Jesus was heralded by an archangel, welcomed by an angel choir, and worshiped by earth's wisest philosophers! How divine was our Lord!

Most young people, when they begin reading Matthew, with its "begats," and Luke 3:23-38, with its "the son of's," wonder what these are all about. We ought to realize that if they were included in Scripture, they were put there for a purpose. We want to look in this lesson at these two genealogies.

A "genealogy" is "the history of the descent of an individual or family from an ancestor" (Webster). There are two genealogies of Christ:

Matthew 1:1-17, and Luke 3:23-38. They are not alike, and the reason is that each traces the descent of Christ back for different purposes.

Matthew traces Jesus' line back to Abraham and David to show that He was a JEW (coming from David). Luke traces Jesus' line back to Adam to show that He belonged to the human race.

Matthew shows Jesus as of royal descent, the King, the Messiah, the Lion of the tribe of Judah, the promised Ruler of Israel. Luke shows Jesus as of human lineage, the ideal Man, born of woman.

You will find that these pictures of Jesus are kept all through each Gospel—Matthew portraying Him as MESSIAH, Luke as MAN.

THE KINGLY LINE

Why are we concerned about these genealogies? Because they give us the key to the whole LIFE OF CHRIST. They show us, from the very start, that He was not just another man, but that

359

He was descended from a royal family, and there was a king's blood in His veins. If He were not a KING, He could not claim the rulership of our lives. If He were not a MAN, He could not know "our sorrows" and "be acquainted with our griefs."

Go through Matthew and follow this trail of the King.

Behold How Much Like a King He Was!

A KING'S NAME—*They shall call his name Emmanuel* (1:23).

A KING'S POSITION—*Out of thee shall come a Governor, that shall rule my people Israel* (2:6).

A KING'S ANNOUNCEMENT—*Prepare ye the way of the Lord, make his paths straight* (3:3).

A KING'S CORONATION—*This is my beloved Son, in whom I am well pleased* (3:17).

A KING'S DUE RESPECT—*Thou shalt worship the Lord thy God, and him only shalt thou serve* (4:10).

A KING'S PROCLAMATION—*And he opened his mouth, and taught them* (5:2). *He taught them as one having authority . . .* (7:29).

A KING'S LOYALTY—*He that is not with me is against me; and he that gathereth not with me scattereth abroad* (12:30).

A KING'S ENEMIES—*From that time forth began Jesus to show unto his disciples, how that he must go unto Jerusalem, and suffer many things of the elders and chief priests and scribes* (16:21).

A KING'S LOVE—*The Son of man came not to be ministered unto, but to minister, and to give his life a ransom for many* (20:28).

A KING'S GLORY—*When the Son of man shall come . . . then shall the King shall say unto them . . . Come, ye blessed of my Father, inherit the kingdom* (25:31,34).

A KING'S SACRIFICE—*And they crucified him . . . and set up over his head his accusation written, THIS IS JESUS THE KING OF THE JEWS* (27:35,37).

A KING'S VICTORY—*He is not here: for he is risen, as he said* (28:6).

Matthew alone tells of the visit of the wise men from the East. These were Persian magi, scholars, students of the stars. They came to worship and honor a King. These wise men did not come inquiring, "Where is He that is born the Saviour of the world?" but *Where is he that is born King of the Jews?*

Mark, Luke and John are silent about the wise men because they are not recording the birth of a king. The holy, sacred star had halted over a manger in Bethlehem to tell of Christ's birth. The whole world at this time was expecting the advent of some great One. *Where is he that is born King of the Jews?* was the question on every lip. With all the prophecies that had been made to Israel, neither the world nor Israel could be criticized for expecting a King who would rule the earth from David's throne! (Jeremiah 23:3-6; 30:8-10; 33:14-16,25,26; Ezekiel 37:21; Isaiah 9:7; Hosea 3:4,5).

The priests knew where Christ was to be born, but they did not know Christ when He was born.

The wise men were led to a Person, not a creed.

The adoration of the wise men foreshadowed Christ's universal dominion. Some day *every knee should bow, . . . every tongue should confess that Jesus Christ is Lord, to the glory of God the Father* (Philippians 2:10,11). *He shall have dominion also from sea to sea, and from the river unto the ends of the earth* (Psalm 72:8).

Paul tells us, in Galatians 4:4,5, *When the fulness of the time was come, God sent forth his Son, made of a woman, made under the law, to redeem them that were under the law.* Jesus came to be the world's Saviour.

The birth of Jesus was followed by twelve years of silence until His visit with the doctors in Jerusalem. Then silence shut Him in again, with only the word "carpenter" to throw any light upon the next eighteen years, and let us know what He was doing. Jesus took thirty years of preparation for three years of ministry.

PROCLAMATION OF THE KINGDOM
(Read Matthew 3:1–16:20)

John the Baptist had another name, for, as the prophet Isaiah began to unfold the real message of his book, the coming of the Messiah, Servant of Jehovah, he introduced a character known

PALESTINE
NEW TESTAMENT

SIDON
ITURAEA
ABILENE
SAREPTA
DAMASCUS
TYRE
MT. HERMON
CAESAREA PHILIPPI
PHOENICIA
TRACHONITIS

MEDITERRANEAN
SEA
GALILEE
GAULANITIS
CHORAZIN
PTOLEMAIS
CAPERNAUM
BETHSAIDA
CANA
SEA OF
MAGDALA
GALILEE
RIVER
TIBERIAS
KISHON
NAZARETH
GERGESA?
RIVER
MT. OF
GADARA
KISHON
BEATITUDES
NAIN
RIVER
JORDAN
DECAPOLIS
SALIM?
CAESAREA
AENON?
SAMARIA
SAMARIA
PLAIN OF
SYCHAR
SHARON
MT. GERIZIM
ANTIPATRIS
BETHABARA?
JOPPA
ARIMATHEA
PERAEA
RAMAH
EPHRAIM
LYDDA
EMMAUS
JERICHO
BETHPHAGE?
BETHANY?
AZOTUS
JERUSALEM
MT. OF OLIVES
BETHANY
BETHLEHEM
JUDAEA
DEAD SEA
GAZA

IDUMAEA
EGYPT
ARABIA

simply as "a voice." *The voice of him that crieth in the wilderness, Prepare ye the way of the LORD, make straight in the desert a highway for our God* (Isaiah 40:3). It is this "voice" which, although unnamed here, is to be the herald of Jesus Christ. His two functions: that of voice and that of messenger (Malachi 3:1), are all that the Old Testament tells us of John the Baptist. But it is much. It is indeed wonderful not only that Christ should have been foretold all through the Scriptures, but that His forerunner, John the Baptist, also is described.

In Matthew we hear the "voice": *Repent ye: for the kingdom of heaven is at hand. For this is he that was spoken of by the prophet Esaias [Isaiah], saying, The voice of one crying in the wilderness, Prepare ye the way of the Lord, make his paths straight* (Matthew 3:2,3).

The King must be announced! It was the duty of this herald to go before the King, as a Roman officer before his ruler, and command that the roads be repaired over which his Master would travel. John the Baptist did this. He showed that the spiritual roads of the lives of men and nations were full of the chuckholes of sin and sharp turns of iniquity, and needed rebuilding and straightening.

We see the King stepping from His personal and private life into His public ministry (Matthew 4). He is facing a crisis. Satan met Him. After the benediction the Father had put upon Him at His baptism, when He said, *This is my beloved Son, in whom I am well pleased;* we see Jesus coming forth to carry out the plans for which He came into the world. He was led into the wilderness to face the first major conflict of His public ministry.

Notice that Satan offered Jesus a short cut to that universal Kingdom which He had come to gain through the long and painful way of the cross, but Christ came to be a Saviour first, then a King. How strong is the temptation to take a short cut to our ambitions! Jesus stood victor, His shield undented and untarnished. He went forth to conquer all other temptations until His final victory and ascension to heaven as Lord of all. (See I Cor. 10:13.)

363

THE KINGDOM LAWS

Every kingdom must have its laws and standards to control its subjects. The Kingdom of Heaven is no exception. Jesus declared that He came not to destroy the law but to fulfill it. The old law was good in its day. Moses and the prophets were far in advance of their time. They were pioneers. Jesus did not destroy this old law, but He treated it as rudimentary and not as perfect and final.

Jesus says that any reform that starts on the outside and works in is beginning at the wrong end. Christ starts on the inside and works out. The only way of getting a good life is first getting a good heart.

From the lofty pulpit of a mountain, Jesus preached the sermon that contains the laws of His Kingdom (Matthew 5,6,7). Read through these chapters and refresh your memory about this most wonderful of Jesus' discourses. It is freighted with teaching. After over 1900 years this Sermon on the Mount has lost none of its majesty or power. The teachings of this sermon overtop all human teachings. The world has not yet caught up with its simplest ideals and requirements. Many a person who is not a Christian claims that the Sermon on the Mount is his religion. How little he understands the depth of its meaning. It is important that we do not simply praise this rule as a wonderful theory but that we actually practice it in our own lives. If we let this rule operate in our lives, it will change all of our personal relations, heal our social wounds, solve every dispute between nations, yes, set the whole world in order. The root of this law is kindness. It is true, if human society would have its standards as theirs, the world would be set in order. One day filled with it would be a bit of heaven. Love would reign instead of lawlessness. Christ shows us that sin lies not just in committing the act but in the motive behind it as well. (See Matthew 5:21,22,27,28.) No one can expect forgiveness who does not forgive (Matthew 6:12,14,15). Has anyone yet ever fathomed the depth of Matthew 7:12? It is easy to read; it is hard to do.

Jesus defines the nature and limit of the Kingdom, the condition for entrance, its laws, its privileges and rewards. The Sermon on the Mount sets forth the Constitution of the Kingdom. Fourteen times the King says, "I say unto you." Mark them in your Bible. This will reveal Jesus' authority as He deals with the law of Moses. Men must not only keep the law outwardly but in spirit as well. Notice the effect upon the people. *And it came to pass, when Jesus had ended these sayings, the people were astonished at his doctrine: For he taught them as one having authority, and not as the scribes* (Matthew 7:28,29).

THE KING'S POWER

We find the King proved the special miracles which He wrought (Matthew 8,9). He met human needs. There are twelve astonishing miracles in these two chapters. What were they? After Jesus had performed the miracles in chapter 12, we read, *And all the people were amazed, and said, Is not this the Son of David* (Matthew 12:23)?

The critical scribes now thrust themselves into the scene and passed their hostile judgment on the actions of Jesus (Matthew 9:3).

The Kingdom was proclaimed "at hand" because the King Himself was there.

THE KING'S CABINET

Jesus not only preached Himself, but He gathered others around Him. It was necessary to organize His Kingdom, to put it on a wider and more permanent basis. A king must have subjects. He would reflect His light through human instruments. He says, *Ye are the light of the world* (Matthew 5:14). Jesus still has a great message for the world, and He needs us to carry it. Spiritual ideas cannot stalk alone through the world and be of any value. They must be clothed with men and institutions who will serve as hearts and brains, hands and feet to carry them out. This is what Jesus was doing. He was calling men into His companionship to train them to carry on His work.

Where did Jesus find His helpers? Not in the temple, among the doctors or priests, nor in the colleges of Jerusalem. He found them on the seashore mending their nets. Jesus did not call many mighty or noble, but rather chose the foolish things of the world to confound the wise (I Cor. 1:27).

A list of the disciples is given in Matthew 10:2-4. This is probably the most important catalogue of names in the world. These men were given a work to do which would make winning battles and founding empires seem of small consequence. We find their great message was the Kingdom of Heaven. *And as ye go, preach, saying, The kingdom of heaven is at hand* (Matthew 10:7). Their tremendous mission was to start it.

Note some of the warnings and instructions for the disciples which Jesus stated in Matthew 10. What were they? If these requirements of discipleship hold true today, could you call yourself a disciple? Consider Christ's words thoughtfully in Matthew 10:32,33.

THE KINGDOM OF HEAVEN

The word kingdom occurs some 55 times in Matthew for this is the Gospel of the King. The expression, "kingdom of heaven," is found 35 times here and nowhere else in the Gospels. Of the fifteen parables recorded in Matthew, all but three begin, *The kingdom of heaven is like . . .*

The Jews well understood the term, "kingdom of heaven." Neither Jesus nor John defined it. At Sinai, God said to Israel, *Ye shall be unto me a kingdom of priests, and an holy nation* (Exodus 19:6). Israel at first was a theocracy. God was their King; they formed His kingdom. The prophets had referred to the Messianic Kingdom again and again.

Jesus likened the Kingdom of Heaven to: (Matthew 13)

The Sower	Leaven in the Dough
The Tares	A Hid Treasure
A Mustard Seed	A Pearl of Great Price

A Dragnet

These parables, called *the mysteries of the kingdom of heaven* (Matthew 13:11), describe what the result of the presence of the Gospel of Christ in the world will be during this present age until the time of His return when He will gather the harvest (Matthew 13:40-43). We see no bright picture of a

366

converted world. There shall be tares mixed with the wheat, good fish and bad, leaven in the loaf. (Leaven is always a type of sin. The Spirit never uses leaven as a type of anything good. Look this up in your concordance and determine this for yourself.) Then there is an abnormal growth of the mustard seed, that admits "fowls of the air" to lodge in its branches. This is Christendom. Only Christ can determine what is good and what is bad, and at the harvest He will divide. If we are to have a kingdom on this earth, with the laws which Christ set down, then we must have the King. Some day Christ will come in power and great glory and establish His throne on this earth. We will have peace when the Prince of Peace reigns!

REJECTION OF THE KING (Read Matthew 16:21–20:34)

The sad story reads that Christ *came unto his own, and his own received Him not* (John 1:11). The Kingdom was first presented to the rightful heirs, the children of Israel (Jews), but they refused the offer, rejected the King, and finally crucified Him. From Matthew 12 on, we see much controversy among the leaders concerning Jesus.

Jesus announced that the Kingdom should be taken away from the Jews and given to another nation. *Therefore say I unto you, The kingdom of God shall be taken from you, and given to a nation bringing forth the fruits thereof* (Matthew 21:43). The announcement offended the rulers, and *they sought to lay hands on Him* (Matthew 21:46).

Our Lord told Nicodemus the requirement for entrance into the Kingdom of Heaven (John 3:3-7,16). "Whosoever" will believe may enjoy its privileges and blessings. The Kingdom is for the Gentile as well as the Jew.

Why did the Jews refuse the Kingdom? The world today is longing intensely for the golden age. A millennium of peace and rest is the great desire of diplomats and rulers. But they want it in their own way and on their own terms. They desire to bring it about by their own efforts. They have no longing for a millennium brought about by the personal return on earth of the Lord Jesus Christ. It was just so with the Jews in the days of John the Baptist.

367

Have you put Christ on the throne of your life? Have you the peace you long for? Have you accepted Christ's terms for your life?

THE CHURCH PROMISED

We find Jesus with His disciples up north in Caesarea Philippi, apparently with the object of having a private interview with them, in which He would disclose a great truth (Matthew 16).

Only in Matthew's Gospel is the "Church" named. When the Kingdom was rejected we find a change in the teachings of Jesus. He began to talk about the "Church" instead of the Kingdom (Matthew 16:18). Church comes from the word "ecclesia" which means "called out ones." Because all would not believe on Him, Christ said He was calling out anyone, Jew or Gentile, to belong to His Church, which is His body. He began to build a new edifice, a new body of people, which would include both Jew and Gentile (Ephesians 2:14-18).

LIFE'S MOST IMPORTANT QUESTION

When they were far away from the busy scene in which they lived, Jesus asked His disciples the question: *Whom do men say that I the Son of man am* (Matthew 16:13)?

This is the important question today! First asked by an obscure Galilean in that far off solitude, it has come thundering down through the centuries and has become the mightiest question in the world today. What think ye of Christ? What men think determines what they do and are. The ideas men hold about industry, wealth, government, morals and religion mold society and alter lives. So what men think of Christ is the master force in the world today and more than anything else influences its life and thought.

The disciples gave the answers men were giving. The answers then were as varied as they now are. All agreed that Jesus was an extraordinary person, at least a prophet or a person with an element of the supernatural. Men's opinions of Christ are high. The answer that Jesus was a myth, a dupe, or an impostor, is no longer tolerated.

Jesus now turned the general question into the sharp personal inquiry. *But whom say ye that I am?* Ask yourself this question. Important as the general question is, far more important to each one of us is this personal question. No one can escape it. A neutral answer is impossible. He is either God or an impostor.

LIFE'S MOST IMPORTANT ANSWER

Thou art the Christ, the Son of the living God! exclaimed the impulsive, fervent Peter. It grasps Christ as the Messiah, the fulfillment of the prophecies of the old Hebrew prophets. This confession is great because it exalts Christ as the Son of God and lifts Him above humanity and crowns Him with deity. From now on He reveals to this handful of disciples new truths about His teachings. He said to Peter and the disciples, after this answer concerning who He was, *Upon this rock I will build my church.* This is what Christ was going to do—build a Church of which He Himself was to be the chief cornerstone. This Church was born on Pentecost (Acts 2).

For the first time the fateful shadow of the cross fell across the path of the disciples. From this time on Jesus began to draw back the curtain that veiled the future and to show His disciples the things that would come to pass. He saw His path running to Jerusalem into the awful hatred of the priests and Pharisees and then on to the terrible cross, but He saw the glory of the resurrection morning. (See Matthew 16:21.)

Jesus did not reveal these things until His disciples were ready to bear it. God often in His mercy hides the future from us.

TRIUMPH OF THE KING (Read Matthew 21:1–28:20)

On the morning of Palm Sunday there was a stir in Bethany, and along the road leading to Jerusalem. It was understood that Jesus was to enter the city that day. The people were gathering in crowds. A colt was procured and the disciples, having thrown their robes over it, placed Jesus upon it, and the procession started. This little parade could not have been compared in magnificence with many a procession that has attended the coronation of a king, or the inauguration of a president; but it meant much more for the world. Jesus for the first time permitted a public recognition and celebration of His rights as Messiah-King. The end was approaching with awful swiftness, and He must offer Himself as Messiah, even if only to be rejected.

In their enthusiasm the people tore off branches from the palm and olive trees, and carpeted the highway, while shouts rang through the air. They believed in Jesus, and with all their warm Oriental enthusiasm were not ashamed of their King. In answer to the crowds who asked, "Who is this?" they boldly answered, "This is the prophet, Jesus, from Nazareth of Galilee." It took courage to say that in Jerusalem. Jesus was not entering the city as a triumphant conqueror, as the Romans had done. No sword was in His hand. Over Him floated no blood-stained banner. His mission was salvation!

In the evening the crowds dispersed, and Jesus quietly returned to Bethany. Apparently nothing in the way of making Jesus King had been accomplished. His Kingdom came not with observation or pageantry. His hour had not yet come. Christ must be Saviour first, then come again as King of kings and Lord of lords.

Christ's authority was brought into question as He went into the temple and ordered the merchants out, overturning their tables and telling them that they had made the house of God a den of thieves. A bitter controversy followed. *Then went the Pharisees, and took counsel how they might entangle him in his talk* (Matthew 22:15). He bade farewell to Jerusalem until He would come again to sit on David's throne.

THE FUTURE OF THE KINGDOM

He delivered His Mount Olivet discourse. He foretold the condition of the world after His ascension until He comes back in glory, to judge the nations as to their treatment of His brethren, the Jews (Matthew 25). This is not the judgment of the Great White Throne, which is the judgment of the wicked dead. Neither is it the judgment seat of Christ (II Cor. 5:10), which is the judgment of saints according to their works. It is the judgment of Gentile nations concerning their attitude toward God's people.

370

Much of Jesus' discourse in Matthew 24 and 25 is devoted to His second coming. He exhorts men to be ready, in the parables of the faithful servant, the ten virgins, and of the talents.

THE DEATH AND RESURRECTION OF THE KING

We have been passing through some of the highlights in the life of Jesus; now we step into the shadows as we enter Gethsemane. We see the Son of Abraham, the Sacrifice, dying that all the nations of the earth might be blessed by Him. Jesus was slain because He claimed to be the King of Israel. He was raised from the dead because He was the King (Acts 2:30-36). Although a large number of disciples believed in Jesus and followed Him, the opposition of the Jews was bitter and they determined to put Him to death. On the grounds of blasphemy, and of claiming to be the King of the Jews, thus making Himself the enemy of the Roman Emperor, Jesus was delivered up by Pilate to be crucified.

Matthew is not alone in his record of the terrible circumstances of the Saviour's passion; but he makes us feel that in the mock array, the crown of thorns, the sceptre, the title over the cross, we have a witness, though it be only scorn, to the kingly claim.

After hanging on the cruel tree for six hours, the Saviour died, not from physical suffering alone but of a broken heart, for He bore the sins of the whole world. We hear His triumphant cry, "It is finished!" He paid the debt of sin and became the world's Redeemer!

REDEMPTION COST A GREAT PRICE!

The mode of the Messiah's death had been foreshadowed by various types and symbols in the Old Testament. The brazen serpent in the wilderness signified that He was to be lifted up; the lamb upon the Jewish altar that His blood must be shed. His hands and His feet were to be pierced; He was to be wounded and tormented; His ears were to be filled with revilings, upon His vesture were lots to be cast and vinegar was to be given Him to drink. All of these incidents at the Messiah's death had been foretold in Jewish prophecy. But this is not all of the redemption story. Jesus was put in Joseph's tomb, and on the third day He arose, as He had said. This is the supreme test of His kingship. Men thought that He was dead and His Kingdom had failed. By His resurrection Christ assured His disciples that the King still lived and that one day He will come back to establish His kingdom on earth.

The ascension of Jesus is not recorded in Matthew. The curtain falls with the Messiah still on earth, for it is on earth and not in heaven, that the Son of David is yet to reign in glory. The last time the Jews saw Christ, He was on the Mount of Olives. The next time they see Him, He will be on the Mount of Olives! (See Zech. 14:4, Acts 1:11.)

A WORLD-WIDE COMMISSION

Jesus announced His program and a crisis hour was struck in the history of Christianity. The climax is found in His great commission, *All power is given unto me in heaven and in earth. Go ye therefore, and teach all nations, baptizing them in the name of the Father, and of the Son, and of the Holy Ghost: Teaching them to observe all things whatsoever I have commanded you: and, lo, I am with you alway, even unto the end of the world* (Matthew 28:18-20).

On what mission were they sent? To overrun the world with armies and make men submit under the sword? No, but to "make disciples of all nations."

From the mountain top of His ascension His disciples started forth on this mission, radiating from that center, and they have gone on until they have everywhere reached the rim of the world. Christianity is no national or racial religion. It knows no bounds of mountain or sea, but it envelops the globe.

372

Minimum Daily Requirements/Spiritual Vitamins

Sunday: THE KING BORN Matthew 1:18–2:23
Monday: THE KING BEGINS WORK Matthew 4:1-25
Tuesday: THE KING STATES KINGDOM LAWS
  Matthew 5:1-17, 41-48; 6:19-34
Wednesday: THE KING AND HIS FOLLOWERS
  Matthew 10:1-33
Thursday: THE KINGDOM MYSTERIES
  Matthew 13:1-52
Friday: THE KING OFFERS HIMSELF AS KING
  Matthew 21:1-11
Saturday: THE KING WILL RETURN
  Matthew 25:14-16

CHAPTER 29

UNDERSTANDING MARK

*Mark
Portrays Jesus Christ,
the Servant of God*

THE WRITER

John, whose surname was Mark, is the writer (Acts 12:12,25). He was the son of Mary, and cousin of Barnabas (Colossians 4:10), and likely a native of Jerusalem. He accompanied Paul and Barnabas to Antioch, and was the cause of some trouble between them (Acts 12:25; 13:5). Then he left them, probably on account of hardships (Acts 13:13). Finally he became a great help to Paul (Colossians 4:10,11; II Timothy 4:11). It is believed that the disciples met in the upper room of Mark's mother's house in Jerusalem. Peter was the means of his conversion, and affectionately speaks of him as "my son" (I Peter 5:13). We see the influence of the teaching of Peter in this Gospel.

THE PURPOSE

If we turn to Mark 10:45 we can quite easily determine Mark's object in writing his Gospel. *For even the Son of man came not to be ministered unto, but to minister, and to give his life a ransom for many.* Unlike Matthew, Mark was not trying to prove certain statements and prophecies concerning Jesus. His only object in writing was to tell clearly certain facts about Jesus, His deeds more especially than His words. That Jesus is the Son of God he proves, not by declaring how He came to earth, but by showing what He accomplished during His brief career on this earth, how His coming changed the world.

There is a general agreement that Mark's Gospel was written for Roman readers. The Roman was different from the Jew. His genius was his strong common sense. His religion must be practical. He would have no interest in tracing beliefs back into the past. Legal genealogies and fulfillments of prophecy would leave him cold. Jewish dogmas were not in his line. He might say, "I know nothing of your Scriptures, and care nothing for your peculiar notions; but I should be glad to hear a plain story of the life this man Jesus lived. Tell me what He did. Let me see Him just as He was."

Mark differs widely from Matthew in both character and scope. Mark's Gospel is the shortest of them all.

Matthew has 28 chapters, abounds in parables, and portrays Christ as the Son of David with kingly dignity and authority (28:18).

Mark has 16 chapters, and gives four parables. Mark portrays Christ as the humble but perfect Servant of Jehovah. We find the angels ministering unto Him.

GENERAL CHARACTERISTICS OF THIS GOSPEL

The skill of an artist may lie in what he leaves out. An amateur crowds everything in. In strict harmony with Mark's central purpose of emphasizing Jesus as the Servant, we note the omissions.

There is nothing about the virgin birth. No reference to His birth is made in the whole Gospel. This is significant. No one is interested in the pedigree of a servant.

There is no visit of wise men. A servant does not receive homage.

No account of Jesus as the boy in the temple is given. In this practical age, as in the age of Jesus, men demand a Christ who can do things. They are not interested in Jesus, the boy, but Christ the man, who is able and willing to accomplish today what He did of old.

There is no Sermon on the Mount. Matthew devotes three whole chapters to this sermon which sets forth the laws of the kingdom, and describes the character of its subjects. Mark presents Christ as a perfect "Workman"; a servant has no kingdom and frames no laws.

No quotations from the prophets are imparted. Mark's one direct quotation from the prophets is found in Mark 1:2. Matthew quotes on every page.

No divine titles are used. Jesus is never owned as "King" in Mark, except in derision. Matthew says, "They shall call His name Emmanuel,"—"God with us." Not so in Mark. Mark calls Him "Master"—other evangelists call Him "Lord."

Matthew says, "Lord, save us; we perish." Mark says, "Master, carest thou not that we perish?"

There is no statement that His work was finished at His death. In John 19:30, He said, "It is finished." This is not found in Mark. It is not for a servant to say when his work is done.

There is no introduction in Mark. The other Gospels have lengthy openings, but there is none in Mark. The opening verse says "Gospel of Jesus Christ." Mark adds, "Son of God," to guard His divine glory. How different this is from Matthew, where we found the Gospel of the Kingdom.

The word "gospel" is used twelve times in Matthew, Mark, Luke and John together, and eight of those times are in Mark. Yes, the Servant is to bear good news!

Another term is the Greek word "eutheos," which is translated "forthwith," "straightway," "immediately." Mark them when you find them. In all, this word is found no less than forty times in Mark's Gospel. This is a servant's word.

If you glance at the word which opens twelve out of sixteen chapters, you will see the little word "and." His service was one complete, perfect whole, with no pause or breaks in it. His service was continuous. We slacken up, but not our Lord.

One of the first things that impresses us, as we look at Mark's Gospel, is its brevity. It is much shorter than any of the other Gospels. Very little is found here that is not found in the others. It moves off with precision.

Matthew records fourteen parables; Mark only four—the Sower, the Seed growing secretly (peculiar to Mark), the Mustard Seed, and the Wicked Husbandmen. Not only do you find omission in number but in type. There is nothing about the "householder," or the marriage of the "king's son," or "talents."

Miracles have a leading place in Mark, as parables have in Matthew. A servant works; a king speaks. Mark describes more of Jesus' miracles than he records Christ's parables. Twenty miracles are given in Mark in detail.

THE SERVANT PREPARED (Read Mark 1:1-13)

The Book of Mark skips over the first thirty years of Jesus' life, but these years were all needful for His human preparation for His life's work. He grew in sympathy with daily toil. He wrestled, like Jacob, with life's problems. He fought many battles in the arena of His heart. He meditated upon the needs of His nation, till His heart burned within Him.

Preparation in life is needed. Jesus' life illustrated this. The foundations of the lighthouse are so necessary though unseen beneath the surface. The coral colony builds the foundations for an island and its tropical growth. The plant sends its roots into the dark soil before it can bring forth the flower and leaf. Look at the forty years which Moses spent in the desert before he entered upon his great work; the long period of Elijah's youth before he appeared before King Ahab; the youth of Amos spent on a farm; John the Baptist's thirty years of training. So with Jesus! He spent thirty years in obscurity in Nazareth before He appeared for the three years of public ministry. Getting ready for our life's work is of tremendous importance. Don't chafe if Christ uses time in preparing you for life.

PREPARATION BY JOHN THE FORERUNNER

This Gospel begins with John the Baptist making ready for the coming of the Messiah. John's coming was in fulfillment of a Messianic prophecy, *as it is written in the prophets* (Mark 1:2). This quotation is from Malachi 3:1. Verse four refers back to Isaiah 40:3. Isaiah says he is known simply as "a voice." *The voice of him that crieth in the wilderness, Prepare ye the way of the Lord, make straight in the desert a highway for our God* (Isaiah 40:3). It is this "voice" which is to be the herald of Jesus Christ.

We see this strange man, who appears on the scene in an almost sensational way, *clothed with camel's hair, and with a girdle of a skin about his loins.* His food, too, was strange, for *locusts and wild honey* were his diet.

There is a lesson here for us. God does not always choose the kind of men we would select. He often picks *the foolish things to confound the wise,* and the *weak things . . . to confound the things which are mighty* (I Cor. 1:27,28). No doubt, if we were left to select a herald for Christ, we would have chosen one of high birth, university trained, a man of wide reputation. He would have to be eloquent and a fearless champion of great causes. Not so with God. Graduated from no outstanding school, of humble birth, little known, dressed like a desert hermit, John the Baptist was approved of God (Matthew 11:11).

John's message was as startling as his appearance. He went before his Monarch, as any Roman officer would go before his, demanding that the road be repaired and the highway reconstructed. *Prepare ye the way of the Lord, make his paths straight*. A true revival is always a revival of righteousness.

PREPARATION BY BAPTISM

John and Jesus met one day. John recognized immediately that this Man was not a subject for the baptism of repentance that he was preaching. There was in this face a purity and majesty which smote John's heart with a sense of his own unworthiness. He was the Son of God. John hesitated, and said, *I have need to be baptized of thee, and comest thou to me* (Matthew 3:14)?

Jesus was baptized with John's baptism in obedience to an appointed ordinance. *Thus it becometh us to fulfill all righteousness* (Matthew 3:15). He set a seal of approval on John's message and work, and acknowledged him as the true forerunner of Christ. The baptism by John was ordained of God and therefore was binding on all those that acknowledged God and meant to keep His commandments.

Christ was the standard and example of righteousness. He would fulfill every duty He required of others (I Cor. 10:13).

PREPARATION BY RECEIVING THE HOLY SPIRIT

And straightway coming up out of the water, he saw the heavens opened, and the Spirit like a dove descending upon him (Mark 1:10). The Spirit descended not only in the manner of a dove, but in the bodily shape of a dove (Luke 3:22). This was a symbol. The coming of the Spirit Himself was a reality. Every event in Jesus' life had significance. In any service for

God, the Spirit always prepares the life by giving power and equipment. He is God's great agent for spiritual warfare.

Because Jesus went down into the baptismal water of obedience to God, He could come up under an opened sky with the Holy Spirit descending upon Him, and hear the voice of His Father declaring Him to be His beloved Son.

Jesus came up out of that water a new Man into a new world. His relationship to His Father and His mission were proclaimed.

PREPARATION BY A DIVINE CALL

There came a voice from heaven (Mark 1:11). God endorsed Jesus and His mission, and showed to the Jewish nation that He was the Messiah. *God anointed Jesus of Nazareth with the Holy Ghost and with power; who went about doing good, and healing all that were oppressed of the devil; for God was with him* (Acts 10:38). This has been called "Mark's Gospel in a nutshell." Later we hear this same Voice at His transfiguration. *This is my beloved Son, hear him* (Mark 9:7).

PREPARATION BY TESTING

Baptism and temptation are here crowded together. Hardly had the Voice from heaven died away than we hear a whisper from hell. Out of the baptismal benediction of the Father, Jesus stepped into a desperate struggle with the devil.

Mark says, *Immediately the Spirit driveth him into the wilderness,* which shows how quickly the Spirit moves (Mark 1:12). "And" indicated continuity, showing that temptation was as much a part of the preparation of the Servant for His work, as His baptism. Suffering and trial are as much God's plan as thrills and triumphs. Jesus was "led" to be tempted. It was no accident or evil fate, but a divine appointment. Temptation has its place in this world. We could never develop without it. There is nothing wrong in being tempted. The wrong begins when we begin to consent to it. We are not to run into temptation of our own accord. Jesus did not go of Himself, but was led of the Spirit. We will find that the path of duty often takes us through temptations but *God is faithful, who will not suffer you to be tempted above that ye are able; but will with the temptation also make a way to escape, that ye may be able to bear it* (I

Corinthians 10:13). He always makes a way of escape! This subject is of great importance. Be sure you understand it.

THE SERVANT WORKING (Read Mark 1:14–8:30)

There is a continuous, unbroken service of the Servant recorded in this Gospel. We read, "And He did this, and He said that." He must teach men; they were in darkness. He must cheer men; they were without hope. He must heal men; they were sick and suffering. He must free men, because they were under the power of Satan. He must pardon and cleanse men, because they were sinful.

We see Jesus preaching by the seashore, and selecting four of the fishermen to become His first disciples, to learn under His guidance how to become "fishers of men." Who were they? (See Mark 1:16-20.) They were to turn all the practical knowledge and skill that they exercised in the art of catching fish into the work of catching men. What disciple was called in Mark 2?

It is interesting to note that Jesus never called any man from idleness. He called busy and successful men to follow him. Everyone can turn his business into a channel of service for Christ. How was Christ's call received? *Straightway they forsook their nets, and followed him* (Mark 1:18). Too often there is lost time between our call and our coming; our doing lags far behind our duty.

Jesus is introduced at once as "anointed with power," and as fully engaged in His work. You will find no long discourses in these next chapters, but many mighty deeds. Demons were cast out (1:21-28); fever put down (1:29-31); different diseases healed (1:32-34); lepers made whole (1:40-45); palsied man made to walk (2:1-12); withered hand cured (3:1-5); multitudes healed (3:6-12); storm at sea quelled (4:35-41); maniac's mind restored (5:1-15); woman's hemorrhage of blood stopped (5:21-34); Jairus' daughter brought back to life (5:35-43); five thousand fed (6:32-44); the sea was made His sidewalk (6:45-51); all that touched Him were made whole (6:53-56); deaf and dumb heard and spoke (7:31-37); four thousand fed (8:1-9); blind man healed (8:22-26).

The action is rapid, and events appear to be happening before our very eyes. His descriptions are abrupt and outspoken, but Mark preserves many things for us that would have been lost. It is only in this Gospel that we are told Jesus was a carpenter. Mark tells us He *took* one *by the hand,* and little children *in His arms.* Mark tells us that Jesus was *grieved;* that He *sighed,* He *wondered.* He *loved,* He was *angry.* He was *touched with the feelings of our infirmities.*

Let us spend the Sabbath with Jesus that is recorded in Mark 1:21-34, going with Him to church, listening to His preaching, watching Him when interrupted by a maniac, casting out the unclean spirit and making the healing a powerful aid to His teaching. Then, after service let us go with Him to Peter's house, and see Him heal Peter's wife's mother of a severe fever, and then let us spend the Sabbath afternoon in quiet rest and friendly conversation. Toward evening we shall look out in the beautiful twilight and see men coming toward the house, bringing great numbers of people, sick with every kind of disease, and watch them as Jesus lays His tender hands upon them and heals them. The lame jump from their stretchers and leap for joy; the blind open their eyes and see their Healer; lines of suffering are turned to an expression of unbelievable happiness as others are delivered from their painful diseases.

Mark records a wonderful statement concerning the Sabbath, in 2:27, *The sabbath was made for man, and not man for the sabbath.* This great saying of Jesus is the central principle of Sabbath observance. The Sabbath is not made to annoy mankind, to confine them, to impoverish them, but to enrich and bless them! Try spending one Lord's day as Jesus did. I believe you will like it, and the Lord will be pleased.

Christ answers the question of Sabbath-keeping with a practical illustration (Mark 3:1-5). His conclusion is that whatever deed is really helpful to man is proper for the Sabbath, and is in perfect harmony with God's design of the day. He illustrated this truth with this miracle of healing. Seven of Jesus' recorded miracles were performed on the Sabbath. The Sabbath was "made." It is God's gift to man.

THE SERVANT AT WORK

The miracles of Jesus were proofs of His mission from God. They showed that He was the promised Redeemer and King, the One that we all need. Because Jesus was God, miracles were as natural to Him as acts of will are to us! Through His miracles, Jesus inspired faith in many of those who saw and heard Him.

The Servant is always found "working." *I must work the works of him that sent me, while it is day,* are His words. Read this memorandum of the full days of our Lord's ministry. How empty our own lives will seem in comparison!

THE SERVANT AT PRAYER

The morning following the great Sabbath day of preaching and healing, in which we followed Jesus, He arose very early and went out of the city to a lonely place and prayed (Mark 1:35). His work was growing rapidly, and Jesus needed heavenly communion. The seeming answer was a larger work, the entrance upon His first Galilean tour of healing and preaching (Mark 1:37-39). Only one healing event of this tour, which lasted several days, is recorded—that of a leper, whose disease was incurable (Mark 1:40-45).

If the Son of God needed to pray before He undertook His work, how much more should we pray. Perhaps our lack of success in life is because we fail at this point. We have not because we ask not.

THE SERVANT FORGIVES SIN

After some days . . . it was noised that He was in the house (Mark 2:1). It is remarkable how rapidly news spread in the East, without newspapers, television, telephones, or radios. But in another part of the city a man sick with the palsy had heard of this new Prophet and His gospel of healing. His four friends brought him to Jesus and let him down into the presence of the Master. We find in this healing the test and proof of Jesus' power not only as a physician of the body but as a healer of the soul. *Who can forgive sins but God only* (Mark 2:7)? Sins are against God and therefore He only can forgive. Jesus said, *That ye may know that the Son of man hath power on earth to forgive sins, . . . I say unto thee, Arise, and take up thy bed, and go thy way into thine house* (see Mark 2:9-12).

God endorsed Jesus' claim to be the Messiah in this miracle. The man arose, took up his bed, and went forth before them all, a living witness to Jesus' power over sin, a visible illustration of the work which Jesus came to do. Jesus came to give His life a ransom for many that He might forgive men their sins. *All have sinned,* and all need a Saviour. (See Romans 3:23.)

We find the account of the choosing of the twelve apostles in Mark 3:13-21. Notice the fourteenth verse. It tells why Jesus chose these men, *that they should be with him.* Mark it in your Bible. This is what Jesus wants of His disciples today—that they will take time to be in His presence and commune with Him. In John 15:15, He says, *I call you not servants; . . . but I have called you friends.*

As you turn to Mark 4, notice once again that the opening word is "And." *And he began again to teach,* as on former occasions. (See Mark 2:13; 4:1.) What a wonderful teacher is Jesus!

The parable of the sower sets forth the hindrances to the Gospel that dwell in the hearts of the hearers (Mark 4:3-20).

Everyone should master these parables of the Kingdom in chapter 4. They were a special teaching instrument of Christ. The interpretation of the sower is given in Mark 4:13-20. Jesus used this method of instruction because of the growing hostility to Him and His message. He was surrounded by enemies who tried to catch Him in His words, but no one could object to a simple story. Besides, stories are remembered by the dullest of hearers.

A parable is an analogy. It assumes a likeness between higher and lower things. "Parable" comes from the Greek word meaning "beside" and "to throw." A parable, then, is a form of teaching in which one thing is thrown beside another.

Beside the parable of the sower, our Lord spoke other parables:

1. The parable of the candle............................Mark 4:21-25
2. The parable of the seed springing secretly....Mark 4:26-29
3. The parable of the mustard seed.................Mark 4:30-33

After interpreting the parables, Jesus took a ship to escape from the crowd. On the way, as the weary Teacher fell asleep, a violent storm arose on the Sea of Galilee. About to perish, the frantic disciples awoke Jesus. At a word from His lips, the sea became calm. He had power over the elements (Mark 4:35-41).

Mark 5 begins again with "And." Jesus is still working. What does He do now? Read parallel accounts in Matthew 8:28-34; Luke 8:26-39. Compare this miracle with other recorded cures of demoniacs, in Matthew 9:32,33; Mark 1:23-26; Matthew 17:14-18; Luke 9:38-42.

The miracle recorded in Mark 5, like all others, tested the character of men. It took them off their guard and disclosed their true natures. Notice the contrast in the way men receive the work of Christ.

Some shun the Saviour. *They that fed the swine fled.* Others *were afraid* (verses 14,15) and *began to pray him to depart out of their coasts* (verse 17). Doubtless there were other herds of swine, and they feared the loss of them. What a true picture of the attitude of many toward Christ! There is some gainful business they do not want to give up. There is some sin that lies close to the heart. It is for these reasons that men thrust away Christ.

Some seek the Saviour. The healed man begged Him not to depart out of his coast but *that he might be with him.* It is so with men today. Either men ask Jesus to "depart" because they want to keep their sin, or they ask that He might remain "with" them because they want to lose their sin. Do you want to keep or lose your sin?

"And" starts another episode in Jesus' miracles (Mark 5:21). After healing the demoniac, Jesus returned to Capernaum. He heals a woman long sick, and *while he yet spake* (5:35), He was called upon to raise a child already lying in death, Jairus' daughter.

Jesus started out on a third preaching tour of Galilee (Mark 6). He sent forth the twelve disciples, two and two, on independent missions. (See Mark 6:7-13.) Matthew 10 records the instructions they received. As they preached, Herod heard them and we read of his uneasy conscience, thinking that the man he had murdered was back to haunt him (Mark 6:14-29). How much men recklessly give away for passing pleasures. For a glass of wine, a moment of passion, a little more money, a position of empty honor, they give away half—yes, all the kingdom of their souls, their health, home, friendships, peace, happiness and eternal life. Like Esau, they sell their birthright for a mess of pottage. Like Judas, they sell their Saviour for thirty bits of metal.

After the apostles had been trained, Jesus sent them out on an extensive missionary tour among the villages of Galilee (Mark 6:12,13). On returning they *gathered themselves together unto Jesus* (6:30), probably at their regular rendezvous, Capernaum. They reported upon their sermons, the number of conversions, and the miracles which were wrought. No Christian work can be carried on long without frequent talks with Christ. We need His sympathy, approval, guidance and strength.

We must hasten if we would follow this mighty Servant, this Workman of God. Jesus had gone apart in a desert to rest awhile (6:31) but the multitudes followed Him. The feeding of the 5,000 follows without an interval (Mark 6:32-44). This is one of the most important miracles. Evidently it made a special impression upon the writers of the Gospels, as it is the only one of the thirty-five miracles that is recorded by all four. Review it carefully. Notice Jesus served in an orderly way.

What miracles are next? (Mark 6:45-52 and 53-56). Follow Jesus in what He does and says (Mark 7:1-23; 7:24-30; 7:31-37; 8:1-9; 8:22-26).

Peter's confession of faith should be mastered by everyone —Mark 8:29. Jesus does not tell His disciples who He is. He waits until they tell Him. When He asked, *Whom say ye that I am?* the climax of His ministry was reached. He was testing the aim of all His training of the chosen twelve. Peter's answer gave Him the assurance that His goal had been attained.

What did the Pharisees think of Jesus? Already they had agreed to put Him to death.

What did the multitude think of Him? Already they were deserting Him.

What did the disciples think of Him? Peter gives the answer. What do you think of Christ?

THE SERVANT REJECTED (Read Mark 8:31–15:47)

Even before Mark sets forth Christ's direct claim to be King of the Kingdom, he reveals the way the King is to be received. His is a pathway of suffering and rejection. Jesus said, *The Son of man must suffer* (Mark 8:31). The evangelists write it down in plain language that He was to be rejected by the rulers of Israel, and killed, and was to rise again the third day.

Jesus tells His disciples He is to be rejected by the elders, chief priests and scribes (Mark 8:31).

He is to be delivered by treachery (Mark 9:31).

He is to be put to death by the Romans (Mark 10:32-45).

He is to rise again the third day (Mark 9:31).

Jesus, nevertheless, claimed the Kingdom by presenting Himself as the Heir of David, at Jerusalem, according to the prophecy of Zechariah 9:9. (See Mark 11:1-11.)

How did the people accept this King? At first they welcomed Him, because they hoped that He might deliver them from the yoke of Rome and free them from the poverty they were enduring. But when He entered the temple and showed that His mission was a spiritual one, He was hated by the religious leaders with a satanic hatred that led to the plot to put Him to death (Mark 14:1).

THE WORLD'S GREATEST SIN

The greatest sin of this age, as of every age, is the rejection of Jesus Christ. Yet, remember that everyone who has heard the Gospel must either accept the Lord as Saviour, or trample Him underfoot. The people of Jesus' day made their choice and the people of our day must make theirs.

This wonderful Presence that shines forth in the Gospels, this vision of God in the flesh—are you to look and then pass on, as though you had but seen a work of art? This Voice that sounds throughout the centuries, are you to listen as though it were just the voice of a gifted orator? What is Jesus to you? A name? or your Master? If you cannot answer the question as Peter did, will you not sign this covenant, worded by Dr. R. A. Torrey?

"I promise to examine carefully the evidence that the Bible is God's book, and Jesus Christ is God's Son and man's Saviour; and if I find reason to believe that this book is true and He is man's Saviour, I will accept Him and confess Him before men, and undertake to follow Him."

(Signed) ....

After Christ's public ministry, described in Mark 10:46–11:26, we read of His last conflict with the Jewish authorities and of His triumph over the leaders (Mark 11:27–12:44).

Jesus sought to persuade the Jews to receive Him as the Messiah (Mark 11:15–12:44). It was a busy Tuesday, occupied from morning till night in one great and powerful effort to induce the Jewish nation to acknowledge Him, and thus become that glorious nation, blessing the world, for which it had been set apart.

In the beautiful temple courts the simple Galilean met the Jewish authorities, arrayed in all the pomp of their official regalia. There was a sharp and prolonged controversy on puzzling questions.

The scribes and chief priests ask Him, *By what authority doest thou these things? and who gave thee this authority to do these things* (Mark 11:28)?

The Pharisees and Herodians try to catch Him in His words, *Is it lawful to give tribute to Caesar, or not* (Mark 12:14)?

The Sadducees, who say there is no resurrection, ask Him, *In the resurrection . . . whose wife shall she be of them? for the seven had her to wife* (Mark 12:23).

The scribes ask Him, *Which is the first commandment of all* (Mark 12:28)?

After Jesus had answered them all, we read, *And no man after that durst ask him any question* (Mark 12:34).

It would seem that He could not escape treason to the Roman government in answering them, but He came out unscathed. Hour by hour Jesus met the attack.

All the way through, the perfect Servant of God was dogged by His enemies. The Enemy is not dead! God's servants today are called to tread a similar path. Jesus silenced His enemies, but their hearts would not yield. Then He exposed all their hypocritical practices in words that fell like bombs. He tried to break through their walls of prejudice, and cause them to repent before it was too late, but all seemed to be in vain.

Before He goes to the cross, Jesus reveals the future to His troubled disciples, in the Olivet discourse (Mark 13). He tells them of the end of this age, and of the great tribulation, and climaxes it with the promise of His return in power and glory.

The plotting of the chief priests, how they might take Him by craft and put Him to death, and the anointing of His "body to the burying" by His friends, opens chapter 14. Then the ever sad story of His betrayal at the hand of His own disciple (Mark 14:10,11), the celebration of the Passover and the institution of the Lord's Supper all are crowded into twenty-five short verses. Adding insult to injury, we read of the denial of his Lord by Peter (Mark 14:26-31, 66-71).

Isaiah's great message is that the Son of God shall become the Servant of God in order that He might die to redeem the world. Mark records how the sufferings of Jesus in Gethsemane and on Calvary fulfilled the prophecies of Isaiah (Isa. 53).

Jesus was sold for thirty pieces of silver, the price of a slave. He was executed as only slaves were! Yes, Christ was the suffering Servant and died for me! He bore my sins in His own body on the tree.

No reference is made by Mark that in the garden He had the right to summon twelve legions of angels, if He so willed. No promise of the Kingdom is given to the dying thief on the cross. These claims are made by a King (in Matthew), but they are not mentioned by a Servant.

THE SERVANT EXALTED (Read Mark 16:1-20)

After the Servant had given His life a ransom for many, He arose from the dead. We read again the great commission (Mark 16:15), also recorded in Matthew 28:19,20. Compare the two. In Mark, we do not hear a King say, *All power is given unto me in heaven and in earth,* as in Matthew. In Mark, we see in Jesus' words that His disciples are to take His place, and He will serve in and through them. He is yet the Worker, though risen (Mark 16:20). The command rings with urgency of service. Not a corner of the world is to be left unvisited; not a soul to be left out!

Finally He was received into heaven, to sit on the right hand of God (Mark 16:19). He who had taken upon Himself the form of a servant, is now highly exalted. (See Philippians 2:7-9.) He is in the place of power, ever making intercession for us. He is our Advocate.

But Christ is with us. The Servant is always working in us and through us. We are laborers together with Him. (See I Cor. 3:9.) He is still "working with us" (Mark 16:20). Let us, being redeemed, follow our Pattern, and go forth to serve also!

Therefore, my beloved brethren, be ye steadfast, unmoveable, always abounding in the work of the Lord, forasmuch as ye know that your labor is not in vain in the Lord (I Cor. 15:58).

Minimum Daily Requirements/Spiritual Vitamins

Sunday: THE SERVANT'S COMING AND TESTING
    Mark 1:1-20
Monday: THE SERVANT WORKING   Mark 2:1–3:25
Tuesday: THE SERVANT SPEAKING   Mark 4:1–6:13
Wednesday: THE SERVANT'S MIRACLES
    Mark 6:32–8:26
Thursday: THE SERVANT'S REVELATION
    Mark 8:27–10:34
Friday: THE SERVANT'S REJECTION
    Mark 11:1–12:44
Saturday: THE SERVANT'S DEATH AND TRIUMPH
    Mark 14:1–16:20

CHAPTER 30

UNDERSTANDING LUKE

Luke
Portrays Jesus Christ,
the Son of Man

The writer of this third Gospel was Dr. Luke, Paul's companion (Acts 16:10-24; II Timothy 4:11; Col. 4:14). He was a native of Syria and apparently was not a Jew, for Colossians 4:14 places him with the other Gentile Christians. If this is true, he was the only Gentile writer of the New Testament books.

It is easily seen that Luke was an educated man, and a keen observer. We learn from Acts 1:1 that the Acts was written by the author of this third Gospel.

Luke's Gospel was written for the Greeks. Beside the Jew and the Roman, the Greek was another who had been preparing for Christ's coming. He differed from the other two in many particulars. He possessed a wider culture, loved beauty, rhetoric, and philosophy. Luke, an educated Greek himself, would be well fitted for this task. Luke presents Jesus as the ideal of perfect manliness.

Notice that inspiration does not destroy individuality. In the introduction, verses 1-4, the human element is seen in connection with God's revelation. Luke addressed his Gospel to a man named Theophilus. It is thought he was an influential Christian layman in Greece.

Matthew presents Christ as King, to the Jews.

Mark presents Him as the Servant of Jehovah, to the Romans.

Luke presents Him as the perfect Man, to the Greeks.

This is the Gospel for the sinner. It brings out Christ's compassionate love in becoming man to save man.

In Luke we see God manifest in the flesh. Luke deals with the humanity of our Lord. He reveals the Saviour as a man with all His sympathies, feelings and growing powers—a Saviour suited to all. In this Gospel we see the God of glory coming down to our level, entering into our conditions, and being subject to our circumstances.

Luke's Gospel is the Gospel of Christ's manhood. This we must know, however; although He mingles with men, He is in sharp contrast to them. He was the solitary God-Man. There was as great a difference between Christ as the Son of Man, and we, the sons of men, as Christ, Son of God, and we, the sons of God. The difference is not merely relative, but absolute. Make this fact plain. Read the words of the angel to Mary: *That holy thing which shall be born of thee* (Luke 1:35), refers to our Lord's humanity. It is in contrast to ours. Our human nature is unclean (Isaiah 64:6), but the Son of God, when He became incarnate, was "holy." Adam in his unfallen estate, was innocent, but Christ was "holy."

In keeping with the theme of his Gospel, Dr. Luke has given us the fullest particulars concerning the miraculous birth of Jesus. We are grateful that our chief testimony concerning this fact should come from a physician. Christ, the Creator of this universe, entered this world like any other man. It is a mystery of mysteries, but enough facts are given to let us see that the predictions are true.

Luke alone tells the story of the visit of the shepherds (Luke 2:8-20).

We learn from this Gospel that as a boy, Jesus developed naturally (Luke 2:40,52). As a child, He was subject to Joseph and Mary (2:51). There was no record of unhealthy or supernatural growth. Only Luke tells of Jesus' visit to the temple when He was twelve years old.

As a man He toiled with His hands; wept over the city; "kneeled in prayer," and "knew agony in suffering." All is strikingly human. Five out of six of the miracles were miracles of healing. Luke alone tells of healing Malchus' ear (Luke 22:51).

Luke is the Gospel for the outcast on earth. It is Luke who tells of the Good Samaritan (10:33), the publican (18:13), the prodigal (15:11-24), of Zacchaeus (19:2), and the thief on the cross (23:43). He is the writer who has most to say for womanhood (Chapters 1 and 2). Luke records Jesus' compassion for the woman of Nain, and the depths of His mercy to the woman who was a sinner. His regard for women and children is shown in 7:46; 8:3; 8:42; 9:38; 10:38-42; 11:27; 23:27.

Luke alone tells us that when our Lord beheld the city of Jerusalem, He wept over it; of the bloody sweat in Gethsemane; of the Lord showing mercy to the dying thief on the cross. Luke alone mentions the walk with the two to Emmaus. He also tells of Jesus leading His disciples out as far as Bethany and that as He lifted up His hands and blessed them, He was parted from them.

Luke is a poetic book. It opens with a song, "Glory to God!" It closes with a song, "Praising and blessing God." The world has been singing ever since. Thank God for such a Gospel! It preserves the precious gems of Christian hymnology:

The Magnificat—Mary's hymn of rejoicing (1:46-55).

Song of Zacharias (1:68-79). Song of the Angels (2:8-14).

Luke speaks more of the prayers of our Lord than any other Gospel writer. Prayer is the expression of human dependence on God. Why is there so much working and activity in the church, and yet so little result in positive conversions to God? Why so much running hither and thither, and so few brought to Christ? The answer is simple. There is not enough private prayer. The cause of Christ does not need less working, but more praying.

The hardest thing that the Jew and the early Christians had to learn was that the Gentile would have full and free admission into the Kingdom and into the Church. Simeon taught this. Read Luke 2:32. Christ sent the seventy disciples not to the lost sheep of the house of Israel alone, as Matthew says, who wrote especially for the Jews, but "to every city and place" (10:1). All of Jesus' ministry over the eastern side of Jordan was to the Gentiles.

THE PREPARATION OF THE SON OF MAN
(Read Luke 1:1–4:13)

The opening of this beautiful book is significant. A Man is to be described, and the writer, Luke, will draw his good friend, Theophilus, into it. He tells him of his own personal knowledge of his subject—*having had perfect understanding of all things from the very first.* He seems to bring something warmly human into his task of presenting the Man, Christ Jesus.

The opening chapter is characteristic, too. John, as befits his theme, begins, *In the beginning was the Word, and the Word was with God, and the Word was God.* His tone throughout is not of this world. But Luke, so different, begins like a simple story touching men, with *There was in the days of Herod, the king of Judaea, a certain priest.* As the story progresses, we are introduced to human sympathies and relationships that none of the other Gospels tells us. We learn all about the circumstances that accompanied the birth and childhood of the Holy Babe, and about the one who was sent as His forerunner. The birth of John the Baptist (1:57-80), the angels' song to the shepherds (2:8-20), the circumcision (2:21), the presentation in the temple (2:22-38), and then the story of the boy Jesus, twelve years of age (2:41-52), are all recorded here.

In chapter 2, Luke notices that *in those days . . . went out a decree . . . that all the world should be taxed* (see Luke 2:1-3). Then comes a fact that we would never find in Matthew, that Joseph and Mary *went up to be taxed* with the rest, who went each to his own city. Luke is not showing here One who has claims to rule, but One who is coming down to take the place man then occupied.

God brings to pass what the prophets had spoken. Micah said that Bethlehem was to be the birthplace of Jesus (Micah 5:2-5), for He was of the family of David. But Mary lived in Nazareth, a town one hundred miles away. God saw to it that Imperial Rome sent forth a decree to compel Mary and Joseph to go to Bethlehem, just as the Child was to be born. Isn't it wonderful how God uses the decree of a pagan monarch to bring to pass His prophecies! God still moves the hand of rulers to do His bidding.

Now look on! We hear the message of the angels to the watching shepherds, but we do not find the kings of the East asking for One "who is born King." The angel tells the poor shepherds, *Behold, I bring you good tidings of great joy, which shall be to all people. For unto you is born this day in the city of David a Saviour,* (not a King) (Luke 2:10-12).

Why did the Father allow His blessed Son, now incarnate in the flesh, to be born in this lowly place? Luke is the only one of the four evangelists who touches this point concerning His humanity.

BOYHOOD DAYS

The *child grew . . . and the grace of God was upon him* (Luke 2:40). When He was twelve years old, He went up with His parents to Jerusalem to the feast, as every Jewish boy did at that age. *The child Jesus tarried behind, . . . and his mother knew not of it.* How characteristic of a boy this is! He was found *sitting in the midst of the doctors, both hearing them, and asking them questions* (Luke 2:46). How intensely human this is! Yet we read, *And all that heard him were astonished at his understanding and answers.* Luke says that He was filled with wisdom. Side by side with the human, there is evidence always that He was more than a man. We find Jesus' first words here: *Wist ye not that I must be about my Father's business?* It is the first self-witness to His deity.

Again we read, *He went down with them, and came to Nazareth, and was subject unto them*—these earthly parents (Luke 2:51). *Jesus increased in wisdom and stature, and in favor with God and man* (Luke 2:52). All of these things are peculiar to Jesus as man, and Luke alone records them. It is important that we notice Jesus was a "favorite" in Nazareth. It is not a sign that we are in the grace of God when we are out of favor with man.

Eighteen years of silence followed. We read of John the Baptist, preaching *repentance for the remission of sins* (Luke 3:3). Then Jesus came to be baptized. Only Luke tells us that *When all the people were baptized, it came to pass, that Jesus also being baptized, and praying, the heaven was opened* (Luke 3:21). He is linked with "all the people." He came down to the level of man. Matthew and Luke record the baptism of Jesus, but John omits it, for Christ is viewed as the only begotten Son of God. Here only do we read of the age at which our Lord entered His public ministry (Luke 3:23).

GENEALOGY

The genealogy of Jesus in Luke is given at the time of His baptism, and not at His birth (Luke 3:23). There are noticeable differences between the genealogy in Luke and that found in Matthew 1. In Matthew we have the royal genealogy of the Son of David, through Joseph. Here it is His strictly personal genealogy, through Mary. There it is His legal line of descent through Joseph; here it is His lineal descent through Mary. There His genealogy is traced forward from Abraham; here it is followed backward to Adam. Each is significant! Matthew is showing Jesus' relation to the Jew, hence he goes back no further than to Abraham, father of the Jewish nation. But here in Luke is His connection with the human race; hence His genealogy is traced back to Adam, the father of the human family.

In Luke our Lord's line is traced back to Adam, and is, no doubt, His mother's line. Notice in Luke 3:23, it does not say Jesus was the son of Joseph. What are the words? *As was supposed.* In Matthew 1:16, where Joseph's genealogy is given, we find Joseph was the son of Jacob. Here it says he was the son of Heli. He could not be the son of two men by natural generation. But notice this carefully—the record does not state that Heli begat Joseph, so it is supposed that Joseph was the son by law (or son-in-law) of Heli. Heli is believed to have been the father of Mary.

The Davidic genealogy goes through Nathan, not Solomon. This too is important. The Messiah must be David's son and heir (II Sam. 7:12,13; Romans 1:3; Acts 2:30,31), and his seed *according to the flesh.* He must be a literal flesh and blood descendant. Hence Mary must be a member of David's house, as well as Joseph (Luke 1:32).

And Jesus being full of the Holy Ghost returned from Jordan, and was led by the Spirit into the wilderness, being forty days tempted of the devil (Luke 4:1,2). Only here do we learn that the Saviour was *full of the Holy Ghost* as He returned from His baptism. Then follows the account of His temptation. We may

396

also notice that Luke is the only one to tell us that *Jesus returned in the power of the Spirit into Galilee* (Luke 4:14), showing that the old Serpent had utterly failed to break the fellowship of the Son of Man on earth with His Father in heaven.

As Jesus came forth from the fire of testing in the unabated *power of the Spirit* so can we. It is only as we are filled with His Spirit that we can overcome temptation with the power of the Spirit.

The purpose of the temptation was not to discover whether or not Jesus would yield to Satan, but to demonstrate that He could not; to show forth the fact that there was nothing in Him to which Satan could appeal. Christ could be tried and proven. The more you crush a rose, the more its fragrance is recognized. So the more the devil assaults Christ, the more will His perfections be revealed.

THE MINISTRY OF THE SON OF MAN
(Read Luke 4:14–19:48)

Scan through Luke from chapter 4:14, and find the events in Jesus' life as they are recorded in succession.

MINISTRY AROUND GALILEE—Luke 4:14–9:50

Ministry in Nazareth, His hometown.........................4:16-30
Preaching in Capernaum...................................4:31-44
Call of Peter, James and John............................5:1-11
Call of Matthew 5:27-39
The Pharisees 6:1-11
The Twelve Apostles Chosen...............................6:12-16
Disciples Taught 6:17-49
Miracles 7:1-17
Discourses of the Teacher................................7:18-50
Parables 8:4-18
Real Relatives...8:19-21
The Sea Calmed...8:22-25
The Maniac Healed..8:26-40
The Woman Made Whole.....................................8:41-48
Jairus' Daughter Restored................................8:49-56

This list is not complete, of course, but it gives a bird's-eye view of the busy life of the Son of Man on earth. The key word of His ministry is "compassion."

Following the temptation, Jesus *came to Nazareth, where he had been brought up: and, as his custom was, he went into the*

synagogue on the sabbath day, and stood up for to read (Luke
4:16). He went to the place where He had been "brought up."
Bringing up is an important thing in life. We find that Jesus was
accustomed to go to church on the Sabbath day. He had been
reared in a godly home.

Jesus here stated that God had anointed Him to preach deliverance to the captives, and bring good tidings to the poor and
brokenhearted (Luke 4:18,19). He selected a text from Isaiah
61:2, which announced the object of His whole mission on
earth. He was commissioned and sent of God, and divinely
qualified for His work. He is our Kinsman-Redeemer. He was
made like us, that He might deliver us. He became man that He
might bring man close to God.

Early in Jesus' ministry we see those of His own home town
determining to kill Him (Luke 4:28-30). They said, *Is not this
Joseph's son?* This is the first hint of His coming rejection. He
proclaimed Himself to be the Messiah (Luke 4:21). They were
angered that He should hint that their Jewish Messiah would
also be sent to the Gentiles. (See Luke 4:24-30.) They believed
God's grace was to be confined to the Jews, and so they were
ready to kill Him. He refused to work miracles for them, because of their unbelief. They attempted to cast Him down the
brow of the hill, but He escaped and went to Capernaum
(Luke 4:29-31). (By comparing Luke 4:16 with Matthew
13:54, it would seem that He made another visit to Nazareth
some months later, but with no success.)

A WORLD GOSPEL

The Jews hated the Gentiles for their treatment of them when
they were captives in Babylon. They regarded them with contempt. They considered them unclean and enemies of God.
Luke pictures Jesus as tearing down these barriers between Jew
and Gentile, making repentance and faith the only condition of
admission to the Kingdom. *And that repentance and remission
of sins should be preached in his name among all nations, beginning at Jerusalem* (Luke 24:47). The Gospel of Jesus Christ
is not just one of the religions of the world. It is the living

truth of God, adapted to all nations and to all classes. Read Romans 1:16.

As the Son of Man, Christ is looking at the needs of the Gentiles, as He is looking at the needs of all men. In Luke 6, which in substance is the same as the Sermon on the Mount in Matthew, we find simply broad moral teachings, suited to the needs and wants of all men. He condenses what Matthew puts into chapters 5 through 7 into a few verses, Luke 6:20-49. He makes no reference to "the law and the prophets," as in Matthew's Gospel.

Jesus spoke choice words here to His disciples. The beatitudes are a picture of the Christian. "Blessed are" each one of them begins. It is not what you are striving to be, but what you are in Christ that brings you joy. The beatitudes are a picture of Christ. They are the picture of the face of Jesus Himself, not boastingly but truly describing the perfect Christian.

DISCIPLES COMMISSIONED

When the twelve are commissioned (Luke 9), we see a broader field of ministry given. In Matthew we hear the Lord saying, *Go not into the way of the Gentiles, but go rather to the lost sheep of the house of Israel* (Matthew 10:6). Luke omits this and says, *He sent them to preach,* and that *they departed, . . . preaching the gospel . . . everywhere* (Luke 9:2,6).

Wherever this Man, Christ Jesus, went, a whole multitude followed Him and *sought to touch him: for there went virtue out of him, and healed them all* (Luke 6:19). He gave of Himself. Our service must be of this kind.

We find Jesus' power over disease and death (Luke 7:1-17); we find Him the sinner's friend. He had *come to seek and to save that which was lost* (Luke 19:10). He is called a *friend of publicans and sinners* (Luke 7:34).

JESUS CHRIST, THE TEACHER

THE SCHOLARS—Jesus was a teacher. His disciples were taught and trained to carry on His message (Luke 6:12-16).

THE SCHOOL—Matriculation in this school is guarded. Requisites are demanded. Yet, on the other hand, entrance is easy.

There is no barrier of age, sex, race or color. (Read Luke 14:25-33.)

ENTRANCE REQUIREMENT—*Whosoever doth not bear his cross, and come after me, cannot be my disciple* (Luke 14:27). *Whosoever he be of you that forsaketh not all that he hath, he cannot be my disciple* (Luke 14:33).

EXAMINATIONS—Jesus knows the ability and weakness of each student in His school. His examinations are not the same for everyone. He gives individual tests. It is easy to follow Jesus' tests with Peter. In Luke 5, He is testing Peter on obedience (5:5). In Luke 9:18, Jesus "sprang an examination" upon this impetuous fellow, and Peter gave a startling answer (Luke 9:18-20).

RULES TO BE OBSERVED—Right relationship with the Teacher must be maintained at all times. Many think that just because they have at one time entered into a relationship with the great Teacher, that is all that is necessary. But this is false. There must be a constant study of His Word, a laboratory time of prayer (Luke 11:1-4), a gymnasium of spiritual exercise (Luke 9:59; 5:27).

A PRACTICE SCHOOL—Jesus not only taught them, but He made them try out the great facts which He presented (Luke 10:1-12,28,36,37; 11:35; 12:8,9; 14:25-33; 18:18-26).

THE COURSE—The course included a study of the Kingdom and the King (Luke 7:28; 8:1; 9:2,11,62; 13:20,21; 12:32; 19:12,15; 22:29; 13:28,29; 17:20; 18:29).

THE SUFFERING OF THE SON OF MAN
(Read Luke 20:1–23:56)

Jesus is sitting with His disciples, around the table, celebrating the feast of the Passover. At this time He institutes what we call the "Lord's Supper." Listen to His words: *My body which is given for you: . . . my blood, which is shed for you* (Luke 22:19,20). This is different from the account in Matthew and Mark. They say, *My blood which is shed for many.* His love is expressed in such a personal way in Luke. The evangelist adds: *This do in remembrance of me.*

See the sad record of events in connection with His death. We find the disciples arguing over which one of them would be counted greatest in the Kingdom (Luke 22:24-27). We follow Peter from that moment and we read a lamentable story—one which ends in denial of his Lord and Master (Luke 22:54-62).

GETHSEMANE

Look into the Garden of Gethsemane. Jesus is praying, and "as it were" great drops of blood were on that holy brow. Luke tells us that the angels came to minister to Him, the Son of Man. Matthew and Mark omit the mention of the ministering angels.

In the shadow of the garden, a band of soldiers were approaching; leading them was Judas. He stepped up to kiss Jesus. Why, yes, he was a disciple. But the Scriptures had said that Jesus would be betrayed by a friend, and sold for thirty pieces of silver (Luke 22:47-62; Psalm 41:9; Zechariah 11:12).

Worst of all, His friends deserted Him. Peter denied Him, and all forsook Him and fled except John the beloved. Luke alone tells us that Jesus looked on Peter, the denier, and broke his heart with that look of love.

We follow Jesus into Pilate's hall; then before Herod (Luke 23:1-12). We follow along the Via Dolorosa to the cross (Luke 23:27-38). Only Luke gives the name Calvary, which is the Gentile name for Golgotha. Luke omits much which Matthew and Mark record, but he alone gives the prayer. (See Luke 23:13-46.)

There were three crosses on Calvary's hill. On one of them was a thief, dying for his crimes. Luke tells us this story, too (Luke 23:39-45). The way this thief was saved is the way every sinner must be saved. He believed on the Lamb of God, who died on the cross that day, to pay the penalty of sin.

The scene closes with the Son of Man crying with a loud voice, *Father into thy hands I commend my spirit*. The centurion, in keeping with this Gospel, bears this witness, *Certainly this was a righteous man*.

402

THE VICTORY OF THE SON OF MAN
(Read Luke 24:1-53)

We turn with great relief from the sorrow and death of the cross, the darkness and gloom of the tomb, to the brightness and glory of the resurrection morning.

Luke gives us a part of the scene that the others leave untold. It is the story of the walk to Emmaus.

He shows these disciples that as their resurrected Lord, He is just the same loving, understanding friend that He had been before His death. After His walk and conversation with them, we hear these disciples urging Him to come in and spend the night with them. He revealed who He was when He lifted up those hands which had been pierced on the cross and broke the bread. Then they knew Him, but He vanished out of their sight. On returning to Jerusalem they found abundant proof of the resurrection. He proved to them that He was a real man with flesh and bones. All these details belong to the Gospel of Luke.

No less than eleven appearances of Jesus are recorded, following His resurrection—not only to individuals but to companies and crowds. First, to the women, to Mary and then to the others (Mark 16; John 20:14); then to Peter alone (Luke 24:34); then to two men walking to Emmaus (Luke 24:13); to ten apostles in Jerusalem (Thomas being absent) (John 20:19); and subsequently to the eleven remaining disciples (John 20:26,29); yet later to seven men at the sea of Tiberias (John 21:1). Yet again to the whole number of the apostles on a mountain in Galilee (Matt. 28:16); and afterward to 500 brethren at once (I Cor. 15:6). Then to James (I Cor. 15:7), and finally, to the little group on the Mount of Olives at His ascension (Luke 24:51).

Three times, we are told, His disciples touched Him after He arose (Matthew 28:9; Luke 24:39; John 20:27). He ate with them, too (Luke 24:42; John 21:12,13).

As Jesus put out His hand to bless them, He was *carried up into heaven* (Luke 24:51). The fact that He was "carried up" reveals again that He was a man.

He is no longer a local Christ, confined to Jerusalem, but He is a universal Christ. He could say to His disciples, who mourned for Him, thinking when gone He could be no more with them, *Lo, I am with you alway.* How different was the hope and joy of those chosen followers, from their despair and shame at the crucifixion! They return to Jerusalem with great joy.

Minimum Daily Requirements/Spiritual Vitamins

Sunday: THE MAN "MADE LIKE UNTO HIS BRETH-REN" Luke 1:1–3:38

Monday: THE MAN "TEMPTED LIKE AS WE ARE" Luke 4:1–8:3

Tuesday: THE MAN "TOUCHED WITH . . . OUR INFIRMITIES" Luke 8:4–12:48

Wednesday: THE MAN "ABOUT MY FATHER'S BUSINESS" Luke 12:49–16:31

Thursday: THE MAN "NEVER MAN SPAKE LIKE THIS MAN" Luke 17:1–19:27

Friday: THE MAN, OUR KINSMAN-REDEEMER Luke 19:28–23:56

Saturday: THE MAN IN RESURRECTION GLORY Luke 24:1-53

CHAPTER 31

UNDERSTANDING JOHN

*John
Portrays Jesus Christ,
the Son of God*

MESSAGE OF THE BOOK:
"The Word of God" John 1:1

The author indicates the purpose of his book in the opening eighteen verses, called the Prologue, and states very plainly in John 20:31.

John wrote to prove that Jesus was the Christ, the promised Messiah (for the Jews), and the Son of God (for the Gentiles), and to lead believers into a life of divine friendship with Him. The Key word is "believe." We find this word 98 times in this book.

The theme of John's Gospel is the deity of Jesus Christ. More here than anywhere else His Divine Sonship is set forth. In this Gospel we are shown that the "Babe of Bethlehem" was none other than the "only begotten of the Father." There are evidences and proofs given without number. Although *all things were made by him,* although *in him was life,* yet He *was made flesh, and dwelt among us.* No man could see God; therefore Christ came to declare Him.

Omissions in John

No genealogy is recorded—neither His legal lineage through Joseph (as given by Matthew), nor His personal descent through Mary (as given by Luke).

No account of His birth—because He was "in the beginning."

Nothing about His boyhood.

Nothing about His temptation. Jesus rather is presented as Christ the Lord, not the One tempted in all points like as we are.

No transfiguration.

No appointing of His disciples.

No parables in John.

No account of the ascension.

No Great Commission.

His Titles Are Significant

Only here is He called "the Word"

The Creator

The only begotten of the Father

The Lamb of God

The revelation of the great "I AM" (See Exodus 3:14.)

THE WRITER

The author was John, "son of thunder," "the disciple whom Jesus loved." His father was Zebedee, a fisherman in good circumstances; his mother was Salome, a devout follower of the Lord, who may have been a sister of Mary, the mother of Jesus (Mark 15:40; John 19:25). His brother was James. His position was probably somewhat better than that of the ordinary fisherman.

John may have been about 25 years of age when Jesus called him. He had been a follower of John the Baptist. In the reign of Domitian, John the Disciple was banished to Patmos, but afterward he returned to Ephesus and became the pastor of that wonderful church. He lived in that city to an extreme old age, the last of the twelve apostles. During this time he wrote his Gospel concerning the deity of the Christ, co-eternal with the Father.

John wrote nearly a generation after the other evangelists, somewhere between 80 and 100 A.D., at the end of the first century, when all the New Testament was complete except for his own writings. The life and work of Jesus was well known at this time. The Gospel had been preached; Paul and Peter had suffered martyrdom, and all the apostles had died; Jerusalem had been destroyed by the Roman legions under Titus, 70 A.D.

All the Synoptic Gospels, Matthew, Mark and Luke, were written before 70 A.D., the fateful year of the overthrow of Jerusalem. Already false teachers had arisen, denying that Jesus Christ was the Son of God, come in the flesh. John, therefore, wrote emphasizing those facts, and gave the witnesses and recorded the words and works of Jesus that reveal His divine power and glory.

John is more elevated in tone and more exalted in view than the other Gospels. In each of the first three Gospels Christ is viewed in human relationship, with an earthly people, but in John we find spiritual relationships with a heavenly people. Let us look at them again.

In Matthew and Luke, "Son of David" and "Son of Man" link Christ to the earth. In John, "Son of God" connects Him with the Father in heaven.

As in Luke, Divine care was taken to guard our Lord's perfection in His humanity; so in John, His deity is guarded. In these days of widespread departure from the truth, the deity of Christ Jesus must be emphasized.

In John, Jesus is shown dwelling with God before ever a creature was formed (John 1:1,2). He is denominated as *the only begotten of the Father* (1:14). *This is the Son of God* (1:34, etc.).

Thirty-five times He speaks of God as "My Father."

Twenty-five times He says, "Verily, verily"—speaking with authority.

Beside His own affirmations, 6 different witnesses avow His deity.

His Deity Revealed in Every Chapter

Chapter

1. In Nathanael's confession, *Thou art the Son of God* (vs. 49).

2. In the miracle of Cana, He *manifested forth his glory* (vs. 11).

3. In His word to Nicodemus, He said He was *the only begotten Son* (vs. 16).

4. In His conversation with the woman of Samaria, He stated: *I that speak unto thee am he* [the Messiah] (vs. 26).

5. To the impotent man, He disclosed that *the voice of the Son of God* would give life (vs. 25).

6. In the "Bread Chapter," He admits that *the Bread of God is he* (vs. 33).

7. In the "Water of Life Chapter," He proclaims, *Let him come unto me, and drink* (vs. 37).

8. To the unbelieving Jews, He disclosed, *Before Abraham was, I am* (vs. 58).

9. The blind man was told that *He that talketh with thee is the Son of God* (vs. 37).

10. Jesus stated, *I and my Father are one* (vs. 30).

11. Martha's declaration, *Thou art the Christ, the Son of God* (vs. 27).

12. To the Greeks, *I, if I be lifted up from the earth, will draw all men unto me* (vs. 32).

13. At the supper, He said, *Ye call me Master and Lord: ... so I am* (vs. 13).

14. In His statement, *Believe in God, believe also in me* (vs. 1).

15. Likening us to branches on a vine, He says, *Without me ye can do nothing* (vs. 5).

16. In promising the Holy Spirit, He says, *I will send him unto you* (vs. 7).

17. In this "Prayer Chapter," He says, *Glorify thy Son* (vs. 1).

18. In His trial He states, *Thou sayest that I am a king* (vs. 37).

19. In His atonement He had the right to say, *It is finished* (vs. 30).

20. In his confession, Thomas the doubter exclaimed, *My Lord and my God* (vs. 28)!

21. In demanding obedience, *Follow thou me* (vs. 22).

SEVEN WITNESSES

The Book of John was written that men might believe that Jesus Christ was God. John brings seven witnesses to the stand to prove this fact. Here they are. Turn to the Scripture and hear each one making his own statement.

What do you say, John the Baptist? *This is the Son of God* (1:34).

What is your conclusion, Nathanael? *Thou art the Son of God* (1:49).

What do you know, Peter? *Thou art that Christ, the Son of the living God* (6:69).

What do you think, Martha? *Thou art the Christ, the Son of God* (11:27).

What is your verdict, Thomas? He is *My Lord and my God* (20:28).

What is your statement, John? *Jesus is the Christ, the Son of God* (20:31).

What do you say of yourself, Christ? *I am the Son of God* (10:36).

SEVEN MIRACLES

Besides the seven witnesses in John, we find seven signs or miracles, which prove that He is God. *For no man can do these miracles that thou doest, except God be with him,* were Nicodemus' words (John 3:2).

Look over these signs as they occur throughout the book.

Turning water into wine 2:1-11
Healing the nobleman's son 4:46-54
Healing the man at Bethesda 5:1-47
Feeding the 5,000 .... 6:1-14
Walking on the water 6:15-21
Healing the blind man 9:1-41
Raising of Lazarus 11:1-57

SEVEN "I AM'S"

There is another proof of His deity running through John. He reveals His God-nature in the "I AM'S" of this book. He says:

I AM the bread of life 6:35
I AM the light of the world 8:12
Before Abraham was, I AM 8:58
I AM the good Shepherd 10:11
I AM the resurrection, and the life 11:25
I AM the way, the truth, and the life 14:6
I AM the true vine 15:1

John, only, records the triumphant shout, "It is finished!" The finished work of salvation is accomplished only by the Son of God (John 19:30).

John says that he wrote his Gospel that men might believe that Jesus was the Christ. This part is especially for the Jews, to lead them into a personal belief in the historical Jesus "as the Messiah," who came in fulfillment of all the Old Testament prophecies.

In John, Christ the Messiah is revealed. Messiah means God's anointed One, to come as King.

Nathanael says, *Rabbi, thou art the Son of God; thou art the King of Israel* (1:49).

To the woman at the well, Jesus declared Himself to be the long-expected Messiah (4:26).

To Pilate, Jesus testified that He was King.

There are various ways of remembering the contents of the Book of John. We will state several. One gives us man's estimate of the Son of God.

What individuals thought about Christ..................................1-5
What Christ said about Himself..6-10
What crowds thought of Christ..11-20

THREE KEYS

Dr. S. D. Gordon suggested: "There are three keys that unlock John's Gospel."

BACK DOOR KEY—John 20:31

This key unlocks the whole of the book. It states the purpose of the Gospel.

SIDE DOOR KEY—John 16:28

At the side, a bit toward the back we find a second key. At the last supper with His disciples, Jesus reveals this truth to them: *I came forth from the Father, and am come into the world: again, I leave the world, and go to the Father.* His constant thought was that He used to be with the Father. He came down to earth on an errand and stayed for 33 years. He would go back again to His Father.

FRONT DOOR KEY—John 1:11,12

This key hangs right at the very front, outside, low down, within every child's reach. *But as many as received him, to them gave he power to become the sons of God, even to them that believe on his name.*

This is the Great Key—the Chief Key to the whole house. Its use permits the front door to be flung wide open. Any one who believes may enter.

THE GREAT PROLOGUE (Read John 1:1-18)

We open the Book of John with this question in mind—*What think ye of Christ?* (See Matthew 22:42) Is He only the world's greatest teacher, or is He actually God? Was He one of the prophets, or is He the world's Saviour, whose coming was foretold by the prophets?

All that John is to discuss in his book he crowds into these first eighteen verses.

Let us study this Gospel with John's purpose clearly in mind. Read it over again, John 20:31. Let us see how the plan is developed and how the purpose is shown, as we read the book.

THE SON OF GOD

John begins his wonderful record with Jesus the Christ, before His incarnation. God did not send His Son into the world in order that He might become His Son, for He IS the eternal Son.

Comparing the first verses of John with the other three Gospels, we see how differently it opens, how exalted is its theme. Omitting the birth of Jesus, the Son of Man, John begins "before all worlds." Read John 1:1-18 carefully. It opens like the Book of Genesis. Jesus is portrayed as the Son of God.

Our Lord had no beginning. He was in the beginning. He is eternal. Christ was before all things, therefore Jesus is no part of creation—He IS the Creator (Col. 1:16; Heb. 1:2).

The Word was with God. He is a Person of the Godhead. He is called "The Word." He came to declare God, to tell out God. As words utter thoughts, so Christ utters God. Words reveal the heart and mind; so Christ expresses, manifests and shows God.

Jesus said to Philip, *If ye had known me, ye should have known my Father also* (John 14:7).

Then comes the wonderful announcement that *All things were made by him,* and *In him was life; and the life was the light of men;* yes, He *was made flesh, and dwelt among us.* The full claims of Christ are given here, as truly God, Light of Life, Declarer of God the Father, Baptizer with the Holy Spirit.

THE SON OF MAN

John does not open at the manger in Bethlehem, but before all worlds were formed: "In the beginning." Jesus was the Son of God before He became flesh and dwelt among us. *In the beginning was the Word.* How like Genesis this book opens!

Christ became what He was not previously—a man. But Christ did not cease to be God. He was God-Man. He lived in a tabernacle of flesh here in this world for 33 years. Incarnation comes from two Latin words, "in" and "caro" meaning "flesh." So Christ was God in the flesh.

Man had sinned and lost the image of God, so Christ *the image of the invisible God* (Col. 1:15) came to dwell in man. No man could see God; therefore the only begotten Son, who was *in the bosom of the Father,* came to declare Him to us.

Even the witness of John the Baptist is different in John's Gospel. In Matthew, he tells of the "coming Kingdom." In Luke, he preaches repentance. In John, the Baptist is a witness to the Light, that all men might believe (1:7). He points to "the Lamb of God" (1:32-36). These are all characteristics of this Gospel.

Jesus is God Himself in human form, coming to earth. Jesus is the Witness of the Father to men. Jesus knew the Father. He lived with Him from the beginning. He came down to tell what He knew. He wanted men to know the Father as He knew Him.

He told by His words, His deeds, His character, His love, but most of all by His dying on the cross and His rising the third day. All this was a declaring, a witnessing, a telling.

How was Christ the Word received? Read John 1:11. *He came to his own* [the Jews] and *his own received him not.* He presented Himself as King to His people, but He was rejected.

412

All through the book we see Jesus dividing the crowds. As He comes out and speaks the truth, the crowds listen. Some believe and some reject. Tragedy indeed! But not all rejected Him. John presents the results of faith.

All of this Prologue deals with Christ before His incarnation. God did not send Christ into the world in order that He might become His Son. Christ is the eternal Son. He is the eternal Word. Jesus is none other than the Jehovah of the Old Testament, "God manifested in the flesh." In Luke we see Christ going down to man's needs; in John, we see Him drawing men up to Himself (12:32).

Remember that John is writing to prove that Jesus is the Son of God.

THE WAY OF SALVATION

What We Must Do for Salvation: (John 1:12)

WHAT TO DO: "Believe" and "receive."

RESULT: You become a child of God.

What Not To Count On for Salvation:

Sometimes the way to better understand what a thing is, is to find out what it is not. In John 1:13, John tells us what salvation is not. *Which were born, not of blood, nor of the will of the flesh, nor of the will of man, but of God.* All of these things are what people are counting on today for eternal life. The "new birth" makes us "sons of God."

Not of blood—heredity. How much we depend on good birth!

Nor of the will of the flesh—culture and education. It is not what we know but *Whom* we believe that saves us.

Nor of the will of man—prestige or influence.

But of God—by the power of the Holy Spirit of God. God comes down and redeems us, if we will only believe and receive Him as Saviour and Lord.

PUBLIC MINISTRY (Read John 1:19–12:50)

When John the Baptist stepped on the scene, the great drama of John's Gospel began. *Among them that are born of women there hath not risen a greater than John the Baptist,* Jesus declared. He was the Forerunner of the Messiah. In this Gospel, the Baptist is not described. He merely bears his witness that Jesus is the Messiah (1:18-34).

A delegation of Jews and priests were sent to ask John who he claimed to be. He told them he was not the Messiah; he was not even Elijah or any other prophet Moses spoke of, but merely *the voice of one crying in the wilderness, Make straight the way of the Lord.*

The next day, on seeing Jesus, John points to Him and says, *Behold the Lamb of God!*

Finally, John the Baptist indicates another sign. He would know the Messiah because he would see *the Spirit descending, . . .* and *it abode upon him* (1:33). So John adds, *I saw, and bare record that this is the Son of God.*

Jesus' disciples were convinced of His deity by His first miracle, turning water into wine. He spoke and it was so. This was one of the big factors which brought faith into the hearts of the disciples. This was the first "sign" to prove that He was the Messiah. (See 2:11.)

There was only one place where Jesus could start His ministry—in Jerusalem, the capital city. The night before the Passover, the Lord entered the temple, and taking a scourge of cords, as a badge of His authority, cleansed the sanctuary, which He declared was His Father's house. By this act He claimed to be the very Son of God.

When the rulers asked for a "sign" to prove His authority, when Jesus cleansed the temple and drove out the money-changers, He said, *Destroy this temple, and in three days I will raise it up.* The rulers were shocked, for it had taken forty-six years to build this edifice. *But he spake of the temple of his body,* John explains (2:19-22). The supreme proof of Christ's deity is the resurrection.

Jesus gave to Nicodemus the wonderful teachings about eternal life and His love (John 3:16) and the new birth (John 3:6). Nicodemus was a moral, upright man; yet Christ said to him, *Ye must be born again.* If Jesus had said this to the woman of Samaria, Nicodemus would have agreed with Him. She was not a Jew and could not expect anything on the ground of her birth as a Samaritan. But Nicodemus was a Jew by birth and he

414

had a right to expect something on this ground. But it was to him that Jesus spoke, *Ye must be born again* in order to enter the Kingdom of Heaven. Have you been born again?

Like the Jews of his day, Nicodemus knew God's law, but nothing of God's love. He was a moral man. He recognized Jesus as a Teacher, but he did not know Him as a Saviour. This is just what the world does today. They put Jesus at the head of the list of the teachers of the world, but they do not worship Him as very God.

Jesus revealed to one woman the truth of His Messiahship. This story gives us Christ's estimate of a single soul. He brought this immoral woman face to face with Himself and showed her what kind of a life she was leading. Her loose view of marriage is not unlike the view taken today by many people. Christ did not condemn her or pass judgment upon her, but He did reveal to her that He is the only One Who could meet her needs. Christ revealed the wonderful truth to her that He is the water of life. He alone can satisfy. The wells of the world bring no satisfaction. Men are trying everything, but they still are unhappy and restless. Did the woman believe Christ? What did she do? Her actions spoke louder than any words could have done. She went back and by her simple testimony brought a whole town to Christ (4:1-42).

In healing the son of the nobleman, we see the second sign of Christ's deity. During His interview with the centurion, we find Jesus bringing this man to an open confession of Christ as Lord—yes, and his whole household joining with him (4:46-54).

The miracle of the feeding of the 5,000 was an acted parable. Jesus Himself was the Bread from heaven. He wanted to tell them that to all who put their trust in Him will He give satisfaction and joy (6:35)

The people wanted to make Christ their King because He could feed them. How like men today! They long for someone who can give them food and clothing. But Christ would not be King on their grounds. He dismissed the excited multitude and departed into a mountain. Men were disappointed that He would not be a political leader, and so they *walked no more with him* (6:66).

415

The people were divided because of Jesus (7:40-44). We find unbelief was developing into actual hostility, but in His true followers faith was growing. Some people said, "He is a good man." Others said, "Not so." Men must say one or the other today, when facing Christ's claims. Either He is God, or an impostor. There is no middle ground.

The healing of the blind man led Jesus to reveal to this fellow who He was. When "they cast him out" because of his confession of Christ, Jesus gave a great discourse on the Good Shepherd (chapter 10). See the opposite results produced by His words in 10:19-21. Notice the accusations of blasphemy they made of Christ, when He said, *I and my Father are one,* and they *took up stones again to stone him* (10:31). What happened in face of all this criticism and opposition? (10:42).

The raising of Lazarus is the final "sign" of John's Gospel. The other Gospel records give the raising of Jairus' daughter and the son of the widow of Nain. But in this case Lazarus had been dead four days. In reality, would it be any harder for God to raise one than the other? Nevertheless it had a profound effect on the leaders (11:47,48). The great claim which Jesus made for Himself to Martha is recorded here, *I am the resurrection, and the life: he that believeth in me, though he were dead, yet shall he live: And whosoever liveth and believeth in me shall never die. Believest thou this* (John 11:25, 26)?

This scene closes with Jesus' triumphant entry into Jerusalem. His public ministry had come to an end. It is recorded that many of the chief rulers believed on Him, without making an open confession.

JESUS' STARTLING CLAIMS

Claims to Be Equal with God:

Calls God *My Father* (5:17). The Jews knew what He meant. "He made Himself equal with God," they said. They knew that He claimed God as His Father in a sense in which He is not the Father of any other man.

Claims to Be Light of the World:

I am the light of the world: he that followeth me shall not walk in darkness, but shall have the light of life (John 8:12).

Claims to Be Eternal with God:

Verily, verily, I say unto you, Before Abraham was, I am (John 8:58). This claim of eternity with God was unmistakable. He was either the Son of God or a deceiver. No wonder the Jews "took up stones to cast at Him."

PRIVATE MINISTRY (Read John 13–17)

Here we leave the multitude behind and follow Jesus as He lived the last week of His life on earth, before His crucifixion. We call it Passion Week.

Sunday—the triumphant entry into Jerusalem.

Monday—the cleansing of the temple.

Tuesday—the conflicts in the temple.

Evening—the discourse on the Mount of Olives.

Thursday—preparation for the Passover.

Evening—the Last Supper with His disciples.

THE LAST EVENING TOGETHER

Last words are always important. Jesus is leaving His disciples, and is giving them His last instructions. This passage, chapters 13 to 17, is called the Holy of Holies of the Scriptures. Read it all at one sitting.

The Jews had rejected Jesus completely. Now He gathered His own around Him, in an upper room, and told them many secrets before He departed from them. He wanted to comfort His disciples, for He knew how hard it would be for them when He was gone. They would be sheep without a shepherd.

It is wonderful that Jesus should have selected and loved men like these. They seem to be a collection of "nobodies," with the exception of Peter and John. But they were "His own," and He loved them. One of Jesus' specialties is to make "somebodies" out of "nobodies." This is what He did with His first group of followers, and this is what He has continued to do, down through the centuries.

What a picture we have in John 13:1-11! Jesus, the Son of God, is girded with a towel, a basin of water in His blessed hands, washing His disciples' feet! He wanted us to serve in the same spirit. He taught us that greatness is always measured by service. There is no loving others, without living for others

417

(16, 17). Christ said, *He that is greatest among you shall be your servant.* The biggest merchant in the city is the one who serves the greatest public.

Jesus foretells His betrayal by Judas (13:18-30), and Judas goes out into the night. It was night in Judas' heart, too. Fellowship brings light. Sin brings darkness. What a pitiable picture Judas is. His opportunities of knowing Jesus were unsurpassed, but he rejected the Lord. This is what unbelief can do. Belief means life; unbelief means death.

After announcing His going, the Lord gives His disciples "a new commandment," that they love one another. *By this shall all men know that ye are my disciples.* Discipleship is tested not by the creed you recite; not by the hymns you sing; not by the ritual you observe, but by the fact that you love one another. The measure in which Christians love one another is the measure in which the world believes in them or their Christ. It is the final test of discipleship. He mentions this "new commandment" again in John 15:12.

CHRIST'S ANSWER FOR A LIFE BEYOND

I go to prepare . . . I will come again, and receive you unto myself (14:2,3). This is Jesus' cure for heart trouble—faith in God. We see there is no break between the 13th and 14th chapters. Jesus goes right on with His discourse. How many hearts have been put to rest, and how many eyes have been dried, by these words in John 14!

Jesus had spoken of His Father, but now He speaks of the other Person of the Godhead, the Holy Spirit. If He (Christ) is to go away, He will send the Comforter, and He will abide with them. This is a wonderful promise for the child of God! Jesus repeats the promise in chapter 15 and again in 16. Look them up (15:26; 16). Few know of this Presence in their lives. It is by His power that we live. Never call the Holy Spirit "it." He is a Person. He is One of the Godhead.

Peace I leave with you, my peace I give unto you. This is Christ's legacy to us. The only peace we can enjoy in this world is His peace.

Jesus reveals the real secret of the Christian life to His

disciples in John 15. *Abide in Christ*. He is the source of life. Abide in Christ as the branch abides in the vine. The branch cannot sever itself and join itself whenever it will, to the trunk. It must abide if it will bear fruit. This is the picture of our lives in Christ. Live and walk in Christ, and you will bear fruit. If you are not abiding in Christ, the fruit will soon disappear.

After He ended His talk with the eleven disciples, Jesus spoke to the Father. The disciples listened to His loving and solemn words. How thrilled they must have been as He told the Father how much He loved them, and how He cared for them! He mentioned everything about Himself that He had taught them. He would keep them (17:11); He would sanctify them (17:17); He would make them one (17:21); and finally, He would let all His children share in His glory some day (17:24).

If you would know the beauty and depth of these wonderful words, kneel and let the Son of God lead in prayer as you read this seventeenth chapter of John aloud.

Let us look at the teaching about the Holy Spirit as given by John.

1. The Incoming Spirit (3:5).

This is the commencement of the Christian life, the new birth by the Spirit. We are born by the Spirit into the family of God.

2. The Indwelling Spirit (4:14).

He fills us with His presence and brings us joy.

3. The Overflowing Spirit (7:38,39).

Out of his inmost being shall flow rivers of living water—not just little streams of blessing, but rivers—Mississippis and Amazons if the Holy Spirit dwells within us.

4. The Witnessing Spirit (14—16).

He speaks through us. This is the particular task of the Christian through the Holy Spirit—to testify of Christ.

SUFFERING AND DEATH (Read John 18; 19)

Immediately following His prayer, Jesus went into the Garden of Gethsemane, knowing all things that should come upon Him. The change from the scene in the upper room (chapters 13-17 to chapter 18) is like going from warmth to cold, from light to darkness. Only two hours had passed since Judas

419

left the supper table. Now we see him betraying his best Friend. Remember, Judas did not have to betray his Lord to fulfill prophecy or carry out God's plan. Nothing happens because it was prophesied to happen. It was prophesied because it was going to happen. No man ever had to sin to carry out any of God's plan.

"The hour" had come! The mission of our Lord on earth was ended. The greatest work of Christ remained to be done. He was to die that He might glorify the Father and save the sinful world. He came to give His life a ransom for many. Christ came into the world by a manger and left it by the door of the cross.

Jesus was now ready to give them the real sign of His authority in answer to the question in chapter 2: *What sign showest thou unto us, seeing that thou doest these things?* He answered, *Destroy this temple, and in three days I will raise it up.*

We see Jesus, always poised, always gentle. He knew His hour had come. He was not surprised when He heard the soldiers approach. He stepped forward to meet them. The men retreated and fell before the majesty of His look.

Follow Him, bound as a captive, to the hall of the high priest. Jesus was the One in command of the situation all through this terrible drama. He went forth (18:4), a voluntary sacrifice. He deliberately tasted death for every man.

Almost as sad as Judas was Peter, the deserter in the hour of need, denying three times that he had any connection with his best Friend! This is a lesson for us—over-confidence. Poor Peter is to be pitied, for he really loved the Master.

Peter did not know that the supreme trial of his life would come in the question of a servant maid. It is so often thus. We lock and bolt the main door, but the thief breaks into a tiny window we hadn't thought of. We would die at the stake but deny Christ in our speech.

All the disciples but John deserted Jesus in the hour of His greatest need. In that fleeing nine is James of the "inner circle," Nathanael the guileless, and Andrew the personal worker. Yet here they were, running pell-mell down the road together, away from their Friend. A sorry sight! Wait! Don't start blaming them. Suppose you look up and see where you are. Are you following Jesus closely? Remember, majorities aren't always right. Be sure you are right! Can Christ count on you?

MISSION COMPLETED

Jesus has come to the supreme, crowning act of His life on earth. It was not a crisis, but a climax. He came to earth to *give his life a ransom for many.*

Finally the make-believe trials are over. It is morning at last, and yet it seems like night. It is the world's blackest hour. The courtyard is deserted. The fire at which Peter warmed himself is only gray ashes. The soldiers' jeers and Herod's sneers and Pilate's vacillation are over.

The brief interval between Peter's denial and Jesus' climbing the hill to Golgotha was crowded with incidents. The night trial before Caiaphas and the Sanhedrin probably preceded the last denial of Peter. Then came the awful treatment up to the morning session of the Sanhedrin.

Often the cruel scourging of the Romans was so severe that prisoners died under the torturing blows. The crown of thorns, which was thrust upon His holy brow, was only another act of cruel torture. When He comes again He will bring many crowns (Rev. 19:12).

Finally Pilate led Him forth and said, *Behold the man!* What a sight! To see the Creator of this universe, the Light and Life of the world, the Holy One treated so! But Satan energized the rulers of the Jews, and they cried, *Crucify Him! . . . he made himself the Son of God!*

At the cross we have hate's record at its worst, and love's record at its best. Man so hated that he put Christ to death. God so loved that He gave men life.

Our religion is one of four letters instead of two. Other religions say, "Do." Our religion says, "Done." Our Saviour has done all on the cross. He bore our sins and when He gave up His life, He said, *It is finished!* This was the shout of a conqueror. He had finished man's redemption. Nothing was left for man to do. Has the work been done in your heart?

Jesus was crucified on Golgotha, "place of a skull." He is crucified there today—in men's minds. They crucify Him afresh and put Him to an open shame. Salvation is costly. *Christ died for our sins* (I Cor. 15:3). It cost Him His life.

VICTORY OVER DEATH (Read John 20; 21)

We have a Saviour who is victorious over death. He "ever liveth."

On the third day the tomb was empty! The grave-clothes were all in order. Jesus had risen from the dead, but not as others had done. When Lazarus came forth, he was bound in his grave-clothes. He came out in his natural body. But when Jesus came forth His natural body was changed to a spiritual body. The changed body came right out of its linen wrappings and left them, as the butterfly leaves the chrysalis shell. Read what John says, in 20:6-8.

Jesus' appearances, ten in all, after His resurrection, helped His disciples to believe that He was God. Read the confession of the seventh witness, Thomas the doubter (John 20:28). Jesus wanted every doubt to be removed from each one of His disciples. They must carry out His great commission and bear the Gospel into all the world (John 20:21).

Jesus gave the disciple who denied Him thrice, Peter, an opportunity of confessing Him thrice. He restored him to full privileges of service again. Christ only wants those who love Him to serve Him. If you love Him, you must serve Him. No one who loves Christ can help but serve.

What are Jesus' last words in this Gospel? *Follow thou me.* This is His word to each one of us. May we all follow Him in loving obedience "till He come"!

"This Gospel opens with Christ in the bosom of the Father, and closes with John in the bosom of Christ."—A. J. Gordon.

422

Minimum Daily Requirements/Spiritual Vitamins

Sunday: CHRIST BECAME FLESH   John 1:1-51
Monday: CHRIST SO LOVED   John 3:1-36
Tuesday: CHRIST SATISFIES   John 4:1-54
Wednesday: CHRIST, THE BREAD OF LIFE
          John 6:1-59
Thursday: CHRIST, THE LIGHT OF THE WORLD
          John 9:1-41
Friday: CHRIST, OUR SHEPHERD   John 10:1-39
Saturday: CHRIST PROMISES THE COMFORTER
          John 14:1-31

UNDERSTANDING ACTS

*Acts
Portrays Jesus Christ,
the Living Lord*

Luke, in his Gospel, shows what Christ "BEGAN to do" on earth; Acts shows what He CONTINUED to do, by the Holy Spirit.

The ascension of our Lord is the closing scene in Luke. It is the opening fact in Acts. (See Luke 24:49-51 and Acts 1:10,11.)

GOSPELS AND ACTS

The Gospels set forth the Son of Man, who came to die for our sins. The Acts shows the coming of the Son of God in the power of the Holy Spirit.

The Gospels set forth what Christ began to do. The Acts shows what He continued to do by the Holy Spirit, through His disciples.

The Gospels tell of the crucified and risen Saviour. The Acts portrays Him as the ascended and exalted Lord and Leader.

In the Gospels we hear Christ's teachings. In the Acts we see the effect of His teachings on the acts of the apostles.

Acts is not a record of the acts of the apostles, as no extensive accounts are given of any apostles except Peter and Paul. It records the acts of the Holy Spirit through the apostles. His name is mentioned about seventy times. Look for some work of the Holy Spirit in every chapter of this book.

The word "witness" is used over thirty times.

Ye shall be My witnesses is the heart of the Book of Acts. Salvation comes to this world through Christ alone (Acts 4:12), hence men must know Him. Christ's plan includes us. Are you witnessing for Christ? If not, why not? It is true that Christ alone can save the world, but Christ cannot save this world alone. This is His plan. If you have no witness for Christ, look into your heart. *For out of the abundance of the heart the mouth speaketh* (Matthew 13:34).

Christ had told His disciples that He would send the Spirit, and *He shall testify of me: and ye also shall bear witness, because ye have been with me from the beginning* (John 15:26,27). This promise of Christ's was fulfilled on the day of Pentecost when He poured forth the Holy Spirit upon the disciples (Acts 2:16,17,33), and from that moment, as they bore witness to the Saviour, the Holy Spirit bore witness at the same time in the hearts of their hearers, and multitudes were brought to the Lord.

It is a wonderful thing to know that when the Spirit prompts you to speak to someone about Christ, He has been working in that heart and making it ready to receive your witness. There is a perfect example of this in Acts 8, where Philip was sent to speak to the Ethiopian. Read this ever-thrilling story!

What was the result of the first sermon on the day of Pentecost? (Acts 2).

In each widening circle of influence we find a marked outpouring of the Holy Spirit. Isn't it amazing that in one generation the apostles had moved out in every direction and had preached in every nation of the then known world? (Col. 1:23).

The infant church was slow to realize what was the extent of their commission. They confined their preaching to Jerusalem until persecution drove them out. The blood of Stephen, the first Christian martyr, proved to be the seed of the growing church.

The book opens with the preaching of the gospel in Jerusalem, the metropolis of the Jewish nation. It closes with the gospel in Rome, the true metropolis of world power.

Although we call this book the Acts of the Apostles, we find that it is for the most part the acts of the Holy Spirit working through Peter and Paul and their companions.

In Acts 1 through 12, we find Peter witnessing to the Jews. Peter says, "Repent" (Acts 2:36-38).

In Acts 13–28, we find Paul witnessing to the Gentiles. He says, "Believe" (Acts 16:30,31).

There are two natural divisions in Acts. In 1-12, Peter says to the Jews, "Repent." Why? Because they needed a definite change of mind about the Messiah. In 13-28, Paul says, "Believe." Why? Because the Gentiles needed not to change their minds concerning the Messiah; they needed to believe on Him.

This book tells of the extension of the Gospel to the Gentiles. All through the Old Testament we find God dealing with the Jew. In the New Testament we find Him working among all nations.

A GUIDEBOOK TO MISSIONS

No doubt Acts is the best guide book to missions that has ever been written. We find in it the motive for missions. Their one aim was to bring men to a saving knowledge of Jesus Christ. He was their one theme, and the Word of God their one weapon.

We find the first church pursuing a definite program in carrying out its plans. They chose some great radiating center of population for a base from which the influence of their work might spread to the surrounding area.

The disciples were simple, straightforward and successful. They depended entirely upon the power of God, through His Spirit. They moved with a zeal that could not be quenched, and a courage that was unflinching.

POWER FOR WITNESSING (Read Acts 1-2)

What a wonderful forty days after the resurrection of Jesus the disciples spent with the Lord before His ascension! How anxious they were to hear His last words of instruction! He was speaking of the *things pertaining to the kingdom of God*. It was then that Jesus *commanded them that they should not depart from Jerusalem, but wait for the promise of the Father* (1:4).

The first 26 verses of the first chapter are introductory to the rest of the book. They tell of:

The great commission..6-8
The ascension 2,9,11
The promise of Christ's return..10,11

The disciples still were not satisfied as to the time when Christ would set up His Kingdom on earth. They still expected a

427

MEDITERRANEAN LANDS

PAUL'S MISSIONARY JOURNEYS

BLACK SEA

CAPPADOCIA

DAMASCUS

PALESTINE

GALATIA

CILICIA

SELEUCIA

ANTIOCH

SYRIA

CILICIAN GATES

TARSUS

SIDON

TYRE

PTOLEMAIS

CAESAREA

LYDDA

JOPPA

JERUSALEM

GAZA

BITHYNIA

SALAMIS

PHRYGIA

ANTIOCH

PISIDIA

ICONIUM

LYSTRA

DERBE

CYPRUS

PAPHOS

MYSIA

ASIA

ADRAMYTTIUM

PHILADELPHIA

PAMPHYLIA

PERGA

ATTALIA

MYRA

LYCIA

THYATIRA

LAODICEA

COLOSSE

SARDIS

PATARA

MITYLENE

ASSOS

TROAS

PERGAMOS

SMYRNA

EPHESUS

MILETUS

TROGYLLIUM

CNIDUS

RHODES

ALEXANDRIA

CHIOS

COS

PATMOS

SAMOTHRACIA

PHILIPPI

NEAPOLIS

AMPHIPOLIS

APOLLONIA

THESSALONICA

BEREA

AEGEAN SEA

MACEDONIA

ATHENS

CORINTH

CENCHREA

ACHAIA (GREECE)

SCALE OF MILES

0 50 100 200 300

CRETE

LASEA

FAIR HAVENS

CLAUDA

SALMONE?

ITALY

PUTEOLI

RHEGIUM

APPII FORUM

ROME

THREE TAVERNS

SICILY

SYRACUSE

MELITA

AFRICA

MEDITERRANEAN SEA

kingdom that would give them political independence and establish them in a place of leadership in the world (1:6). What was Jesus' answer? (1:7).

One day Jesus *led them out as far as to Bethany, and He lifted up his hands, and blessed them* (Luke 24:50). He told them their power was not to be political but spiritual. Listen to His words (Acts 1:8).

At the ascension of Christ, our Lord went "out of sight," but stayed with men in a far more real way. After He had spoken His last words to his disciples (recorded in Acts 1:8), He was taken up *and a cloud received him out of their sight.* Think of so great an event told in such few words! The Father took His Son back to glory.

CHRIST SHALL RETURN

This same Jesus, . . . shall so come in like manner as ye have seen him go into heaven (Acts 1:11). How will His "coming" be, as spoken of here? Will it be merely at death? Is it merely as He comes to dwell in our hearts? No. The promise is that He shall come "in like manner." If this is so, we should examine how He went. Then we shall know how He will come back. See the Scriptures. It will be:

Personal ....I Thess. 4:16
Visible ....Revelation 1:7
Bodily ....Matthew 24:30
Local ....Luke 24:50

Picture the disciples as they returned from the Mount of Olives to Jerusalem. They went into "an upper room." It might have been the very same room where Jesus had eaten the Last Supper with them (Luke 22:12). They "all continued in prayer" for ten days. Jesus had told them to tarry in Jerusalem until they should receive power from on high (Luke 24:49). Even though they had been three years in training with the Lord, they needed the presence of the Holy Spirit, whom Jesus said He would send to empower them. They had proved to be a weak lot in themselves.

Christ had told them not to depart from Jerusalem, but to wait there. It would have been natural for them to have fled from that place where their Lord had been crucified, and to have gone back to Galilee. But Christ said, "Tarry at Jerusalem," because it was the center of widest influence. We cannot always choose our place of service.

Next in importance to the coming of the Lord Jesus Christ to this earth, is the coming of the Holy Spirit. The Church was born on that day of Pentecost. Become familiar with this account, given in Acts 2:1-13. Pentecost was one of the most popular of the feasts, and Jerusalem would be crowded with pilgrims from everywhere. It was fifty days after the crucifixion. From this time Pentecost was not to be a Jewish feast, but the dawn of a new day, the birthday of the Church of Christ.

The scene opens with the disciples assembled together, with their hearts fixed on Christ, waiting for His promise to be fulfilled. The Holy Spirit, Himself, descended that day. Luke does not say there was wind, but sound was a symbol, as were the "tongues of fire." The mighty wind represented heavenly power. The luminous tongues conveyed the symbol of fire, and tongues expressed power to witness. See the results of this advent in Acts 2:6,12. Fire is a symbol of divine presence. It illumines; it purifies.

THE HOLY SPIRIT AT PENTECOST

The Spirit fell on them (2:1-3). The Spirit came in them (2:4). The Spirit worked through them (2:41-47).

They were filled with the Holy Spirit and thus endowed for special service. They not only were enabled to preach in power, but could speak in the different tongues represented that day at Jerusalem (2:2-4). Was the speaking in new languages a jargon not understood by anyone, or were those present able to understand and benefit? (2:6).

The wonderful thing about Pentecost was not the *rushing mighty wind,* or the *tongues like as of fire,* but the disciples being filled with the Holy Spirit that they might be witnesses to men. If we do not have the desire to tell others of Christ, it is evident that we do not know the fullness of the Holy Spirit.

Do not think that at this Pentecost the Holy Spirit came for the first time to the world. All through the Old Testament we see an account of how He had been guiding men and giving them strength. Now the Spirit was to use a new instrument, the Church, which had been born on that very day.

They were all amazed, and were in doubt (2:12). Men by nature are unbelieving. Is it not a great exhibition of God's grace when men come to believe God truly, and really accept His word?

Some mocked. *These men are full of new wine* (2:13-15). Men always try to explain away the miracles of God on natural grounds. But rationalism can never give a reasonable explanation of anything that is Divine. Also, it was only nine in the morning, and no Jew could touch wine till then. Read Peter's defense against this false charge in Acts 2:15-21.

PETER'S SERMON

The theme of this first Christian sermon was that Jesus is the Messiah, as shown by His resurrection.

Peter is the outstanding figure in the first twelve chapters of Acts. The real power of the Holy Spirit was shown when Peter, the humble fisherman, rose to speak, and 3,000 souls were saved! How can we account for cowardly Peter's boldness as he stood that day to preach before a multitude on the streets of Jerusalem? What was the secret of Peter's ministry?

It is a serious thing to charge men with murder; yet Peter did just this (Acts 2:36). Will he get away with it? Will he be stoned? The last verses in chapter 2 answer the question (Acts 2:37-47).

What a Church was this First Church of Jerusalem, organized with a membership of 3,000 on the day of Pentecost! What glorious days followed, in "teaching" and "fellowship," and "signs and wonders," and, above all, salvation! *The Lord added to the church daily such as should be saved* (Acts 2:47). This is the real objective of the Church. Are we seeing it today in our churches?

Just as marvelous as the gift of tongues was the daily life of this first church. It is not surprising that they found "favor with all the people," and that additions were made "day by day."

First Christians—"Regular Christians"

Regular in church going—*All that believed were together.*
Regular in church giving—Acts 2:44,45.
Regular in church's mission—Acts 2:46,47.

WITNESSING IN JERUSALEM (Read Acts 3:1–8:3)

Chapter 3 opens at the Beautiful Gate of the temple. Peter healed an incurable cripple, lame from birth, who had been carried daily to this place to beg for his living. The miracle attracted the notice of the Jewish leaders and resulted in the first real opposition to the Church.

When a great crowd had gathered around the lame man who had been so miraculously healed, Peter took advantage of the circumstance to preach his second recorded sermon. He did not spare the Jews. Again he told them that Christ, whom they had crucified, was the long-promised Messiah. So powerful were the words of Peter and John that a total of 5,000 men had now turned to this Christ!

The leaders were aroused because the apostles taught the people that this Jesus whom they had crucified, had risen from the dead, and would appear again (4:2). They commanded the apostles not to preach, but opposition only made the Church thrive. Opposition should never be a matter of amazement, not even a matter of surprise to any Christian. The work of the Spirit is always a signal for Satan to work. Whenever the Spirit comes to bless, the Adversary comes to curse. But martyrdom is an aid to the Church, and whenever the truth is faithfully preached, fruit will be brought forth. (See Acts 4:3,4.)

As soon as Peter and John were released by the rulers, they sought their friends and reported their experiences and united in prayer and praise. The Church must expect opposition but in all circumstances we can find courage and help in God. *The place was shaken where they were assembled together; and they were all filled with the Holy Ghost, and they spake the word of God with boldness* (4:31).

We find that this kind of preaching brought unity in the

Church. They *were of one heart and of one soul* (4:32). They went out to tell, "Jesus is risen." (See v. 33.) Let us tell it out! Dying men need it; the day demands it!

No man was compelled to part with his personal possessions. It was not expected of him. If he brought what he had, it was a purely voluntary act. The sharing of property was voluntary, not obligatory; individual, not general; confined to Jerusalem; temporary; limited to believers.

The Church became so unselfish that many sold all they had and gave it to the apostles to distribute "as each had need." But even this act of love and generosity was open to abuse and deception. Barnabas' liberality was an illustration of the spirit of love. Ananias and Sapphira were an illustration of deception in that they deceived themselves and the apostles as well. But the Holy Spirit revealed the truth about it all. They wanted glory without paying the price. They wanted honor without honesty. They were punished with instant death, for, while claiming to give all to God, they had kept back part (Acts 5:4,5).

As Christians, we claim to give all to Christ. Complete surrender is the condition He sets down for discipleship. *Forsake all and follow me,* is His condition. (See Luke 14:33.) Do we hold anything back from Christ? Are we hypocrites in our testimony?

The power in the apostles' story was in the fact that their lives fitted in with the life of their risen Christ. "You've got to show me," is the attitude of the world today. Those early Christians did show the world. Do you show by your life and conduct that you are a Christian?

When signs and wonders were wrought among the people, the crowds came to see. When the Holy Spirit was in the midst, the people saw the power of God. The same is true today. When churches present Christ in His winsomeness and the Holy Spirit in His power, the people will come. Christ draws all men.

Miracles commonly result in converts. Look in this Book of Acts. When the miracle of tongues appeared, the people "thronged to the place" (Acts 2). When Peter healed the man at the Gate Beautiful, *the people ran together unto them in the porch that is called Solomon's* (Acts 3:11). When the miracle of judgment came upon Ananias and Sapphira, *believers were the more added to the Lord, multitudes both of men and women* (5:14). So we will find instances all through the book.

Thousands of articles have been written as to how to put men to work in the churches. There will be plenty of service in the church when we give place to the Holy Spirit. The Spirit-filled church will be a serving church.

Then the high priest rose up, and all they that were with him, . . . And laid their hands on the apostles, and put them in the common prison (Acts 5:17,18). Again we see that the wonderful work of the apostles aroused the opposition of the Sanhedrin (a court of 70 religious rulers). A few unlearned fishermen had risen up to teach, and multitudes were listening and following after them; hence they were disturbed. Even though the apostles were beaten with rods, and prohibited to preach, we find them rejoicing that they were counted worthy to suffer shame for His name! *And daily in the temple, and in every house, they ceased not to teach and preach Jesus Christ* (Acts 5:42). We find their boldest words in this statement: *We ought to obey God rather than men* (5:29). Is this the conviction of your life?

Let us have the spirit of these apostles! Let us not be discouraged when opponents multiply.

A meeting of the Church was called, and seven members elected as deacons. There were two offices in the Church now. One was to "serve tables," to attend to the benevolence and to care for the needy. The other office was to devote itself to preaching and prayer.

The first two deacons named were Stephen and Philip (6:5). These two men were mighty in their influence over the Church, perhaps more than any beside Peter and Paul.

The opposition was centered around Stephen. Read the experiences as recorded in Acts 6 and 7. Stephen was just a layman, but he was one of the first deacons. He is described as a man *full of faith and power* (Acts 6:8). We have a record of but one day of his life—the last. What an account it is! It is not the length of time we live that counts, but how we live. Someone has said, "A Christian is always on duty." This means that every minute of his life is important and under God's direction.

Stephen was just a layman. Like thousands of other laymen since his time, he *did great wonders* because he was *full of faith and power!*

The layman Stephen's life and death had an incalculable effect upon the history of the world, in his influence upon Saul of Tarsus. Who can tell what your life may do in its influence upon some friend?

The leaders in the synagogue *were not able to resist the wisdom and the spirit by which he spake* (6:10). Their anger flared into murderous hatred. Stephen was the first martyr of the Christian Church. To Stephen's death we may trace, without doubt, the first impressions made by the followers of Christ on Saul.

WITNESSING IN JUDEA AND SAMARIA
(Read Acts 8:4–12:25)

The disciples had been witnesses in Jerusalem, but Jesus had told them they must go into Judea and Samaria.

If you were quite sure that you would lose your life by remaining in your own hometown, but would be safe in some nearby village, do you think you would go to that village? This is the very problem that faced the early Church in Jerusalem. There were religious leaders there who thought they were doing God's will when they tried to wipe out Christianity by killing the Christians. Paul said: *I verily thought with myself, that I ought to do many things contrary to the name of Jesus of Nazareth* (Acts 26:9).

Paul really began his work of spreading the Gospel then but he didn't know it. Read Acts 8:3. He thought he was stamping out Christianity. Instead, he was spreading it. Just laugh when you see anyone opposing Christianity. Persecution always has spread Christianity like wind spreads fire. This has been true all down through the centuries since our Lord lived on the earth.

See what kind of a Church this early Church was. *Therefore they that were scattered abroad went every where preaching the word* (Acts 8:4).

This is the reason the Gospel spread at first. What commission did the disciples have? *Go ye into all the world, and preach the gospel* . . . How many did Jesus train for His work? Just twelve, and one of them forsook Him.

Well, here were the rest of the twelve, sitting down at Jerusalem and "all the world" needing the Gospel. Saul's persecution, like the confusion of tongues at the tower of Babel, scattered the Christians throughout the world. Cowardice did not prompt them to flee, for every place we find them preaching the Gospel.

PHILIP, THE EVANGELIST

Philip (not the apostle), one of the seven who had been chosen as a deacon (Acts 6:5), was an evangelist. He had settled in Samaria, as a result of the persecution. Jesus had said, "Ye shall be witnesses . . . in Samaria." Philip preached Christ. Multitudes were following him in his evangelistic campaign. But God called him to leave his successful work, and *Arise, and go toward the south unto the way that goeth down from Jerusalem unto Gaza, which is desert* (Acts 8:26). Philip obeyed and left and on the way he met an Ethiopian. "By chance," you say? When you are in the will of God, things do not just happen. No friend crosses your path by accident. No joy or sorrow comes into your life except by God's permission.

This story brings up the question as to which brings the larger results, preaching to men in great numbers, or telling men individually about the Lord. Some people think that winning just one person at a time to Christ would be a slow process, but listen to this!

There are over 190,000,000 people in the United States. Suppose you were the only Christian among these one hundred ninety million today. You win one soul of the one hundred ninety million today. Then tomorrow you two win one soul each, for Christ. On the following day each one of you four do the same; next day the eight of you win one apiece. Here is a startling fact. If each of these Christians and the newly won

436

Christians should win one soul a day to Christ, how long would it take to win one hundred ninety million? Just less than one month from the day the first one began! Wouldn't it be a good thing for your class to form a G. O. Club? Each one G-E-T O-N-E. This is Christ's method of soul-winning.

Philip's convert no doubt preached the Gospel in Africa. There is nothing to show that Africa previously had any knowledge of the Son of God. The Gospel was on the way to *the uttermost part of the earth.*

SAUL

It was at Stephen's death that we have the first mention of Saul. Stephen's martyrdom seemed to have inflamed this persecutor of the Church. Saul was struggling with an aroused conscience. He knew he was in the wrong, but he wouldn't give up. That is why Jesus told him in his vision that it was hard for him *to kick against the pricks* (Acts 26:14).

Saul made havoc of the Church! The more moral and intelligent a man is, the more harm he can do when controlled by Satan.

The story of Saul's conversion is one of the most thrilling accounts in history. Become familiar with this great story. He was a man *breathing out threatenings and slaughter against the disciples of the Lord* (Acts 9:1,2). Then we find him preaching *Christ in the synagogues, that he is the Son of God* (Acts 9:20).

Every step of his three great missionary journeys Paul made known Christ's will with unmistakable clarity. There is no doubt that Paul holds the most important place of any man in the New Testament. He was converted and made an apostle by Christ Himself. It was to him that Christ gave first-hand revelations of truth, and to him Christ committed the doctrine of the Church. To what people was Paul especially sent? He was the apostle to the Gentiles, as Peter had been to the Jews.

What had Peter done since Pentecost? It is not only what a man believes but what he is doing about it, that counts. Christ had told Peter that he was to be a witness. Peter helped start the

437

first Church, worked miracles, and baptized thousands. His work had been among the Jews.

We find Peter now in the house of Simon the tanner (Acts 10:5,6). God was going to show Peter that the Gospel was for the Gentiles as well as the Jews (Acts 10:9-16). The high wall of religious difference between Jew and Gentile must be broken down. Peter was the man God used to start leveling it. Christ was building a Church and He wanted both Jews and Gentiles to be the living stones of which it is to be formed (Eph. 2:20-22).

At Pentecost, Peter had used the "keys of the kingdom" entrusted to him, to open the door of the Gospel to the Jews. While Paul was in Tarsus, Peter in the house of Cornelius put the key into the lock of the door that had barred the Gentiles, and opened it (Acts 10:1-48). Read this account. What about race prejudice today? Do you think that what God told Peter to do was easy? (Acts 10:14-16). What is the Church doing today?

WITNESSING IN THE UTTERMOST PART OF THE EARTH
(Read Acts 13–28)

The death of Stephen was only the beginning of great persecution of the Christians. How did they ever get to Antioch? (Acts 11:19-21). Someone has called Christianity in the early days, "A Tale of Two Cities"—Jerusalem and Antioch.

Up through Acts 12, we have seen the beginning of the Church, with Peter as its leader, in Jerusalem. From Acts 13 through 28, we are going to see Paul and the Church at Antioch. Antioch is the new base of operations. All the wonderful missionary journeys of Paul started from here, not from Jerusalem. It became the new center of the Church for carrying out Jesus' commission.

The Jewish Christians, who had been compelled to leave Jerusalem because of persecution, were naturally thrown with all the Gentiles. These early Christians could not help but talk about that which interested them most. The power of the Lord was so manifest that a great crowd joined the Church (Acts 11:21).

438

It was here in this church that a new name was given to Christ's disciples. They were first called "Christians" at Antioch (Acts 11:26).

It is interesting to note here that the Church had lost track of Paul. They did not care what had become of him, but Barnabas looked him up (11:25). He had kept track of him all these years. If it had not been for Barnabas, Paul might have remained in obscurity all his life! Think of what the world would have missed had Paul not been discovered! Many a person is waiting to be discovered for God.

BEGINNING OF FOREIGN MISSIONS

Do we realize that we Americans might have been pagans, living in heathen darkness and superstition, while the Chinese and Japanese would have been Christian nations if the first missionaries had gone East instead of coming West? Wouldn't you think that Americans, above every people, ought to believe in missions? Think of what our condition might have been today, if missionaries had not brought Christ to us.

We see Paul and Barnabas, the first foreign missionaries, starting westward from Antioch (Acts 13:2,3). The greatest enterprise in the world is foreign missions, and this is the very start of this great movement. The whole idea began just the way it should, at a prayer meeting.

While Paul and Barnabas were preaching the Gospel and suffering all kinds of persecution and hardship, there were many at home at Jerusalem stirring up the most troublesome question that the Church had ever faced. It was this: "Must a Gentile become a Jew, and accept his laws and ceremonies, before he can become a Christian?" (15:1). Paul and Barnabas had said nothing about the law of Moses. They had stated: *Believe on the Lord Jesus Christ, and thou shalt be saved* (Acts 16:31). The law doesn't save anyone.

Luke now joined the missionary party (16:10). The first convert in Europe was not a famous scholar or some mighty ruler, but a business woman, Lydia, a seller of purple dyed garments.

In Philippi, we find Paul and Silas in prison. Why do we find men like these locked behind iron bars? Read Acts 16:16-24. The second Christian in Europe was very different from the first. Lydia was converted in a prayer meeting, but it took an earthquake to arouse the jailer. The jailer's question is one of the most important questions in all the world (Acts 16:30).

Paul's experiences in the greatest cities of his day are crowded with interest. He founded a church at Thessalonica (17:4).

In famous Athens, Paul preached his immortal sermon on Mars Hill. This is one of the great scenes in history. What effect did it have on those listeners? (Acts 17:32).

Paul was not only giving a wonderful message to the Athenians, when he preached that day, but he was speaking to you and to me. Paul tells us that God is near. He seems so far away to some, that they do not even try to reach Him, yet God hears our faintest whisper if we speak to Him.

Paul left Athens and arrived at Corinth, very much discouraged. We do not know whether he was successful in starting a church in Athens, but in Corinth, one of the most wicked cities of the ancient world, he founded a church and remained there eighteen months to establish the people in the faith (Acts 18:8). It was here Paul found Aquila and his wife Priscilla, who afterward became his loyal friends.

After an absence of three or four years, Paul returned to Antioch by way of Ephesus. In Antioch he reported his entrance into Europe.

PAUL'S THIRD MISSIONARY TOUR

Now we find Paul spending three years in one of the greatest cities of his day. Ephesus was perhaps the world's largest and most cosmopolitan city, except Rome. Multitudes of Jews and Gentiles of Asia heard the Gospel preached. Ephesus was notorious for its luxury and licentiousness, and the worship of the goddess Diana. The years spent here are so crowded with interesting details that it is hard to choose the most important. Enthusiastic converts burned their books on "the black art," magic, and threw away their silver idols. There was a great bonfire in Ephesus. It almost seems as though we can see the flames burning to this day. It represented the burning of their old lives. Paul has taught us that every idol must be torn down from its place in our hearts and the Lord alone must occupy the throne. Is there anything in our lives that calls for a bonfire? Don't be afraid of bringing yourself face to face with your own inner life.

Such blessings as these could not last long without opposition. If we read on to the end of the chapter, we will see the results of Paul's work. The silversmiths stirred up a riot, and the apostles were rescued from danger only by the help of the city officials.

As Paul traveled, he kept writing his wonderful letters. We read them today with great profit and interest. From Ephesus Paul sent his First Epistle to the Corinthians (I Cor. 16:8). During his third journey Paul wrote Second Corinthians, Galatians and Romans.

PAUL'S FAREWELL

Paul's last missionary journey must have been a heart-breaking experience. He had to say farewell at every place. He knew it was a final farewell. Read Acts 20:37,38. They all wept and "fell on Paul's neck," the Oriental expression of sorrow, knowing they would never see him again. Think of this sad experience repeated a dozen times over. Probably no man, except David, has ever inspired such intense personal love in so many hearts.

Sailing out of the harbor of Ephesus, Paul bids his friends a last farewell. He is headed for Jerusalem, and from now on he is seen as "the prisoner of the Lord." Paul makes his last visit to Jerusalem and here one of those swiftly formed mobs, which gather so quickly in the excitable Orient, rushed against the apostle and bound him, declaring he was teaching the Jews to forsake Moses. No doubt he recalled the fact that outside that city, he himself, twenty-six years before, had assisted in the murder of Stephen. Finding that Paul was a Roman citizen, the chief captain promised to give him a fair trial. Paul made his defense before the Roman governor, Felix, at Caesarea. After two years' imprisonment, Paul was tried a second time before the new governor, Festus, and appealed from him to Caesar himself, the emperor (Acts 21:27–26:32).

After a most exciting voyage, in which his ship was wrecked in a terrific storm off the coast of Malta, Paul arrived in Rome. Here he was kept a prisoner in his own hired house for two years. Even in prison the great preacher and evangelist led the servants in Nero's own palace to Christ. Service for the Master can brighten life's darkest hours. When we seek to lift others' burdens, we lighten our own (Acts 27:1–28:24).

During his imprisonment, Paul wrote many of his epistles, Philemon, Colossians, Ephesians and Philippians. It was while he was in a dungeon in Rome, expecting at any hour to be beheaded, that he wrote his second epistle to Timothy.

Finally (according to tradition) the beloved apostle was condemned and beheaded. His heroic soul was released and the feeble body buried in the catacombs.

Paul changed Christianity from its Jewish tribal confines to a worldwide influence. He tried to break down the barriers between Jew and Gentile and between slave and free.

This is the only unfinished book in the Bible. Notice how abruptly it closes! How else could it close? How could there be a complete account of a Person's life work as long as He lives? Our risen and ascended Lord still lives. From the center, Christ, the lines are seen proceeding in every direction, but *the uttermost part of the earth* is not yet reached. The book is evidently a fragment. The Gospel of Christ moves on! You are still living the Acts.

Minimum Daily Requirements/Spiritual Vitamins

Sunday: FIRST CHURCH IN JERUSALEM
Acts 1:1–4:37
Monday: WITNESSING IN JERUSALEM
Acts 5:1–8:3

Tuesday: WITNESSING IN JUDEA AND SAMARIA
Acts 8:4–12:25
Wednesday: PAUL ESTABLISHES THE CHURCHES
(FIRST TOUR) Acts 13:1–15:35
Thursday: PAUL REVISITS THE CHURCHES
(SECOND TOUR) Acts 15:36–18:21
Friday: PAUL ENCOURAGES THE CHURCHES
(THIRD TOUR) Acts 18:22–25:9
Saturday: PAUL SENT TO ROME
Acts 25:10–28:31

CHAPTER 33

UNDERSTANDING ROMANS

*Romans
Portrays Jesus Christ,
Our Righteousness*

We now begin a study of the Epistles in the New Testament. Thirteen of the twenty-one were written by Paul, hence they are called the Pauline Epistles. He wrote his letters to the churches at Thessalonica, Galatia, Corinth and Rome during his missionary journeys. It was while he was a prisoner in Rome that he wrote his letters to the church at Ephesus, one to the Colossians, one to Philemon and one to the Philippians. After his imprisonment he wrote two letters to Timothy and one to Titus.

Paul was born at Tarsus, of pure Jewish stock. His teacher was Gamaliel, the great teacher of the Pharisees. Like all Hebrew boys, he learned a trade—he was a tentmaker. At Jerusalem he was present at the stoning of Stephen, the first Christian martyr. No doubt this scene made a tremendous impression upon the young Saul. On the way to Damascus, on a mission of persecution of the Christians, the young Pharisee had a head-on collision with Jesus Christ! After his miraculous conversion, he was baptized, and received his commission to preach the Gospel. He retired to Arabia, and spent three years there in study and preparation.

After laboring in Tarsus for three years and one year in Antioch, directed by the Holy Spirit, Paul became the great missionary to the Gentiles. On his three missionary journeys he founded many churches, and wrote his epistles. The combination of Roman citizenship, Greek education and Hebrew religion wonderfully qualified him for his great work, but you will find that he trusted alone in the grace and apostleship which he received direct from Jesus Christ (1:5).

After a life filled with sacrifice and suffering, he sealed his testimony with his own life's blood. Tradition says he was beheaded at Rome, and his body buried in the catacombs.

THE CHURCH AT ROME

Who founded the Church at Rome we do not know. It was not founded by Peter. Peter's ministry was to the Jews (Gal. 2:9). Visitors from Rome, in Jerusalem for the Passover and converted at Pentecost, went back to the capital, carrying the seed of the Gospel, and established this new center in Rome. During the twenty-eight intervening years many Christians from all parts of the East had migrated to Rome, some of them Paul's own converts.

Paul was eager to visit this church, and sent them this letter from Corinth, from the home of Gaius, a wealthy Corinthian Christian, while he was on his third missionary journey. It was written in the fourth year of Nero, then Emperor of Rome. In this epistle he sets forth his gospel (1:16,17).

Paul, the servant (1:1), writes to the saints at Rome (1:7), concerning the Saviour (1:3,4).

Paul the Servant Is

Separated unto the Gospel..1:1
Serving in the Gospel 1:9
Saved by the Gospel...1:16

Is the Gospel of Christ gripping you this way? Are you saved by it, separated unto it, and serving in it?

After Paul's greeting to the church, he thanks God for their faith (vs. 8). Notice Paul's expression of obligation to this church (vs. 14,15):

I am debtor 1:14
I am ready to fulfill my obligation 1:15
I am not ashamed of the message 1:16

Why was Paul not ashamed of the Gospel of Christ? Because it reveals what the sinner needs, and what he may have on the ground of simple faith. A *righteousness of God*—the righteousness of Jesus Christ.

The Gospel has dynamic power. It is the power of God unto

446

salvation. Do you realize that nothing short of the power of God could make one Christian?

Paul was not ashamed of the Gospel of Christ, even in Rome. The terrible sinfulness of man, as pictured in 1:18-32, had reached its climax in Rome.

Paul spoke from the white-hot conviction that is born of experience. On the road to Damascus, at one blow, he had all the props of works, of race and of character knocked out from under him. He caught a full glimpse of the glorified Christ. Thenceforth he had but one message—faith in the crucified and risen Lord. He would hear nothing else; he spoke nothing else; he lived nothing less. He proclaimed that henceforth *The just shall live by faith.* One must simply believe. Salvation is not of works—works are damning; not of race—the race is under the curse of death; not of character—because our character is as filthy rags! There is only one salvation, and that is by the acceptance of the Gospel of Christ. For therein is a righteousness from God revealed—from faith to faith. This righteousness God gives or "imparts" to us when we believe in Christ. He does not say we are made righteous, but declared righteous. God gives to us the righteousness He demands of us. Why is God's righteousness necessary? Because we have none of our own.

RIGHTEOUSNESS OF GOD NECESSARY

After Paul states the subject of the Book of Romans, in 1:16,17, he then reveals man's need of this righteousness. *For all have sinned,* and *all the world may become guilty before God.* From his elevated pulpit, Paul looks around and sees zealous Jews, proud Greeks, boastful Romans and a multitude of ordinary, common sinners like ourselves. What a terrible picture he presents in 1:18-32! First the unrighteousness of the Gentiles is portrayed; then the Jews.

The Book of Romans tells us of God's method of making guilty men good. The key of this great thesis is found in Romans 1:16,17:

Romans in a Nutshell

The Person of the Gospel ....Christ
The Power of the Gospel ...."Power of God"

447

The Purpose of the Gospel ....“Unto Salvation”
The People to whom sent ....“To everyone”
The Plan of acceptance ....“To everyone that believeth”
The Particular result ....“The just shall live by faith”

Paul was proud of the Gospel, because he had proved its power in his own life, and in the lives of all who would believe.

Good news! These words will command the attention of anyone. Say, “I have good news for you!” and one can always secure a listener. The real value of “good news” depends on the source—who said it. That is why the Gospel Paul presents is so welcome. The news comes from God. Romans is Paul's shout of joy to a lost world.

The first three chapters describe the “Hell of Sin.” The last five chapters describe the “Heaven of Holiness.” Intervening chapters describe “Christ, the Way.”

In Romans, Paul shows us God's method of making a guilty man good. He reveals a sinner's needs and then presents what he may have by faith: “A righteousness from God”—Christ, our righteousness. The righteousness of God is a Person. The righteousness which God demands is in a Person, Jesus Christ. No one will ever get into heaven with any less righteousness than Christ's righteousness. When you look at Jesus, you see the righteousness which God requires.

WHAT WE ARE BY NATURE (Read Romans 1:1–3:20)

Why does man need salvation? Because he is a sinner. God has X-rayed the human heart and has given us the picture. He shows us what He finds in us all. The findings are so terrible that they cannot be read in a mixed audience. But remember, this is the picture of us that God sees. I know your picture is there because it says, *There is none that doeth good, no, not one.* This fact Paul proves conclusively in the first three chapters of this Book of Romans. This is the picture of man without God. Read every word of Romans 3. You will believe then that the natural heart is desperately wicked. Have you ever asked the Holy Spirit to throw a searchlight on your own heart? If you have, you know today that you need a Saviour.

The Book of Romans presents a courtroom scene. God, the

Judge of all the earth, summons Jew and Gentile before the bar of justice. Prisoner after prisoner is brought up.

The general charge is stated—"All under sin" (Romans 3:19). Both the Gentile (2:1-16) and Jew (2:17–3:8) are given the opportunity for a hearing. Their special pleas of "not guilty" are carefully considered and answered, clearing the way for the final verdict from the Judge.

Finally the Judge pronounces the verdict. *All the world . . . guilty before God* (Romans 3:19). If this were today, newspapers everywhere would blaze this headline. All the television newsmen would be announcing it. Can't you hear them? "ALL - THE - WORLD - FOUND - GUILTY!"

Against all this there is no defense. The Judge says, "Is there anyone to plead the cause of the prisoners?" And there is no answering voice. Every mouth is stopped (Romans 3:19). There is no room for excuse.

The condemnation of the world is settled. The next step in order will be to reveal the plan of God to save a lost world. Remember, the Book of Romans tells us God's method of making men good.

Do not say, "God is love. He will not condemn me." Listen to God's words here: *The wrath of God is revealed from heaven against all ungodliness* (Romans 1:18). He has already passed sentence on everyone. "All . . . guilty." There is no chance of appeal. It is the decision of the Supreme Court of the universe. Sin is universal—*All have sinned!* Hence we need a world's Saviour. Because God is a God of love, He has provided just this One! Repeat aloud John 3:16. The Judge on the bench says, "Is there anyone to appear for the prisoners?" Then the Son of God says, "Yes, I am here to represent these. It is true that they committed these sins. It is true that they are guilty, but I bore their guilt on the cross. I died in their place that they might go free. I am their righteousness." And the Judge sets them free.

We get an awful picture of sin in these first three chapters of Romans. Remember, SIN is a marksman's word. It means "missing the mark"—the standard that God has set for us. God's Word says, *All have sinned, and come short.* In our

449

good deeds? No—*of the glory of God.* Do not measure your life by any other standard but this. Do not "compare yourselves among yourselves." Of course you may not have fallen as short as some others you know, but you are "short" as far as God is concerned.

We are all sinners because we were born into a sinful race. We are all "sons of Adam." But we were not only born into sin; we have sinned ourselves, for "all have sinned." Remember this —we sin because we are sinners. This is our nature. A plum tree bears plums, because it is a plum tree. The fruit is the result of its nature. Sin is the fruit of a sinful heart. *The heart is deceitful above all things* (Jer. 17:9).

Christ not only saves us from the penalty of sin, but He is able to free us from the consciousness of guilt and the power of sin. The result of sin is a sense of guilt. When one has broken the law he feels guilty and seeks to hide. This is what the first man, Adam, did. The guilty conscience brings a fear of punishment. The sinner is always trying to flee from the consequences of the broken law. He fears the judge. This is why a man's sins and his consciousness of guilt banish him from the presence of God. God does not need to banish the sinner. He flees of his own accord. This is what will happen in the day when the wrath of God shall be revealed (Rev. 6:15,16).

The first thing that is necessary for the freedom of the sinner is that the dreadful consequences of his guilt be taken away. He needs more than pardon, for that would leave him with his guilt. Any president or governor or king can pardon a criminal, but not one has the power to remove the guilt. Proper punishment for the deed must be given. This is what Christ has done. *The wages of sin is death* and since all of us "have sinned," Christ came to die and bear the penalty for the sins committed against a holy God.

HOW TO BECOME A CHRISTIAN
(Read Romans 3:21–5:21)

Question: How does God save sinners? Answer: *Through redemption . . .* in *Christ Jesus* (3:24).

God's plan of salvation runs through the entire Scriptures. It is like the cordage of the British Navy with a scarlet line interwoven through it that you cannot take out without destroying the cord. There is a scarlet line of salvation running through Scripture. You can see it very plainly in certain portions of the Bible. Romans 3 is one of them.

When God looks at us, He sees no righteousness. (See Romans 3:10.) When God looks at us "in Christ," He does not see an improvement but perfection, for God sees only His own Righteousness, Jesus Christ.

You have become acquainted with one great word of Scripture, "salvation." Here is another—"justification," "just-as-if-I'd." Everything that Christ has done has been credited to my account. His righteousness is mine!

When Christ's righteousness is reckoned as ours, this is called "justification"—a man made just (righteous) before God. *The just shall live by faith.* A man is not made just by his works but by believing on Christ. (Read Romans 3:28.) This great truth gave birth to the great Reformation. It freed the believer from the idea that men were saved by works to a life of faith and liberty in Christ. Not only are we saved by faith, but we must live by faith, trusting in Christ.

Paul gives us illustrations of justification by faith from the Old Testament. Especially does he tell us of how Abraham's faith was counted for righteousness (Romans 4). Abraham received three things by faith: Righteousness, inheritance, posterity (Romans 4:3,13,17).

We too have great benefits when we are justified by His grace. Grace is unmerited favor. In this life we find that faith is followed by peace, pardon and promise, (Romans 5:1-5) and more than all, an assurance of salvation (Romans 5:6-11).

How can a man be justified by God? Read Romans 3:24-28. God imparts His righteousness to man in the following way:

1. By grace—(Rom. 3:24) The source of it. Grace means unmerited favor.

2. By God—He is the giver of it. Rom. 3:26; 8:33.

3. By blood—The reason for it. Rom. 3:24; 5:9.

4. By faith—The means by which it is received. Rom. 3:22.

5. By works—The way it is shown. James 2:21-23.

6. By experience—The blessings that we enjoy from it. Rom. 5:1-4.

When I look into heaven and remember that God who sits upon His throne has condemned me, I would be in despair. But I see One standing at His right, holding up a wounded hand, and presenting His pierced feet and side. With these wounds Christ pleads for me, and I have His own assurance that they are efficacious, sufficient to meet my needs.

SALVATION

You will find the stream of sin and the river of salvation running along together, from Romans 1 through 16. *Where sin abounded, grace did much more abound.* Paul shows sin in all its squalor, and salvation in all its splendor. Some simple steps in these next paragraphs will show you "How to become a Christian!"

One does not have to be a sinner in the sight of men to be lost. Of course there is a difference in the degree of sin, but not in the fact of sin, and its results, for *the wages of sin is death.* One may be drowned in seven feet of water and be as dead as if he had been submerged in seventy feet of water. In our inability to save ourselves, we are all on the same level—*There is no difference* (Romans 3:22).

We are saved by Christ's righteousness. He has made it available for us by His death. *Being justified freely by his grace through the redemption that is in Christ Jesus: Whom God hath set forth to be a propitiation through faith in his blood, to declare his righteousness for the remission of sins that are past* ... (Romans 3:24,25).

I am a person condemned to die because of my sin, for *the wages of sin is death.* But I can look on the cross and see that Christ has already died for me. I believe that He died for my sin. And so in exchange for my poor, sinful, condemned life, I can accept His righteousness and His life (I Peter 2:24).

He that believeth on the Son hath everlasting life (John 3:36). *But now the righteousness of God without the law is mani-*

fested, . . . even the righteousness of God . . . which is by faith of Jesus Christ unto all and upon all them that believe (Romans 3:21,22). Apart from man's effort to be good, God has provided his righteousness, the Lord Jesus Christ. Our righteousness is as filthy rags (Isaiah 64:6).

Your sin is on Christ. He has borne it for you. Have you accepted Him as your Saviour and *passed from death unto life* (John 5:24)? If you have decided to let Christ be your sin bearer, you now have His salvation. (Read Romans 3:24.)

JUSTIFIED BY FAITH

A murderer may stand at the bottom of a mine and you on the highest peak of the Rocky Mountains, but you are as little able to touch the stars as he. You cannot attain unto the righteousness that God demands, no matter how far you climb.

Forgiveness is the removal of our unrighteousness, an unclothing or putting away of sin.

Justification is the act of being clothed with the righteousness of God's own providing. It is perfect.

The person who put his faith in Christ an hour ago is just as much justified as the oldest Christian living. We never become any more justified than the minute we received Christ. Justification depends upon something done outside of us, something done on the cross of Calvary.

Justification takes care of all the sin and guilt upon us, buries all this sin and guilt in the grave of Jesus Christ, and then sets us in heavenly places with Christ our Saviour.

There is a question that many ask: "How could one man die for the whole world?" One man might take another man's place and be his substitute. That is all right, you say, but for one to die for the whole world—that is nonsense! Let us see if this is true!

None of us like the idea of being called a "sinner," but we must face what we are. Listen to what Paul says in Romans 5:12-21. We were born sinners. We were not asked if we wished to come into this world. We woke up to the fact one day that we were subject to a sinful nature. Adam, the head of our race, was not created that way (Genesis 1:26). He deliberately sinned and his sinful nature was passed on to us all. We sin because we are sinners.

But over against Adam, the head of the natural race, we find Christ, the Head of a spiritual race—"a new creation." When I was born in this body, I was born a descendant of Adam. I have his nature which is sinful. When I am born into the family of God, by Christ Jesus, I have Christ's nature which is holy. In the words of Scripture, *As in Adam all die, even so in Christ shall all be made alive* (I Cor. 15:22). I did not choose to be a descendant of Adam. I may choose to be a child of God. If one man's sin made it possible for all the race to die, one Man's righteousness made it possible for all the race to get out of this condition. (Read Romans 5:15.)

Have you received "eternal life by Jesus Christ our Lord"? Are you a sinner "in Adam," or are you a son "in Christ"?

HOW TO LIVE A CHRISTIAN LIFE (Read Romans 6–8)

We have learned how to become a Christian. Now we must find out how to live like a Christian. It is one thing to accept what Christ has done for you. It is another thing to experience it as personal and real.

In Romans 6 there are three important words. Mark them.

KNOW that Christ died for us (Romans 6:3-5,10).

We died with Christ (Romans 6:8).

RECKON on this! *Likewise reckon ye also yourselves to be dead indeed unto sin, but alive unto God through Jesus Christ our Lord* (Romans 6:11). If a relative told you that he had put $500 in the bank for you for a trip and you could draw it any time you needed it, you would count on it, I am sure, though you never saw the money. If you should question it, and not draw it out, the money would never be yours. If you reckon it yours by signing a check and passing it through the bank window, that which you have never seen becomes a reality. Reckoning makes things real! Since we are dead to sin and alive unto God, how shall we live? (See Romans 6:13.)

YIELD—*Neither yield ye your members as instruments of unrighteousness unto sin: but yield yourselves unto God, as those that are alive from the dead, and your members as instru-*

ments of righteousness unto God (Romans 6:13).

This means "let go" of your life and "let God" live through you. This is the surrendered life. This is the right way to live a life of victory and blessing. Let Him work His will in you and through you.

The Christian soon finds a new standard for his life. He does not try to live up to the Law, for he is no longer under it. He strives to please the One who dwells within him. *For to me to live is Christ,* and I *do all to the glory of God.*

Romans 6 reveals the secret of a life of victory. I am living in Christ! Dead to sin, but alive to God! It tells me how "I" can lead a Christian life. Self, we have learned, was a condemned thing, unable to be good, never righteous (Romans 3). Now when self becomes a Christian and tries to live a Christian life, it finds this to be impossible. We are saved by faith, and we cannot live by our own efforts.

This sad truth is revealed in Romans 7. It tells us how we cannot live a victorious life. Mark the little word "I" and you will find it is used thirty-eight times in the twenty-five verses of this chapter. The Holy Spirit is never mentioned. Although "I" tries, it finds only defeat.

Dr. Griffith Thomas said, "It is not hard to live a Christian life; it is impossible."

Paul said, *It is not I that live, but Christ that lives in me.*

Listen to the words of the man who tries to live by his own effort. *O wretched man that I am! who shall deliver me from the body of this death? I thank God through Jesus Christ our Lord. So then with the mind I myself serve the law of God; but with the flesh the law of sin* (Romans 7:24, 25).

Finally, "I" finds that there is One who is sufficient. Struggling yields to power, defeat is changed to victory, misery is transformed into joy. When "I" goes out, Christ comes in.

THE SPIRIT-FILLED LIFE

The life "in Christ" is a wonderful thing. Paul says, *The law of the Spirit of life in Christ Jesus hath made me free from the law of sin and death.* This is what happens. When I step into an airplane, I am free from the law of gravity. The higher law operates in the plane to lift it above the clouds, although the law of gravity a few minutes before held me fast to the earth. The law of gravity is not destroyed but rendered inoperative. This is what happens in my life when I step "in Christ." The law that operates by the Spirit in my life lifts me above the world and sin, and sin no longer has dominion over me. I am free. I am without condemnation. Have you stepped into Christ? Are you living on a plane far above evil principalities and powers?

Have you come to the end of "self"? Remember, "I" never brings anything but failure. It is the "I" in "s-I-n" that must be removed. Put "O" in its place and you have "SON." He will give you victory!

Step out of the self-life into the Spirit-filled-life. In Romans 8 instead of the word "I," we find the word "Spirit" used twenty-one times. We must "yield" our lives to Him. This is our part. Then He will fill us with His Spirit. That is Christ's part.

This glorious chapter opens with "no condemnation," and ends with "no separation." This is a picture of our life "in Christ." The Christian is safe: Christ is around him; the Spirit is within him; and God is for him.

WHY ISRAEL IS SET ASIDE (Romans 9–11)

The story of the Jews' being set aside and scattered throughout the world without a homeland, without a king is a warning for us (Romans 9,10,11). God is a sovereign God, and He will do what He will. He has a perfect right to turn to the Gentiles, because the Jews would not seek the righteousness of God which is by faith (Romans 9:32). They tried to set up their own righteousness. But man does not build up righteousness. He only receives it. If God will set aside His chosen people, will He not set us aside if we are disobedient?

Let us be careful lest we become self-willed and disobedient as the Jews, not heeding God's commandments.

Ask Christ to take control of your life and guide you in His path. There are wrecks outside His divine course. The Jews are a solemn lesson to us. Read the wonderful description of God's mercy in Romans 11:32-36.

HOW TO SERVE GOD (Read Romans 12–16)

I beseech you therefore, brethren, by the mercies of God, that ye present your bodies a living sacrifice, holy, acceptable unto God, which is your reasonable service (Romans 12:1).

In this appeal, Paul urges us to have our life measure up to our belief. He shows that the doctrine of justification by faith will not allow laxity in life or conduct. We are saved to serve. The Christian life must be lived in its relation to God, self and others.

It may surprise you to find out that up to this point we have not had to do a thing but believe on Christ and yield ourselves to Him to use as He will. Now we are to serve!

Until we have been saved by His grace and transformed by His love, we can do little for God. Read I Corinthians 13. But when we present ourselves to Christ and become filled with His love, we can find much to be done. Christ wants a "living sacrifice," not a dead one (Romans 12:1). Many will die for Christ. Few will live for Him. There are many of you who might rather be burned at a stake than stand the ridicule of your associates. One definition of a modern Christian is "a person who will die for the church he will not attend." How many of us say nothing when Christ's name is brought into question or is used in vain!

Let others see Jesus in you! Live for Him, then you will be ready to die for Him.

The first part of Romans is what God did for us. The last part of Romans is what we may do for God.

We find our Christian service in

Church ....Romans 12:3-8
Government .... Romans 13
Questionable Things...............................Romans 14:1–15:3
The Whole World..Romans 15:4-13

Minimum Daily Requirements/Spiritual Vitamins

Sunday: WHAT WE ARE BY NATURE
Romans 1:14-23; 3:9-20

Monday: HOW TO BECOME A CHRISTIAN
Romans 3:21–5:21

Tuesday: HOW TO LIVE A CHRISTIAN LIFE
Romans 6:1-23

Wednesday: A STRUGGLE   Romans 7:1-25

Thursday: THE LIFE OF VICTORY
Romans 8:1-39

Friday: THE JEWS SET ASIDE
Romans 9:30–11:12

Saturday: THE CHRISTIAN'S SERVICE
Romans 12:1-21

CHAPTER 34

UNDERSTANDING I CORINTHIANS

I Corinthians Portrays Jesus Christ, Our Lord

The name "Lord" is very prominent in this book (I Cor. 1:31; 2:8,16; 3:20; 4:4; 5:4,5; 6:13, etc.). This is full of meaning, because much of the confusion that had crept into the church at Corinth had come because the believers failed to recognize Jesus Christ as Lord.

The archaeologist's spade is making Corinth live again! Corinth was the most important city of all Greece in Paul's day. Its wealth was fabulous. Men spent their days in tournaments and speeches. Luxury, dissipation and public immorality were rampant among this great industrial and seafaring population. Corinth attracted great crowds of foreigners from the East and West. Their gods were gods of pleasure and lust. There was, besides, much culture and art. The city abounded in studios of language and schools of philosophy.

As in most cities, there was a large colony of Jews who had kept a strong moral standard and held to their religious beliefs. But the city itself was the center of a debased form of the worship of Venus.

If we read Acts 18, we find how the Gospel reached this wicked city. The apostle Paul, then a man about fifty years of age, in the garb of a working man, entered the busy metropolis and went through its streets in search of a workshop where he might earn his own living. There were no billboards advertising the coming of a world-renowned evangelist. This tradesman came into town and began his tentmaking. This was a leading industry in that day like building is today. He went into business with the well-to-do tentmakers, Aquila and Priscilla. He was always able to support himself, making enough to carry on his missionary work. A wonderful work was done in Corinth during the year and a half that Paul was there. He began by speaking in the synagogues to mixed congregations of Jews and Greeks.

I Corinthians is a difficult book to outline, but it takes up many wonderful subjects. *In him you have been enriched with everything* (I Cor. 1:5, Weymouth). In Romans, Paul told us that it was by Christ that *we have access by faith into this grace wherein we stand* (Rom. 5:2). Then follows these riches of grace in Christ Jesus, our All in all. I Corinthians deals with Christian conduct.

CORRECTIONS IN CHRISTIAN CONDUCT
(Read I Corinthians 1–11)

The wonderful church at Corinth, the brilliant jewel in the crown of Paul's labor, was failing. It all was because the worldliness (carnality) of the city had gotten within its walls. It was all right for the church to be in Corinth, but it was fatal when Corinth got into the church. It is a glorious sight to see a ship launched into the sea, but it is a tragic sight when the sea gets into the ship. The church of Christ should be set as a light in a dark place, but woe unto the church when the wickedness of the world invades.

Practices common to this wicked city soon crept into the church. There were divisions among them; Christians going to law with Christians before heathen judges; behavior at the communion table was disgraceful; the women of the church no longer observed standards of modesty, the church membership was arguing over marriage and even spiritual gifts. Finally the church wrote Paul about these things, and asked his advice on the matter. These two letters to the Corinthians were written in answer to their requests.

After the usual greeting (I Cor. 1:1-3), Paul refers to the coming again of our Lord Jesus Christ (I Cor. 1:7,8). Then he plunges right into the question of the failure of the church, about which he had been told. The source of his information he gives us in I Cor. 1:11.

Men had lost sight of God. Three kinds of selfishness had blinded them:

SELF-ADMIRATION, their intellect had been perverted.

SELF-WILL, their conscience had been darkened.

SELF-INDULGENCE, their passions had been given full reign.

The greatest danger to the Corinthian church was from within.

Paul speaks first of the divisions and cliques about which he had learned from friends and travelers. Nothing eats out the heart and life of the church like party politics.

The Greek spirit of party politics had entered into the church, dividing it into four parties, each trying to get the mastery. Their names are given in I Cor. 1:12. Paul, Apollos and Peter (Cephas) were parties named for their favorite teachers. The Christ Party held to that Name as if it did not belong to everyone in the church.

This dissension about religious leaders meant that the Christians at Corinth had slipped off center. There is only one Leader in every church. That Leader and center is Christ. If the church gets off center here, it goes off all down the line. A great flywheel on center moves quietly; off center it shakes the building to pieces. Christianity must be Christ-centered. If it is Christ-centered it is powerful. Christ Himself is the "good news." He did not only bring God's message; he was God's message. The Corinthians had slipped off center. Paul, Peter, Apollos were all good men, but not God-men. How many are following religious leaders today rather than Christ Himself! *For me to live is Christ* (Philippians 1:21).

Jesus Christ is the only cure for division (I Cor. 1:13). Every eye, every heart, every spirit must be turned to one object —Jesus Christ, our personal Saviour. Paul said, in effect, "Your party spirit is a sin. Can you follow a mere man, hoping that he can give you life? Was that man crucified for you? Trusting in what man has to say is foolish. Men see nothing in the cross of Christ. Christ alone has all the power and wisdom of God."

Youth and old age alike follow Christ to the cross and then stumble at the "blood" of the sacrifice. This is what the Jews and Greeks of Paul's day did. Shall we remove the cross from the Gospel because people do not like it? If we do, we remove the world's only way of salvation. We must preach "Christ crucified."

THE CROSS

Unto the Jews a stumblingblock, something they could not get over (I Cor. 1:23). They could not understand how such a display of weakness could be a source of power. A man dying on a cross did not look much like a world Saviour to them. The scribes and Pharisees scornfully turned from the cross. To them, the cross meant failure. The Jews needed signs of power. They demanded something they could see and grasp. The Messiah must be a world prince, a miracle worker. A multitude of Christians are like this today. They worship success as much as did the Jews. They despise weakness and admire force. These people tell us that men of science are apt to stumble at the cross because they cannot explain how the blood of one Man could wash away the stain of sin.

Unto the Greeks foolishness. The Greeks regarded with contempt the unscientific religion first taught in an unschooled corner of the world like Nazareth, by the son of a carpenter who never studied at Athens or Rome. The Greeks idolized "brains." But God has never despised the humble things.

Either the cross is the "power of God" or it is "foolishness." If "foolishness" then you think it is unfit to do any good in your life. But listen! That condemns you, not the cross.

No man ever leaves the cross in exactly the same condition as he came to it. He must receive it or reject it. If he receives it, he becomes a son of God (John 1:12); if he rejects it, he is lost (John 3:36). If he neglects it, he is in effect rejecting it.

Paul did not preach Christ the conqueror, or Christ the philosopher, but Christ crucified, Christ the humble. Read his words in I Cor. 2:2. Paul remembers that his words will be tried by fire (I Cor. 3:13). To know Christ crucified is the maximum of knowledge.

THE MINISTER

One objection to Paul was that his preaching was too simple. He answered that he could not preach any differently because they were mere babes in Christ. They could not stand anything but a milk diet. The proof of their childish state (carnality) was in this division among them (I Cor. 3:1-4).

462

Paul points out that the Christian minister is not the head of a school or a rival sect, as the Greek philosophers. He is the servant of God, not a master of men. Paul always called himself a servant of the Lord Jesus Christ. Christian service is only acceptable to God when done in the spirit of Christ, for His glory.

Everyone is four men—one the world knows, one our friends know, one we know ourselves, one God knows. Paul describes this in I Cor. 4. There are three courts before which we stand:

Men .... I Cor. 4:3
Our own conscience.. I Cor. 4:3
Jesus Christ .... I Cor. 4:4

Do not depend on man's judgment. The world judges our character upon a single act. The voices of criticism may be loud, but if you go high up on the hilltop with God, you will see the bustle of the crowd but you won't hear it.

Beware of your friend's judgment because he may be too favorable in his opinion of you. We like to believe all the good things said about us and resent unfavorable criticism.

Paul says, *I judge not mine own self* (I Cor. 4:3). Beware when you stand at the bar of your own conscience. When your conscience says to you, "You may do it," it is always well to go to Jesus Christ and say, "May I?" It is hard to be fair with ourselves. No man, no matter how honest he is, is permitted to judge in his own cause.

Paul says there is one judgment to which he will submit—one that is always right. *He that judgeth me is the Lord* (I Cor. 4:4). I am Christ's steward and to Him am I ultimately responsible. From His judgment there is no escape. His calm eyes are upon me.

Seek praise from Him which is praise indeed. If He says, "Well done, good and faithful servant," what else matters!

VICE IN THE CHURCH

In Paul's letter to the Romans, we find his theme to be the righteousness of God. In Corinthians, he enlarges it into the life of righteousness in the Christian. We, as Christians, must act out in our lives what we believe in our hearts. It is a serious thing

463

to profess to live the life of a Christian. If we lower the standard Christ has set, we give the wrong testimony to the world. You are an epistle open and read of all men. What kind of a gospel is "The Gospel According to You"?

Do not let your life be so near the edge of questionable things that some day you will slide off. If you fall, others will fall with you. Watch your testimony.

Righteousness comes from God, but it must be shown in our daily walk. The Corinthians, living in the Hollywood of their day, needed admonition just as we do. Righteousness is from Christ, and for Christ. "What would Jesus do?" should be the query to every questionable thing of life. Christ in you is the secret and the way of life.

In the church at Corinth, a member actually married his own stepmother, which was socially immoral among the pagans, to say nothing of Christians. Paul reproves them for being puffed up with pride, while this scandal existed in the church. He urges them not to tolerate evil among them, while calling themselves Christians. Just as leaven spreads through all the dough, so a bad man's spirit spreads through all the church. The church should exclude the wrongdoer so as to prove that it does not condone sin (5:13). Discipline in the church should always commence with mourning and sympathy, not anger, or pride, or revenge (5:2).

Paul then makes a personal application, useful in our own lives. *Therefore let us keep the feast, . . . with the unleavened bread of sincerity and truth.* Self-examination is often the most difficult thing we do, but it is one of the most important.

Know ye is one of Paul's expressions. His faith was built on facts. He wanted to know things. Underline the "know ye's" in chapter 6. What are we supposed to know?

First, Paul makes the statement, that although it might be necessary at times for Christians to go to law, Christians never should quarrel with each other and then drag this quarrel before a worldly court. What a terrible impression of Christianity this gives to the world! We say when we do it, "We, as Christians, are just as bad as other folk. We want our way. We are covetous and just as ambitious for our own rights as you are." Paul says, "Dare you do such a thing?"

Paul then gives us a picture of the Corinthians as he found them, in 6:9. When we finish verse 11, we find what grace has done!

Christ has paid a great price to purchase us, and it is His purpose to make us like Himself (I Cor. 6:19,20).

If our bodies have been redeemed by the Lord Jesus Christ, then they no longer belong to us but to the One who purchased us with His precious blood. *Ye are bought with a price.*

God used to have a temple for His people; now He has a people for a temple. When a man steps into the church, off comes his hat, for he realizes he has stepped into the sanctuary. But has he forgotten that the real sanctuary in which Christ dwells is his body? We are taught as boys and girls not to be noisy or boisterous in the church, for it is the house in which we meet God. How much more important that we remember that our body is His dwelling place and that we should do nothing to grieve Him.

LIBERTY NOT RECKLESSNESS

The Scripture does not lay down little rules for our conduct and tell us just the things we ought to do or not do, but rather states principles which should guide the Christian's actions. Someone has well said that Christian liberty does not mean the right to do as we like, but rather to do as we should. Paul puts it, *All things are lawful unto me, but all things are not expedient: all things are lawful for me, but I will not be brought under the power of any* (I Cor. 6:12).

A man was walking down the street swinging his arms out from his chest and by mistake, struck a passer-by in the face. The man struck was furious and started to strike the man back. "Hey, isn't this a free country? Can't a fellow do his exercises on the street if he wishes?" "Yes," was the answer, "but remember where my nose begins, your liberty ends."

Let this be in your mind constantly as far as your conduct is concerned. If your liberty harms another, then your liberty has gone too far.

Yes, I can do anything I want to, but I must be sure my desires are to please Christ. What I do is an example to others, and may harm or bless them. I should not only answer the question, "Does my action harm weaker Christians?" but "Does it glorify God?"

MARRIAGE

Paul discusses the subject of marriage for the Christian. Controversy had arisen between the Jewish and Greek philosophers about the importance of marriage. Paul would keep the church from scandal, hence his words in 7:2. Society is pure and virtuous in proportion as marriage is deemed honorable. Some of the church tried to discourage marriage, and others thought that when one became a Christian he should divorce a heathen mate. But Paul was wise. He knew the evil condition in Corinth and advised every man to have his own wife and every woman to have her own husband. He did not believe in a Christian divorcing a pagan partner. He told them that it would be very likely that the Christian would lead his unbelieving mate to Christ (7:16).

Mark I Cor. 7:9,13 in your Bible. Think over these verses. They will tell us much of our Christian responsibility to those who are not Christians.

THE LORD'S SUPPER

Paul gives a careful account of the beginning of the Lord's Supper, and then tells of its value.

It was established on the night in which Christ was betrayed.

It is celebrated in remembrance of His undying love for His followers.

It was a symbol of His body which was broken for them (10:16).

It was a new covenant in His blood.

It was a pledge of His coming again (11:26).

We should be careful not to eat or drink in an unworthy manner. "Let a man prove himself," and never eat without self-judgment and thankful love.

466

"And as oft as ye do, in remembrance of Me." (See 11:25.)
Christ wants us to remember Him! Think on Christ when you
go to His table. He longs for your love!

It was the custom of the Corinthian church to eat a meal in
connection with the Lord's Supper. Each person brought his
own food. Often this led to excesses among the rich, while the
poor had nothing. What an unworthy observance of the Supper
itself this led to! Paul reminds them of the deep spiritual significance of this Supper, and of the scandal of such behavior as
theirs.

Paul closes this scene with these words: *The rest will I set in
order when I come* (11:34). There were other things to be
straightened out, but he would leave his corrections and go on
with his instructions.

INSTRUCTIONS IN CHRISTIAN CONDUCT
(Read I Corinthians 12–16)

In I Corinthians 12, we see the gifts that the Spirit gives to
believers. In verses 1-3, he tells of the change that had come
into the lives of these Corinthian Christians when they turned
from worshiping dead idols to the living Christ. In order that
they might develop in their Christian life, Christ gave them the
gifts of the Spirit (I Cor. 12:4-7). The Holy Spirit is the Giver
of spiritual gifts (I Cor. 12:8-11). One cannot teach the Scriptures unless the Spirit gives him wisdom. One must pray "in the
Spirit" and to sing acceptably to God "in the Spirit." Sometimes
we say when we look at a successful Christian, "My, he is a
man of natural abilities," when really he has received many gifts
from the Spirit.

Many people in Paul's day were making much of the spiritual
gifts which Paul mentions. They were coveting the more showy
gifts, such as speaking with tongues.

The Corinthian Christians were using these gifts as ends in
themselves. Many people today, like the Corinthians of old,
pray constantly for the power of the Spirit. They forget that all
the gifts which God gives were given that Christ might be exalted and others blessed. If God gives me any little gift at all,

He gives it not that I may gather people about myself, but that it may, through me, be a blessing for others. God gave these nine gifts mentioned in I Corinthians 12 to assist in the founding of the new church, but they were being used by people to gratify their pride. Paul shows that the purpose of the gifts is for the building of the church (I Cor. 12); that they should be used in love (I Cor. 13); and that their value was to be measured by their usefulness to the church.

God gave gifts like healing, miracles and tongues, we believe, for "sign" gifts (II Cor. 12:12), to prove to the world that Jesus was the true Messiah, and that the apostles were divinely appointed. These miracles, tongues, visions and signs were given to put the stamp of authority upon the apostles and their preaching. Today we are to believe and walk by faith. We are to covet the best gifts of wisdom, knowledge and faith. If it is God's will for us to have any of these gifts, He will give them to us; otherwise He will not. The Holy Spirit divides *to every man severally as he will* (I Cor. 12:11).

The way to use these gifts that the Spirit gives is beautifully told in I Corinthians 13. This chapter is called the Hymn of Love. Gifts without love are poor things. People talk of love but they do not live it. Until the love of Christ is in a heart it is impossible for men to love one another with any degree of permanency. Men seem to worship force. But history shows us that the victories of force do not last.

THE PILLARS OF THE GOSPEL

No doubt there was a group in the Corinthian church who did not believe in the resurrection of the dead. Paul in answering this starts out by giving a wonderful statement of what the Gospel is in I Cor. 15:1-11. Paul did not give a new Gospel. It was the old Gospel, given in Genesis, Exodus, Leviticus.

1. Christ died for our sins according to the Scriptures (15:3).
2. He was buried (15:4).
3. He rose again the third day according to the Scriptures (15:4).
4. He was seen by many witnesses (15:5,6).

If we deny the resurrection, we deny one of the greatest of all truths of the Gospel. Preaching is vain; faith and hope are all vain. But more than all that, no resurrection would mean no Gospel at all for we would be worshiping a dead Christ. There would be no "good news," for there would be no proof that God had accepted Christ's death as an atonement for our sins. If a sailor on jumping overboard to rescue a drowning man were drowned himself, then we would know that he did not save the man after whom he went. If Christ did not come out from the grave, then He could not bring anyone with Him from the grave. Christ's body died, and it was His body that was raised again. His soul was committed into the hands of the Father.

Because Christ lives, we shall live also. *O death, where is thy sting? O grave, where is thy victory?*

Paul gives the many proofs of Christ's resurrection in I Cor. 15.

1. Christ's resurrection.
2. His coming again.
3. Resurrection of believers.
4. Overthrow of Christ's enemies.
5. His glorious reign.
6. Our mortal bodies shall be changed to immortal.

Minimum Daily Requirements/Spiritual Vitamins

Sunday: DIVISIONS IN THE CHURCH
I Cor. 1:10-31
Monday: HUMAN WISDOM   I Cor. 2:1-16
Tuesday: WORLDLINESS IN THE CHURCH
I Cor. 3:1-23
Wednesday: IMMORALITY IN THE CHURCH
I Cor. 5:1-13
Thursday: THE LORD'S SUPPER   I Cor. 11:1-34
Friday: HYMN OF LOVE   I Cor. 13:1-13
Saturday: THE RESURRECTION   I Cor. 15:1-58

UNDERSTANDING II CORINTHIANS

II Corinthians Portrays Jesus Christ, Our Sufficiency

Paul was somewhat worried as to how the church at Corinth would receive his first letter. He wondered how they had accepted his rebukes, so he sent Titus, and perhaps Timothy, to Corinth to find out the effect of his epistle. During Paul's third missionary journey, while he was in Philippi, Titus reported that the majority of the church had received the letter in the proper spirit. But there were those who doubted his motives, and even denied his apostleship, saying that he did not have the proper credentials for an apostle. Perhaps they questioned this because he was not one of the original Twelve.

Under these circumstances he wrote his second epistle, to express his joy over the encouraging news of how his first epistle had been received, and to defend his apostleship.

Paul gives more of his personal history in this letter than in any of his other epistles. He reveals his courage and his self-sacrificing love. He speaks of glorying or boasting thirty-one times, because he was compelled to. Read II Cor. 12:11.

Paul tells us of some things which happened in his life, that are revealed only in this letter.

His escape from Damascus in a basket (11:32,33).

His experience of being caught up to third heaven (12:1-4).

His thorn in the flesh (12:7).

His unusual suffering (11:23-27).

He told none of these until he was compelled to, to prove that if he wanted to boast, he had good reason.

Jesus Christ, Our Comfort and Our Sufficiency

THE EPISTLE BEGINS WITH "COMFORT": *Blessed be God, even the Father of our Lord Jesus Christ, the Father of mercies, and the God of all comfort* (II Cor. 1:3).

471

It Closes with "Comfort": *Finally, brethren, farewell. Be perfect, be of good comfort, be of one mind, live in peace; and the God of love and peace shall be with you* (II Cor. 13:11).

In the Middle We Find the Reason for Comfort: *That ye, always having all sufficiency in all things, may abound to every good work* (II Cor. 9:8).

The Source of This Comfort Is: *My grace is sufficient for thee* . . . (II Cor. 12:9).

PAUL'S MINISTRY (Read II Corinthians 1–7)

Paul opens this second epistle with his usual greeting and thanksgiving (II Cor. 1:1-3). Everyone loves a true story. Paul tells so many personal experiences of his life in this letter that it makes everyone love to read it. He begins by telling of the great trouble through which he had been passing. Through all of his trials he had learned to know God better. God is always made more real to us in times of sorrow. We find that God never fails.

Paul's sufferings in Asia were of a very serious nature. Very likely he went through a dangerous sickness in which they despaired of his life (II Cor. 1:4-11). He appreciated their prayers and now he was appealing to their love and sympathy. He wanted them to be ready for much that he was to write about, concerning the defense of his apostleship.

Paul had a clear conscience as to his sincerity and faithfulness while he labored among them. He explained that he sent his first letter instead of coming himself, that when he did come he might be able to praise and not scold them. (II Cor. 1:23-2:4). To this statement he calls God to witness.

The Judaizing teachers (or law teachers) of Paul's day always carried letters of introduction with them. They were Paul's chief trouble-makers. They tried in every way to fight him. We hear them asking, "Who is this Paul? What letters of recommendation from Jerusalem does he have?" How foolish this question was to Paul! Did he need a letter of recommendation to a church which he himself had established? He answers, *Ye are our epistle written in our hearts, known and read of all men* (II Cor. 3:2).

The lives of true Christians at Corinth served as letters to recommend both Paul the servant and Christ the Lord. Men read men. Living epistles are read when Bible epistles are not. Remember your life is an open letter. Christian lives are about the only religious books the world reads. They do not study God's Word, but they do study church members. This gives us a great opportunity for good, for we may lead men to Christ.

Paul's Gospel was a triumphant and transforming Gospel (II Cor. 3:18).

Paul's ministry was a triumphant one, but it was filled with suffering. Warfare always is full of illustrations of triumph through suffering. Victory costs! Paul tells us much about his tribulations (chapters 4; 6; 11). When he was so gloriously converted, the Lord said, *I will show him how great things he must suffer for my name's sake* (Acts 9:16). It seems as though the trials began immediately, and followed his pathway for thirty years. But Paul was always optimistic because he knew that afflictions here would increase glory beyond (II Cor. 4:17,18).

"The pessimist sees a difficulty in every opportunity.

The optimist sees an opportunity in every difficulty."

Paul could sing as he suffered, for he knew the wonderful grace of God. He was always conscious of the presence of the Lord Jesus Christ. He knew that the greater the suffering in this present world, the greater the glory of eternity (II Cor. 4:8-18). Paul lived with his eye on the future!

Christ nowhere promises that a Christian will be free from suffering or sorrow. Rather do we hear that *in the world ye shall have tribulation* (John 16:33). Christ allows us to get into trouble that He may deliver us. He allowed Daniel to be put into the den of lions that He might pull him out. He allowed Shadrach, Meshach, and Abednego to go into the fiery furnace that He might deliver them. He allowed Paul to be shipwrecked that He might save him. Our God is able to deliver!

Paul finds his comfort through all his troubles in the fact of the resurrection. He lived under the inspiration of the fact that one day he was to have a changed, glorified body. Our suffering bodies will soon be exchanged for painless glorified bodies.

Whether we live or die, we must keep this reward in view (II Cor. 5:10).

The aim of Paul's ministry is that men may be reconciled to God (II Cor. 5:20). Men are God's greatest concern. As Christ's ambassador he makes his appeal to men of the world.

He follows this with an appeal to holy living (6:11–7:16). Holy living means wholly unto God. Read these verses, everyone! He appeals to his fellow-workers not to receive God's loving kindness in vain, but to open their hearts to Him. God demands a clean and separated life. He wants Christians to separate themselves from unbelievers.

LIBERAL GIVING (Read II Corinthians 8; 9)

Paul tells the church at Corinth of the generosity of the churches of Macedonia to the Palestine Famine Fund. Although poor themselves, they begged for an opportunity to give, and they gave liberally because first they gave themselves to the Lord. The fund was gathered from all the churches of Asia Minor and Greece. It had been started a year before (8:10). Paul was in Macedonia at the time he wrote this. He had accepted no pay for his work from any of the churches except Philippi. Christ was the example for these early Christians (II Cor. 8:9). The Lord knows that if He gets us He will get our gifts and our service.

How To Give

Give out of your poverty	(8:2)
Give generously	(8:3)
Give willingly	(9:7)
Give proportionately	(8:12,13,14)
Give cheerfully	(9:7)
Give bountifully	(9:6)

God has ever promised to reward the generous giver (9:6). He enriches us with spiritual graces as well as with material things. These gifts strengthened the ties of brotherhood between the Jewish and Gentile Christians. *Thanks be unto God for his unspeakable gift* (II Cor. 9:15).

This is the reason for our giving, *for God so loved the world, that he gave his only begotten Son.* God Himself delights to give.

474

PAUL'S APOSTLESHIP (Read II Corinthians 10-13)

The charge against Paul by some in the church was that he was a coward. He was bold in his writings, but was weak in personality. The New Testament gives us no suggestion as to what Paul looked like. To imagine that this man, who turned city after city upside down, was weak is absurd. He was a powerful and dominating person. He was a man of outstanding gifts and had a keen and inquiring mind. Beside this, Christ lived in him and worked through him.

His enemies said that no apostle would work with his own hands and support himself. They pointed to the other apostles but Paul explained that he had the right to receive pay, yet refused it lest his example be abused by these false teachers who would commercialize the ministry. He declared that at least he founded his own churches and did not go around troubling churches founded by others, as they were doing.

Paul stated also that if these false teachers could boast of their power and authority, then he would boast too. In a dramatic manner he challenged these critics to compare themselves with him, in every way. He was a loyal Hebrew; he had worked more than all the rest of them put together; as a martyr he had suffered more than they all, on land and sea. He realized the poor taste of boasting about oneself, and he disliked to do it, but they had forced him to it. When Paul boasted, it was for the glory of God.

They measuring themselves by themselves, and comparing themselves among themselves, are not wise (II Cor. 10:12). We all have a tendency to take a wrong standard for measuring character. We compare ourselves among ourselves. We conclude we are "as good as the average." But average Christians are not what the Bible requires. Let us pray Wesley's prayer, "Lord make me an extraordinary Christian."

Paul was caught up into "Paradise," even to the third heaven. You recall that Jesus went into Paradise at His death (Luke 23:43). There Paul had been given marvelous visions and revelations, and heard things that could not be put into speech (12:4). No doubt no human language could describe the glory.

475

It would have been like trying to picture a sunset to a man born blind. Paul had nothing to compare it with that we could understand.

It seemed as though because of these heavenly experiences God allowed Paul to suffer a physical weakness. The Lord knows the danger of pride of heart after such an experience, and so He permitted "a messenger of Satan to buffet him." He himself called his affliction *a thorn in the flesh* (12:7). There have been many speculations as to what this "thorn" really was. It would appear that God has not told us what it was, so that all might know that the grace which was sufficient for Paul in his trouble would be enough for any thorn given to man.

PURPOSE OF TESTING

Many wonder why God does not remove "thorns" from the flesh when we pray to Him. We must learn that God always answers prayer, but sometimes the answer is "No." He knows it will be better for us to bear the thorn than be without it. "Thorns" in the flesh have made many a man lean on Christ.

Dr. Moon, the brilliant young man whose blind eyes made him give to the world the system of reading that others with blind eyes might know the joy of acquiring knowledge, came to the realization that his "thorn" was a blessing. Sometimes a "thorn" is a warning to keep us from sin and failure. God proved to Paul that no matter what his weakness was, His strength was sufficient.

A minister one day buried his only child. He went into his study the next day to prepare his message for Sunday, but he could not. His grief was too great. Through his tears, which would insist upon coursing down his cheeks, his eyes fell on these words: "My grace is sufficient." It seemed to read this way: "My grace IS sufficient." He wrote it that way on a card and hung it in front of his desk. He learned to know a God who is always present. Every word is important.

MY—means God.

GRACE—unmerited favor. I bring Christ what I have, my sin. He brings me what He has—His righteousness. The exchange is made. He takes my sin and gives me His righteousness. This is grace, wonderful grace!

Is—the present, always.

SUFFICIENT—enough and to spare. *Our sufficiency is of God* (3:5). Here is where Charles Haddon Spurgeon laughed out loud. "To think," said he, "that our little cups could exhaust the ocean of His grace."

We are satisfied with Jesus. Is He your personal comfort? God gives us unusual strength for unusual tasks. Paul says, *When I am weak, then am I strong* (12:10). There is strength and courage in the heart in which Christ is dwelling.

THE DUTY OF SELF-TESTING

Examine yourselves, whether ye be in the faith; prove your own selves (II Cor. 13:5). In this second letter, Paul emphasizes that the Corinthians might know themselves—test themselves to make sure of their faith. He was anxious that none of them should be deceived. Use every means to know where you really stand spiritually.

Do not depend on a mere profession of religion. Do not rely on church membership. Joining the church saves no one. Joining Christ saves us. Examine your standing.

Do not trust a past experience. Live only for today. Trust only in a present love, a present faith, and a present service. This gives you the test of your spiritual life in Him.

Do not rest upon mere approved methods of conduct. One may go through the forms of religious worship and not be religious. Wax museum figures wink and blink and seem to breathe, but there is no particle of life in them. Some people go through the motions of religion. Examine yourself as to the motives that move your life. Is it to please God or man? What do you love? The Adversary always tells us we are "good enough," but Christ says we must be perfect. Here are some tests to use:

Do I love to think of Christ?

Do I love to pray?

Do I love to study God's Word?

Do I love Christian friends?

Do I love the church?

Do I love to serve Christ?

II Corinthians closes with the benediction which today brings to a close many a church service (II Cor. 13:14).

Minimum Daily Requirements/Spiritual Vitamins

Sunday: CHRIST OUR COMFORT   II Cor. 1:1–2:17

Monday: LIVING EPISTLES   II Cor. 3:1–4:18

Tuesday: AMBASSADORS FOR CHRIST
          II Cor. 5:1–6:18

Wednesday: THE HEART OF PAUL
          II Cor. 7:1–8:15

Thursday: CHRISTIAN GIVING   II Cor. 8:16–9:15

Friday: PAUL'S APOSTLESHIP   II Cor. 10:1–11:33

Saturday: GOD'S STRENGTH   II Cor. 12:1–13:14

UNDERSTANDING GALATIANS

*Galatians
Portrays Jesus Christ,
Our Liberty*

This epistle shows that the believer is no longer under the law but is saved by faith alone. *Stand fast therefore in the liberty wherewith Christ hath made us free* (Gal. 5:1). The "law" is that portion of God's Word found in the first five books of Moses (Genesis–Deuteronomy) by which every phase of Israel's life was to be guided.

During Paul's second missionary journey (Acts 16:6), he was delayed in Galatia by sickness (Gal. 4:13). Though ill, this tireless servant of the Lord could not remain silent, but kept on preaching the Gospel. The theme of his sermon was *Christ crucified* (Gal. 3:1). It was at this time that he succeeded in founding the Christian churches in Galatia (Gal. 1:6). They were scattered over a rural district and the people were country folk. Teachers of the law had followed Paul, teaching salvation by works, claiming that even if Christianity were true, Christians should be circumcised, and do all the works of the law. These teachers explained that the reason Paul had not taught the Galatians this was because he was not a true apostle and had learned his doctrines from others. This had upset the new converts.

Circumcision was the initial rite of the Jewish religion. If a person born a Gentile wished to become a Jew, he must observe this ceremonial law. It was much like a foreigner in our country taking out citizenship papers. If he actually takes out papers, although he was born on foreign soil, he is just as much a citizen as one born here.

False teachers had begun to "bewitch" the people by telling them they must keep all kinds of ceremonies. Paul wanted them to know that nothing, no fetishes, or works, or ceremonies, could bring them to Christ. Salvation comes by believing on Christ—nothing else.

Being very fickle and loving something new and a change, the Galatians were on the verge of accepting the views of these false teachers. When Paul heard it, so urgent did the matter seem that, since no one was with him to write it, he wrote the letter himself (Gal. 6:11).

It has been said that Judaism was the cradle of Christianity and very nearly its grave. God raised up Paul as the Moses of the Christian church to deliver them from this bondage. This epistle has done more than any other book in the New Testament to free our Christian faith from Judaism (law), and from the burden of salvation by works, taught by so many false cults, which has threatened the simple Gospel of the Lord Jesus Christ. So many people want to do something to be saved. The question of the Philippian jailer, *What must I do to be saved?* is the question multitudes ask. The answer is always the same. *Believe on the Lord Jesus Christ, and thou shalt be saved* (Acts 16:31).

A religion without the cross is not Christ's religion. Christ did not come merely to blaze a trail through a tangled forest, or to set us an example of true living. He came to be a Saviour.

The Power of the Cross

To deliver from sin.....................................Gal. 1:4; 2:21; 3:22
To deliver from the curse of the law........................Gal. 3:13
To deliver from the self-life..............................Gal. 2:20; 5:24
To deliver from the world..................................Gal. 6:14
In the new birth...Gal. 4:4-7
In receiving the Holy Spirit...............................Gal. 3:14
In bringing forth the Spirit's fruit.......................Gal. 5:22-25

This epistle of Galatians is the Christian's Declaration of Independence. Our battle hymn is "Christus Liberator." *If the Son therefore shall make you free, ye shall be free indeed* (John 8:36). Folks imagine that restrictions destroy liberty. The opposite is true. On entering a free public park, the first thing we see is, "Don't walk on the grass," "No dogs allowed," "Don't pick the flowers." And yet this is a free park! We do not complain. These laws preserve the park. Were they not enacted it would be no more a park than any vacant lot in the neighborhood. Thus it is with society at large. If we revolt against God and His order, civilization would lapse into barbarism. This is what is happening in the world today. Liberty is not freedom from law—that is recklessness. Liberty is freedom in law. Paul speaks of the liberty we have "in Christ" (Gal. 2:4), for *where the Spirit of the Lord is, there is liberty* (II Cor. 3:17). This is the one great secret of liberty.

This is the liberty that is told of in this book, so get hold of Galatians and let Galatians get hold of you. In Galatians, we are not servants working for a living, but sons working in our living. Learn what it is to be free in Christ! Christ said, *I call you not servants, but friends* (John 15:15).

This Book Contrasts Law and Grace

In Romans we find our STANDING.

In Galatians we take OUR STAND.

Paul Tells Us:

In Romans to use our HEADS to grasp the great facts of Christianity.

In I Corinthians to put out the HAND to grasp our privileges in Christ.

In II Corinthians to lift our HEARTS to receive the comforts that are ours.

In Galatians to stand on our FEET in the liberty that Christ gives.

INTRODUCTION (Read Galatians 1:1-11)

This is the only time in all of Paul's writings in which he does not express his thankfulness. Rather he says, "I marvel." This is the only church of whom he does not ask prayers. How could he, seeing they were bringing dishonor upon the Lord? (Read Gal. 1:1-5.)

Paul marvels that these new Christians could give up the Gospel of liberty so quickly and accept a Jewish message that was no gospel at all. Twice he pronounced a curse upon those causing the trouble. He says if an angel from heaven were to preach any other Gospel than the one he preached *let him be accursed* (Gal. 1:8,9).

481

What was this Gospel Paul preached? Paul's Gospel shuts out all works. *Knowing that a man is not justified by the works of the law, but by the faith of Jesus Christ, . . . for by the works of the law shall no flesh be justified* (Gal. 2:16). The difficulty about salvation is not that we should be good enough to be saved but that we should see that we are bad enough to need salvation. Christ can only save sinners. Grace cannot begin until the law has proven that we are guilty, as the Book of Romans showed each of us to be. Then Christ offers us His righteousness.

A Gospel of mixed law and grace has no power. The false teachers of this kind of gospel are "accursed" because they pervert (not deny) the Gospel. They admitted that Christ must die upon the cross, but denied that faith alone in His sacrifice was sufficient for salvation. They taught that to be saved one must keep some part of the law at least. They thought that simple faith according to the Gospel which Paul preached was not sufficient for salvation. People like this kind of preaching because they feel they can do something to obtain merit before God.

Paul shows us the seriousness of our condition outside Christ. When a medical specialist says, "Your only hope is this or that," you know what a critical and serious condition you must be in. Here are the words of a great Gospel expert. Paul declares that our position is so serious that the Gospel of the grace of God is our only hope. There is no other.

Paul introduced the atonement (1:4), a truth once so dear to them, but now practically rejected. Christ *gave himself for our sins*.

PAUL DEFENDS HIS APOSTLESHIP
(Read Galatians 1:12–2:21)

Paul's teaching was authorized by God Himself (1:11-24). He proves that he received his Gospel directly from the Lord. Only God could have changed him from a murderer to a preacher.

There are many things we can learn by experience but that is not so with the things of God. To know them they must be revealed to us. *For I neither received it of man, neither was I taught it, but by the revelation of Jesus Christ* (Gal. 1:12).

Paul did not consult with any one as to what he should preach but retired to the wilds of Arabia for three years and there listened to God. He was taught by the Spirit. He had only been with Peter and James fifteen days after the three years in Arabia so he couldn't have learned much from them.

The authority behind Paul's Gospel is shown by his rebuke of Peter (2:11-21). To prove that Peter was not a greater apostle than he, he points out in Galatians 2:11-21 how he had openly rebuked Peter for being two-faced about Jewish customs when he was in Antioch. He made no secret attempt to undermine Peter's authority. Paul was not dominated by this strong apostle to the Jews. Verse 11 is an unanswerable argument against the supremacy of Peter. *I certify you, brethren, that the gospel which was preached of me is not after man* (Gal. 1:11). It is good to know that the friendship between Peter and Paul was so real that it stood this severe test. (See II Peter 3:15.)

What does justified mean? God credits to my account what Christ has done—just-as-if-I'd done it. A criminal is pardoned though he cannot be regarded as righteous. But justification is that act of God whereby He not only forgives us but puts Christ's righteousness to our account. God justifies the sinner without justifying his sin. He gives us a righteousness not our own but Christ's.

How are we justified? *Not by works* (Gal. 2:16,17). Works are excluded! We are not justified by the works of the law but by the faith of Jesus Christ.

There are no degrees of justification. The moment we believe on Christ we are made just.

Justification Is

By God	Romans 3:26; 8:33
By Grace	Romans 3:24
By Blood	Romans 3:25; 5:9
By Faith	Romans 3:21-28

Paul ended his great apology by a personal word of testimony which gives us a complete picture of the Christian life both positively and negatively. *I am crucified with Christ: nevertheless I live; yet not I, but Christ liveth in me: and the life which I now live in the flesh I live by the faith of the Son of God, who loved me, and gave himself for me* (Gal. 2:20). It is a paradox.

This verse is true of every believer. We do not need to be crucified with Christ. We have been crucified with Him. He died in my place. Now we live not by law but by faith. Christ was our sacrifice for sin and now is our sufficiency for the new life. The Christian life is a dying life—dying daily to self and sin. It is the crucified Saviour who lives in those who have shared His crucifixion.

PAUL DEFENDS THE GOSPEL (Read Galatians 3:1–4:31)

"I've tried religion for the past five years and it hasn't worked. I gave it up," were the words of a young man when a preacher asked him to accept Christ. "Why I tried religion for fifteen years and it did nothing for me. I gave it up, too," the preacher said. A pause followed. "Then why are you a minister?" the youth asked. "Then I tried Christ, and He fully met my needs. It is not religion I am recommending to you but a living, loving Saviour."

Religion, a word once so commonly used among Christians, is fast becoming out of vogue because it has been twisted and misapplied. A religious person now means one who has accepted a creed or observes certain ceremonies, or attends certain places of public worship. But all this is not sufficient. There must be a living faith in a living Saviour. It is possible to have a religion without the Gospel. This was the peril that faced the Galatian Christians. So many people count on their sincerity in believing some creed they have worked out to save themselves. They say, "The golden rule is my religion." But there is no salvation in that for *without shedding of blood is no remission* of sin (Heb. 9:22).

People who do not believe in foreign missions say that the heathen have their own religion and why disturb them? Yes, they have so much religion that they are bowed down under the weight of the load, but no "good news" of the Gospel. It is the Gospel we are commanded to preach to every creature.

Religion is the best man can do. Christianity is the best God can do. See the results of man's best. *For by the works of the law shall no flesh be justified* (Gal. 2:16). How can a man be made just? *By the faith of Jesus Christ* (2:16). Christianity is God's best. Christ is no sheriff. He is *the Lamb of God, which taketh away the sin of the world* (John 1:29). We are pronounced righteous not by works of the law but by faith in Him.

Paul is defending the Gospel of Christ. He describes his own preaching as having so fully set forth the cross that it was as if they had seen Christ crucified in their midst (3:1). He shows what the law could not do but what grace had done.

Paul puts a challenging question to these "foolish Galatians." He cries, "O foolish Galatians, I have brought you the true Gospel, and you received it with eagerness and gratitude. Now suddenly you drop the Gospel. What has got into you?

"Come on now, my smart Galatians, you who all of a sudden have become professors, while I seem to be your pupil, did you receive the Holy Spirit by the works of the law, or by the preaching of the Gospel?" Paul asked. This question was a challenge to them because their own experience proved the truth of Paul's preaching to them.

"You cannot say you received the Holy Spirit because you kept the law. Nobody ever heard of such a thing. But as soon as the Gospel came, you received the Holy Spirit by the simple hearing of faith," Paul adds.

It is hard for us to believe that the priceless gift of forgiveness of sins and the gift of the Holy Spirit are not gained by real effort, but God offers them to us free of charge. Why not take them? Why worry about our own unworthiness? Why not accept them with thankfulness?

Immediately foolish reason says, "If people don't have to do a thing for their salvation or for an atonement for their wrongdoings then they will become shiftless and will not even try to do good." But we have found that when we have accepted the Gospel with a thankful heart that then we get busy on good works. We want to please God. Those who think we ought to be saved by our works think faith is an easy thing but we know from personal experience how hard it is to simply believe.

Luther tells us that a Christian is not sinless, but God no longer chalks sin against him because of his faith in Christ.

Even as Abraham believed God, and it was accounted to him for righteousness (Gal. 3:6). Abraham may have had a good standing with men for his upright life, but not with God. In God's sight, Abraham was a condemned sinner. You see righteousness had been given to Abraham on the ground of his faith, not his works. If faith without works was sufficient for Abraham, why should we turn from faith to law? "Abraham believed." That is faith. Faith says to God, "I believe what you say."

It must have startled the proud and troublesome Jews when Paul told them that not those born of Abraham's flesh and blood but those who believe in Christ Jesus are the true sons of Abraham (Gal. 3:26-29). Though born in obscurity, through the new birth, all can sit down with Abraham as a son of the father of the faithful (Gal. 3:14,29). Abraham believed God and it was accounted to him for righteousness. (See Gal. 3:6,7.)

THE CURSE OF THE LAW

The curse of God is like a flood that swallows everything that is not of faith. Remember, the law Paul is talking about is not civil law. Civil law has its place, but civil righteousness will never deliver a person from the condemnation of God's Law. Just because I am a law abiding citizen does not mean that I am a Christian. Governmental laws are blessings for this life only but not for the life hereafter. Otherwise many infidels would be nearer heaven than some Christians, for infidels often excel in civil righteousness. A guilty man would never come before a court and plead innocent because he is a good church member, a fine giver, a member of a Sunday school class. Neither can a sinner come before the court of heaven and plead that because he is in public office, or a good citizen, or a moral man, that God should accept him. The civil courts require that you keep the law. The court of heaven requires that you have faith in Jesus Christ.

The law cannot give righteousness but it does bring death

upon all those who do not keep it (3:10). Law demands perfect obedience. Many think that they should get something for keeping the law. Really they should get nothing. Men ought to keep the law and get nothing for doing so. You live in a city all your life and during your lifetime you keep the laws of that city. Will the city council present you with a gift because you have not broken the laws? Of course not. You ought to keep the law. But suppose after twenty years of law-keeping you then commit a crime. The authorities will then give you something—a jail sentence for breaking the law. The Bible tells us that a curse (a sentence) is upon all who break the law, while a blessing is upon all those who live by faith.

Christ hath redeemed us from the curse of the law, being made a curse for us (Gal. 3:13). As all had broken the law, all had come under its curse. But Christ has redeemed us. Don't turn back to the law from which Christ redeemed us. O foolish Galatians, who hath bewitched you, that ye should turn from the blessing of faith to the curse of law?

The law deals with what we are and do, while grace deals with what Christ is and does. What good is the law? We find the answer in Gal. 3:19,20. Everything has its purpose. Let us see the purpose of the law. The law is given to restrain the wicked by giving punishment for crime, just as civil laws keep men from murder and theft because of the fear of jail or the electric chair. These restraints do not make men righteous but they do restrain them from crime.

Another purpose of the law is spiritual. The law reveals to a person his sin, and blindness and contempt of God. As long as a person is not a murderer, or thief, he would swear that he is righteous. How does God show such a man what he really is? By the hammer of the law. As long as a person thinks he is right, he is proud and despises God's grace. This monster of self-righteousness needs a big axe, and the law is just that. When anyone sees by the law that he is under God's wrath, he begins to rebel and complain against God. The law inspires hatred of God. What does this beating by the hand of the law accomplish? It helps us to find the way of grace. When the conscience has been thoroughly frightened by the law, it welcomes the Gospel.

487

Law reveals sin but does not remove it. The law proves that every man is a sinner by nature and directs him to Christ! We so often think that we become sinners when we commit some sinful acts. But it is because we are already sinners that we commit the act. A man lies because he is a liar. He steals because he is a thief. He does not become a liar when he utters the lie. It only proves he is a liar.

The law, too, was given to drive us to Christ by showing us our need. The Gospel tells us that Christ is the only One who can meet that need (Gal. 3:23–4:11). Paul says that the law was our schoolmaster to shock us into a sense of our need of Christ that we might be justified by faith in Him (3:24). God's law is not like the cruel schoolmaster of former times, a regular tyrant. His law is not to torment us always. God's law is like the good schoolmaster who trains his children to find pleasure in doing the things they formerly detested.

The law really has a place in leading us into a Christian experience. Did you ever see anyone trying to sew without a needle? That person would make poor speed if she sewed with only a thread. This is like God's dealing with us. He puts the needle of the law first, for we sleep so soundly in our own sins that we need to be aroused by something sharp. Then when He has the needle of the law fairly in our hearts, He draws a lifelong thread of Gospel love and peace and joy.

SONS OF GOD

Paul tells us that all are not the children of God. We find that it is faith in Christ, not works of the law, nor the Fatherhood of God, nor the brotherhood of man that makes us children of God. *For ye are all the children of God by faith in Christ Jesus* (Gal. 3:26). It is faith not works that puts us into the family of God.

As long as an heir is underage there is no difference between him and a slave, for he is under the control of his guardian. So Paul shows us in Galatians 4:5,6 that all believers are children of God, yet all children are not "sons"—grown-up ones. "Adoption" is a Roman legal word and means "the placing of a son" in a son's legal position. It might be receiving into a family one who does not belong to it by birth, or the legal act of acknowledging his "coming of age." Christ came to ransom us, so we would be no longer slaves, under the law, but possess all the privileges of full-grown sons and heirs.

As another illustration of their state as free men in Christ, Paul reminds them that Abraham had two sons—one Ishmael, the child of Hagar the bondwoman, and the other Isaac, the child of Sarai, the free woman. Ishmael did not enjoy the blessings of a son in Abraham's house but was left out in the cold although he was the first born, and Isaac was called. This is what happens to those who seek to be saved by keeping the law. But Isaac, the child of promise and faith, was the heir of all things. So we are heirs of a spiritual promise.

PAUL DESIRES THE GOSPEL BE APPLIED
(Read Galatians 5; 6)

The first application of the Gospel pertains to one's own personal freedom from the law. Paul wants the Galatians to hold fast to their personal liberty. It is the Gospel of God's grace which gives true liberty (5;1-12). *Stand fast therefore in the liberty wherewith Christ hath made us free* (Gal. 5:1). If the Galatians seek to be saved by keeping the law, they are bound by the law. Their liberty should be prized because it cost so much, the blood of Christ.

"Stand fast." This is one of Paul's favorite expressions. Maintain your position of erectness!

1. In the faith .... I Cor. 16:13
2. In the liberty .... Gal. 5:1
3. In the Spirit .... Phil. 1:27
4. In the Lord .... Phil. 4:1

The Gospel of Grace guards against recklessness (5:13-15). Many people are afraid to live under grace instead of law for fear it will lead men to "live as they please and do as they like." Grace will always lead a man to live as God pleases and like what He likes.

We Abuse Our Liberty

By Lack of Love—Galatians 5:13-15. *Love one another* for all the law is fulfilled in one word, *thou shalt love thy neighbor as thyself*. Use love!

By Unclean Living—Galatians 5:16-26. See how the flesh "acts up." Read this list of her seventeen evil works, 5:19-21. These are sins of the mind as well as the body. This is what we are by nature and these are the things that we do. Christ has given the Holy Spirit to make us free from these. *Walk in the Spirit, and ye shall not fulfil the lust of the flesh*. Let the Holy Spirit rule your life.

A child begins to walk by someone holding on to his hand. We begin our walk by the Spirit holding on to us. But He is not only a help outside as in the case of the child but He helps within. Think of walking arm in arm with the Holy Spirit! This means no running ahead or lagging behind (5:16).

Nine Graces

Toward God	Toward Others
Love	Longsuffering
Joy	Gentleness
Peace	Goodness

Toward Myself

Faith

Meekness

Temperance

In contrast to the work of the flesh we see the ninefold fruit of the Spirit (5:22-23). If we abide in Christ (John 15), we shall be free to bear fruit with God. Are we showing this cluster of fruit in our lives?

SOWING AND REAPING (Galatians 6:7-9)

Whatsoever a man soweth, that shall he also reap (6:7).

If we sow to the Spirit, we shall reap a spiritual harvest. If we sow to the flesh (the lower appetites), we will reap moral weakness (6:7-8).

The harvest will not be according to how much we know, but how much we sow. We may have a large supply of seed in the

490

barn of the mind but unless it is planted in suitable soil it will bear no harvest. Sow the seed of thoughts in word and deeds. God's Word always brings forth seed after its kind.

Sow the seeds of your life in the soil of the Spirit, not the soil of the flesh. In the Spirit it will honor God but in the flesh the seed will rot and bring forth corruption. The Spirit brings forth only good fruit, the flesh only evil.

So many deceive themselves by saying, "It doesn't matter what I sow if I am sincere." Would that be good advice for a farmer? Self-life will never produce the fruit of the Spirit. Sowing and reaping are agricultural terms. The Christian worker is not likened to a salesman or mechanic, but to a farmer. Christian work is not buying and selling, but sowing and reaping. When dealing with souls we are not mechanics. We are not just to fix over "run-down" lives, but we are to plant the living Word.

Paul bore in his body the "slave marks of Jesus." These were marks of:

Ownership—I belong to another. The Greek word "stigmata" means a brand, a mark, sometimes burnt into the face, body or arm of a slave, or criminal.

What were Paul's stigmata? They were scars he had received by persecution and hardship endured for Christ (II Cor. 6:4; 11:23).

The rough hands of a laborer tell he is the slave of hard toil; the weatherbeaten face of a sea captain, the wounds of a soldier, the lines in a mother's brow are all honorable. The slave marks of Christ speak first of a changed character and second of a labor of love for Him.

Devotion—What scars had the false teachers received for Christ? None. They have saved themselves. But behold me!

Commission—The false teachers had come armed with letters of authority. I am without letters of recommendation. But behold my scars! They constitute my commission.

In Christ we are free to know the boundless life that is in Him. In Him we are "new creatures" (Gal. 6:15). We are a new creation; we have a new life in Christ. No wonder Paul cries out, *God forbid that I should glory, save in the cross of*

*our Lord Jesus Christ, by whom the world is crucified unto me,
and I unto the world* (Gal. 6:14). "Let the world go by! I have
Christ, and having Him, I have all things," Paul is saying. Oh,
the joy of a free, full life in Christ Jesus.

CONTRASTS IN THE BOOK OF GALATIANS

Grace and Law

The one thing that distinguishes our Christian faith from all
others is the grace of God. Grace is unmerited favor of God to
us when we are undeserving.

Law shows us our need.

Grace shows God's provision to meet that need.

Law says we must work for our salvation—"Do."

Grace says salvation is free, a gift—"Done."

Faith and Works

Faith makes us receive salvation by believing.

Works keep us striving to earn it.

Fruit of the Spirit and Works of the Flesh

The Spirit gives us daily victory over sin.

The flesh makes us prone to sin.

Cross and the World

The cross means love and sacrifice.

The world suggests force and selfishness.

Minimum Daily Requirements/Spiritual Vitamins

Sunday: ONLY ONE GOSPEL   Galatians 1:1-24

Monday: JUSTIFIED BY FAITH   Galatians 2:1-21

Tuesday: THE LAW POINTS TO CHRIST
Galatians 3:1-29

Wednesday: LAW AND GRACE   Galatians 4:1-31

Thursday: STAND FAST IN CHRISTIAN LIBERTY
Galatians 5:1-16

Friday: FLESH VERSUS SPIRIT
Galatians 5:17-26

Saturday: SOWING AND REAPING   Galatians 6:1-18

UNDERSTANDING EPHESIANS

Ephesians
Portrays Jesus Christ,
Our All in All

In this epistle we enter the Holy of Holies in Paul's writings. Paul speaks in II Cor. 12:2 of being "caught up to the third heaven." Well, here, as it were, he gives his report. He seems to be carried away as he tells of it. It is the greatest revelation of truth that God has given to man. It is the mystery that has been hidden from before the foundation of the world.

This book shows us the great mystery of the Church. The real Church is the Body of Christ, and believers are members of that sacred Body of which Christ is the head. The Father not only prepared a body for Jesus Christ to suffer in, but He prepared a Body for Him in which He should be glorified. The Greek word for church is "ecclesia," which means an assembly of called-out ones. Christ is taking out a people for His name (Acts 15:14). The Church is an organism. It is the Body of Christ. Every believer is a member of Christ's Body, and He is the head of the Church.

Imagine for a moment that the Body is like a great building. The "stones" are redeemed human beings. Christ occupies the great throne room, or "Head." All the parts are like "rooms" in the building. With this picture in mind, it is easy to see the whole story of the mystery of the Church. The suffering of Christ in an earthly body is now to be made up for by erecting a spiritual body, or "building." Come with Paul through this glorious structure.

Outline of the Book of Ephesians

Paul seems to present a picture of "Christ's Temple of Ephesus" which the Christian may enter. It is *an holy temple in the Lord* (2:21). We approach in these chapters, one after another, six magnificent rooms in this great temple. They are all "in Christ." Let the scenes of this book be laid in each of these rooms successively.

THE ANTEROOM (Read Ephesians 1)

Let us enter this sacred Temple with hushed voices and bared heads. Christ is going to allow us to go into His holy presence. The door opens into the spacious Anteroom, where we read upon the walls our standing with God through Jesus Christ. *Blessed . . . with all spiritual blessings. Chosen . . . in him before the foundation of the world. Holy and without blame before him in love. Accepted in the beloved.* These are some great wall mottoes for Christians. It will tax every spiritual energy to live up to them.

The blessings of the Christian are not only "heavenly" but "in the heavenlies." Go through this first chapter and mark all you find "in Christ."

Our Blessings "In Christ"

We are in Christ Jesus.....................................(1:1)
Blessed in Christ..(1:3)
Chosen in Him..(1:4)
Adopted by Christ ....(1:5)
Accepted in the beloved...................................(1:6)
Redeemed and forgiven in Christ.........................(1:7)
Revealed His will in Himself..............................(1:9)
Everything centered in Christ.............................(1:10)
Inheritance in Christ ....(1:11)
Glorified in Christ ....(1:12,13)
Faith in Christ ....(1:15)
Wisdom in Him ....(1:17)

494

Was this always our position? (2:11-13).

We learn on entering this Temple that our calling and position have been planned and worked out by God the Father, the Son, and the Holy Spirit before the foundation of the world (1:4). Every Christian should know his calling above everything else (1:18). The true knowledge of it will govern his life.

Our Salvation

The Father planned it......................................1:4-6

The Son paid for it..1:7-12

The Spirit applied it..1:13,14

In whom we have redemption through his blood, the forgiveness of sins, according to the riches of his grace (Eph. 1:7).

Redemption is the most glorious work of God. It is greater far than His work of creation. He spoke a word and worlds were formed, but it cost Him the life of His beloved Son to redeem the world. Paul delighted to dwell on this theme. The reason was that he had experienced Christ's redeeming love. He had been redeemed from sin, from the curse and bondage of the law. He had been washed clean in the blood of Christ, and anointed by the Holy Spirit. Well might he glory in his Redeemer.

To redeem means to buy back, to pay the ransom price. This is what Christ did for us when we were captive under sin. Let us consider:

The Necessity for Our Redemption

The sinner is a captive:

1. To sin.

Jesus answered them, Verily, verily, I say unto you, Whosoever committeth sin is the servant of sin (John 8:34). We feel that bondage. We know sin rules our lives.

2. To Satan.

Paul speaks of sinners, recovering *themselves out of the snare of the devil* (II Tim. 2:26).

3. Under law.

We have broken the law and for this reason God *hath concluded all under sin* (Gal. 3:22). The literal meaning is "shut up in prison." We have been put under arrest for violating the law.

The captive is in a miserable state and needs to be redeemed.

The Provision for Our Redemption

Christ is our Redeemer! *In whom we have redemption.*

The Means of Our Redemption

In whom we have redemption through His blood. We are "not redeemed with corruptible things, as silver and gold . . . but with the precious blood of Christ." (See I Peter 1:18,19.) Christ voluntarily took our place. He stood charged with our sins and paid the penalty with His blood.

The Fruits of Redemption

Even *the forgiveness of sins* is the result of redeeming love and this is *according to the riches of his grace.* Grace is unmerited favor. His forgiveness is according to His abounding favor, without limiting it by our demerit.

He casts our sins behind His back. He blots them out of His book of remembrance. He sinks them into the depths of the sea. He removes them as far as the east is from the west. Yes, He forgives *according to the riches of his grace.*

We hear a great prayer in this Anteroom. Think of hearing Paul pray (1:15-23)! Paul wants every one of us who are believers to realize fully his privileges in Christ. He wants the eyes of our understanding to be enlightened that we might behold the glory of Christ. There is no use of showing a gorgeous sunset to a blind man. So we cannot understand the greatness of God until the Great Physician has healed our spiritual eyes.

There are three "what's" in this prayer which each believer should know. Do you know the answers?

What is the hope of His calling?

What are the riches of the glory of His inheritance in the saints? Think of Christ's inheritance in us. He has suns and stars, but He wants sons and saints.

What is the exceeding greatness of His power? What the Church needs today is power. She is shorn of her real strength.

THE AUDIENCE CHAMBER OF THE KING
(Read Ephesians 2)

Next we are conducted into the glorious Audience Chamber of the King, into the Divine Presence. We *have access by one Spirit unto the Father* (2:18). We would tremble as we entered if we did not hear the gracious words sound out, *You hath he quickened, who were dead in trespasses and sins: ... hath raised us up together, and made us sit together in heavenly places in Christ Jesus* (2:1,6). But best of all, there is a sweet Voice sounding through the corridors, Welcome here! *Now therefore ye are no more strangers and foreigners, but fellow citizens with the saints, and of the household of God* (2:19). All of this is in sharpest contrast to what we were "in time past" (2:11-13). We once were "far off." Now we are "nigh."

In this Audience Chamber, we find that God has made both Jew and Gentile "one" in Christ. We can better understand this by an illustration from our day. Dr. Keller, formerly of Hunan Bible Institute in China, tells of a barber who was marvelously converted. He had been an opium addict and a moral degenerate. In desperation he had come to the missionaries, and prayer was answered for him. His appetite for opium left and he became a living witness for Christ.

During the barber's stay in the mission, a young man of "the student class" came as an inquirer but, seeing the barber, he refused to go in. (A barber's occupation was held in contempt in China.) One day, thinking the barber had gone, he entered the mission and met the barber. Being too polite not to speak to him, he engaged in conversation. The barber told of the wonderful change that had come into his life through Christ.

Class barriers melted away. The barber soon was a guest in the student's home, surrounded with wealth and culture. Christ had "made both one." This is what Christ will do with both Jew and Gentile, slave and free man. Christ makes each one a new man and gives him access and approach into the very Audience Chamber of the King.

This New Man has access to God through the blood of His Son (2:13). He is our Mediator, and He says, *No man cometh unto the Father, but by me* (John 14:6). Then when we have been redeemed, the Holy Spirit introduces the New Man at the Court of Heaven. He does not ask Peter for the privilege, nor does He consult the saints, nor does He invoke the "Mother of Jesus." There is only one Mediator and that is the Lord Jesus Christ. The Father rejoices in the New Man and welcomes us into His very presence.

THE MASTERPIECE PLANNED

God is producing a Masterpiece, His Church. Paul says, *For we are his workmanship* (2:10). This comes from the Greek word "poiema"—poem or masterpiece.

In Ephesians 1, we find how God planned and worked in the production of this Masterpiece. We were "chosen in Christ" to be holy and blameless (1:4). In the ages of past eternity God was thinking about us, loving us, and planning to bless us. Know this, before Satan ever appeared to spoil the happiness of man upon this earth, God made plans to make all who would believe on Him to be blameless.

Then in Ephesians 2:1-10 we find how it was produced. Look at the material He used. Read these verses. How does God take us up and produce a Masterpiece out of such material? We see:

What the nature of man is 2:1-3

What the walk of a natural man is 2:2

"But God"—see God act! He changes all by His touch! This "But God" is the bridge which leads men out of their dark and hopeless condition (2:4). When all human strength is at an end—"But God." Remember Christ comes to give life to the dead.

498

A quaint old legend tells of a piece of marble crying from a pile of material which had been left as rubbish after a great building had been erected. It was saying, "Glory, glory!" A passer-by hearing the cry, stopped. He learned from the marble half-covered with dust and rubbish that Michelangelo had just passed by and said, "I see an angel in that stone." Now he had gone to get his mallet and chisel.

Humanity was like that stone in the heap, broken and useless, but the great Sculptor saw it and began His Masterpiece. As Michelangelo saw the angel in the old stone, so God sees the image of His Son in wretched humanity. The grace of God carved a Mueller out of the family black sheep, a John B. Gough out of a barroom wreck.

The greatest proof of Christianity is that it has produced a New Man who is approved unto God. Only God could make a Paul out of Saul.

DESTINY OF THE MASTERPIECE

What a destiny it is (2:7)! What is a little suffering with a few trials here in comparison to the glory in the "ages to come"! He will show the "exceeding riches of His grace." He will tell the universe what He has accomplished.

Salvation is the gift of God. *For by grace are ye saved through faith: and that not of yourselves: it is the gift of God* (2:8). Faith is a gift, too. *Faith cometh by hearing* (Rom. 10:17). Faith is the channel of salvation. It is the hand that receives the gift. It connects man with God.

THE THRONE ROOM (Read Ephesians 3)

Standing at the doors of the Throne Room are the stalwart guards of Law. They demand: "Who goes there? Why do you come? What are your credentials?" I answer feebly, "A sinner; I come to see the Lamb. I have nothing to recommend me for admittance." Then I hear the Voice of the Lamb from within, the call of the Son of Grace. "It is one of my sheep. Invite him in. My blood covers all. He needs no credentials." And Grace brings me past the stern guards of Law unto the throne of His mercy.

We have boldness and access with confidence by the faith of him (3:12). What a piling up of words to persuade us of our privilege and position as Christian believers! We are *accepted in the Beloved* (1:6).

Here we behold the King! With Paul, we bow our knee *unto the Father of our Lord Jesus Christ, of whom the whole family in heaven and earth is named* (3:14,15). Is posture a small thing? Kneeling is the attitude of humility, confession and entreaty. Remember the holiest of all men have approached God this way. David, Solomon, and Daniel knelt upon their knees. These men stooped to conquer, knelt to prevail.

Paul tells how God had held back from the Gentiles the secret that they should be heirs and shareholders of the gospel and have admission into the Church (His Body) on the same terms as the Jews (3:8-10). To *gather together in one all things in Christ* was God's plan (1:10).

The word "mystery" which occurs three times here does not mean something mysterious. It merely means it is hidden until the appropriate time comes for God to reveal it.

The mystery of the Church is that the Gentiles are to have an equal position with the Jews, God's chosen people (Ephesians 3:6). All this was "by faith" (Rom. 15:9,10; Gal. 3:8,9). This is a radical thing that God would make the Gentiles with the Jews "co-heirs" of Christ and "co-members" of His Church.

Paul prays again and his prayer is recorded in Ephesians 3:13-21. The first prayer recorded in chapter one gave us three "what's." This prayer gives us four "that's," and is steeped in the love of Christ.

That they should be strengthened by His Spirit.

That they might have Christ dwelling in their hearts.

That they might understand what is the breadth, length, depth, and height of the love of Christ.

That they might be filled with the fulness of God.

Paul enjoys the "riches" of the gospel. It is so bountiful in its gifts and so inexhaustible in its resources.

If we are to enjoy this life in the Temple of God, we must be yielded in obedience to Him. If we yield to His plan for our lives as willing subjects, we will find that in His hand our lives will be filled with joy and beauty.

THE JEWEL ROOM (Read Ephesians 4)

Here amid the flash of the Jewel Room, we will get our epaulets and our garments of holiness—*all lowliness and meekness, with longsuffering.* Here are our banners and escutcheons —*one Lord, one faith, one baptism.* Here are the brilliant gems of the graces as we will take them—*But unto every one of us is given grace according to the measure of the gift of Christ* (4:7). We must "put off," or lay aside, the old life as we would lay aside a garment, and "put on" the new life as a new garment (4:22-25). We must be different, but how? In what respect? What are the things we should be very careful about? We must put away lying. Our speech shows our spirit. We must put away all bitterness and anger and harsh words. Be kind to each other. We must not have anything to do with deeds of darkness for we are children of light. Read all of Ephesians 4:31,32.

We must go into God's robing room, not to make the garments but to put them on. God is the Tailor and He makes our dress to conform to our position and purpose in life. God wants His sons to wear suitable garments.

We have discovered as we have come into this Temple what our riches are in the heavenlies (1:18-21). Now we must *"walk worthy of the vocation wherewith ye are called.* The way we live must correspond to our creed. A heavenly calling demands a heavenly conduct.

What is a "walk"? It is not a path, or a way of moving about over the earth, or even a sphere of work. A Christian's walk includes his conduct, attitudes, consecration; it is, in short, "a way of living before men."

We are to walk (Ephesians 4:1-3):

Humbly—*with all lowliness and meekness.*

Lovingly—*with longsuffering, forbearing one another in love.*

Peacefully—giving diligence *to keep the unity of the Spirit in the bond of peace.*

We know that our spiritual lives affect our social lives. But so many turn it around and attempt to create a social life that will create a spiritual life. This cannot be. When man is in right relation to God, he will be in proper relation to man.

When God puts upon us His jewels of grace, He seals us by His Spirit (4:30). It is like a young man putting a diamond upon the engagement finger of one whom he has promised to marry. The Lord knoweth them that are His and we are sealed unto the day of redemption. The seal is the mark of ownership. "They are mine." A seal is set for security. We are sealed unto the day of redemption. Have you the seal? Show it then!

THE CHOIR AND ORATORY ROOM (Read Ephesians 5)

In the Jewel Room we were bedecked as children of God and enjoined to walk worthy of our calling. We were sealed with the seal of ownership. Now we are to go out and be followers of God, as dear children. A Christian is "I" following Christ–Christ-I-an.

The Walk of a Christian

Walk in love 5:1,2
Walk in light...5:8
Walk carefully 5:15,16

Be not drunk with wine, wherein is excess; but be filled with the Spirit (5:18). The body, mind and spirit cannot function without outside stimulants. No one will think clearly or feel deeply unless something without excites him. But this is where the tragedy comes. The world has plenty of powerful stimulants which give quick and joyous reactions. But the results are devastating. Our bodies and minds are not made for such ruinous flames and are destroyed. Our bodies are for God's altars. *I beseech you therefore, brethren, . . . that ye present your bodies a living sacrifice* (Rom. 12:1), is God's plea. The Holy Spirit fires our bodies and spirits and sets them aglow but never destroys. Therefore God commands, *Be not drunk with wine . . . but be filled* [set aflame] *with the Spirit*. We can burn and never be consumed. We may live dangerously for God and never be in danger.

It is just as great a sin not to be filled with the Spirit of God as it is to be drunk with wine. Don't think that only ministers and missionaries need to be filled with His blessed Presence, but all! God's Spirit is waiting that He might fill His temples (5:19,20).

Speaking to yourselves in psalms and hymns and spiritual songs, singing and making melody in your heart to the Lord (5:19). Sing, Christian, sing! Christ wants it so. A singing heart guarantees a transformed life. When the Spirit fills the heart, the lips overflow with praise. We will walk the Christian life as we sing and talk about Christ.

This joyful praise of Christian meetings is in contrast to the noisy drunken revellings of Ephesus. Singing is the most natural joyous expression of the Christian life. Have much of it in your church groups. There is music in God's house. God does not delight in sighing and groaning or weeping, but in songs of praise and adoration, in rejoicing and thanksgiving. He is the One who inspires the poet, the hymn writer, the artist in the world. The devil is the author of distress and discord.

There is social life in this great music room of God's Temple. We find it in relationship to everyone.

The Lord not only tells us to walk carefully in the spiritual sphere of our lives but in every other field. How is your walk as a Christian before your family, your friends, and your acquaintances? God demands a walk worthy of Him every place and everywhere. How practical all of this is! How simple yet how spiritual! Only men who believe that the Christian life "is not I but Christ" could fulfill such demands. Christ is the key to a life of victory in the Son of God. He teaches that a child of God can and must, under all circumstances, be a living witness of the power of Christ in his life.

THE ARMORY (Read Ephesians 6)

Now we stand in a room hung with the whole armor of God. The armor is His, not ours! But He tells us to put it on. We must put on the whole of it if we will be safe. The armor is not for a museum where we can go and look over its strength, but it is for the battlefield. Polished armor hanging up in the hall of our creed will not save us in the day of battle. What a relief to know that we do not have to provide the armor! How ignorant we are of the strength and stratagem of the enemy. How inadequately we judge our own ability and weakness.

Paul says, *Finally, my brethren, be strong in the Lord, and in the power of His might* (6:10). You can be strong! You must be strong! But remember this! Be strong in the Lord and in the power of His might! As soon as we are brought into communion with God, we need to be fitted for the fight of faith. All who belong to the Kingdom of God's dear Son have the forces of the Kingdom of Satan against them, so they need to be covered with the whole armor of God.

The Christian's walk includes a warfare. Let us know the wiles of the forces marshalled against us! We have been raised to the heavenly places of fellowship with Christ. Let us maintain the honor of our calling and the wealth of our high estate. As good soldiers let us stand and defend our interests. The crying need of our day is for strong men. In Ephesians 5, we were asked to put on clothing suited to the New Man, moving in society. Here we are to put on armor necessary to the soldier, the man of war.

You must come to Calvary for each piece of this wonderful armor. When we come and take it for ourselves, we can see that our whole body is covered. We are to "be able to stand against" the enemy. Stand, Christian, in the victory Christ wrought on Calvary. But you notice there is no armor for the back. The Christian is never supposed to run from his enemies but fight the good fight of faith, praying always!

"The Whole Armor of God"

Girdle of truth.
Breastplate of righteousness.
Shoes of readiness to bear
   the gospel.

Shield of faith.
Helmet of salvation.
Sword of the Word.
Prayer.

Minimum Daily Requirements/Spiritual Vitamins

Sunday: THE BELIEVER'S POSITION
Ephesians 1:1-23
Monday: SAVED BY GRACE   Ephesians 2:1-22
Tuesday: A MYSTERY REVEALED
Ephesians 3:1-21
Wednesday: A CHRISTIAN'S WALK
Ephesians 4:1-32
Thursday: FOLLOWING CHRIST   Ephesians 5:1-20
Friday: LIVING WITH OTHERS   Ephesians 5:21–6:9
Saturday: CHRISTIAN WARFARE
Ephesians 6:10-24

UNDERSTANDING PHILIPPIANS

*Philippians
Portrays Jesus Christ,
Our Joy*

This epistle was written to the first church founded in Europe. Paul was called there by the vision and the cry, *Come over into Macedonia, and help us* (Acts 16:9).

Paul urges the Church to have Christian unity and joy. This letter shows how unity among Christians can be broken. Christ is the secret of joy. *Finally, my brethren, rejoice in the Lord* (Phil. 3:1). Then there is a pause. Paul is trying to think of some better last word to speak, but he can't find it. Presently he cried out, "And again I say—well—just rejoice, that is enough" (Phil. 4:4). This is joy in the midst of trouble and problems.

Paul and Silas, you remember, sang in the jail there at Philippi at midnight when their backs were bleeding and sore! He is rejoicing now as he writes this letter, chained to a Roman soldier, for he knows that his very chains are helping him to spread the gospel. He could reach some in Caesar's household that he never otherwise could have brought to Christ. He urged his Philippian converts to rejoice because they were allowed to suffer for Christ (1:29).

The joy of the Lord is your strength. The word "joy," or "rejoice," occurs in this epistle sixteen times. Paul seems to laugh out loud for sheer joy in this letter. He is the rejoicing apostle. "Joy" and "rejoice" and "all" are the words to underline. "Be glad" is Paul's exhortation. We are commanded to rejoice. We break a commandment if we rejoice not, for joy drives out discord. It helps in the midst of trials. "Joy is a bird; let it fly in the open heavens, and let its music be heard of all men." Sinners are attracted to Jesus by the joy of Christians.

It hardly seems possible that Paul is writing from prison with chains holding him. His words seem to come from a light heart.

It is evident that the soul of this great apostle is free! There is an atmosphere of joy even from prison.

This letter has no definite plan, but it is the sweetest of all Paul's letters. There is no scolding. It is more of a love letter.

Paul mentions the Saviour's name forty times in this short epistle. Some of the most wonderful things concerning Christ and the Christian life are here. In order that your life may be purified, dangers avoided and progress made, Christ must be your joy, your trust, and your aim in life. Paul tells us of his joyful triumph over trying circumstances because of his trust in Christ.

JOY IN LIVING (Read Philippians 1)

Paul loved to call himself the servant (really "bond servant") of Jesus Christ. He had been made free by Christ and now he wanted to serve Him as long as he lived. He starts his epistle, "Paul, a slave of Jesus Christ." That is the reason he says, *For to me to live is Christ.*

You notice when Paul writes his letters he puts his name first. How sensible this is, for the first thing you do in opening a letter is to turn to the end and find out who wrote it.

Although in prison, Paul could pray for his friends. *I thank my God upon every remembrance of you, always in every prayer of mine for you all making request with joy* . . . (1:3,4).

Paul lived to intercede for others. So should every true Sunday school teacher, Christian friend, father, mother, brother or sister remember others in their prayers without ceasing. Have you a "prayer list"? Do you talk to the Lord about your friends? *Making request with joy.* Why can we rejoice in prayer? What is your answer?

Although Paul was in prison, chained to a soldier, people came to hear him preach. The Roman guards were so interested in the gospel that they spread it around. This encouraged others to be bold in preaching and many found Paul's Christ.

There is great power in the witness of a consistent life. You may be bound to unsympathetic companions, but by your life you may win them for God. Your obstacle may become your pulpit. The Christian who works for Christ when everything is against him stirs others up.

For to me to live is Christ (1:21). Can you say this? Is Christ everything to you? Do you live for Him? Is your one aim and purpose to glorify Him?

Listen to the cries of the men of this world. What are they? To the successful businessman it is, "To me to live is wealth." To the scholar it is, "To me to live is knowledge." To the soldier, it is, "To me to live is victory." To the young man, "To me to live is pleasure." To the man desirous of recognition, "To me to live is fame." To the high school student, "To me to live is recognition." So we could go on and listen to all the voices of the world, but one is heard over them all—"To me to live is not wealth, nor knowledge, not fame nor glory, but Christ. Christ first, last, midst all, and always Christ."

Paul, What Do You Mean?

Christ is the giver of life—*I am come that they might have life* (John 10:10).

Christ is life itself—*I live; yet not I, but Christ liveth in me* (Gal. 2:20).

Christ is the model of my life—*Be ye therefore perfect, even as your Father which is in heaven is perfect* (Matt. 5:48).

Christ is the aim of my life—*I desire to make known . . . the power and coming of our Lord Jesus Christ* (II Peter 1:16).

Christ is the reward of my life—*Thanks be unto God for his unspeakable gift* (II Cor. 9:15).

Paul Says

When I travel, it is on Christ's errands.

When I suffer, it is in Christ's service.

When I speak, the theme is Christ.

When I write, Christ fills my letters.

JOY IN SERVICE (Read Philippians 2)

Paul gives us the wonderful Example of the Christian life that we may follow in His steps. We must imitate Christ for although He is Lord of all He became servant to all! Paul urges the church to complete his happiness by living together in love and unity. Is there anything more Christ-like for Christians to do? *Fulfil ye my joy, that ye be likeminded* (2:2). This is not an easy thing to do. It means love without compromise.

What is the most important social grace? Elegance of manners? The gift of saying agreeable things? No, it is courtesy of heart and not mere fashion. Moody says, "Strife is knocking others down; vainglory is setting oneself up." *Each esteem other better than themselves* (2:3) is an astonishing phrase; in other words, "I am willing to be third."

We must always bear in our thoughts the example of Jesus Christ (2:5-11). Paul says, "Have the mind of Christ," which is self-forgetting love. Although He was God, He humbled Himself. Not only did Christ take on Himself the form of man but the form of a servant. Then He humbled Himself more. He who was author of life became obedient unto death. But even more than this, He faced an ignominious death, *even the death of the cross*. This must be our spirit. (See Matt. 16:25.)

Paul is practical as well as profound. He never leaves us in the clouds. He never separates knowledge from action. Christianity is both life and creed. The creed without the life amounts to little. After Paul has scaled the heights in Christ's exaltation, he has no idea of leaving us there. *Wherefore, my beloved, . . . work out your own salvation* (2:12). "Work out" means live out—not working for salvation but showing the works of salvation. God has a plan for each of our lives as He had for Jesus. We must live it out. It is an absolutely personal matter. No one can do it for you. God plants in our hearts salvation in Christ, great, divine and wonderful to be lived out. Can you go about it without "fear and trembling"? Happy is the person who finds God's plan for his life and falls in with it.

Christian experience is not something that is going on around you but in you. *Christ liveth in me!*

Do all things without murmurings and disputings (2:14), Paul is saying. "Don't be grouchy! You can't glow if you are!"

Having committed our lives to the control of the Lord, we are under orders. Don't murmur or complain! "If God is supreme, why did He allow this thing to happen?" should never pass your

510

lips. You cannot ask your Commander-in-chief the "why" of anything he asks you to do.

Paul shows us, too, that there is a sacrificial side of the Christian life. That which costs nothing amounts to nothing. Paul feared his work might be "in vain." So much in life is done "in vain." Are we running "in vain," or working "in vain"? So many days are spent in vain! So many books are written in vain! So many sermons are printed in vain! So many gifts are given in vain! The Christian life should be a sacrifice if we are to follow Christ. Does your faith cost anything?

But if Christ is our Example then we see that there is no cross without a crown. If we suffer with Him, we shall also reign with Him. We are God's luminaries in a dark age. No flame can shine brightly when it is filthy. The Christian who brings honor to the Lord must be "faultless," "innocent," and "unblamable."

JOY IN FELLOWSHIP (Read Philippians 3)

Paul tells the Philippians that the duty of every Christian is that he be joyful. A long-faced Christian is the worst advertisement against Christianity. The world doesn't want a greater burden, it wants a light heart. How can a Christian be joyful in a world so full of sorrow? Paul tells us in the first verse—*Rejoice in the Lord.*

Saul of Tarsus, a man rich in religious background, seeking for the best, had gone from one religion to another. He was an earnest searcher after truth and blameless as far as the law was concerned, but he had found nothing that satisfied him. One day Christ found him, and in this marvelous paragraph we see the change that he underwent in evaluating things (3:4-9). He gladly sacrificed everything and counted the treasures of this world as nothing in comparison with Christ. He set a new standard of values. He had a new reason for life. Christ had stepped in between Paul and his old ideals and made him change the headings at the top of his ledger. He erased "gains" (credits) and wrote "loss" (debit). This was his choice in life.

Paul weighed both the world and Christ and remembered the words of the Lord Jesus, *For what is a man profited, if he shall gain the whole world, and lose his own soul* (Matt. 16:26)?

In Philippians 3:12-14, Paul tells us that every man's life is a plan of God! The one thing I do should be to carry out this plan. Neither the successes nor failures of the past must keep me from "pressing on" today. *I am ready for anything and equal to anything through Him Who infuses inner strength into me,* [that is, I am self-sufficient in Christ's sufficiency] (Amp. N. T.).

When Paul met the Lord on the way to Damascus (Acts 9), his whole being was changed. His eyes were opened. He discovered in Christ a store of spiritual wealth which made him count all that he had as trash (3:7). He had boasted of lineage and pedigree; he was blameless in the law; he had every honor and privilege, but now he was willing to lose everything to gain Christ.

THE SOUL'S QUESTS

Here are some of the ambitions of Paul's heart. Mark these in your Bible.

That I may win Christ (3:8). Christ had won him (Acts 9). Now he wished to win Him as a daily prize.

That I may know him (3:10). There are degrees of knowing Him.

And be found in him (3:9). To be found in Christ means we are blameless and complete.

That I may know . . . the power of his resurrection (3:10). The power of the gospel is in a risen Christ.

That I may know . . . the fellowship of his sufferings (3:10). This means a life consecrated to Him, conformable unto His death.

That I may apprehend that for which also I am apprehended (3:12). He wanted to know Christ's purpose for seizing him on that road to Damascus.

I press toward the mark for the prize of the high calling of God in Christ Jesus (3:14). The higher the calling, the greater the prize.

Do you know that your citizenship (conversation) is in heaven, that you have been born from above? (3:20,21). Therefore we should live as citizens of "a better country," a heavenly kingdom. Love not the world nor the things of this world, but be loyal to Him who rules in the "Heavenly Jerusalem." When Christ comes, He will change these bodies of ours into bodies like unto His own fit for His heavenly kingdom.

Christ's residence was for thirty-three years here on earth, but it did not naturalize Him as a citizen of earth. Let us not forget where our citizenship is. *Be not conformed to this world: but be ye transformed by the renewing of your mind,* Paul puts it (Rom. 12:2).

JOY IN REWARDS (Read Philippians 4)

Rejoice in the Lord alway: and again I say, Rejoice. Let your moderation be known unto all men. The Lord is at hand (4:4,5). This blessed hope of Christ's coming again casts its gracious influence over all of life. Paul prays that the Christian may have joy at all times and not be worried by cares.

Moody says of verse six:

"Be careful for nothing;
Be prayerful for everything;
Be thankful for anything!"

Yes, the way to be anxious about nothing is to be prayerful about everything. The prayer of faith must be a prayer of thanksgiving because faith knows how much it owes to God. Put your prayers into God's hands and go off and leave them there. Do not worry about them. Give them completely as the farmer gives the wheat to the soil, after the soil has been properly plowed. If you do this, then the peace of God will stand guard over your heart and mind.

Guard your thoughts! Paul tells us what to think about and remember, *as a man thinketh in his heart, so is he* (Prov. 23:7). Thoughts determine your life! Therefore whatsoever things are true, . . . honest, just, pure, lovely, of good report, virtuous, praiseworthy, think on these things!

Paul expressed his gratitude for the loving thought which had promoted the church at Philippi to send him gifts. He was especially happy about their gifts, not because he was in want, for he had learned to be content in any circumstance with Christ. He could do all things through Christ Who strengthened him. But their gifts meant *fruit that may abound to your account.* He opened God's bank account to them. *My God shall supply all your need according to his riches in glory by Christ Jesus.*

Minimum Daily Requirements/Spiritual Vitamins

Sunday: JOY TRIUMPHS OVER SUFFERING
Philippians 1:1-30
Monday: JOY IN CHRIST   Philippians 2:1-11
Tuesday: JOY IN SALVATION   Philippians 2:12-30
Wednesday: JOY IN CHRIST'S RIGHTEOUSNESS
Philippians 3:1-9
Thursday: JOY IN CHRIST'S WILL
Philippians 3:10-21
Friday: JOY IN CHRIST'S STRENGTH
Philippians 4:1-7
Saturday: JOY IN CHRIST'S PROVISION
Philippians 4:8-23

A QUICK LOOK AT THE NEW TESTAMENT

MATTHEW THROUGH PHILLIPIANS

INFORMATION PLEASE

1. Which of the Gospels portrays the Manhood of Jesus?
   a. Matthew ....
   b. Luke ....
   c. John ....
2. In which Gospel is the plan of salvation best presented?
   a. Matthew ....
   b. Mark ....
   c. John ....
3. The Sermon on the Mount is stated at greatest length in:
   a. Matthew ....
   b. Mark ....
   c. Luke ....
4. The genealogy of Jesus is given in:
   a. Matthew ....
   b. Mark ....
   c. Luke ....
   d. John ....

WHAT'S THE ANSWER?

1. Name five outstanding miracles of Jesus.
   ....
   ....
   ....
   ....
   ....

2. Name three persons with whom Jesus had a personal interview.
   ....
   ....
   ....

515

3. In which one of Paul's letters is the "Love Chapter" found?

....

4. How is Jesus portrayed in each of the four Gospels?

....

....

....

....

5. How is Jesus portrayed in each of the six of Paul's epistles we have studied so far?

Romans: ....

I Corinthians: ....

II Corinthians: ....

Galatians: ....

Ephesians: ....

Philippians: ....

6. Why did Paul call the Galatians "foolish"?

a. Because they followed other leaders. ....

b. Because they turned back from their liberty in Christ to the bondage of the law. ....

c. Because they formed a new church. ....

7. A Christian's "works" count before God:

a. For his salvation. ....

b. For rewards. ....

c. For escape of punishment. ....

8. Name the epistles of Paul in their order from Romans to Philippians. ....

....

....

....

9. Trace the spread of Christianity from Jerusalem to Rome as given in the Book of Acts...

....

....

....

....

516

COMPLETION TEST

1. Matthew was written especially for the..

2. The only Gospel that tells the story of the wise men is...............

3. The two greatest preachers in the Book of Acts whose names begin with "P" are...................................and...................................

4. The greatest event in the Book of Acts begins with "P" also. What is it? ....

UNDERSTANDING COLOSSIANS

Colossians Portrays Jesus Christ, Our Life

Ephesians and Colossians were written about the same time, while Paul was a prisoner in Rome. They both contain great doctrines of the gospel, and were to be read aloud in the churches. They are very similar in style, yet very different in emphasis.

Ephesians talks about all believers, calling them the "body of Christ." Colossians talks about the "Head" of the body, Jesus Christ.

In Ephesians, the Church of Christ is the important item. In Colossians, the Christ of the Church is emphasized.

Both are needed. There cannot be a body without a head, nor a head without a body. Notice this all the way through Colossians—"Christ," "Christ," "Christ."

Heresy had broken out in the church at Colosse, misleading the young believers, calling for the worship of angels (2:18), and a strict observance of Jewish ceremonies (2:16,21). This heresy was a mixture of Jewish, Greek and Oriental religions, and all this called forth this statement of the truth of the supreme Lordship of Christ. This epistle draws a faithful portrait of Christ in all His glory and dignity.

Christ is all in all. The failure of the Colossians was at this very point, "not holding fast the Lord." The place that Christ holds in any religious teaching determines whether it is true or false. Some thought in Paul's day, as now, that Jesus was but a man, and Christ was the divine Spirit which came at His baptism and left Him at the cross. This meant that Christ did not die but simply that Jesus died. You can see that this is the root error of many cults today. Every modern cult is based on just the same old heresy and misrepresents the truth in regard to Christ and His Person and work. It is good for us, in reading the

Colossian letter, to examine our own belief and see that we always put the Head, Christ Jesus, in His rightful place in our thinking and glorify this wonderful One.

Have you noticed that many of the epistles were used to answer the heresies that crept into the early churches everywhere?

This letter begins, like twelve others, with the name of Paul. They are addressed to Gentile believers.

The church was likely founded by Epaphras (1:7) in the town of Colosse, about 100 miles east of Ephesus. It consisted of Gentile Christians. Philemon was a member. Paul kept in close touch with the people and was greatly beloved.

Epaphras went to Rome to tell Paul of the heresies that were creeping into the church. These false teachings took Christ off the throne, and denied His headship of the Church. To help answer them, Paul sent this letter back by Epaphras. He writes especially on the pre-eminence and deity of Christ, for Christ is very God.

The gospel, by this time, had been brought to "all the world" (1:6), and had been "preached to every creature" (1:23). Thirty-two years after Christ's death, the gospel had reached the whole Roman world. It needed only one generation to establish the Church as a world-wide fact.

Church's Position "in Christ"

United in Christ 2:2
Complete in Christ.. 2:10
Dead in Christ.. 2:20
Buried with Christ...Rom. 6:4
Risen with Christ 3:1

CHRIST OUR LIFE

And your life is hid with Christ in God (3:3). This epistle tells us that Christ is our life, and we are complete in Him (2:10).

The Christian life is not a "creed" nor a "system of doctrine," nor a certain kind of worship, but a life that is Christ's very own within you.

Christ is All in All

IN HIS DEITY—The image of the invisible God (1:15).

IN CREATION—Sovereign Creator of the universe (1:15,16).

IN PRE-EMINENCE—Before all things (1:18).

IN REDEMPTION—Reconciling the universe through His blood (1:20-22).

IN HEADSHIP—Over all principalities and powers (1:18; 2:14).

IN HIS CHURCH—The Head of the body (1:18; 2:19).

IN HIS INDWELLING PRESENCE—The Christian's hope (1:27).

God has given Christ pre-eminence in all things (1:18). We dare not give Him a lower place!

In Romans, we are justified in Christ; I Cor., we are enriched in Christ; II Cor., we are comforted in Christ; Galatians, we are free in Christ; Ephesians, we are quickened in Christ; Philippians, we are happy in Christ; Colossians, we are complete in Christ.

Colossians presents the glorious culmination of it all. We are *complete in him*. We are *rooted and built up;* we are *grounded and settled*. We discover the facts of this building process in the four chapters of this book.

Building "downward," rooted in Jesus, *grounded and settled* 1:23

Building "upward," *built up in him*..................................2:7

Building "inward," *hid with Christ*.................................3:3

Building "outward," walking *in wisdom toward them that are without* 4:5

The DEEPER LIFE is rooted in eternity. It begins in Him Who was *in the beginning with God*. God gives us eternal life.

The HIGHER LIFE is the life Jesus is living for us at the right hand of God, and living in us, for it is no longer I that live, but Christ that lives in me (Galatians 2:20).

The INNER LIFE is all the life we have as Christians. It is the life *hid with Christ in God*. It is life real and sufficient, for we are *complete in Him* (2:10).

The OUTER LIFE is that expression of life that makes Christ known to others. "What you are speaks so loudly, men cannot hear what you say."

521

THE DEEPER LIFE (Read Colossians 1)

Paul opens this letter as he opens so many: *We give thanks* (1:3). He rejoices in the good news from the brethren scattered abroad in the various churches which he founded.

Notice Paul's favorite words, "faith," "love," and "hope" (vs. 4,5), which he so often uses. He wants everyone to have faith in Christ, love toward others and hope of heaven.

Paul tells us the secret of the deeper life that we as Christians should have in Christ. Dig downward first, and become *grounded and settled* in Christ (1:23). Send the taproot of your Christian faith down deep into His life, as the great oak sends its root into the heart of the earth. We find that storms may beat against the solid oak, but it stands fast, for it is rooted deep. In sharp contrast is the California redwood. It may have acres of roots, but they are spread close to the surface of the earth. The giant redwood lifts its head several hundred feet into the air, but it has no taproot. Its roots cannot hold. When the storm beats against it, it topples.

Send your roots down into Christ. The source of your life is in Him. The Japanese have a way of cutting the taproot of the trees of the forest and confining them in miniature gardens and flower pots. The tree gains its life from the little surface roots and only grows to a few feet in height. Every soul is stunted until it puts its taproot into God and begins to draw on Him.

Next Paul presents a glowing description of the mighty Christ, the Superior One. He is ALL IN ALL.

We find in this first scene, that not only are we in Christ, but Christ is in us. *Christ in you, the hope of glory* (1:27). This is what it is to be a Christian, living in Him, this glorious, wonderful Person, the Creator of this universe, in whom we have redemption through His blood, and having Him live in us.

In closing this scene, notice Paul's beautiful prayer for the Church, given in Col. 1:9-14. He expresses his desire for all Christian believers:

That they might be filled with a knowledge of Christ's will. He wants us to know how to live a Christ-like life, for the fullness of Christ's wisdom will keep us from error.

That they might walk worthy of the Lord, fruitful in work, increasing in knowledge.

That they might be strengthened with might so as to be able to withstand all temptations.

That they might be thankful.

THE HIGHER LIFE (Read Colossians 2)

As ye have therefore received Christ Jesus the Lord, so walk ye in him: rooted and built up in him (2:6,7). Paul is always practical. Again he says, "Act out what you believe." You commenced well. Go on as you have begun! We have received Christ, and have been grounded and settled in Him (1:23). Let us therefore walk in Him. Paul always wants our walk and life to correspond with our belief. It is sad when a Christian believes in Christ and acts like the devil. No one will accept his profession as sincere. If we have received Christ, let us walk as He would have us. If we have been rooted in Him, let us grow up in Him. If we have been founded on Him, let us be builded up on Him. All of these are outward evidences of a changed heart. "Walking" expresses life. "Growing" exhibits an inner power. "Building up" shows progress of character until the structure is complete.

We have to do a great deal more than just believe truths about Christ. We must receive Christ if we are to have life. We cannot earn it or purchase it. It is a free gift (2:6). We are rooted in Christ. That means we draw our nourishment from Him. A plant cannot grow unless it is in touch with the lifegiving soil. We are built up in Him. We have our foundation in Him. Every structure needs a foundation. All this must be our experience if we would be built up. The Christian life is starting in Christ, and then growing in His grace and gifts. We must be as dependent on Christ for steadfastness of walk as we were for our assurance of salvation.

All the life we have as Christians is the life "in Him."

Walking in Him 2:6
Rooted in Him 2:7

This is the life—real and satisfying, eternal life. We find in this chapter that Christ is all-sufficient, for *in him dwelleth all the fulness of the Godhead bodily*. This is a tremendous truth for us to grasp. In this Jesus, who walked on the earth, dwelt the whole Godhead. But more than this—in Him was the fulness of the Godhead.

Let us look again. *In Him dwelleth all the fulness of the Godhead*. This Jesus was very God in all of His fulness. Neither angels, nor prophets, nor saints rank with Him—for He is the very embodiment of the divine fulness!

Our life must first be built downward, "rooted in Christ." Next we must build upward, *built up in him, and established in the faith* (2:7), rearing a stately structure to His praise, and of course, wholly by His grace. This is the higher life.

The higher you go with the Lord, the steadier is your disposition, the less disturbing are temptations, and the smoother is your everyday life.

We see Paul's personal concern for the Church at Colosse. He longs for the Christians to be established and kept firm in their convictions, so that the shrewd philosophers and legalists of their day would not deceive them. The best way to be protected from the snares of the world and its philosophy is an understanding of the perfection of Christ, for He is all and in all. Be rooted and grounded in the Word lest you be swept away by false teachers.

Some of the popular street-corner philosophers of the day were teaching that man is unworthy to approach Christ directly. He needed to approach Him by means of angels (2:18). There are some in our day who teach that we need to approach God through the virgin Mary or through some other person. Christ says He is the only mediator between God and man. He adds, *I am the way, . . . no man cometh unto the Father, but by me*

(John 14:6). Paul rebukes the Colossians for their failure to recognize the supreme Headship of Christ and the only mediator between God and man.

Paul reminds the Christian that when Jesus died on the cross He freed us from the law. We need not keep fast days. There is nothing Christian in punishing the body or in fasting, as the ascetic has done through the centuries and is still doing. The sacrifice that God asks is a broken spirit, not a beaten body. A sinful heart can dwell in a fasting body. Self-imposed hardships are of no value in offsetting the thoughts of a sinful heart. We like to think that when we have done something bad we can erase our record by doing something which we feel is good. But we must remember that only what Christ does is good, for *there is none that doeth good, no, not one* (Rom. 3:12). If "God" is taken out of "good," nothing—"o"—is left.

THE INNER LIFE (Read Colossians 3)

The building of our life cannot be only downward, *rooted in Christ,* upward, *built up in him,* but our building must also be inward. Let us know that Christ is the believer's life. Many believe that Christ gave us life as one would put a living seed into a flower pot. The pot would hold a detached thing—life. But Christ is more than that. He Himself is in the believer. The life that is in Christ is in the believer. The illustration He gives, *I am the vine, ye are the branches* (John 15:5).

We find that our new life in Christ makes us less interested in the things the world offers. We become "dead to the world." We find ourselves *hid with Christ,* and as we know Him we discover, one by one, the beauties of the Lord Jesus. Mercy, kindness, humbleness of mind, meekness, longsuffering (3:12). *Let the word of Christ dwell in you richly* (3:16). It will make a difference.

The Brown family lived in a house that was an eyesore in the neighborhood. Weeds grew over the porch; the shades were always torn; the curtains were sagging and soiled. One day in passing by the house, we saw the grass cut; fresh white curtains were hung at the windows. The broken steps were mended.

"When did the Browns move?" we ask. "Why, they haven't moved," answered our neighbor. "O, yes they have. The Browns don't live in that house any more. A new family has moved in. I haven't seen the people yet, but I know by the appearance that a new owner occupies the house." Yes, our outward life will be different. Others will see Christ living in us.

Since we are rooted in Christ, and our life is in Him, we are not only identified with Him in His death, but we are in union with Him in His resurrection. In Christ's death we died to sin, and in His resurrection we rose to walk in a new life. Since we are *risen with Christ,* we should seek those things which are above, and show to the best of our ability the goal of our lives.

For example, the submarine is made to travel under the water. Yet, every submarine is equipped with a periscope by which it seeks those things which are above. It travels in the water but the well-being of those in it depends on a knowledge of what is above.

We live in the world, but we must set our minds (affections) on things above, for we are citizens of a heavenly country. Look upon Christ and He will draw you upward.

THE CHRISTIAN'S WARDROBE

First we must "put off" the old nature. Paul tells us to put it to death (3:5-9). After we receive our new life in Christ Jesus, then we must "put off" the old man and his deeds. It should not be necessary to tell Christians that they must put off things that are more like the devil than the Saviour!

Any self-denial or asceticism not built on our union with Christ, whether practiced by the priests of India, or the Buddhists of Thailand, or the monks of Catholicism or a Protestant layman, is condemned at the start.

Christianity is not a series of "giving-ups"; it is a new life. Women do not give up playing jacks; they outgrow it. As we come to know Christ better, we find that some things no longer interest us. Christ adds so much to our lives that there is no room for the old things. The first thing we know, we have lost interest in the old and are busy with the new life in Christ.

Paul admonishes us to destroy our old nature and "put off"

all its vices. Read over Paul's black catalogue. There is immorality, impurity, passion, greed. Then there are passionate anger and wrath, and the many sins of speech. Let us forever give up these sins. It is possible in Christ.

Can you imagine how ridiculous you would look if, when you went to buy a new suit, you refused to take off the one you had on, but rather insisted that the new one should be tried on without "putting off" the old one! This is what many Christians do. They try to put the garment of a new life on over their old nature. It just doesn't fit. We must lay aside sin first, then "put on" the new man.

A Christian's conduct is what men see you do. As clothes indicate what kind of a person you are—they tell whether you are careful or careless; they tell whether you are a soldier or civilian, a king or a commoner—so outward expression will show *whose you are, and whom you serve* (Acts 27:23).

Now Paul thinks of our new nature in Christ. *Put on the new man.* This new nature we receive from Christ is ever being renewed as we grow in the knowledge of our Lord and Saviour. But we must not become so absorbed in our great privileges in Christ that we neglect our duty to our fellow men. Our knowing Christ should make us much more thoughtful of others. The new Christian not only puts away, but puts on or adds to, his life. Let us "put on" the excellences of this new life, such as tenderness, kindness, humility, patience, forgiveness and love (3:12-14). Yes, these are the things with which we are to adorn ourselves. If we lived like this, we would find perfection on earth. Paul says all these virtues are like pieces of clothing, all held in place by a belt of love. This fills our life with the peace of God.

Do you remember how Luther Burbank took the little wild daisy and developed it into a bloom five to seven inches in diameter, and the little poppy developed into a blossom ten inches across? So our Christian graces must be cultivated and enlarged. Too often they perish for want of care. Too often the fruit of our lives looks only like the ordinary fruit of the world. We must grow into the full stature of the fullness of Christ. As long as we live, there is something new for us to learn. We should never stop growing.

Set down all the commands given to you in this chapter.

CHRIST IS OUR ALL OR NOTHING

Yes, *Christ is all, and in all* (3:11). If Christ is not all in your life, He is nothing. No surer test can be given to any false teaching of today than this: Where does it put Jesus Christ? The Bible says: *Every spirit that confesseth that Jesus Christ is come in the flesh is of God* (I John 4:2). This is the test of every creed. Does it proclaim that *we have redemption through his blood, even the forgiveness of sins* (1:14)? If so, it is true; if not, it is false (I John 4:1-3).

A Christian heart is a singing heart (3:16). Christ wants us to be taught in His word, and then He wants us to express our joy in Him by singing hymns.

THE OUTWARD LIFE (Read Colossians 4)

This chapter introduces another phase of our life in Christ, the outward life. We found we must build within, cultivating the virtues of the new life in Christ. But there is something more. We want our new life to be seen and felt among others (4:5). This is the way we present Christ to the world. Remember, Christians mean "little Christs." The life of Christ is not written only by great authors like Farrar or Edersheim. It was not ended when the Gospels were completed. Christ is living in us. His life is told today in living epistles, that are known and read of all men.

When there were just a handful of Christians in the early days, they felt a great gulf between them and the pagans of the country. They were "without." Paul says, *Walk in wisdom toward them that are without.*

528

Minimum Daily Requirements/Spiritual Vitamins

Sunday: PAUL'S GREETING AND PRAYER
Colossians 1:1-14
Monday: SEVEN SUPERIORITIES OF CHRIST
Colossians 1:15-29
Tuesday: CHRIST EXALTED   Philippians 2:1-16
Wednesday: COMPLETE IN CHRIST
Colossians 2:1-19
Thursday: OLD AND NEW MAN
Colossians 2:20–3:11
Friday: CHRISTIAN LIVING   Colossians 3:12-25
Saturday: CHRISTIAN GRACES   Colossians 4:1-18

UNDERSTANDING I THESSALONIANS

I Thessalonians Portrays Jesus Christ, the Coming One

The second coming of the Lord Jesus Christ is the truth that Paul is presenting in these two letters to the Thessalonians and it would be missing the mark not to recognize it. The two epistles contain twenty different references to the coming of the Lord. This is the hope of the Church. It is mentioned in the closing of every chapter: *To wait for his Son from heaven* (1:10); *In the presence of our Lord Jesus Christ at his coming* (2:19); *At the coming of our Lord Jesus Christ with all his saints* (3:13); *Caught up together with them in the clouds, to meet the Lord in the air* (4:17), and in the last chapter, *I pray God your whole spirit and soul and body be preserved blameless unto the coming of our Lord Jesus Christ* (5:23). In view of all this, should anyone raise the question, "Will Christ come again?"

Christ's first coming was sudden and a surprise to the philosophers of His time. We learn that His second coming will be no less surprising.

Paul, accompanied by Timothy and Silas, had spent only three Sundays at Thessalonica, on his second missionary journey, but during that time he had not only founded a church, but had grounded it firmly in the faith. In the short time he was there, Paul had created a great stir. His enemies accused him of "turning the world upside down" (Acts 17:6). On account of this great stir, the brethren sent the Apostle away. He went on to Berea and Athens and Corinth. It was from here he wrote this first letter to the Thessalonians and sent it by Timothy. We know he had only been gone a short time, for he said he was *bereaved of you for a season of an hour*.

It is an unprecedented thing even in the ministry of Paul, this establishment of a flourishing church in less than a month. He preached to them for three Sabbath days, although no doubt he continued his meetings during these weeks. Paul's success in Thessalonica has not been the usual experience of missionaries among the heathen. Carey in India, Judson in Burma, Morrison in China, Moffat in Africa waited each seven years for his first convert. But here, the Holy Spirit allowed Paul to reap a sudden harvest.

During this short stay in Thessalonica a great number of Greeks and women believed (Acts 17:4). He began at once to feed this church with the meat of the Word. He talked of the Holy Spirit (I Thess. 1:6), of the Trinity (1:6) and of the second coming of Christ (1:10). The church was composed mostly of Gentiles, rather than Jews. Being greatly concerned about the young converts, Paul sent Timothy from Athens to strengthen their faith, and to bring him news of how they were getting along. Timothy brought back a favorable report that was a great comfort to the Apostle-founder of the church. However, Timothy had discovered that there were some faults to be corrected. They held some false views concerning the Lord's coming. They were worried about some who had died, fearing that they would not have any part in the rapture and glory of the Lord's return. Others were so overwhelmed by the truth of Christ's return that they had neglected their daily tasks (4:10-12). Wishing to correct these wrong views and to inspire and comfort these new converts, Paul wrote this epistle.

This is an intimate epistle. The letter is a "heart-to-heart talk." Paul gets very close to "his brethren." This word occurs fourteen times. It is a message of comfort and instruction to those who are in the midst of persecution.

There should be nothing doubtful or divisive about this "blessed hope" of our Lord's return. No one can read the Word without finding the teaching. Let us not quarrel with one another about so sweet a message as our Lord's "I will come again." This is the Christian's hope. Let us rather be watchful, for we know not the day nor the hour when the Son of man comes.

CHRIST'S COMING (Read I Thessalonians 1)
"An Inspiration to Young Christians"

If you wish to know how to get on with other folks in Christian work, just go over the things that are said by Paul himself, under the guidance of the Spirit. This is the kind of service that the Lord Jesus would have us render in His name.

Paul did not try to please men in ways that displeased God.

Paul did not try to capture men by flattery.

Paul was not covetous of what they had.

Paul was not seeking glory for himself out of his work.

Paul kept at his task day and night.

Paul always encouraged men.

In Paul's greeting, he includes his fellow-workers, Silvanus (Silas) and Timothy. Silvanus had been with him when he founded the Church at Thessalonica, and Timothy had been his special messenger to them, carrying the good news of their progress, and reporting their needs back at Corinth. We can learn much from Paul. He knew the secret of friendship, that so many would like to possess. He loved people. The Bible tells us how to have friends. *A man that hath friends must show himself friendly* (Prov. 18:24). This is just what Paul did. He always acknowledged others in his service, and expressed appreciation of their part in every work done.

PRAYING AS PAUL PRAYED

We give thanks to God always for you all, making mention of you in our prayers (1:2). Do we follow up our new converts as Paul did? Teacher, do you? Paul's converts were in more than a score of different cities, yet he carried them "all" in his heart and kept in touch with them.

Do you have a prayer list? Do you pray for others by name? Do you "make mention" of your friends before God? If you find it difficult to speak to others about Christ, try speaking to Christ about others, and soon you will be speaking to others about Him. All of us can do this, even the most timid.

Are we realizing as Christians what we are in the world for?

How seriously are we taking our task? Have we any evidence that we have been "approved of God" to be entrusted with the gospel? Paul sets forth in this letter the intensity of his ministry; his willingness to die for his new converts; and his dealing with "each one."

Paul thanks God for this church. The beauty of this church did not consist of a gorgeous building of mortar and stone, but a people who are *in God the Father and in the Lord Jesus Christ* (1:1). He is very pleased over the wonderful growth these young converts have made. He held them up as an example everywhere he went (1:7). Already their zeal had made a profound impression all over Macedonia and Achaia (Greece), and everyone was talking about the wonderful way God had worked in this young, vigorous church at Thessalonica.

Ye were ensamples to all that believe (1:7). This is what everyone in the world is looking for—Christians who live the Christian life, who act what they believe. This is just what the Thessalonians did. Nothing was mentioned of the financial condition of their "annual budget." But their faith in God was known everywhere (1:8). Their missionary enthusiasm in sounding forth the Word of God had been felt all through Greece. They were what every church should be.

LIFE IN THREE TENSES

PAST TENSE—"Turned to God"

The believers at Thessalonica "turned to God from idols." There must be a personal turning to God from sin and unbelief, if one is to become a child of God. The idols of our lives are numerous and varied. To turn to God is to forsake everything that would divide our affections or hinder us in following Him with our whole heart.

PRESENT TENSE—"To Serve the Living God"

They *turned to God from idols to serve the living and true God* (1:9). What a change! Serving a living God instead of going through a dead ritual that only mocked their needs by a dead silence!

FUTURE TENSE—"To Wait for His Son from Heaven"

They were serving and waiting! These early Christians believed that Christ would come again, as He Himself had promised. This was called "that blessed hope." The prophets of old waited for the coming of the Messiah long ages before He came, but "in the fulness of time" Christ did come. The Church may have to wait long for His promised coming again, the second time. Many have lost the vision and hope. But in the fulness of time He will come, as He said. Mark in your Bible these blessed promises: John 14:3; Acts 1:11; I Thess. 4:16; Rev. 1:7.

Paul feels that his one reward for all his toil and pain and suffering will consist in presenting these converts of his ministry to Christ when He comes again.

CHRIST'S COMING (Read I Thessalonians 2)
"An Encouragement to the Faithful Servant"

Paul gives us these descriptions of his services at Thessalonica.

"Not in vain" 2:1
"Bold" in spite of contention 2:2
Not of deceit, nor of uncleanness, nor in guile 2:3
"Pleasing God" 2:4
No flattery 2:5
For God's glory 2:6
"Gentle" 2:7
"Affectionate" 2:8
"Laboring night and day" 2:9
Backed by holy living 2:10-12
Successful in its results 2:13-18

What a man was Paul! He preached to please God and lived to convince men of the truth of his preaching. His conduct commended his preaching. The Thessalonians became an eager missionary church. He was not a flatterer, neither did he seek wealth. He came as simple as a child, and as gentle as a nurse caring for little children. He was never idle, but toiled night and day. Giving them this example of his own life, he pleaded with them to make their daily lives worthy of the name Christian.

Paul urges *that ye would walk worthy of God* (2:12). A Christian's walk is a Christian's life. An Indian pastor who was worried over the inconsistent lives among some of his flock, said to a missionary, "There is much crooked walk by those who make good talk." Our walk and our talk should be twins going along on the same trail.

It is so true for young people that this life holds such strong interests, such demanding problems, such vital experiences, that even this most blessed hope for the future is not the only teaching we must help them find in God's Word. Paul's letter to the Thessalonians proves how well Paul knew this, for it abounds in plenty to do right now, while we wait for that day of Christ's appearing. All the way through Paul enjoins us to "work" and "labor" while we "hope."

Paul looked forward during these trying days to the *Lord Jesus Christ at his coming.* His greatest reward, after he has seen his wonderful Saviour's face, will be to present the young converts of his ministry to Christ, letting them share in the glory of His advent. They will be his *crown of rejoicing* (2:19,20).

CHRIST'S COMING (Read I Thessalonians 3:1–4:12)
"An Incentive to Love Among Christians"

This scene describes Paul's "labor of love" among the brethren. Paul was aware of the strain under which the members of the church at Thessalonica were living. He sent Timothy from Athens to encourage them under their bitter persecution.

Timothy had brought back the good news of their "faith" and "love." This report filled Paul with unbounded joy. How glad Paul was to hear of their firm stand in the faith and to know that they thought kindly of him and his fellowworkers and longed to see them. In the midst of their persecution and suffering Paul flashed the light of that wonderful day when they should be made perfect and unblamable, when they shall be changed in a moment, and be holy before God. (See 3:13.)

The test of any hope that a man holds is what it does for him *now.* Paul told them that the coming of the Lord should be an incentive to

Right living 3:13
Consistent walk 4:1
Purity 4:3-7
Love 4:9,10

536

Paul urges personal purity, and a life that is consistent with their testimony (4:1). This is the place where most Christians fail. Let us strive to have our ideals beyond reproach. Our attitude toward each other should be one of love. You remember the two commandments Jesus gave. First, *Thou shalt love the Lord thy God,* and second, *thy neighbor as thyself.* Paul charges us to *abound in love one toward another* (3:12; 4:9,10).

We discover that looking for His glorious appearing does not mean a life of idleness. (Read I Thess. 4:11,12.) Looking for Christ never makes idle hands. If we were expecting a loved one to return home after a long absence, we would not just sit down as the day of his return approached. Rather would we be busy getting everything ready, doing the things he wanted done. Can you imagine a mother waiting for her son to come home from the service, just sitting down and letting everything go! She would be fixing up her son's room, making his favorite cake, and preparing his favorite food, as she listened for his footsteps. This is the true Christian's attitude concerning our blessed Lord's return.

CHRIST'S COMING (Read I Thessalonians 4:13-18)
"A Comfort to the Bereaved"

A little band of Indian converts in Canada came to a missionary with a strange request. "We are always hearing what God has done," they said. "Now tell us what He is going to do."

Where would you find an answer to that wise request? We have it in our Bibles. He shall come again (4:16)! If one of your best friends said he was coming to see you, you would not rest until you found out when he was coming and how. But our wonderful Lord and Saviour says He is coming and He will transform the whole world and glorify all humanity. Can it be possible that we would be less curious about His coming than we would be about the fleeting visit of an earthly friend?

There is so much in these few verses that end with, *Wherefore comfort one another with these words* (4:18). There is comfort because of His sure return.

The Christians at Thessalonica were disturbed because of

537

their mistaken ideas about Christ's coming. They were under the impression that Christ's coming was soon and they were worried as to what would happen to those who had died. What part would they have in His glorious coming and kingdom?

When Christ returns to earth, He will not come alone. Our loved ones who have fallen asleep in Christ *will God bring with him*. What a meeting that will be! Death does not end all. Parents and children, husbands and wives, loved ones and friends will be united. How anxious we are to know that "ours" will be in that happy throng.

The Lord himself shall descend from heaven (4:16). Christ does not say He is going to send the messenger of death to bring His bride (the Church) home. He is coming Himself for her! *This same Jesus, . . . shall so come in like manner as ye have seen him go into heaven* (Acts 1:11). And *They shall see the Son of man coming in the clouds of heaven with power and great glory* (Matt. 24:30). What a marvelous hope this is.

THE DEAD SHALL RISE

Those who have Christian loved ones who have died should not give way to undue sorrow when they lay them in the grave for they have a double assurance from Christ's Word. There is the hope that one day all the dead in Christ shall rise and the additional assurance that He may come again at any time. When Christ comes He will greet the believers who are dead first and bring them with Him (4:13,14). When the archangel shall sound the trumpet call of God, announcing the Lord's coming, then *the dead in Christ shall rise first* to meet Him. Then those that are alive and remain shall be caught up in the clouds to share with them the glory of His coming, and to be forever with the Lord (4:17,18).

The second coming of Christ was the bright hope of the early Church. The greatest fact of the past is that Christ came the first time, as a man, and died on the cross to free us from the penalty of sin. The greatest fact of the future is that He is coming again, as a King, to free us from the presence of sin (Matt. 24:42).

THE LIVING SHALL MEET HIM

Then we which are alive and remain shall be caught up together with them in the clouds, to meet the Lord in the air (4:17). Paul assures us that all shall not die before He comes. *We shall not all sleep* [die], *but we shall all be changed, in a moment, in the twinkling of an eye, at the last trump* (I Cor. 15:51,52).

And so shall we ever be with the Lord (I Thess. 4:17). Made like Him, we shall ever be with Him. He has gone to prepare a place for you. *I will come again, and receive you unto myself* (John 14:3). Heaven is where Christ is now. There we will be. This is heaven's greatest honor conferred on mortals.

This is the order of these great events:

The Lord's descent from heaven

The dead in Christ raised

The living believers changed

The whole company caught up to meet the Lord in the air.

The truth of Christ's coming again thrills us. He went away in the clouds (Acts 1:9). He will come back in triumphal glory (Rev. 1:7). The angels will be with Him (Matt. 25:31). The believers of the past ages will be raised, those that are alive will be changed, and as Enoch and Elijah were translated into heaven, so will the whole Church be caught up, to give a joyful welcome to the returning Saviour!

Discuss the thoughts and habits one must cultivate in himself to make his life count for Christ—physical, mental, spiritual. Discuss methods of cultivation.

Be ye therefore ready also: for the Son of man cometh at an hour when ye think not (Luke 12:40). Every morning when we rise we should say to ourselves, "Be ye ready for your Lord's return for He may come today." Every night our closing question should be, "Would I be ready for my Lord if He should come before I wake?" (I Thess. 3:12,13). Don't live to be ready to die, but live that you may be ready for Christ's coming (5:4-8)!

CHRIST'S COMING (Read I Thessalonians 5)
"A Challenge to Holy Living"

Christ's second coming will be like the coming of a thief in the night or like the flood in Noah's time. The world will know nothing of His return. They scoff at the idea. But Jesus said there would be "signs" before His coming so that watchful believers may know when the time is drawing near. Over and over again Jesus had told them that His coming would be as a thief in the night (Matt. 24:36,42; 25:13; Mark 13:32-37; Luke 12:40; 21:25-35). He warned His disciples to be ever on the watch. This should be their duty and their attitude. Christians need have no fear of that glorious day.

Don't fix dates! We should live watchful lives. We should not live lives of sleepy indulgence but of wakeful watching (I Thess. 5:6). The hope of Christ's coming does not mean a life of idleness. Activity should be the theme of our lives as we find it in this chapter.

While you wait, Paul gives you a grand octave upon which to play great melodies of hope. Strike every note on this wonderful octave. If you do, your life will be rich.

Rejoice evermore 5:16
Pray without ceasing 5:17
In everything give thanks 5:18
Quench not the Spirit 5:19
Despise not prophesyings 5:20
Prove all things 5:21
Hold fast that which is good 5:21
Abstain from all appearance of evil 5:22

Have you ever thought of Paul as a human example of what it means to follow Christ? Paul was "as straight as a shingle" and "as clean as a hound's tooth." Paul could challenge a critical examination of his record as a Christian. Paul had a brilliant mind, and a highly cultured one. We are apt to say, "How hard it is for a brainy man to remain loyal to his Maker!" But Paul humbly prostrated his wonderful intellect at the feet of his Master. The only explanation of such a life is that it was entirely yielded to Christ. You can't be perfect in this life, young people. But there is one thing you can do one hundred per cent. It is what Paul did. You can give yourselves totally and without reserve to the Master.

Discuss the thoughts and habits one must cultivate in himself to make his life count for Christ—physical, mental, spiritual. Discuss methods of cultivation.

Be ye therefore ready also: for the Son of man cometh at an hour when ye think not (Luke 12:40). Every morning when we rise we should say to ourselves, "Be ye ready for your Lord's return for He may come today." Every night our closing question should be, "Would I be ready for my Lord if He should come before I wake?" (I Thess. 3:12,13) Don't live to be ready to die, but live that you may be ready for Christ's coming! (5:4-8)

Minimum Daily Requirements/Spiritual Vitamins

Sunday: CHRIST'S COMING AN INSPIRATION TO YOUNG CHRISTIANS I Thessalonians 1

Monday: CHRIST'S COMING AN ENCOURAGEMENT TO THE FAITHFUL SERVANT I Thessalonians 2

Tuesday: CHRIST'S COMING AN INCENTIVE TO LOVE AMONG CHRISTIANS I Thessalonians 3:1–4:12

Wednesday: CHRIST'S COMING A COMFORT TO THE BEREAVED I Thessalonians 4:13-18

Thursday: CHRIST'S COMING A CHALLENGE TO HOLY LIVING I Thessalonians 5

Friday: CHRIST'S SUDDEN COMING Matthew 24:1-27

Saturday: TRIBULATION DAYS Matthew 24:29-51

541

UNDERSTANDING II THESSALONIANS

*II Thessalonians
Portrays Jesus Christ,
Our Returning Lord*

This is the second epistle on the "blessed hope," or the coming again of our Lord Jesus Christ. These Thessalonians were forward-looking people. Paul talks to them about what is uppermost in their minds and thoughts. The first epistle says, "He is surely coming again." The second epistle says, "But work and wait till He comes."

The second coming of Christ is mentioned 318 times in 260 chapters of the New Testament. From this we see how important this subject is. We read the prophecies of the Old Testament with deepest interest, to find out about our Lord's first advent upon this earth. We should be just as interested to discover what the New Testament teaches regarding His second coming "in power and great glory." He said He was coming again. Here are His words: *And if I go and prepare a place for you, I will come again* (John 14:3). He intended that His disciples should understand that His second coming would be in as literal a sense as His going away.

I Thessalonians tells about Christ coming for His Church. The "coming of Christ" should be cleared up a bit in our minds. One day Christ will come to take away His bride, the Church. He will not be seen of the world at that time, but those who are His, including the dead in Christ, shall be "caught up" to meet Him. This is the teaching of I Thessalonians. After a period of seven years of tribulation for those left on the earth, Christ will appear to the world, with His Church, to establish His throne upon the earth. Then He will be seen of all men. His "coming," then, includes both of these two events, seven years apart. We, as Christians, are looking for the first event. The world will not see Him until the end of the seven years (II Thess.)

II Thessalonians tells about Christ coming with His mighty angels. The two events, Christ coming for His Church and His coming with His mighty angels, are really two aspects of but one occurrence. Between these two aspects, the Jews occupy their own land of Palestine; the gathering of the Gentile nations against them takes place; the Antichrist becomes the world ruler; he makes a covenant with the Jews and breaks it. Following this is the great tribulation. (See Matt. 24:21,22.) Then Christ will come with His saints and set up His kingdom on this earth with Jerusalem as the center. Christ will come first and receive His own unto Himself, before that great and terrible day "of His revelation" in judgment upon His enemies.

This second letter was written almost immediately after I Thessalonians. In addition to their trials and persecutions, the Thessalonian Christians were "shaken in mind" and "troubled" by deceivers who made some believe that they were already passing through the great tribulation and that "the day of the Lord was already here." Paul tries to clear up the difficulty. Always, when war is threatening and sorrow seems to cover the earth, people wonder if they are in the end "tribulation" time. This second epistle to the Thessalonians is good for all to read, so that these errors in our thinking shall be cleared up.

The church at Thessalonica was carried away with the expectation of Christ's glorious return. Who can help but be thrilled when he thinks about His triumphant coming? But we must keep our feet on the ground. We must work while we wait, and pray as we watch, for there is much to do while Christ tarries.

The message here is something like our Lord's word to His disciples in Acts 1. You remember their eager question, *Lord, wilt thou at this time restore the kingdom?* "Leave that with the Father," Jesus in effect replied. "Do your day's work and wait. The kingdom is coming."

CHRIST'S COMING (Read II Thessalonians 1)
"Comfort in Persecution"

We find that Silas and Timothy are mentioned again in the salutation of this letter. From this we judge that this letter followed the first rather quickly. These two aides were still with Paul. Paul commends the young Christians at Thessalonica warmly before he rebukes them. Let us always look and see if we can find something to commend in those we would criticize. Paul did this so often. He noticed that the promise of the Lord's coming again had inspired them to a "growth in faith" (1:3), and "patience" (1:4). They knew that when Christ came, wrongs would be righted and the Lord would deal with those who had oppressed them, for this was a much persecuted church (1:5-7).

How does Paul describe this event of the coming of Christ? It is sudden and startling. *The Lord Jesus shall be revealed from heaven with his mighty angels, in flaming fire taking vengeance.* This is no mild appearing for "them that know not God." It will be very different for His own. We read about *the presence of the Lord, . . . the glory of his power; when he shall come to be glorified in his saints, and to be admired in all them that believe* (1:9,10). What a wonderful day this will be for them! Yes, He is coming. Remember the promise of the two as Jesus went into heaven. Read Acts 1:11. What a sharp contrast is shown between the glorious destiny of believers when Christ comes and the punishment of the wicked (II Thess. 1:7-12).

Many believe that Christ will not come to set up His kingdom till all the world is converted, but verses 7-12 of this first chapter seem to destroy this view. Read them carefully and you will find that the thing emphasized is that the coming of the Lord will be a terror for the disobedient, and Christ says, *When the Son of man cometh, shall he find faith on the earth?*

The world has never seen our Lord Jesus since it crucified Him. He has been hidden from its view. But one day He will appear to the whole world. In I Thessalonians chapter four, Paul says that at first Christ will descend from heaven and, with the shout of the archangel, the Church will be caught away to be forever with the Lord. At that time He will be seen only by His own. He is coming for His Church. Paul says, *For the Lord Himself shall descend from heaven with a shout, . . . and the dead in Christ shall rise first: then we which are alive and remain shall be caught up together with them in the clouds, to meet the Lord in the air: and so shall we ever be with the Lord* (I Thess. 4:16,17).

Here in II Thessalonians, Paul says He will appear to the world with the angels of His power *in flaming fire, taking vengeance on them that know not God* (1:7,8). First He comes to take His own out of this world. They will be caught up to meet Him in the air (I Thess. 4:17). Then He appears for judgment (Jude 15). *For unto every one that hath shall be given, and he shall have abundance: but from him that hath not shall be taken away even that which he hath. And cast ye the unprofitable servant into outer darkness: there shall be weeping and gnashing of teeth* (Matt. 25:29-30). Christ is coming in the air for His saints, and later He is coming to the earth with His saints to set up His kingdom. *When the Son of man shall come in his glory, and all the holy angels with him, then shall he sit upon the throne of his glory* (Matt. 25:31).

CHRIST'S COMING (Read II Thessalonians 2)
"Instructions for Those in Confusion"

The Thessalonian Christians were suffering great persecution, and some of them had begun to think that they were passing through "the great tribulation" of which Christ spoke as the terrible time which should precede His coming and that the day of the Lord was already present. They were disturbed about the time of the Lord's coming and were entertaining wrong views as to the nearness of His return. The reason for this was that a forged letter and report, both supposed to have come from the apostle Paul, had confused the church and added fuel to the fire (II Thess. 2:2). Jesus had told the disciples, *Take heed that no man lead you astray* (Matt. 24:4, A.S.V.).

The coming again of Christ to the earth is the great future event that the Church has looked forward to since Christ ascended from the Mount of Olives and the two men in white apparel said that this same Jesus would so come in like manner as He went into heaven. (See Acts 1:11.) Because of its greatness it has overshadowed all other events.

One day we traveled up the western highway to Mount Rainier. The morning of the day we arrived the air was clear. The vision was perfect. There was the majestic snow-covered mountain. It seemed so near that it would only be a few minutes until we would be climbing up its side. We ate our breakfast and started off in anticipation. We rode on and there it was, but we hadn't reached it. Every once in a while a low hill and a turn in the road would cut it off from our vision, but though it would reappear in all its glory, we weren't there yet. For three hours we traveled. There it was, the greatest thing on our horizon. Other things fell into insignificance in proportion to its grandeur and importance. Lunch time came and still we had not arrived, but it kept beckoning us on. Finally it was upon us. We were there! This is a picture of Christ's coming again in glory. It has loomed big on the horizon of every Christian's life since the early Church. It is the "blessed hope" of the Church. His coming is "at hand" because it is the greatest future event, but it may not be immediate because God must finish His plan before Christ comes. Do not be anxious. God will take care of His own program of the ages. But know this—the "Man of Sin must be revealed" first, and the "mystery of iniquity" work itself out.

The Man of Sin is the same as the Antichrist spoken of by Daniel the prophet, and by the Lord in Matthew 24:23,24. In Revelation 13:1 John tells about him.

The Antichrist is a counterfeit Christ. Satan in a last desperate effort will try to imitate Christ. The world would not have God's Man; now they must have Satan's man.

BEFORE THE DAY OF THE LORD'S JUDGMENT

The Lord's coming will be "sudden" but sudden does not necessarily mean "immediate." They were to wait anxiously for this time when the Lord will gather His children to Himself. Christ tells us always to be ready. The "day of the Lord" is "at hand" but it will not come until certain things take place. God always follows out a program. Paul warns the people against confusing the hope of Christ's coming for His Church, with the day of the Lord's judgment. Before this "day of the Lord's judgment," the following things must happen:

A great falling away from the faith (II Thess. 2:3)

How true this is, in the day in which we are living! People are leaving *the faith which was once delivered unto the saints* (Jude 3), and *denying the Lord that bought them* with His own precious blood (II Peter 2:1), and crucifying the Lord afresh, and putting Him to shame (Heb. 6:6). The world acknowledges Christ to be a teacher but not the Saviour. *Because iniquity shall abound, the love of many shall wax cold* (Matt. 24:12). These are perilous times. Scoffers will arise and ridicule the idea of Christ's coming.

The "lawless one" must be revealed

He will be revealed before Christ appears to the world. But not until the Lord has caught up His own will the lawless one come into public view (II Thess. 2:8). This "lawless one" is described in 2:4. He will oppose God; he has the title "Antichrist."

The "man of sin" will open his awful campaign against the Lord

When Christ comes, He will find the Antichrist ruling with all power and signs and lying wonders. It will be a time marked with strong delusions. This is Paul's prediction of the Antichrist. "The sin of man has its final outcome in the Man of Sin." Read Matthew 24:24. He will be destroyed by Christ.

The Antichrist—"Christ's Counterfeit"

Will establish himself in Jerusalem........................Matt. 24:15
Will make war with the saints.................................Rev. 13:7
Will be worshiped as God....................................II Thess. 2:4
Will do signs and lying wonders.........................II Thess. 2:9
Will work for only three and a half years............Rev. 13:5,6
Will be cast into the lake of fire at Christ's coming..Rev. 19:20

IS THE WORLD GETTING BETTER?

Does Paul teach that the world is getting better? Is it true that the preaching of the Gospel is going to win the whole world for Christ? If so, has the gospel failed? What is God's plan for this present age?

The gospel has not failed. It is accomplishing just what Christ intended it should accomplish—the gathering out from the world of a people for His Name, the Church. On the other hand, there is this "mystery of lawlessness" working (2:7), a development of anarchy among all classes of society. Don't be disheartened. Paul gives us a picture of the state of the world at the close of this age when Christ shall come again. There will be a great departure from the faith. In fact Christ says when He comes shall He find faith on the earth? This is the picture of the Church preceding Christ's return—a falling away, a great apostasy. Does Christ really mean this? We should judge so from His description of the end days in Matthew 24:1-14, 36-42.

When Christ returns, He will find Antichrist (the man of sin) carrying out his satanic plans. From the description of the Man of Sin in the Scriptures and his diabolical role of mighty works and lying wonders, we do not see how that and the millennial glory could exist together. It is just as God said it would be. Indeed, the darkest clouds that are gathering are but harbingers of the golden day that is surely coming, when our Lord Himself shall return to take up the reins of government.

CHRIST'S COMING (Read II Thessalonians 3)
"Practical Preparation in Service"

The time of this glorious event is to be left with God. The delay in the Lord's coming gives us real opportunities for service. There are two wrong views of the Lord's coming that we might have. Either we become restless and troubled because of having to wait so long, or grow idle because we know that when He comes, He will right every wrong and overthrow iniquity. But both of these attitudes are wrong. We are not just to stand and wait, but rather have "our loins girded" for service, making ready for the glorious day when He shall come. Let us not abandon the work that Christ has given us to do.

Paul gives some instructions to the Thessalonians.

Stand fast—don't be influenced by false teaching.

Hold that which you have been taught—don't lose any of your foundation truth.

Comfort your hearts.

Establish yourselves in every good word and work.

Then Paul asks for their prayers (3:1). His heart was burdened and he needed their fellowship. He had great confidence in their faith.

The hope of Christ's coming stimulates without exciting; sobers without depressing. It is a balancing doctrine. We find in this epistle that our Lord's delay gives us opportunities of

Being loyal to Him 2:15
Evangelizing the world 3:1
Praying for His servants 3:1,2
Patiently waiting for Him 3:5
Living a holy life...3:6-14

Some thought, because Christ was coming, they would just withdraw from business and not work, claiming the right to be supported by the brethren who had money. Paul was very drastic in his dealing with these lazy fellows. The attitude on the part of these men was absolutely wrong, and he asked them to look to him for an example. He never ceased to labor while he was preaching to them. He laid down a great principle of life that *if any would not work, neither should he eat.* Any view of Christianity that makes a man neglect working for his livelihood is not of God. Although Paul always advocated charity toward those in need, and spent much time in taking up offerings for the poor, yet he was very severe in condemning the able-bodied fellow who could but would not work. He forbade the Church to support these folks, and even urged them to withdraw fellowship from them.

Minimum Daily Requirements/Spiritual Vitamins

Sunday: PAUL'S SALUTATIONS   Eph. 1:1,2;
Phil. 1:1-4; Col. 1:1-3; I Thess. 1:1-3;
II Thess. 1:1-4
Monday: CHRIST'S COMING OUR COMFORT
II Thess. 1:5-12
Tuesday: EVENTS PRECEDING CHRIST'S COMING
II Thess. 2:1-12
Wednesday: AN APPEAL TO SOUND DOCTRINE
II Thess. 2:13-17
Thursday: THE CLOSE OF THE AGE   Matt. 24:13-31
Friday: WARNINGS TO THE WICKED CONCERNING
HIS COMING   Matt. 24:30,31; Mark 8:38;
II Thess. 1:7,8; Jude 14,15; Rev. 1:7
Saturday: CONSISTENT CHRISTIAN CONDUCT
II Thess. 3:1-18

CHAPTER 43

UNDERSTANDING I TIMOTHY

*I Timothy
Portrays Jesus Christ,
Our Teacher*

The key verse is 3:15, *that thou mayest know how thou oughtest to behave thyself in the house of God.* Realizing that behavior is based upon belief, Paul stresses sound doctrine.

First and Second Timothy and Titus are the three "pastoral epistles," written to ministers in charge of important churches instead of to the churches themselves. Both Timothy and Titus were given explicit directions for shepherding the sheep, for guarding the churches after Paul should be called "home," as he knew he soon would be (II Tim. 4:7,8). Timothy had been entrusted with the government and supervision of Ephesus, and Titus of the church at Crete. How inadequate both of these young men felt!

Because Timothy was a young man, we may expect to find in the writings of the apostle to him valuable suggestions for other young men who are living the Christian life, and we are not disappointed in this expectation; but we also find helpful suggestions for those who are older in years. It would be interesting for your class to select from the two letters to Timothy the admonitions that are "up-to-date." It would be helpful for those who think the Bible is out of date.

In this day of modern education it is well to offer to young people a commendation of the faith of their fathers, and to warn them against "science falsely so-called." It is well to enjoin them to *fight the good fight of faith . . . holding . . . faith in a pure conscience.* And when athletic contests threaten to consume the major portion of interest and time in scholastic circles, it is good for a young Christian to remind himself that though *bodily exercise profiteth* for a while, *godliness is profitable unto all things,* both here and hereafter. And who can hear Paul's words to his young associate without hearing him say across the years to our own young people, "And whatever it costs, keep yourself pure."

It was a real honor for the young Timothy to enjoy the friendship of the apostle Paul. He was one of Paul's own converts, and Paul calls him his *beloved son, and faithful in the Lord* (I Cor. 4:17). It was during the impressionable days of Timothy's boyhood that Paul visited Lystra, when the people first tried to worship the apostle, then sought to take his life. How Timothy had listened to the gospel preached by Paul! He saw him heal the cripple, heard him as he appealed to the multitude and then saw him stoned and left for dead. But the next day Paul rose and came again into the city. Among the most enthusiastic converts of that city were Eunice and her son Timothy.

When Paul came back to Lystra on his second missionary journey, he took Timothy as his companion. What a wonderful thing for so young a man! After long years of training under this mighty man of God, Timothy was left in charge of the important church at Ephesus. This brought the timid young man face to face with serious problems. Think of this inexperienced young fellow being left in that big church to take the place of a man like its founder, Paul! How unworthy he must have felt! How he leaned on the apostle for advice and direction! It was while Timothy was acting as pastor in Ephesus that Paul wrote his two letters to Timothy, as letters of instruction and guidance indeed to Timothy, but also as a handbook for Christian pastors through the centuries. Paul instructed Timothy to deal severely with false teachers, to direct public worship, choose church officers, and to work with all classes found in the church. But most important of all, he must lead a life which would be an example to all. Timothy had a hard task.

Paul had won a vast multitude to Christ during his stay in Ephesus. In the succeeding years the number of converts increased tremendously. Within the next 50 years so many of the non-Christians turned to Christ that their heathen temples were almost forsaken.

One of the things to remember about this time of the early

Church is that there were no church buildings. Groups of Christians met in homes. No churches were built until about 200 years after Paul's day, and not until Constantine put an end to the persecution of Christians. This meant that there would be hundreds of small congregations, each with its own pastor. These pastors were called "elders" (Acts 20:17). In these letters to Timothy they are called "bishops" (3:1). Timothy's work was with these various pastors. Remember, there were no seminaries to prepare leaders. Paul had to train his own men. But in spite of no buildings and no theological seminaries, and also in spite of continued persecution, the Church grew by leaps and bounds.

WARNING AGAINST FALSE TEACHING
(Read I Timothy 1)

Paul calls Timothy his "son in the faith." It is clear that the boy was led to Christ by Paul. He was an example of one accepting Christ as a child because he had been brought up in a home where the Scriptures had been taught. This is the kind of Christian experience which we need to emphasize today as not only possible, but as that which should be the normal experience.

There has never been a day when the Church has been free from false teachers who present new and strange doctrines. They are hard to combat since they base their teachings on parts of God's Word, and do not "rightly divide" and interpret it as a whole. What the Church needs today is instruction in the vital truths. Over against the teaching of the Law and *fables and endless genealogies,* Paul puts *the glorious gospel of the blessed God.* Therefore Timothy must safeguard against any other doctrine. Don't mix fables and legends with the Gospel!

Paul warns Timothy to hold *faith and a good conscience* because these save men from spiritual shipwreck. It is a thrilling sight to see a ship loosened from her moorings and plunging into the ocean. But it is a solemn sight, too, considering the many storms she is likely to meet. If this is true of a ship, how much more so of a Christian starting out on the voyage of life.

Paul speaks plainly of some who, having put away faith and a good conscience, have caused spiritual shipwreck and are wrecked for two worlds. Let us pay heed to his warnings.

DANGER OF INCONSISTENCY

Even in that First Century Church, Paul was called upon to warn his young co-worker Timothy against the false teaching which is much like the false doctrine of the Twentieth Century. Paul had warned them when he left Ephesus seven years before, that grievous wolves would ravage the flock (Acts 20:29,30). Now they had come in full force and presented young Timothy with his worst problem.

Paul's charge to Timothy included more than soundness in doctrine. He wanted soundness in life. Paul realized that a man can believe the Word of God completely and yet live a life far from its truth. It is sad when one's life and one's belief are poles apart!

In this letter Paul says that the best way of fighting error is with a life that measures up to the standards set down in God's Word. Remember, many of us are the only Bibles others ever read. Christians have to live better than other men in this world if their testimony is to count. We either commend Christ to others by our lives, or we drive them away from Him. How often have we heard, "Well, if that's what Christianity does for a man, I don't want any of it!"

Paul wants Timothy to live a life that will vindicate the truth he preaches. He challenges him to be a good soldier of Jesus Christ. Let us remember that we will not fight very hard for a truth that we do not live. As with Timothy, so with us. "What Timothy will preach will be empowered and made mighty by what Timothy is." Timothy is charged to "fight the good warfare" (1:18). This presents the thought of a campaign and all the responsibilities of the officer in command.

Paul humbly declares: *This is a faithful saying, and worthy of all acceptation, that Christ Jesus came into the world to save sinners; of whom I am chief* (1:15).

Here we catch a glimpse of the man who probably did more for Christ than any other throughout the ages since the world began, bowed to his knees with the feeling of his own unworthi-

556

ness. Although Paul was once a blasphemer, now God in His grace had appointed him an apostle, and although he had persecuted Him, now he could proclaim His love. The closer we get to the heart of Christ, the more we realize our own unworthiness. A singer may feel that he has a very good voice but let him compare himself with a Caruso and he feels as if he could never sing again. The reason many people today do not have a sense of sin is because they are not near to Christ. Just to stand in Christ's presence is enough to make us feel condemned. Paul did not realize how sinful he was until he was brought face to face with his Lord and Saviour. He felt his miraculous conversion was intended to be an example of how God can save and use the chief of sinners. Read 1:2-15.

DIRECTIONS FOR THE CHURCH (Read I Timothy 2; 3)

The Church has a great calling. We are not only called upon to plead with men to turn to God, but to plead with God the cause of men. Read what Paul says: *I exhort therefore, that, first of all, supplications, prayers, intercessions, and giving of thanks, be made for all men: for kings, and for all that are in authority* . . . (2:1,2). Yes, he tells us to pray for rulers. It is well to remember that Nero was the emperor of Rome at this time! It was under this wicked despot that Paul was imprisoned and he knew that soon he was to be beheaded. This proves to us that we must pray for bad rulers as well as good, *that we may lead a quiet and peaceable life in all godliness and honesty* (2:2).

Remember when we pray that God *will have all men to be saved, and to come unto the knowledge of the truth, for there is one God, and one mediator between God and men* (2:4,5). Paul makes it clear that when we pray for one we can go straight to God for him. We need no saint or virgin to approach near to God, only the One who gave Himself a ransom for all. Our blessed Lord Himself stands in God's presence pleading for us.

Do you remember the story of Aeschylus who was condemned by the Athenians and was just about to be executed? His brother Amyntas, the brave warrior who had just gained a victory for Athens, came into the court. Without a word he held up the bleeding stub of the arm which had been severed in the battle. As the judges looked upon the wound, they said, "For the sake of Amyntas, Aeschylus is counted innocent and set free!"

When we look to heaven and remember that God has condemned us because of our sin, we would despair. But we see Jesus standing at the right hand of the throne on high, holding up His nail-printed hands, and presenting His pierced feet and wounded side, pleading for you and me.

Finally, let all who pray be clean in conduct and pure in character (2:8-10). Let us lift up "holy hands" when we pray. That means that we should not fill our lives with worthless pleasures or needless things that absorb, but come to the Lord with a heart that is cleansed (I John 1:9).

CHURCH OFFICERS

When we think of church officers, we immediately think of the "official board." Paul tells us the kind of people that really ought to be on the church board. If the Church shall fulfill her mission of proclaiming the gospel and praying for all, then she must be governed properly and know the real reason for her existence. There are two officers described, who shall direct the Church, bishops and deacons. Paul outlines the requirement for both groups.

After Paul stated the excellence of the office of bishop or pastor, he states the qualifications of the pastor's life. We see he must be a man well balanced. Read I Timothy 3:1-11.

We find as we look this over that the pastor must be a man of blameless character, having only one living wife, not quarrelsome, not greedy for money. He must be a skillful teacher, and one who makes his own children obey. He must not be a new convert, lest his head be turned with pride. He must have a good reputation in his community. It is important that the Church have the right leadership. Good pastors lead a church forward. How we need good and faithful shepherds today!

Deacons must have the same moral qualifications as elders or pastors. This office is not inferior, but different. The two offices were to be complementary to each other. A deacon must be as carefully chosen. Sometimes it may be necessary to appoint women to this office.

Paul shows us the need of Christian conduct. Church manners are a lost art in most places today. It makes a great deal of difference how we behave, for behavior reveals character. It is not "do-havior" but "be-havior" that counts. It is what we are that speaks so loudly that men cannot hear what we say.

THE CHURCH

Paul gives us a beautiful description of the Church and states her purpose. He tells you how you should *behave thyself in the house of God, which is the church of the living God, the pillar and ground of the truth* (3:15). The Church upholds all truth in the sight of men. She is the only earthly institution to which Christ committed the preaching of the gospel.

DIRECTIONS FOR THE PASTOR (Read I Timothy 4-6)

Picture the young pastor Timothy awed by his instructor, the fifty-year-old Apostle Paul, as he says, "Now in these last days some shall depart from the faith, giving themselves up to spiritualism and all of its teachings. They will tell you if you would be holy, you must not marry, neither should you eat certain kinds of food. But let us not put a ban on that which God has given for our good. Turn a deaf ear to foolish 'isms' filled with 'do this' and 'don't do that.' Men are always trying to find what they can 'do' to inherit eternal life."

Lead a godly life. *Godliness is profitable* (4:8). Religion is an appeal to common sense. God says it pays. In one way, Christianity is a business. It asks us to get out our account books, to study the current prices, to consider the possibilities of profit and loss, and decide, *What shall it profit a man, if he shall gain the whole world, and lose his own soul?* Paul, after taking account, found that what he had counted as "gain" was "loss."

Does it pay to invest in the Christian life? Does it pay from the standpoint of life right now? God says it does. Christ says, *Seek ye first the kingdom of God, and his righteousness; and all these things shall be added unto you* (Matthew 6:33).

A noted Puritan once said that God had only one Son, and He made Him a minister.

Paul says to the young minister and to those of you who may be ministers, "Don't think entirely in terms of the physical, how you can please your body." Everyone is thinking in terms of "having fun," of "doing things." The body must be fed, clothed, entertained and pleased! "Bodily exercise is profitable for some things," says Paul, "but godliness is profitable both for this life and the life to come." Start living for eternity!

Be an example in both word and deed, in your love, faith and purity. Carry conviction and command respect. In order to do this, give much attention to your reading and preaching and teaching. The best way to combat any error is by reiterating the simple gospel truth. The Bible itself will do the job, if only you give it a chance. *Give thyself wholly to them* [the Scriptures]. If a man is to succeed in the ministry, he must pour all his strength into it. It demands the whole man, the whole time. Godliness does not starve real living. You will not become a "sissy" if you are good. Godliness is not "goody-ness."

The way a minister treats his flock is of vital importance. He must deal wisely and fairly with each one. The widows must be cared for. Elders must be honored and supported, but they must also be reproved, even in public, if they are found guilty, that others may be warned. In other words, sin can never "get by" in the Church, no matter who is guilty of that sin.

Paul even remembers the Christian slaves. They must be taught. Those who serve unbelieving masters are to let their service be a testimony to these unbelievers. Those who serve Christians should not take advantage because of their spiritual relation. Love should make us serve the better.

Fight the good fight of faith (6:12). Christ makes His appeal to the heroic in a man or woman. The Christian life is not a thing to be entered into lightly. We will not be carried into heaven on flowery beds of ease. We must fight if we would be conquerors. But it is a "good fight."

Minimum Daily Requirements/Spiritual Vitamins

Sunday: PUT UP A GOOD FIGHT   I Timothy 1:1-20
Monday: PRAY FOR ALL MEN   I Timothy 2:1-15
Tuesday: THE OFFICIAL BOARD   I Timothy 3:1-16
Wednesday: THE GOOD MINISTER OF JESUS CHRIST
    I Timothy 4:1-16
Thursday: A MINISTER'S TASK   I Timothy 5:1-25
Friday: BRIEFING THE CHRISTIAN MINISTER
    I Timothy 6:1-21
Saturday: THE WHOLE BOOK   I Timothy 1:1–6:21

CHAPTER 44

UNDERSTANDING II TIMOTHY

II Timothy
Portrays Jesus Christ,
Our Example

Therefore endure hardness, as a good soldier of Jesus Christ (2:3). Be loyal to Christ and His Word!

In I Timothy, Paul enjoins a straight Gospel, in II Timothy, a straight life.

In I Timothy, Paul says, "Guard the doctrine which is our message from God." In II Timothy, Paul says, "Guard the testimony which is our life from God."

I Timothy seems to say, "Shoulder arms! Polish the metal! Ammunition ready!" II Timothy says, "Attention! Onward march! Face front, shoulders square, keep step with our Leader, who is Christ!"

The walk is as necessary as the weapon. The sons of Wilberforce said of their father, "After a while father gave up preparing his discourses and simply prepared himself." Guard the witness diligently.

We are reading a letter of Paul's written from his last imprisonment in Rome, in which he himself says his course is "finished" here on this earth. What ground had he covered? Note every city or province and island in answering this question. To how many thousands had he preached his Christ, do you suppose, in those at least thirty different localities? In how many languages had he testified for Christ? How many of his letters have found a place in the Christian Bible? Are these letters still being read?

PAUL IMPRISONED

After writing his first epistle to Timothy, Paul was arrested again, in Greece or Asia Minor, and hurried back to Rome, this time as a criminal (2:9). While waiting in the Roman dungeon for "the time of his departure," he wrote this last letter to his

563

beloved son in the gospel, Timothy. His arrest had been so sudden and unexpected that he had had no time to collect his valuable books and parchments, or even to take his warm cloak with him (4:13). This second imprisonment was very different from the first. Then he had his own rented house; now he was kept in close confinement. Before, he was the center of a large circle of friends, accessible to all, but now he was alone (4:10-12). Before, he had hoped for freedom; now he was expecting to die (4:6). Paul had already appeared before the wicked Nero, but his case had been postponed (4:16,17). He expected to appear again in the winter and wrote urging Timothy to come immediately and bring Mark with him. He asked him to bring the things that were left (4:9,11,13,21). Being uncertain whether Timothy could get there before his death (and he did not, for his trial probably took place in June rather than the next winter), he wanted to give him his last words of warning and encouragement.

It is well to remember that this is Paul's last writing! His pen was to be dried forever. This epistle is very personal. He mentions twenty-three individuals. Although alone and facing death, yet he forgot himself in thinking of others. The Bishop of Durham said, "I have often found it difficult deliberately to read these short chapters through, without finding something like a mist gathering in my eyes. The writer's heart beats in the writing."

ENDURE IN THE CAMP — THE HOME (Read II Timothy 1)

Parental example is the greatest answer to the problem of juvenile delinquency. We must first guard our testimony in the home, which is the training center of the Christian life. This is the hardest place to begin. So many young people today do not have a strong Christian influence in their homes. The problem of youth today is so often the problem of parents. Parents are never found in church; they never hear the Word preached or taught and the family altar is unheard of. This kind of a home produces spiritual and social illiterates.

Timothy had been reared in a sweet Christian home, with his mother Eunice and his grandmother Lois. Paul mentions these wonderful Christian women and commends Timothy for having had early training at a consecrated hearth (3:15).

Paul remembers Timothy's pure faith that *dwelt first in thy grandmother Lois, and thy mother Eunice; and I am persuaded in thee also* (1:5). Someone said, "When you want to make a great person, start with his grandmother." Whatever may be the value of that observation, one thing is sure—when you want to build a Timothy you must begin in the Primary Department.

Paul calls Timothy his "son in the faith" (1:2). It seems clear that the youth was led to confess Christ by Paul during his first missionary journey. He was a Christian from childhood. It is no surprise that Paul saw in Timothy a lad of promise as a minister in the early Church. He became Paul's "understudy," and at the end of the apostle's life, he was the best man to whom Paul could turn over his work.

Timothy possessed fine qualities, but he had excellent training as well. He was a thoroughly Christian young man. He had a splendid reputation in his own church. He was the constant companion of the great apostle Paul. He knew the Word of God and made use of it in his life and teachings (3:14-16). He demonstrated a splendid spirit of unselfishness in his service. He was given great responsibilities by Paul. All this was instrumental in a large degree in his training (II Tim. 1:3; 3:15; 4:6-12).

Timothy is addressed, "Man of God." What does that mean? Godliness comes from the Word and prayer, God speaking to us and our speaking to God. Manliness includes truth in the mind, love in the heart, and righteousness in the life. Manliness is due to godliness. The grace of God makes a man godly, and then proceeds to make him manly.

No man ever lived a life of such constant abiding in Christ, as Paul. Now that he was about to leave the church which he had established, he is concerned as to its future. He is warning the youthful and timid Timothy that henceforth he must stand alone in comforting and directing the Church. Paul's son in the gospel, now perhaps thirty-five years of age, must emphasize above all things a doctrine that is true and sound, for "grievous wolves" had already begun to play havoc with the Church.

The key verse is II Timothy 1:13. *Hold fast the form of sound words, which thou hast heard of me, in faith and love which is in Christ Jesus.* Paul's life was characterized by an unceasing effort to guard in its purity the priceless treasure of the Christian faith. He wanted it kept untarnished. We live in a day when it is being said that it is deeds not doctrine that count, but Paul's teaching was that conduct must be based on creed. "As a man thinketh . . . so is he." Wrong thinking makes for wrong acting. World War II was brought about by men possessed with wrong creeds. These creeds soon became conduct, and millions died to correct it.

STIR THE GIFT

How easy it is for us not to make use of our gifts and natural endowments. How many lose all initiative. How few people think! Timothy had one of the gifts of the Spirit (I Cor. 12). He seems to have been neglecting to use it. In the first letter (4:14) Paul says, *Neglect not the gift that is in thee,* and in the second letter (1:6), Paul writes, *Stir up the gift of God, which is in thee!* How about our gift? Have we ever let God tell us what it is? Cultivate whatever God has given. Remember everyone has some talent. To be sure, some have five talents, others two and others only one. But stir up the gift you have.

Two men had been discussing the possibility of permanently destroying weeds in the garden, and failed to agree. A third person who had been listening said, "You differ, my friends, concerning the possibility of utterly destroying the weeds in the garden plot. One thinks fire will permanently destroy the weeds, while the other is sure fire will only increase their next growth. But in one thing you will agree with me. We must all agree that no weeds will spring up in that garden so long as the fire is kept burning." Young people, stir up the fire in your heart. It is easy to let it die down. This will keep down the weeds in your life. Keep your love constantly burning for Christ by serving Him.

We find in this first chapter one of the apostle's "I know's." It is a verse which gives us great assurance. *I know whom I have believed, and am persuaded that he is able to keep that which I have committed unto him against that day* (1:12).

What is your persuasion? Will your answer come swift and strong as Paul's, *I am persuaded that He is able to keep that which I have committed unto him against that day?* Make it very personal. Don't say, "I know IN whom," as the verse is so often quoted, but "I know WHOM I have believed."

I know One who is able to keep. Put your life in His hands. He will hold you fast. The Psalmist said, *Commit thy way unto the LORD; trust also in him; and he shall bring it to pass* (Ps. 37:5). II Timothy 1:12 is the sequel.

ENDURE IN THE FIELD — AWAY FROM HOME
(Read II Timothy 2)

We must *endure hardness, as a good soldier* away from home, in the school, in the office, in the place of business. This is our field of service and discipline. Here we are to stand the test as one who "needeth not to be ashamed."

Paul says as a faithful steward entrust the truths you have learned from him to reliable men who in turn will teach others. As a brave soldier, endure hardships. A soldier does not become entangled with ordinary affairs, but is under the authority of his superior officer. He leaves his business and friends to serve in the army. Let that be our attitude. The athlete, too, must observe this if he will gain the wreath of victory. As the farmer is the first to enjoy the fruit of his harvest, so will it be with you. Avoid business entanglements that will keep you from rendering the best service. Watch, too, lest the comforts of life and the common enjoyments make us to love ease too well.

Endure your hardships manfully and with the spirit of a hero. Don't just endure!

For one who was a good man, Paul was enduring the cruelest of suffering. He was charged as a criminal, and was being put in chains. But he was glad to suffer anything, just so the gospel would not be chained. He reminds Timothy that he is worshiping a living Christ. *Remember that Jesus Christ . . . was raised from the dead, according to my gospel,* he said. Even though his body was bound, his mind was on "eternal glory."

Paul urged the people to keep away from foolish discussion, for these only breed quarrels and a Christian should not quarrel (2:24). Do not argue about the Christian life. Live it! Outlive the world—live better than they do—and they will soon listen to what you have to say. The best argument for Christ is a victorious life.

God gives us a "sure foundation" upon which to build our lives—the foundation laid of God (2:19). "It standeth sure," for that Rock is Christ. All who build on it are sealed for Him. This is the inscription: *The Lord knoweth them that are his*. It is wonderful to know that we are known personally by Him. This is not true of any other religion under heaven. In Christianity we are God's children and He knows every one of us. *The very hairs of your head are all numbered* (Matthew 10:30). He calls us by name.

God's work needs real gentility. It was said of the Messiah, *Thy gentleness hath made me great* (Ps. 18:35). Gentleness and conviction in the ministry will break down hatred for the Church, and give the Church its rightful place. Study to be gentle. Don't send people away by your cruel criticism but draw them to Christ by love.

ENDURE IN THE FIGHT — WHEN THE SHARP BATTLE IS ON (Read II Timothy 3)

When the battle is on, and our faith is assailed, stand firm and strong. Fight effectively with a life which is lived *godly in Christ Jesus*. During every engagement let us wield the Word which is the sword of the Spirit. Let us be soldiers *throughly furnished unto all good works*.

There is but one way to be strengthened against all of these vices today. We find it in verses 14 through 17. The Scriptures will make us wise unto salvation (3:15). Jesus met His temptations by the Word of God. We can do no better.

Have you ever heard anyone say, "I was a drunkard, a disgrace to my family, a nuisance to the world, until I began to study mathematics and learned the multiplication table, but since then I have been happy as the day is long. I feel like singing all the time, for my heart is at peace!" Have you ever heard a person ascribing his salvation from drunkenness and sin to the multiplication table or to science? Of course you haven't. But thousands have said, "I was unhappy and heartbroken. I had no reason for living until I heard God speak to me through His Word, and now I know the living Saviour."

The Word of God is the only thing that will keep the Church in this terrible day. The Church of Rome put aside the Word and the Dark Ages was the result. The Protestants brought it back into circulation, but Christians everywhere are neglecting it. The ignorance of the Word today is appalling.

CATALOGUE OF TWENTIETH CENTURY VICES
(II Timothy 3:1-5)

Lovers of themselves more than lovers of God.

Covetous—men will do anything to gain possession of what they want.

Proud and boastful—pride fills the natural heart.

Blasphemers—taking God's name in vain.

Disobedient to parents—there seems to be no respect today in the home.

Unthankful—no gratitude, taking everything for granted.

Unholy—men care for neither God nor man.

Without natural affection—mothers taking the lives of their own children; divorce courts full.

Truce-breakers—promises mean nothing.

Lovers of pleasure—this age has gone pleasure-mad.

Having a form of godliness but no power—there is only one source of power and that is in the Gospel of Christ Jesus.

ENDURE TO THE DEATH — WHEN LIFE IS ENDING
(Read II Timothy 4)

To endure to the end and look back over a hard and bitter fight and say, "I have won!"—that is enduring as a good soldier. Life's last hours for Paul were full of glory. He forgot that the lions in the arena or the flames at the stake or a cruel cross might end his earthly life at any moment. His good fight was ended, his long hard race was run, and now only the memories of a noble life gave him great peace.

He closes this letter with a solemn farewell charge to Timothy, before God and Christ, who will judge him and who soon will appear to spread the gospel everywhere. *Preach the word; be instant in season,* for a time is coming when men will not listen to sound teaching.

PAUL'S VALEDICTORY

This is the grandest utterance of the grandest mortal who ever lived. Where can we match Paul's words which he wrote from his dungeon to Timothy, his own true son in the faith? Let us picture the old battle-scarred hero of the cross, standing in the gloomy dungeon, bound with chains, and looking up through the one opening in the roof of his cell through which only a tiny shaft of light could enter, but which reveals his countenance with the expression of perfect peace. His lips are moving, and we hear him say, *I have fought a good fight, I have finished my course, I have kept the faith; henceforth there is laid up for me a crown of righteousness, which the Lord, the righteous judge, shall give me at that day: and not to me only, but unto all them also that love his appearing* (II Tim. 4:7,8).

Ever since Jesus had laid His hand upon him, Paul seemed to have been contending in the arena and running in the stadium. There had been scarcely a moment of rest. It was an intense training, and a strenuous wrestling all the way through. But within, peace reigned. His questions were answered; his sins were forgiven. His wants were supplied. Peace within, but the athlete's contest without. This is the true Christian life.

COMING WITH CROWNS

The crown is for Paul, but it is also for us—*for all them that love his appearing.* You and I, whose achievements are so much less than Paul's, may yet be partakers of Paul's heaven.

Surely the "crown" which gleams before us should spur us on to a new diligence in service. Do we love His appearing?

The last verses of this letter give us a glimpse of the loneliness of this great wrestler and runner. Many were leaving him, under the stress of persecution. But *the Lord stood with me, and strengthened me; that by me the preaching might be fully*

570

known. This is the secret of Paul's success. This is why he could fight a good fight and finish the course. His greatest opportunity seemed to be reserved for the end. He stood in Nero's courthouse, face to face with the "lion," as he designated him (4:17). He was alone, as far as human help was concerned. The great basilica was crowded, and every eye was fastened on the forsaken old man at the bar. Did he quail? Was he afraid? No, indeed! He leaped to the height of the momentous occasion. He was not content in defending himself. That he did, but much more. To the multitude, curious and hostile, he told out clearly the Gospel of Christ, and all the Gentiles heard.

Minimum Daily Requirements/Spiritual Vitamins

Sunday: STIR UP THY GIFT   II Timothy 1:1-9
Monday: HOLD FAST TO THE TRUTH
II Timothy 1:10-18
Tuesday: ENDURE HARDNESS AS A SOLDIER
II Timothy 2:1-15
Wednesday: FOLLOW RIGHTEOUSNESS
II Timothy 2:16-26
Thursday: KNOW THE SCRIPTURES
II Timothy 3:1-17
Friday: BE FAITHFUL TO THE END
II Timothy 4:1-22
Saturday: RECEIVE A CROWN   I Cor. 9:25;
II Tim. 4:8; James 1:12; I Peter 5:4;
Rev. 2:10; 3:11

UNDERSTANDING TITUS and PHILEMON

Titus and Philemon
Portray Jesus Christ,
Our Pattern;
Our Lord and Master

The importance of good works is stressed in this epistle. Not that we are saved by good works, but we are saved unto good works. God presents His ideal for the Church and its officers and members.

The epistle to Titus was written by Paul. Titus was Bishop of Crete, a hard post (1:12,13). Paul had given Titus the difficult task before of settling the differences at Corinth, and tactfully persuading the Church to do the right thing in the matter of divisions. Paul's second letter to the Corinthians shows how successful Titus was in this mission. Titus was a Gentile. No doubt he was one of Paul's converts during the early years of the apostle's ministry. He accompanied Paul and Barnabas to Jerusalem seventeen years after Paul's conversion.

When Paul heard that Apollos was about to go to Crete, he took the opportunity to send a letter to Titus. It is full of practical advice to the young pastor and directed him in his administration, and warned him against the heretics of his day. He asks Titus to come to him and to report on the condition of the church in the island. Although this is a personal letter, it undoubtedly was to be read to the church also.

The letter is very much like Paul's first letter to Timothy, being written about the same time, and dealing with the same subjects.

WORKS FOR CHURCH OFFICERS (Read Titus 1)

Paul presents himself in this scene as the "bond servant" of the Lord Jesus Christ, then as His apostle. Paul loves to call himself a bondslave of Christ. Another time he says of Christ, *whose I am and whom I serve.* It is terrible to be a slave to most anyone or anything but to be a slave of Jesus Christ—to be bought by Him, that is wonderful! It is a slavery of love.

"In grace," Spurgeon once said, "you can be under bonds yet not in bondage. I am in bonds of wedlock but I feel no bondage. On the contrary it is joy to be so bound."

Paul kept his eyes steadfastly on heaven as he neared the end of his earthly life. Read what he says of his apostleship, *according to the faith of God's elect, . . . in hope of eternal life.*

STARTING A CHURCH

Paul left Titus in Crete to superintend the work of the church organization there. It was a hard situation, but Paul had given him a difficult task before at Corinth and he had worked out the problem. In Crete he was to set things in order and ordain elders in every city (1:5).

What kind of officers the Church should have was well described. These qualifications are stated carefully. Only men of character should even be considered. He must be blameless in his home life (1:6), blameless in his personal life (1:7,8) and true to the Word (1:9).

How do you act at home? What kind of a Christian are you there? This is so often the test of your Christianity. It is the home life that counts. The Christian household is the main evangelizing agency everywhere. When the home is Christian, the community is Christian. For this reason, the bishop and pastor are enjoined to set a good example before the people. He must have but one living wife, but he is not compelled to be married as is demanded of the priests of the Greek Church. On the other hand, he is not to refrain from marriage, as the Roman Catholic Church decrees. Because a minister is judged by his family life, he must rule his own children well, for he who cannot rule his own household well cannot rule the church of God (I Tim. 3:5). He must be a man of moral courage and sympathy. He must be a good teacher, and encourage others in his teaching.

The Cretan churches were being upset by outside teachers who, for the sake of making money, were working havoc in "whole houses" (1:11). This probably meant whole congre-

574

gations, for the early Church met in private homes. Paul calls these fellows "abominable" and "disobedient" (1:16) and said they must be stopped in their teaching. He demands severity in dealing with them. How much false teaching there is today everywhere! There are more cults and sects which men and women are starting, by which they make themselves rich.

A Sure Foundation

During the California earthquake an old saint in San Francisco remained in her room, joyously rocking back and forth in her chair, singing while all around her people were running in dread of death. After all was over someone asked her how she could have had such a feeling of joy. "Oh," replied the old saint, "I was so happy in the thought that my God was mighty enough to rock the world like that, while He held me securely in His hand. I did not have time to be frightened."

So in this day in which we are living, when all is being shaken in confusion about us, and there are *many unruly and vain talkers and deceivers, . . . who subvert whole houses, teaching things which they ought not, for filthy lucre's sake* (1:10,11), who *profess that they know God; but in works they deny him* (1:16), so let us, I say, rest our faith not on the reasonings and opinions of men, but on the infallible Word of God. By this Word alone judge new and strange doctrines, and stop the mouths of those who handle the Word of God deceitfully (1:9-11).

WORKS FOR CHURCH MEMBERS (Read Titus 2; 3)

Paul believed that doctrine must be expressed in life, and so he had a word to Titus about the aged (2:2,3), the youth (2:4-6) and the slaves (2:9,10).

The Aged:

Men . . . be temperate, serious, discreet; be sound in faith, love and patience.

Women . . . be in conduct as becomes a consecrated person (2:3); be reverent, avoid drink and scandal, teach good things, become good wives and mothers.

Youth:

Exercise self-control, be examples of a noble life.

Servants:

Obey masters, be diligent and faithful, give satisfaction; don't contradict, don't steal.

LIFE WITH A CAPITAL "L"

Leave the old life.

Live the new life.

Look for that blessed hope and glorious appearing of Christ. (2:11-13)

How essential that this be our foundation! Then can we *adorn the doctrine of God our Saviour in all things* (2:10). To think that we in any way can adorn the wonderful gospel by our lives! As we put a frame on a beautiful picture, to enhance its beauty and make it more conspicuous, so we must adorn and make more beautiful the gospel of Christ. A king in his royal robes is more easily recognized as such, than one in ordinary clothing. How we can either make or mar the gospel! What is the "gospel according to you"? In all things show thyself a pattern of good works (2:7). The test of fellowship is not warmth of devotion, but holiness of life. One cannot live on strong "feelings." Some mistake religious feeling for holiness and good thoughts for good conduct. There is use and abuse in religious emotion.

Be so faithful in your attitudes and obligations of life that critics of your religion will be silenced (2:8). Make others say, "If this is what Christ can do for you, there must be something to your religion."

Not that we are saved by good works, but we are saved unto good works. Paul says we are saved by His mercy (3:5), and justified by His grace (3:7). But because we have been saved at such a cost, we should show it by "good works."

"God our Saviour" did not save us as a result of our good works, but through His kindness and according to His mercy. He cleansed us by His blood and gave us a new life by His Holy Spirit.

Good Works

A pattern of good works 2:7
Zealous of good works..2:14
Ready to every good work...3:1

576

Careful to maintain good works...3:8
Maintain good works for necessary uses............................3:14

Paul urges citizens of the heavenly kingdom to be good citizens of the country under whose flag they live. Every Christian should be submissive to rulers and authority (3:1,2; Rom. 13:1-7; I Peter 2:13-17).

Don't say anything of a person if you can't say something good, is a wonderful admonition to follow. Paul said it long ago. *Speak evil of no man*. Don't be quarrelsome. Show a gentle spirit in your dealing with others. It is well for us to remember that *we ourselves also were sometimes foolish*. Yes, we had all the faults we hate in others. It is well to remember that the things we criticize in others are very apt to be our own weaknesses. We like to call attention to these faults in others to take eyes off of ourselves. Try this test on yourself.

Avoid controversies and foolish discussions. They are always useless and futile. So often an argument only strengthens a person in what he believed before. Do all you can to correct a person, but if he persists in causing divisions among you, after warning him once or twice, have nothing more to say to him. Reject him (3:10). Devote your time in doing good.

UNDERSTANDING PHILEMON

Christian love and forgiveness are given prominence in this book. It shows the power of the gospel in winning a runaway thief and slave, and in changing a master's mind. This is a book in "applied Christianity," a text book of social service.

The Rev. Sir W. Robertson Nicoll once said: "If I were to covet any honor of authorship, it would be this: That some letters of mine might be found in the desks of my friends when their life struggle is ended."

We don't know whether Paul coveted this honor or not, but tucked away in your New Testament, between Titus and Hebrews, you will find a model letter written by a master of letter writing. It is a personal letter from Paul to Philemon. Only one chapter, of twenty-five verses, but containing such strong and beautiful statements and so well expressed, that it stands out as a gem, even in the Book of books.

Notice the courtesy and tactfulness of Paul's letter. Our letter writing can be a ministry for God, if we make it so. Some who find it hard to speak to anyone about Christ can write about Him. Then, too, a letter is good for the one who receives it, for he has a chance to read and re-read and think it over. Use the pen in witnessing to your friends. Remember all that has been preserved to us of Paul's ministry has come mainly through his epistles. What a heritage his letters are for all Christians today! In order to appreciate what God thought of correspondence, see how many letters He kept for us in Holy Scripture.

In this letter Paul intercedes with Philemon (who was an outstanding member of the church at Colosse), for a runaway slave by the name of Onesimus, who had stolen from his master and made his way to Rome. There he had been providentially brought face to face with Paul, and had found Christ as his Saviour. He became endeared to the apostle by his devoted service. But Paul knew he was Philemon's lawful slave and so he could not think of keeping him permanently. So Paul sends him home and pleads with Philemon to take him back. He makes himself personally responsible for the debts that Onesimus owes, asking that they be charged to his (Paul's) account. He wished to save the runaway slave from the severe and cruel punishment he deserved according to Roman law. Paul feels that the slave must not encounter his outraged master alone.

This letter deals with the question of slavery. Paul does not demand the abolition of slavery, but he shows that slavery can never be the fruit of Christianity. This beautiful letter from God's aged servant, in bonds for the gospel, foreshadows the time when the bonds of Christ's love should break the bands of slavery.

Onesimus was merely one of a world of slaves belonging to a handful of masters. In 300 B.C., 21,000 citizens of Athens owned 400,000 slaves. It was not so different proportionately in the days of the Roman Empire, at the time of the writing of this epistle. Roman masters owned from ten to two hundred, even a thousand or more slaves, who had no rights of life or liberty!

PAUL'S PLEA FOR ONESIMUS (Read Philemon 1–25)

Here is a letter from Paul, the aged (v. 9). It is not always the passing of years that brings old age. The apostle had become prematurely old through work, anxiety and eagerness of spirit. He was only about sixty, but he was a prisoner, and as such he appealed to his friend, Philemon.

Paul speaks of himself as a prisoner, not, as in the letter to the Colossians, with the authority of an apostle. He writes as a friend to a friend. He says, *Our dearly beloved and our fellow-laborer*. He does not say these kind things just to flatter his friends, but because he always looked for the good in others.

This letter is addressed to a man and his wife and presumably a son, in Colosse. A little meeting of Christians was held at their home. Paul gives us a beautiful picture of a Christian home in the time of the early Church. This family was the nucleus of that home-church and doubtless other believers in Colosse gathered there for worship. One of the causes for the spiritual decline today is the lack of *the church in thy house*. Is there one in your house? It begins around the family altar.

Paul always begins his letters with commendations unless there is a reason for not doing it, as in Galatians. He speaks of love and faith, and tells of the joy he finds in fellowship. Even though he was separated by a great distance from his friend Philemon, nevertheless this man's loving helpfulness to others had done Paul good in that far-off prison in Rome. He prays that Philemon's faith may ever grow.

Paul was a wonderful student of human nature. The picture he portrays of himself as the bent and battered *prisoner of Jesus Christ* (v. 9), opens a well of sympathy in the heart of Philemon as he reads his friend's letter. Onesimus, whose name means "profitable," had robbed his master and run away to the big city of Rome. In some way he fell in with the little band of Christians surrounding Paul and was converted. Paul sends the boy back to his master, with this friendly, personal note. He takes pleasure in playing with the fellow's name. The "unprofitable" servant now will be "profitable." Christ makes a man profitable to others.

579

In approaching the main purpose of the letter, Paul does not blurt it out at once. He anticipates anger, and so he uses the finest tact. He admits that Onesimus had been good for nothing in the past, but playfully alludes to his name, hoping to put the reader into a favorable mood.

While Philemon's voice trembles, Mother Apphia is wiping her eyes on her apron, and son Archippus is clearing his throat. All three read on into the letter. Paul has his little joke and pun, and the faces of the trio break into smiles. Onesimus, meanwhile, nervously fumbles with his cap in back of the door, then breaks into a broad grin, and the tension is over.

Paul's action with regard to Onesimus is an illustration of the Lord's work on behalf of the sinner. Paul does not minimize the sin, but he pleads for forgiveness for the sinner on the ground of his own merit in the eyes of Philemon, his friend. More than that, he makes himself personally responsible for the debts of Onesimus. *Put that to mine account.* This is the message of the gospel. For Christ bore our sins in His own body on the tree. This is what Christ does—takes the sinner's place.

SOCIAL MANAGEMENT

The secret of the solution of the capital-labor problem lies in the love of Christ, such as undoubtedly existed between Philemon and Onesimus after the slave returned home.

This epistle gives a clear idea of the attitude of Christianity to the social organization of the world. The subject of the epistle is slavery, which was widespread in that day. If slavery is wrong, why did not Paul say so, instead of apparently condoning it in this letter to the owner of the runaway slave? If Paul had made slavery an issue, he would have torn society to shreds. Instead he presents principles which would surely undermine slavery and in time actually did so. Brotherhood in Christ is more than emancipation. Christianity does not merely free the slaves, but teaches them that they and their masters are one in Christ.

Has Christianity yet driven slavery from the world? Here began the abolition of slavery. This terrible menace has been vanquished wherever brotherly love of Christ has been shed abroad. But there are still portions of the world in which slavery is practiced. Sometimes it is disguised by other names, but wherever human life is sold, wherever forced labor is carried on, it exists. It takes changes in people's thinking to destroy slavery. Christ came to change men; He frees us from sin's slavery and sends us forth to abolish slavery of every kind.

If Timothy or Tychicus took Paul's dictation of this letter, Paul took the stylus or quill and wrote in his big, near-sighted scrawl: *I, Paul, write it with my own hand, I promise to repay it [in full]—and that is to say nothing [of the fact] that you owe me your very self* (Amp. N.T.)!

Minimum Daily Requirements/Spiritual Vitamins

Sunday: CHURCH OFFICERS   Titus 1:1-9
Monday: CHURCH ENEMIES   Titus 1:10-16
Tuesday: CHURCH INFLUENCE   Titus 2:1-8
Wednesday: CHURCH RULE   Titus 2:9-15
Thursday: CHURCH WORKS   Titus 3:1-15
Friday: A CHRISTIAN GENTLEMAN   Philemon 1–7
Saturday: A PRISONER'S PLEA   Philemon 8–25

UNDERSTANDING HEBREWS

*Hebrews
Portrays Jesus Christ,
Our Intercessor
at the Throne*

We as Christians have that which is better—better in every way. The key word to the book of Hebrews is "better." It occurs thirteen times.

There are words in this book that help us in understanding it. Trace the words "eternal," "perfect," "once," "blood" (mark this in red), "without," "better," and the expression "we have . . . therefore let us," "sat down," and "heavenly."

The author of this epistle is unknown. Many have speculated but there is no certainty. Hebrews is attributed to Paul, and although many question his authorship, there is abundance of evidence in his favor.

This book has been called the "Fifth Gospel." The four describe Christ's ministry on earth; this one describes His ministry in heaven at God's right hand.

The glories of our Saviour are exhibited in this epistle. Our eye is fixed upon Jesus, the *author and finisher of our faith* (12:2). He is set before us *crowned with glory and honor* in the heavens (2:9).

This book was written, first of all, to Jewish Christians, probably of Jerusalem, who were wavering in their faith. Because of the taunts and jeers of their persecutors, the Jewish Christians were beginning to think they had lost everything, altar, priests, sacrifices, by accepting Christianity. The apostle proves that they had only lost the shadow to be given the substance (Jesus Christ). They were undervaluing their privileges in Christ, and were engaged in self-pity and discouragement. They were in danger of even giving up their faith (5:11,12). They had started well (6:10), but had not made progress (6:11). The Christian life is like riding a bicycle—if you do not go on, you go off. The writer is trying to lead them from an elementary knowledge to a mature grasp. He exhorts them to be loyal to Christianity. He shows them the superiority of Christianity over Judaism. The writer wanted to keep them from drifting back into their Jewish rites and ceremonies. They were urged to let go of everything else, in order to hold fast the faith and hope of the gospel.

The book is also a timely warning and a word of comfort to all, especially in this day when many have so little instruction in the things of Christ, and are inclined to be led astray by so many fads and cults.

Hebrews shows skill in dealing with the discouraged Jewish Christians. The writer tells all that we have in Christ.

How often when you take a trip for the first time over a new road, you drive straight along anticipating where it will lead, and what difficulties you may encounter. It seems to be the thing to do. Coming back over the same road, you look around and notice things. Do this in studying the Book of Hebrews. Read it through, and do not be over-anxious about the things you cannot understand. Then you can go back over the road in your reading, and take notice of the many things along the way. You could spend months in Hebrews. It presents so many wonderful truths. At the first reading you will be impressed by one fact above all others: that Jesus Christ is prominent on every page. This is not true in all the other books of the New Testament. In Acts, the apostles, disciples, the Jews and pagans are predominant. In Romans, a great doctrine attracts our attention. In the other letters the Church and its problems are considered, but here it is our Lord Himself.

Jesus Christ

Greater than prophets 1:1-3
Greater than angels..1:4—2:18
Greater than Moses 3:1-19
Greater than Joshua 4:1-16
Greater than Aaron..5:1—10:18

The reason the writer uses these comparisons stated above is because each of these held a place of great importance in the religion of the Jews. They were the framework of their worship, and it must be proved that something or some One "better" had come to take their place, if their followers are to transfer allegiance.

This book was written to strengthen the faith of wavering Christians. Paul's great argument is the superiority of Christ over all others.

Do we know the real difference between having Christ as a Saviour and as a Priest? Well, this book answers the question.

The Book of Hebrews proves that we can never understand the Old Testament without the New, nor the New without the Old.

THE SUPERIORITY OF THE PERSON OF CHRIST
(Read Hebrews 1:1–4:13)

Nowhere is our Lord's deity and humanity so emphasized as in Hebrews 1 and 2. As our great High Priest, Christ is able to understand all our need, because He is perfect Man. He is *touched with the feeling of our infirmities.* He is able to meet all our need, because He is perfect God. He is able.

The opening sentence of the Book of Hebrews (1:1-4) is one of the grandest in the Bible. It ranks with the opening words of Genesis, and of John. We find Jesus there, His deity, His glory, a Creator, Heir of all things, superior to all things, and Saviour.

Write down all that you find about Christ in Hebrews 1 and 2. If you knew nothing more about Him than you found in these two chapters, you would know much.

Two great truths are taken for granted—the existence of God, and that He reveals Himself to men. He revealed Himself before, *in time past . . . by the prophets; . . . in these last days . . . by his Son.* The Bible records a series of stories of how God speaks to man and reveals His will and His plan to them. How marvelous to hear His only begotten Son speak!

Remember, this letter is written to correct the erroneous idea that the Christian Jews had lost some things because they had taken up Christianity. The letter is written to remove this misconception. Christianity is not "giving up" but "receiving," receiving the greatest gifts of life, in fact Life itself, for Christ is Life.

ARGUMENT FOR CHRISTIANITY
Superiority of the Person of Christ

The Lord Jesus Christ is greater than any human leader (prophets). (1:1-3)
> He is God's Son.
> He is Heir of all things.
> He created the world.
> He is Himself very God.
> He upholds all things.
> He cleansed us from sin.
> He is set down at the right hand of God.

The Lord Jesus Christ is greater than angels. (1:4—2:18)
> He has a more excellent name of Son. (1:4,5)
> Angels worship Him. (1:6)
> He is the eternal God. (1:7-12)
> His throne is forever. (1:8)
> He is the ruler of the coming age. (1:11-13)

The Lord Jesus Christ is greater than Moses. (3:1-19)
> Moses was a faithful servant.
> Christ is the Son over His own house.

The Lord Jesus Christ is greater than Joshua. (4:1-16)
> Joshua was a great leader. He led the Hebrews into the promised land, but he did not lead the people into rest. What he failed to do, the Son accomplished. Jesus is greater, for He alone gives real rest.

It is well to notice that angels and human spirits (of those who die) are not the same. Human life is a different order of creation than angels. We do not become angels when we die. Angels are a separate creation of God. They are now and always will be, in heaven, our servants (1:14). Angels worship Christ just as we do.

When God wanted to save man from his sin, He did not send an angel, but His Son. God came not in the form of an angel but in the form of a man. He became Man to redeem man. He suffered as a man and died as a man that He might be our

586

Redeemer (2:10). Jesus tasted the bitterness of death for us, in order that He might render the devil powerless, who has the power of death. He came up from the grave with the keys of hell and of death; no longer can the devil lock any of us in death.

CONSIDER JESUS

This is our weakness. We look at ourselves and our own weakness. Consider Him (3:1). This is the astronomer's word. Set your telescope to the heavens and gaze upon Him.

Many Christian Jews were confused about Christ's ministry on earth. They thought that He came to enforce the laws that Moses had given. Moses was the law-giver, and Christ must enforce them. This was their interpretation. But Christ is His own Law-giver. The old Mosaic system was imperfect and weak (7:11,18). It had served its purpose. Now Christ has a "better way." Christ is over Moses. Moses was only a servant; Christ is a Son, the Master, in His own house. He is the Heir (3:6).

Canaan, the land that flowed with milk and honey, was the Promised Land into which Joshua led the children of Israel. But this is only a picture of the rest of faith in God Himself, that every Christian should enjoy. St. Augustine said that no soul found rest until it found its rest in God. Joshua could not lead the children of Israel into this perfect rest and trust in God, but Jesus did. Cease from self-effort and yield yourself to Christ (4:10). Trust Jesus as your Joshua and "enter in" to His land of promise. Cease struggling and place all in His hand. (Read Psalm 37:5.)

Two Great Warnings

Warning 1. Give heed not to neglect so great salvation as is offered to us, not by angels but by the Lord Himself. Take heed to what the Son speaks (2:1-4).

Warning 2. Take heed not to depart from the living God (3:12).

Hebrews 4:12 shows the power of God's Word. Let the Word search and try you! Let God's Word have its proper place in your life. It searches out every motive and desire and purpose of your life, and helps you in evaluating them. Christ is the living Word of God. He is alive (quick) and powerful and all-wise and all-knowing.

THE SUPERIORITY OF THE PRIESTHOOD OF CHRIST
(Read Hebrews 4:14–10:18)

Here begins the main theme. *Now the main point of what we have to say is this: We have such a High Priest* (Amp. N.T.). Christ has been compared with all others, the prophets, angels, Moses and Joshua, but the most important comparison is with Aaron, the high priest. The writer shows that the priesthood of Christ is greater than the priesthood of the Levitical law.

The central point in the book is Christ's eternal priesthood and His sacrifice which availed for the sin of the world. The epistle dwells upon the supreme importance and power of the blood of Christ in obtaining redemption for us. He has purged us from our sins, and opened the way into the heavenly sanctuary and to the very throne of God.

Christ is Himself a priest. Listen to the Word: *Seeing then that we have a great high priest, that is passed into the heavens, Jesus the Son of God, let us hold fast our profession. For we have not an high priest which cannot be touched with the feeling of our infirmities; but was in all points tempted like as we are, yet without sin. Let us therefore come boldly unto the throne of grace, that we may obtain mercy, and find grace to help in time of need* (4:14-16).

Jesus Christ not only had the qualifications of a priest like Aaron, the earthly high priest, but He is a High Priest forever after the order of the eternal Melchizedek priesthood, because this priesthood is continuous and will never end. The Aaronic priests could not make men perfect, because they themselves were sinful, but Christ is eternal and sinless.

CHRIST'S PRIESTHOOD
like Melchizedek's—Genesis 14

A Royal Priesthood—
Both were kings of peace and righteousness.

Was Universal—
Not alone for the Jews.

Had No Human Ancestry—
"Without father or mother."

Had No Successor—
When Melchizedek passed away no one stepped into his place. So Christ is a priest forever.

Let us find an important fact here. Christian ministers are nowhere called "priests" in the New Testament, except as all Christians are called "priests" (I Pet. 2:9). We have learned from Paul's letters that Christian ministers are called teachers and pastors.

The glories of our Saviour are exhibited in this epistle. There are three great "betters" connected with our High Priest.

CHRIST IS A PRIEST

Of a Better Covenant. (8:13)
A better covenant because it is based on better promises. These promises are written on the heart, not on tables of stone (8:10).

Of a Better Tabernacle. (9:1-12)
Christ officiates in heaven. The tabernacle was of this world. The high priest entered into the holy of holies once a year, but Christ has entered into the heavenly sanctuary "once and for all."

Of a Better Sacrifice. (10:18)
He Himself is the sacrifice. He offered Himself as a lamb without blemish, to cleanse us. The sacrifices of the Old Testament were calves and goats. They could not take away sin. They were but the shadow. This Sacrifice needed to be offered only once.

Christ is called our High Priest. What does that mean? We are taught very plainly in the Word that sin has cut men off from God. No sinner can approach God. The way has been closed. In the Old Testament a representative, the high priest, whom God appointed, could come into God's presence only once a year, after sacrifice for the sins of the people had been made. He must offer the blood of calves and goats not only for the sins of the people, but for his own sins, for he too was a sinner. He then would go into the holy place, then on beyond the veil into the holy of holies where the Ark of the Covenant rested. Here was the mercy seat, and here God met man through the mediator, the high priest.

How can we approach God today? Christ has made that possible. He is our High Priest, our Representative before the Father. He entered into the heavenly sanctuary, God's presence, bearing the blood of His own sacrifice to cleanse us from our sins and to give to us eternal salvation. His blood had to be shed, for *without shedding of blood is no remission* (9:22). *But this man, after he had offered one sacrifice for sins forever, sat down on the right hand of God* (10:12). *It is finished,* He said on the cross. All His work of redemption had been completed, hence we see Him sitting. We find this picture of Christ often in Hebrews.

Our High Priest is at the right hand of the Father at this minute, making intercession for you and for me (7:25; 8:1; 10:12). He has gone *to appear in the presence of God for us* (9:24). This is why we can have boldness to enter into the holiest by the blood of Jesus, by a new and living way (10:19,20). Avail yourself of this glorious privilege.

CHRIST'S GREAT APPEARINGS

In Hebrews 9, our Lord's three great appearings stand out:

Past—

On the cross—*Once in the end of the world hath he appeared to put away sin by the sacrifice of himself* (9:26).

Present—

At the right hand of the throne—*Now to appear in the presence of God for us* (9:24).

Future—

In the clouds of glory—*Unto them that look for him shall he appear the second time without sin unto salvation* (9:28).

CHRIST — A BETTER SACRIFICE

Christ offered Himself as the sacrifice, a Lamb, without blemish or spot. The priest offered the lives of calves and goats, but they could not take away sin. This better Sacrifice had only to be offered once and for all (10:10-18).

Since Christ has made this new and living way into the presence of the Father, let us come boldly to the throne of grace. The sin question is settled forever.

Let us not only approach the throne of grace, but let us not neglect *the assembling of ourselves together* (10:25). There is nothing like Christian fellowship to make us grow. D. L. Moody visited a woman who had grown cold in her Christian life. She said she had not been able to come to church, but otherwise she could not understand what had happened to make her feel as she did about spiritual things. Without saying a word, Mr. Moody arose and lifted out a live coal from the grate and placed it on the hearth. In a few moments the glow was gone, and the coal was black. "I see it," she said. You cannot continue to glow in your Christian life alone. You need the warmth of fellowship with other Christians. This is a command to us.

THE SUPERIORITY OF THE LIFE IN CHRIST
(Read Hebrews 10:19–13:25)

From now on, the writer tells us the kind of life we should live, because of Christ's work as High Priest for us. We know He is at the right hand of God and that He *ever liveth to make intercession for us.*

After one has accepted Christ, there are levels of Christian living. Some Christians live in the basement of Christian experience, merely inside the building, but where it is dark, dismal and gloomy. Others live on the ground floor. They leave the first foundations and go on. Some sunlight enters but their outlook is upon the circumstances about them. They live very close to the world. Still others live up higher. Sunlight and warmth flood the rooms. The noise and attractions of the worldly street do not disturb them. The air is pure. The outlook is toward the blue skies and distant mountains. These live above the world, hid with Christ in God. It is in this high realm that God wishes us all to live continuously.

Let us look at a few men and women of God whose names are given in Hebrews 11, who lived with a high look. The Holy

Spirit tells us the secret of each life is faith, yet it is not so much his or her faith as their reliance upon our faithful God.

A WORKING FAITH

The secret of Christian living is simply allowing Christ to meet our needs. Some say, "I have no faith; I can't believe." Yet we constantly place faith in our fellow men. You want to go to New York from San Francisco. You buy your ticket and get on the airplane. In the course of your journey, a pilot will guide your plane. Without seeing him or knowing a thing about his ability, you trust your life to him. Faith is just trusting God, believing Him. There is nothing mysterious about faith. It is a simple act of the will. Either we will believe God, or we won't. We decide. It is as simple as turning an electric light switch. This is not a difficult, or baffling, or mysterious thing to do. But the result? Light and power. When we decide to believe God absolutely, then supernatural life and power enters our lives. A miracle is wrought within us. One of the practical results of faith is that it makes weak men strong (11:34).

To live in the Hall of Faith forever we need to do two things. First, like anyone entering a race, "lay aside every encumbrance." Yield everything to Christ. Second, we are really to believe that Jesus is trustworthy. When we do, we have given up the sin which so easily besets us—for that is the sin of unbelief. We give up that sin by "looking unto Jesus."

There is only one kind of human being in the world that can please God. Who is it? (Heb. 11:6) It is not what we do for God, but what God does for us that makes a life of power and strength. Our great God, rather than our great faith, is the thing to think most about. It is fashionable to be doubtful rather than sure about the great facts of God and Christ and salvation. Remember, this cannot please God.

> F—orsaking
> A—ll
> I
> T—ake
> H—im

Christ is the belief which brings salvation.

Because of the great company of witnesses on the bleachers watching from heaven, let us run the race of life God has set before us. As any athlete would, when he is preparing for a race, let us lay aside every sinful habit, and anything that would hinder us (12:1,2).

To Run Life's Race . . .

Let us have patience..12:1
Endure chastening 12:11
Follow peace and purity of heart.....................................12:14

Always looking to Jesus, the author and finisher of our faith.

A life well-pleasing in His sight will be made possible by the Lord Himself.

Now the God of peace, that brought again from the dead our Lord Jesus, that great shepherd of the sheep, through the blood of the everlasting covenant, make you perfect in every good work to do his will, working in you that which is well-pleasing in his sight, through Jesus Christ; to whom be glory forever and ever. Amen (Hebrews 13:20,21).

Minimum Daily Requirements/Spiritual Vitamins

Sunday: CHRIST SUPERIOR TO PROPHETS AND ANGELS Hebrews 1:1-14

Monday: CHRIST SUPERIOR TO MOSES Hebrews 3:1-19

Tuesday: CHRIST SUPERIOR TO AARON Hebrews 5:1-14

Wednesday: CHRIST'S SUPERIOR COVENANTS Hebrews 8:1-13

Thursday: CHRIST'S SUPERIOR ATONEMENT Hebrews 10:1-25

Friday: CHRIST'S SUPERIOR FAITH LIFE Hebrews 11:1-40

Saturday: CHRIST'S SUPERIOR PRIVILEGES Hebrews 12:1–13:25

UNDERSTANDING JAMES

*James
Portrays Jesus Christ,
Our Pattern*

The law of Christ for daily life is found in the word "doers."
But be ye doers of the word, and not hearers only (1:22).

The author of the book is no doubt James, the brother of our
Lord. He may well be called the practical apostle. He stands for
efficiency and consistency in life and conduct.

There are three men by the name of James mentioned in the
New Testament—the son of Zebedee, the son of Alphaeus, and
James the Great, our Lord's brother. Although James refers to
his own brother Jesus only twice, he does it in a most reverent
manner. Though he knew Him so well, there was no familiarity,
for he called Him Lord and Christ. He associates his brother
with God, so as to imply an equality with the Almighty. If Jesus
were not Deity, this would be blasphemous.

GUIDEBOOK FOR EVERYDAY RELIGION

The Book of James is the most practical of all the epistles,
and has been called "A Practical Guide to Christian Life and
Conduct." This book is the Proverbs of the New Testament. It
is filled with moral precepts. It states the ethics of Christianity.
It is full of figures and metaphors. It is often quite dramatic in
style. It compels real thought. Hebrews presents doctrine; James
presents deeds. They go together in vital Christianity. There is no
conflict between Paul and James. Only superficial reading of
both would bring that indictment. Paul says, "Take the gospel
in." James says, "Take it out." Paul saw Christ in the heavens,
establishing our righteousness. James saw Him on the earth,
telling us to be perfect, even as His Father in heaven is perfect.

Paul dwells on the source of our faith. James tells of the fruit
of our faith. One lays the foundations in Christ; the other builds
the superstructure. Christ is both "author and finisher" of our

faith. Not only believe it, but live it! But although Paul lays great stress upon justification by faith, we have noticed in his epistles, especially in Titus, that he lays great stress on good works. It is an astounding fact that while Paul uses the expression *rich in good works* (I Tim. 6:18), James uses *rich in faith* (2:5). It is well to notice, too, that when James seems to speak in a slighting way of faith, he means a mere intellectual belief and not a "saving faith" that is so essential. James exalts faith. He says its trial worketh patience. His epistle opens and closes with a strong encouragement to pray (1:6; 5:14-18). He only denounces the spurious faith which does not produce works.

James calls himself a "bondman of Jesus Christ." He proudly accepts this title as a description of what his relationship was to Jesus. This speaks of real humility because James nowhere refers to the fact of his earthly relationship to the Lord Jesus Christ, a brother.

James mentions the name of God seventeen times, but he repeats the name of Jesus only twice. James was bitterly opposed to Jesus and His claims up to the time of His death, but after the resurrection he was converted by a special and private interview with the risen Lord (I Cor. 15:7). This adds value to James' testimony as to the deity of our Lord. Immediately he became a man of prayer, and was made bishop of the church at Jerusalem (Acts 15:13-21). His life work was to win the Jews and to help them understand Christianity. At the end he was slain by the Jews in A.D. 62. We are told that he was probably forced to the roof of the temple by the high priest and rulers, and commanded to blaspheme the name of Christ. He, rather, boldly proclaimed the fact that he is the Son of God. James was hurled from the roof to instant death.

James says his epistle is written *to the twelve tribes which are scattered abroad,* to those who lived outside the holy land. Then there were no lost tribes, for he addressed his letter to the twelve whose location was well known at the time. Like Hebrews, it is addressed to the Christian Jews. The Jews to whom he wrote had not ceased to be Jews, although they had embraced Christianity. Many of them had been converted on the day of Pentecost, and had carried home only a partial understanding of Christianity. In their enthusiasm at having found the true Messiah, they neglected the graces and virtues that should accompany the Christian life. They taught that all that was necessary to have salvation was to believe that Jesus was the true Messiah and Saviour. They were in great danger of being discouraged in their Christian life by the persecution of their own unbelieving countrymen.

FAITH VICTOR OVER TEMPTATION (Read James 1:1-21)

After the briefest of greetings, James plunges straight into his subject. Realizing that these Christian Jews scattered everywhere outside of Palestine were undergoing severe testing of their faith, he begins by telling them how they must meet temptation and tries to encourage and comfort them.

Spiritual arithmetic is of value. The arithmetic of the Bible is important and none of us can afford to ignore it. James invites Christians to "count." *Count it all joy when ye fall into divers temptations* (1:2). We usually count it joy when we escape temptation and sorrow. Instead we should count testing as a glorious opportunity of proving our faith, just as the automobile manufacturer knows that the best proof of the car's worth is the road test. Why we must count it joy is not because of the trial itself but what it will work out. In other words, use your trials. What is the purpose of the testing? God makes our trials the instrument of blessing (1:3). Too often our trials work impatience, but God will give grace that His real purpose may be accomplished. Patience is more necessary than anything else in our faith life. We forget that time is nothing with God, for with Him a thousand years is as one day, and one day as a thousand years. Christ's purpose in our lives is that we shall be perfect and entire, wanting nothing.

Let us be careful where we lay the blame of temptation. Read 1:14 carefully. Testings of character come from God (Genesis 22:1), but temptations to evil never come from Him, but from the adversary through our own corrupt nature (1:13), and the appeal is made to meet a proper desire in an improper way (1:14). Instead of wrong things coming from God, we find that only good and perfect gifts come from above, from the Father of lights, who never changes (1:17). Our God is a God who loves to give. Alexander the Great said to one overwhelmed with his generosity, "I give as a king!" Our Father in heaven gives to us as the infinite God.

HOW TO BE WISE

It is hard to behave wisely, but God's wisdom will help you to do it. Put together the teaching on wisdom in this short letter. Pray for wisdom to behave wisely in time of trial. When you are wronged and insulted, ask God how you shall act. *If any of you lack wisdom, let him ask of God, that giveth to all men liberally, and upbraideth not; and it shall be given him* (1:5). What a sad lack! What a mess such a lack can lead us into. Does James say, "If you lack wisdom, sit down and think or study"? No, he says the wisdom we need is from above.

Did it ever occur to you to thank God for temptations? Do you think of your temptations as blessings? Yet James says, *Count it all joy when ye fall into divers temptations* (1:2). Do you count it so? Then he adds, *Blessed is the man that endureth temptation* (1:12). How spineless and weak you would become without temptation. Valueless is the character that knows no testing. There is a joy of overcoming. There is no greater satisfaction than to know we have resisted temptation victoriously.

James begins and ends with prayer (1:5-8; 5:13-18). Prayer is one of the easiest subjects to talk upon, but one of the hardest to practice. Find all you can on this subject in this epistle. What about his practice? Tradition tells us that on his death they discovered that his knees were worn hard as a camel's through constant habit of prayer.

FAITH SHOWN IN OUR ACTIONS (Read James 1:22–2:26)

Don't be merely listeners to God's Word, but put the Gospel into practice. What is the good of a man saying that he has faith, if he does not prove it by actions? We must not be satisfied with only "hearing." We must go on "doing" (1:22). If anyone is a hearer and not a doer, he is like a person looking at himself in a mirror and then going away and forgetting how he looked (1:24).

Try this experiment to prove the truth of this statement. Look in a mirror and then turn away. Close your eyes and try to remember how you look. You can't picture yourself. Now try to recall how your best friend looks. It is easy to remember another face, but not your own. That is the reason James says we must keep looking into the mirror of God's Word to remember how we look, to find out the sin in our life. He who looks carefully into the Scriptures and practices them, will be blessed in what he does. If anyone thinks he is religious and doesn't control his tongue, this man's religion is vain. The religion that does not influence the tongue is not a true or vital one. An uncontrolled tongue in a Christian is a terrible thing—guard it. Control your temper. It is dangerous. Under trial, be slow to speak. Keep the draft closed and the fire will go out (1:26).

WHAT SHALL WE DO WITH THE WORD?

Receive it 1:21
Hear it 1:23
Do it 1:22
Examine it 1:25

WORKS ARE RESULTS

Works do not save us, but they are a pretty good evidence that we are saved. *Inasmuch as ye have done it unto one of the least of these my brethren, ye have done it unto me* (Matt. 25:40) is not a "saving" text, but a "sign" text. What He has done is our salvation; what "ye have done," the proof of it. Keep faith and works in their proper place.

Because of all this, James says in effect, "The faith you have is the faith you show." *Pure religion and undefiled before God and the Father is this, To visit the fatherless and widows in their affliction, and to keep himself unspotted from the world* (1:27).

Christianity is a brotherhood that has no "respect of persons" (2:1-4).

How the world today ignores James' command not to show favoritism of persons! The world worships the successful, strong and wealthy, and despises the man who is poor. A Christian must not show partiality to the man of wealth and position, James tells us, but it seems that money and honor are the only things that men worship today. Showing favoritism is not only a breach of good manners and discourtesy to the poor, but it is a sin to worship rank and insult the poor. By doing this we break the law of God. *Thou shalt love thy neighbor as thyself.* This law of love is a royal law (2:8). It comes from heaven's Royalty. We are not only to admire and respect others, but to love them as we do our own selves (2:1-13).

WHAT IS SIN?

To disobey God's law is sin. It is human to gloss over sin. A little girl said when excusing herself for something she had done, "I haven't broken the commandment; I only cracked it." James says that whosoever obeys the whole law, and only makes a single slip, is guilty of everything (2:10,11). He is a lawbreaker. If a man is brought into court for violating a traffic ordinance, he does not plead that he has kept all the others. The judge is interested only in the fact of whether he has broken this one with which he is charged. That classifies him as a lawbreaker. We may have a fine chain, but of what use is it if all the links are good except one? That broken link renders the entire chain useless.

It is clear that the one sin thought of here is mentioned in 2:9—"respect of persons."

Faith which does not express itself in works is of no value. Faith is revealed by what we do. What is the use of anyone's saying that he has faith if he does not prove it by his actions? Just as a body without a spirit is dead, so faith is dead without actions (2:17).

Has the phrase, "friend of God," ever gripped you? God evidently needed a friend, and He found in Abraham the friendship which He desired. What is essential to become a friend of God? (See 2:23)

FAITH SHOWN IN OUR WORDS (Read James 3:1-18)

Our speech reveals what and whose we are. It expresses our

personality more than anything else. Anyone who controls his tongue, James says, is a perfect man (3:2). If he has mastery over that difficult member, the tongue, the rest is easy. He is able to curb the whole nature. Just as we control a spirited horse by a firm hand on the bridle, so the hand of the Man, Christ Jesus, can grip and firmly use the bit and bridle on our tongues. Even as a great ship is controlled by a very small rudder and turned in any direction the captain determines, so the pierced hands of Jesus can firmly control and wisely use the helm of our lives—our tongue. The tongue, though small, is very powerful. It can determine the course of human life.

Remember, this same tongue can be used to testify for Christ and praise His holy name. It is the instrument that the Holy Spirit uses to magnify the Lord (3:9,10). We should not praise God and curse men who áre made in His likeness! Cruel words have wrecked homes, broken friendships, divided churches, and sent untold millions to ruin and despair. There are so many people who call themselves Christians who seem not to make the slightest effort to control the tongue.

FAITH SHOWN IN OUR PURITY OF CHARACTER
(Read James 4:1-17)

The Devil has organized this world system upon principles opposed to God in every way. They are principles of force, greed, ambition, selfishness and pleasure. The believer should be crucified to this world (Gal. 6:14). We should count its passing pleasures, its honors, its treasures as of little value, and remain unmoved by its attractions. The world is that system of things about us, or that spirit within us, which is blind and deaf to the value of spiritual things and cares nothing about doing the will of God. Because we live in the world, surrounded by all its attractions and the things needful to our daily living, we must be very watchful to keep our affections above the border line of the world (4:4).

Men keep asking, "How can we end war?" But James goes back farther and tells us what causes war. A cause of most of the wars which have devastated the earth has been some nation's desire to get what does not belong to it. This has always been the cause of quarrels between individuals. Selfishness is the root of it all. Next, men fail to pray or if they do, it is with a wrong motive, to spend what they get upon themselves instead of having their lives glorify God (4:1-3). God promises to answer prayer, but He will not give to those who would consume it on their own pleasures. It is common to see worldly minded Christians praying for purely selfish reasons. So often you hear people say, "I don't believe in prayer. I prayed for a new car, and God didn't give it to me," or "My husband was sick and I prayed that God would heal him, and he died." In either case the answer might easily have led the person farther away from God. The car would have been used to carry him to the beach and not to church. The family circle restored could make the wife find her joy in her husband rather than in her Lord.

PLEASURE MAD

Four times the word "lust" is found in the first five verses of James 4. Dr. Jowett defines it as "anything that steams the windows of the soul and blurs our vision." This word "lust" can be translated "pleasures." This helps give meaning to these verses and furnishes the clue to the teaching they contain.

Over-Indulgence in Pleasure Is Sinful:

First, there are wars and fighting (brawling) among you. The newspapers are filled with horrible pictures of this every day.

Second, pleasure wars in your members. If pleasure is allowed to have its own way in us, a war is on and we are mastered by it.

Third, *Ye ask, and receive not, . . . that ye may consume it upon your lusts* [pleasure] (4:3). Overindulgence in pleasure always affects the prayer life. We stagnate in our Christian life.

Fourth, *Ye adulterers and adulteresses*—how a pleasure-lover degenerates in his Christian walk! He becomes a friend of the world, an enemy of God (4:4).

What Is the Cure for All This?

Examine 4:6-10

Submit to God. (4:7) We have made a mess of our lives because of a lack of surrender to God.

Draw nigh to God and he will draw nigh to you (4:8,9). Come with clean hands and a pure heart.

Humble yourself in the sight of the Lord (4:10). Remember yourself as a sinner and take the lowly place. Then God will lift you up.

To be friends with the world means to be at enmity with God (4:4). Jesus said, *Ye cannot serve God and mammon* (Matt. 6:24). Therefore surrender yourself to God, and be not subject to the devil. When the devil is resisted by those who have surrendered themselves to God, he flees.

How easy it is for us to plan without God, yet how futile! Let us submit all of our plans to the Lord, and see what His will is in the matter. *If the Lord will* (James 4:15). One of the most amazing things in all of God's Word is that though He holds the whole universe in His hands, yet He has a definite plan for each one of our lives. Our life is a series of surprises. We live just one day at a time. We know not what shall be on the morrow. What a wonderful God we have!

FAITH SHOWN BY OUR PRAYER LIFE (Read James 5:1-20)

Evidently many of the humble folk among the Christian Jews were being oppressed by the rich and their hard earnings were being *kept back by fraud* (5:4). James warns the rich! *Ye have heaped treasure together for the last days* (5:3). How true this is today—heaped up millions, yes, billions. The coffers of the rich are full indeed. They are charged with fraud and injustice. How much goes on today under the cloak of Christianity! It is true there are some great Christian souls among the rich, but for the most part, James' picture of wealth holds good. You remember that Jesus said it was easier for a camel to go through the eye of a needle than for a rich man to enter heaven.

Here again the tongue is brought in. It is amazing how many Christians, in ordinary conversation, take the name of the Lord in vain (5:12). God says, *The Lord will not hold him guiltless that taketh his name in vain*. This is a serious indictment.

A KEY TO REAL RICHES

Prayer is a golden key, which, kept bright by constant use, will unlock the treasures of earth and heaven.

James gives us a series of short phrases of advice. If anyone is in trouble, he should pray. If anyone is merry, he should sing. If anyone is sick, he should send for the elders of the church and let them anoint him with oil and pray for him (5:13,14). The Bible says, *And the prayer of faith shall save the sick, and the Lord shall raise him up; and if he have committed sins, they shall be forgiven him* (5:15). If anyone has wronged another, he should confess his fault to that one (5:16). The prayer of faith demands confession of sin, and a will surrendered to God. Elijah's mighty prayer that opened and closed the heavens is an example to us, for *the effectual fervent prayer of a righteous man availeth much* (5:16).

This epistle closes abruptly on a high plane. It is with the gracious act of a Christian who finds someone erring from the truth, and converts him. Although only God can save a soul, He uses human instruments to accomplish it. That one *shall save a soul from death, and shall hide a multitude of sins.*

Minimum Daily Requirements/Spiritual Vitamins

Sunday: FAITH TESTED   James 1:1-21
Monday: FAITH LIVED OUT   James 1:22-27
Tuesday: FAITH AND BROTHERHOOD   James 2:1-13
Wednesday: FAITH DEAD WITHOUT WORKS
        James 2:14-26
Thursday: FAITH AND TONGUE CONTROL
        James 3:1-18
Friday: FAITH REBUKES WORLDLINESS
        James 4:1-17
Saturday: FAITH IN PRAYER   James 5:1-20

UNDERSTANDING I PETER

*I Peter
Portrays Jesus Christ,
Precious Cornerstone
of Our Faith*

Jesus lived the kind of life described in this letter of Peter's and *he that saith he abideth in him ought himself also so to walk* (I John 2:6). To "abide in Christ" is to rest quietly where we are. We, who have received Christ as Saviour, are "in Him" (Col. 3:3). The secret of walking "in newness of life" (Rom. 6:4) or victorious Christian living, is simply to "remember Jesus Christ" (II Tim. 2:8), and to rest on the blessed eternal fact of His sufficiency.

Unto you therefore which believe he is precious (I Peter 2:7).

Seven Precious Things

Precious trial of faith _____1:7
Precious blood _____1:19
Precious Cornerstone _____2:4,6
Precious Christ _____2:7
Precious spirit _____3:4
Precious faith _____II Peter 1:1
Precious promises _____II Peter 1:4

Mark these in your Bible.

Peter has been called "The Apostle of Hope," as John was "The Apostle of Love," and Paul "The Apostle of Faith." The word "hope" is found in I Peter 1:3,13,21; 3:15.

Another word (or its equivalent) is used 14 times in this short epistle, and that is "suffering," the suffering of Christ and of Christians in following Him.

Try a complete reading, at one sitting, of this short four-page letter, preferably in Weymouth or Moffat or the American Standard. Mark in two colors each mention of joy and grace and glory (in red perhaps), and of suffering (in black). At least

26 times does Peter dwell on the joy and glory that are ours who have received God's grace, against the 14 times he mentions the suffering of Christ and the Christian following Him.

Try to see that Peter was enlarging on the statement that *Jesus the author and finisher of our faith; . . . for the joy that was set before him endured the cross, despising the shame, and is set down at the right hand of the throne of God* (Hebrews 12:2). He knew the connection between suffering, and joy and glory.

This book was written by Peter toward the close of his busy life (around A.D. 67). He was staying at Babylon on the Euphrates (5:13) where a Christian church had been established. The letter was sent by Silas (5:12), one of Paul's companions. Peter had become a leader of the apostles. He was the spokesman. He belonged to the "inner circle" of the three friends of Christ. He was the preacher at Pentecost. The first twelve chapters of Acts are centered around this apostle and his ministry. He went about preaching to the Jews. At last he died a martyr's death, being crucified under the Roman emperor, Nero. According to tradition, at his own request, he was crucified with his head downward, considering himself unworthy to even resemble his Master in death.

The picture of Peter in the Gospels is amazingly different from that found in his own writings. In the Gospels we see Peter, the impulsive, restless soul, sometimes fearless but again a coward, even going so far as to deny his Lord with a curse! In his own epistles, we see him patient, restful, and loving, with a courage purified and strengthened by the indwelling Spirit. This is a wonderful illustration of the transforming work of God in a human life.

The Christians to whom Peter is writing were suffering "fiery trials" from the hostile Jews and fanatical Gentiles. The Christians would not join their pagan neighbors in idolatry and drinking and lust, so they were called "haters of the human race" and were classed with thieves and murderers. Lives today are on the auction block, sold to the highest bidder. The world is bidding high. Let Christ have a chance. (See I Peter 1:18,19.)

This letter was evidently written at a time when general dislike of Christians was threatening to pass into active persecution (2:15; 3:13-17; 4:12). It was about the time of Nero's persecutions. Peter himself suffered under this cruel emperor not later than A.D. 67. Read 1:1-3, 6-9; 2:13-17; 4:12-19.

A subject repeatedly mentioned is the "reappearing" of our Lord and Saviour. Mark this as the letter is read. The influence of this "blessed hope" on the Christian's way of life cannot be escaped. This short epistle is full of golden nuggets of truth, which can be marked and memorized. Try it!

Let us discover what this letter has for our own lives as we read it. We are not enduring persecutions of heathen emperors, but we are meeting on every side the alluring temptations of that same adversary, the devil, who is seeking those whom he may win away from Christ, who endured all for us. Although we are not witnesses of the suffering of Christ as was Peter, we may be taught by the same Holy Spirit. Ask the Holy Spirit to teach you today!

This book gives us good plain advice from Peter on how we ought to live. Read it and take heed! We find here how Peter has been growing in his experience. This letter shows him some twelve or more years after the last record of him in Acts 15. He wishes to encourage the believers and so he gives his own personal testimony. He adds assurance because he could prove from his own experience all he was saying. There is power in personal testimony. This personal note sounds through all the letter. The Christians were experiencing a time of trial (1:6). They needed encouragement from one who knew what trial meant. Peter points away from the trials to the future glory which awaited them (1:7), to the example of Christ (2:21), and the reward which would follow (4:13).

PRIVILEGES OF THE CHRISTIAN (Read I Peter 1:1–2:10)

Peter, who is an apostle of jubilant hope, addresses this epistle to the "strangers" scattered everywhere. It is a letter to homesick Christians. He tells these persecuted and discouraged ones of a near and precious Saviour. Let it lift you up and fill you with joy! This is the purpose of the book.

What are our privileges as Christians? First, we are redeemed by the precious blood of Christ. This is our position in Christ (1:18,19). Because of this relationship to Christ, we have everything in Him which God desires us to possess. If God has given us His Son, will He not freely with Him give us all things?

The life of faith is described at the beginning. We are born of God (begotten) (1:3). At the end there is an inheritance for us (1:4) and to assure us of it we are "kept" by the power of God (1:5). What a life this is!

All This and Heaven Too!

We have been begotten by Jesus Christ
into a lively hope..1:3
We have in reserve an incorruptible inheritance........1:4,5,10
We are kept by the power of God.....................................1:5
We are being purified to fit us to stand with Christ..........1:7
We have salvation for our souls...1:9
We have a gospel that angels desire to look into.............1:12
We have a great hope...1:13
We have redemption through His blood.....................1:18,19
We shall not be confounded (ashamed)............................2:6
We are born again by His Word.......................................1:23
We are built up a spiritual house.......................................2:5
We are a chosen people..2:9
We shall have a crown of glory..5:4

Peter gives good plain advice on how we ought to live (1:13-16). Here he says, *Gird up the loins of your mind, be sober, and hope to the end.* Fashion your life after the Lord Jesus Christ. Don't live your life after the old pattern. *Be ye holy; for I am holy.* Love one another (1:22). Seeing you are "born again" (1:23), live like it. You are a new creature in Christ Jesus.

How can anyone *put away all wickedness,* as Peter commands? (Chapter 2) Not by effort! Not by trying! Not by practice! Not by setting our will power against sin! But by trusting that God by His grace can do it. The only person who can "put away" sin, is the one who, having received Christ as Saviour, knows that Christ has "put away" his sin.

First, we must "lay aside." Peter summons us to abandon

some ugly things—wickedness, guile, hypocrisy, envies, evil speaking (2:1). From the root of wickedness all these noxious weeds spring. These must go from our hearts if we would grow. Weeds always choke out the plant, if we allow them to spread. All that challenges the supremacy of the Lord Jesus Christ must go, whether it be our sin or our righteousness. Sometimes even good things keep us from God's best. *Seek ye first the kingdom of God, and his righteousness, and all these things shall be added unto you* (Matthew 6:33). We must be careful of this. The choices you must make are not always between bad and good, right and wrong, but between the good and the best. *As for God, his way is perfect* (Psalm 18:30).

CHRISTIAN INFANTS

We are called "newborn babes." Newborn babes have no treasury of supplies in themselves. They are helpless and dependent from morning till night. They need food, clothing, shelter, the tireless care of a mother and protection of a father. It is a parable of Christian men and women. A Christian has nothing in himself, but he has access to the unsearchable riches of Christ, and they are filled with all the fulness of God. As new Christians we have a new longing in our hearts, a new hunger. We are not self-sustained; we are God-sustained. We are newborn babes the whole way through. Peter describes the attitude as desiring the spiritual milk, *the sincere milk of the word.* Food makes a difference. Spiritual milk makes us grow unto salvation. So that's the thing we live on. The Word as "milk" suggests that it is a perfect food for children, containing all the elements for building up the body. So the Word is perfect for the building up of the soul.

"Word" in 2:2 might be spelled with a capital "W," meaning Christ as well as His Word, for in the third verse we read that if you have once tasted of the Lord you will find He is gracious. He is the nourishment of our souls.

Peter says that when we become "children of God" (John 1:12), we are like newborn babies (1:23). We need food to make us grow. This is just what God has provided in His Word. Desire the Word as newborn babes, and eating it, grow thereby.

You will find that it tastes good. Christ will become real and gracious to you (I Peter 1:23; 2:2,3).

A STUDY IN STONES

Right here Peter turned to another figure and called Christ a "stone," rejected by men, but precious in God's sight (2:4). Everyone in this world has to do something with this "Stone," Christ Jesus. He is in every man's path. We can lift Him up and put Him in as the chief Cornerstone of our lives, which is God's will. But if we do not, we must stumble headlong over Him, tragically, to our death. To the Jews He was a stumbling-block and a rock of offense. To many today He is just that. What have you done with this precious "Cornerstone"? Is He in His rightful place in your life?

And we are stones, too, laid up on Christ as the foundation and cornerstone, to make a spiritual temple to God. This makes it very important for each one of us to find our right place in God's plan, and stay in it. The "spiritual house" (2:5), built up of believers, is the corporate temple of the Holy Spirit, as the individual Christian is the individual temple of the Holy Spirit (I Cor. 6:19).

We are not only "living stones" in a spiritual temple but each of us is a priest in this temple. Priests represent God to men, and men to God. Christians are a "holy priesthood" (2:5). Are you representing God to men by your life, and men to God by your intercessory prayer? As priests we cannot offer lambs and goats today, but Paul tells us to offer ourselves a living sacrifice (Romans 12:1).

A PRECIOUS SAVIOUR

Unto you therefore which believe he is precious (2:7). Charles Spurgeon's wonderful preaching started here. When only a youth in his teens, he was walking out with a friend to an appointment in the country. "I hope the Lord will bless you," said his companion. "Me!" exclaimed the young fellow, "I never preached." "Well, if you don't preach this time, there will be no preaching." Right there the young man, appointed of God, all unaware of the fact that he was to be the greatest preacher of his age, bowed his head. In a few minutes he rose and addressed the crowd in the words of this text. God was there. It was his first text and the theme of all his gracious ministry. Christ was ever precious to him and his sermons were precious to the people.

DUTIES OF THE CHRISTIAN (Read I Peter 2:11–4:11)

Peter is giving us wise counsel by telling us how to behave in the game of life. Up to this point he has been exhorting the Christians to walk worthy of their new calling. Now he urges them to glorify God before an ungodly and persecuting world. A greenhouse religion is of very little value to others. It is good for us to be compelled to justify our faith before our fellows.

Peter offers a simple program. Anyone can follow it. Any earnest seeker can find the way that Peter commends. His first suggestion is that we remember that we are "pilgrims." We are not settled here, but we are on our way to an eternal city. It is important that we keep this in mind, otherwise we will be tying our lives to stakes that will be shaken loose some day.

But for the Christian who has followed Peter's plan, all is different. He has invested time and thought and money in the pursuit of Christ's plan for his life. He finds life "sweeter as the years go by," and the end is the best of all!

The greatest satisfaction that can come to a Christian is to realize that he is pleasing his Lord and Saviour. In the power of the Lord, live for Christ in all phases of your life. Do not shut Him out of even the most insignificant parts. It will not be easy; the devil will see to that. He will use every weapon against you. But Christ has already won the victory over him and that victory may be yours for the asking. Read again I Corinthians 15:57.

Christians are not at home in this world. They are away from home, *as strangers and pilgrims* (2:11), for our *conversation* (citizenship) *is in heaven* (Phil. 3:20). We are in the world, but not of it (John 17:11,14).

Peter makes an earnest appeal in this scene. First there is a call to purity of life. Christians are warned against all fleshly appetites, for they are like an infection in our blood. If we once let them have a place in our lives, they will contaminate our souls and pollute our characters, worse than any disease harms our bodies. There is no health, strength or manhood left in us and all on account of sin. The soul may be dragged down to hell or lifted up to heaven. The body is the main channel through which debasing influences affect the soul. A Christian's life is to be true in the presence of those who are not yet Christian. This will disarm opposition and glorify God. Peter says *I beseech you . . . abstain from fleshly lusts* (2:11).

THE POWER OF INFLUENCE

We are to influence others by what we say and do. *Having your behavior seemly among the Gentiles* (2:12 A.S.V.). People are not reading much religious literature on paper, but they are doing a lot of reading in religious (or anti-religious) works by those professing Christ. It seems trite to say but it is true that more are won to Christ by the true Christian life of the believer than by any other means. If it is true that what you are speaks so loudly I cannot hear what you say, then it is equally true that your deeds speak so loudly that I cannot help but believe what you say.

This subject of the way a Christian lives is discussed from 2:12–4:11. It was the all-important topic in Peter's mind for those Christians who were the only "Bible" known or read of the world in their day.

Whereas they speak against you (2:12). The Christians were accused of horrible crimes. They were called atheists because they denied the heathen gods. They were regarded as unpatriotic because heathenism was the official religion. To reject the state religion was considered an outrage against the state itself. The Christians would often be obliged to depart from social customs and often bore the stigma of malefactors. The answer to all this must be in the superior moral life of every Christian. They must live beyond reproach.

Today some of you are subjected to severe tests. There are many things your companions do, both in business and recreation, that you as a Christian cannot do. Your action will be misunderstood and misrepresented. You will be called "narrow" or a "killjoy" or a "wet blanket." The best way to meet all such criticisms is not to assume an air of superiority or "holier than thou" attitude. Don't regard yourself as a martyr but accept the position with a smile and try to be helpful to those who are finding fault with you. Nothing cools opposition like a gentle laugh of love.

FREEDOM DEFINED

As free, and not using your liberty for a cloak of maliciousness (2:16). There is an amusing story of the early days of the Russian Revolution. After the Czar had abdicated, a stout old woman was seen walking leisurely down the middle of one of the busiest streets in St. Petersburg, at no small peril to herself and to the great confusion of traffic. A policeman pointed out to her that there was a walk for pedestrians, and that the street was for wagons, automobiles and horsemen. But she was not to be convinced. "I am going to walk just where I like," she said. "We've got liberty now." When we assert to "do as we like," we are as thoughtless and foolish as the old woman. Freedom is not a question of doing as we like. It is rather a question of doing as we should.

Squaring Your Life (I Peter 2:17)
Honor all men!
Show respect for others.
Love the brotherhood.
Every social problem could be solved.
Fear God.
The fear of the Lord is the beginning of wisdom.
Honor the king.
Show respect for your government.

One of the most convincing and powerful demonstrations that a Christian can give that he has a "newborn" life is the enduring of wrong and injustice patiently (2:19,20). That is when we show forth the grace of God. That is what Christ did while He was on earth, and in submitting to His crucifixion and death. This is what His followers are to do as we *follow his steps* (2:21).

Patience in undeserved punishment is one way of testifying for Christ. A wicked crowd in his regiment took a violent dislike to one Christian soldier because he wouldn't swear or gamble or travel a loose life with them. His days were made miserable. But he never lost his temper nor gave in nor tried to pay them back, and in the end he led one of the worst of the fellows to Christ.

Such suffering by Christians, from injustice, without retaliation or defense, is a reflection of the vicarious atonement of Christ (2:24). *With men this is impossible; but with God all things are possible* (Matt. 19:26). We are to suffer "patiently." Patience is "noble" because it is Christlike (I Peter 3:17,18; 4:12-16). Peter points to the example of his Master. The secret of patience is always found in divine grace (James 1:3,4).

THE MAN WHO SUFFERED FOR ME

Christ also suffered for us (2:21). A lady was visiting in a hospital. She went up to a bed on which lay a wounded soldier, and said gently, "Thank you for being wounded for me." The young man's face brightened. That was a new thought to him. It made the pain more bearable to look upon it in that light. Do you realize that many years ago One was wounded for you? And that "One" was the Son of God Himself? Yes, He was wounded for my transgressions, by His stripes I am healed (2:24).

Spurgeon puts it this way: "The remedy for your sins and mine is found in the substitutionary suffering of the Lord Jesus Christ, and in this only. But if I say of a certain ointment that it heals, I do not deny that you need a bandage with which to apply it to the wound. Faith is the linen which binds the plaster of Christ's reconciliation to the sore of my sin. The linen does not heal; that is the work of the ointment. So faith does not heal; that is the work of the atonement of Christ."

We find in chapters 2 and 3 some instructions for the various relationships of our lives. First, there are some personal instructions (2:1-12). Next we find our social relationships. Servants should obey their masters with respect, not only those who are good and considerate, but also those who are arbitrary. In 3:1-7 our home relationships are mentioned. Naturally the home begins with the marriage relationship. *Wives be in subjection to your own husbands.* This means unselfish devotion, so as to win his love and admiration. This might sound unreasonable if we did not hear the injunction to husbands (3:7) that they *dwell with their wives according to knowledge.* This makes a wife subject to love which acts in knowledge and not according to selfish desires. It is manly for one to be tender toward his wife. God's plan is that the love of husband and wife should be a mutual thing. Each one shall consider the other. The result of all this will be a marriage relationship in which prayers are not hindered (3:7). Prayer is the surest secret of success in any married life.

The Christian

"A babe" (2:2), desiring the milk of the Word.
"Living stone" (2:5), built into the temple of life.
"Priest"—offering spiritual sacrifices.
"Stranger"—to keep himself unspotted from the world.
"Pilgrim"—good deeds along the way.
"Citizen"—render obedience to rulers.
"Man"—honor all men, in the fear of God.
"Servant"—subject unto Christ.
"Sufferer"—to be patient, committing all to Christ.
"Steward" (4:10)
"Oracles" (4:11)

Peter gives the way to be happy in a world that is wretched. *For he that will love life, and see good days, let him refrain his tongue from evil, and his lips that they speak no guile: let him eschew evil, and do good; let him seek peace, and ensue it. For the eyes of the Lord are over the righteous, and his ears are open unto their prayers: but the face of the Lord is against them that do evil* (3:10-12). He quotes Psalm 34:12-14. This is a remedy that works today as well as it worked in David's time. The best way of making this life happy and prosperous is to keep from speaking evil and from slander and to be always ready to overcome evil with good.

A READY ANSWER

Another important command is given in 3:15. This is for everyone of us. *Be ready always to give an answer to every man that asketh you a reason of the hope that is in you.* Have you an intelligent answer to give to others of your trust in Christ? If not, stop right here and get one ready. What does Christ mean to you?

Christ's sufferings in the flesh were physical and literal. *Who his own self bare our sins in his own body on the tree* (2:24). The Christian's suffering, spoken of in 4:1, is spiritual. Christ suffered when He was put to death on the cross. He *suffered for sins, the just for the unjust, that he might bring us to God* (3:18). The Christian takes up his cross and follows Christ, denying himself (Matt. 16:24). The phrase, *Arm ye yourselves also with the same mind,* means the same as the words, *If any man will come after me, let him deny himself and take up his cross and follow me* (Matt. 16:24). Such a high resolve will involve a measure of actual suffering, for God's will may cut across our desire to gratify some bodily craving. Very few in this world escape suffering, either mental, physical or spiritual. We cannot choose the way we shall suffer.

Often God allows us to go through life denied the one thing we wish for more than anything else. But we should be comforted in this that whom God loves, He chastens. If He grinds down the surface of our lives, it is that the stone may shine the more brilliantly. It is the many facets of the diamond that make it dazzling. Know that the greater the suffering in this world, the greater the glory in heaven. This is what Peter means in 4:2.

The Christian sometimes has to forego the gratification of even right desires. The natural cravings of the body for food and drink, for example, are not to be considered merely as ends in themselves. They come to have a spiritual meaning, that whether we eat or drink, or whatever we do, we do all to the glory of God. (See I Cor. 10:31.) *If meat make my brother to offend, I will eat no flesh while the world standeth* (I Cor. 8:13). Sometimes we must refuse for the sake of others. This is "the mind of Christ."

618

Be careful not to follow the world, *the will of the Gentiles* (I Peter 4:3). What the heathen world desired the Jewish Christians to do, Peter names here. "Lasciviousness" is mentioned. The Greek word means "that which disgusts"; the English word, "anything which excites impure desire."

TRIALS OF THE CHRISTIAN (Read I Peter 4:12–5:14)

Nero was subjecting the Church to awful persecutions. Trials resulting from loyalty to Christ are inevitable. Christ sits as a refiner before the fire. It is with the most precious metals that the assayer takes the most pains, as he subjects them to the heat. Such fires melt the metal, and only the molten mass releases the alloy or takes its new form in the mold. Christ allows us to be subjected to the heat until all the dross is burned out and as the assayer sees his face in the molten mass and knows it is pure, so Christ can see His own face reflected in our life.

Christians were burned every night in Nero's gardens. It looked as if the devil were about to devour the Church (5:8). It was a "fiery trial," but God would use its very heat to burn out the dross and leave the pure gold (1:7). History is replete with the record of the many persecutions of Christians. Some have been even more brutal than Nero's. Millions of Christians through the centuries have been subjected to every conceivable kind of torture. These words have been for them too. How ashamed we should be even to mention our little troubles in the light of these!

Don't be surprised when you are tried in the fire, as if some strange thing were happening to you. (See 4:12.) Don't think that Christ has promised that we, as Christians, shall be spared from pain, or misfortunes, or death. In fact Christ says, "In this world ye shall suffer persecution." This means no doubt that men will persecute the real Christian, because the world hates Christ and anything called by His name.

Peter exhorts the leaders of the Church to care for the flock. He tells them not "to lord it over them" (5:3), but to serve them. Jesus had told Peter to "feed my sheep" (John 21). Under-shepherds are to receive their rewards from the Chief

Shepherd when He shall appear (5:4). His crown of glory shall be fadeless.

The Christian life is like a jungle battle. Peter tells us who our enemy is. He is the devil. His work is opposed to all that is good in this world. He is pictured as a roaring lion, seeking his prey (5:8). This Adversary is cagey, appearing sometimes as an angel of light, at another time as a serpent, coiled for the strike. He is always *seeking whom he may devour*. He is watching for the vulnerable spot, for the unguarded door to our hearts. Paul tells us what armor we should wear in Ephesians 6. But we need not be afraid, for *the God of all grace, who hath called us unto his eternal glory by Christ Jesus, after that ye have suffered a while, make you perfect, stablish, strengthen, settle you.*

Minimum Daily Requirements/Spiritual Vitamins

Sunday: PRECIOUS FAITH   I Peter 1:1-12
Monday: PRECIOUS BLOOD   I Peter 1:13-25
Tuesday: PRECIOUS CORNERSTONE   I Peter 2:1-10
Wednesday: PRECIOUS SAVIOUR   I Peter 2:11-25
Thursday: PRECIOUS IS A MEEK AND QUIET SPIRIT
       I Peter 3:1-22
Friday: PRECIOUS SUFFERING OF CHRIST
       I Peter 4:1-19
Saturday: PRECIOUS CROWNS   I Peter 5:1-14

UNDERSTANDING II PETER

II Peter
*Portrays Jesus **Christ**,*
Our Strength

The first letter was to console; the second to warn.

In his first letter, Peter was trying to encourage Christians who were suffering terrible persecutions from without. In his second letter, he is warning them of danger within the Church.

Christians need moral courage even more than physical courage. It is our duty to do right under all circumstances, with no qualification and no hesitation. "A Christian is never off duty." To stand up for truth is often more difficult than to go into battle. Illustrations from the Bible are found in Joseph (Gen. 39:9), Nehemiah (5:7; 6:1-16), Daniel (1:8), Paul. History is full of instances, too: Polycarp, Luther, Latimer, Wesley. They were never ashamed of Christ because they knew Him.

Paul, in warning against the dangers from within, urges them to grow strong in "the grace and knowledge" of Christ. Christian knowledge is the best way to overcome the false teaching that was creeping within the walls. We obtain knowledge of Christ through His Word. Don't neglect the Word of God! It is indeed *a lamp to our feet, and a light to our path.* In I Peter we hear much about suffering. In II Peter we hear much about knowledge. Shallow knowledge makes superficial Christians. Paul said, "I know Whom I have believed." It is not what you believe that gives you strength, but WHOM you believe. Peter knew that heresy often leads to immoral living. Christianity must have a creed if right conduct is to be assured. Leaders were using the church for money-making schemes. Leaders in the church were permitting wrong-doing of every sort. The false teachers were laughing at the

Lord's coming, and the church could easily cease from looking for that "blessed hope."

Simon Peter, a servant and an apostle of Jesus Christ, is the writer. The first name, Simon, suggests his old, unstable nature. The name Peter (meaning a rock) suggests the new nature that Christ had given him, strong and true. He calls himself a bondslave (servant). Slavery is the happiest life in the world when the slave has the right master. There is only one right Master, and He is Jesus Christ. His slaves know the only true meaning of freedom.

Peter, the Apostle of Hope, speaks again to the younger Christians in the faith. He urges them to look toward heaven while dwelling for only a season in a very bad world. He stirs up their pure minds *by way of remembrance* (3:1). He talks about the readers as those who have obtained *like precious faith with us* (1:1). We remember how Peter's faith was kept through Christ's prayer for him. *But I have prayed for thee, that thy faith fail not; and when thou art converted, strengthen thy brethren* (Luke 22:32). This is how our faith can be preserved also.

CHRISTIAN VIRTUES (Read II Peter 1:1-21)

Do the days seem dark to you and does sin seem to abound everywhere? That is the way the world looked to the young Christians of Peter's day. So that they would not be discouraged by this outlook he showed them how to escape *the corruption that is in the world through lust* (1:4). Here it is. God has *given unto us all things that pertain unto life and godliness* (1:3).

Look at a criminal condemned to be hanged. Suppose a messenger comes to him and says: "The governor has taken your case into consideration, and I have brought you a purse of a thousand dollars." The criminal will say, "What good will it do me? I am to be hanged tomorrow." "Well, I have another message. He has considered your case and sent you the deed to a million dollar estate." The condemned man despairingly shakes his head and says, "What can I do with that? I must be hanged tomorrow." But the messenger goes on.

"Stop! I have another offer to make. I have brought you the governor's own inauguration robe for you to wear with special favor." The condemned man bursts into tears, as he says, "Do you intend to mock me? How would I appear ascending the steps of the gallows, wearing the governor's own robe?" Then the messenger says, "Wait, I have one more message. The governor has sent you a pardon. What do you say to that?" The poor man looks at him and says he doesn't believe it. But the messenger hands him the pardon, signed by the governor, with the official stamp upon it. Then the man leaps for joy, while tears of gratitude run down his face. Then the messenger says, "I am not through yet. I have brought you the pardon, the purse of gold, the deed, and the royal robe which are yours in addition." These are the "all things" God has given us in Christ, His Son. With these, nothing can defeat the young Christian.

The way I can escape the awful sins in this world every day and all the day is by partaking of His nature and letting Him live through me. Lay hold of the *great and precious promises: that by these ye might be partakers of the divine nature.* I am a sharer in the very nature of God (1:4). Everyone has not the nature of God. The divine is not in all men. His image remains in us, though marred (I Cor. 11:7), but not an atom of His life. We are dead and lifeless apart from Christ. The "divine nature" of God becomes ours only when the divine Saviour becomes ours. This is a wonderful truth. We ought to take courage when we remember that with Christ in us, "the divine nature" also is within us. The "exceeding great and precious promises" are before us. We ought to go straight ahead, fearing nothing (II Peter 1:4).

The "divine nature" which God has given us should be shown in the everyday practices of the Christian life. That is all Christian character is. It is no more or less than the practice of Christian virtues. If we turn to Galatians 5 we will find that Christian virtues are only the fruit of the Spirit.

Do others know that you are a Christian by the way you look and act? You remember that night by the fire, when a smart young girl recalled that Peter had been with Jesus, Peter gave her some of the choice language of the Galilee fishing trade to try to prove otherwise. The crowd picked him out by his accent (Mark 14:66-71). He gave himself away by a word. Later, the rulers picked him out as a companion of Jesus by his appearance and talk. The world recognizes us in exactly the same way. There is something about a person's whole bearing that proclaims him as a companion of Jesus Christ. As soon as we hear a man speak about Christ, we can tell what he is.

Although God gives us a changed, divine nature, He wants us to do our part in developing this priceless gift (1:5-11). We are sharers in the very life of God, therefore we should press on to possess more. God says, "Add one grace to another."

The Bible's Math Chapter

Multiplication—*Grace and peace be multiplied* (1:2)
Addition—*Add to your faith* (1:5)
Subtraction—*Purged from his old sins* (1:9)

STEPS TO HEAVEN

There are seven steps going up from faith, and the last one is love. These steps are the Christian virtues that every Christian should have. Let's climb slowly and thoughtfully up this flight of stairs, and see how far we have gone. To your faith, add virtue, knowledge, self-control, patience, godliness, brotherly kindness, love. This is the result of our precious faith.

The fuller the measure of these virtues, the greater will be our knowledge of Jesus Christ our Lord. Know Christ, for to know Him is life eternal, and in none other is there salvation. (See Acts 4:12.)

Someone has said this is a seven-story-and-basement building. Add story to story, but be sure to put faith at the foundation. If you try to build without the proper base the building will become top-heavy. To be sure, faith is the foundation grace. But a foundation is of little use if no building follows. During the days of the depression it was a common sight to see the framework of a great building standing stark and gaunt, with weeds growing around it, abandoned by the men who had begun a good work but for some reason ceased before it was finished. The foundation was substantial and adequate, but for years was entirely useless because nothing was added to make it habitable.

Peter, like Paul, warns Christians from standing still. Don't remain babes in Christ, tripping over every teaching, but grow strong.

But he that lacketh these things is blind, and cannot see afar off (1:9). Near-sighted Christians we will be, "unfit" for enlistment in God's army, if we do not have these virtues. Be sure of your position in Christ. Don't ever doubt your calling in Him. Spare no effort to put God's call and choice beyond all doubt. Spare no effort in prayer, in study and in talking with older Christians. Life is full of so much uncertainty, but you do not have to be uncertain in spiritual things. A spiritual certainty produces a stability in life, and *ye shall never fall* (1:10).

A Christian's ambition should be to have a full life. Peter wants you to have an abundant entrance into the Haven of Rest, Christ's eternal kingdom (1:11).

FOLDING OUR TENTS

Peter, like Paul, was conscious of his approaching death. He has a beautiful name for death, *put off this my tabernacle* (1:14). Moffatt says, "The folding up of my tent." Because he knew he was about to leave them, he wanted to stir them up by putting them in remembrance of what he so well knew. His memory pictured before him the great Transfiguration scene. There he had witnessed the glory of Christ. Any doubt as to His reality or of His coming again in power was forever banished from his mind. God Himself had borne testimony of His glory and honor, and a Voice said, *This is my beloved Son, in whom I am well pleased*. He heard the Voice from above. This is the testimony of Deity. Now Peter knew. He was sure. He wanted them to know that he was not telling them fairy stories when he told them of the power and coming of the Lord Jesus Christ, but he was an eyewitness of His majesty.

Remember, Peter suffered and died for this truth he was telling. At one time he said, *We cannot but speak the things which we have seen and heard* (Acts 4:20).

People depend too much on feeling instead of knowledge based on facts. Peter didn't want these Christians to rest on feelings. When the devil sees a poor soul in agony on the waves of sin, getting close to the Rock of Ages, he just holds out the plank of feeling to him and says, "There, get on that. You feel more comfortable now, don't you?" And while the man stands there getting his breath again, out goes the plank from under him and he is worse off than ever.

Added to the evidence of the Transfiguration is the *more sure word of prophecy* (1:19), rather, prophecy made sure. This does not put Christian experience (the vision on the mount) over against prophecy, but it says the word of prophecy is confirmed by experience. They go together. Peter throws much light on the inspiration of the Scriptures. See I Peter 1:10-12; II Peter 1:4,16-21; 3:15.

Remember the divine origin of the Scriptures. Dr. Gray says, "Private interpretation means private origin. God is the One who has spoken" (1:21).

A native in India, writing to a friend about a great revival they were having said, "We are having a great 'rebible' here." Not a bad idea. The Church needs to be re-Bibled!

CHRISTLESS TEACHERS (Read II Peter 2:1-22)

Are the times in which we live hard, and temptations strong, and opposition powerful? Expect it and rise above it. We are warned that it shall be so. The world always has been and always will be full of antagonism to the truth, and to those who speak it. But God will bring it to naught. In the meantime, *The Lord knoweth how to deliver the godly out of temptations* (2:9).

Peter tells of the coming, the influence, and the doom of the false teachers, in this dark and appalling chapter. We need not be surprised at their coming, for Christ warned us of that in Matthew 7:15; 24:11,24, and we have listened to Paul's words about them to Timothy (I Tim. 4:1-3; II Tim. 3:1-9).

What a black list is this account which Peter gives us of their deeds. There is no softening of the shade from one end to the other. It is a black picture indeed. Read it! No wonder Peter warned the Church of false prophets!

Bring in damnable heresies..2:1
Deny the Lord that bought them..2:1
The way of truth evil spoken of..2:2
With feigned words make merchandise of you.................2:3
Walk after flesh in the lust of uncleanness.....................2:10
Despise government 2:10
Presumptuous, self-willed 2:10
Speak evil of dignities..2:10
Natural brute beasts..2:12
Speak evil about that which they understand not...........2:12
Pleased to riot in the day...2:13
Spots and blemishes in society.......................................2:13
Revel in their deceivings while they feast with you.........2:13
Eyes full of adultery that cannot keep from sin.............2:14
Enticing unsteadfast souls..2:14
Hearts filled with covetousness.......................................2:14
Children of cursing..2:14
Gone astray 2:15
Wells without water...2:17
Clouds carried about with a tempest................................2:17
Utter great swelling words of vanity.................................2:18
Entice through the lusts of the flesh.................................2:18
Servants of corruption...2:19

The false teachers of today do just what is told here. First, they *privily . . . bring in damnable heresies.* They do it subtly. They don't believe in the deity of Christ—that Jesus, who was born of a virgin, was actually God. Peter describes the "damnable heresy" they bring in. This is it—*denying the Lord that bought them.* It does not say that they deny the Lord that TAUGHT them. Practically every false religion acknowledges Christ as a great teacher, but they will not accept Him as Saviour, the One who BOUGHT us with His own precious blood. They deny the blood atonement.

627

Blood Test—This is the mark by which to test and reject the false teacher. Ask for credentials of teachers who are abroad today. When any teacher does not put the cross at the center of his teaching, beware! Turn from him. Our redemption is in the blood. Jesus bought us with His blood.

Popularity Test—These teachers are popular. *Many shall follow their pernicious ways* (2:2). Don't think it strange that false religions, of which there are many varieties, are able to procure a large following. Peter told us they would. Men do not want to be told that they need a Saviour. That makes them admit that they are sinners. They only want to be taught, not "bought." *The way of truth shall be evil spoken of* (2:2). All of these false teachings talk about "truth" but they forget that Christ said, *I am the way, the truth, and the life: no man cometh unto the Father, but by me* (John 14:6). He is not just a part of truth—He IS TRUTH. He is not a "way-shower"—He is THE WAY. He does not come to show us how to live. He is LIFE.

Vocabulary Test—*With feigned words make merchandise of you* (2:3). Words mean so little in many of these false religions. There is a new meaning given to so many words. They say they believe in everything; but when we ask them what they mean by it, it is far from what the Scripture says. They keep the form of words, but the meaning is pumped out. It is like an egg. We put holes in either end and then blow out all the inside. The form of the egg is there, but the real substance is gone. Christ said that men would even say, "Lord, Lord," but He would say, "Depart from Me; I never knew you." Words mean nothing unless there is heart in their meaning. *Make merchandise of you* is added. How these false religions prey upon the people for money! You cannot have healing unless you pay. A "practitioner" demands a price. God says we may come to Him *without money and without price* (Isaiah 55).

There is only one thing God can do with these kinds of men, and that is to destroy them. "Light that is trifled with becomes lightning." Peter declares with no uncertain sound that that shall be the end of false teachers who cover themselves with the

628

cloak of the Church (2:3-9). They shall certainly be punished. God did not even spare the angels who sinned! He sent a flood upon a godless world in Noah's day. Sodom and Gomorrah were reduced to ashes. All of these were as a warning to the godless of every generation of what God has in store for him. One thing we can be sure of, no matter how severe the judgment for the false teacher may be, the deliverance of God's people is promised. Leave the punishment of the wicked with God.

As we read on, we find much else that these wicked teachers will do. They will malign Christ's apostles; they will ensnare weak men, promising them freedom, while as a matter of fact, they are enslaving them in corrupt habits (2:2-22).

CHRIST'S COMING (Read II Peter 3:1-18)

False teaching about Christ, which denies His Deity and power, results in false thinking. The first question it raises is about the coming of Christ. To help the Church in this, Peter reminds them of the things Jesus had said. Men misunderstood Him and thought His return might be in that generation. Peter tells them that time is nothing with God—*that one day is with the Lord as a thousand years* (3:8). He will keep this promise as He has kept all of His promises, but according to His own time.

The Lord is not slack concerning his promise . . . [He is not] *willing that any should perish, but that all should come to repentance* (3:9). The last days are to be sad days, for scoffers shall make fun and say, "Ha, ha, where is the promise of Christ's coming? As far as we can see, everything is going on just as it has from the beginning of creation. Nature goes along in the even tenor of her way. There have been no signs of any radical change. The promise of His coming has failed." These scoffers were evil men, but the sad truth today is that good men scoff at the promise of His coming. They make sport of the great hope of the Church. How illogical was their reasoning about Christ's not coming. Here they are! He had not come, hence He was not coming. Nothing different had happened, hence nothing unusual was going to happen. Because our Lord has not come as yet, shall we give up hope? No, indeed. Rather, rejoice in the fact that His return comes nearer every day.

FLOODS AND FIRES

Peter reminds these skeptics that a mighty flood did drown the world once, and Christ likened His coming to the flood in Matthew 24:37,38. No doubt Peter heard Him say it. But next time God will destroy the earth by fire. Will it be literal fire? Was the flood literal? Stored within the earth are oils and gases and fire enough to burn it up. Volcanoes are the release of these elements. Scientists now tell us we are sitting on a crust of earth only thirty miles in depth. Beneath this is a mass of molten matter. At a word, God could release a spout which would bury the earth in literal fire. The devastation caused by the atomic bomb has proved the possibility of such catastrophe. Or our earth may collide with some other heavenly body.

We know that, when God's clock strikes the hour, the earth will melt with a fervent heat. The earth shall be burned up and in the great explosion the heavens will pass away. Then *new heavens and a new earth* will emerge (3:13).

Today men are heady and high-minded. They think they know everything. But all this is to be expected. Satan will not give up his hold on this earth without protest. But his days of liberty are numbered and "Jesus shall reign." *Knowing this first, that there shall come in the last days scoffers, walking after their own lusts, and saying, Where is the promise of his coming? . . . but the day of the Lord will come!* Scorn and scoffing did not hold back the flood when it was unloosed. The angel's mighty trumpet will make short work of men's foolish "I don't believe it," and "I don't think it is true," or "I don't see it." Nevertheless we, according to His promise, look for new heavens and a new earth, wherein dwells righteousness. It will not be entirely a destruction, but a new earth will be constructed. Look toward the East, for *the Sun of righteousness arise with healing in his wings* (Malachi 4:2).

What effect should all this have on our lives? Peter answers in verse 14. We will be diligent in our service, striving always to be peaceable, spotless and blameless in character. Don't grow careless because He is delaying, for one day the Lord will come suddenly. Be patient while He delays, knowing that He does it because He is longsuffering and would give the last man, woman and child a chance to accept Him.

What lives we ought to live while we wait for His coming! We may hasten it by our holy living. Faith in the return of our Lord must lead to this. Then we may hasten it by a holy conversation. Watch your speech. Don't forget to look forward with an eager gaze. Then be diligent that you be "found of Him" (3:14). Are you looking forward to His coming? What effect has this hope had upon your life and conversation?

Peter's last word of warning is "Beware!" This is a note of caution. Beware lest ye also, *being led away with the error of the wicked, fall from your own steadfastness.*

KNOW AND GROW

The remedy against falling back is to "grow"—make progress. *Grow in grace and in the knowledge of our Lord and Saviour Jesus Christ.* Are you growing in your knowledge? Christian knowledge is an effective weapon against heresy. Christianity without a creed cannot stand against the attacks of the critics. If you are not growing, beware lest you fall by the way, for we are living in a wicked world where men are enemies of God and His truth. A living thing ought to grow. When there is no growth, there is no life. The foundation of growth is the knowledge of Christ. As we grow in this, we grow in likeness to Him.

Minimum Daily Requirements/Spiritual Vitamins

Sunday: CHRISTIAN VIRTUES   II Peter 1:1-14

Monday: CHRIST'S WORD EXALTED
II Peter 1:15-21

Tuesday: CHRISTLESS TEACHERS   II Peter 2:1-14

Wednesday: CHRIST AGAINST THE BACKSLIDER
II Peter 2:15-22

Thursday: CHRIST'S COMING SCOFFED
II Peter 3:1-9

Friday: CHRIST'S COMING ASSURED
II Peter 3:10-18

Saturday: CHRIST OUR HOPE   II Peter 1:1–3:18

CHAPTER 50

UNDERSTANDING I, II, III JOHN and JUDE

Jesus Christ, Our Life; the Truth; the Way; Our Keeper

This letter was written by the aged Apostle John in the year A.D. 90, probably in Ephesus. Unlike the other apostles, he does not address his letter to any church or any particular person. He writes to all Christians, old and young (2:12-14). He calls Christians by a tender word "teknia"—which means "born ones" or "bairns." God is dealing with His very own born-again children.

John told us why he wrote his Gospel—that *ye might believe that Jesus is the Christ, the Son of God; and that believing ye might have life through his Name* (John 20:31).

He wrote his epistle that those who believed in Christ might KNOW that they have eternal life (5:13).

Turn to the Gospel of John 20:31 and read it with I John 5:13. The Gospel was written to show men how they might receive eternal life. The Epistle of I John was written to assure those who have believed that they HAVE eternal life, by believing "that Jesus is the Christ." The Epistle of I John appears to have been intended as a companion to the Gospel of John. Thus we find the word "believe" running all through the Gospel of John, and the word "know" running through the Epistle. The word "KNOW" is used over thirty times in this short letter. Underline it each time you discover it.

John wrote for four reasons:

That they might be happy 1:4
That they might not sin 2:1
That they might be on guard against error 2:26
That they might KNOW 5:13

Someone has well named this the "Really and truly Epistle."

633

It has a confident, exultant tone all the way through. John was the disciple whom Jesus loved. He stood close to Him on the cross at Calvary. He looked into the empty tomb on that morning of the resurrection. On Patmos he was lifted up by the Spirit and saw a door opened into heaven. This one gives us his witness of these facts. "We know," he says. "There is no possibility of doubt about it." *That which was from the beginning, which we have heard, which we have seen with our eyes, which we have looked upon, and our hands have handled, of the Word of life*—JESUS! John gives us evidence for his knowledge. He has heard and seen and handled the Word of life. He longs to bring his hearers into intimate fellowship with the Father and His Son, that their joy might be full (1:3,4,7; 2:-13,14).

Christ, who was God, took on flesh and dwelt with men so they could hear His voice, see His face, and feel the touch of His loving hand. This brought God down to man, that we "may have fellowship." To walk in fellowship is to live in agreement.

God wants us to have fellowship with Him and in Him to have fellowship with one another (1:3).

John says that we not only must believe like Christians, but we must act like Christians. In chapters 1–3, we find out whether we are living like Christians. In chapters 4 and 5 we discover whether we are believing like Christians. Striking lightning is accompanied by thunder. So "striking" faith is accompanied by life and testimony (2:3). Some people say they believe God, but act more like the devil. This cannot be. We must be as orthodox in our behavior as we are in our belief. Do the truth and believe the truth. *If we say that we have fellowship with him, and walk in darkness, we lie, and do not the truth* (1:6).

God in the Epistles of John

God is Truth ....II John
God is Good...III John

RIGHT BEHAVIOR (Read I John 1:1–3:24)

John gives us seven tests of Christian behavior. Read these and find what your "rating" is as a Christian. They are easy to find because each of these tests is introduced by *if we say* or *he that saith*. The test is this—*if we say* one thing, and do another, we are not living as Christ would want us to, in full fellowship with Himself. How much easier it is to talk than it is to do. As Moody said, "We talk cream and live skim milk." For *truly our fellowship is with the Father, and with his Son Jesus Christ* (1:3). We are to walk together, talk together, and live together. We are to eat at the same table (Rev. 3:20). We are one family (Eph. 3:15). God is my Father because Jesus Christ my Elder Brother has made me a child of the King. Therefore I must behave that way. Fellowship brings joy (1:4). There is no joy greater than fellowship with a friend.

I walk with a God of light. *God is light, and in him is no darkness at all* (1:5). If my walk is with Him, I will walk in the light of His love and grace.

SEVEN TESTS OF OUR WALK WITH GOD
First Test—Walk in the Light

If we say that we have fellowship with him, [the God of light] *and walk in darkness, we lie, and do not the truth* (1:6).

Is there known sin in your life? If there is, you are not walking with Christ. His presence throws light on your conscience and heart and shows the presence of sin in the life (Eph. 5:13). A Christian who is walking in fellowship with God will enjoy fellowship with other Christians (I John 1:7). Have you ever picked up a stone that has been lying on the ground for a long time? The minute you lift it, loathsome things move in every direction to flee from the light. Light reveals sin. Known sin will keep you from fellowship with Christ, but fellowship with Christ will keep you from sin. Do you ask Him to throw His searchlight upon your heart?

Second Test—Admit You Are a Sinner

If we say that we have no sin, we deceive ourselves, and the truth is not in us (1:8). You cannot walk with God and practice sin in your life at the same time. God keeps showing us the sin in our lives. On the cross He redeemed us from the penalty of sin once and for all. But let us know, too, that if we confess our sins He keeps cleansing us from the sins that creep into our lives by our contact with this world.

When a farmer plows his field he throws out every stone that he finds. But the next year as the plow goes deep in the furrow, he finds other stones that had remained hidden the year before. He throws these aside as they turn up. Then the next year the same thing occurs. So in our lives! God will reveal by the plow of His Spirit the sins that are hidden in our lives, that we did not know were there. Don't be discouraged, but use His remedy.

If we confess our sins, he is faithful and just to forgive us our sins, and to cleanse us from all unrighteousness. Don't pray in an indefinite way. Name it before God. Is it pride, lack of trust, anger, love of pleasure more than God? Well, whatever it is, lay it out before God and tell Him what it is. Call it by name. Then claim God's promise. *He is faithful and just,* not only to *forgive us our sins* but *to cleanse us from all unrighteousness.* A human parent can forgive our misbehavings, but only God can cleanse us from sin.

Third Test—Obey God's Will

He that saith, I know him, and keepeth not his commandments, is a liar, and the truth is not in him (2:4). Obedience is a real test. God makes a very strong statement. If you say you are a Christian and do not obey Him, you are a liar. The man that is a Christian keeps God's commandments.

What are Christ's commandments? Love the Lord thy God with all thy heart, soul and mind, and thy neighbor as thyself. Do you love God that way? Put yourself to a few tests. Do you spend more time watching television than you do with God? Then you don't love Him with all your heart. Are you ambitious to carry out some plan in your life that you hope will bring you fame or wealth or just enjoyment? Don't say you know God when you won't keep His commandments. Do you know His will for your life? Do you want to? This is a test of your Christian life. Are you obedient to His Word? His still small voice? Many times we do not want to let God talk to us. We will not listen to Him because we are afraid of His will for us. Youth looks for a career. God has a career for each one of us. He has a plan for every step of our lives, for "the steps of a good man are ordered of the Lord." We must obey in everything for "whatsoever is not of faith is sin."

You will begin to know what God wishes as you grow to know Him better. A group of fellows were going to a nightclub of bad reputation. They stopped to ask a young chap to go along. "I can't go," he said. "Why not?" his associates asked. "Well, because my mother wouldn't want me to." "How do you know she wouldn't? She doesn't even know we are going." "Because I know my mother," was his very wise reply. This is true when you learn to know God—you will know what His desires are (3:24).

Christ says, *If ye love me, keep my commandments,* and *Ye are my friends, if ye do whatsoever I command you* (John 15:14). His command is in that very chapter: *These things I command you, that ye love one another* (John 15:17).

Fourth Test—Imitate Christ

He that saith he abideth in him ought himself also so to walk, even as he walked (2:6).

We should be Christlike in all our life. Christ says, *Ye are the salt of the earth.* Salt preserves food from spoiling. Are you the preservative of your crowd? Do you keep the language clean? Do you refrain from using God's Name in vain? Does your presence keep them from doing questionable things?

A little Chinese girl said, "I know why Christ said, *Ye are the salt of the earth.* Because salt makes folks thirsty and Christians should make others thirsty for Christ." Are you making folks thirsty?

People are too lazy to look up. Few try to find Christ. So Christ wants others to see Him reflected in us. In the famous Sistine Chapel in Rome, the beauty of the art is in the ceiling.

As you enter you are given a mirror. It seems strange to see people walking around looking down when the paintings are above. But they see all the glory reflected in the mirrors before them, without breaking their necks. Be a reflector. Let the beauty of Jesus be seen in you.

Fifth Test—Love Others

He that saith he is in the light, and hateth his brother, is in darkness even until now (2:9).

Another acid test of the Christian life is love (2:7-11). Love changes a person. Love makes us have a concern for the welfare of others.

God speaks of love to others, personal attitudes. There are three chief attitudes toward others: hatred, which is murder (3:15); indifference—a feeling akin to hate—no concern (4:20-21); love. Love shows itself in different ways (2:9-11; 3:14); physically—concern for welfare (3:16-18); spiritually—concern for another's soul.

Sixth Test—Relationship to the World

If any man love the world, the love of the Father is not in him (2:15).

We live in a present evil world (Gal. 1:4). The scheme of things as they exist today is not the standard for the Christian. Whenever you find him obeying them, he is walking on forbidden ground.

All sins may be put into three categories: 1. *Lust of the flesh;* 2. *Lust of the eyes;* 3. *Pride of life.*

1. *Lust of the flesh*

Temptations come through the body and its appetites and passions. The devil tempted Jesus in this way first. Jesus had been fasting forty days, and every atom of His being cried for bread. How plausible was Satan's temptation! It was the same appeal to appetite that Satan made to Eve. In all these thousands of years the devil has invented no new weapons of attack. *Command that these stones be made bread.* The temptation for self-gratification is one of the strongest that can assail us. Appetite is still one of the most vulnerable points when Satan attacks us. The necessity for bread and pleasure is supposed by some to justify any means to get them. It is not necessary that we should live at all! There is only one moral necessity—to trust God and keep His commandments.

2. *Lust of the eyes*

Foiled with one weapon, Satan quickly drops it and tries another. Taking Jesus into a high mountain, he showed Him *(lust of the eyes)* all the kingdoms of the world in a moment of time. *If thou therefore wilt worship me, all shall be thine* (Luke 4:7). Satan was working his second trick.

How men worship at the altar of riches and honor, because they long for what their eyes see of this world!

Your eyes can blacken your soul! Be careful what you see. If you throw a white tennis ball against a sooty wall, there will be a black mark left upon it. If your eye is thrown against impure objects, be sure a mark will be left upon your mind and heart. Be careful what you see!

3. *Pride of life*

Everyone wants spectacular success. The devil took Jesus to the pinnacle of the Temple and told Him to cast Himself down and if He was the Son of God, He would be kept by angels. It was a proposal to leap from the pinnacle of the Temple into immediate popularity. It is a temptation for any person to be popular. We all have human ambitions. How many men of genius have been led astray because the glittering prize of ambition has been held up before them! We want to win it at a single stroke. How strong is the temptation to take a short-cut to our ambition whether of education or wealth or position and power. We are in danger of selling our very souls to gain our end! Even Jesus saw the world spread before Him and saw how short and alluring was the step that was promised Him, but to become the subject of the "prince of this world" would have ended His mission as the Saviour of the world.

Seventh Test—Prove Christ Is Righteous by Your Life

Do we acknowledge Christ by our life? (2:22) *If ye know that he is righteous, ye know that every one that doeth righteousness is born of him* (2:29). Others watch us to see if we "do righteousness." He who abides in Christ will bear the same fruit in his life that Christ bears and that is righteousness.

There are a few verses in chapter 3:1-10 that are difficult to understand unless we know what the original text means.

Everyone who commits (practices) sin is guilty of lawlessness; for [that is what] sin is, lawlessness. This is The Amplified New Testament translation of 3:4. If we know Christ as God dwelling in our lives, we will not "practice sin." *Whosoever sinneth* [keeps practicing sin] *hath not seen him, neither known him* (3:6), and in verse 9, *Whosoever is born of God doth not commit* [practice] *sin*. It is possible for a Christian under strong temptation, to fall into sin for the time, but he will not keep practicing it. If a man continually practices sin, he may well doubt his conversion! We should consider sin as God does. Sin cost God His Son!

RIGHT BELIEF (Read I John 4:1–5:11)

We need a creed by which to live. The word "creed" comes from the Latin word, "credo"—"I believe." There are sins of the body which we all commit, but there are sins of the heart and disposition as well. God is as interested in what you believe as in how you act.

You cannot believe things that are not true about Christ and at the same time have fellowship with Him. It is absurd to say that it doesn't make any difference what you believe as long as you are in earnest. This statement is unsound. We cannot believe what is false and have it affect our life and then go out and live a life that is true. This is not any more possible than that we can believe that an eight o'clock train leaves at nine o'clock and not miss the train. Neither can we sincerely believe a bottle contains a healing medicine when really it is a deadly poison and taking it find anything but death.

The unsound teachers of John's day were denying the fact that Christ truly suffered and truly rose again. They said He was only a mystery man who appeared and vanished but He was not God.

You cannot deny the death of Christ on the cross and find a pardon for your sin. You cannot deny the resurrection of Christ and enjoy the privileges of Christianity that are found in a living

Christ. You cannot deny that Christ is God and find any access to the Father.

Your sin can start in your intellect. What do you believe? Christ wants to be our only Teacher. What we believe determines how we act.

Is a creed necessary? Read John 3:16 and see if you think it is. It says *Whosoever believeth hath everlasting life*. Christianity is Christ-centered. Christ out of Christianity leaves nothing. This means death. If we believe not, we shall die, but if we believe we shall live (Rom. 10:9,10).

So many Christians are spiritual babes in Christ. They are led astray with every new "wind of doctrine." They are susceptible to all about them. When doubt fills their minds they sink in despair. Hence everyone ought to be given a way whereby he can test every religion to see if it be true. Especially is this true in this day of so many religious beliefs. John states the test very clearly in 4:1-3. *Beloved, believe not every spirit, but try the spirits whether they are of God: because many false prophets are gone out into the world. Hereby know ye the Spirit of God: Every Spirit that confesseth that Jesus Christ is come in the flesh is of God: and every spirit that confesseth not that Jesus Christ is come in the flesh is not of God: and this is that spirit of antichrist.*

WHAT SHALL WE BELIEVE?

John makes some plain statements in these verses above.

1. That Jesus Christ is come in the flesh—"in carnis" (4:1,2; 5:20,21).

This is the first thing we must be sure of. We must believe that when Jesus walked this earth He was God clothed in human flesh. He took upon Himself the form of a man that He might die in man's place, and bare his sins in His own body on the tree.

John records, *And the Word was made flesh, and dwelt among us, (and we beheld his glory, the glory as of the only begotten of the Father,) full of grace and truth* (John 1:14). Christ's earthly life was thirty-three years, but that is not His whole existence. Christ was with the Father from the beginning.

Over 1900 years ago this Man of the ages came to this earth at His first advent. He did not begin life at the manger. He merely took upon Himself the form of a man. Then He remained on this earth thirty-three years. He died and was buried and rose again. Then He went back to where He came from.

Think how Christ was received on the earth the first time He came! *He came unto his own, and his own received him not* (John 1:11). They did not think that this One "in the flesh" before their eyes was God. They called Him a blasphemer when He claimed to be equal with God, saying, *I and my Father are one* (John 10:30). For this they put Him to death. They would not believe that Jesus Christ was God come in the flesh!

2. We must believe in the deity of Christ (4:15; 5:5). That He is the Son of God, the only begotten Son.

The liar is the one who denies that Jesus is the Christ, the promised Messiah (2:22). The Old Testament prophets told us the Messiah was coming. The angel chorus said that the Babe, born in Bethlehem, was this Messiah who was prophesied. Simeon saw Christ in the Babe (Luke 2:25-35).

3. We must believe that God is love (4:8).

There is no force in the world to compare with Christian love. Its power is seen in the great fact that "God is love." All through this chapter it isn't our love that is the definition of love at its best, but God's love which is the measure. Listen! *For love is of God; God is love; Herein is love . . . that he loved us; His love is perfected in us; We love him, because he first loved us.* Love turns our hearts away from ourselves. We cannot really love God without loving others. So we become channels of blessing to others around us, because of what God is in us.

Nothing could influence our lives as much as the love of God. For *God dwelleth in us* (4:12). A man went to a pastor and said, "Sir, I want to enter into your religion." "My friend," said the pastor, "our religion must enter into you." God's love was shown in the gift of His Son to be a sacrifice for our sins (John 3:16; I John 4:9,10). When we look at the cross we catch a glimpse into God's heart of love. The cross was the only way God had of showing us His heart. It is a picture of infinite love poured out in all of its fullness. Christ did not die to make God love man. He died because God had loved man always with an everlasting love. *For God so loved.* Our salvation does not depend upon what we are, but upon what God is, and God is love!

God's love is first directed toward the individual. Then the individual must affect society. God is unseen and there are many who need God's love. So we will show it to others when we love. And when we love, we are like God. *We ought also to love one another.*

4. We must believe that Christ is our Saviour (5:10-12).

Christ was sent to be "the propitiation for our sins" because sin barred man from God's love, for *the wages of sin is death* (Romans 6:23). So Christ took the judgment of sin upon His own body on the cross and made it possible for God to show mercy righteously. Propitiation is the satisfaction by Christ's death of the whole demand of the law upon the sinner. Propitiation is the cause of life, for it is through the sacrifice of Christ that we have everlasting life (4:10).

He that believeth on the Son of God hath the witness in himself: he that believeth not God hath made him a liar; because he believeth not the record that God gave of his Son. And this is the record, that God hath given to us eternal life, and this life is in his Son. He that hath the Son hath life; and he that hath not the Son of God hath not life (I John 5:10-12).

GOD AND LOVE

Love is the supreme test of our Christian faith. *We know that we have passed from death unto life, because we love the brethren. He that loveth not his brother abideth in death* (3:14). The word "love" occurs 48 times in this first epistle of John. We find out how "love" acts in I Corinthians 13.

He that loveth not knoweth not God; for God is love (4:8). Love is the first instinct of the renewed heart. Where do we get our love? From within? No, from above. *We love him, because he first loved us* (4:19). What if we do not love? God says, we *knoweth not God.*

We should show our love to Him by loving one another (I John 4:7). He who has love in his heart has fellowship with God (4:16). But where there is no love, there is no fellowship (4:19-21).

RICH REWARDS (Read I John 5:12-21)

The rewards of a life in Christ are stated in the last verses:

Assurance of eternal life 5:13
Power of prayer 5:14,15
Power of intercession 5:16
Victory ....5:18 and 5:4,5

Underline the word "know" in verses 12-20. We can have confidence when we know Christ. John uses the word "know" over forty times in his epistles. True Christianity is more than a creed—it is something that can be known and felt. We know that Christ was manifested to take away our sins. We know that we have passed from death unto life. We know that whatsoever we ask we shall receive. John assures us of these truths.

II JOHN

This is a good example of John's private correspondence. This letter was addressed to an unknown Christian woman. This is the only book in the Bible addressed to a woman.

The word "truth" is found five times in this short letter of but thirteen verses. It is the key word. "Love" occurs four times. Truth and love are inseparable.

We must test all the teachings in the world by the Scriptures, *for the truth's sake* (v. 2). This is the final test. Test your experience by the Word of God, but never test the Word of God by your experience!

The truth that John speaks of is from above, the Truth as it is in Christ Jesus. We are to walk in the truth, not just admire it. Then we will love one another (v. 5). This love is genuine and not subject to change. *The love of Christ constraineth us* (II Cor. 5:14). The proof of our love is in our walk. *This is love, that we walk after his commandments* (v. 6).

THE DOCTRINE OF CHRIST

He that abideth in the doctrine of Christ, he hath both the Father and the Son (v. 9). This is the test of the gospel. Not what I think, or what someone else has thought, or said or done, but what has Christ said? What is He to you? Is He the Son of God?

Many false teachers were traveling among the churches (vs. 7-11) who would not confess that Jesus Christ was here in the flesh. These were deceivers and an antichrist (v. 7). See also I John 4:1,2. They did not believe in the humanity of Christ. They denied His incarnation. If you call Him "Lord" and deny His deity, you are a liar and an antichrist. John says this.

Apply this test to some of the popular religious movements of our day—Christian Science, Spiritualism, Unity, Jehovah's Witnesses and other similar movements. They deny the "Christ doctrine" mentioned here.

Don't be friendly with these false teachers, John commands, or entertain them, for thus you share in their wicked work.

III JOHN

Do you remember what Christ said of Himself in John 14:6? *I am the way, the truth, and the life.* We find Him portrayed in I, II and III John:

I John—Jesus the Life
II John—Jesus the Truth
III John—Jesus the Way

This letter was written to his generous and warmhearted friend called Gaius. This man was the type of the true Christian layman who has dedicated his wealth and talent to the Lord. His purse strings are loose and his latchstring is out. All he has belongs to Christ. He is the picture of the man who has found Christ to be the "Way," and in his everyday life, he tries to show that gracious "Way" to others. Such men, scattered here and there, have through the years, kept not only the Church alive in an unfriendly world, but have kept Christ's love burning brightly in the midst of God's people when all seemed dark.

Gaius was noted for his loving hospitality. John urges him to continue entertaining the traveling preachers in spite of bitter opposition of an autocratic and blustering church official named Diotrephes. Hospitality is a manifestation of Christian love.

You can be either a Gaius, helping in the Kingdom, or a Diotrephes, hindering the cause.

What a splendid thing to be rich and powerful, and to choose to lay all your gifts and talents at Jesus' feet, like Gaius and Demetrius!

UNDERSTANDING JUDE

Jude was a brother of the Lord. He knew Peter. They walked with the Master and no doubt talked together after His departure. They evidently thought much alike on the great issues of the day. II Peter and Jude are very similar in thought and language. Both men were dealing with the dangers confronting the doctrines of the Church.

No doubt certain persons had "joined the Church." They were not outside but inside the Church. They had crept in unawares.

Alas! What church is without them today? They are with us, but not of us. Christ will judge these evil men as He did the fallen angels.

These intruders had begun to teach error in the church (vs. 3,4). There was a leaven of evil at work among the readers.

In contrast to these evil fellows we find the true followers of the faith, lifting high the cross of Christ (vs. 20-23).

THE INTRUDERS

Ungodly men—worldly
Turning the grace of our God into lasciviousness—carnal
Denying the only Lord God—skeptical
Despise dominion, and speak evil of dignities—lawless
Murmurers, complainers—critical

Having men's persons in admiration—flattery
Sensual, having not the Spirit—aliens

A Christian's Building Program

Build your faith
Pray in the Holy Spirit
Keep in God's love
Look for God's mercy
Win souls for Him
Rest on His keeping power

Thank God for this noble army of faithful ones! Of these God says that their reward shall be that here they will *keep you from falling* and up there *present you faultless* (v. 24).

Minimum Daily Requirements/Spiritual Vitamins

Sunday: WALKING IN FELLOWSHIP
I John 1:1–2:14
Monday: WALKING AS CHILDREN OF GOD
I John 2:15–3:24
Tuesday: WALKING IN LOVE   I John 4:1-21
Wednesday: WALKING IN KNOWLEDGE
I John 5:1-21
Thursday: WALKING IN TRUTH   II John 1–13
Friday: WALKING IN THE WAY   III John 1–14
Saturday: WALKING WITHOUT FALLING
Jude 1–25

647

UNDERSTANDING REVELATION

Revelation Portrays Jesus Christ, Our Triumphant King

Revelation is the only book of prophecy in the New Testament. It is the only book in the Divine Library that especially promises a blessing to those who read and hear. "Blessed" is a strong word. *Blessed is he that readeth* is what the book of Revelation says of itself, but after reading the first chapters about the churches, and the last chapters describing heaven, not many of us read much in this book.

Revelation presents a glorious, reigning Christ. The Gospels presented Him as a Saviour, One who came to take the curse of sin, but in this last book we see no humiliation. In one way Revelation is the most remarkable book in the whole sacred canon. Revelation tells us about the reign of Christ on this earth which Satan wants to control. It tells of Christ's complete and eternal victory over Satan. It describes Satan's defeat and punishment, first for a thousand years, then eternally. It tells more about Satan's final doom than any other book. No wonder Satan doesn't want men to read it!

UNRAVELLING THE RIDDLE

Does "revelation" mean a riddle? Most people seem to think it does, when speaking of this book. No, it means just the opposite—"unveiling." It is written in symbols. "It was sent and signified" by the angel to John. The deaf and dumb have a sign language. Each gesture is filled with meaning. So is every sign in Revelation. There are 300 symbols in this book, and each has a definite meaning. Symbols are wonderful and speak great truths.

The content of the book seems to indicate that most of its events are yet to be fulfilled.

This book is the Revelation of Jesus Christ, not the revelation of John. It is not the revelation of the growth of the Church and the gradual conversion of the world, but it is the Revelation of Jesus Christ! It was given by Christ Himself to John (1:1,2). The book deals with the return of the Lord to this earth. It describes the readiness or unreadiness of the Church for this great happening (3:20). There are descriptions of the tremendous events on earth and in heaven just before, during and after His coming.

What is meant by *the time is at hand* (1:3)? Almost 2,000 years have passed since these words were spoken, but the idea is "the next on the program." No matter how much time may intervene, the next thing after the day of grace is the kingdom age to be ushered in by our Lord's coming.

There are few people with any imagination who have not sat down and thought, "I wonder how it would feel to be a king." But Christ says when He comes He will make us reign as kings (1:6)!

Then *those that pierced him* shall see Him (v. 7). While that means especially the Jews who at Christ's coming will turn to Him as a united people and be saved (Romans 11:25,26), at the same time it means many others who have pierced Christ will see Him. Have YOU pierced Him?

Christ is the theme of this wonderful book. It gives an authentic portrait of the Lord Jesus as the Triumphant One. No less than twenty-six times do we find in it Christ's sacrificial title "Lamb" (5:6). In addition we see a vision of the future of the Church and the world in relation to Him.

It has been said that the saving blood of Christ runs through the entire Bible like a red cord. It has also been said that the second coming of Christ runs through the Bible like a golden cord. We are saved and washed clean in His blood, in order that we may be ready and eager for His return.

A TO Z

Revelation is a wonderful way to finish the story which was begun in Genesis. All that was begun in the Book of Beginnings (Genesis) is consummated in Revelation. In Genesis the heaven and earth were created. In Revelation we see a new heaven and a new earth. In Genesis the sun and moon appear; in Revelation we read that there is no need of the sun or moon, for Christ is the light of the new heaven. In Genesis there is a garden; in Revelation there is a holy city. In Genesis there is the marriage of the first Adam; in Revelation the marriage supper of the second Adam, Jesus Christ. In Genesis we see the beginning of sin; in Revelation sin is done away. So we can follow the appearance of the great Adversary, Satan, and sorrow and pain and tears in Genesis, and see their doom and destruction in Revelation.

Things are very black in the world today. No one living has ever known such uncertainty as to the future of human events. But things were black when the apostle John, an old, old man, was exiled to the Isle of Patmos. He had been banished for his testimony of Jesus (1:9). While on the island, John was forced to labor hard in the mines and quarries. But his Commander-in Chief appeared to him and delivered a ringing message and ultimate glory.

God had determined from the beginning that His Son would be the Ruler of this universe (Isa. 9:6,7).

GOD'S LAST DRAMA

Revelation is the greatest drama of all time. The plot is tense throughout; the final scene is glorious, for Christ comes unto His own. The Hero is our Lord Himself; the villain is the devil. The actors are the seven churches. The characters unloosed by the seals of chapters 6 and 7 are introduced by the "four horsemen." Then those summoned by the trumpets in turn leave the center of the scene of action, and we see the Antichrist, the world ruler, stalking across the stage (chapter 13). This incarnation of the devil himself is determined to set up his own kingdom and be worshiped by men. But Christ brings all to naught. This majestic Actor, bringing His hosts with Him, comes forth—the long-looked-for King of kings and Lord of lords. He drives His enemies from the stage in utter defeat (chapter 19).

After all the struggle has ended, and the beasts have been destroyed and the devil bound, and *the former things are passed away,* then we hear these words, full of hope, *Behold, I make all things new* (Rev. 21:4,5). This book brings to a climax the great story commenced in Genesis, and as all good stories should, it ends "And they lived happily ever after."

NOTICE THE 7's IN THIS BOOK

- Seven Churches
- Seven seals
- Seven trumpets
- Seven signs
- Seven last plagues
- Seven dooms
- Seven new things

PAST—THE THINGS WHICH THOU HAST SEEN
(Read Revelation 1:1-18)

Here is the last picture of Jesus Christ given in the New Testament. Many artists have tried to portray Him, but they have failed. Here is an authentic portrait (1:13-16). He is standing in the midst of the seven golden lampstands, representing the churches (v. 20). Lampstands prove that the Church is to be a light-bearer. *Ye are the light of the world.* How many churches today are for entertainment, bazaars, and to promote money-making schemes, instead of lights to shine in a dark place!

Christ is likened to a "son of man," but it is clear from the vision that the One whom John saw was more than human. He was the Son of Man. Everything symbolizes majesty and judgment, and this thought of judgment strikes the keynote of the book. Christ is presented to the whole world as Judge:

Clothed with a garment down to the foot—flowing robes a token of dignity and honor

Hair . . . white like wool—He is the Ancient of Days

Eyes . . . as a flame—intelligence; bringing hidden things to light

Feet like unto fine brass—brass symbolizes judgment

Voice as the sound of many waters—power and majesty

Hands—in these are kept the ministers of Christ

Mouth—out of it went judgment

Countenance . . . as the sun shineth in his strength (1:12-18).

John's vision was not of this age in which we are living, but of a future day when men shall appear before Christ to be judged (John 5:27-29). Now, we may have all of God's grace, mercy and forgiveness for the taking. Now, Christ is before us to be judged. We can reject Him if we choose. In Revelation, John is picturing Christ in judgment. The day of mercy is past, when we stand before the Judge.

When John saw this glorious One, he fell at His feet as dead, so overpowering was the vision (1:17). But Christ's words were reassuring. He said He was the Living One, and though He had been dead, He was alive for evermore, and held the keys of death and Hades. Then follows the command to write what is found in this book (1:19). We do not have the usual picture of Christ starting in Bethlehem and ending at the Mount of Olives, but here we have His life in heaven, as the crown and culmination of all.

Have you ever seen the Lord? When Moses saw Him his face shone. Job abhorred himself and repented in ashes. Isaiah saw himself unclean. Saul (Paul) fell down and worshiped Him as Saviour. What would happen to us if we really saw the Lord?

PRESENT — THE THINGS WHICH ARE
(Read Revelation 1:20–3:22)

In the second and third chapters we find Christ's love letters to His churches. These letters are alike in pattern. Christ dictated them to the ministers (angels) of the seven churches to whom He addressd these letters. In each, look for the speaker, praise, reproof, exhortation, and promise.

The churches named were churches which actually existed in John's day. In dealing with them, He seems to give us a brief church history from the First Century Church to the Church of Today, in seven periods:

Ephesus—the church of the first-love, the Apostolic Church (2:1-7)

Smyrna—the persecuted church—Diocletian to Constantine (2:8-11)

Pergamos—the church under imperial favor—under Constantine (2:12-17)

Thyatira—the Papal church—the Dark Ages (2:18-29)

Sardis—the Reformation church—Protestantism, 16th and 17th Centuries (3:1-6)

Philadelphia—the missionary church—period ushered in by the Puritan movement (3:7-13)

Laodicea—the rejected church—church of the final apostasy (3:14-19)

Discover where you find Christ at the end of this Church Age. *Behold, I stand at the door, and knock: if any man hear my voice, and open the door, I will come in to him, and will sup with him, and he with me* (3:20). He is outside, knocking to get in. The Church will not let Him in, but He pleads with the individual: *If any man . . . open the door, I will come in.* Have you opened your heart's door to Christ?

Let us take heed to words like those found in this letter: *Nevertheless I have somewhat against thee . . . But I have a few things against thee . . . Notwithstanding I have a few things against thee* (2:4,14,20). These are the warnings of a faithful Saviour.

Discover how Christ is set forth in these two chapters. Remember, this book is the Revelation of Jesus Christ. What are the promises to the overcomers? See if you can find seven.

FUTURE — THE THINGS WHICH SHALL BE HEREAFTER
(Read Revelation 4:1–22:21)

The great revelation proper, unfolds with the sound of trumpets, *a door is opened in heaven* and a Voice says, *Come up hither, and I will show thee things which must be hereafter.*

First the throne of God comes into view (4:1-3). Revelation becomes the "Book of the Throne." This is the great central fact which pervades the book. This throne speaks of judgment. The throne of grace is no longer seen. The scene is a courtroom. The Judge of all the earth is on the bench; the twenty-four elders are the jury, representing the twelve patriarchs of the Old Testament and the twelve Apostles of the New (4:4). The seven spirits of God (4:5; 5:6) are the prosecutor, and the four living creatures are court attendants, ready to carry out the will of the Judge.

Next in importance to the Lamb Himself is the sealed book (5:1). Who can possibly open the book? None, save One. He *hath prevailed to open the book*. Christ prevailed in the wilderness after forty days. He prevailed in Gethsemane. On Calvary, He prevailed when He dropped His divine head on His pulseless breast and said, "It is finished." On the third day He arose from the dead and conquered death, sin, hell and Satan. This same Christ now claims the kingdom of the world by right of conquest.

The day of tribulation begins with the opening of the seven seals (chapter 6). This describes the Great Tribulation period spoken of by the prophet Jeremiah in Jeremiah 30 as the *time of Israel's sorrow*. Christ also referred to it as a great tribulation, such as has never happened upon the earth (Matt. 24:21). During the Great Tribulation God will allow sin to work out its tragic results. God's hand will be lifted from man and beast. The earth will be filled with war, hunger, famine and pestilence. Judgment must come on those who have rejected the Son of God and put Him to an open shame. We as Christians can look for Christ, not for calamity, because our Saviour is coming to receive us to Himself and free us from this day.

FOUR HORSEMEN

In the sixth chapter we see the famous "four horsemen" (6:1-8). Restraint is removed as the seals are broken. The forces of evil have been held in check. When the seals are torn away, war and destruction are set loose. Man is reaping what he has sown himself. The anguish and horror of the period will be the result of human ambition, hatred and cruelty.

First, we see the white horse of religious witness come before the final catastrophe upon the earth. Then comes the red horse, and universal war breaks upon the world, when peace will be taken from the earth. The black horse of famine and scarcity follows upon universal war. Lastly, the pale horse of pestilence and death comes forth with merciless tread.

The sixth seal (6:12-17) brings social chaos, the complete breaking up of society and a boasted civilization. Darkness, falling stars, heavens rolled up as a scroll, islands moving, is the picture presented. Then the most tragic prayer meeting on earth with kings and priests, rich and poor, fleeing from God in a general stampede, praying for death, for *the great day of his wrath is come.*

There is a momentary pause (chapter 7), while the saved of the tribulation period are presented. These are "a great multitude" with their garments washed and made white in the blood of the Lamb. The "sealed" are all Israelites—God is starting to gather His people unto Himself (Hosea 1:9,10). The "great multitude" is from all nations. This proves that the Gospel preached in the tribulation period will be most effective.

THE SEVEN TRUMPETS

Silence in heaven for thirty minutes! Orchestras cease! Seraphim and cherubim fold their wings! All is still! It is as though all heaven were waiting in breathless expectation. This is the calm before the storm (chapter 8). War, famine and pestilence have devastated the earth. Now His judgments have come upon the earth and Satan, knowing his time is short, is exceedingly wrathful. We find unprecedented activity of demons, 200,000,000 demons sweeping across the earth. Hell is let loose! Sin is allowed its full sway, and death is preferable to life (9:1-21). Satan does his last work upon the earth.

Finally we see Satan incarnating himself in the Antichrist. His portrait is given in Revelation 13. See also Daniel 12:11; Matthew 24:15; II Thess. 2:3. This Antichrist will be a world ruler. He demands the honors due to Christ Himself. He will be the political ruler of this world. He is the embodiment of wickedness. He will be shrewd and clever and a real leader of men. The Antichrist will be a Caesar, an Alexander, a Nero and a Hitler all in one. Men can neither *buy or sell, save he that had the mark.* Mergers and trusts of great proportion are in the world today. Such mergers and trusts were unheard of a few years ago. The "mark of the beast" is like the brand mark of ownership, or the token of allegiance like the swastika. It will be impossible for man to buy or sell without permission. The number 666 is "the number of a man." 6 is the number of evil.

So three 6's express a trinity of wickedness.

The final doom of the Antichrist will be the lake of fire at Christ's coming (19:20). There will be plagues like those of Egypt—blood, hail, fire, locusts, darkness, famine, sores, earthquakes, war and death. In these plagues is summed up the wrath of God upon a Christ-rejecting world.

THE SEVEN GOLDEN BOWLS

In the trumpets, Satan is releasing his power to accomplish his objectives. The bowls are God's power released against Satan. The bowls are God's answer to the devil. The "bowls" blast the dominion of Satan. Satan has dared to challenge God's power. God is now answering the challenge. Satan is forced into action. His kingdom is shaken to its foundations and he is undone. This event ends in the Battle of Armageddon (16:13-16). This battle is described in chapter 19. In the closing scene of the war, Christ takes the leadership of His armies, and brings His foes to their doom.

THE DOOMS

The seventh "bowl" announced the "dooms" which were to follow. Civilization has come to utter collapse. Even though God has revealed its utter evil, nevertheless men blaspheme God and repent not (16:9,11). Today, amid the luxuries of invention, men are dissatisfied and far from God. Hatred has turned into wars of colossal dimension. God pronounces seven "dooms" (chapter 17-20). First the doom of great systems—ecclesiastical (chapter 17), commercial (chapter 18), political (19:11-19); then the beast and the false prophet (19:20,21), followed by the nations (20:7-9), and the devil (20:10), and finally, the doom of the lost is pronounced (20:11-15).

THE MARRIAGE OF THE LAMB

The "Hallelujah Chorus" announces the coming of the long-promised King, our Lord Jesus Christ, the heir of David's throne, to catch away His bride (I Thess. 4:17). Hell has been let loose on earth. Satan and his cohorts have done their worst, and Christ has finally triumphed. Righteousness, long on the scaffold, is now to mount the throne. The marriage of the Lamb is come (19:7). The marriage supper of Christ will take place in the air. The saints will be rewarded in the air, according to their works. This time of rejoicing will continue until Christ returns to the earth with His bride, to set up His millennial kingdom.

After the Battle of Armageddon (19:17-19), Christ having subdued all His enemies, will take alive Antichrist (19:20) and the false prophet and cast them with a strong arm into the lake of fire. This is a name for Gehenna, the place where torment never ceases and from which none return. Christ will make an end of Satan's entire system.

THE MILLENNIUM

This is the time when Christ, the Prince of Peace, will establish His kingdom upon the earth for a thousand years. The devil is to be bound for a thousand years (20:3); the saints that Christ brings with Him will reign with Him for a thousand years (20:4,6); the wicked dead will not rise until the end of the thousand years (20:5).

There will be a thousand years of peace and joy upon the earth, when *the earth shall be filled with the knowledge of the glory of the LORD, as the waters cover the sea* (Hab. 2:14). It will be a glorious time to live. No wars, no weeds, no wild animals, no taxes, neither the heartache of death! When this period has come to an end, then the devil will be released again. He will come to test the nations (20:7-9). We discover their real attitude, and learn that they prefer Satan to Christ. We can hardly believe it, but read 20:7,8 *And when the thousand years are expired, Satan shall be loosed out of his prison, and shall go out to deceive the nations which are in the four quarters of the earth, Gog and Magog, to gather them together to battle; the number of whom is as the sand of the sea.*

Satan is the author and instigator of war. After a thousand years of peace, Satan gathers them to "the war." Not a few gather, but a countless number, like *the sand of the sea*. But *fire came down from God out of heaven, and devoured them* (20:9). Men's rebellion against God seems almost unbelievable but *the heart is deceitful above all things, and desperately wicked: who can know it* (Jer. 17:9)?

SATAN'S DOOM

Satan is treated too lightly by the average person. He is mighty! He is the deceiver of the whole world. He fell from the highest place, next to God Himself, to the lowest depths—*the lake of fire.* Christ described it as *the everlasting fire, prepared for the devil and his angels* (Matthew 25:41). The devil is given a life sentence (Rev. 20:10).

The blazing white throne of the final judgment is set. The One sitting upon it shall judge all men. Read Revelation 20:11-15. The "dead" are brought before Him. The sea gives up its dead. The grave gives up its dead. Hades gives up the dead. The dead are judged according to their works (20:12,13). Final doom is pronounced. The Saviour is now the Judge. *Whosoever was not found written in the book of life was cast into the lake of fire* (20:15). Judgment must come before the Golden Age of glory can be ushered in. Someone has called hell the penitentiary of the universe, and the universal cemetery of the spiritually dead.

SEVEN NEW THINGS

A new heaven and earth 21:1

A new people 21:2-8

A new bride 21:9

A new home 21:10-21

A new temple 21:22

A new light 21:23-27

A new Paradise 22:1-5

HAPPILY EVER AFTER

Yes, God's story ends "and they lived happily ever after." Read the triumph of God in Revelation 21 and 22. Satan has not been victorious in his attempt to separate man from fellowship with God by sin, ever since his meeting with the first man and woman in the garden of Eden. He has utterly failed and we will be with Christ forever and ever!

Don't try to analyze or interpret this. Rather, meditate upon it. This is heaven! How limited words are in explaining its glory! The fellowship between God and man is restored. God "dwells with His people." Every purpose is realized and every promise is fulfilled. Heaven is the opposite of what we experience here. All is beautiful!

The last words of Christ in His Revelation are *Surely I come.* (22:20) Our response should ever be, *Even so, come* (22:20).

Minimum Daily Requirements/Spiritual Vitamins

Sunday: CHRIST AND THE CHURCHES
Revelation 1:1–3:22

Monday: CHRIST'S THRONE AND THE SEVEN SEALED
BOOK   Revelation 4:1–6:17

Tuesday: CHRIST'S TRUMPETS SOUNDED
Revelation 7:1–9:21

Wednesday: CHRIST AND THE WOES
Revelation 10:1–12:17

Thursday: CHRIST AND ANTICHRIST
Revelation 13:1–15:8

Friday: CHRIST'S FINAL TRIUMPH
Revelation 16:1–18:24

Saturday: CHRIST THE LORD OF ALL
Revelation 19:1–22:21

CHAPTER 52

A QUICK LOOK AT THE NEW TESTAMENT

COLOSSIANS THROUGH REVELATION

OUTSTANDING TRUTHS

Christ's Second Coming
Twentieth Century False Religions
Christ the Head of the Church
The Power of a Christian Life
The Word "Better" in Hebrews
Power of the Tongue

WHAT EPISTLES ARE SUGGESTED BY THE FOLLOWING WORDS?

Righteousness   Christ's coming again
The unruly tongue   Christian love
                The good fight (the wrestler)

BIOGRAPHIES

Timothy   James
Philemon   Peter
Titus   John, the apostle

WHAT WAS THE OCCASION OF EACH OF THE FOLLOWING STATEMENTS?

In What Book Is It Found?

I have fought a good fight, I have finished my course, I have kept the faith: henceforth there is laid up for me a crown of righteousness, which the Lord, the righteous judge, shall give me.

The Lord Himself shall descend from heaven with a shout, with the voice of the archangel . . . and the dead in Christ shall rise first . . .

I am not ashamed of the gospel of Christ: for it is the power of God unto salvation to every one that believeth.

All things work together for good to them that love God.

Come boldly unto the throne of grace.

Blessed is he that readeth, and they that hear the words of this prophecy, and keep those things which are written therein: for the time is at hand.

GREAT SENTENCE REVIEW

This gives a study of the most notable sentences in the epistles. Pick out the ones that seem most important to you. (Use concordance if necessary.)

All scripture is given by inspiration of God.

Now faith is the substance of things hoped for, the evidence of things not seen.

Faith without works is dead.

Unto you therefore which believe He is precious.

Add to your faith virtue; and to virtue knowledge.

If we confess our sins, He is faithful and just to forgive us our sins, and to cleanse us from all unrighteousness.

LAST WORDS ARE IMPORTANT

What Were The Last Words Of

Christ?	Luke 24:46-53
Paul?	II Timothy 4:1-9
Peter?	II Peter 3:10-18
James?	James 5:10-20
Jude?	Jude 17-25
The Bible?	Revelation 22:8-21

CHECK IN THE SQUARE YOUR CORRECT ANSWER

Thessalonians tells □ the sin of the tongue; □ of Christ's second coming; □ of Christ, the High Priest.

The heroes of the faith are found in □ Timothy; □ Hebrews; □ Revelation.

Timothy was □ Paul's son; □ an early missionary; □ Paul's convert.

God's future plans are revealed in □ Hebrews; □ Titus; □ Revelation.

662

TEACHING SUGGESTIONS

The primary purpose of this book is to give the Bible student a panoramic view of the Bible, so that he sees it as a cohesive whole instead of a series of unrelated stories set down in archaic English. The Bible is the story of what God is doing in history. Like any good story, it has a beginning and an ending. It starts with the creation; conflict is introduced with the workings of Satan and the fall of man, introducing the dilemma. The rest of the story is the solving of that great dilemma by God, and the final triumph of His purpose at the second coming of Christ. All the events in between fit into that story and contribute to the unfolding of the "plot." The Bible has one main theme—redemption—and many sub-themes which run through the entire book. Redemption is hinted at in the beginning—Genesis 3:15—and developed as the main theme, coming to a climax with the advent of Christ. The sub-themes, interwoven into the narrative, and all dependent upon the main theme of redemption are all defined and illustrated in the events of the Bible. For instance, the innate rebelliousness of sinful man is played up and becomes a major chord in the story of the wandering in the wilderness and in Judges, as well as in other minor episodes. The mercy of God is portrayed in Hosea; the victory He gives, in Joshua.

Fortunately, twentieth-century thirst for knowledge includes a wholesome curiosity about what the Bible teaches. In accompaniment to churches' expanding Sunday school enrollments, home Bible-study groups are springing up, and churches gladly respond to desires for weekday classes.

For the use of students in such classes, *A Look at the Old Testament* and *A Look at the New Testament* are available. These are abridgments of this parent volume, *What the Bible Is All About.* They may be secured from religious bookstores.

If you are teaching the Bible, there are two things to remember about your class or home study group:

1. Chances are they *do not* have any systematic knowledge of the Bible. Most of your students will not have attended Sunday school consistently enough to be really well informed. They see

663

the Bible as a collection of unrelated stories with morals, interspersed with long, dull passages they have never bothered to read; some beautiful poetry; some outstanding verses. The *pattern* of the Bible will be new to them. The history will certainly be a hazy impression of dignified characters in flowing garments either wandering in the wilderness or tending sheep in Palestine.

2. You can get across *one* main idea each lesson—and only one.

Now, with those two facts firmly in mind each time you teach, you want to do these things: give your class a picture of the whole of God's pattern, emphasizing how the particular book you are teaching fits into that whole, and drive home the major lesson of that book.

There is ample material provided for you to use any of several different approaches, but there are a few very broad principles that apply, whatever method you pursue.

First, always keep the whole scope of the Bible in mind. To begin with, read through this book for main impressions and emphases—quickly, just picking out the main points. Details will come later, as you work on each chapter.

Second, begin preparing each lesson a week in advance. You may have had some issues raised during the last class session that need to be clarified. Write those down. It's better to work on the lesson a little bit each day, and then put the final touches on it at the end of the preparation period. You will find that preparing a lesson this way is a little bit like making a pot of stew—the longer it simmers the better it gets.

Third, though by no means third in importance, do as much reading as you can in the book of the Bible you are teaching. This book has the most important passages listed. For instance, in the chapter on Genesis, we find a list of the beginnings that are noted in that book, along with the Scriptures. In each chapter the outline covers the major events of the book.

Fourth, constantly bring your thinking back to the central theme of each book. This is the thing you want to get across to your students! There may be other lessons drawn—other "themes" you'll mention—but keep referring back to this *main* theme. Cohesiveness ought to be the watchword of the teacher using this material.

Fifth, bear in mind the character and needs of the students you are teaching—they are not all alike. You may have a class of young adults, all wearing that brittle mask of self-sufficiency which cracks so easily to show the uncertainty underneath. They need absolutes, and they will respond to the absolutes of the Bible. They also need love and understanding, and they will open up like flowers to the understanding grace of God. Teach to those needs. A middle-aged group is another thing entirely. They may still have many of the same needs as the young adults, but added to this is the new dimension of attainment and power. It's up to the teacher to present the Bible in a manner suited to its importance. This age group especially needs to be buttressed against the persuasively presented false philosophy that security is to be found in "things." We ought to stress that God's kingdom must always have priority.

Finally, do remember that you are teaching, primarily, and not giving a devotional. Because we are all aware, as we ought to be, of the need to know Christ better and to love him more, we tend to forget that one of the major means to achieve these ends is to teach what the Bible says. There is no substitute for real teaching. There are all kinds of inspirational meetings designed to impel Christians to action, to move them to decision, help them with their devotional lives—but the Bible study is to give knowledge and directive to their faith. Anything that makes your teaching clear and explicit, that clarifies and explains, is good. If you use stories and illustrations to bring out your point, be sure they *do* just that. If they have an emotional punch, well and good; but beware of mere sentimentality. You may move a class to the edge of tears with a touching little story of a dying child, but if there isn't a real solid Bible truth in that story the effect is not so lasting.

Now, there are three basic methods that might be used with this material:

1. Student preparation method.
2. Class discussion method.
3. Lecture method.

Each method has some advantages and certain disadvantages; consider them, and see which one will best suit your class and its needs.

1. **Student preparation.** This requires real work by the pupils. For instance, on the week preceding the study of the chapter on Genesis, you might assign sections to the students. Tell each one to read the section assigned, study the Scriptures, and then give in his own words, at the next session, the lesson to be drawn from that story. Give each one a specified time to speak, allowing yourself at least ten minutes to sum it all up and bring out the main theme of the book.

The advantages are obvious—this encourages interest and Bible study on the part of the students. Most of them love to have a part, and unless you have an entire class of introverts you should be able to find enough each week to participate. There are some drawbacks to this. Unless your people are dependable they may either prepare poorly or be absent from the class when they are supposed to shine. This may be avoided by a telephone check during the week. Occasionally you'll get the original thinker who becomes so entranced with an obscure passage that he dwells on it to the exclusion of the main part of the story, sometimes drawing some very odd conclusions from the Scripture! Also, the time can get away from the speakers and you may be left with one minute for summing up. Experiment with this way of teaching—perhaps you will want to modify it a bit, or use it once in a while. It requires just as much preparation on the part of the teacher, for you must be on your toes to see that the lesson is rightly presented.

2. **Class Discussion.** This can be done in one of several ways. You might hand out discussion topics for the following week. These topics should be worked out from the lesson material, not simply using the questions at the end of the chapter. For example, in the lesson on Genesis you might find the following topics: What is God's answer to man's disobedience? How did sin enter the world? How does the Abrahamic Covenant illustrate the grace of God?

It is amazing how many people are seriously concerned about a question such as the origin of sin; they may ask some searching questions, and want to go far beyond the pointing out of Satan as the tempter. They may well ask you, "Yes, but if Satan was originally created by God, how could he be evil? How can a good God create something evil?" Be prepared to treat such a question with respect. A quick answer is not always the best answer, and such a profound issue demands more than a facile reply. Sometimes it may be a good thing to tell the class you will bring the answer next week, rather than hurry through.

In using this class discussion method, the teacher must be sure to keep the talk from wandering far afield. Remember, you have a point to put across, and you can't do justice to more than one major lesson. If the discussion dribbles off into pointlessness, keep pulling the class back to the main theme. One great secret in teaching is to know when an issue raised by the class is vital to their faith—something they've wondered about, puzzled over, and need an answer to—or when it is merely an oddity to quibble over. If, in the course of the lesson, your students seem concerned about a point you are making, don't be hesitant about taking more time to clarify that point. You may have to skim lightly over the rest of the lesson because of it; but you remember the fifth basic principle—that you are *teaching to their needs*. As you can see, this kind of classroom work requires a nice balance between adherence to the main purpose of your lesson and flexibility within that framework. Such a method is very demanding on the teacher, but the rewards are great.

Another way of using the discussion method is to ask the students to hand in the questions they would like to have answered, and then guide the discussion. This assumes a great deal of interest and intelligence on the part of your students, and there is one caution: you may have two or three very precocious and uninhibited students; they are all too willing to speak at length on their ideas about the lesson. *They* may be getting a great deal out of being so verbose, but the rest of the class is not. Regardless of the brilliance of the few vocal ones, the others don't want to listen to them; they want to hear from someone "in the know"—someone with more authority behind his statements than simply "Joe, who always talks too much anyway." Frequently these extroverted pupils are the ones who linger after class with special questions, or problems. They do need attention, but not to the exclusion of the rest of the class and some of the quieter students who need to be gently coaxed into sharing their ideas.

3. **Lecture.** This does not mean a rigid, formal presentation at all. It can be as flexible as either of the other methods, or used in combination with one of them. After you have established a good rapport with your class they'll feel free to interrupt the lesson when they have questions.

Let's take the chapter on Genesis, again, as our example. Read over this chapter carefully. Read through the book of Genesis, not stopping for details, but simply reading to get the broad outline of the book. This can be done, remember, at the first of the week. Let the lesson build, slowly, in your thinking.

Now you are ready to begin thinking about the emphasis you want to give the chapter. There is enough written material in the book so that if you merely read through it, your class time would be consumed. But what you have been provided with is the raw material of the lesson; it is up to you to shape it and give it emphasis.

First, think of the whole scope of the Bible as you want to present it. Beginnings are vitally important, and Genesis contains the plot, in germ, of the whole story of the gospel. Read over the first portion of the chapter carefully, until it becomes your own.

Second, go over the rest of the material and decide where you want to stress a point, where you can cover lightly. Since all of the stories are referred to again and again in the Bible as examples, they need to be well told. You may wish to dwell longer on one than on the others, in order to make a point. These should be related, not as different stories, but as parts of the whole. You have a double purpose in each lesson—to present the book in its proper relation to the entire scope of the Bible; and to bring out one grand truth, one practical lesson, from each book. Of course, you may cover several sub-themes, but keep coming back to the main lesson.

Third, go over your lesson, tie up any loose ends, and decide how you are going to sum it all up. The closing portion of your lesson is of prime importance. Here is where many a good speaker goes wrong. There is, as you know, a kind of "timing" that is the one main source of effective speaking or teaching. Some fortunate people have a built-in sense of timing—they know just how to build interest, when to hesitate the merest fraction of a second before uttering the punch line of a funny story, just when to move in fast for a climax, and, most important of all, when to *stop*. There *is* a Spirit-chosen time to stop—when you have made your point, *don't embellish it*. After you have said, in the most effective way you can, what you want them to remember, *that's all*. Resist the temptation to add just one more effective little sentence; it will not be at all effective if it's said after the psychological stopping time. Your audience has already mentally left; you might as well close.

Now, here are some reminders—little tips to tuck away in the back of your mind. It would be ideal if your students remembered everything you gave them each week, but be realistic—they will not. Recapitulate a little—not in detail, which would bore them terribly, but *briefly* go over the material covered. Do this in a positive way, so you won't make them conscious of their failure to remember. Say, "Of course you recall . . . " and then tell them what of course they did not recall. Since none of us assimilates knowledge in wholesale gulps, the teaching process consists largely of telling and retelling the same truths in different ways, so that gradually—very, very gradually—they become a part of the life of those who are learning.

Because this is a discussion of methods, we have not mentioned the very obvious things that underlie successful teaching—your desire to present Christ in a winning way, your constant dependence on prayer, and your utter reliance on the guidance of the Holy Spirit.

Beyond and above all the timeworn and timeless truths about teaching—our duty to do it, the satisfaction it affords, and all the reasons for devoting the time and the work and the energy to it—lies the deep and abiding pleasure of handling the Word of God, to which we are all committed.

GUIDING THE PRAYER TIME

Begin each class session with prayer.

Prayer is the keynote of success. Neither a class nor an individual can succeed in Christ without it. Prayer is the breath of the Christian. We are commanded to *pray without ceasing* (I Thessalonians 5:17). As natural as breathing is to a natural man, so natural should prayer be to a spiritual man. Does all of this describe you? Does the time of prayer in class have meaning or is it just a part of the normal procedure? It is a true statement that the class will go no further spiritually than you as teacher lead them.

What does prayer mean to *you?* To guide the time of prayer in class, you must be completely sold on its necessity yourself. You might make it a standard practice to ask the Lord daily for His guidance as you lead your students. Ask Him to give you a love and understanding of them that is like unto His love and understanding of you. Pray for the individuals, by name, if possible. Prepare your lesson, with prayer receiving an important part in your consideration.

As you come to class have an attitude that shows your complete dependence upon the Holy Spirit to guide your thoughts and words. Before you teach, ask that God will lead you. Do not rush through the opening prayer time, but do not prolong it to the place of boredom. Give opportunity for the students to take part if they desire. Encourage, but do not force participation. Be careful that neither you nor any other more mature Christian monopolize the prayer time. This is a time to talk to God, not the time to preach a sermon. When you pray, *really pray.*

VISUAL TEACHING AIDS

Visual aids for adults may be divided into four main types: projected, chalkboard, diagrams and charts, and maps. Use the aid (or combination of aids) that best illustrates a particular lesson.

PROJECTED AIDS

Preview the film before class. In this way you can prepare for the discussion which will follow the presentation and foresee any difficulties which the film may create. Projected aids should not be looked upon as "teaching crutches," but should be used either to introduce the lesson or to summarize that which has been taught.

Set up the projector and the record player well in advance of the presentation. Be sure that all is in good working order. The projector should have a 500-watt bulb and a cooling fan. If the room is small, a 300-watt bulb may be adequate, but test first to be sure. The projector should be placed on a rigid stand at the back of the room and high enough to avoid head shadows on the screen.

Place the screen in line with the projector and high enough to allow clear view by the class. Where it is not feasible to use the screen and darken the room, the projector may be placed at the front of the room and a sheet of white paper suspended between projector and class. The film should be turned around so the class can read the titles.

The record player should be placed near the projector. If at all possible use an auxiliary speaker at the front of the room. Ideally the operator should adjust the sound level and synchronize the sound and the picture as the showing progresses.

CHALKBOARD

A chalkboard may be purchased, or you can make it yourself. Use a piece of Masonite, the size appropriate to your class, and paint it with chalkboard paint. Or you can put a piece of clear plastic over a piece of cardboard (covered with white paper) and write with a grease pencil. If you would like to keep the outlines so that you can refer back to them in later lessons, use a flip chart. Fasten several pieces of paper or cardboard together at the top and then turn each piece as you complete the writing on it. Suit the size of the board to the size of your class. Often a portable board is sufficient.

The chalkboard is an indispensable part of teaching equipment. It provides an economical aid because it can be re-used repeatedly. It serves to center the student's interest on the point under discussion. But, needless to say, if the chalkboard is to be used successfully it must be wisely and efficiently used. All representations placed upon it should be definite and immediately purposeful; meaningless "doodlings" are confusing and distracting and are evidences of the teacher's lack of skill. In order to be easily readable, the material should be clearly and accurately reproduced with a minimum degree of artistry. Not too much material should be used at any one time because this clutters up the board and gives it a messy appearance. It also tends to reduce the space left for writing and makes it less intelligible.

Generally speaking, it is a good idea to erase material that is not needed in order to avoid distraction.

When outlines, summaries or similar materials are to be used by the group immediately, they should be placed on the board before the class convenes. If the teacher writes on the board while the class waits, valuable time is lost and the interest wanes. Do not be afraid, however, to use the chalkboard as the lesson develops. Put certain points on the board. Make a list of ideas that a discussion has brought forth. Write the reference for some Scripture that you are using. Let the students do some of the writing.

Use the chalkboard often in your lesson presentation. It will assist in keeping the development clearly in mind.

DIAGRAMS AND CHARTS

A good diagram must maintain two standards. First of all, it must be technically correct; it must be correctly and neatly drawn in the proper proportion and completely titled, labeled and explained. Nothing can be left to the imagination. In the second place, it has to be artistic because it must command the student's respect and thus encourage his interest and under-standing.

The diagram must be adequately explained or interpreted and a definite application made from it.

Various types of charts may be used. For example, a chronological chart which lists events in the proper sequence is often a help in getting an over-all view of the book or topic under study. The use of titles, labels, columns, lines, arrows, numerals, colors, variations in sizes of charts, light and heavy type, diagrams, illustrations, pictures, maps, appended explanatory notes, and other devices help to clarify the material and make it more readable and meaningful.

Charts may be shown to clarify genealogy or to trace historical sequences. A time-line chart will serve to keep specific events within the right general periods (see the chart on page 675. Charts may be used effectively to show the relationship of one main thought to its several component parts.

Charts and diagrams may be prepared on poster board, on flannelboards, or on chalkboards. Flip charts may be made in which each event or thought has its own specific representation.

MAPS

Maps are indispensable to man. He is continually making and using maps—either mentally or graphically. When taking a long trip by car, he uses a road-map until it is thumbworn.

As educational devices, maps help the student to visualize and localize important geographical areas.

Make sure that the student comprehends the purpose of the map—what is intended to be made clear with the use of the map. Is it the distance between two places? Or is it the extent of territory covered? Or is it the type of terrain which is present in certain sections?

Use maps at the opportune moment. The map should be used when it is most needed to answer questions, solve problems or supply information or data. Studying a map apart from an actual situation makes it a meaningless exercise that lacks purpose and life.

Do some map work. For example, trace the spread of the

church throughout the world. A world map will show the mission work that is being done on the foreign and home fields. A map of Paul's journeys would be helpful. To show the spread of Christianity throughout the world, shade the area on the map. Areas of non-Christian influence can be indicated also, perhaps with overlays of plastic. You may want to show the mission areas to which your own church has contributed.

Visual teaching need not be elaborate to be effective. A simple statement of what is being taught is all that is required. Use a variety of methods to impress these great truths upon the minds of your students.

TIME LINE – GENESIS to NEHEMIAH

—to 2000 B.C.	**GENESIS 1–11** Period: The world before Abram (Creation—Sin—Flood—Babel) People: Adam—Eve—Cain—Seth—Noah—Shem—Ham—Japheth
2000–1700 B.C.	**GENESIS 12–50** Period: Age of the patriarchs (Call of Abraham—Migration to Egypt—Growth of Israel) People: Abraham—Isaac—Jacob—Joseph
1700–1450 B.C.	**EXODUS – DEUTERONOMY** Period: Oppression in Egypt (The Exodus—The Law—Worship—Wilderness) People: Moses—Miriam—Aaron—Joshua
1450–1100 B.C.	**JOSHUA – I SAMUEL 7** Period: Conquest of Canaan and time of the Judges (Invasion of Canaan—Bondage and deliverance) People: Joshua—Caleb—Othniel—Ehud—Shamgar — Deborah — Barak — Gideon — Jephtha — Samson — Eli — Samuel
1100–600 B.C.	**I SAMUEL 8 – II CHRONICLES** Period: Monarchy—united, divided, declining (Kingdom established — Temple built — Kingdom divided — Destruction of Samaria — Discovery of the Law — Destruction of Jerusalem) People: Saul — David — Solomon — Jeroboam — Rehoboam — Ahab — Asa — Jehu — Elijah — Elisha — Jehoshaphat — Joab — Amaziah — Jeroboam II — Hoshea — Uzziah — Jotham — Ahaz — Hezekiah — Manasseh — Josiah — Jehoiakim — Zedekiah
500–400 B.C.	**EZRA – NEHEMIAH** Period: Return from the Exile (Decree of Cyrus — Close of Old Testament History) People: Zerubbabel — Ezra — Nehemiah

675